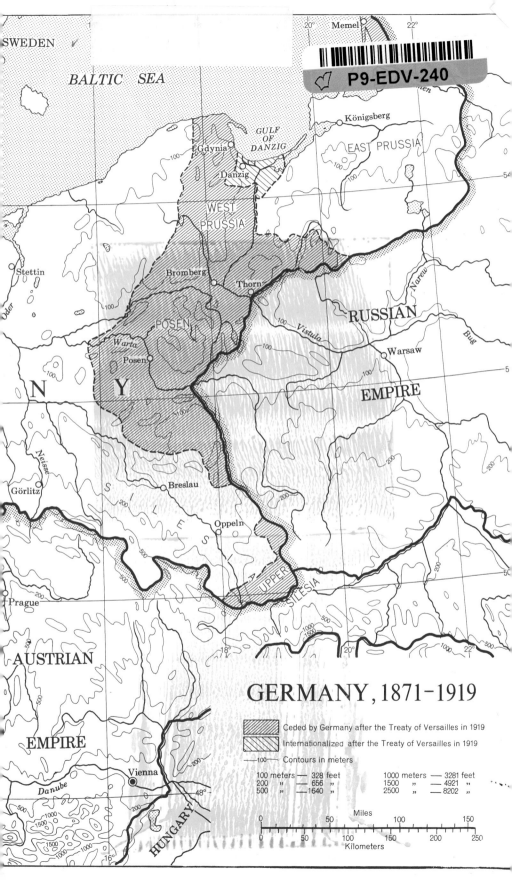

SWEDEN

BALTIC SEA

Memel
20°   22°

Königsberg

EAST PRUSSIA

GULF OF DANZIG

Gdynia

Danzig

WEST PRUSSIA

54

Stettin

Bromberg

Thorn

Narew

RUSSIAN

Oder

POSEN

Vistula

Warta

Posen

Warsaw

Bug

N   Y

EMPIRE

5

Neisse

Görlitz

S I L E S I A

Breslau

Oppeln

UPPER SILESIA

Prague

5

AUSTRIAN

18°   20°   22°

GERMANY, 1871–1919

Ceded by Germany after the Treaty of Versailles in 1919

Internationalized after the Treaty of Versailles in 1919

—100— Contours in meters

EMPIRE

Vienna

Danube

HUNGARY

48°

16°

100 meters	—	328 feet	1000 meters	—	3281 feet
200 "	—	656 "	1500 "	—	4921 "
500 "	—	1640 "	2500 "	—	8202 "

Miles
0   50   100   150

0   50   100   150   200   250
Kilometers

Modern Germany

ITS HISTORY AND CIVILIZATION

𝕸𝖔𝖉𝖊𝖗𝖓 𝕲𝖊𝖗𝖒𝖆𝖓𝖞

ITS HISTORY AND CIVILIZATION

SECOND EDITION

𝕶𝖔𝖕𝖕𝖊𝖑 𝕾. 𝕻𝖎𝖓𝖘𝖔𝖓

Chapter XXIII by
KLAUS EPSTEIN

MACMILLAN PUBLISHING CO., INC.
New York
COLLIER MACMILLAN PUBLISHERS
London

To

CARLTON J. H. HAYES
Distinguished Historian, Inspiring Teacher, Devoted Friend

Library of Congress catalog card number: 66–16925

MACMILLAN PUBLISHING CO., INC.
866 Third Avenue, New York, New York 10022

COLLIER MACMILLAN CANADA, LTD.

Printed in the United States of America

Printing   14 15 16 17 18   Year   6 7 8 9

Preface to the Second Edition

Professor Pinson was planning to revise *Modern Germany* before his untimely death. To bring the work up to date, I was asked to write Chapter XXIII, covering the history of the Bonn Republic from its foundation in 1949 to the present. A bibliography of works on Germany history in English has also been added; considerations of space precluded, however, the inclusion of most biographies and military studies dealing with the Nazi era. Dr. Edgar Alexander has kindly added a list of recent documentary collections and reference works in both English and German. The original General Bibliographical Note remains as an aid to students. Some changes and corrections of material in the first edition have been made from notes left by Professor Pinson, and I have added a table of Bundestag election results from 1949 to 1965.

This edition of *Modern Germany* is entirely the work of Professor Pinson through Section Five of Chapter XXII; responsibility for the latter part of Section Six and all of Chapter XXIII is mine.

KLAUS EPSTEIN

Introduction

In these days when books roll off the presses in greater numbers than newspapers and periodicals did in years gone by, every author owes it to himself and to his readers to justify the addition of another title to be flourished before a critical and sophisticated public. The reasons which prompted me to undertake the preparation of a history of Germany in the nineteenth and twentieth centuries were many. The key position of Germany in world affairs today hardly needs to be labored. It is my profound conviction, however, that the so-called German problem of today is unintelligible without an adequate understanding of German historical developments during the past 150 years.

Despite the importance of modern Germany, attempts at synthesis of its history and culture are on the whole not very numerous. This is true not only for historical literature in the English language but equally so for historical scholarship in Germany. The first great attempt at a history of Germany in the nineteenth century was made by Heinrich von Treitschke at the end of the last century. Despite its aggressive nationalism and its violent assault upon the very values most cherished by me, I count the work of Treitschke among the most brilliant achievements of modern historiography both for its scholarship and for its literary style. With all its five volumes, however, it remained but a torso, ending with the period before the revolution of 1848. The second great attempt at a synthesis of modern German history was begun by Franz Schnabel in 1932. Inspired by quite a different set of spiritual, political, and intellectual values than those of Treitschke, Schnabel's work gave promise of being the definitive and most objective account of German history and culture. It too, unfortunately, remained a torso. The Nazi revolution of 1933 brought Schnabel's work to a halt, and his magnificent four volumes likewise end with the 1840's.

Perhaps more important than chronology is the fact that almost all academic scholarship in the field of German history has until recently been dominated by the conservative and nationalist schools of German historians. This was obviously so inside Germany. But the same influence predominated in America and Britain as well. American and British scholars trained in Germany assimilated this point of view directly by contact with the German academic world and indirectly by their dependence upon the German historical literature which breathed this dominant spirit. During the wars with Germany the call of patriotic duty brought forth propaganda diatribes by Anglo-American historians against the Germans and their "Kultur," only to be followed after the wars by remorseful pangs of conscience and guilt feelings which often resulted in panegyrics of Germany and the German cause that were just as bereft of sound scholarship and balanced view as were their propaganda tracts of the war days.

A definitely new trend in German historiography set in with the advent of the Weimar Republic in 1919. Scholars who because of political or religious reasons had been excluded from German academic life now were afforded opportunities to make their contributions to German culture. They brought with them a broader, more humane, more socially minded and more liberal outlook. A new school of young German historians began to emerge who had little or nothing of the traditional "Prussian" point of view. New areas of German life hitherto considered unworthy of attention by the learned scholar began to be studied; the light of historical investigation was turned on movements and figures of the German past hitherto forgotten or distorted by the official schools of history; a vast amount of new source materials and a great number of monographs dealing with the nineteenth and twentieth centuries were published. All this, however, was cut off by the advent of Hitler in 1933, before these materials could be digested and utilized for purposes of broader synthesis. These materials have been used by me in the preparation of this work, and they have contributed enormously to make my task more rewarding.

Like the famous nineteenth century English historian J. R. Green, I have studiously avoided making this a "drum and trumpet history." Emulating Green, I can say that "I have preferred to pass lightly and briefly over the details of foreign wars and diplomacies . . . and to dwell at length on the incidents of that constitutional, intellectual, and social advance in which we read the history of the nation itself." The wars and diplomacy of modern Germany are the very subjects covered most adequately and in greatest detail in the older German and non-German historical literature. What has received far more inadequate attention are the internal domestic developments in Germany, especially as seen by Germans themselves and not through the eyes of foreign travelers or of the more internationally minded Germans who often were erroneously received by the non-German world as typical or representative of the German nation.

I have attempted also to integrate developments in German culture and German thought into the process of historical development. Because of this desire for integration, however, I found it necessary to exclude automatically from consideration here the artistic and literary creations in the German language in Austria and Switzerland. This often, I am aware, produces the effect of mechanical excision. But to proceed otherwise would lead to the extension of the political framework beyond the confines of the German Reich, and thus beyond the limits set for this work. Figures like Mozart, Jakob Burckhardt, Gottfried Keller, Carl Spitteler, Hugo von

Hofmannsthal, Artur Schnitzler, Karl Kraus, and other such Swiss-German and Austro-German intellectual and artistic personalities were no doubt of great significance for German intellectual life, but they could not be dealt with within the framework of this volume.

I make no claim to Olympian aloofness or to *absolute* scientific impartiality in this work. With Croce I believe that all history is inevitably contemporary history, and I am quite conscious of the fact that my selection of data, the emphasis and evaluation I have given to materials, are colored by my own *Weltanschauung,* my political views and my interests. This work is written frankly from the standpoint of one who finds liberal democracy, humanitarianism, and the ethical ideals of the Judeo-Christian tradition most congenial to his own frame of mind; I am also aware of the fact that I use these values as the criteria wherewith to gauge the historical significance of men and events. It is my conviction that the writer of history who frankly avows his philosophical point of view approximates more closely the canons of objective and impartial scholarship than those who cloak their concealed biases and their hidden sets of values either beneath the mantle of "scientific" objectivity or more arrogantly under the guise of a "tragic" view of history, according to which all men and events are the products of hidden and superhuman forces ruled over either by Fate or by Providence, with the historian himself occupying usually an exalted seat alongside these cosmic arbiters of human destiny.

If there is a unifying theme to this work, it is that of the tragic efforts made by liberalism and democracy to assert themselves in modern German history, of how they have been inundated time and again by the opposing forces, especially those of militarism and nationalism, and of how, nevertheless, these efforts recur to start the struggle anew. There is also the conscious perspective of one writing in our own times, and hence the more extended treatment of the more recent periods of German history or of those issues in the older periods which are relevant to our own contemporary interests. Despite such conscious and deliberate "myopia," I believe, nevertheless, that this work is a sincere attempt to present the pattern of German developments on a broad canvas and with a sympathetic awareness of the manifold complexity of the forces and factors at work in the fashioning of modern Germany.

It has not been my deliberate aim to present here any startling revelations or to be novel for the sake of novelty. The primary purpose of this work is to present the results of the best scholarship to date and to utilize the vast amount of German source materials and monographic literature for the purpose of a broad synthesis of the history of Germany during the past century and a half. In some instances this has involved correction and revision of hitherto accepted conclusions; in other instances it meant but a reaffirmation of established points of view. Similarly, while I am fully sympathetic to the utilization by the historian of techniques and concepts developed in the other social sciences, I cannot refrain from recalling the words of John Locke in the introduction to his *Essay Concerning Human Understanding.* "Vague and insignificant forms of speech, and abuse of language, have so long passed for mysteries of science; and hard and misapplied words, with little or no meaning, have, by prescription, such a right to be mistaken for deep learning and height of speculation, that it will not be easy to persuade either those who speak or those who hear them, that they are but the covers of ignorance, and hindrance of true knowledge." Too much of the new jargon developed in some of the social sciences serves not to illuminate the factors in human and social behavior but rather to introduce obfuscation and obscurity, or else merely to substitute novelty of verbiage for originality of ideas.

This work is the product of over twenty years of preoccupation with German history and culture. It began with my studies of the influence of religious currents in the seventeenth and eighteenth centuries upon the rise of German nationalism in the nineteenth century. The five years I spent as a member of the editorial staff of the *Encyclopaedia of the Social Sciences,* during which time I was delegated with chief responsibility for all materials pertaining to German history, politics, and culture which went into those fifteen volumes, provided me with a unique opportunity to become familiar with German scholarship and German life in their broadest aspects, and I shall always look back with grateful recognition to Dr. Alvin Johnson and my fellow editors for this rich and fruitful experience. I had the good fortune to see Germany at first hand before Hitler (1932), during Hitler (1935), and after Hitler (1945–1946). The year I spent as Educational Director for Jewish Displaced Persons in Germany and Austria under the auspices of the Joint Distribution Committee and UNRRA enabled me to observe Germany in collapse and under Allied occupation. Through the kind assistance of the Social Science Research Council I was able to spend a summer at the Hoover War Library in Stanford, California, and to make use of its rich collection of source materials for the period during and immediately following World War I.

The manuscript has been read by three persons to whom I am greatly indebted for my intellectual growth and stimulation: by my inspiring teacher, Professor Carlton J. H. Hayes, under whom I first began my studies of German nationalism; by Professor Hans Kohn, who by personal contact as well as by his published works has helped to give direction as well as stimulation to much of my thinking; and by Professor Waldemar Gurian, of the University of Notre Dame, who matches his wealth of knowledge and understanding by his breadth of view and his broad intellectual tolerance. To all of these I am deeply grateful for their valuable suggestions and help. No student of modern German history can escape the profound and almost bewitching effect of the works of the late Friedrich Meinecke, dean of contemporary German historians. It has been my rare privilege and good fortune to have also benefited by personal contact with him and to have drunk from his deep philosophical understanding of the process of history. Despite differences in political outlook, this work no doubt shows many evidences of his intellectual influence. My wife, Hilda Pinson, labored with unwearying effectiveness and has been a tower of strength to me throughout all the stages of this work. I also wish to express my appreciation to Mona Shub and Franz Bibo for their kind assistance in the technical preparation of this manuscript. Needless to say, final responsibility for the end product rests with no one but the author himself.

I am indebted to Mr. Wickham Steed for permission to use the lengthy description of William II by Eça de Queiroz taken from his *Through Thirty Years*.

KOPPEL S. PINSON

Table of Contents

xiii

𝔐𝔬𝔡𝔢𝔯𝔫 𝔊𝔢𝔯𝔪𝔞𝔫𝔶

ITS HISTORY AND CIVILIZATION

CHAPTER I

Germany and the Germans
The Problem of Europe

Germany is powerful in everything, in evil as in good.

MAX NORDAU

Germany has been a problem not only for the world at large; it has also been a problem for Germans themselves. Among no other people, with the possible exception of the Jews, has there been so much speculation, so much painful thinking on the why and wherefore of being German and on the "essence" of Germanism. "It makes me miserable," said Goethe, "to think of the German people. They are valuable as individuals, but hopeless as a whole." No one has castigated the Germans in such realistic and almost brutal fashion as did Friedrich Nietzsche, the German philosopher who in his own person illustrates so clearly the tragic and fateful union of brilliant genius with ominous and demonic amoralism of purpose—a characteristic found all too frequently in modern Germany. Nietzsche knew his own soul too well, and as he looked into it he saw mirrored there the tragic destiny of Germany and the Germans.

The German soul [wrote Nietzsche] is above all manifold, varied in its source, aggregated and superimposed, rather than actually built; this is owing to its origin . . . As a people made up of the most extraordinary mixing and mingling of races, perhaps even with a preponderance of the pre-Aryan element, as the "people of the center" in every sense of the term, the Germans are more intangible, more ample, more contradictory, more unknown, more incalculable, more surprising, and even more terrifying than other peoples are to themselves. . . . It is characteristic of the Germans that the question "What is a German?" never dies out among them. . . . The German soul has passages and galleries in it; there are caves, hiding-places and dungeons therein; its disorder has much of the charm of the mysterious; the German is well acquainted with the by-paths to chaos. And as everybody loves its symbol, so the German loves the clouds and all that is obscure, evolving, crepuscular, damp and shrouded: it seems to him that everything uncertain, undeveloped, self-displacing, and growing is "deep." The German himself does not *exist:*

1

he is *becoming,* he is developing himself! "Development" is therefore the essentially German discovery and hit in the great domain of philosophical formulas, a ruling idea, which, together with German beer and German music, is laboring to Germanize all Europe.[1]

Thus Nietzsche, one of the most German of modern German thinkers, described the complexities and contradictions inherent in the problem of Germany in the modern world.

Germany has become a world problem particularly during the past century. Today it is still destined to occupy a central role in the politics of Europe and the world for generations to come. The advent of National Socialism in 1933 in particular made the problem of Germany one of universal concern and gave rise to varied and conflicting theories regarding German mentality, German national character, and German social structure. Cataclysmic and magical interpretations of German history have been particularly abundant. The Marxist-Leninist theory of the "last stage of capitalism";[2] the Freudian interpretation of a nation of paranoiacs;[3] the "fruits of Versailles,"[4] all have been invoked to provide oversimplified and monistic explanations of the so-called German problem. While these theories have much to offer in high-lighting certain aspects of German behavior, none are adequate without the long-range factor of historical perspective and historical evolution. Physical, environmental, biological, and psychological factors all play their role, but the chief reason for Germany's being what it is is found in its history. In some instances it is necessary to go back into the very remote German past; in most instances it is the transformations that have taken place, particularly since the close of the eighteenth century. The most important thing to remember is that Germany is what it *is* today because of the way it has *become,* that is, because of its history.

Physically, Germany is the "land of the center," without natural frontiers on either east or west. Its boundaries have always been fluid, either as a result of the push of foreigners into German lands, or more often as a result of the pressing onward of German colonists, especially to the east. Hemmed in on all sides, the Germans, when confronted with the pressure of population, sought expansion on the Continent rather than overseas. The Germany of the Hanseatic towns did not join in the overseas expansion movement of the Age of Discovery in early modern times. German colonization movements extended eastward into Poland, Rumania, the Baltic, and Russia as far east as the Volga, and formed islands of German language and German culture and German loyalty that were to create grave problems in later days.

Situated in the heart of Europe, Germany has been the meeting ground as well as the battleground of the Romanic and Slavic peoples of Europe. Nor is there a single focal point for Germany as a whole. Berlin is not the heart of Germany as is Paris of France. Berlin is a relatively modern city, and the inhabitants of Munich, Dresden, or Cologne can well point with pride to the time when their cities were already old centers of culture while Berlin was still raw and primitive. Nor is the river Rhine, despite its prominence in nationalist literature, the focal point of Germany. In Roman times the Rhine was the dividing line between the Roman world and the barbarians. Then it served for a while to hold together the Carolingian Empire. After the break-up of the Carolingian Empire, the Rhine was the center of internal and external strife. It never achieved a central position in Germany. The romantic halo of a national shrine did not come to it until relatively late in history. Poets did not sing about it nor idealize it until the end of the eighteenth and beginning of the nineteenth century.[5] Physically, therefore, Germany lacked the requisite centrical forces necessary to develop a cohesive and well knit national state.

Ethnically, too, Germany was far from homogeneous. Goths, Vandals, Franks, Alemanni, Burgundians, Frisians, Anglo-Saxons, and Slavs all mingled to form the population of modern Germany. Nordic Pomeranians and Alpine Bavarians, "cold" and humorless Prussians and "warm" and witty Rhinelanders, semi-Slav Silesians and near-Romanic or Franco-German types in Baden and Westphalia—all these together are Germans. The nation that was to exalt the racial principle to a dogma of official state policy shows the widest variety of ethnic origins. Perhaps that is why the idea of *Zerrissenheit* (a word difficult to translate into English but which denotes a "torn condition") has exercised such a profound and almost mystical influence not only upon the literary but also upon the political and social thought of the Germans. No lines are more often quoted than the famous soliloquy of Goethe's *Faust:*

> Two souls, alas, reside within my breast
> And each withdraws from and repels its brother.
> One with tenacious organs holds in love
> And clinging lust the world within its embraces.
> The other strongly sweeps this dust above
> Into the higher ancestral places.*

The idea of cleavage permeated German political thinking. There were religious disunity and political disunity, cultural cleavages and class cleavages. And the more the Germans reflected on these divisions, the greater and more vehement were the attempts to overcome them. In no other country in modern Europe did this struggle between centripetal and centrifugal forces take on such enormous proportions and attain such a quasi-psycho-

---

* Nietzsche went even further. "A German," he wrote, "who would embolden himself to assert: 'Two souls, alas, dwell in my breast,' would make a bad guess at the truth, or more correctly, he would come far short of the truth about the number of souls." (*Beyond Good and Evil,* Modern Library ed., p. 175.)

pathic condition, and in no other country in modern Europe did such vehement nationalism develop to resolve this struggle.*

In the realm of religion there were cleavages which affected profoundly the entire course of German history. The opposition between Christianity and paganism runs a steady course throughout all German history. It has been said, and rightly so, that Germany was never completely and thoroughly Christianized. The eastern parts of Germany accepted Christianity only under duress. The Christian Charlemagne overwhelmed the pagan Saxons under Widukind and offered them the alternative either to embrace Christianity or to be annihilated. There have always been many Germans for whom the real hero of that epoch was not Karl der Grosse but the pagan Widukind, and precisely because he resisted the Christian might of Charlemagne. When National Socialism ruled Germany the historic coronation chapel of Charlemagne at Aachen ceased to occupy public attention; history and literature textbooks now sang the praises of the Saxon Widukind.[6] This pagan tradition burst forth time and again in German life. It appeared on the scene during the Protestant revolt, attempting to take advantage of the troublesome times to rid Germany entirely of the "burdensome" Christian faith. It reappeared in the *Sturm und Drang* and romantic periods, in the music dramas of Richard Wagner and in the philosophy of Nietzsche, and it reached its apotheosis in the period of the Third Reich.†

An even greater breach was the religious cleavage introduced by Martin Luther. Germany was the birthplace of the Protestant revolt, and while most other countries became predominantly Protestant or Catholic, Germany remained almost evenly divided between both denominations. Religious wars induced by the spread of Protestantism took place all over Europe, but nowhere did they last as long or leave such deep scars as in

---

* The prominent German economist and "Socialist of the Chair," Adolph Wagner, speaking at the banquet of the Verein für Sozialpolitik on the general subject of labor unions, still felt the need in 1897 to remind his hearers of these German cleavages. "We Germans," he declared, "are called upon on every occasion to remember what Germany has lost through inner cleavage and dissension, and we should always remember what we can lose if we do not stand together. . . . Certainly we Germans have a harder fate . . . than any other modern nation, perhaps than any other great nation in history. . . . Only one thing can actually save us: unity." (*Schriften des Vereins für Sozialpolitik*, vol. lxxvi [1898], p. 422.)

† "In their tentative, many-sided, indomitable way, the Germans have been groping for four hundred years toward a restoration of their primitive heathenism. Germany under the long tutelage of Rome had been like a spirited and poetic child brought up by very old and very worldly foster-parents. For many years the elfin creature may drink in their gossip and their maxims with simple wonder; but at last he will begin to be restive under them, ask himself ominous questions, protest, suffer, and finally break into open rebellion." (George Santayana, *Egotism in German Philosophy*, London, 1915, pp. 149–150.)

"Christianity had the effect of dividing German paganism into an upper and lower portion, and, by dint of repressing the dark underside, it succeeded in domesticating the bright upper portion and adapting it to civilized requirements. But the excluded lower portion still awaits deliverance and a second domestication." (Carl Jung, quoted in Ernst Jäckh, *The War for Man's Soul*, New York, 1943, p. 162.)

Germany. The seventeenth century in France and in England was the great period of national revival and national glory; in Germany it was *Deutschlands trübste Zeit* (Germany's most sorrowful period).

The most obvious manifestation of *Zerrissenheit* in Germany was political disunity. Here we find the long and deep conflict between nationalism and the universal tradition, between greater German nationalism and local patriotism, and between Austria and Prussia. Unlike the other countries of western Europe, royal power in Germany never achieved a central position. Whereas in France, for example, the power of the monarch was consolidated in the struggle against the feudal nobility, and France emerged as a strong, centralized dynastic state, the case was different in Germany. Here the tradition of the Holy Roman Empire dominated political thinking. The medieval German emperors dreamed of universal empire; their attention was more often focused on Italy than on Germany, and their energies were expended in the endless struggle between Empire and Papacy. In this struggle the German emperors were forced to call upon their feudal barons for aid, and had to make concessions to them. Thus, whereas in England, France, and Spain the advent of the modern era brought about the break-up of feudalism and the emergence of closely knit national states, in Germany feudalism and all that went with it lingered for several centuries afterward. The dream of universal empire, despite the disrepute into which it had fallen by the eighteenth century, nevertheless continued to fascinate and charm many German political thinkers.

In the other countries of western Europe the advent of the royal power as against that of the feudal barons also coincided with the emergence of a strong bourgeoisie. This too was lacking in Germany. The economic transformations brought about by the Age of Discovery and the Commercial Revolution, in which Germany, like Italy, did not participate, brought a halt to the nascent capitalist developments in these two countries. Until well into the nineteenth century Germany remained predominantly agrarian and feudal, and without a strong and militant bourgeoisie. Here liberalism as well as nationalism took on a special character which set Germany apart from the rest of western Europe. Here, as in all pre-nationalist societies, there was continuous oscillation between universalism on the one hand and localism on the other.

The map of Germany before 1800 was frequently described as a "carnival jacket." It consisted of 314 states and 1,475 estates, making a total of 1,789 independent sovereign powers. The absolutism which spread over Germany after the Treaty of Westphalia, with its imitation of the court of Louis XIV, took on a ludicrous character in the aspirations of these tiny states to ape the majesty of the court of the "grand monarch." Even after the disappearance of most of the smaller states in 1806, local patriotism still was a powerful force among Bavarians, Saxons, Prussians, Württembergers, and inhabitants of other local divisions.

The effect of these political divisions and tensions was to prevent the emergence of a more normal and more healthy kind of nationalism, such as developed in England and France. To these elements there was added still one other factor. The beginnings of a nationalist spirit in Germany toward the end of the eighteenth century coincided with the emergence of the state of Prussia as a great power. The German national movement was thus confronted with the serious rivalry between Prussia and the Hapsburgs, guardians of the universal tradition of the old empire and rulers over non-German as well as German peoples.

The history of Prussia as an important factor in German history begins with the Great Elector, Frederick William (1640–1688). The original domain of the Hohenzollerns was the district of Brandenburg, centering in and around Berlin. In 1415 Brandenburg was invested as an electorate in the empire and a century later it increased its area by the seizure of the lands of Catholic princes. It was the Great Elector, however, who first began, by thrifty and hard-working administration, to bring efficiency and order into his state. His successor, Frederick I (1688–1713), was the first to take the title of King in Prussia (1701), and his son Frederick William I (1713–1740) initiated the policy of building up an efficient army and a subservient bureaucracy. He also instituted a program of educational reform. It was Frederick II (1740–1786), however, who greatly increased the size of the Prussian state, by the seizure of Silesia and through the partition of Poland. By his signal military and diplomatic successes Frederick made Prussia a state to be reckoned with in Europe, and by his humiliation of Maria Theresa he served notice on the Hapsburgs that the future of Germany could no longer be decided upon without Prussia.

He was a strange man, this Frederick the Great: successful soldier, skilled performer on the flute, and would-be philosopher. He wrote in French instead of German because, as he himself said, "I speak German like a coachman." He regarded himself as the first servant of the state, yet he ruled with autocratic and absolute power, leaving to his ministers merely the function of clerks. Frederick, more than any other German ruler, set the example of military force, a conquering army, for modern Germans to follow. "Negotiations without weapons," he said, "are like music without instruments." By his cult of military force and by his own example of military success, he implanted in Prussia, and through Prussia in Germany, that inordinate reliance on military strength which both the Germany of Bismarck and the Germany of Hitler were to follow. He became the supreme example of the amoral national hero who hovered over and above the everyday concepts of good and evil.

The emergence of Prussia, and above all the triumphant successes of Prussia, impressed upon the rest of Germany a set of values, traditions, and ideals that came to be accepted as being universally German. The special position of the army, the officers' corps, the supremacy of the military over the civil—all these characteristic features of later Germany bore witness to the triumph of the Prussian spirit. In this connection the influence of the Order of the Teutonic Knights is significant. This famous order was founded in 1198 and very soon thereafter was transferred to the eastern frontiers of Germany for the scene of its activities. In 1226 it was made an instrument for Germanization and Christianization. In 1229 it was called upon to aid the Duke of Poland in Prussia. A series of revolts against the order resulted in its loss of West Prussia, but East Prussia was retained. Treitschke describes the ascetic life of discipline, duty, and order which characterized this group.

The "Rules, Laws, and Customs" of the order [writes Treitschke] shows us even today how highly developed was here the art of dominating men and using them. A man became a member of the order by taking the three vows of poverty, chastity, and obedience. . . . And received in return from the order a sword, a piece of bread and an old garment. He was forbidden to wear the coat of arms of his family, to lodge with secular people, to frequent the luxurious cities, to ride out alone, to read or write letters. Four times during the night the brethren, who slept half-clad with their swords by their side, were summoned to choir by the sound of a bell, and four times to the prayers during the day. Every Friday they were subjected to the monastic discipline. . . . If a member was guilty of any misdeed, the secret chapter was convened, which began with a mass and ended with a prayer. The culprit was often assigned to eat at the table of the servants or condemned to receive the discipline. . . . In this terrible discipline, in a world which always revealed the order as grand and illustrious but the individual as insignificant and poor, there developed the spirit of selfless dedication.[7]

For a time the order declined in power and influence, but in 1525, after the triumph of Protestantism, it was secularized and its territory became the fief of the Hohenzollerns. With this secularization of the order the ascetic discipline and servile obedience once attached to the religious and otherworldly life were now turned to the service of the political state, and the code of behavior of the Order of Teutonic Knights became the foundation for the code of the Prussian officers' corps.[8]

Closely related to the influence of the Prussian Order of Teutonic Knights is the enormous role played by the Prussian Junkers. The Junkers have been a persistent and dominant factor in modern German history, and their spirit has contributed to shape and mold German institutions and policies. Ruthless land-grabbers and adventurers in their earlier history, they settled down to become a "noble squirearchy" engaged in large-scale capitalist agriculture and an oligarchy that came to fill most of the important offices in German diplomacy, bureaucracy, and the military. They became the main pillars of Hohenzollern Germany and the chief agents in the Prussification of Germany.[9]

The state of Prussia thus developed as a *Soldaten- und Beamtenstaat*, a state of soldiers and bureaucracy, a product of stern and ruthless wrestling with raw nature, a state formed by and for war, a *Machtstaat* in which mechanical efficiency of the highest order became united with the traditional notions of political obedience and obligations to the divinely ordained ruler. Fashioned from an aggregate of varied and far-flung territories and peoples, the unity of the Prussian state and its centralizing principle rested in the ruling power of the dynasty, in that which the Great Elector, Frederick William I, and Frederick II had constructed. "Through bold and often unscrupulous and aggressive policies and through a personal army, they brought their lands together and through a thrifty and carefully planned administration they secured the means to maintain a military force far greater in proportion to population than that of other states." [10]

In the field of culture, likewise, modern Germany presents a spectacle of spiritual and intellectual *Zerrissenheit*. Germany, in the words of Thomas Mann, is "spiritually forever the battlefield of Europe." [11] The struggles between the classical Greco-Roman tradition and the Germanic, between the Renaissance and the Gothic, between the "Luther in Rome" and the "Goethe in Rome," are forever present. Germany never completely identified itself with Western civilization. There always has been a strong anti-Western tradition. The Russian novelist Dostoievsky saw this in the middle of the nineteenth century. "Germany's aim," wrote Dostoievsky, is "her *Protestantism*—not that single formula of Protestantism which was conceived in Luther's time, but her continual Protestantism, her continual protest against the Roman world, ever since Arminius—against everything that was Rome and Roman in aim, and subsequently—against everything that was bequeathed by ancient Rome to the new Rome and to all those peoples who inherited from Rome her idea, her formula and element; against the heir of Rome and everything that constitutes this legacy." [12]

The most characteristic quality of the Germans, continues Dostoievsky, "ever since their appearance on the historical horizon, consisted of the fact that they never consented to assimilate their destiny and their principles to those of the outermost Western world. . . . The Germans have been *protesting* against the latter throughout these two thousand years." Thomas Mann, quoting these words of Dostoievsky in 1914, gave his full assent to this characterization at that time, and gloried in it.[13] About a century earlier the rebel Börne had recognized this strain in German cultural tradition but had not been as enthusiastic about it as the Thomas Mann of 1914. "Some pride themselves," wrote Börne, "in the fact that we Germans—and we alone—were never subdued by the Romans. Who loves his German Fatherland should rather deplore this fact, for it explains why we have remained far behind so many peoples of Europe." Along with the powerful influence of the classical tradition, as found in Germany from Winckelmann and Goethe to Stefan George and Rilke, there is the equally powerful current of resentment against the intrusion and imposition of the Greco-Roman and Judeo-Christian traditions upon the Germanic. This factor, above all, created that "spiritual dissension," as Croce calls it, between Germany and Europe. With Widukind, leader of the pagan Saxons, Arminius, prince of the Cherusci, was enshrined in the nationalist pantheon of immortal Germans, for it was he who defeated the Roman legions of Augustus in A.D. 9 and prevented their penetration eastward into what is now Prussia.* The concept of "natural law," common to Roman Stoicism and to the teachings of the Christian Church Fathers, which presupposed both the principle of the dignity of human personality and a sense of the "unity of mankind," never became an integral part of German political thinking. It was of relative unimportance in the entire history of German intellectual and political development, as compared with its great historical role in the development of democratic ideology in England and France. This accounts for the weak foundations in Germany of all Western doctrines of liberalism and popular sovereignty that derived from this tradition.

It was this hostility to the West that induced great interest in German literary circles in Russia and Russian literature. If Germany was not of the West, so was Russia not of the West. Dostoievsky, in particular, was a powerful force in German literature and philosophy.† German politics, too, wavered on more than one occasion between East and West. Concluding his observations on World War I, in 1917, Thomas Mann wrote: "I close these notes on the day that news has come of the beginning of armistice negotiations between Germany and Russia. If everything does not change, then the long-desired wish of my heart ever since the beginning of the war will be fulfilled: Peace with Russia! Peace first with it! And the war, if it is to continue, will continue only against the West." [14]

Often this opposition to the West, to the French revolution and to the classical tradition, sought refuge in English influence, which was taken to be Germanic. Witness the enormous vogue of Shakespeare in Germany,

---

* The German historian Richard Laqueur, writing in 1932, said, regarding Arminius and his victory over the Roman legions in the Teutoburg forest, "Whoever speaks German and feels German should never forget whom he has to thank for this." (*Das deutsche Reich von 1871 in weltgeschichtlicher Beleuchtung*, Tübingen, 1932, p. 12.)

† See especially the writings of Karl Nötzel, Moeller van den Bruck, Thomas Mann, and Stefan Zweig.

introduced especially by the romanticist August Wilhelm von Schlegel; witness too the introduction of Burke into Germany to counter the effects of the political ideas of the French revolution.

It was the romantic movement, however, that initiated the most significant cleavage in German cultural life. Romanticism was a general European movement. But nowhere did it permeate all forms of social and political life, in addition to the literary, as it did in Germany; nowhere has it continued to exercise its power consistently through the past century and a half as in the case of Germany. The opposition in Germany between classic and romantic, to this day, connotes not merely esthetic and literary ideals and preferences. It almost invariably goes hand in hand with a general world outlook that reflects itself in the domains of economics, politics, religion and social affairs. Heinrich Heine, discussing Schlegel and Tieck and their romantic medievalism, explained in witty fashion this overpowering effect of German romanticism:

What happened to them [wrote Heine] is similar to what happened to the old chambermaid concerning whom the following is told. She had noticed that her mistress owned a wondrous elixir that restored youth. When the mistress was away she took the little bottle with the elixir out of her lady's toilette. However, instead of taking only a few drops she took such a long and big gulp that, through the powerful and miraculous force of the rejuvenating elixir, she became not merely young again; she became quite a small child again.[15]

Finally, in understanding the evolution of modern Germany one must never forget the enormous effect of the retarding of national unity in Germany. All the larger nations of western Europe attained their national unity in early modern times. Only Italy and Germany had to wait until the middle of the nineteenth century. In the case of both Italy and Germany there were many similar factors that prevented the early realization of national independence and unity. In both, the retarding of national unity also induced a more aggressive and militant nationalism. It is no mere accident, therefore, that fascism and National Socialism, the most extreme forms of modern nationalism, found their most developed forms in Italy and Germany. But there was also a significant and interesting difference between the two. In Italy the chief enemy of national unity was the foreigner—Austria. All the resentment born out of national emotions was directed toward the outside. In Germany the chief obstacle to German unity was the *Zerrissenheit* of the Germans themselves. The resentment was chained inward. This is the psychological explanation for the great touchiness, the more sensitive and sickly character of German aggressive nationalism. The greater the feeling of their own inferiority, the more extreme was the compensation in the form of arrogant superiority. Even after unity was attained in 1870, German nationalists were never quite sure of their Germans. Intensive and persistent agitation had to be continued in order to overcome the internal, centrifugal, and anti-national forces. This fact explains the ever present unity on foreign policy among all political groups in Germany, no matter how divided they were on internal questions.

There is no doubt that the Germany of 1900 was far different from the Germany of 1800 when Mme de Staël called it a land of "poets and thinkers." Politically, economically, socially, and culturally, far-reaching transformations had taken place. The history of Germany since 1800 is a study of the changes (1) from an agrarian to a highly industrialized society, (2) from cosmopolitanism to nationalism, (3) from a nation largely non-political to a *Machtstaat,* (4) from idealism to materialism, (5) from Austrian to Prussian domination. Through all those changes there was the fatal weakness in Germany of all the trends that made for progress in the countries of the West—liberalism, democracy, popular rights, and so on. Before we proceed to study these changes, however, it is important to look at the dominant world view of Germany at the close of the eighteenth century, the period of Germany's greatest cultural glory —the classical humanistic tradition.

CHAPTER II

The Classical Humanistic Tradition

Sapere aude! *Habe Mut, dich deines eigenen Verstandes
zu bedienen!*

IMMANUEL KANT

The most glorious period in German cultural history was undoubtedly the age of classical humanism, the century between the birth of Lessing and the death of Goethe. During this age the foundations were laid for a national German literature, and the fame of German music, German poetry, and German philosophy was carried to the far corners of the world to remain forever a lasting monument of world civilization. It was the tradition from which nineteenth and twentieth century Germany turned away, but its world significance was so profound, and its contribution to the Weimar tradition of Germany, as contrasted with the Potsdam tradition, so deep, that some analysis of this great stream of German culture is necessary before proceeding to the Germany of the nineteenth and twentieth centuries.

We may take as representative of this classical humanistic tradition such figures as Gotthold Ephraim Lessing (1729–1781), noted playwright, critic, and essayist; Johann Gottfried von Herder (1744–1803), philosopher, historian, and literary critic; Friedrich von Schiller (1759–1805), Johann Wolfgang von Goethe (1749–1832), Immanuel Kant (1724–1804), and the titan of music, Ludwig van Beethoven (1770–1827). Obviously the period was not of uniform homogeneity in all respects, and intellectual giants such as these were too individual in their creative talents to be pigeonholed neatly into categories. Nevertheless there are some aspects of their general approach to human problems that may be singled out as characteristic of this classical humanistic tradition.

In the first place this period represented a revolt in the cultural field against pettiness, intolerance, and philistinism. Lessing came to be known as the "Voltaire of Germany" because of his sharp criticism of all the petty intolerances of German society. Goethe's first play to receive attention, *Götz von Berlichingen*, was a similar protest. Goethe, with his usual lack of modesty, recognized this himself. "You may without qualms," he

12

said later in life, "set up a monument for me as for Blücher. He freed you from the French. I from Philistinism." Schiller's *Räuber* and his *Kabale und Liebe* were clarion calls to battle against all the elements of injustice and oppression which he saw dominant in his generation.

Secondly, this classical humanistic movement was definitely bourgeois in character. Not only were all the bearers of this tradition recruited from the ranks of bourgeois society but they also revealed in their personalities and emphasized in their works typical bourgeois values and virtues. Goethe's pecuniary sense was notorious, as was Beethoven's, and Kant always declared his greatest virtue to be that he owed no one a dollar. "With calm and joyous heart," he once said, "I can always call out: 'Come in' when any one knocks at my door, for I am certain that no creditor of mine stands outside." The ideals of *Entsagung,* renunciation, thrift, duty, service, revealed in the poetry as well as in the philosophy of this period, are a reflection of bourgeois ideals and bourgeois virtues.

The eighteenth century was the great period of secularization in Europe. In Germany too it was this classical humanistic tradition that served to bring about the great shift from religious and otherworldly values to secular and worldly ideals. The writers and thinkers of this epoch emphasized the significance of the *human* element in history and the dominance of man's reason. The basic idea in Lessing's religion was that morality was of greater value than theological dogma. Natural religion common to all denominations was for them the true religion. Lessing combated Christian dogmatism for its intolerance, its exclusiveness, and because it contradicted practical Christian morality. Activity was the highest goal for Lessing in life as in poetry. That is why the heart of all religiosity was for him, as it was later for Goethe, to be found in active and persistent striving. It was Lessing's bitter opposition to religious intolerance that led him to become the champion of the Jews, the most abused victims of intolerance. In his plays *Die Juden* (1749) and above all in his *Nathan der Weise* (1779) he brought upon the European stage for the first time the picture of a Jew, not as a villain or as a figure of comic relief, but as a human and noble character. "Are Christian and Jew rather Christian and Jew than Man?" he asked in his *Nathan.* And taking his friend, the Jewish philosopher Moses Mendelssohn, as his prototype, he described him in these noble lines:

> How free from prejudice his lofty soul
> His heart to every virtue how unlocked
> With every lovely feeling how familiar
> O what a Jew he is! Yet wishes
> Only to pass as a Jew.

Herder, himself a Protestant divine, stressed above all the human and moral element in Christianity. One becomes a Christian, he held, by becoming a man and remaining true to the disposition made by God. The Bible must be read in a human way, for it is "a book written by men for men." It is Jesus the man rather than Jesus the God that was emphasized.

Kant, perhaps more than anyone else, was responsible for undermining the supernatural foundations of the traditional world outlook. It was Kant who liberated science from the trammels of metaphysics and theological romanticism. His *Critique of Pure Reason* came to be considered by Germans as the Magna Carta of scientific work. "With this book," wrote Heine, "began a spiritual revolution which has the most marvelous analogy with the material revolution in France. . . . All respect is denied to tradition . . . every thought has been obliged to justify itself. And as the monarchy, the keystone of the old social order of things, fell here, so fell there deism, the keystone of the spiritual ancient régime." [1]

Closely allied with the emphasis on the human and moral aspects of religion was the espousal of the cause of Pelagianism as against the traditional Augustinian view of man. Back in the early days of the beginnings of the Christian view of man, a controversy had taken place between Pelagius the Briton and St. Augustine of Hippo. As against the Augustinian doctrine of the inherent corruptness of man and his absolute dependence upon God alone for grace, Pelagius posed the assertion that man, being free, can of himself choose good rather than evil and can by his own powers save himself. "If I ought, I can," was a favorite sentence of Pelagius. But the doctrine that prevailed in traditional Christian teaching was that of Augustine, and it continued to hold sway until the Age of Enlightenment. The humanism of the Enlightenment took up once again the cause of Pelagius. Man is not inherently corrupt, they said, and he can better himself and save himself. The aspect of striving in man's nature is constantly affirmed. Faust is saved in the end only because of his striving. "Das Streben meiner ganzer Kraft," says Faust, "ist grade Das, was ich verspreche." To which God replies: "Wer immer strebend sich bemüht, Den können wir erlösen." And in *Wilhelm Meister* Goethe hopes for a union of all religions that would

produce what may properly be called the true religion. Out of those three reverences spring the highest reverence—reverence for one's self, and those again unfold themselves from this; so that man attains the highest elevation of which he is capable, that of being justified in reckoning himself the best that God and nature have produced—nay, of being able to continue on this lofty eminence, without being again, by self-conceit and presumption drawn from it into the vulgar level.[2]

The classical humanistic tradition was characterized by the worship of man—man the individual and collective man, humanity. Every individual personality, said Goethe, bears his own law within him, and the highest realization of humanity was to form one's own life out of inner laws.

That is why Goethe, for example, in discussing Oriental poetry said: "You compare it only with itself, you honor it in its own circle, and forget thereby that there ever were Greeks and Romans." This is the emphasis on the unique and the individual that was later to play such an important role in the development of historicism.[3] The full realization of individual personality was the supreme goal of society. Goethe called the totality of his work "chips of a great confession." The essential aspect of his *Wilhelm Meister* is the exalted ideal of personality, transcending all temporal and spatial conditions—personality, which by free self-development, continuous absorption of new life elements, continuous change, strives for a higher type of mankind.

For Schiller, too, the meaning of life was to develop the individual man. The concept of man and mankind was not that of something given by nature; it was a cultural concept. Each individual "becomes" man through education. The individual is to develop his personality through the harmonious cultivation of all his potential capacities. These are what constitute his "individuality." But this "individuality" is most completely realized in universality and totality. It is this ideal of individual personality that leads Hölderlin in his *Hyperion* to exclaim: "I know of no people that is more divided than the Germans. You see artisans, but no men; thinkers but no men; priests but no men; masters and servants, young and mature people, but no men—is it not like unto a battlefield where hands and arms and all the limbs lie strewn about in pieces, while the spilled blood of life runs into the sand?"

It is this supreme importance of the individual that formed the very foundation of Kantian ethics. A free man, said Kant, "is one who is autonomous. Man exists only as an end in himself. The highest maxim of morality and freedom is: Act so that you utilize the humanity in your own person as well as in the person of every other individual at all times as an end and never as a means." Freedom, said Kant, is to "have the cause of one's self-determination within himself," and Kant rejected the dictum of Frederick II: "Reason as much as you want and about anything you want, only obey."

The yearning for the full development of personality was also one of the reasons for such wide preoccupation with classical antiquity during this time. The German poets and thinkers saw around them only the vain glory of the court and servility. And when, under the stimulus of the researches of Winckelmann and Lessing they discovered classical antiquity, they imagined they found in the world of Homer and Greece what they sought for in their own generation and what they wanted to be themselves —men, complete and full individuals. Here was the ideal of an esthetic culture of a true humanity.

Because these poets and thinkers found their own generation lacking in those ideals they cherished, they were on the whole almost entirely non-political in their interests. They were not stirred by the desire to reform the state or any other institutions of their time. The institution of the state they viewed with hostility, suspicion, or complete indifference. Neither patriotism nor nationalism counted in their scale of values. Corresponding to the non-political individual was the universal concept of humanity and that of the world citizen. "The ants," says Ernst in Lessing's *Ernst und Falk,* "have no one who holds them together and rules them, and yet what order!" "Order must therefore also be possible even without government, if each individual knows how to govern himself." The happiness and welfare of the state are merely the sum total of the happiness of all the members of the state, and there is nothing else besides this. Every other supposed happiness of the state, which might bring even the slightest amount of suffering to the individual, was a cloak for tyranny. Patriotism, wrote Lessing, "is a sentiment which I do not understand. It is, as it seems to me, an heroic infirmity which I am most happy in not sharing."

Goethe, reviewing a book by Sonnenfels in 1792, wrote: "If we find a place in the world where we may rest with our possessions, an acre that will supply us with food, a house that will protect us, do we not then have a fatherland? And do not thousands upon thousands have these in every state? And are we not happy within these limits? Why then the useless striving for a sentiment which is not within the possibilities or even desirable, which with certain peoples at certain times was and is the result of many happily converging incidents? Roman patriotism, may God protect us from this. We should find no chair on which to sit, no bed on which to lie." According to the flesh, he wrote to Jacobi, "let us be and remain citizens of the times, because anything else is impossible; but according to the spirit it is the privilege and duty of the philosopher and poet to belong to no nation and no time, but rather to be a contemporary of all times." Lessing, Herder, Goethe, Schiller, and all the rest gloried in the title "world citizen." "I write as a citizen of the world," said Schiller, "who serves no prince. At an early time I lost my fatherland in order to trade it for the whole world."

During the Napoleonic wars, when German nationalism was already in the ascendancy, Goethe was urged to put his poetic genius to the use of the fatherland and to write poems of hate against the French. He refused. Looking back at that period of 1812–1813, he said later to Eckermann in 1830:

How could I have written poems of hate without hate! And between you and me, I do not hate the French, as much as I thank God that we are rid of them. How could I, for whom the only thing that matters is culture or barbarism, hate a nation which belongs to the most cultured on earth and to which I am indebted for so large a part of my own development? National hate in general is a peculiar thing. You will usually find it in its strongest and most vigorous expression at the lowest stages of culture. There is a stage, however, where it is completely non-existent and where one stands over and above the nations and where one experiences the joys or pains of a neighboring nation as one's own.

Goethe created the term *Weltliteratur*. "Instead of limiting oneself to oneself," he said, "the German must take the world into himself in order to influence the world. . . . National literature does not mean much now; the epoch of world literature is at hand, and everyone must now work to hasten it."

Herder, one of the great figures in this classical humanistic tradition, was, it is true, at the same time the first to develop a political philosophy of nationalism.[4] But Herder's nationalism was, in the first place, entirely cultural. Herder, like the other figures in this movement, had no interest in the state. Nor was he swept off his feet by the triumphs of Frederick II. His interest was entirely to free German literature and thought from slavish imitation of the French and to develop an original and native culture based on folk traditions and folk inspiration. He expressed himself in no uncertain terms on militant and aggressive nationalism. "Of all forms of pride," said Herder, "I consider that of national pride as the most foolish. Let us contribute as much as we can to the honor of the nation; let us also defend it whenever it is the victim of injustice. But to glorify it *ex-professo*—that I consider to be a form of self-exaltation without any effective influence." [5]

Herder was most emphatic in his attack upon chauvinism of all kinds whether it was German, British, or any other. "To esteem the Germans God's chosen people in Europe, to whom the world belongs by right of their innate ability, and to whom other nations were destined to be subservient in consequence of this preëminence, would be to display the base pride of a Barbarian." He was equally emphatic in condemning British nationalism with its motto "Rule Britannia, Britannia rules the waves." National pride as well as family pride he considered befitting only the greatest fool. "No single nation is God's chosen people on earth. Truth must be built up by all nations. At the great veil of Minerva all nations shall exert their influence, each one in his place without injury and without proud discord."

Herder, nationalist though he was, did not look upon the nation as the highest point of development. Over and above the various nationalities there were the universal laws of humanity. "That relations between nations are outside the pale of law," he wrote, "is a doctrine of the Demons for Tartarus and Chaos, and not applicable to human society. It is a remnant of the madness and stupidity of the Barbarians."

"As Solyman viewed his empire as a garden full of all kinds of flowers, an orchard full of all kinds of fruits, so is the human race a family of the most various characters and national religions existing and unable to exist otherwise than for one purpose and one aim." [6]

In 1801, after the humiliating peace of Luneville, Schiller sought to comfort his fellow Germans. He drafted a plan for a poem which he never carried out, and only the fragment remains. What he wrote then, taken out of the historical context, may seem chauvinistic. But when understood as the attempt to lift the morale of a humiliated people it breathes quite another spirit.

Can the German [wrote Schiller] in this moment, when he goes forth without glory from this bitter war, when two arrogant nations have their feet on his neck and when the victor determines his fate, can he feel conscious of himself? Can he glory and take joy in his name? Can he raise his head and take his place with self-dignity in the rows of nations? Yes he can! He leaves the battle with misfortune, but that which constitutes his true worth he has not lost! German Reich and German nation are two different things! The majesty of the Germans rests not upon the heads of their princes. Removed from the political field, the German has established his own worth and even if the empire is overthrown German dignity remains unimpaired. It is a moral of greatness, it resides in the culture and the character of the nation and is independent of the political destiny. This *Reich* is blooming in Germany, it is in full growth, and under the Gothic ruins of an old barbarian constitution the living force is developing. . . . The German is chosen by the World Spirit to work amidst the struggle for the eternal building of man's development; not to shine for the moment or play a passing role but to conquer the great process of time. Every nation has its day in history, but the Day of the Germans is the harvest of all times. In the end power will come to him who is formed truly by spirit, if there is any plan at all in the world and if human life has any meaning. In the end morality and reason must triumph over raw force— and the most gradual nation will overtake all the speedy vanishing ones.[7]

It is from this piece by Schiller that the later jingoistic term of *Der Tag* of the Germans was derived. But it was a far cry from Schiller's meaning to the militant and aggressive connotation given to this phrase a century later by William II, the arrogant ruler of a powerful state.

The concept of humanity was also the stimulus to Kant's *Essay on Perpetual Peace.* In this plan for the elimination of national strife and the dream of a world order, Kant's scheme provided (1) that no peace treaty was to be valid if made with the secret intent of preparing for a future war; (2) that no state shall become the property of another state through heredity, exchange, purchase, or gift; (3) that standing armies be outlawed; (4) that no state is to interfere violently with the internal affairs of another state; (5) that each state is to have a republican constitution; and (6) that international law is to be founded upon a federal system of free states.

This concept of universal peace, world citizenship, and common brotherhood was one of the most deeply rooted ideals of the classical humanistic tradition. It was given popular expression in Schiller's *Ode to Joy:*

> Seid umschlungen Millionen
> Dieser Kuss der ganzen Welt
> Alle Menschen werden Brüder.

And the immortal Beethoven set these words to music in the chorale of his Ninth Symphony, which became the most inspiring musical expression of this ideal. It was this tradition, too, that was echoed in the writings of Franz Grillparzer. "Nationality," said Grillparzer, "should show itself in acts but should not be shouted about." "One does not possess what one utters as a command. Peoples that have nationality do not speak about it." When attacked in 1819 for writing poetry about the Argonauts instead of the Nibelungen heroes, Grillparzer replied:

I do not despise your primitive Germanism but I can not use it. First let the nationality of the Germans go from the head to the arteries and flow through with the blood; first give me the assurance that when I sing it will re-echo in you, then German subject matter will be more welcome to me than any other. As long as it has not reached this far yet, however, I will leave the national as such to the literary road-makers and street cleaners and I shall pursue my goals on the generally practical highway of all-human in the tested forms of its centuries-long wonted ways.[8]

Summarizing the characteristics of the classical humanistic tradition, we may say (1) that it was primarily bourgeois in character; (2) it was secular, (3) tolerant, (4) optimistic, (5) individualistic, (6) humanitarian, and (7) cosmopolitan.

This intellectual tradition came to be regarded as the noble German tradition. It was the Weimar tradition as opposed to the militaristic Potsdam tradition of Frederick II and of Prussianism. It was the set of values which most of the subsequent liberal and progressive forces in Germany, those most oriented to the West and those representing moderate or humanitarian nationalism, looked to for inspiration and guidance. With all these noble elements, however, this tradition was also marked by several serious weaknesses that proved well-nigh fatal to the cause of German liberalism.

Classical humanism, like the idealistic philosophy which developed within it, was dualistic in character. A far too sharp division was made between matter and spirit. Kantian ethics, with all its emphasis upon the autonomy of the individual, also created the fatal dichotomy of the realm of morality and legality. In the realm of the pure spirit, all these noble ethical and political ideals were the only true and proper ones. They represented the highest realization of the human spirit. But there was the everyday mundane, ordinary world of human life. In that domain the idea of legality held sway. There Frederick's dictum of "only to obey," as inferior as it may be to the highest realm of the spirit, was none the less supreme.[9] There are noble values in the ideal world, but one must reconcile himself to the fact that in the world of brute matter they have no influence.

> In des Herzens heilig stille Räume
> Musst Du fliehen aus des Lebens Drang!
> Freiheit ist nur in dem Reich der Träume
> Und das Schöne blüht nur im Gesang.

Freedom, says Schiller, was to be left to the world of dreams, and one had better realize that it is vain to aspire to find it in the world of reality.

The cleavage between the world of spirit and the practical world, introduced by German idealism, was to paralyze all movements for liberalism and democracy in Germany. Mme de Staël, who described the Germany of the late eighteenth century in her *De L'Allemagne,* noted:

The Germans, who cannot endure the yoke of rules in literature, require everything to be traced out for them in the line of their conduct. . . . They know not how to deal with men; and the less occasion is given them in this respect to decide for themselves, the better they are satisfied. . . . The nature of the government of Germany was almost in opposition to the philosophical illumination of the German. From thence it follows, that they join the greatest boldness of thought to the most obedient character. The pre-eminence of military states, and the distinctions of rank, have accustomed them to the most exact submission in the relations of social life. Obedience with them is regularity, not servility; they are as scrupulous in the execution of orders they receive as if every order became a duty.

German intellectuals, she wrote, "dispute vehemently among themselves in the domain of speculation and will suffer no shackles in this department; but they give up without difficulty all that is real in life to the powerful of the earth."

Germans themselves realized this divorce of thought from action. Jean Paul, long before modern technology was to give his words a significance of which he never dreamed, said: "To the French, God has given the land; to the English, the sea; to the Germans only the air." And Heinrich Heine, more under the influence of the French revolutionary tradition, drew a satire of this character of German intellectuals in his *Germany—A Winter Fairy Tale.*

> Man schläft sehr gut und träumt auch gut
> In unseren Federbetten;

Hier fühlt die deutsche Seele sich frei
Von allen Erdenketten.

Sie fühlt sich frei und schwingt sich empor
Zu den höchsten Himmelsräumen;
O deutsche Seele, wie stolz ist dein Flug
In deinen nächtlichen Träumen!
. . . .
Franzosen und Russen gehört das Land;
Das Meer gehört den Britten;
Wir aber besitzen im Luftreich des Traums
Die Herrschaft unbestritten.

Hier üben wir die Hegemonie
Hier sind wir unzerstückelt;
Die andern Völker haben sich
Auf platter Erde entwickelt.*

What interested the bearers of the classical humanistic tradition more than anything else was the realm of esthetics and beauty. It was an estheticism that was also bound to be aristocratic in spirit, if not always in the literal political sense. The "esthetic culture" which Schiller prized more than anything else was the monopoly of limited aristocratic circles. Goethe was a fighter and liberator in matters of culture and the spirit, but he was anything but a fighter in civic or political matters. Like his followers after him, he looked down upon the world of everyday life as from Olympian heights, with an attitude of utter indifference to practical needs. There was an almost inhuman coldness and lack of conviction in Goethe which stemmed from his naturalistic pantheism and from his amoral conception of the genius. "From one eye," a contemporary wrote of him, "blinked an angel, from the other a devil, and his speech was deep irony concerning all human affairs." He was tolerant but not kindly. To a young man who had vowed that he would live and suffer for art, Goethe said, "One cannot speak of suffering in art." Every poem, wrote Goethe, is a kiss given to the world, "but kisses do not make any children." Goethe's works, wrote Heine, "adorn our literature as beautiful statues adorn a garden, but they are only statues. You can fall in love with them but they do not bear seed."

This aristocratic estheticism not only contributed to the strengthening of anti-democratic trends and bore fruit in later figures such as Lagarde,

---

* We sleep very well and dream very well in our featherbeds. Here the German soul feels itself to be free of all earthly chains. It feels itself to be free and soars aloft to the highest realms of heaven. Oh German soul, how proud is your flight in your nightly dreams. . . . To the French and Russians belongs the earth, to the Britons the sea. We, however, possess unchallenged supremacy in the airy realm of dreams. Here we exercise hegemony, here we are not divided up, while other nations have developed upon the flat earth.

Nietzsche, Spengler, and George, but created in those very circles which depended most on this tradition for their inspiration, a hesitant attitude that never dared to risk the full-hearted acceptance of democratic ideology and popular government. Humanistic cul*ure, for these circles, meant music, metaphysics, psychology, poetry, and a contemptuous exclusion of everything political. This was the basis for the absence of political maturity and criticism among intellectual classes of modern Germany who drew their inspiration and sustenance from the golden age of classical humanism.

CHAPTER III

(Germany, the French Revolution, and Napoleon

Nur in der Sehnsucht finden wir die Ruhe.
SCHLEGEL, *Lucinde*

1. CULTURAL NATIONALISM BECOMES POLITICAL

The French revolution as a movement that transcended the borders of France was injected into the life of the German people more immediately and more directly than into that of any other European nation.[1] Friedrich Gentz, writing in 1794, called the revolution "one of the events which belongs to the whole human race" and "of such magnitude that posterity will eagerly inquire how contemporaries of every country thought and felt about it, how they argued and how they acted."[2] In Germany, however, the French revolution was of much greater consequence for eliciting a negative reaction against all that the revolution stood for rather than for positive revolutionary influence. The contagion of revolution in the German states was slight and of little consequence. Minor disturbances occurred in Silesia, Saxony, and Mecklenburg and in Treves, Cologne, and Speyer. At no time, however, was there any organized movement in Germany that sought to emulate the events in France. Neither revolutionary sentiment nor a revolutionary situation was present in any of the German states. Whatever revolutionary ideology did find vocal expression was confined to a small group of intellectuals. The great tradition of the Enlightenment which in France served to pave the way for the revolutionary upheaval exercised no such influence in Germany. Neither the doctrine of natural law nor that of the social contract and the revolutionary implications derived from these by Locke and Rousseau found echo in the literature of the German Enlightenment. Here the political theory of the *Aufklärung* took as its own the ideal of the enlightened despot. In sovereigns like Frederick II of Prussia or Joseph II of Austria the enlightened German "liberals" saw the road to the solution of the world's ills. They had no sympathy for, or any real understanding of, the meaning of

23

revolution. The initial reaction among Germans to the events of 1789, as
we shall see later, was therefore that of purely intellectual and ideological
spectators. It was like the reaction of a seismograph registering a distant
earthquake.

The political reaction in Germany to the French revolution was really
a reaction not to the revolution proper but to the revolutionary wars and
especially to Napoleon and his conquests. Its end result was the War of
Liberation of 1813. German involvement with the French revolution,
therefore, was predominantly concerned with the Napoleonic era. Goethe's
remark that "Napoleon was the expression of all that was reasonable,
legitimate and European in the revolutionary movement" is expressive of
the fact that it was Napoleon rather than either the ideas of 1789 or
Jacobinism which the Germans identified with the French revolution.
Baron vom Stein and Prince Hardenberg always considered the wars
against Napoleon as a continuation of the French revolution. German
engagement with the revolution and Napoleon, therefore, became essentially one of nationalist resistance, and the whole struggle against the
revolution became the fountainhead for the quickening of German national consciousness and national feeling.

It has often been alleged that the French revolution marked the birth
of German nationalism. This is not so. German national consciousness
showed perceptible signs of growth long before 1789. German Pietism,
beginning with Philipp Jakob Spener and August Hermann Francke at the
close of the seventeenth century, had initiated a trend of psychological
reactions and intellectual processes which introduced into German life
many of the necessary ingredients of the sentiment and theory of nationalism—the emphasis upon enthusiasm and irrationalism, the feeling
for individuality, the attention to the needs of the common man, and a
greater emphasis upon popular education.[3] The revived classicism popularized the ideal of civic patriotism and civic virtue. Lessing, Klopstock,
Hamann, and Herder had destroyed the dependence of German literature
and German thought upon French models and had laid the solid foundation for a national literature and national education. Herder had elaborated
a complete philosophy of nationalism long before the outbreak of the
French revolution. But all these manifestations were purely in the realm
of cultural nationalism; they were not yet carried over to the domain of
the national state. It was the French revolution that provided the shock
that quickened all these trends and that, above all, served to politicize the
German intellectual classes, to make them politically conscious and politically active. The participation of intellectuals like Arndt, Görres, Fichte,
Schleiermacher, and others in the War of Liberation would have been
unthinkable a generation earlier. Only Goethe, true to the earlier tradition, remained "above the battle" in his Olympian aloofness.

The Enlightenment, with its secularizing direction, had loosened the bonds of the individual to otherworldly ties and to religion. The coming of the French revolution coincided with the time when the influences of all these other currents and movements converged to interact upon one another. The secularized Pietist, psychologically still given to enthusiasm, to irrationalism, to the *zelo ardentissimo* of the older Pietism, but released by the force of the Enlightenment from his ties to traditional religion, now found a worldly outlet for his emotional attachment—the nation and the state—and the wars of the revolution created the situation for the transfer of this emotion. Nationalist consciousness is the product of a feeling of kinship within the group and a feeling of apartness from those outside the group. Internal developments in Germany during the eighteenth century were bringing about a greater feeling of kinship within the German people. The wars of the French revolution stimulated their national feeling by contrast, by the effect of hate. Nationalism before the French revolution was entirely cultural; German political nationalism was born out of the struggle against the foreigner. And although the achievement of political unification was still to wait for half a century, it was the struggle against France that first made German intellectuals and political leaders acutely aware of the need for some form of political unity.

2. THE REVOLUTION AND GERMAN INTELLECTUALS

German intellectuals were almost unanimous at first in their acclaim of the revolution. Only a few, like the old Prussian patriot and bard of the Frederickian conquests, Wilhelm Ludwig Gleim (1719–1803), the Osnabrück archivist and historian Justus Möser, who had long battled against the doctrine of natural rights, and the Pomeranian royalist admirer of Gustavus Adolphus and Frederick the Great and champion of George III against the American revolutionists, Ernst Moritz Arndt, viewed the revolution from the start with open hostility or cool disdain. Goethe expressed his sovereign contempt for all champions of liberty, while Wilhelm von Humboldt, "as cold and as bright as the sun in December" (as Görres described him), found more to interest him in Paris in the creations of the "spirit" than in the revolutionary events.

Apart from these few exceptions all prominent figures in German letters were stirred profoundly by the coming of the revolution. Some were wildly enthusiastic like young Hölderlin, who as late as 1792 was inspired by the revolution to write his "Hymn to Humanity" and "Hymn to Liberty" and who in the war of 1792 asked his sister "to pray for the French, the champions of human rights." Others like Wieland were distinctly mild in their reaction. But almost all the great figures in German cultural life expressed positive appreciation of the revolution. The philosophers Kant, Fichte, Schelling, Hegel, and Schleiermacher; the literary lights Klopstock, Herder, Schiller, Wieland, Tieck, Hölderlin, and Jean Paul; scholars and journalists like Campe, Hennings, Stolberg, Johannes Müller, and Georg

Forster, all joined the chorus of rejoicing over the events of 1789. Even the subsequent arch-enemy of the revolution, Friedrich Gentz, was, up to 1790, an admirer of the events in France. Hegel and Schelling participated in 1791 in the planting of a tree of liberty in Tübingen. Fichte proclaimed that "the dark ages are over"; Klopstock hailed the revolution as "the noblest deed of the century," and in his ode *"Sie und nicht wir"* bemoaned the fact that it was France and not his own nation that had heralded the call for liberty. Young Ludwig Tieck, in his enthusiasm for the revolution, declared: "I salute the genius of Greece, which I see hovering over Gaul. France is now my thought day and night." The historian Johannes Müller, writing on August 14, 1789, said: "July 14 in Paris was the most wonderful day since the decline of the Roman empire. . . . Let them fall, those who tremble, unjust judges and exalted tyrants! It is very good that kings and councils become aware that they too are only men." [4]

Geographically, the revolution found sympathetic echo, especially in the state of Brunswick, in the free city of Hamburg, and in the Rhineland. The enlightened régime of the Duke of Brunswick, himself a disciple of the *philosophes,* made that state a center of pro-French sentiment. There, thanks to the freedom of the press, J. H. Campe edited the liberal *Braunschweiger Journal,* in which he published his famous letters from Paris. Another contributor to this journal, Major Jakob Mauvillon, friend and collaborator of Mirabeau and later of Benjamin Constant, underscored the social foundations of the revolution and pointed out that when there are 16 million serfs in Germany, "then such curiously minded persons as we are fondly desire a revolution." [5]

Hamburg was also a center of pro-French sympathies. There Klopstock made his home; there too hovered the liberal Protestant tradition of Lessing and Reimarus, with a more highly developed and politically conscious bourgeoisie. There the Hanseatic merchant prince Georg Heinrich Sieveking (1751–1799) arranged a public celebration of the first anniversary of the fall of the Bastille, and there the journalist August Hennings (1746–1826) published a German translation of the *Marseillaise* and in the journals *Genius der Zeit* (1794–1800) and *Annalen der leidenden Menschheit* (1795–1801) he championed the cause of the French revolution but pointed out the need for "Protestantizing" France in order to make the revolutionary principles secure.

In the Rhineland the corrupt and absolutist conditions which existed, especially in the ecclesiastical states, were responsible for the enthusiasm with which not only the news of the French revolution but also the French revolutionary armies were greeted. Here it was that the renowned scientist and traveler Georg Forster (1754–1794) welcomed the French troops as the bearers of the ideas of German and Anglo-American Enlightenment and formed the Rheinischdeutscher Nationalkonvent to bring about secession from Germany and federation with revolutionary France. The so-called "Klubists" carried on similar activities under Michel Venedy in Cologne and under young Joseph Görres in Coblenz.

Most of the other official circles, including Prussia and the South German states, were hostile to the revolution. From Hanover especially emanated a great deal of the theoretical opposition to the ideas of the revolution. This state, still joined by a personal union with England, was a center for cultural contacts with Britain. There, under Burke's influence, Brandes, Rehberg, and Spitteler, centered at the University of Göttingen, developed their intellectual arsenal of attack against political rationalism and revolution along the same lines as Mallet du Pan, De Rivarol, and De Bonald.

In official government circles the French revolution soon took on the character of a world conspiracy spearheaded by France but aided by fellow conspirators in all European states who "bored from within." Especially suspect were the Freemasons and the Illuminati as allies of the Jacobins. The Prussian envoy von Stein reported to Frederick William II from Mainz on July 23, 1791, that Germany was being flooded with secret revolutionary propaganda and that the Illuminati were to blame. He complained that Göttingen, Gotha, and Brunswick were full of these *"éclaireurs de genre humain,"* who, under cover of cosmopolitanism, were hiding their designs "to subvert all order." [6] In Saxony the government imposed strict control over "subversive" literature, and pro-French travelers were barred from entry into the country. In this campaign against "subversion" a leading role was played by ex-Illuminati who revealed the names of their former comrades and who urged battle against Jacobins, Masons, and Illuminati. Together with charges of world conspiracy were added reports of atrocities and immorality. Especially shocking to the solid German burghers was the report that French women had supposedly ceased wearing undershirts. [7] Interestingly enough, most of these official circles, especially in the smaller states, became sycophant admirers of France and Napoleon after the Eighteenth Brumaire.

What was it that attracted German intellectuals to the revolution and what was it that brought about their subsequent revulsion? For some it was the earth-shaking character of the event that inspired their admiration. Herder compared the revolution to the birth of Christianity or to the Barbarian migrations; Franz Dautzenberg, editor of the *Aachener Zuschauer,* felt that it "promised the blessing of all mankind"; for still others it evoked memories of Luther's revolt in Germany. Some, like Kant and young Fichte, inspired by Rousseau with a love of liberty, saw in the revolution the realization of this ideal; others, like young Görres, championed it because of their hatred of the old empire; and still others, like Tieck, found it to be the embodiment of the classical spirit. Enthusiastic youth, like Hölderlin, saw in the revolution the spirit of Schiller's robbers Moor, while older cosmopolitans, like Forster and Campe, hailed it as the inauguration of a truly united and enlightened humanity. These reasons, singly or jointly, actuated the intellectual classes to adopt a position of sympathy with the events in France. But whatever their reasons, they were all united in their desire to keep the "experiment" confined to France. They had no desire to see anything like it occur in Germany. "Heaven forbid," wrote Johannes Müller in 1791, "that similar revolutions occur in other lands; but I do wish that it should serve as a mirror and that its influence should be felt. And that it is doing." [8] Herder, while declaring that it was impossible to exclude the mighty event of the revolution from the minds and souls of men, nevertheless went on to point out the difference between France and Germany. Germany, he wrote, was never subjected to evils like those that plagued the French under the old régime, and therefore, said he, "We can watch the French revolution as we watch a shipwreck at sea from the safety of the shore." On the whole, German writers of the time found the *Kleinstaaterei* of Germany superior to the huge centralism of the French. In their enthusiasm for the classical *polis* or for the Swiss cantons they did not wish to see Germany follow the French model. Above all, however, German political theory of the Enlightenment was committed to the ideal of "enlightened despotism." The spirit of obedience of the subject to his lawful ruler was part and parcel of their political ideology. While admiring from afar the advent of "reason" in France, they could not bring themselves to urge their own fellow citizens to revolutionary action, especially when they believed that the spirit of Enlightenment, while absent from the old régime in France, was securely anchored in the German states. Enlightened officials in Prussia, as well as the leading *philosophes* in Berlin, expressed the view that the French revolution in 1789 was after all only the application of the principles obtaining in the "enlightened state of Prussia" under Frederick II. Karl Mangelsdorff, professor of history in Königsberg, published a pamphlet, *Ueber den Geist der Revolution* (1791) in which he maintained that for Prussians, "a people fortunate beyond expression," disobedience would be odious, but in France, where the yoke had become unbearable, revolt was justified. Similar sentiments are found in other political tracts of the time.

The reaction against the French revolution set in among German intellectuals with the increase in violence in France. The September massacres and especially the execution of Louis XVI turned the hearts of former sympathizers against the new régime. "Our golden dream is shattered," lamented Klopstock. German supporters of the revolution had been largely pro-Girondist. The influence and contacts of Abbé Sieyès were also widespread. The triumph of the Jacobins and the ensuing reign of terror, therefore, served to heighten the reaction against the revolution. Some, like Johannes Müller and Dautzenberg, were shocked by the Jacobin attack on religion and on "property." The influence of Burke's *Reflections on the French Revolution* was also an important factor in crystallizing anti-revolutionary thinking in Germany. Friedrich Gentz translated Burke into German in 1792, and it immediately became a fountainhead for anti-revolutionary ideas. The Hanoverian Whigs Rehberg and Brandes, and the journalists Görres and Gentz, sought to emulate Burke. Above all, Burke was a profound influence on the romanticists, who took over his traditionalism and organicism but left out completely the Whig concepts of "public spirit" and traditional "British liberty." "There have been many anti-revolutionary books written *for* the revolution," wrote Novalis, "but Burke has written a revolutionary book *against* the revolution." And Friedrich Schlegel, writing retrospectively in 1815, said:

> Burke, that consummate statesman and orator, shed abroad over the whole of Europe, and, judging from the frequent use made of it, over Germany especially, a copious store of political sagacity and moral experience drawn from the primitive source of all political wisdom. He was the deliverer of his age when it was involved in the storms of revolution.[9]

The major factor which turned German intellectuals against the revolution was their disillusionment with the cosmopolitan character of the revolution. The French revolution in its initial stages meant for German intellectuals the triumph of universal good. As good cosmopolitans they hailed the achievements of the revolution as their very own. As soon as the French revolutionary armies, however, began to extend their domain outward, these universal humanitarian aspects began to lose their meaning. It became difficult to distinguish between universal revolutionary propaganda and French imperialistic conquest. Dautzenberg's paper reported on April 25, 1792, the French declaration of war and declared, "France's lot is finally cast—to the mourning of humanity." The universal dream proved to be only imperialist conquest. It was not that the German nationalism of these intellectuals reacted against France but rather that French nationalist expansion purged the German intellectuals of their eighteenth century cosmopolitanism and induced instead the rise of a German national spirit, either alongside or replacing their previous cosmopolitanism. Joseph Görres, on his return from Paris in 1800, gave such expression to his feelings:

> When liberty, which we saw France striving for, was still universal liberty; when it still gave praise to the God of all the nations, then its interest was also the interest of all the nations who were mature enough to improve their condition; then it was the duty of everyone to embrace this universal cause with enthusiasm, over and above all other considerations, quite apart from all private interests, and severed from all local connections. It was one's duty to unite with all others to work for the same goals with all the energy he

possesses and to lose sight of sacrifices and less significant inconveniences for the sake of the great cause. In this way he would add his striving to the great mass of forces which nature had awakened for its experiments. . . .

As soon as that nation, however, renounced this solemn office, as soon as it is concerned only with its own egotistical liberty, as soon as it gives praise to its own national good and fashions its constitution to its own climate, at this moment the bonds of world citizenship that bound it to other peoples are dissolved; their interests diverge from its interests, and considerations that did not previously obtain, and motivations that previously would have been considered narrow-minded now assume full significance. Now it is no longer individual vs. individual, but state against state, and alongside the question: What does justice demand? the other question poses itself: What does wisdom demand? [10]

Only a few of the German intellectuals persisted in their espousal of the revolution to the end. Georg Forster died in 1794, and it is difficult to say how long his pro-French sentiments would have lasted; but he remained steadfast in his loyalty until his death. He defended the execution of the king, and although he deplored some of the "fury of the Jacobins" he nevertheless declared: "I am rather for than against the Jacobins. Without them the counter-revolution in Paris would already have triumphed. If all the ground gained since 1789 is not to be lost, they had to act as they did. The guilt of all the horrors lies on the Court, the nobility, the priests, and the foreigners." [11] The philosopher Kant continued to uphold the revolution to the very end and lashed out against political "heresy hunting" in Prussia. In his *Streit der Fakultäten,* published in 1798, he recognized the misery and cruelties engendered by the revolution, yet concluded that "it finds in all onlookers a sympathy which borders on enthusiasm." "Such a phenomenon in human history," said Kant, "is never forgotten; for it has revealed such a capacity for improvement in human nature as no politician ever dared to conjure up, and which only nature and freedom in combination can produce." [12]

3. NAPOLEON IN GERMANY

Despite the widespread intellectual reaction against the revolution, there was no enthusiasm for war with France. The Peace of Basel in 1795 between France and Prussia was widely acclaimed. Napoleon's ascension to power was on the whole greeted with favor. The nationalist reaction against France did not reach its full height until 1813, in Prussia's War of Liberation.

Friction between revolutionary France and the German states, particularly Austria and Prussia, came about because of the sanctuary found by French émigrés on German soil and because of the abolition of the feudal and ecclesiastical jurisdictions by the revolution which affected German holdings in Alsace. Prussia joined the first coalition against France in

1792. The Prussian armies suffered military defeats at Valmy and Jemappes, and the French troops under Custine conquered the Rhineland and were received warmly by large sections of the German population. The ruling dynasty, as well as Prussian public opinion, was anxious to have peace, and suspicion of Austria prevented the joint action against France that the situation demanded. In 1795 Prussia signed the separate Peace of Basel giving France a free hand west of the Rhine and receiving in return compensations east of the Rhine. The treaty of Campo Formio with Austria in 1797 formally recognized the cession of the entire left bank of the Rhine to France.

Napoleon's policy in Germany was to play off Prussia against Austria, isolating Austria and trying to throw enough crumbs to Prussia to keep her attached to France but not strong enough to dominate the rest of Germany. His policy toward the smaller states consisted of manipulating them as his satellites and building them up at the expense of the larger states. Thus Bavaria, Württemberg, and later Saxony were raised to the status of kingdoms, and these states, as well as Baden, received additional territory from Austria after the Peace of Pressburg in 1805.

The weakening of Austria was further advanced by the destruction of the old Holy Roman Empire. A preliminary step had been taken by the diet of the empire on February 25, 1803, when it passed the *Reichsdeputationshauptschluss,* whereby 112 estates of the empire were wiped out, all the ecclesiastical states dissolved except the electorate of Mainz, the imperial knights eliminated as independent sovereigns, and the number of free cities reduced to six. All in all, the number of sovereign states in the empire had been reduced to about thirty. The final blow to the empire came on August 6, 1806, when Francis II was forced by Napoleon to renounce his title as emperor and become Francis I of Austria. Without lamentation or the shedding of tears, the old Holy Roman Empire, which had aspired to carry on the glories of Charlemagne, Otto, and the Hohenstaufens, came to an inglorious end. In its place came the wrestling by the Germans with the phenomenon of modern nationalism.

The first semblance of national unification in Germany (as in Italy) was provided by Napoleon when he created the Confederation of the Rhine on July 17, 1806. Under his suzerainty Bavaria, Württemberg, Baden, Hesse-Darmstadt, and twelve smaller German states were united to form what Napoleon sometimes conceived of as a "Third Germany" to balance the states of Prussia and Austria. Subsequently the Kingdom of Saxony entered the confederation. Hanover was occupied by France as part of Napoleon's fight against England. The Rhineland was incorporated into the French empire and divided into four departments. Out of the states of Hesse-Cassel and Brunswick, Napoleon created the Kingdom of Westphalia for his brother Jerome in 1807. The entrance of Prussia into the war against Napoleon resulted in its most disastrous military defeat at Jena on October 14, 1806, and the occupation of Berlin by Napoleon on October 27. The war with Prussia came to an end with the Peace of Tilsit in 1807, and Prussia entered a period of what Germans have come to call "deep humiliation," as well as a period of preparation and strengthening of economic, military, and spiritual resources for eventual liberation.

Napoleonic policy in Germany represented a combination of the attempt to exploit the country for French interests with a missionary and civilizing aim to bring to Germany the benefits of what Napoleon had selected from the revolutionary heritage. In Berlin and in his triumphal tours through the other German states, Napoleon acted as the vulgar conqueror. He collected tribute and requisitions and ordered raids on "undesirable" persons and against alleged conspiracies. His execution of the bookseller Palm in Nürnberg because of the latter's publication of the pamphlet *Deutschland in seiner tiefen Erniederung* engendered considerable resentment, and still more was aroused by the cold-blooded murder of the Duc d'Enghien. But Napoleonic rule in Germany was also responsible for immediate and direct reforms that lasted on into the restoration period. With Napoleon, despite his own dictatorial rule, the old absolutist order came to an end. In the areas administered directly by him, feudalism was abolished and the elimination of the ecclesiastical states in the Rhineland made way for small peasant proprietors. Jewish disabilities were abolished, and freedom of worship both for Protestants and for Jews was recognized. The French system of weights and measures was introduced and freedom of trade established. Above all, the Code Napoléon, with its great civilizing effects, became the legal code for all of western Germany and remained such ever after. Offering his advice to his brother Jerome for the rule of the Westphalian kingdom, Napoleon wrote:

> The benefits of the Code Napoléon, the publicity of procedure, the establishment of juries, will be so many distinctive characteristics of your monarchy. . . . It is necessary that your people should enjoy a liberty, an equality, and a degree of well-being unknown to the people of Germany. . . . What people would wish to revert to Prussian despotism, when it has once tasted the benefits of a wise and liberal government? [13]

The support which Napoleonic rule received from the German people was much more widespread than the impression subsequently created by Prussian writers. In the first decade of the century most German writers and statesmen hailed Napoleon as either "a prince of peace" or as the "regenerator of Germany." The Bavarian writer von Aretin in 1809 identified Napoleon with "true Germanism," and the same view was echoed in Baden. The Prussian parson Bodenburg glorified Napoleon as "the hero that has arisen out of the wondrous days of antiquity." Even the patriot Ernst Moritz Arndt had welcomed Napoleon in his ode *Der Mächtige*. The Chief Prince Primate of the Confederation of the Rhine,

Archbishop Dalberg, said of Napoleon: "Napoleon's genius does not confine itself to making the happiness of France; the great man is intended by Providence for the world." And Hegel wrote on the day before the battle of Jena, "As I formerly, now everybody wishes success to the French army." [14]

4. THE "REGENERATION" OF PRUSSIA

It should be pointed out too that even the architects of the regeneration of Prussia and of ultimate victory over Napoleon were, with all their hatred of the French, impressed by the way in which the unity and strength of France had been advanced by the revolutionary ideas, and they sought to adapt many of these reforms for the strengthening of their own country. This was true of Prince Hardenberg in particular, but it was similarly true of Gneisenau, Scharnhorst, and Stein. Hardenberg, like so many of the German leaders, identified the French revolution with Napoleon. He advocated "the application of the ideas of the French revolution to Prussia" combined with the traditional monarchy. In his Memorial of 1807 to Frederick William III, Hardenberg wrote: "Your Majesty! We must do from above what the French have done from below." Earlier in 1794 he had elaborated his political ideas which indicate the close affinity of his thinking with that of Napoleon. He wanted to open the paths to a career to men of talent, to secure equal distribution of burdens, security of property and person, and the combination of "true liberty with religion and civil order."

> The French revolution [wrote Hardenberg] . . . has brought the French people a new vigor, despite all their turmoil and bloodshed. . . . It is an illusion to think that we can resist the revolution effectively by clinging more closely to the old order, by proscribing the new principles without pity. This has been precisely the cause which has favored the revolution and facilitated its development. The force of these principles is such, their attraction and diffusion is so universal, that the state which refuses to acknowledge them will be condemned to submit or to perish. . . .
>
> Thus our . . . guiding principle must be a revolution in the better sense, a revolution leading directly to the great goal, the elevation of humanity through the wisdom of those in authority and not through a violent impulsion from within or without. Democratic rules of conduct in a monarchical administration, such is the formula . . . which will conform most perfectly to the spirit of the age. [15]

Gneisenau, in July, 1807, attributed French greatness to the fact that the "revolution had aroused all the forces and had apportioned to each force its appropriate sphere of influence. That is why the armies came to be led by heroes, the highest positions in administration were held by statesmen and at the head of a great nation it took the greatest man out of its midst." [16] From the revolution Gneisenau and Stein learned to know "what endless forces not developed and not utilized slumber in the bosom of a nation," and they wanted to muster the same totality of energy for the strength of the Prussian state. It was not the ideals of liberty that inspired them, but the totalitarian and authoritarian aspects of French nationalism—the united nation, the nation in arms, and the subordination of the individual to the nation state. Baron vom Stein, in his *Denkschrift* of September 11, 1807, pointed to the creative energy engendered by the French revolution, and indicated that only the diffusion of the same kind of spirit could overthrow Napoleon. Varnhagen von Ense tells of how Stein had made a study of the French revolution and of his unbounded hatred of it. But he also tells how Stein revealed his admiration for "the prodigious force and unparalleled power with which the Committee of Public Safety ruled France internally, and victoriously defied all external foes. These powerful measures, this fearful rigor, and almost superhuman energy, impressed him; they suited his nature and taste, they were such as he would have liked to turn against the French for the deliverance of Germany." [17]

The legislative reforms actually carried out in Prussia, first by Stein and then by Hardenberg, paralleled in many respects, as Seeley has pointed out, the work of the French revolution and Napoleon. Stein's emancipatory edict was analogous to August 4 in France; the administrative reform followed the pattern of the constitution of 1791, while the military reforms were inspired by the work of Carnot and the armies of the revolution.

The Prussian state, overwhelmed by the military debacles and weakened by the wavering and vacillating policies of Frederick William III, started on the road toward regaining the position in Germany and Europe that it had occupied under Frederick II and toward eventual liberation from Napoleon's rule, through the work of a group of patriotic intellectuals and a number of able statesmen and military leaders. Schleiermacher, Fichte, Arndt, Jahn, Görres, and Wilhelm von Humboldt stirred the patriotic conscience of Germans and directed their patriotic hopes and aspirations toward Prussia as the only possible redeemer from Napoleonic oppression. Stein, Hardenberg, Wilhelm von Humboldt, Gneisenau, and Scharnhorst were the architects of the reforms in the Prussian state that made possible the "regeneration" of Prussia.

Friedrich Schleiermacher, "the enlightened Pietist," who passed from a Herrnhut youth through the Enlightenment to romanticism, served first in Halle and then in Berlin as a university professor and as a preacher. As such he came to be known as "the first great political preacher of the Germans since the time of Luther." From 1804 through 1815 he fought from the pulpit as the armies fought in the field of battle. He addressed the troops before they departed, and in the Dreifaltigkeit Kirche in Berlin he preached some of the most passionate sermons in the history of homiletics. A contemporary has left us a stirring description of Schleiermacher giving young soldiers a parting message before they went off to battle.

His sonorous, clear and penetrating voice [records R. F. Eylert] rang through the solemn silence of the overflowing church. With pious ecstasy and intense conviction he animated every heart, and the full and clear flow of his powerful oration swept everything away with it. . . . His entire sermon was one torrent and each word emanated from the times and was for the times. When, after addressing the young recruits with all the fire of his enthusiasm, he turned to their mothers and concluded with the words: "Blessed be your bodies which bore such sons, blessed be your breasts that gave such children to suck," the whole assemblage was seized with convulsions and amidst loud weeping and sobbing Schleiermacher pronounced his final Amen.[18]

It was Schleiermacher more than any other at this time who elaborated a philosophy of national education intended to infuse a common spirit into the people by transmitting to the succeeding generations the values and spirit that had become part of the national heritage. The way to German patriotism and German nationalism, he believed, must come first by means of educational and moral regeneration. This too was the burden of Fichte's famous *Addresses to the German Nation* delivered in 1807 at the University of Berlin. The former Jacobin and Freemason now joined Schleiermacher in the task of creating among his countrymen the national will to resist the foreigner. It was not the spirit of the peaceful citizen's allegiance to laws and constitution that Fichte now demanded, but "the devouring flame of higher patriotism, which embraces the nation as the vesture of the eternal, for which the noble-minded man joyfully sacrifices himself, and the ignoble man, who only exists for the sake of the other, must likewise sacrifice himself." [19] Fichte's *Reden* did not, at the time they were delivered, create as much of a stir as described in the exaggerated accounts of later historians. Nor was his nationalist feeling as narrow and as chauvinistic as interpreted by later nationalists. In the words of Hans Kohn, "Fichte's patriotism was a call to spiritual regeneration, its effects were something different." Fichte's entire concept of "German" was not the usual nationalist one. He did not divide mankind into Germans and non-Germans, but rather into those who believed in the spontaneous originality and liberty of man and those who did not. The former, Fichte held, were Germans, no matter what their racial or political affiliation; the latter were not.[20] He did, however, develop the concept of a nation as a living community with the living urge to growth and expansion. It is this which, according to Fichte, gives legitimacy to Machiavelli's concept of the state as a power and to the principle of *raison d'état*.

A group of political journalists and pamphleteers began, in the second decade of the century, to rouse public opinion in Prussia and in Austria for the final reckoning with Napoleon. Ernst Moritz Arndt turned from Swedish to Prussian patriotism and entered the service of Baron vom Stein to spread hatred of the foreigner. Görres, converted from his youthful Jacobinism to nationalist traditionalism, but possessed of the same ardor, passion, and magnetism, exercised a tremendous influence on the German youth. His speeches, wrote Eichendorff, were "like the roar of the sea in the distance, rising and falling . . . like an effulgent and powerful storm, rousing and igniting for the whole life." Görres took over the newspaper *Rheinische Merkur* and made it, in the words of Wilhelm Grimm, "a bastion of German liberty." It was disseminated in all regions of Germany and among all classes of the population, and became such a tremendous force that Napoleon labeled it the "fifth great power."

Father Jahn, influenced by Arndt to enlarge his national feeling from Prussia to all of Germany, published in 1810 the famous political pamphlet *Deutsches Volkstum,* in which he demanded a reform of the Prussian army and urged the replacing of a standing army by an army of volunteers. His gymnastic organization, also founded in 1810, spread throughout Germany to become even more influential during the restoration period. But he and his followers carried on their patriotic agitation in a manner which even the nationalist historian Treitschke finds shocking. He manifested, writes Treitschke, "some of the most ludicrous traits which marred the new Germanism: rough and arrogant hatred of the foreigner, noisy boasting, contempt for all that was graceful and refined." Incidentally it was Jahn who coined the word *Volkstum.*

It was as part of this political agitation that the romantic cult of the Rhine emerged. The national romantic adulation of the Rhine as a symbol of German spirit was largely the work of Görres and Arndt during these years. Before this there was little attention paid to the Rhine in German literature. It was only when the Rhine was in the hands of the foreigner that the love of the river became a cult of nationalist enthusiasts. Görres followed the German troops in the Rhineland, encouraging them and proclaiming that "our earliest ancestors never recognized the Rhine as the German frontier"—this in plain contradiction to his proclamation seventeen years earlier that the Rhine was Germany's proper boundary line. After the battle of Leipzig in 1813 Stein and Gneisenau vowed not to make peace before the left bank of the Rhine was liberated, and Stein inspired Arndt to write his "Der Rhein, Teutschlands Strom, aber nicht Teutschlands Grenze," in which he set up language as the primary criterion of nationality. Herder's humanitarian and cultural nationalism was now turned to the cause of political and romantic nationalism. To the query: Where is the German fatherland? Arndt replies: It is wherever the German tongue is spoken, thus transcending all territorial and natural frontiers. This is the beginning of that fusion of culture and politics, of universalism and nationalism, out of which subsequent romantic dreams of pan-Germanism and expansionism were derived.

The chief architect of the reform of the Prussian state, Karl Freiherr vom Stein (1757–1831), was an imperial knight of Nassau, whose passionate hatred of the "foreigner" led him to the service of the Prussian state. His education at Göttingen and his close association with Rehberg brought him into contact with British ideas and institutions, and he always posed British traditionalism and gradualism against the eruptive revolutionary spirit of France. But he wanted to achieve in Germany what the French revolution had accomplished in France—the total mobilization of the moral and physical energies of the German people for the rebirth of the German nation. After the battle of Jena, when he attacked the inefficiency of the Prussian ministers, he was forced to resign, but was recalled in 1807. He served again from October 1, 1807, to November 24, 1808, when once again pressure forced him to resign. During the subsequent period he was engaged in conspiratorial work and then entered the service of Alexander I of Russia. Stein's reform work was then carried on in Prussia by Prince von Hardenberg.

The chief reforms in Prussia were social and economic, administrative, educational, and military. The edict of October 9, 1807, brought about the emancipation of the Prussian peasantry. This edict did not convert the peasantry into laborers or farmer proprietors. It merely abolished the legal aspects of serfdom. The "status" of serfdom was eliminated. Manorial jurisdiction of the landowners remained, and even unlimited manorial police power survived until 1872. Little was done to help the peasants economically. But the nobility lost its rights over the person of the peasant. The peasant could move about freely, marry off his children as he willed, select occupations for his children without interference, and so on. At the same time nobles were permitted to engage in "citizen occupations," and peasants and citizens were allowed to assume mortgages on noble lands. The old *Stände* thus were converted into modern "classes." Hardenberg, who carried on the work of Stein, was much more the follower of the physiocrats and Adam Smith. In a series of edicts in 1810 and 1811 he brought about the elimination of old economic corporations and medieval economic regulations, and established complete freedom of occupation and freedom of contract.

Administrative and municipal reform was also initiated by Stein. The municipal ordinance of November 17, 1808, established a system of municipal self-government with the participation of all the citizens in the town and created "islands of liberal citizenship" in Prussia. The administrative reform of November 24, 1808, established a modern bureaucracy in the Prussian state which became a model of discipline and efficiency. Both Stein and Hardenberg also had plans for some sort of legislative body. Neither of them had in mind a popularly elected body after the

style of the French. Stein conceived of an assembly of representatives of
Stände. The old medieval Reich tradition with its corporations still lived
on in him. Hardenberg wanted a legislative body of representatives appointed by the government. Nothing materialized out of any of these
plans, however, and a legislative assembly was not established in Prussia
until 1848. These legislative reforms, as Seeley has pointed out, came not
out of fear of the oppressive character of government but out of "a pity
for the government, a feeling that it is not fair in the people to wash
their hands altogether of public matters and to discharge the whole
burden upon their rulers. . . . The people are not allowed, but commanded, to govern themselves." [21]

In July, 1807, Gerhard Scharnhorst was appointed head of a committee to reorganize the army that had been so badly mauled by Napoleon.
He was assisted by Gneisenau, Grollman, Boyen, and Clausewitz. The
ideal of these military reformers was to emulate the French revolutionary
"nation in arms" organized by Carnot. The army was no longer to consist of slaves kept down by fear, but of enthusiastic and devoted patriots.
The system of flogging of soldiers was abolished, as was the hereditary
right to the officer class. Similarly, recruiting was eliminated and the en-
listing of foreigners forbidden. According to the terms of the treaty with
Napoleon, Prussia was not to have an army of more than 42,000 men.
Scharnhorst evolved the so-called "Krimper System," whereby the recruits
were drilled for a month and then given a leave of absence, thus maintain-
ing a reserve force of about 150,000. This made possible the army of
Blücher in the War of Liberation and also provided the model for the
German general staff after World War I.

To the social and economic, administrative and military reforms should
be added the educational reforms initiated by Wilhelm von Humboldt,
who served as head of the Prussian education ministry from March, 1809,
to June, 1810. Humboldt, the author of the most extreme *laissez faire*
political treatise and upholder of the supreme importance of the individual, now also turned to help strengthen the power of the Prussian state.
He was influenced by the educational ideals of Pestalozzi, Fichte, and
Schleiermacher, as well as by the national education system of the French
revolution and Napoleon. His educational ideal still remained the development of the free individual personality rather than the pursuit of vocational objectives, hence his labors in behalf of the unified school to replace
the old caste and vocational schools. But he now saw the greater need
for the state to take the initiative in the realization of this educational
ideal. Under Humboldt's régime, too, the final plans were made for the
organization of the University of Berlin, where soon were concentrated
all the great patriotic intellectual forces of the nation, to play their role
in the battle for liberation.

The example of the Spanish revolt against Napoleon in 1808 ignited the sparks of rebellion against Napoleon's rule throughout the countries under his subjection. His invincibility and prestige were badly shaken by this challenge to his power. The retreat from Moscow in 1812 was the last straw to set off the Prussian struggle against Napoleon. The defection of General Yorck, commander of the Prussian divisions of Napoleon's Grand Army, on December 30, 1812, and his agreement of neutrality with the Russian general, marked the beginning of Prussia's final reckoning with Napoleon. The weak-willed Frederick William III now took heart. The work of the patriot-intellectuals and the reforming statesmen bore fruit. Stein came to Königsberg, where the Prussian king had established his court, and brought pressure on the king to sign the Treaty of Kalisch between Russia and Prussia on February 28, 1813. The battle of Leipzig on October 16–19, with the decisive defeat of Napoleon by the Allies, forced Napoleon out of most of Germany and paved the way for the final victorious entry into Paris on March 31 of the following year. "Finally," wrote Stein to his wife on October 21, 1813, "one dares to allow one's self the feeling of happiness. Napoleon is defeated." The goal of the patriots had been achieved. The "villain" and "the enemy of the human race" was overthrown and the "one enemy of German independence, morality and progressive national development" was humbled in defeat. Both the right and the left banks of the Rhine were cleared of the hateful foreigner. The task of German unity loomed larger than ever before. But the realization of this goal was still to wait for half a century.

5. THE WAYS OF GERMAN ROMANTICISM

It was during the Napoleonic period that German romanticism attained its full-grown development. In Fichte and Schleiermacher, Novalis and Görres, Tieck and Wackenroder, Adam Müller and the Schlegel brothers, romanticism went far beyond a literary and esthetic movement to become an all-embracing and comprehensive *Weltanschauung* that left its deep impress on the future course of German history. Romanticism was, of course, a general European movement, and was far from being confined to Germany alone. Nor did it originate as a result of the French revolution. The antecedents of German romanticism go back to the Pietism of the seventeenth and eighteenth centuries, to the intellectual influence from England of Percy's *Reliques* and Ossian, to the enormous stimulus from Rousseau, and to the *Sturm und Drang* movement of the late eighteenth century. Given a normal process of development, German romanticism might well have taken the course of the romantic movements in other European countries. But the fact that the French revolution was identified with the principles of the Enlightenment meant also that romanticism, the movement that revolted against the Enlightenment, came to be identified with the counter-revolution. Because of the French occupation of Germany, therefore, German romanticism became an ideological weapon against the foreigner, against French rationalism, and against the revolutionary spirit. German romanticism, therefore, came to differ in a marked way from the romanticism of Europe at large. It assumed more extreme forms; it acquired a deeper and more lasting hold upon German intellectual life; it spread out over all areas of human activity to embrace not only literature, art, and music, but also science, scholarship, economics, and above all politics. Almost without exception German romanticists came to be identified with political reaction and conservative nationalism. In the history of German romanticism (apart from the special case of Heine) we find no parallels to libertarians like Lamartine and Victor Hugo in France, Mazzini in Italy, or Pushkin in Russia. Romanticism in Germany always maintained a mark of hostility to democratic and republican ideology and sentiment.

Romanticism as a literary movement began during the last years of the eighteenth century. Literary circles were established in Jena, in Berlin, in Dresden, and in Heidelberg. Perhaps no one embodied the romantic ideal in a purer and more ethereal form than the youthful Friedrich von Hardenberg (1772–1801), far better known under his pen name Novalis. He died too young to be able to realize the hopes of his followers that he become the "torchbearer" of the romantic protest against the Enlightenment, and he left a literary legacy that consists mainly of fragments. But his works revealed, wrote Eichendorff, "the whole internal history of modern romanticism, its truth and its errors, in all its main currents." Schleiermacher called him "the all-too-soon departed divine youth, who turned everything that his spirit touched into art, and whose entire view of the world was one great poem." What Novalis did not live to achieve was carried out by Friedrich Schlegel, called by Eichendorff "the real founder of romanticism."

The basic psychological feature of German romanticism was *Sehnsucht,* or yearning—yearning above all for the unattainable, for the lost, for the irrevocable, for the disappearing, for fancy, for dreams. This was symbolized in Heinrich von Ofterdingen's search for the "blue flower" in Novalis's allegorical romance of the same name. The romanticist reacted against the growing materialism and mechanization of the human spirit engendered by the new industrial and democratic age. He sought escape in flights of poetic fantasy, in sentimentality, and in allegory. He indulged in spiritual toying with death, and found greater affinity with the brooding, somber, dark, and opaque recesses of night than with the clarity of the bright day. "Life is a sickness of the spirit," wrote Novalis. And in his famous *Hymns to the Night,* Novalis sings to "Sacred Night, with her unspoken mysteries, who draws me to her." Night, says Novalis, "has aroused me to life and manhood," and "What joys or pleasures can life offer to outweigh the chain of death?" We have here the beginning of that esthetic pessimism, which is later reinforced by the philosophy of

Schopenhauer and the music of Wagner and culminates in the literary creation of Thomas Mann.

Romanticism uncovered the deeper irrational forces of the human spirit. It pointed out the inadequacy and the frequent shallowness of the logical thought processes of the *Aufklärung,* which all too often sacrificed the complexities and contradictions of human psychology for the sake of schematic and unilinear reasoning. Romanticism operated with the principle of polarity, with the reality of opposites. This gave it a richness of content alongside which the geometric rationalism of the Enlightenment looked pale and lifeless. "To the poet who comprehends the nature of his art to its center," wrote Novalis, "nothing appears contradictory and strange. To him all riddles are solved. By the magic of the imagination he can unite all ages and all worlds. Miracles disappear, and everything transforms itself into miracles." [22] Morbid sickliness was in this way combined with the glorification of heroism and might; admiration for pageantry and nobility went hand in hand with the worship of the simple peasant, and wild ecstasy alternated with naïve and serene simplicity. The romanticist was able, no doubt, to plumb the deeper recesses of the human soul, but the door was also thus opened to *Schwärmerei,* to charlatanism, to incoherence, to crackpot ideas, to dangerous irresponsibility that found in the principle of polarity a convenient vehicle whereby to escape the serious challenge of hard thinking. Georg Brandes, in introducing his readers to the romanticism of Novalis, compares his task to that of a guide leading a visitor down the subterranean shaft of a mine. "The shaft to which we are about to descend," writes Brandes, "is that of the German 'soul,' a mine as deep, as dark, as strange, as rich in precious metal and in worthless refuse as any other." [23]

The romantic movement was more, however, than a literary movement and more than a psychological attitude. At the hands of Adam Müller, Schlegel, Görres, Schleiermacher, and Fichte it asserted itself as a system of thought that was to replace the previously dominant rationalism of the *Aufklärung.* As opposed to the dominance of reason, the romanticist posited the all-importance of enthusiasm and feeling. "My soul is a passionate dancer," wrote Bettina von Arnim to her brother Klemens. "It jumps around according to inner dance music, which only I hear and no one else. All shout to me that I should calm down . . . but my soul does not listen to you in its passion for dance and if the dancing stops then it will also be the end of me." [24] This enthusiasm, first brought into German life by the Pietists, came to be transferred to the secular world and above all to the nation. It found an outlet in the patriotic literature of 1813. The *Wiedergeburt* of Spener and Zinzendorf became the national regeneration of Novalis and Fichte. It filled the poems of Arndt, Körner, and Schenkendorf, and through them it permeated the broad masses of the population.

Romanticism stressed inwardness and reflection upon one's self. *"Nach innen geht der geheimnisvoller Weg,"* said Novalis. Schleiermacher's *Monologen* is a superb expression of this delicate and sensitive inwardness. Inwardness, individuality, uniqueness, combined with manifoldness and variety, were to replace the essential oneness and sameness of the Enlightenment. In place of individualism came individuality. Schleiermacher recounts in his *Monologen* how he became disillusioned with the ideals of the Enlightenment.

For a long time I too [he writes] was content with the discovery of a universal reason: I worshipped the one essential being as the highest, and so believed there is but a single right way of acting in every situation, that the conduct of all men should be alike, each differing from the other only by reason of his place and station in the world. I thought humanity revealed itself as varied only in the manifold diversity of outward acts, that man himself, the individual, was not a being uniquely fashioned, but of one substance and everywhere the same.[25]

Rejecting this "general" conception of man, Schleiermacher turned inward to himself. "Only in his innermost activity, wherein his true nature abides, is [the individual] free." "As often as I turn my gaze inward upon my inmost self, I am at once within the domain of eternity." [26] This is what provides the uniqueness of the individual and marks the divine element in each being. Schleiermacher tells how he came to see that "each human element is meant to represent humanity in his own way." Humanity is thus not of one cast and of one mold, but is all the richer for its manifoldness and variety. For the veneration of one's own uniqueness and individuality means also the recognition of legitimate variety. And the romantic individualist felt the strong need of fellowship and community with others. The romanticist was not an individualist anarchist. Far from it. He recognized the need for community feeling, for corporate individualities as well as for single individualities. "Everything I do," said Schleiermacher, "I like to do in the company of others."

I feel the communion with mankind augments my own powers in every moment of my life. Each of us plies his own particular trade, completing the work of someone whom he never knew, or preparing the way for another who in turn will scarcely recognize how much he owes to him. Thus the work of humanity is promoted throughout the world. . . . By the ingenious mechanism of this community the slightest movement of each individual is conducted like an electric spark through a long chain of a thousand living links, greatly amplifying its final effect: all are as it were members of a great organism, and whatever they may have done severally is instantaneously consummated as its work.[27]

Life, wrote Schleiermacher, "is an alternation between an abiding-in-self (*Insichleben*) and a passing-beyond-self (*Aussichheraustreten*) on the part of the subject."

Thus romanticism was easily converted from extreme individualism to the worship of the organic community and from the extolling of free personality to the recognition that true individuality is found only in the collective national individuality. Literary and esthetic romanticism became political romanticism. Seeking satisfaction not in the rational and well established rules of tradition but in the realization of personality and in the untrammeled expression of subjective emotion, it soon came to be recognized that these deep and irrational forces of subjective personality do not come into being spontaneously but are deeply embedded in the individual's early memories, in the songs and tales imbibed in his childhood, and in his entire cultural and physical milieu. Romanticism thus exhibited an ardent interest in all forms of folk creation and in the native countryside. Once these were recognized, it followed that one's individuality was not separate and apart from all other individualities, but integrated into a greater organism of land and nation. This explains the otherwise seeming paradox of the identity of highly developed individualism with collective nationalism, which seem so utterly opposed to each other. The comparative folklore of the brothers Grimm and the popularity of the *Knaben Wunderhorn* were the most marked evidences of this tendency. This interest in folk culture also helped to stimulate a sort of "patriarchal democracy" in which monarch and *Volk* were united into one ideal whole.

We arrive here at what was no doubt the most fundamental and most far-reaching political and social concept of romanticism, the organismic theory of the state. In taking issue with the political theories of the Enlightenment, the romanticists rejected entirely the natural-rights doctrine and the social contract. The contractual nature of the state they regarded as abstract, artificial, and mechanical. The state was for them a living organism, a *macroanthropos,* a living individuality which was not merely a sum of individuals bound together by a rational contract but organically related by blood, by descent, by tradition, and by history. It was to all intents and purposes the corporate *moi* of Rousseau's state after the social contract has been formed, in which each individual is indissolubly linked to the whole like each limb of the body of the individual. The organic state has its spirit, its unique individuality like the unique individual. This becomes the germ of the romantic theory of nationalism. Novalis and Schleiermacher provided the initial suggestive ideas for the theory. It was developed in its fullest form by Adam Müller, who often caricatured the theories of the Enlightenment in order to make his case stronger and who also acknowledged the indebtedness of German romanticism to Burke for the full working out of this theory.

Müller conceived of the state as being more than "an institution of convenience," more than a "cushion of indolence" (*Polster der Trägheit*), as Novalis called it, more than the "neutral commercial, business and insurance company" which receives the civic dues, payments, and taxes of the "citizen stock-holder." The state must absorb the innermost feelings and thoughts of the individual. The body of the state, holds Müller, is not the physical assets and wealth of the state, not the transitory ruler, estates, or bureaucracy. The body of the state is made up of the ancient and hoary traditions that are just as immediate for the present and the future as they are for the past. The individual, therefore, can never and should never act for himself alone and in "absolutely new fashion." His deeds must always be the "continuation of the deeds of his ancestors."

Adam Müller, more than any other of the German romanticists, paid his homage to the Englishman Burke, "the one who first described the state as an immortal family," "the greatest, most profound, mightiest and most human of all statesmen of all times and of all nations." In the same way in which August Wilhelm von Schlegel claimed that the Germans really understood and honored Shakespeare more than the British, so Müller claimed greater appreciation for Burke in Germany than in his native land. "I say it with pride," declared Müller, "he belongs to us more than to the British. I glory in the fact that my own ideas of the state, though perhaps not ripe children, are none the less hopeful children (grandchildren I might call them) of his spirit. He is recognized in Germany as the most influential and happiest mediator between liberty and law, between separation and unity of powers and of labor, between the principle of nobility and that of the bourgeoisie, and thus, no matter how influential his deeds may have been for Great Britain, his glory belongs to the German sphere." [28]

Organicism and traditionalism led romanticism to medievalism. The earliest beginnings of the organic community were traced back to the Middle Ages. The national tradition in its purest form, uncontaminated by foreign and cosmopolitan influences, is to be found in the medieval epoch. Hence the preoccupation of romanticists with the folk tales and folk songs of the Middle Ages. Görres's *Die teutschen Volksbücher,* and Achim von Arnim's and Clemens Brentano's *Des Knaben Wunderhorn* and Tieck's collection *Die altdeutschen Minnelieder,* were expressions of this literary medievalism. But the Middle Ages also provided the best example of an organic society. "For all times," wrote Novalis, "will this society be a model for all societies that feel an organic yearning for unending expansion and eternal existence." "The task of politics," wrote Schlegel, "is to reestablish the constitution of the Middle Ages and to bring it to full realization." This is the foundation for the vogue of the *Ständestaat,* or corporate state idea of political romanticism, as well as for the harking back to the pre-capitalist society as found in the romantic economics of Franz von Baader and Adam Müller. But it was, above all, the religious character of the Middle Ages that captivated the souls of the romanticists. Eichendorff pointed out the religious foundation of the romantic movement. Novalis, in his *Christenheit und Europa* (1799), laments the "fatal decline" of spiritual life in Europe and points to the turning away from religion as the basis for this spiritual poverty. He looks back to "the beautiful and glorious time, when Europe was a Christian land, inhabited by *one* Christianity." In this religious and Christian worship of the Middle Ages Novalis and the romanticists went beyond the merely historical and esthetic rediscovery of the Gothic and the medieval as found in Herder's *Auch eine Philosophie der Geschichte.* It was Luther and Protestantism, declared Novalis, that put an end to the unity of Christendom and opened the way for the deterioration of Christian influence. Only the return to the true religion of medieval society, to Catholicism. with its hierarchical church structure and its theocratic society will bring about "the divine period of eternal peace." This religious medievalism brought about the numerous conversions of romanticists to Catholicism— Novalis, Friedrich Schlegel, Adam Müller, Count Stolberg, and others.

It is to the everlasting credit of the romantic movement to have brought about the deepening of the historical sense and the resulting development of scientific history. The Enlightenment had been "peculiarly unhistorical." History in the eighteenth century was pragmatic and generalizing. Romantic medievalism initiated the more objective study and evaluation of the Middle Ages, hitherto neglected by the rationalist Enlightenment. The chain of connection that binds the present to the earlier generations made investigation of the origins of the European nations a matter of national urgency. One of the achievements of Baron vom Stein was to initiate the collection and publication of the epoch-making series of documents of German history, the *Monumenta Germaniae Historica,* which became the model for scientific editions of historical documents. This aspect of romanticism was not without its precursors. The study of medieval documents had been initiated by the Benedictines of St. Maur in France and by Muratori in Italy. Similarly the philology and epigraphy that emanated from the classical humanistic movement and that reached its apogee in Friedrich August Wolf (1759–1824) developed before and independently of the romantic movement. But German romanticism added to these instruments of scholarly investigation the all-important conception of historical uniqueness and individuality, of what Dilthey was later to call *Einmaligkeit,* and thus breathed into historical scholarship what we have come to call today "historical-mindedness." The purpose of the historian was no longer that of a cosmopolitan philosopher set on learning the lessons to be derived from history, but rather to study origins, connections, and development, and above all to study the unique aspects of a given age in its own terms. World history became national history, and the role of the state and of political institutions supplanted the history of ideas. Out of this intellectual climate came the epoch-making historical scholarship of Barthold Georg Niebuhr (1776–1831) and Leopold von Ranke (1795–1886).

Similarly German romanticism deepened the study of language and speech. Its concern with the basic character of the organic community brought the recognition that language was not just a useful vehicle for communication but that it was the repository of the deepest emotions and traditions of a people. Language is the vehicle of thought, hence the uniqueness of national languages. An individual may know several languages, but only one is peculiarly his own. "Language," wrote Görres, "is the great bond that binds individuals together," and the culture of language is indissolubly linked with the culture of a people. "What is there," asks Schlegel, "more completely characteristic of man, or of greater importance to him than language?" Here too the romantic movement was antedated by the lexicography of J. C. Adelung and by the philosophical analysis of language by J. G. Hamann and Herder. Hamann, especially, anticipated the romantic theory of language. Like the romanticists, Hamann's approach was tinged with a deep religious and mystical tone that came from his pietist background. Language was recognized not only as the expression of the inner character of an individual, but likewise as the expression of the psyche of a people. What was, however, of purely cultural concern for Hamann and Herder now became in the hands of the romanticists a political weapon. We have already seen how Görres and Arndt made language their weapon against French occupation of the Rhineland. The brothers Schlegel and the Grimm brothers took up the work of Hamann and Herder, to lay the foundation for the scientific study of language and comparative language. It was Schlegel who coined the ill fated dictum of *quot linguae tot gentes,* which became the basis for linguistic racialism. But the motivation was not purely scientific. As in the case of history and folklore, language became "national language" and a tool for that process which Carlton Hayes has described as the transmission of nationalist ideology from the classes to the masses.

German romanticism rejected all democratic ideology of popular sovereignty. Yet it developed a kind of populism, or cult of the people of its own. It saw in the common people the healthy core and reservoir of national creative energy. Its interest in folk literature and folk creations sprang from this "populism" and at the same time contributed to it. Joseph Görres, in his introduction to his *Die teutschen Volksbücher,* pointed out how much richer German literature had become since it moved out of the closed circle of the higher classes and identified itself with the lower classes, with the *Volk,* of which "all genius of virtue, art and scholarship . . . are the fruits." Ernst Moritz Arndt aspired to a synthesis of the democratic nationalism of the French revolution with the traditional hierarchical structure of German society. The Germans took from Rousseau and the French revolution the "democratic" idea of state sovereignty, but identified it not with the people but rather with the royal power. Novalis, fortified no doubt by his principle of polarity and law of opposites, posed the otherwise meaningless paradox of the identity of true monarchy with true republicanism. Novalis dreamed of an ideal monarchy which would at the same time be a real republic. Real republicanism was for him "general participation by all in the entire state and inner contact and harmony of all members of the state." But the unity and harmony of all should be embodied in one exemplary individual—the monarch. "The king is the pure life principle of the state in quite the same way as the sun is that of the solar system." The monarch is not the first servant of the state. The distinguishing feature of monarchy, for Novalis, is that it rests on the faith in a higher born individual, on the voluntary acceptance of an ideal man. "I cannot elect a superior from among my equals," said Novalis. "I cannot turn anything over to one who is in precisely the same condition I am in. The monarchy is therefore the only genuine system because it is tied to an absolute center, to a being who belongs to humanity but not to the state." A time will soon come, predicted Novalis, when there will be universal conviction that there cannot be a king without a republic nor a republic without a king, that both are as inextricably linked as body and soul, and that a king without a republic, as a republic without a king, are only words without meaning. This is not too far off from the Führer principle of later years, in which also the older distinction between monarchy and republic lost all meaning.

Finally German romanticism developed a cult of estheticism which looked upon all phases of human existence from the standpoint of art and which saw the solution to all human problems by the extension of the esthetic approach to all realms of existence. This "estheticization" was part of the revolt against reason. It sought to apprehend unity and immediacy in one instantaneous act. This is the typical intuitive approach of the poet. The true historian, according to both Novalis and Schlegel, is likewise a poet, because "poets alone know the art of skillfully combining events." But not only the historian; all life has poetry as its origin. "Poetry creates life." "The kernel of my philosophy," wrote Novalis, "is the belief that the poetical is the absolutely real, and that the more poetical anything is, the truer it is. Therefore the task of the poet is not to idealize, but to cast a spell." As a poet he approached problems of science, philosophy, history, religion, and politics. Some branded this attitude as the way of the dilettante. For the romanticist it was the way of reality and truth. Schelling called the state "a work of art," and Novalis, following him, declared:

A true prince is the artist of artists, the poet of artists. Every individual should be an artist. Everything can become fine art. The materials of the prince are the artist's; his will is his chisel. . . . The regent is the director of an unending and multi-varied play, where stage and parterre, actors and spectators are all one and he himself is at one and the same time poet, director and hero of the play.[29]

It is this estheticization of politics, particularly in the neo-romanticism of later times, that supplied legitimacy to the acts of the dictator. Just as the poetic genius creates best by his own laws and his own intuitive powers, so the Führer and the Duce conceive of their political leadership as emanating from the same sort of intuitive and creative genius that is just as immune from outside analysis and rational argumentation as the work of a Shakespeare or a Goethe.

The French revolutionary epoch thus may be said to mark the beginnings of modern Germany. The old order was completely shattered. Practical reforms introduced by Napoleon or by the Prussian reform leaders radically altered the character of social and political institutions. Liberalism became fixed in German tradition as being identified with the foreigner, while political conservatism and romanticism came to be identified with "higher" German nationalism. National hate against the French expressed itself in a reaction against the *Vernunftrechtliche,* or rationalist legal ideas of the French revolution. The hate motif made its entrance into German consciousness. The deep and passionate hatred which was deliberately propagated by Stein and Arndt, Fichte and Jahn, was not soon forgotten. Perhaps the most extreme form of political passion found expression in Heinrich von Kleist. Kleist more than any other German of the period exemplified the *Zerrissenheit,* that internal struggle with the daemon, which sought resolution in passionate attachment to nation and fatherland, but which, in the period of national catastrophe, could find no way out except suicide. Kleist combined, as no other romanticist did, glorification of the ancient Germanic with anti-Roman, anti-Christian, and anti-French sentiment. His *Katechismus der Deutschen,* and especially his *Hermannsschlacht,* represent the most passionate examples of poetic genius concentrated on the patriotic service of hate. Eichendorff called it "a magnificent poem of hate." A morbid bitterness against the outside world set in, and even after the triumph over the French "there still remained in the hearts of the spirited Teutons a profound rancor against the foreign world. It seemed impossible to dream of Germany's future greatness without railing at the foreign nations which had sinned so often and so grossly against Central Europe" (Treitschke). The toleration of Jews during the Frederickian age and during the epoch of Napoleonic reforms gave way to bitter antisemitic feeling. The heroic and militarist virtues of the ancient Germans and of the *Landsknecht Lieder* were revived. Romanticism glorified war as a virtue in itself. It set up the ideal of the "blond German youth," who despising the *"Strohtod,"* or peaceful death, would be conducted from the warrior's field of honor to Valhalla. "No more noble death in the world than to be smitten down by the enemy" foreshadows by more than mere suggestion the "education for death" of later days, when Philip Gibbs in 1935 reported a German Catholic youth at his first Mass praying that "he might die with a French bullet in his heart."

Most significant of all, this epoch marks the turn from cosmopolitanism to German nationalism, from *Weltbürgertum* to *Nationalstaat*. The politicization of German intellectuals turned them away from the purely cultural nationalism of Herder to the political nationalism of Schleiermacher and Fichte, Arndt and Görres, Müller and Gentz, Stein and Clausewitz. Not that cosmopolitanism had completely disappeared. National feeling, as Friedrich Meinecke has brilliantly shown, was still fused with a large mixture of universalism. *"Deutschheit,"* said Novalis, "is cosmopolitanism mixed with the most powerful individualism." Meinecke points out rightly that the Prussian patriots in 1812–1813 divided Europe into the areas of freedom and unfreedom, and identified Prussian and German national freedom with universal and individual freedom. Stein's conception of a national state was still full of the cosmopolitanism of the eighteenth century, and his notion of the future of Germany was made dependent on the general European settlement. What Meinecke did not see, however, was that it was this very mixture of universalism with romantic nationalism which gave to German nationalism first its chiliastic and eschatological character of a *"Wiedergeburt"* or regeneration, then the foundation for its mission idea, and finally its expansionism beyond its own borders. Novalis as well as Fichte identified Germanism with universalism. But universalism and nationalism are fused through the concept of the mission of Germany to civilize the rest of the world. It was no longer the universalism of Herder and the eighteenth century, that of a garden of many colors blended to create a more diverse and richly colored universe. Out of the defeat and resentment of the Napoleonic wars emerged the superiority notion of Germany as the purest spiritual and cultural nation destined to lead the world to "true universality." Where the dream of a universal European state federation persisted, as in Novalis's dream of a revived medieval Christian Europe, there lurked in the background the notion of German hegemony and leadership. All the nations of Europe are bound together, but, says Adam Müller, Germany is "the mother of the nations of present-day Europe." It is precisely in Germany's capacity for universality that Fichte and Görres, Müller and Schlegel, saw the preeminence of the German spirit. Wilhelmian pan-Germanism, as well as Nazi expansionism, drank deeply from this romantic nationalist universalism.

CHAPTER IV

The Restoration in Germany, 1815-1848

Alle Freiheitsapostel, sie waren mir immer zuwider
Willkür suchte doch nur jeder am Ende für sich.

GOETHE

The period following the downfall of Napoleon was known in Germany, as in the rest of Europe, as the period of the Restoration.[1] The enemies of the French revolution, as well as the opponents of the despotism of Bonapartist Caesarism, were restored to their former and "legitimate" positions. But the forces released by the French revolution and the wars of the revolution could not be completely eradicated. While "legitimacy" triumphed as far as political power was concerned, the conflict between the old and the new continued on in the world of ideas. "There never was an epoch," wrote Wilhelm von Humboldt in 1816, "in which everywhere and at all points the old and the new ages appeared in such sharp contrast."

The tremendous enthusiasm engendered in Germany during the War of Liberation subsided considerably during the years immediately following the settlement of 1815. The hopes alike of radical nationalists and of romantic reactionaries for glorious and "final" solutions of the problems of Central Europe were far from realized, and ideological conflicts continued during the epoch of 1815 to 1848. This was a period in which the heirs of eighteenth century Enlightenment and rationalism fought a losing battle against the great and swelling tide of romanticism. F. C. Schlosser, in his history of the eighteenth century, and Karl von Rotteck, in his political treatises, clung to the worship of reason and the ideas of 1789, which they made the basis of their political liberalism. The aging Goethe still lived on for fifteen years to embody in his person as well as in his writings the gospel of classical harmony and restraint. But as against these came the swell of the much more influential and more widespread torrent of romanticism.

The restoration period also witnessed the continuing battle between conservatism and liberalism. Georg Wilhelm Friedrich Hegel (1770–1831)

50

represented an attempted synthesis of these two currents in much the same way as Goethe symbolized the harmony between the classic and the romantic. Hegel combined the rationalism of the eighteenth century with the new individualizing historicism of the nineteenth. His theory of the dialectic was an attempt to find a logic and inner meaning in the process of history that was open to rational and scientific observation and analysis. His views on constitutionalism were closely akin to the moderate British type of liberalism of the time. But his emphasis on the idea of development and change, his conception of the *Volksgeist,* or unique spirit which is inherent in each national group; his elaboration of the idea of the *Machtstaat,* with its worship of the powerful state as the highest political entity, subject to no other law but its own; and his acceptance of the Prussian patriarchal state of his own time as the concrete realization of his political ideal, all marked a definite break with the liberal, rational, and universal tradition of the Enlightenment and a closer affinity with romantic and historical nationalism and conservatism. The attempted synthesis, therefore, which may be found in Hegel's own system broke up soon after his death into the rival camps of radical young Hegelians and reactionary right Hegelians. While the theory of the dialectic was appropriated by Marx and the radicals, the idea of the *Machtstaat* became one of the chief ideological weapons of the nationalist and militarist tradition of later-day Germany. During the restoration period, too, the older humanitarian nationalism, as represented by Herder and Schiller, continued to give way before the extremism of the Germanomaniacs and the nationalist demagogues.

Destined to relative political impotence during the restoration period, Germany saw a further flowering and flourishing of the arts and a tremendous development of the social sciences. Perhaps Humboldt was right when he said in 1813 that the political division of Germany was the necessary condition for the great variety of its cultural development. True, neither in literature nor in music did this restoration era approach the great period of classical humanism. There were no equals to Lessing, Herder, Goethe, and Schiller, nor to Haydn, Mozart, and Beethoven. But a rich poetic and prose literature brought forth Eduard Mörike (1804–1875), Ludwig Uhland (1787–1862), Friedrich Rückert (1788–1866), Heinrich Heine (1797–1856), and Ludwig Börne (1786–1837), not to mention the romanticists like Tieck, Eichendorff, Chamisso, and Brentano who carried on from the Napoleonic period; and Schubert, Schumann, Weber, and Mendelssohn brought German romantic music to a high peak of development. "If they [the Germans] do not know how to play the grand instruments of liberty," wrote Balzac in his *Une Fille d'Eve,* in 1839, "they know naturally how to play all the instruments of music."

This was also a period of great architectural development. Karl Friedrich Schinkel in Berlin and Gottfried Semper in Dresden carried out grandiose plans for large and imposing public buildings. King Ludwig of Bavaria made Munich one of Europe's architectural showplaces. Metternich after a visit to Munich wrote: "What one sees in Munich exceeds even the most glowing imagination. . . . At this moment they are building the royal palace, the library, the university and I do not know how many other public buildings and four huge churches. And these are not puny enterprises; everything here is tremendous." [2]

The historical and social sciences, in particular, reached a high point of development during this epoch.[3] The philosophy of Kant and Hegel flourished in a more highly subjective form in Schelling and Schopenhauer, and the rationalist emphasis on reason gave way to the quest for the hidden sources of human will. The universalistic and pragmatic historical writing of the Enlightenment was replaced by a more profound and concrete sense of historical individuality, as found in Niebuhr and Ranke. But whereas in Ranke the individuality of historical events and nations was still deeply grounded in the universality of a divine order, thus tempering the sharpness of conflict between the unique and the general, the newer historical school of Droysen and Dahlmann, re-enforced by Hegelian theory, paved the way for a "pure" historicism which no longer could discover any unity in the history of nations. For them, therefore, the highest unity was to be found in the nation and national history, and political and moral relativism followed as a necessary corollary from this basic premise.

In the field of jurisprudence the older school of natural law, never too influential in Germany, was completely eliminated by the new historical and comparative school of Karl von Savigny. The dominant school of classical economics came to be challenged first by Friedrich List with his *Das nationale System der politischen Oekonomie* in 1841 and then by the founder of the historical school of economics, Wilhelm Roscher, who published his *Grundriss zu Vorlesungen über die Staatswirtschaft nach geschichtlicher Methode* in 1843. Jacob and Wilhelm Grimm, Karl Lachmann and Franz Bopp developed the school of comparative literature, and Karl Ritter laid the foundations for scientific geography. In all these fields, quite apart from the underlying philosophy basic to these disciplines, new, precise, and expert methods of research, of collecting data, and of the use of auxiliary disciplines were developed. In the technical institutes and universities of this period were laid the foundations for that renown which German scholarship achieved in the second half of the nineteenth century and which made German scholarship the model for scientific methodology and research throughout the world.

Politically, the period following 1815 was "one of disillusionment, of hopes belied, promises broken and reforms deferred" (Pollard). Germany, following the period of the Napoleonic wars, was confronted with problems which England required ten centuries to solve—the remains of the feudal system, constitutional problems, church and state, and, above all, the all-important problem of national unity.

The Congress of Vienna did away with the Napoleonic Confederation of the Rhine, but no attempt was made to restore the Holy Roman Empire. That institution was gone for good, although the universalist dreams with which it was associated lingered on in various forms for many years.*

In place of the old Reich a Germanic confederation was set up, consisting of thirty-nine sovereign states bound in loose confederation. The imperial knights disappeared completely, as did the ecclesiastical states, and of the once proud free cities only four remained—Bremen, Hamburg, Lübeck, and Frankfurt. Of the thirty-nine sovereign states the chief members were Austria, with a mixture of German and non-German peoples, and Prussia. Elsewhere the old *Kleinstaaterei* still reigned supreme.

The political restoration in Germany was much more complete than in France. True, many of the changes brought about by the revolution remained untouched, but the absolutist princes that were thrown out by the hateful foreigner were welcomed back by a populace that was more deeply attached to order, authority, tradition, and patriarchal rule than to doctrines of natural rights, popular sovereignty, or democratic ideology. "What was our restoration by and large?" asked Ranke. "It consisted in chasing out the foreigners." [4] Princely absolutism once again held sway with all its bureaucracy, inefficiency, extravagance, fiscal oppression, pomp, mistresses, play at soldiery, arbitrary interference with state finances, and open traffic in public interests. The old social supremacy of the aristocracy once more asserted itself over the other classes. Nobles again were to dance only with the nobles, the best seats in the theater and opera were again to be reserved for the nobility, and the upstart bourgeois classes were put back in their former places. The bourgeoisie, moreover, showed little resentment at being restored to its "God-given" inferior status.

Apart from Austria and Prussia, only Bavaria was what might be called a middle-sized state. All other member states of the confederation were but fragments of states. Formally Bavaria was a constitutional monarchy. It had become a kingdom in 1806, and the pro-French King Max Joseph was succeeded in 1825 by Ludwig I, who had openly opposed his father in his pro-French policies. But traditional ties to France persisted side

---

* The poems of Friedrich Rückert and the plays of Ernst Radpach, together with the historical works of Friedrich Raumer and Wilhelm Giesebrecht, served to keep alive and even intensify German romantic interest in the medieval Reich and especially in the Hohenstaufens. "It would be a great mistake to believe that with the creation of new conditions the romantic conceptions of the German past lost their influence. They continued to live on, in a certain measure as ideal complements to the conditions of reality . . . and it would be self-delusion to underestimate their subconscious power" (Robert Davidsohn, "Die Vorstellungen vom alten Reich in ihren Einwirkungen auf die neuere deutsche Geschichte," in Bavarian Akademie der Wissenschaften, *Sitzungsberichte*, Philos.-Hist. Klasse, Munich, 1917, p. 32).

by side with the strong pro-Austrian alignment of the predominantly Catholic population. Ludwig I, an esthetic nature who would much rather have won acclaim as a poet than be credited with political triumphs, tried in the early years of his reign to make Munich and Bavaria not only a center of beauty and art but also a Mecca for liberal writers and scholars. At the opening of the University of Munich, Ludwig declared: "Religion must indeed be the basis of life, but I do not like bigots or obscurantists. The youth should take joy in life and not be hypocritical." The rector of the university went even further on the same occasion. "More decisive than all else for the flourishing of the sciences," he declared, "is the freedom of expression and the free exchange of ideas. . . . Abuse of it is indeed possible, but without it there can be no freedom." [5]

After the revolution of 1830 in France, however, Ludwig became more wary of the liberal currents, and the conservative trend in Bavaria became more marked. Ludwig too became notorious for his amorous adventures. The most famous of these was with the Irish-born Dolores Eliza Gilbert, who swept across the European scene as the Andalusian-Moorish dancer Lola Montez, and who managed in 1846, when she was 26, to captivate the heart of the sixty-one-year-old Bavarian king and to exercise complete sway over him until the eve of the revolution of 1848.

Lola Montez, regarding whom Aldous Huxley has aptly said that "her reputation made you automatically think of bedrooms," aspired to be the Madame Pompadour of the Bavarian court, and she almost succeeded in realizing her aspiration. Public sentiment, especially Catholic sentiment, was aroused against her, but Ludwig stood firm. When the Archbishop of Munich remonstrated with him that Lola was an emissary from Satan sent from England to destroy the Catholic faith, Ludwig said to him, "You stick to your *stola* and let me stick to my Lola." Finally resentment against the foreign lady forced her to flee to Switzerland, and a short while thereafter Ludwig was himself forced to abdicate his throne.[6]

Württemberg, like Bavaria, was also a kingdom. Friedrich List's petition of 1821 to the Chamber of Deputies provides us with a description of political conditions in that state. "Wherever one looks," wrote List, "one sees nothing but councillors, officials, offices, aides, secretaries, notaries, document boxes, uniforms, high living and luxury of officials down to the servants. On the other side of the picture there are low grain prices, business stagnation, decline in commodity prices, bitter complaints against dishonest magistrates, brutal officials, and secret reports, absence of impartiality of higher officials, wailing and distress all over."

The Grand Duchy of Baden had a more enlightened government, influenced by liberal political leaders like Friedrich Bassermann and Karl Mathy. Here the *Deutsche Zeitung* of Heidelberg exercised an important influence on the development of liberal nationalism. In addition to these states there were two Hesses, two Mecklenburgs, two Lippes, and a half dozen Saxonies, each attempting again, as in the eighteenth century, to display the pomp of the court of a grand sovereign.

The chief instrument of government of the Germanic Confederation was the diet (*Bundestag*), which sat in permanent session in the free city of Frankfurt am Main. The Bundestag had two houses, the ordinary and the general assembly. The ordinary assembly had seventeen delegates, while the general assembly, or plenum, had four delegates each from the larger states, three from the middle states, and on down to at least one delegate for each state. Only the plenum could render decisions on fundamental questions. Austria presided over this diet. The members of the diet were bound by government instructions, and there was no executive machinery for carrying out the decisions of the diet. It was mainly the creation of Metternich, and for him it was more a defensive league of German sovereigns against foreign foes than a form of German unity. "Its external function was to protect the German monarchs against the Jacobinism of the French and Russian governments; its domestic business was to save them from German liberalism" (Pollard). Joseph Görres described the diet as "a central power which does not rule, but is ruled by the separate parts; an executive wholly destitute of authority, which cannot proceed against the refractory, and is not in a condition to execute anything whatever because it can never obtain the requisite unanimity; a legislature which will never investigate its own competence; a judiciary which no one is bound to obey; an assembly which ever seeks but never finds authority for its acts in an interminable weaving of diplomacy."

The period after 1815 in Germany was the period of the twilight of Goethe's life, but it was dominated not by the poet of Weimar but by the former Rhinelander, now chancellor of the Austrian Empire, Prince Klemens von Metternich. His opponents coined the expression "system of Metternich" to characterize this period, but Metternich himself denied having a "system" and loved to describe it as a "world order" based on "power through law." Metternich prattled a great deal about "principles," and his memoirs and political writings, carefully sifted by himself and by his literary executors, were deliberately arranged to bring into high-light these "principles."

It has recently become the fashion to "rehabilitate" Metternich from the opprobrium and hostility heaped upon him by a century of political and historical writing, to which radicals, liberals, and Prussian nationalists all contributed. Historians like Guglielmo Ferrero, with the ominous pictures of the late Roman Empire and fascist Italy ever before them; reactionary nationalists, like Ritter von Srbik, who later came to see in Hitler's union of Germany and Austria and the establishment of German hegemony in Europe the true realization of "German unity" and the revival of the old Hapsburg imperialist "Europeanism"; disturbed liberals like Peter Viereck, who are overwhelmed by the confusion, the disorder, and above all the brutalization of contemporary politics and culture—all have joined in constructing a picture of Metternich as a good European and a champion of peaceful reconstruction as opposed to the ravages wrought by insurrection and violent revolution.[7] All these constructions are achieved primarily by reading into the restoration period after the French revolutionary and Napoleonic wars all the hopes and ideals, realized or destroyed, of the tumultuous decades of the twentieth century. Obviously Metternich was not a brutal Genghis Khan or a wild-eyed Adolf Hitler. The decorum of his traditional ways of diplomacy was certainly more agreeable and pleasing than the brutal coarseness of a Vater Jahn in the same way that the polished and traditional old-style diplomacy of von Papen and von Neurath impressed "respectable" circles in 1932 when contrasted with the coarse demagogy of a Goebbels or Hitler. But it is both unhistorical and contrary to fact to set up the juxtaposition between Metternich and Jahn and Arndt as it is false to describe the "core and fire-center" of Metternich's conservatism as being "a humanist reverence for the dignity of the individual soul." [8] The core of Metternich's conservatism was the idea of the social stability of organized society and of the state, and the protection of this "order" and "peace" by any and all means necessary, irrespective of the effects upon the "individual soul."

True, Metternich was in temperament and spirit a child of the eighteenth century. That meant that he had no feeling or sympathy for the romantic spirit, that he was rational and practical-minded in his approach to political problems, and that he preferred the discipline and state order of the classic spirit to the disturbing and dynamic romanticism of the nineteenth century. A story is told of Metternich standing one day in the garden of his castle on the Rhine, watching an eclipse of the sun. A great sense of relief came over him when the moon finally completed its path across the sun and the temporary darkness was dispelled. There was "order" again in the world.

Metternich's attachment to the eighteenth century was to the rationalist justification of the age of absolutism and not to the enlightened political ideas of the *philosophes*. He was indeed heir to the idea of European unity and cosmopolitanism, but it was the unity of the empire of Charles V and not the enlightened universalism of a Condorcet. He fought the "ideas of 1789" not because they had become corrupted and lost their original idealism and intent but because they ran counter to his deep-seated hostility to liberty and equality and to his mistrust of popular sovereignty and the rights of the lower classes. True, he recognized the need of giving some attention to the amelioration of the social conditions of the lower classes, but this came neither from any real concern for general welfare nor even from a patriarchal or paternalistic approach to the lower classes. It was the vehicle whereby the majority of the people were to be made oblivious of their loss of liberty.

Jahn and Arndt and the "Germanomaniacs" were not the only alternatives to Metternich. One has wide choice in the many camps of Metternich's contemporaries of finding alternative philosophies to rampant and brutal nationalism. One could go to the more genuinely spiritual traditionalism of Catholic philosophy like that of Baader or Görres; or to the much more genuine heirs of the Enlightenment like Gervinus and Schlosser; or to the true liberalism of a Börne; or to the flaming and passionate champion of true European unity, Giuseppe Mazzini. Nationalist though he was, Mazzini recognized more keenly than did Metternich the degradation of the "ideas of 1789" and the perils of aggressive nationalism. The ideal of the Association of Young Europe was the *federal* organization of European democracy under one sole direction. And in his "Reply to the German Nationalists," Mazzini declared: "Do not reduce the great question that is being debated in Europe today to a question of determining just how many slaves will pass from the uniform of one master to the uniform of another on this or that area of soil. Do not justify oppression by making the people its sponsors." [9] It is, therefore, not necessary to rewrite the biography of Metternich in order to find a good European in 1815. The record of the Austrian chancellor remains, despite his new apologists, very much the one that has come down to us from his contemporaries—the record of the arch-champion of reaction and political absolutism both in Austria and in the rest of Europe.

Metternich, anti-liberal, anti-national, opposed to the ideals of the French Enlightenment and revolution, set the reactionary pattern of the period. Censorship was rigidly imposed; the country was covered by a network of police and spies; the slightest trace of liberal tendency was immediately suppressed. Liberalism, at the time, was closely identified with nationalism. Both were considered part of the dangerous poison concocted by French Jacobinism. Austria, confronted with a heterogeneous mixture of Slav, Hungarian, and German nationalities, was particularly sensitive to nationalist currents. The traditional Hapsburg dynasty, invoking the spirit of "throne and altar," was to be the only expression of unity. Nationalist activities in the German states as well as in the Slav lands were considered radical and dangerous, and were suppressed along with movements for political reform.

Political conservatism became the official restoration philosophy in Germany, as was also the case elsewhere on the Continent. The influence of the Englishman Burke, popularized in Germany and Austria by Gentz, had more far-reaching effect in Germany than it had in England. These ideas, reinforced by the influence of French writers like De Maistre, Bonald, and Chateaubriand, and given typical German form by romantic political pamphleteers like Adam Müller, the Schlegels, and Franz Baader, constituted the foundations upon which the German restoration philosophy was built. The leading spokesmen for German restoration conservatism were Karl Ludwig Haller (1768–1854) and, somewhat later Friedrich Julius Stahl (1802–1861). Haller's *Restauration der Staatswissenschaften* was published in six volumes in 1816–1834, and the first volume of Stahl's *Die Philosophie des Rechts nach geschichtlicher Ansicht* appeared in 1830. In Prussia this conservatism received a special tinge of Pietistic Lutheranism (far removed from the Pietism of Spener, Francke, and Zinzendorf) combined with Germanism and romantic Teutonism. Here the brothers Gerlach were the central figures in a circle around Frederick William IV of Prussia and his court.[10]

The basic goal of political conservatism was to root out all traces of French revolutionary ideology. Haller said he wanted "to destroy the hydra of the revolution in its roots" and "to crush underfoot the head of the snake of Jacobinism." In contrast to the individualism of the liberal political theories of the Enlightenment, the emphasis was upon the state as an organism and upon the supreme importance of order, tradition, continuity, religion, family, and authority. The model for the state is the family. The sovereign is a *pater familias* and his domain is a *Patrimonialstaat*. He differs from other heads of families only in that he has no superior but God. Haller rejected the distinction made by liberal political philosophers between public and private law. The concept of public law, he held, was nothing but an abstraction, typical of the abstract character of eighteenth century rationalism. Everything was private law because the sovereign is the proprietor of a *concrete* domain. "One God, one king, one father" was his dictum, and the state, a Christian state, is characterized by monotheism, monarchy, and monogamy. Rights and duties derive not from popular will, natural law, or a mere piece of paper called a constitution; they stem from age-old and hoary custom and tradition. The virtues of the subject (*Untertan*, not citizen) to be nurtured most are the passive virtues of obedience, reverence, meditation, faithfulness, and piety. On the other hand it is important to point out that Haller did not advocate a highly centralized and unitary state under the absolutist rule of the sovereign. He harked back, as did the other romantic philosophers, to the corporate ideas of the Middle Ages with their basic notion of contract. He stressed the importance of local provinces and corporations, and he viewed the state as a pyramid of contracts, privileges, and rights which reached its highest pinnacle in the sovereign power of the king.

The ideas of Haller, and particularly of Stahl, were found to be most convenient for the East Elbian Prussian Junker class. Stahl, born a Jew with the name Jolson, was converted to Christianity and became the philosopher of Prussian Christian conservatism. The rabbinic training which he received as a youth left a deep impress on him, especially in his great emphasis on the omnipresence of religion and the significance of traditional cult and ritual. Like Haller, Stahl attacked the natural-law doctrines of the French revolution and proclaimed the dictum that revolution is sin. Kings are crowned by God and are the tools of God on earth. What gives the state its legitimacy is its divine character, and the purpose of the state is religious and ethical. The state exists for the service of God and "for the realization of the ethical realm." This is also what gives legitimacy to the exercise of power by the state over men. Personalistic theism was to take the place of the cold and impersonal law of the age of reason. Monarchy is the most satisfying form of government because it possesses "personality," "unity," and above all "grandeur." Rationalistic ethics and jurisprudence must give way before the commands of a personal God acting through a personal monarch. The true state, therefore, is a Christian state, paternalistic and absolute in character. The conservative principle, declared Stahl, "leads to the true political conclusion that the nation has an identity of condition and consciousness only through its entire history, complete possession of its past by the present, while according to the radical principles the nation of today is altogether different from that of yesterday or of tomorrow." [11] Constitutions were worthless scraps of paper alongside the divine word of a parental king. These political doctrines, so convenient to the political interests of the Prussian ruling classes, became their ideological tools in the fight against constitutionalism, liberalism, and revolutionary nationalism.

German liberalism, during the restoration period, derived from several sources, native as well as foreign.[12] It drew its native sustenance from the classic idealism of Kant and Wilhelm von Humboldt. Here the German liberals got their emphasis on the moral autonomy of the individual and the supreme importance of the free and unfettered development of personality. In his *Essay on the Limits of the Action of the State* (1792), Humboldt had set forth the view that liberty was the necessary condition for the growth of individual powers and that intervention by the state paralyzes the development of the faculties of man. The sole function of the state is to provide for external and internal security. "If the activity of the state is extended beyond this, then man's own independent activity is restricted in an unfavorable way, uniformity is produced and, in one word, the inner development of the individual is harmed thereby." [13]

This native liberal tradition was re-enforced by the powerful influences that came from the French revolution and from the constitutional theories of England. French liberal influence was particularly strong in the Rhineland and in western and southern Germany, areas that had come into direct contact with the revolutionary armies of France and which had been under French rule for longer or shorter periods. North German liberalism, on the other hand, drew its inspiration more from England than from France. From 1714 to 1837 Hanover was ruled by the same sovereign as England. The University of Göttingen, founded by George II in 1737, became a focal point for English cultural influence. Here Friedrich Christoph Dahlmann taught history and his historical studies of English constitutional development helped disseminate familiarity with English political institutions. In contrast to revolutionary Jacobinism in France these German liberals sang the praises of the organic character of the British constitution and the gradualness of its development. They admired the importance of public opinion in England, and its deep-rooted acceptance of trial by jury and freedom of the press, and they found a kinship and affinity between German Protestantism and the ethical character of Protestant British liberalism. German economic liberalism, on the other hand, did not receive the full impact of Smithian and Manchestrian influences until later in the 1850's.

In South Germany the works of Karl von Rotteck and Karl Theodor Welcker were of paramount importance. The nine volumes of Rotteck's *Allgemeine Geschichte* sat on the shelves of every German liberal home, and the famous *Staatslexikon*, first published in nineteen volumes in 1834–1849, in which both Rotteck and Welcker collaborated, "served as a political text for two generations of the educated classes of Germany" (Theodor Heuss). Both Rotteck and Welcker were professors at the University of Freiburg and deputies in the Baden diet at Karlsruhe. From their professorial chairs as well as in the legislative halls they championed the claims of reason and of "healthy and sound common sense"; they invoked the ideas of 1789 and the demands for a constitutional *Rechtsstaat*. They sought to achieve a synthesis between Kantian idealistic philosophy and the political ideas of the French revolution, and they were the defenders of the doctrine of natural rights as against the new school of historic rights.

Most of the leaders of German liberalism before 1848 were professors. In addition to Rotteck and Welcker, Jakob Grimm, Gustav Rümelin, Robert von Mohl, Georg Gervinus, and Friedrich Dahlmann were all professors. As scholars they were particularly interested in the defense of freedom of expression and the freedom of the press. Many of them suffered personal hardships in their professional careers because of their espousal of the principles of liberalism. A *cause célèbre* that aroused German public opinion during this time was the dismissal of seven professors from the University of Göttingen in 1837 because they had protested against the abrogation of the constitution by Ernst Augustus, the new ruler of Hanover. This instance of suppression of academic freedom served as a rallying point for the forces of liberalism throughout Germany. "Must I now teach," asked Dahlmann, "that the supreme principle of the state is that whatever pleases those in power is law? As a man of honor I would rather give up teaching altogether than sell to my audience as truth that which is a lie and a deceit." [14]

The liberal professors found allies in banking and merchant circles. Friedrich Harkort, David Hansemann, Gustav Mevissen, Hermann von Beckerath, Ludolf Camphausen, and other representatives of the bourgeoisie made up the right wing of liberal leadership which was subsequently called to the helm during the revolution of 1848. These liberal leaders were men of historical, juristic, and scientific training and possessed of a great measure of self-sacrifice, idealism, and moral feeling. Some, like Mevissen, also noted the effects of the new industrialization in sharpening the social problem. Historians have often pointed to the fact that there were no truly "great personalities" among them. This is undoubtedly true, but we must not forget that greatness is very often called forth by the historical circumstances into which one is placed. Many a political leader has been pushed into greatness because the position he found himself in called for exertions of a heroic character. German liberalism never was pushed into such historical situations. In the absence of a strong bourgeoisie and of a large proletariat German liberalism never could draw on the powerful social and numerical support these groups gave to the liberal movements in England and France. Furthermore, liberalism in Germany was handicapped by the fact that it was looked upon as an alien doctrine and hence counter to the true political spirit of Germany. Most important of all, German liberalism was always overshadowed by the urgencies of German nationalism and German unity. The struggle for "freedom" from external oppression always asserted its prior claims over the movement for free institutions inside Germany. German liberals, therefore, either were forced to compromise their constitutional principles because of the nationalist problems or else had to face the powerful resistance that came from the extreme nationalists. This does not mean, however, that liberalism was altogether ineffective in Germany. Constitutionalism made wide gains in a number of the local states, especially in southern Germany.

The first German state to receive a constitution was the Duchy of Nassau in 1814. Grand Duke Karl August, the friend of Goethe, gave Saxe-Weimar a constitution in 1816; Bavaria, Baden, and Württemberg received constitutions in 1818 and 1819. All these constitutions, except that of Württemberg (where the constitution in 1819 came as a result of an understanding between the king and the estates), were *"oktroyiert,"* that is, they were presented to the people by the grace of the sovereign and were not derived from a popular assembly. The French charter of 1814 served as the model. In all of them the monarchical principle was explicit. The monarch, of his own free will, invited the participation of other classes of society in the government of the state, but the sovereign still united in his person all the rights of state authority and he administered all the provisions set forth in the constitution. The constitutions all provided for a popular legislature, but this did not mean acceptance of the co-sovereignty of ruler and people. The ruler was still the only source of power. Representation, except in the state of Baden, was in the form of estates and not by general popular election. Legislatures were all bicameral; they were guaranteed the right of periodic assembly, were vested with power of taxation, but otherwise could not initiate legislation on their own. They were merely to co-operate with the sovereign in lawmaking after he had initiated the laws. Apart from these attempts at constitutional states all other states in the confederation were absolutist in character.

The prevailing conditions in Germany during the restoration period did not fail, however, to call forth opposition—opposition in the political, social, and cultural fields. The predominant movement of protest was centered upon the national question. The nationalist movement continued to gather strength from all classes of the population, but divergences still existed as to the best method and most agreeable form of German unity. For many the tradition of the Holy Roman Empire, with its combination of Christian universalism and Germanic hegemony, continued to feed the imagination and fantasy. But it was also more realistic in the sense that such an arrangement was most feasible for the inclusion of the Austrian Empire. The great difficulty in this scheme, however, was the inclusion in the Austrian Empire of non-German peoples. The co-existence of Germans and Slavs in one state ran counter to the nineteenth century principle of nationality, active both among Germans and Slavs.

This elicited a second school of national unity, which proposed a purely Germanic confederation which was to include only the German parts of Austria, leaving out the Hungarians and Slavs. This plan obviously did not find favor among the ruling circles of Austria. A third plan was the "trias" idea, which proposed to set up three federal states in Germany —Austria, Prussia, and a state made up of all the rest of the German states. The trias idea found its most ardent advocates in the Kingdom of Württemberg. A fourth proposal, one that was ultimately to triumph, was that of Prussian hegemony. National unity was to be achieved through the action and leadership of Prussia. Already in 1813 Clausewitz had written: "Germany can achieve political unity only in one way, that is, through the sword, when one of its states will bring all the others under its sway." The Prussian movement, however, was still weak, and the Prussian monarchy did little to encourage it. The number of Germans looking to Prussia for national leadership began to increase after 1830. Paul Pfizer's pamphlet *Briefwechsel zweier Deutschen,* published in 1831, was a significant factor in stimulating this movement. In addition to all these views of national unity there was the ideal of a democratic German republic, in which all the old local states would be eliminated and all the Germans would enter into the centralized national state on the basis of universal suffrage and popular sovereignty. The advocates of this scheme, needless to say, constituted a tiny minority on the extreme left of the political groupings. Their influence remained insignificant.[15]

The chief center of nationalist activity during the period after 1815 was in the universities. Students and professors combined to carry on the struggle for German national unity. In this movement the most active agents were the *Burschenschaften*. The Burschenschaft was a student organization first founded at the University of Jena in 1815. The Burschenschaften movement represents the political activization of the academic youth of Germany. Born out of the experiences of the War of Liberation, it was a reaction against the traditional student corps of the German universities. It aimed to regenerate the moral virtues of the young people of Germany, but above all it strove to break down local allegiances and to kindle a huge nationalist flame that would engulf all of Germany. Turnvater Jahn, Ernst Moritz Arndt, and the historian Heinrich Luden were the spiritual progenitors of the Burschenschaften movement.[16]

Friedrich Ludwig Jahn, known as Turnvater Jahn, had already before 1815 achieved fame and notoriety by the organization of his *Turngemeinden*, or sport associations. He urged the physical and national regeneration of German youth for the cause of the fatherland. His was a combination of moral idealism and crude and vulgar rowdyism, of folk populism and antisemitism, of racialism and patriotism. The wearing of gray shirts, which he prescribed for his followers, was intended to break down class distinctions and create a feeling of national unity in all who wore them. But they are also a sinister anticipation of the twentieth century brown shirts. Similarly so was also the rowdyism with which Jahn's followers invaded the universities and broke up the classes and lectures of professors whom they considered anti-national.[17] In 1811 Jahn had submitted to the rector of the University of Berlin a plan for the formation of the Burschenschaften to supplant the organization of students along state lines. The plan was rejected at that time. But in Jena, where the nationalist historian Heinrich Luden was active, the first Burschenschaft was formed on June 12, 1815, under the slogan of "Honor, Liberty and Fatherland," with the twofold goal of national unity and the strengthening of moral virtues. The Burschenschaft at Jena adopted red and black as the colors for its banner. The flag was of three stripes of red, black, red, with a gold oak branch. The uniform adopted was that of the Lützow regiment—a black coat with red lapels and gold oak leaves. This is the origin of the combination of red, gold, and black that later became the colors of the German nationalist movement. Paul Wentzcke, who has made the most detailed study of this movement, has definitely shown that the association of red, gold, and black with the old imperial colors was a myth that began to be disseminated some years after the start of the movement. The first organizers of the Burschenschaft at Jena had no such association in mind. They followed the colors of the Lützow regiment, in whose ranks many of them had served.

Jena was followed by the universities of Giessen, Heidelberg, and

Erlangen. Soon Burschenschaften were formed in many other South Ger man universities. The idea did not take hold in northern Germany nor in Catholic Bavaria and Austria.

The first great general assembly of the Burschenschaften was called for October 18, 1817, at the Wartburg, near Eisenach. It was the 300th anniversary of Luther's revolt, and October 18 was the date of the battle of Leipzig. Thus Luther and Blücher were made the heroes of the movement. The former was hailed for the "internal liberation" of the German spirit, while the latter was exalted for the "external liberation" of Germany. A group of 468 young people gathered at Eisenach and marched to the Wartburg, which was placed at their disposal by the Duke of Weimar. There the keynote speaker proclaimed the purpose of the meeting to be "to recall the picture of the past before our souls, to draw strength from the past for living actively in the present, to take counsel with each other on our activities and program, to exchange views, to reveal to us the pure life of the *Burschen* and finally to show our people what it may hope for from its youth." In the evening a huge torch procession was staged. After the formal ceremonies were over, a group of Jahn's followers acted out a scene that harked back three hundred years but that was also to serve as the model for a similar scene a century later. Remembering Luther's public burning of the papal bull, these "gray shirts" collected the books of conservative and anti-nationalist writers and burned them in a huge public bonfire. This event, in particular, aroused the resentment of the government officials and the adherents of the *status quo*.

In October, 1818, a general *Burschentag* was convoked in Jena and the "Allgemeine deutsche Burschenschaft" was formed. Fourteen universities were represented. One of the problems which aroused most controversy was the Jewish question. Ernst Moritz Arndt, in keeping with his general hostility to Jews, had included in his original plan for such organizations a provision limiting membership to Christians only. A similar plank was introduced by the committee in 1818. But some of the delegates from Heidelberg, Königsberg, and Breslau, those who represented the "enlightened" wing of the movement, protested vigorously and pointed to the patriotic record of German Jews in the War of Liberation. A substitute provision was thereupon adopted which called for "Christian-German development by every spiritual and physical force for the service of the fatherland." The Jena Burschenschaft, largest and most influential of the chapters, adopted a provision for membership of only "Christians and Germans." In the Heidelberg Burschenschaft the ex-Jew Friedrich Julius Stahl helped draft a constitution which barred Jews and foreigners from membership.

The climax of the Burschenschaften movement came with the assassination by one of its members of the reactionary poet and journalist Kotzebue. Karl Ludwig Sand, fanatical follower of the radical Burschenschaft leader, Karl Follen of Giessen, and imbued with the zeal of self-sacrifice for the fatherland, decided to murder one of the writers most hated by the nationalist students. On March 23, 1819, he made his way into the home of Kotzebue in Mannheim and with the words "Here, you traitor to your fatherland!" thrust a knife into the unsuspecting poet. Sand then attempted to kill himself as he shouted, "I thank thee O Lord for the victory." He was temporarily saved by medical attention only to be later condemned to death. On May 20, 1820, he was executed. Metternich, long suspicious of this student movement, now determined to act. Frederick William III of Prussia was likewise none too pleased with these student activities. Together they planned a set of decrees, which came to be known as the Carlsbad Decrees, which they put through the Bund on September 20, 1819. These provided for rigid censorship and press control and for the supervision of universities and schools in order to ferret out all subversive elements. The Burschenschaften were ordered dissolved. Thus came to a close the official career of this nationalist student movement. Nothing concrete or tangible emerged from this movement; but its greatest achievement was to politicize the German academic youth and to provide a reservoir from which were drawn many of the most active political leaders of Germany during the next generation.

A movement of protest that included much more genius, maturity, and political sagacity but which exercised much less influence upon German developments was that of Young Germany. Chronologically it coincided with similar "Young" movements in Europe like Young Italy, Young Poland, and Young Ireland, but it differed from these movements in many significant ways. These other "Young" movements became the spearheads of the nationalist movements of their respective countries and mustered the national energies of their people against the foreigners ruling their country. Their leaders were likewise the representatives of romanticism, and they became national idols to later generations. In Germany this movement, owing to the peculiar conditions there, assumed quite a different character. Like the other European movements it too was motivated by a thirst for liberty and drew its inspiration from French revolutionary ideals. But it was directed not against a foreigner, for there was no foreigner oppressing Germany; while aspiring toward a united Germany its main attack was centered upon the racialist, aggressive nationalism in its own country; while romantic in many ways and counting one of the greatest lyric romantic poets in its ranks, it was, at the same time, directed against the excesses of romanticism in Germany, and it expressed itself more in sober and realistic prose. And unlike Mazzini in Italy or Mickiewicz in Poland, these men did not become the national heroes of Germany. If anything, they came to be looked upon as "un-German" and hostile to the "true spirit" of their country.[18]

In the very narrow and traditionally accepted usage in literary histories, the term Young Germany is applied only to a group of literary figures of which the leaders weie Ludolf Wienbarg (1802–1872), Karl Gutzkow (1811–1878), Theodor Mundt (1808–1861), and Heinrich Laube (1806–1884). To these were also added the political and revolutionary poets Count August von Platen (1796–1835), Georg Büchner (1813–1837), Georg Herwegh (1817–1875), and Ferdinand Freiligrath (1810–1876). In the broad historical sense the movement of Young Germany also embraced the philosophical radicals in the circle of Arnold Ruge (1802–1880) and above all the towering figures of Ludwig Börne (1786–1837) and Heinrich Heine (1797–1856). The term Young Germany became popularly known largely as a result of the action taken by the Diet of the Germanic Confederation on December 10, 1835, in passing a resolution calling upon all German states to "bind themselves to bring the penal and police statutes of their respective countries and the regulations regarding the abuse of the press in their strictest sense to bear against the authors, publishers, printers and disseminators of the writings of the literary school known as Young Germany . . . as also by all lawful means to prevent the dissemination of the writings of this school by booksellers, lending libraries or other means."

With few exceptions the leading figures in the Young Germany movement came from the petty artisan classes, from the lower bourgeoisie, or from the Jewish group, which was still outside the pale of accepted German society. In fact their opponents often sought to discredit the whole movement by labeling it a Jewish movement or, as Menzel called it, "Young Palestine." Most of them were men without family, without secure income, without degrees, and without established standing in society. Despite individual differences existing between many of the leading figures they all aspired toward "spiritual emancipation." They proclaimed the rights of youth and aspired to literature which would be identified with life. Much of their political inspiration came from the July revolution in France. The Young German authors introduced a more sober realism into the intellectual climate of Germany, saturated as it was with romanticism. This despite the fact that some of its members were themselves the products of romanticism. They were the innovators of realistic political journalism in Germany. The published letters by the exiles Börne and Heine from Paris disseminated French revolutionary ideas in Germany and created a pattern for subsequent liberal journalism in Germany. Georg Büchner's *Hessischer Landbote,* with its call for "peace to the hut,—war to the palaces," has been called the first socialist pamphlet in Germany.

The general literary vehicle of expression for this movement was prose rather than poetry. After the July revolution of 1830, in particular, there arose in these circles a disgust with verse. They were weary of singing about maidens and moonlight, about roses and nightingales, and above all they sensed the identification of romanticism with reaction. They strove to create a German public opinion that would be politically conscious, critical, and mature. They sanctified the individual and his political and social rights; they called for a *Rechtsstaat* of all Germans based upon popular sovereignty; and they declared war upon the despotism of the ruling powers. Count Platen, Börne, and Heine had to live in exile because of their fierce attacks upon German absolutism.

Börne, born in the ghetto of Frankfurt am Main, suffered all the disabilities of being a Jew, and became a rebel spirit. His *Briefe aus Paris,* pungent and bitter in their attack upon the German despots, made him a hero for the small group of German radicals as it made him a renegade for the dominant political and literary circles both of his own and subsequent times. Börne was particularly critical of the twin gods of German literature, Schiller and Goethe. He condemned them both as a pair of confirmed aristocrats. Goethe, he said, "might have been the Hercules who could have cleansed the Augean stables of his country; but he rather elected to fetch the golden apples of the Hesperides, and to keep them for himself." He chastised Goethe for not following the examples of other notable literary figures who used their positions of literary eminence not as an Olympian retreat but as a vehicle for the championing of moral and political causes. He pointed to Dante, Alfieri, Montesquieu, Voltaire, Milton, and Byron as fighters for justice and liberty, and then, addressing Goethe, he wrote: "A mighty mind was given to thee, didst thou ever employ it to oppose baseness? Heaven gave thee a tongue of fire, didst thou ever champion justice? Thou hadst a good sword, but it was drawn to defend thyself alone." [19]

To those who attacked him as a Jew and accused him of being hostile to German patriotism, Börne replied:

It is like a miracle! A thousand times have I experienced it and yet it is eternally new to me. Some reproach me because I am a Jew; others excuse me for it; a third praises me for it. But all of them think of it. They are as though they were fixed by the spell of this magic Jewish circle and no one can get out. I also know quite well where this evil charm comes from. The poor Germans! Living in the lowest floor, oppressed by the seven floors of the upper classes, their anxiety is made lighter by speaking of people who are still lower than they are and who live in the cellar. Not being a Jew provides them with consolation at not being a state councillor. No, the fact that I was born a Jew has not embittered me against the Germans and has never deluded me. I would indeed not be worthy to enjoy the light of the sun if I paid with scornful grumbling for the great act of grace that God has shown me of letting me be both a German and a Jew. Only because of the derision that I have always scorned and because of the suffering that I have long since ceased to feel . . . yes, because I was a bondsman, I therefore love liberty more than you. Yes, because I have known slavery, I understand freedom more than you. Yes, because I was born without a fatherland my desire for a fatherland is more passionate than yours, and because my birthplace was not bigger than the *Judengasse* and everything behind the locked gates was a foreign country to me, therefore for me now the fatherland is more than the city, more than a territory, more than a province. For me only the very great fatherland, as far as its language extends, is enough. . . . And because I am no longer the bondsman of citizens I also do not wish to remain any longer the slave of princes. I want to be completely free again. I have built my house of freedom from bottom up; do as I have done and do not feel content with covering the roof of a rotten political edifice with new tiles.[20]

Börne's style was clear and incisive. His words were understood by all, especially the young, and were always marked by a deep honesty of conviction.

Karl Gutzkow in his *Wally, die Zweiflerin* and *Uriel Acosta* exalted free thought and speech; Heinrich Laube in his *Das junge Europa* and *Die Karlsschüler* preached a free political life; Theodor Mundt in his *Madonna, Unterhaltungen mit einer Heiligen* idealized free love; and Georg Herwegh in his most famous poem *Aufruf* preached a war on tyrants and philistines. Herwegh, perhaps more than other figures in this movement, retained the greatest amount of militant nationalism. With the characteristic German aspiration to overcome *Zerrissenheit,* he summoned the Germans to become *"Ein Herz, Ein Volk, Ein Wappen,"* and in his poem "Die deutsche Flotte" he anticipated Tirpitz and the pan-Germans. He urged the German women to spin linen for a German navy so that "You shall win the world." Anchors aweigh, he calls, for "You are the shepherd of the great herd of nations"; the sea, he sings, "will wash away from our hearts the last rust of tyranny."

Closely associated with the Young Germany group in many ways, but towering over and above them all in literary genius, was Heinrich Heine, one of the most controversial figures in the history of German literature. Together with Goethe, Heine is the greatest lyric poet of modern Germany. His poems, translated into almost all European languages and many of them set to music by Schubert, Schumann, Mendelssohn, and Brahms, have made him even more universally known than the poet of Weimar.* "I search vainly through the kingdoms of all ages," wrote Nietzsche of him, "for anything to equal his sweet and passionate music." Deeply rooted in romanticism, medievalism, the folklore of the Rhine and other German folk literature, many of Heine's poems, especially "Die Lorelei," achieved the position of German folk songs until the advent of Hitlerism in 1933 changed the authorship of "Die Lorelei" from that of Heine to Anonymous. With the publication of his *Harzreise* his reputation was likewise established as a great prose writer.

To his remarkable lyrical quality Heine added keen wit, pungent irony,

* Heine's poems have been used in more than 3,000 musical compositions. Goethe's lyrics accounted for only 1,700. One authority counted 160 settings of "Du bist wie eine Blume," 83 each of "Ich hab' im Traum geweinet" and "Leise zieht durch mein Gemüth," 76 of "Ein Fichtenbaum steht einsam," and 37 of "Ich weiss nicht was soll es bedeuten." (Cf. Georg Brandes, *Main Currents in Nineteenth Century Literature,* vi, 35.)

and sharp satire. He directed the biting shafts of his intellect against himself, against the ruling powers, and against some of the most hallowed traditions of German social and cultural life. But as Graetz points out, "Behind his banter there was often more earnest conviction than in the litany of a morose moralist," and while he often changed his opinions he did not play with his convictions. A French wit once called Heine "an unfrocked Romantic," and Heine himself accepted the designation as apt. No one did more to expose the literary emptiness, the intellectual sickliness, the vain pomposity, and the reactionary feudalism of the excrescences of German romanticism than did Heine, yet he himself admitted that "I always remained a Romantic at heart." Born of a Jewish family in Düsseldorf, Heine embraced Christianity in 1825, primarily, as he said, to acquire "an entrance card to European culture." But the conflict between Hellenism and Hebraism went on in Heine's innermost being until his last days, and it was only in his later years that he came to recognize the moral grandeur of Jewish ethics and Jewish tradition.

Heine waged a continuous war against the extreme manifestations of German nationalism, much to the chagrin of the professional patriots. Yet, as he himself confessed, his yearning for Germany and German traditions was greatly heightened once he crossed the Rhine and became an émigré. He refused to accept the offer of French citizenship and preferred to remain a *German* poet in exile. "My marriage with my dear Frau Germania, the blond, bearskin savage," wrote Heine, "had never been happy . . . but it never came to an actual breach. I could never bring myself to renounce my domestic cross. . . . I have not lost the birth of my German nature, not a single bell of my German cap. . . . Naturalization may do for others . . . but it is not fitting for a German poet, who has written the most beautiful German poems. It would be a horrible, insane idea for me to have to say that I am a German poet and at the same time a naturalized Frenchman." [21]

While in Paris, Heine came into contact first with the Saint-Simonians, then with the early communism of Marx and Engels. "The Silesian Weavers," in which he drew attention to the woeful conditions of the Silesian weavers in 1844, was one of the first and one of the finest examples of poetry of social protest. But his esthetic nature made him, in the last analysis, skeptical of all mass movements and led him to turn away from the organized socialist and communist movement. He remained devoted most passionately and most consistently to the ideals of liberty and enlightenment, and he threw all his talents of wit, satire, and gifted political journalism in the service of this cause. He recognized no holier spirit than that of emancipation, and called himself a *Ritter* (knight) of this spirit. As Arnold Ruge well pointed out, Heine "conceived of this emancipation not in dogmas and laws but rather in the casting off of dogmas and laws through wit and creative originality." [22] That is why

France, French culture, and above all the French revolution played so important a role in Heine's thinking and writing. "Freedom," he held, "is a new religion, the religion of our age. . . . The French are the chosen people of this new religion. . . . Paris is the new Jerusalem and the Rhine is the Jordan which divides the land of freedom from the country of the Philistines." But in his innermost being Heine yearned for a truly free Germany which would combine the emancipation of Luther and of Kant with the emancipation of 1789. A free France and a free Germany could then become the core of a free and emancipated Europe. In his last testament Heine wrote:

It has been the greatest task of my life to work for a cordial understanding between Germany and France, and to frustrate the plots of the enemies of democracy, who exploit national prejudices and animosities for their own uses. I believe that I have deserved well of my fellow countrymen and of the French, and the claims which I have on their gratitude are no doubt the most valuable legacy which I can bequeath to my universal heirs.[23]

Both during and after his lifetime Heine was "famous and disliked." All his life he was pursued by hatred and resentment. He was hounded by Metternich's agents in Paris, and Prussian officers swore they would kill him if he dared to set foot on German soil. The hostility continued after his death. Conservative literary critics down to the National Socialist writings of Bartels, Rosenberg, and Streicher poured invective and derision upon him. A monument which his admirers wished to set up for him in his native Düsseldorf wandered, unwanted, from Düsseldorf to Mainz to Hamburg to Berlin, until it found a resting place on the Grand Concourse in the Bronx, in New York City.[24]

There are many reasons for this antagonism. His espousal of the revolutionary cause, his pro-French sympathies—often at the expense of German sensibilities—his lack of reverence for commonly accepted mores in religion, in sex relations, and in politics, his socialist leanings, and his life of estrangement as an émigré—all these facets of his life and work gave his opponents ample reasons for hostility. But, as Max Brod has brilliantly demonstrated,[25] examples of the same tendencies can be found in Arnim, Rückert, Uhland, Bettina Brentano, Lessing, Grillparzer, and Nietzsche. Yet none of these writers suffered the fate of Heine. It is the added factor of Heine's Jewishness that distinguishes him from these others. And all of these factors combined are indications not of Heine's weakness and failing but rather of the dominance of romantic nationalism over enlightened and humane liberalism in the history of Germany. He was rejected by the dominant cultural leaders of nineteenth and twentieth century Germany because the things he stood for ran counter to the dominant and all-pervading cultural and political traditions in Germany. That is why he has always evoked so much more sympathy and enthusiasm outside Germany than within and why he is closer to the twentieth century than to his own contemporaries of the nineteenth.

A movement of radical protest against prevailing religious and intellectual currents emanated from the left-wing followers of Hegel, who came to be known as the Young Hegelians.[26] Some of these, like David Friedrich Strauss, remained radical only in their religious views, while accepting the *status quo* in all other areas of social existence; some, like Bruno Bauer, actually made their religious radicalism serve the cause of political reaction; others, like Arnold Ruge, used religious radicalism as a convenient device to cloak their democratic and republican political views, and served as a bridge between the revolution of reason and humanism to the social revolution of Marx and Engels.

The point of departure for these philosophical radicals was the philosophy of Hegel. As Engels pointed out, the famous dictum of Hegel that "what is real is rational and what is rational is real" allowed for two different interpretations.[27] A static construction of this thesis served as a justification for all existing institutions. This was the view taken by the right-wing Hegelians who defended the rationality of the *status quo* by the reality of its existence. On the other hand a dynamic explanation of the same principle led to an interpretation of all reality of today as the "irrational" of tomorrow. Those that emphasized the system in Hegel were the conservatives, and those that made the "dialectic method" their chief point of departure were the radical Young Hegelians. Existing rigorous censorship combined with the generally dominant idealistic and spiritualistic tradition accounted for the fact that the initial outlet for attack by the Young Hegelians came in the field of religion. It was directed against ultramontane Catholicism, against the revived Pietism of orthodox Lutheranism, of which Hengstenberg and his *Evangelische Kirchenzeitung* were the chief spokesman, and against the romantic Christian-Germanic cult of the Prussian court.

The first attack came with the publication in 1835 of David Friedrich Strauss's *Life of Jesus*. Strauss (1808–1874) applied the Hegelian dialectic to the study of the New Testament and destroyed the credibility of the Gospels as historical evidence. These, said Strauss, were not historical facts but rather "myths" which were the result of the myth-making consciousness of the early Christian community that was brought up in the traditions of the Old Testament. Jesus was therefore merely the personification of an Idea, and all the miraculous elements in the New Testament story were eliminated from the picture. Strauss's book created a sensation throughout Germany, so much so that the author was himself scared by the full import of his work and he modified his conclusions in the subsequent editions of the work and in his other theological writings.

Bruno Bauer (1809–1882) went even further than Strauss in his religious radicalism. In 1841 he published his *Kritik der evangelischen*

Geschichte der Synoptiker, in which he denied both the divinity and the historicity of Jesus. The same year witnessed the appearance of *Das Wesen des Christentums* by Ludwig Feuerbach (1804–1872), the most significant philosopher of this humanist school. Feuerbach, going back to the English and French materialists of the eighteenth century, tried to show that nothing existed outside Man and Nature. It was he who coined the famous expression "Ein Mann ist was er isst" (A man is what he eats). The essence of religion, according to Feuerbach, is found in man and in man's desire for happiness. Gods are but the projection of man's thoughts and ideals. It was not God who created man but man that created the gods. The secret of theology is anthropology. Supernatural religion, therefore, wrote Feuerbach, should be replaced by a religion of love between human beings.

While often classed as a materialist, Feuerbach was really a humanist and not a materialist. But he helped clear the intellectual atmosphere of *Vormärz* Germany of the dogmatic, vapid and nebulous spiritualism that was the product of the religious romanticism of Schleiermacher, the speculative theology of Hegel and Schelling, the revival of Pietism, the union of Christianity and Teutonism in conservative Prussian circles, and the dogmatic orthodoxy of Hengstenberg. As such, Feuerbach had a tremendous influence on the "true socialist" circle of Moses Hess and Karl Grün and on the founders of "scientific socialism," Marx and Engels. "One must have personally experienced the liberating influence of this book," wrote Engels many years later, "in order to have a proper conception of it. The enthusiasm was universal, we all immediately became Feuerbachianer." [28] It was "refreshing after the long years of abstract and abstruse *Hegelei.*" And Karl Marx, even though he subjected Feuerbach to a severe critique in his *Heilige Familie,* yet in the same work he also expressed his indebtedness to this humanist philosopher. The significance of Feuerbach for the radicals of his day has best been summarized by Sidney Hook:

What was there in Feuerbach's approach to religion to fire the rebellious hearts of the time . . . ? It was his theory of the natural fetishism of human activity—a fetishism which could be applied to illumine almost every social institution. If the religious fact *par excellence* is the alienation of man from himself, the erection of a *product* of man's own emotional and intellectual activity into an objective norm claiming *a priori* validity, then it could be shown that the whole of society was pervaded by a religious principle. . . . The same formula was extended from religion to politics, to ethics, to economics. . . . The transcendence of God meant in ethical terms the hypostasis of principles which were once functionally justified into oppressive absolutes and the cramping of progressive social tendencies by outworn institutions. The simple truth that ethical commands are demands of man's own nature made it impossible to accept the theory that man existed as a means to the state.[29]

It was Arnold Ruge who was the central figure of the Young Hegelians and the philosophical radicals in Germany on the eve of the revolution of 1848. He was not an original or creative thinker but, in the words of Moses Hess, "he always was able to sense with proper tact what was true and what was in keeping with the times, what was healthy and what was sick in the movement of his day. . . . He was less of a philosopher than a representative of the idea of progress and in his person he embodied the essence of Young Hegelianism, which formed the transition from German philosophy to socialism, from thought to action." [30] Ruge was above all an enterprising and able journalist. The *Hallische Jahrbücher,* which he edited together with Theodor Echtermeyer from 1837 to 1841, made him the recognized leader of philosophical-political journalism in Germany. He enlisted the collaboration of most of the leading liberal thinkers and publicists of Germany. When the Prussian government put pressure on the government of Saxony to close down this journal, he carried it on for a while under the name of *Deutsche Jahrbücher* but was finally forced to emigrate to Paris, where he collaborated for a short period with Karl Marx in publishing the *Deutsch-Französische Jahrbücher.*

In the columns of these journals Ruge declared war on Pietism in religion and reaction in politics and culture. He saw the close relationship between liberalism and the rationalism of the Enlightenment, and he extolled the virtues of Lessing; even more so did he point out the intimate connection between political reaction and literary romanticism, and he made the romantic movement the special butt of his sharp and witty pen. He defined the romanticists as "those writers who use the vehicle of our culture to oppose the epoch of Enlightenment and revolution and who reject and combat in science, art and ethics the principle of a self-sufficient humanity." [31] He espoused the cause of democratic republicanism and in his "Selbst-kritik des Liberalismus" subjected German liberalism to a most realistic and critical analysis. Pointing out that German liberalism had been purely theoretical and abstract and more in the nature of a spectator on the side lines rather than an active participant, he called for the transformation of liberalism into democracy. Anticipating the self-criticism of Thomas Mann in the twentieth century, Ruge deplored the non-political character of the Germans. Their political activity, he wrote, is not their real business but rather "time lost out of their essential interests, *i.e.* their private business. Politics does affect them but only in the same way that the weather affects them. In both instances they have nothing to do with producing it. When they want good politics as when they want good weather they gaze upward silently and with implicit faith." Liberty, declared Ruge, cannot be granted as a gift. It is a condition of being that can only be attained by battling for it and conquering it. The Germans lack and need what the French possess—"political understanding and political courage." And Ruge called upon the Germans to "refresh your slothfulness with French spirit." Like Börne and Heine, he looked for the synthesis of English and French radicalism with the liberating philosophies of German culture. He published a German translation of the letters of Junius and he served as a disseminator of the ideas of the French revolution. But, he pointed out in a review of Schlosser's *History of the 18th Century:* "We want the French principle not because it is French but because it is the principle of the century. We want it as the demand of reason, of history, of justice; in a German form and with thoroughness and reliability." [32]

Ruge examined the feeling of patriotism in a very sober and interesting analysis.[33] While he found a great deal to admire in the spirit of the War of Liberation as expressed in 1813, he considered the revival of this spirit in the 1830's and 1840's as reactionary and opposed to the spirit of liberty. He characterized it as "Francophobia and old-German rubbish" and as a "dangerous reaction against reason and history." [34] He recognized the "tragic conflict between German patriotism and liberal ideas" which is "a source of the most bitter pain for the true patriot." "Triumph over France and political reaction or defeat and national humiliation—that is the sad alternative which calls forth in us an elegiac sorrow." [35] This sad alternative was one that was to confront German liberalism all through its history and thus paralyze its energy and its drive.

Such was the nature and content of the radicalism of the Young Hegelians. Interesting as their ideas were, they did not become the possession of more than a small fringe of the German youth. And most of the members of this group were obliterated from the records of German history by the subsequent nationalist historians who dominated German historical writing throughout the nineteenth and twentieth centuries. But this democratic movement was an integral part of the complex of forces that brought on the revolution of 1848. More important still, it was this intellectual climate that gave birth to Marx and Engels and to the beginnings of Marxian socialism. Marx and Engels believed that they went beyond the critical philosophy of self-consciousness of Feuerbach and Ruge to develop a revolutionary philosophy of "social activity." But they did it at the expense of the humane quality, the true spirit of liberalism, and the deep ethical sense which characterized the thought of Ruge and Feuerbach as it did of Moses Hess.* Before coming to the beginnings of German socialism, however, it is necessary to look at the economic and social conditions of Germany on the eve of the revolution.

---

* Complementing the democratic movement of Ruge in western Germany was the democratic movement led by Johann Jacoby in East Prussia. Whereas the former was inspired by Hegel, the latter derived from the ethics of Kant. In 1841 Jacoby published his *Vier Fragen beantwortet von einem Ostpreussen,* in which he called upon the estates "to demand as a demonstrable right what they had previously solicited as an act of grace." The pamphlet made Jacoby a hero in liberal circles but aroused the ire of the conservatives and of King Frederick William IV. Writing to Schön, the king said: "I would that you could secure uncircumcised men of proved fidelity, men who are devoted to me, to undo the shame which the circumcised of East Prussia have inflicted." (Cf. Treitschke, *History of Germany,* vi, 463.)

Economic and social conditions in Germany on the eve of the revolution of 1848 were still backward as compared with developments in the other countries of western Europe. Agriculture was still the most important industry, employing more than two-thirds of the population. Peasant emancipation had taken place during the revolutionary period, but the patriarchal feudal social order still lived on in large areas of Germany. In the Rhineland, following the French revolutionary pattern, the large estates had been parceled out to the peasants; Bavaria had medium- and small-sized holdings, and the northwest had mostly large- and medium-sized peasant holdings. In Mecklenburg, Pomerania, Brandenburg, Saxony, Silesia, Bohemia, and Moravia there still were knightly estates and feudal latifundia. Here the Junkers, descendants of the old conquerors and colonizers, now became capitalist cultivators. Liebig's work in agricultural chemistry, published in 1840, initiated the development of scientific agriculture, but the social patriarchal relationship between free peasant and landowner still continued. The feudal nobility was the first "estate" in the country, and it contributed most of the army officers and officials in the state bureaucracy.

A small middle class consisted largely of more prosperous peasants, artisan masters, small manufacturers, hotel keepers, merchants, officials, and professional classes. The bourgeoisie in Germany was "neither as wealthy nor as concentrated as in France and England." The old manufacturing establishments were ruined by the introduction of steam and the competition of the products of the industrial revolution in England. The industrial centers were sparse and widely scattered, and transportation facilities to trading centers were poor. After 1835 an increase in industrial and economic activity set in. The textile industry was the most important industry. It was still characterized by small handicraft installations. In 1831 there were in Prussia 252,000 linen looms, but only 33,500 of these belonged to weavers who were engaged in no other pursuit. About the same situation existed with respect to wool. More professional workers were to be found in the silk and cotton industries. On the whole there was very little use of machinery. Linen manufacture increased in Silesia, Westphalia, and the Swabian Alps; woolens in Austria, Saxony, and the Rhineland; cotton in Bohemia, Silesia, Saxony, Vienna, and Berlin. There was also an increase in liquor production in the south, and in oil, beet sugar, and tobacco production in the west. The iron and steel industry also showed increased activity with the beginning of the working of the Ruhr fields after 1815 and the founding of the Krupp works in 1810. In 1846 Krupp still employed only 140 workers.

Despite the beginnings of industrial advance Germany was still a relatively poor country. Capital still had to be raised in England; the Berlin bourse was very small, and communication both within Germany and with foreign countries was still primitive. When Goethe wished to send a parcel of gifts to Carlyle in England, he had to wait several months until some skipper announced a sailing to Edinburgh. The roads within Germany were very poor, and large cities like Leipzig were still without paved sidewalks.

The most epoch-making economic event during this period was the establishment of the German customs union, known as the Zollverein, in 1834. The prevalence of customs barriers between the various German states in the confederation had been a severe handicap to German economic development. It was deplored by the adherents of Smithian liberal economics as running counter to *laissez faire* principles, and it was denounced by nationalist economists who saw in it a serious bar to national unity. The petition of the Deutscher Handels und Gewerbsverein, drawn up by Friedrich List, to the Bundestag on April 20, 1819, gives a picture of the prevailing situation:

Thirty-eight customs and toll boundaries in Germany [wrote List] paralyze communication within and result in approximately the same effect as if every limb of the human body was tied up so as to prevent the flow of blood from one to the other. In order to carry on business between Hamburg and Austria or between Berlin and Switzerland, one must traverse 10 states, master 10 customs and toll systems and pay transit duties 10 times. Whoever is so unfortunate, however, as to live where three or four states come together, spends his whole life amidst hostile customs officials and is a man without a fatherland. This situation is most lamentable for those who wish to carry on activity and business. They look across the Rhine with envious glance and see one great nation from the channel to the Mediterranean, from the Rhine to the Pyrenees, from the frontiers of Holland to Italy, carrying on trade along free rivers and open roads without once meeting a customs official. The powers of those Germans, who at the time of the Hansa carried on world trade under the protection of German warships, is going to destruction through 38 customs and toll systems.[36]

The first free-trade action had been taken in Prussia in the Tariff Law of May 26, 1818, drafted by Karl Georg von Maassen. It eliminated all duties within the state of Prussia and proclaimed Prussian adherence to the principle of free trade, which was to be regulated according to the commercial policies of other nations. This inspired commercial treaties with neighbor states and provided the pattern for the later establishment of the Zollverein. The first such treaty was signed on February 14, 1828, between Prussia and Hesse-Darmstadt. In the meantime a South German customs union of a limited character was established in January, 1828, and an even more limited commercial union was set up by the middle German states in December, 1828. Both of these associations were eventually swallowed up by the Prussian customs union. After several years of rivalry and negotiations the Zollverein came into being on January 1, 1834. Eighteen of the German states were the original members, with an area of 162,870 square miles and a population of over 23 million. Outside the union were the three Hanse towns in the north, the two Mecklenburgs, Schleswig, Holstein, and Lauenburg. In the south and southwest the Austrian empire was excluded, as were Nassau, Baden, and Frankfurt am Main. Subsequent negotiations brought all these other political units into the orbit of the Zollverein, with the exception of Austria. The Zollverein thus became the economic framework upon which subsequent political unification was grafted. It proved to be a powerful stimulus to the development of German industry and trade which began in the 1850's, but it also furthered the increased intensity of national sentiment.

The establishment of the Zollverein coincided with the beginnings of railroad construction in Germany, and in that, too, Friedrich List was one of the most active promoters. Before List the cause of railroad construction had first been launched by Josef von Baader (1763–1835), brilliant scientist and mining engineer and brother of the famous Catholic philosopher Franz von Baader.[37] Baader had spent many years in England and had begun his public advocacy of railroad construction in 1814, ten years before George Stephenson's first line in Liverpool. List, who acknowledged his indebtedness to Baader, was also inspired by the railroad development he had seen in the United States, and projected a plan for a line between Dresden and Leipzig. He envisaged a national system of railroads. The first railroad line actually established, however, was between Nürnberg and Fürth in 1835. The Leipzig-Dresden line was not completed until 1839. In 1838 a railroad was opened between Berlin and Potsdam; in 1841 between Berlin and Anhalt, in 1842 between Berlin and Stettin, and in 1843 the Rhenish railroad from Antwerp to Cologne was opened. The poet Karl Beck celebrated the railroad construction in the following verse:

> Diese Schienen—Hochzeitsbänder
> Trauungsringe, blank gegossen;
> Liebend tauschen sie die Länder
> Und die Ehe wird geschlossen.*

All the early railroad construction was carried out by private enterprise, and there was as yet no integrated system for the entire country. But together with the beginnings of telegraph and steamboat construction, the building of railroads not only stimulated the great industrial and commercial development which was to commence in the 1850's but also helped to shake the country out of its lethargy and bring the various parts of Germany closer to each other to make possible eventual national unification.

The increased industrial and economic activity resulted also in the beginning of a proletarian and socialist protest. This movement was still

---

* "These glittering rails are nuptial bonds and wedding rings, and lovingly they exchange states and the marriage is completed."

weak and insignificant, but it is worth mentioning. Ludwig Gall (1791–1863), a state official and chemist in Trier, had noted the economic distress of the Rhenish workers following the Napoleonic wars and had pointed out that the reason for their poverty was not to be found in the paucity of goods but rather "in the worthlessness of human labor in relation to the all-dominant value of money." In Munich the Catholic social philosopher Franz von Baader (1765–1841) called attention to the growing seriousness of the social question and urged the church to take the lead in its solution. The doctrines of Saint-Simon, Fourier, Cabet, Lamennais, and other French reformers and utopian socialists were spread in Germany by the writings of the political émigrés from Paris, especially Heine and Börne. In more scholarly fashion Lorenz von Stein's *Der Sozialismus und Kommunismus des heutigen Frankreich,* published in 1842, brought to Germany familiarity with the socialist currents in France.* Economists like Karl Marlo, Hildebrand, and Rodbertus elaborated various theoretical aspects of state socialism. These were all works by scholars and theorists rather than expressions of social protest from within the working classes. Wilhelm Weitling (1808–1871) was the first real proletarian leader in Germany. A tailor apprentice, he became the first to dedicate his life to the liberation of the working classes, and his were the first attempts to go beyond utopian socialism and to organize larger masses of the proletariat. In Paris he had become familiar with the ideas of Cabet, Fourier, and Lamennais, and he returned to Germany to preach a communism that was based on the social gospel of primitive Christianity. Weitling carried on most of his agitation among German journeymen from across the German border in Paris and Switzerland. His anti-militarism and anti-nationalism were of greater influence than his communistic views, and his whole system of thought was more closely identified with the old handicraft workers than with the new industrial conditions. His influence declined after 1844, and he emigrated to the United States after the failure of 1848–1849.[38]

The most important socialist movement developed in Westphalia and the Rhineland. Closer to France and in the midst of the more advanced economic sections of the country, this region gave birth to the most active socialist group. Intellectually it derived from the Young Hegelian group discussed above. Here the ethical or "true" socialism of Karl Grün and Moses Hess, and the propaganda carried on by Karl Heinzen, paved the way for Karl Marx and Friedrich Engels, who were just beginning to emerge from religious and intellectual radicalism to develop a doctrine of

---

* Franz Mehring denies the commonly accepted view regarding the influence of Stein's work (cf. *Aus dem literarischen Nachlass von Karl Marx und Friedrich Engels 1841–1850,* ed. Franz Mehring, 2 vols. Berlin, 1923, i, 186). But Moses Hess, a contemporary of Stein's, writes: "Who knows how many years would have gone by until Germany would have given serious attention to socialism had this book [by Lorenz von Stein] not appeared at the right time and hour? . . . Stein made it legitimate to concern one's self with this dangerous and shunned 'outgrowth' of the French spirit" (*Socialistische Aufsätze,* p. 121).

historical materialism and a philosophy of social revolution. But epoch-making as it was for the later history of Germany and Europe, the communist movement, organized by Marx and Engels on the eve of the revolution of 1848, found but very few adherents within the borders of the German Confederation. Marxian socialism, developed largely while its leaders were in exile, did not come to play a significant role in Germany until after the founding of the Bismarckian Reich.

Friedrich Engels, in the series of articles he wrote for the *New York Tribune,* as ghost writer for Karl Marx, on the revolution of 1848, brilliantly summarized the social conditions in Germany on the eve of the revolution:

With growing wealth and extending trade, the bourgeoisie soon arrived at a stage where it found the development of its most important interests checked by the political constitution of the country, by its random division among thirty-six princes with conflicting tendencies and caprices; by the feudal fetters upon agriculture and the trade connected with it; by the prying superintendence to which an ignorant and presumptuous bureaucracy subjected all its transactions. At the same time the extension and consolidation of the Zollverein, the general introduction of steam communication, the growing competition in the home trade, brought the commercial classes of different states and princes together, equalized their interests, centralized their strength. The natural consequence was the passing of the whole mass of them into the camp of the liberal opposition, and the gaining of the first serious struggle of the German middle classes for political power.[39]

The number of workers was relatively small and most of them were employed more like the medieval journeymen than like modern factory workers. But insurrections in Silesia and Bohemia in 1844 indicated a growing social unrest. Between the upper bourgeoisie and the workers was the numerous class of petty bourgeoisie which aspiring, in the words of Engels,

to the position of the first, the least adverse turn of fortune hurls the individuals of this class down into the ranks of the second. . . . Thus eternally tossed about between the hope of entering the ranks of the wealthier class, and the fear of being reduced to the state of proletarians or even paupers . . . the class is extremely vacillating in its views. Humble and crouchingly submissive under a powerful feudal or monarchial government, it turns to the side of liberalism when the middle class is in the ascendant; it becomes seized with violent democratic fits as soon as the middle class has secured its own supremacy, but falls back into abject despondency of fear as soon as the class below itself, the proletarians, attempts an independent movement.[40]

Such was the state of Germany when news came of the revolution of 1848 in Paris and when the "sneezing" of France once again hurled Germany as well as the rest of the European continent into the turmoil of political and social revolution.

CHAPTER V

The Revolution of 1848

Eine Revolution ist ein Unglück, aber ein noch grösseres Unglück ist eine verunglückte Revolution.

HEINE

The year 1848 was a historic year for most peoples of Europe. By this time the effects of the industrial revolution were fully apparent. A class of wage workers was created, the antagonism between bourgeoisie and proletariat sharpened, and the tension heightened between the remains of the old order and the increasingly powerful middle classes. All this brought eruptions throughout Europe. The national movements of oppressed peoples also tested their strength in this fateful year. Italians, Poles, Irish, Czechs, southern Slavs, Hungarians—all were aroused to varying degrees of nationalist action, and the "romantic exiles" in London, Paris, Brussels, and Zurich streamed back to their homelands to try their hand at redrawing the map of Europe and fashioning a new world of free peoples. Germany was no exception. Here too 1848 proved to be a historic year. The various strains of the German movement of 1848, however, are most difficult to unravel.[1] There is a complexity of movements and counter-movements, of currents and counter-currents. The revolution of 1848 was a social revolution—a movement of repressed peasants, of a rising bourgeoisie, and of an exploited urban proletariat. Radical social ideas in gestation since the turn of the century were brought to the fore and they penetrated into liberal and democratic circles. The revolution was a political-constitutional movement of the more politically conscious elements of the German middle classes, who demanded constitutional reform and guarantees of political and civil liberties. Further complexity resulted from the multiplicity of political units in Germany. For there was not only a *German* revolution of 1848 but there were also revolutions in each of the local states; variations of a local character, therefore, must be taken into consideration. Over and above all these other aspects loomed the national question—the revolution to bring about a unified Germany. And with this phase all other social, political, and constitutional aspects came to merge and be lost.

80

Finally, the revolution in Germany was intertwined with events in the Austrian Empire, hence with the revolutions of the Hungarians and the various Slavic nationalities.

Because of its tragic failure the revolution of 1848 in Germany has not occupied an exalted place in the annals of German historiography. Apart from the controversies occasioned by bourgeois versus proletarian conflicts, it has been the butt of much ridicule and derision because it did not succeed in bringing about the national unity subsequently achieved by Bismarck. Nevertheless the years 1848–1849 represented a decisive turning point in the history of Germany. The words *Vormärz* and *Nachmärz,* introduced into German political terminology to designate the periods before and after the revolution, were not merely a formal device to indicate the profound and lasting cleavage produced by the events of 1848–1849 in the evolution of modern Germany. Liberal and democratic movements of the nineteenth and twentieth centuries recognized the historical significance of the "unfulfilled revolution." It remained the starting point for all subsequent movements to democratize Germany and it was accepted as the prototype of the Weimar Republic by the republican leaders of 1918 to 1933.

The German revolution of 1848 was a product of the interaction of internal and external causes. Developments within Germany combined to bring events to a head, and the news of the revolutionary events in France served to ignite the spark and give impetus, confidence, and courage to the revolutionary groups and leaders in Germany. The antecedents of the revolution are to be found first of all in the liberal and constitutional movements of the South German states. Liberal deputies of the parliaments of the South German states established the custom of meeting together and exchanging information, views, and commiseration. The more radical members also met together to frame their social and political demands. Sometimes such programs combined radical political and social slogans with antisemitic charges against Jews. As frequently happened in many of the cruder expressions of social protest in Europe, the Jews were looked upon as the chief agents of commercial and capitalistic exploitation. Early Fourierist and Saint-Simonian literature is full of such "socialist antisemitism." [2] It found its way similarly into some of the declarations by radicals in Germany.

On September 12, 1847, a group of southern radicals met in Offenburg, Baden, under the leadership of two lawyers and politicians of Mannheim, Gustav von Struve (1805–1870) and Friedrich Hecker (1811–1881). The platform they drew up listed the following demands: (1) universal arming of the populace, (2) a German parliament freely elected by the people, (3) universal suffrage, (4) freedom of press, (5) freedom of religion, conscience, and teaching, (6) trial by jury, (7) universal German citizenship, (8) just taxation according to income, (9) universal instruction, (10) protection of labor and the right to work, (11) adjustment of relations between capital and labor, (12) popular and economical administration, (13) responsibility of all ministers and officials, (14) abolition of all privileges.[3]

Liberal opposition deputies from Baden, Württemberg, and Hesse met in Heppenheim (near Frankfurt) in October, 1847, under the leadership of Heinrich von Gagern, David Hansemann, Friedrich Bassermann, and Karl Mathy. They demanded a constitutional monarchy for Germany as a whole and constitutional governments for each of the member states. On February 12, 1848, Bassermann introduced a motion in the Baden parliament calling upon the various state delegations to the imperial Bundestag to take steps to bring about unified German laws and institutions and a general German parliament. This action received added strength from numerous petitions that began to come in demanding (1) free press, (2) trial by jury, (3) a national militia, and (4) a national assembly. "Free speech, secure laws and a people's army," declared Karl Mathy on March 1, "these we consider to be the foundation stones for the erection of a free and great German fatherland."

The people of Prussia, in the meantime, also began to clamor for constitutional reform. Promises of a constitution had frequently been made to them in 1810, 1811, 1814, 1815, and 1820. But despite the efforts of Hardenberg, Humboldt, Boyen, and others, nothing was ever done to that end under the rule of Frederick William III, who looked upon all who aspired to political liberty as subversive Jacobins. In this attitude Frederick William was supported by the old Prussian aristocracy, the bureaucracy, and the military caste. When Frederick William IV came to the throne in 1840 hopes for political reform were raised. But the new monarch, too, was strongly anti-democratic in his views and was, moreover, emotionally unstable and psychopathic.

On February 3, 1847, the Prussian king issued a patent calling for the convocation of all provincial diets to a "united Landtag" in Berlin on April 11. It was to consist of two curial assemblies, a noble curia of 72 high-ranking nobles and a curia of the three estates, made up of 231 nobles, 182 urban representatives, and 120 peasant representatives. The powers of this body were to be extremely limited. It was to have only consultative powers; its taxing power was to be limited only to new or increased taxes; and its approval for loans was to be limited only to peacetime. Addresses to the king were to require a two-thirds vote; sessions were to be secret, but stenographic reports of the meetings were to be published. The king opened the sessions of this Landtag with the words: "You have been called together to represent rights—the rights of your estates and those of the throne. It is not your task to represent opinions." He expressed his views on constitutions in no uncertain terms when he declared that no written piece of paper was ever to come between him and the Lord God in order to govern the country with "its paragraphs" and thus supplant the "old fealty."

Amidst all these political brewings came the stormy news of the events of February, 1848, in Paris. Liberals as well as radicals in Germany now felt that the hour for Germany had arrived. Everywhere a wave of political enthusiasm was set loose. In some instances the resulting action was a very vague and undeveloped expression of social protest. This was true particularly among the peasants of southern and western Germany, who were suffering from the effects of the agricultural revolution. Many of their friends and relatives had emigrated, for economic reasons, to the United States. The success of the German immigrants in the republic of the New World made a deep impression on their friends remaining in the fatherland. Material prosperity came to be identified in their minds with a republican form of government. Very frequently these economic and political aspirations were combined with antisemitic agitation against the Jews. Peasant revolts broke out throughout rural Germany in the early months of 1848. The most serious occurred in the Odenwald and Black Forest regions. This area, decidedly feudal in character and peopled by a heavily burdened peasantry, began its agrarian revolts with anti-Jewish outbreaks. Such anti-Jewish manifestations also occurred in Neckarbischofsheim, Breisgau, and Mühlheim. One peasant leaflet proclaimed the goal of the revolution to be (1) the destruction of the nobility, (2) the banishment of all Jews from Germany, (3) the elimination of all kings, dukes, and princes and the conversion of Germany into a free state like America, and (4) the execution of all officials. "We want it to be as it is in America," declared the leaflet. "We want to elect our president and be able to depose him if he is bad. Then the taxes will immediately fall away, like rotten apples off a tree. The Americans are smart people in having arranged things in this way and that is why they are so well off." [4]

From liberal and radical intellectuals and political leaders everywhere came the same pattern of political demands—a free press, trial by jury, national militia, and a German parliament. The first organized initiative was taken in Mannheim. There a great political meeting was held on February 27. Struve drew up an address to the Baden government in Karlsruhe. "A tremendous revolution has transformed France," it declared. "One idea has flashed across Europe. The old system is waning and falling into ruins. Everywhere the peoples have taken into their own powerful hands the rights which their masters had withheld from them. Germany dare no longer look on patiently while it is being trod underfoot. The German people have the right to demand well-being, education and freedom for all classes of society without distinction of birth and class."

The Mannheim meeting was followed by one in Heidelberg on February 29. Street demonstrations took place. A poster calling upon the people to assemble read: "France is a republic. The hour has struck for us too! . . . Give us what we want, Freedom, or we shall take it." [5]

On March 19 another large meeting was held in Offenburg under the leadership of Struve, Hecker, and the Nestor of the radicals, the venerable Adam von Itzstein. The program adopted called for (1) expression of lack of confidence in the government, (2) the elimination from parliament of all reactionary elements, (3) the fusion of the army with a civil militia, (4) a progressive income tax, (5) the separation of the church from the school system, and (6) the abolition of appanages. The meeting called upon each community in Baden to form a political club charged with the mission of organizing the mobilization of the political and social education of the people, and to carry the responsibility for realizing the rights of the people. The network of such clubs would then serve as an expression of the popular will of the state.

The plan for organizing a network of political clubs throughout the country reveals the essentially Jacobin character of the South German radicalism. For the plan was consciously patterned after the Jacobin clubs of the first French revolution. The social-radical movement in southern Germany, like the French Jacobin movement, was not socialist or communist in character, even though some of the leaders proclaimed themselves to be "social democrats." It was a movement of artisans, petty bourgeoisie, and uprooted intellectuals rather than of an organized industrial proletariat. It combined the goal of a democratic republic with vague social and economic demands to ease the social distress caused by the beginnings of the industrial and agricultural revolutions. Proximity to France and to republican Switzerland provided not only an ideological background but also a base for revolutionary operations and a reservoir for supporters from the various groups of radical nationalist exiles, both German and non-German.

The leaders of the South German radicals were the two Mannheim lawyers Hecker and von Struve. Hecker was the more flamboyant, erratic, and bombastic of the two. His opponents dubbed him a "fresh kid" (*frecher Bub*) and "loudmouth," but as a popular orator, with long, brown hair, full beard, and powerful baritone voice, he became the idol of the republican youth of South Germany. He would set up a republic, he declared, with the aid of a portable guillotine. He refused to wait for the action of the constitutional assembly to be convened in Frankfurt, and he led an abortive Putsch, proclaiming a German republic on April 12, 1848. Within eight days his motley band of followers had been overpowered by the forces of the Bund. The legion organized by the poet Herwegh in Paris was dispersed at the Swiss border, and Hecker escaped to the United States. Here he became a farmer in Illinois, later served in the Union army during the Civil War, and died in St. Louis in 1881.

Gustav von Struve, son of a Russian diplomat, was a much more intellectual figure than Hecker. Cooler and more deliberate, he was often impatient with the impulsive Hecker. Deeply imbued with the spirit of Rousseau and the Jacobins, Struve was known as the "monk of the German republic." He vehemently renounced the aristocratic designation "von" of his family, was ascetic in his personal habits and appearance, and was passionately devoted to the cause of an egalitarian republic. Influenced in part by French and Marxian socialist ideas, he put to the fore the social aspects of the revolution. In the editorial of the first issue of his paper *Der deutsche Zuschauer,* Struve wrote:

The great distress of the people and the numerous outbreaks caused by this distress, which have occurred most frequently and have been most serious in those states which have the least amount of popular government, indicate clearly and distinctly to all who look deeply into these problems that the masses are set into motion not by the question of forms of constitution but by distress of the people, not by ideological but rather by the material interests of the people. The solution to the riddle of our times is therefore to be sought directly in those political institutions which will guarantee the alleviation of the needs of the people.[6]

Struve was not a communist, but he wanted a "social republic" with "well-being, education and liberty for all." By conviction he was a terrorist, but he lacked the essential ruthlessness and drive to carry through a policy of violent revolution. Together with idealistic republicans like Karl Heinzen, Karl Blind, Otto Corvin, and Franz Sigel, he also allowed all sorts of disreputable elements to gather round him. He too, like Hecker, attempted a radical Putsch on September 21, 1848, and proclaimed a republic for all of Germany. This revolt was no more successful than that of Hecker. Struve, too, later emigrated to the United States. He lived there for a while, became a devoted apostle of phrenology, and finally died in Vienna on August 21, 1870.

The social protest of a more organized industrial proletariat found its outlet in the Rhineland, especially in Cologne, and in Berlin. Here the direct influence of Marx and Engels was of paramount importance. Marx and Engels, exiles in Brussels, had in 1847 converted the Federation of the Just, in which they were active, into the Communist League, and at a meeting of the league in London in November, 1847, had been entrusted with the task of drawing up a platform for the league. The result, completed in German in January, 1848, and sent to the printer a few weeks before the Paris revolution, was the epoch-making *Communist Manifesto.*

"The Communists turn their attention chiefly to Germany," declared the *Manifesto,* "because that country is on the eve of a bourgeois revolution that is bound to be carried out under more advanced conditions of

European civilization and with a more developed proletariat than that of England in the seventeenth, and of France in the eighteenth, and because the bourgeois revolution in Germany will be but the prelude to an immediately following proletarian revolution." While their realization of the imminence of revolution in Germany is testimony to the intimate acquaintance of Marx and Engels with German conditions, their prediction of a future proletarian revolution proved to be more than premature.

After the March revolutionary outbreaks in Vienna and Berlin, Marx and his friends issued a declaration of seventeen demands "in the interests of the German proletariat, the petty bourgeoisie and the peasantry." Among other things they called for a unified German republic, the arming of the people, the nationalization of the feudal lands of the princes, of mines and of the means of transportation, the establishment of national workshops and free public education. Marx and several hundred German revolutionaries returned to Germany. On June 1, 1848, Marx began to edit the *Neue Rheinische Zeitung* in Cologne. In the columns of this paper Marx, Engels, and the Communist League carried on revolutionary propaganda in the spirit of the *Communist Manifesto*.[7] They attacked the bourgeois ministers and the Frankfurt Assembly, heaped abuse and vituperation upon the "naïve" and "moralistic" democrats, called for a revolutionary war against Russia, championed the cause of the Poles, and supported the German national claims in Schleswig-Holstein. From the very beginning Marx and his followers carried on a policy that was to become the pattern for communistic activity throughout the subsequent history of Marxian socialism and communism. Communist agents, often using aliases, made it their business to aggravate antagonisms, to break up the bourgeois liberal movements, to arouse suspicions of the liberal and bourgeois democratic leadership, to spread unrest and to inspire terrorist inclinations. All this was intended to sharpen the class struggle, "abridge and concentrate the hideous death agonies of society," and thus to pave the way for the imminent social revolution proclaimed in the *Communist Manifesto*. The *Neue Rheinische Zeitung* managed to continue until May 19, 1849, when it was suppressed by the Prussian authorities and Marx was forced into exile again.

In Berlin the revolutionary activity of the workers was heightened by a serious economic crisis and widespread unemployment in the early part of the year 1848.[8] Most of the workers in Berlin were still artisans and handicraft workers rather than factory workers. Those factory workers that did exist still looked upon themselves as being no different from the old "mechanics." An incipient workers' movement had started in 1844 in which the book printers assumed the most active role. The events in France in February and the revolutionary activity of the radical bourgeoisie and the academic youth inspired the artisans and workers to social protest and action. There as elsewhere in Germany the lines between the various factions were not too clearly drawn; terms like "democrat" and "socialist" were used very loosely, and representatives of the various groups often mingled together at meetings and demonstrations. Several different groups nevertheless can be identified among the Berlin proletariat. There was a group of some 600 to 700 unemployed workers, known as the "Rheberger." They were a crude group of huskies who were used by the radicals for their demonstrations. The call would come: "Rheberger, let's go! Liberty is in danger!" and the Rheberger, wearing their round, yellow straw hats and red feathers, would march out in closed column formation to strike fear and terror into the hearts of the "enemies of liberty."

Wilhelm Weitling was active in Berlin and published a weekly, *Der Urwähler.* Friedrich Wilhelm Held was particularly popular among machinists with his publication *Lokomotive.* A small republican group, after the pattern of the South German radicals, combined republicanism with social-revolutionary aims and with a pan-European orientation. One of their leaflets, calling for a "mass-meeting in the park in honor of the great European revolution," announces speeches to be delivered in "German, English and French." Urging the Berliners to come to the meeting, it declares: "Frenchmen and Poles, Italians and Swiss, Irishmen and Englishmen, all the peoples of Europe, will take each other's hand in brotherly fashion in the park to give a thunderous welcome to liberty throughout the world." It concludes with the slogans "Long live the European revolution" and "Long live the new world." [9] Another group of Berlin radicals was led by Gustave Adolf Schlöffel, a student and son of a famous Silesian manufacturer, who preached an undisciplined and exaggerated communism in his paper *Der Volksfreund.*

The most intelligent, most significant, and most lasting of the workers' groups in Berlin was that led by Stephan Born. Born was influenced by the writings of Marx and Engels and was in touch with them. But he was no dogmatic follower of the Communist League. He gave evidence of independence of mind and he had an intelligent appraisal of the situation. Born was the chief figure in organizing a Central Committee of Workers, with the publication *Das Volk* as its organ. It was the most mature of all the labor papers. In his introduction to the constitution of the workers' organization Born wrote:

We take our affairs into our own hands and no one will ever again tear them from us. But together with this feeling of our strength we also know that in our fatherland there are as yet no two sharply divided classes of capitalists and workers, but that each of these still contains other elements. . . .

We know that the German people is dependent in its historical evolution upon the development of those nations who have already completed this process; we also know that in a nation where there are workers, poor people, oppressed and burdened individuals but as yet no working *class,* no revolution can be carried out by such a class.

Any attempt, declared Born, at a new revolution will only bring anarchy. Peace is in the interests of both workers and capitalists, but the workers must organize to assert their power.[10]

The first issue of *Das Volk,* published on May 25, 1848, carried the following declaration of the aim of the paper:

> On the one hand we shall support the bourgeoisie in its struggle against the aristocracy, against medievalism, against the powers by grace of God. On the other hand we shall aid the independent artisans as well as the workers against the power of capital and of free competition, and always, wherever possible, help the people secure their political rights so that they have the means with which to attain more speedily social freedom and an independent existence. . . . In doing so we will stay clear of the hollow declamations of the fanatical zealots who foam with rage and are always reaching out for the rope of the guillotine because they themselves have no head to lose, as well as from a dewy-eyed and love-sick kind of socialism.[11]

When the National Assembly convened in Frankfurt, the Berlin workers under Born submitted a petition which, among other things, made the following demands: (1) a law establishing minimum wages and maximum hours of labor, (2) the right of association for workers, (3) progressive income taxes, (4) state control of education, (5) free public libraries, (6) the regulation of the number of apprentices taken by a master, (7) the abolition of all travel restrictions for workers, (8) the reduction of the age requirement for voting to 24. In August, 1848, Born took the lead in establishing the first all-German workers' organization. It was called the Arbeiterverbrüderung, and its official publication, edited by Born, was named *Verbrüderung.* Subsequently the headquarters of this organization was moved to the more progressive center, Leipzig, and there it helped prepare the ground for the future activities of Ferdinand Lassalle.

Despite the importance of these proletarian movements for the history of the subsequent labor movement and notwithstanding the subsequent historic significance of the *Communist Manifesto* and its authors, neither the Communist League nor the *Manifesto* assumed a leading place in the German revolution of 1848. For many years after, Marxism was better known outside than in Germany. On the other hand the general role of the workers in the revolution of 1848 has, on the whole, been played down by the nationalist and bourgeois historians of Germany. Friedrich Meinecke has indicated how the events of March 18 in Berlin and the social-revolutionary aspects of 1848 were avoided by the respectable elements of German society in his generation as an ugly and unmentionable page in German history that had best be forgotten.[12] The problem still needs more detailed study than it has as yet received. But the tremendous amount of proletarian pamphlet and leaflet literature, and the rich abundance of caricature and satire, testify to a much more active proletariat than had hitherto been assumed.

A few contemporaries outside the radical world recognized at that time the significance of the proletarian movement. The young physician and subsequently distinguished scientist and Progressive leader Rudolf Virchow, writing to his father in May, 1848, from Berlin said: "I believe that you in the provinces do not realize sufficiently that this revolution is not simply a political one but essentially a social one. All our political activity, the entire constitution, is indeed only the form in which social reform will be realized, the means whereby the conditions of society will be transformed in its very foundations. After we are through with the political the really great work will then begin." [13]

In a letter to King Frederick William IV of March 16, 1848, Radowitz, royal emissary to Vienna at the time, lists "the socialist movement, the struggle of the proletariat for security and organization of labor," as one of the four powerful forces behind the revolution. This new and "enormous force," continued Radowitz, "has been derided as utopian or else merely referred to the police. If left to itself it will most certainly destroy the entire structure of modern states, no matter what political constitutions they assume. But just because this movement stands outside the realm of doctrinal politics, it offers new and powerful means in the hands of the monarchical principle and can serve as a strong counter-force even within the representative system." [14] In his *Denkschrift* of March 28, 1848, Radowitz continued along the same lines: "The proletariat is in itself not republican; this is a widely accepted error. Any form of government that will take up the interests of the proletariat in wise and bold fashion and will embrace a program calling for progressive taxation, a central system of poor relief and the regulation of conflict between capital and labor, will win over the common man to its side and thus acquire an enormous source of power." [15] Here we have in clearly stated form the social-monarchism later found in both Bismarck and Lassalle. Bismarck undoubtedly was familiar with these state papers of Radowitz, and they no doubt played their part in helping to fashion his ideas of social reform legislation.

While Marx, Engels, and other proletarian leaders clamored for a republic at this time, it is also true that neither political democracy nor a republican constitution were as important for them as economic and labor reform. The most consistent and most earnest advocates of political democracy were to be found among the bourgeois democrats and liberals rather than among the communists of 1848. "Democracy and saber rule," declared Weitling, "are all the same. Reason is to be realized only in the immediate establishment of a communist state."

The effects of the February revolution in Paris and the resulting wave of social and political demonstrations throughout Germany were soon

manifested in the changes in complexion of the various state governments. In Baden the liberal constitutionalist Karl Mathy became prime
minister, and the distinguished political theorist Welcker was named the
Baden representative to the Bundestag. Freedom of the press and a
citizens' militia were granted. Liberal ministries were likewise formed in
Württemberg, Hanover,-Brunswick, Saxe-Weimar, and Oldenburg. Heinrich
von Gagern became prime minister in Hesse-Darmstadt. In Bavaria the
revolutionary temper, previously fed by the hostility toward the dancer
Lola Montez, mistress of King Ludwig I, forced the king to abdicate.

In Saxony the liberal historian Karl Biedermann and the democrat
Robert Blum took the lead. Biedermann prepared an address to the king
in Leipzig and presented it to the monarch in Dresden. The king at first
resisted the Leipzig demands, but mass demonstrations in Leipzig forced
him to yield and to place the reins of government in the hands of a
liberal ministry.

These early changes in the governments of the local states were not
brought about by bloody revolutions. Mass demonstrations were usually
sufficient to serve notice upon the reigning princes that a new spirit was
in the air and that their own monarchical interests would best be served
by accepting some form of constitutional government. The changes in the
local states also were reflected in the Bundestag of the Germanic Confederation. A large number of new representatives from the member
states gave the diet a more liberal complexion. The imperial diet, up to
now the focal point of reaction, made a last desperate attempt to save itself by swimming with the new liberal tide. On March 3 it voted to allow
member states to abolish censorship and establish freedom of the press.
On March 9 it proclaimed the black, red, and gold flag as the official
colors of the confederation.

In Vienna the news of the Paris revolution created a panic on the
bourse. Two organizations took the initial lead in the revolution in the
Austrian capital—the Gewerbeverein, a petty bourgeois association of
independent artisans, and the Leserverein, made up of wealthier elements. Petitions for political reforms were presented to the emperor. The
news of the revolutionary triumphs of Kossuth in Budapest further encouraged the Vienna liberals. Demonstrations, ringing with the cry of
"Down with Metternich," filled the streets. Metternich, the architect of
the counter-revolution of 1815, was forced to flee and seek refuge in
London. The government promised reforms, but the new ministry was
still made up of the old ruling groups. Under the pressure of the workers
of Vienna the new government organized national workshops on the
style of those established in Paris. On April 25 a royal edict transformed
Austria into a constitutional state. A bicameral legislature was set up
consisting of an upper chamber that included 150 representatives of the
landowners and an unspecified number appointed by the emperor, and a

lower house elected by popular suffrage. The electoral edict of May 9 gave the vote to all adult males except those in domestic service or those working by day or week. Ministerial responsibility to parliament was recognized. The new constitution, however, satisfied no one. The opposition set up a political committee to fight for a more democratic constitution. When the government sought to suppress this committee, a mass demonstration took place on May 15 and forced the revocation of the constitution and the promise to convoke a constitutional assembly. The emperor retired from Vienna to Innsbruck. Anarchy prevailed in the city, barricades were erected, and a security commission of 100, headed by Adolf Fischhof, a Viennese doctor, was set up with dictatorial powers.

In Prussia the first revolutionary reverberations were heard in the Rhineland. On March 3 the local Communist League drafted a petition to the king. Similar movements took place throughout the Rhineland. But the most important events took place in Berlin. There the revolution coincided with the dismissal by the Borsig works of 400 workers in the first days of March. Thousands of other Berliners were thrown out of work. Unrest increased in the city, and on March 14 the streets of Berlin were filled with soldiers. On March 15 crowds gathered around the royal palace. Several persons were killed and wounded, and barricades were erected in the streets. On March 16 the news of the revolution in Vienna came to the Berliners. This increased their enthusiasm, and they pressed the king for political reform. The king's brother Wilhelm, Prince of Prussia, was strongly opposed to any concessions to the revolution, and he urged the king to remain firm.

On Saturday morning, March 18, a deputation from Cologne was received by the king. The Berlin municipal council at the same time dispatched a deputation to demand the dissolution of the ministry, the granting of a moderate constitution, the establishment of a militia, and the removal of the soldiers from the streets. The king received the people's representatives cordially and showed them the patents he was to issue. At two o'clock the same afternoon he issued patents removing censorship and ordering a general Landtag to be convened on April 2. In the meantime, however, the milder General Pfuel was replaced by the more militant General Prittwitz as commander of the Berlin troops. As the courtyard of the royal castle was filled with people who were shouting for removal of the soldiers, the order was given to Prittwitz to clear the yard. The soldiers marched on the crowd with naked sabers, but the orders were not to shoot. When the courtyard was almost empty, two shots were fired. The story of the shots, where they came from and who ordered them to be fired, has never been cleared up. But the shots were the signal for a wild outburst. Force was answered with force. The street fighting was renewed with increased fury, and for eight hours it continued without abatement. The populace had no experienced, trained leaders. The more important popular leaders were literati such as Dr. Rutenberg, Dr. Löwenberg, Dr. Woeniger, and Lewin Weiss, known as "the philosopher Weiss." Weiss fell on the barricades on the Königstrasse. The number of casualties caused by the fighting has never been definitely established. Figures for the number of soldiers killed varied from the obviously exaggerated figure of 1,100, given by the Bavarian ambassador, to the equally obvious underestimate of the Ministry of War, which gave the figures as 20 killed and 225 wounded. Of the populace 255 were killed in the fighting or died of wounds received.* Of these the overwhelming majority were artisans and factory workers.

King Frederick William issued a proclamation to the people which he entitled "To My Beloved Berliners." The blame for the unfortunate events of the 18th was placed upon foreign agitators, and he called upon "the inhabitants of my beloved native city" to return to peace. "Clear away the barricades that are still standing," he declared, "and send to me men of the genuine old-time Berlin spirit with words fit to address to your King, and I give you my royal word that all the streets and squares shall at once be cleared of troops." [16]

Prittwitz then received an order from the king to withdraw all the troops to the garrison except those from the castle, the armory, and a few other buildings. The king later denied having given this order, but Prittwitz carried it out and gathered all his troops at the royal square. Not getting any further orders during the day, he ordered most of his soldiers back to their barracks, thus leaving the king unprotected and exposed to the populace. The mass demonstration of March 19 in honor of the fallen dead paraded before the royal castle and the marchers forced the king to participate in the symbolism of the revolution. He was obliged to don the black, red, and gold colors and to view the parade of the biers of those that had fallen in the fighting. The comrades of the revolutionary martyrs carried the bodies past the royal balcony, and the voices of the crowd intoned the name of the hero and the manner in which he met his death: "Father of a family of five infant children. Hewn down on the barricades at the Cologne Rathaus"; or "Stabbed without mercy, after he had surrendered"; or "Age 15, shot down at my side, my only son." †

---

* Veit Valentin gives the number of civilians killed as 230. Our figure of 255 is derived from the pamphlet *Vollständiges Verzeichnis von sämmtlichen im Friedrichs-Haine Beerdigten welche als Opfer für die Freiheit am 18. und 19. März in Berlin gefallen sind*, published after the burial of those that had fallen. The names, ages, occupations, and addresses of all the individuals are listed. According to this list 208 were killed instantly, and 47 died of wounds inflicted during the fighting.

† The revolutionary poet Freiligrath described the scene which gave the revolutionary populace so much satisfaction:

> So war's! Die Kugel in der Brust, die Stirne breit gespalten
> So habt ihr uns auf schwankem Brett auf zum Altan gehalten!
> "Herunter!"—und er kam gewankt—gewankt an unser Bette;
> "Hut ab!" er zog—er neigte sich! (so sank zur Marionette
> Der erst ein Komödiante war!)—bleich stand er und beklommen!
> Das Heer indes verliess die Stadt, die sterbend wir genommen!
> Dann "Jesus meine Zuversicht" wie ihr's im Buch könnt lesen;
> Ein "Eisen meine Zuversicht!" war passlicher gewesen!

In the evening the king issued another proclamation "To My People and to the German Nation." In it he declared that salvation from internal and external danger can come only out of the union of the German people and the sovereign princes under one direction. "I take over today," he said, "the leadership for the days of danger. . . . I have embraced the old German colors today and placed myself and my people under the honor-worthy banner of the German Reich. Prussia will merge itself forthwith into Germany." The March demands were all agreed to and the Landtag of April 2 was to become part of a general national assembly. The Rhenish merchant Ludolf Camphausen was called to form a new liberal ministry.

The apparent success of the revolutionary Berliners served to quiet the situation, but it also served to make the leaders of the liberal bourgeoisie more panicky and mistrustful of the social demands of the proletarian elements. The cleft between right and left widened. For very many contemporaries of the revolution there did not appear to be any difference between the agitation of Marx, the social-revolutionary activity of Hecker and Struve, the labor organization of Born, and the evolutionary democratic movement of Robert Blum. The social-revolutionaries were but a small minority among the active elements in the revolution, and the communists were even less numerous. But their activities served to disturb the entire bourgeois world and to weaken the position of the democratic elements of the left bourgeoisie. These had derived a good deal of their strength from the popular movements, but the various proletarian outbreaks, with their attacks upon order, property, and authority, also discredited the evolutionary democrats and served to solidify the ranks of the right and center. Fortified later by the September uprisings and then by the triumph of reaction in Vienna, the counter-revolution set in as a reaction to the more radical and social expressions of protest. Rudolf Virchow, who had helped build barricades on Friedrichstrasse during the uprising in Berlin on March 18, wrote to his father six days later: "The reaction against the workers has already begun among the bourgeoisie. They are already talking once again of the rabble and are already considering how to distribute the political rights unequally among the various members of the nation." [17]

The Camphausen-Hansemann ministry in Prussia, mistrustful of the workers, began to seek ways and means to strengthen the shaken foundations of authority. They thought, wrote Engels, that "every danger of a restoration of the old system had passed away; and thus they made use of the whole of the old state machinery for the purpose of restoring 'order.' Not a single bureaucrat or military officer was dismissed; not the slightest change was made in the old bureaucratic administration. . . . There was nothing altered in Prussia but the persons of the ministers; even the ministerial staffs in the different departments were not touched upon." The throne was considered the "last existing obstacle to anarchy." In the

Frankfurt assembly only lip service was rendered to the problem of social reform.* All the energies of the liberal bourgeoisie were now concentrated on the problem of German unity and on constitutional reform. The social and libertarian aspects of the revolution now recede completely into the background. We must now retrace our steps to study the development of the national question.

The revolution of 1848 represents the only attempt in German history to solve the problem of German unity not by kings or the sword but by liberal-democratic action of the people. As such, its record as well as its ultimate failure are of crucial significance for German national history. The initial step toward national unity was taken on March 5, 1848, when fifty-one self-appointed individuals were called together to meet in Heidelberg. Friedrich Römer was the instigator of the meeting, and Adam von Itzstein sent out the invitations. The Heidelberg assembly called for immediate general elections to a national assembly. Seven men were appointed to prepare for the convocation of a national assembly.

On March 30, 1848, a larger assembly convened in Frankfurt. Over 500 delegates sat in session until April 4. They too were not elected representatives, nor were they convened by a duly constituted authority. They were a congress of notables who came together, in revolutionary fashion, and decided to call a general election, based on universal suffrage, to determine the future of Germany. From Austria came 2 delegates, from Prussia 141, from Württemberg 52, from Baden 72, from Hesse-Darmstadt 84, from Bavaria 44, from Saxony 26, and from Hanover 9. They met in St. Paul's Church in Frankfurt. This assembly, which came to be known as the *Vorparlament* (Pre-Parliament), included about 150 republicans; the rest were monarchists. There were no feudalists and no communists. The South German social-revolutionaries, led by Struve, represented the most militant republican group, and they drew up an elaborate social and political program. The majority of the Vorparlament, however, were moderate constitutionalists who were not interested in extending the revolution but in merely consolidating the constitutional gains and unifying the nation. Struve, Hecker, and their followers were primarily interested in society, the majority in the state. This majority was lured by the magic charms of constitutionalism. The preparatory decisions

---

* Exception must be made for some of the Catholic deputies like Bishop von Ketteler, who already recognized the urgency of meeting the problems created by industrialism (see Chapter IX). Several members of the democratic left were also deeply concerned with the social problem. Of these the most interesting was the Saxon industrialist Bernhard Eisenstuck. On May 24, 1848, Eisenstuck declared in the assembly that the Frankfurt parliament had two main problems to solve, namely, the constitution and the labor question, and that both must go hand in hand. Eisenstuck championed the cause of the workers and advocated the creation of a Ministry of Labor. He proposed in the *Vorparlament* the setting up of arbitration courts to settle disputes between capital and labor and the establishment of a sort of pension fund supported chiefly from contributions by the employers. Needless to say these proposals were not accepted. See Hans Krause, *Die demokratische Partei von 1848 und die soziale Frage* (Frankfurt, 1923).

of the Vorparlament were of no revolutionary character. The "respectable, orderly, political revolution had triumphed over the ideas of a social-revolutionary upheaval" (Valentin).

The Frankfurt Vorparlament formulated the plans for the convocation of a German National Assembly. The date for elections was set for May 1, 1848. Elections were to be held from electoral districts with one deputy for every 50,000 persons. A controversy developed over the interim status of the Vorparlament. The left groups demanded that this assembly stay in session until the National Assembly convened. In this way they wanted to eliminate the Bundestag from the picture. They were outvoted, however, 368 to 148, and instead a committee of fifty was delegated to carry on in the interim period. Voting regulations for the assembly were to be in accordance with the rules in force in each state. Thus Hanover, Kurhessen, and Württemberg barred workers and servants from voting; in Bavaria only those paying a direct tax voted. Unrestricted suffrage was carried out in Austria, Prussia, Hesse-Darmstadt, Schleswig-Holstein, Brunswick, and Nassau. There was no real secret ballot, and there were many election irregularities. Political clubs were organized by the various party groupings to carry on the election campaign.

The National Assembly convened in St. Paul's Church in the old imperial city of Frankfurt am Main, on May 18, 1848, amidst wild jubilation and high hopes and aspirations of the entire German nation.[18] Donoso Cortes, writing later in 1850, said: "The German people greeted its National Assembly of 1848 like a Goddess of Liberty—a year later it let it finish like a prostitute in a saloon." For the first and only time, before and after, an assembly freely elected by the German people of all the states met as one national parliament. All the dreams of German patriots seemed to be realized; all the aspirations of liberals who longed to see a parliamentary and constitutional *Rechtstaat* in Germany seemed to be on the verge of finding concrete embodiment. However, from the very beginning the assembly was impeded by the envy of the local states and by the lack of parliamentary experience of the German people. Like so many other aspects of German liberalism, it was magnificent in its ideal conception but proved to be woefully weak in its concrete realization.

The official composition of the assembly totaled 831 representatives. Only 330 came to the opening session on May 18, and the average attendance later was between 400 to 500. Of the deputies there were 4 master workers, 11 post-office officials, inspectors and the like; 46 merchants, many bankers, industrialists, and printers, and 60 landowners. In addition there were 49 university professors and teachers, 57 teachers of other schools, 157 judges and other government officials, 66 lawyers, 20 mayors, 118 higher officials, 3 diplomats, 5 librarians, 18 doctors, 33 ministers, and 43 writers—all told, 569 academicians out of a total of 831 deputies. There came the leading scholars, writers, and publicists of Germany—the historians Rohmer, Dahlmann, Droysen, Biedermann, Gervinus, Waitz, and Döllinger; the political theorists Zachariä, Welcker, Robert and Moritz von Mohl; the writers Rudolf Haym, Friedrich Theodor Vischer, and Uhland; the patriots Jahn and Arndt; the Jewish liberal Gabriel Riesser; the Catholic leader Bishop von Ketteler; the radicals Blum and Ruge; the statesmen Radowitz, Römer, Bassermann, Gagern, and Vincke. It was a most unusual galaxy of brilliant personalities who were chosen for their individual qualities rather than as representatives of class, group, or political party. But they were primarily theoreticians rather than practical politicians and statesmen; "many famous names but few political heads, very many dependent officials, few independent men of the people" (Gutzkow).

There were as yet no clearly defined political parties in Germany, so that the political complexion of the Frankfurt assembly cannot be described in terms of party affiliations. The assembled deputies came to be grouped under the broad designations of right, center, and left. Factions split into further factions, and eventually there were such designations as extreme right, right "in the English sense," right center and left center, left and extreme left. The various factions came together in particular hotels, and they soon got to be known by the names of their meeting places. The extreme right (Steinernes Haus), consisting mainly of pro-Austrian deputies, numbered 40. The other right faction (Milani), mainly of Prussian officials and numbering 122, was led by Radowitz, Vincke, Detmold, and von Lassaulx. The right center (Kasino), chiefly academicians and North German in composition, numbered 40 and included such notables as Dahlmann, Droysen, Bassermann, Mathy, Welcker, Simson, and Zachariä. The left center, split up into three groups, was made up of younger people, especially from South Germany, who wanted a monarchy but were also in favor of popular sovereignty. These numbered 132. The left (Deutscher Hof and Nürnberger Hof) numbered 56, and included such figures as Robert Blum, Carl Vogt, the Saxon industrialist Bernhard Eisenstuck, and Löwe-Calbe. The extreme left or democratic party (Donnersberg) numbered 47 deputies, among them Lorenz Brentano, Ludwig Simon, Julius Fröbel, and Arnold Ruge.[19] A considerable number of deputies remained unaffiliated.

Heinrich von Gagern, who came as prime minister of Hesse, was elected president of the assembly, and the Mannheim lawyer Alexander von Soiron was named vice president. Von Gagern was a man of imposing appearance, oratorical ability, and energy. But he lacked the experience to judge and appraise accurately the realities of a situation. Bismarck sneeringly called him a "phrase watering can." Over the chair of the president was placed the motto:

The fatherland's greatness, the fatherland's happiness
To create it and restore it to the people.

The parliament was beset with grave difficulties from the start, the most serious being the traditional particularism of the local states. Religious differences also stood in the way. The dualism of Austria and Prussia loomed ominously in the background, and there was no clear majority in the parliament for any specific program or platform. The evaluation of the Frankfurt assembly by Engels is undoubtedly too severe, but it also is in many respects justified. "An assembly," he wrote, "which, while it pretended to embody the very essence of German intellect and science, was in reality nothing but a state where old and worn-out political characters exhibited their involuntary ludicrousness and their impotence of thought as well as action before the eyes of all Germany."

The first problem confronting the parliament was the creation of a central executive power for Germany as a whole. On June 29 it created the position of imperial vice regent (*Reichsverweser*) and named to the post Grand Duke Johann of Austria. Johann was by no means a distinguished person. But he had attained popularity by marrying a middle-class girl and by making a speech on German unity—and he was an Austrian. Provision was also made by the assembly for an imperial ministry. Thereupon the old diet of the Germanic Confederation declared itself ended and turned over to the imperial vice regent all its functions. At the same time, however, it stipulated that it would resume its activities if the official did not discharge his duties to the satisfaction of the states. All the separate states accorded recognition to the new office. Much more serious difficulties arose when a war minister of the parliament was named to take over all the military forces of the separate states. Austria ignored the action altogether; Prussia indicated that it would retain control of its own army but would render assistance to the central government if necessary. All the other states likewise refused to place their military forces under the command of the new central office. Thus from the start the executive weakness of the assembly became obvious and apparent.

The executive weakness of the assembly and of the central authority it set up was also displayed in various phases of German foreign policy during the years 1848–1849. Here there was a curious and interesting mixture of political impotence with expressions of aggressive nationalist sentiment. Comparable to the Marxist historians who have attempted to explain the defeat of the revolution of 1848 in terms of its failure to deal adequately with the social problem, a more recent school of historians has essayed the thesis that the ill-fated end of the revolution was the result of the pan-German and expansionist aspirations of the majority of the assembly.[20] In both cases there is enough in the record to give the historian food for thought but not enough to warrant the extreme formulations of either school.

The nationalist temper of the assembly was tested in numerous instances involving relations with Germany's neighbors, its borders, and minority nationalities. Those that aroused the greatest reactions pertained to

Bohemia, Poland, and Schleswig-Holstein. The Frankfurt assembly, taking for granted that Bohemia was a "German land," was shocked when it was confronted by the refusal of the Czech nationalists, under the leadership of Palacký, to participate in elections for the assembly and come to Frankfurt. Instead Palacký and his associates convened in Prague an all-Slav Congress of all the subject Slavic nationalities in the Hapsburg Empire. German liberals as well as radicals took the view that Czech nationalism was without logical foundation and was reactionary in character. The deputy Höfken, in the assembly on June 14, 1848, called Bohemia "an original German land inextricably bound to Germany by reason of nature, history, culture, law and justice." The venerable patriot Ernst Moritz Arndt warned against allowing every subdivision of the Reich to declare itself an independent nationality. "Where will we be," he said, "if we grant to every small individuality equal right to life?" [21] Marx and Engels, outside the assembly, originally attacked the assembly for its Czech policy * but later expressed their open hostility to Czech nationalism. "The Moravians and Slovaks," wrote Engels, "had long since lost every vestige of national feeling and vitality. . . . Everywhere capital, industry and mental culture were in the hands of the Germans. . . . But as it often happens, dying Tschechian nationality, dying according to every fact known in history for the last four hundred years, made in 1848 a last effort to regain its former vitality—an effort whose failure . . . was to prove that Bohemia could only exist henceforth, as a portion of Germany." [22]

To counter the action of Palacký and the Slav Congress, a Styrian deputy to the assembly, Titus Mareck, introduced a resolution on May 27, 1848, according to which the new Germany would declare (1) that it would not lend its hand to the suppression of any nationality; (2) that all non-German nationals would enjoy the same rights as German citizens and that their nationality would be respected; (3) that although German was the language of the state, legal recognition would be given to other languages in the areas in which a majority of the population do not speak German. After being referred to committee, the Mareck resolution, rephrased by Dahlmann but accepted in the revised form by Mareck, was passed by a large majority. On July 1 the assembly adopted another report which called upon Austria to force the Slavs to vote for represent-

* See Marx's article on the Prague revolution in the *Neue Rheinische Zeitung* of June 18, 1848, reprinted in *Marx-Engels Gesamtausgabe*, pt. I, vol. vii, pp. 68–70. Most interesting is the final paragraph:

"Those to be pitied most are the brave Czechs. Whether they win or are defeated, their decline is certain. Through the persecution by the Germans for four hundred years, which is now being continued in the street battles in Prague, they have been driven into the arms of the Russians. In the great battle between eastern and western Europe which is due to come in a very short time—perhaps within a few weeks, an unfortunate fate places the Czechs on the side of the Russians, on the side of despotism against the revolution. The revolution will triumph and the Czechs will be the first to be suppressed by it."

atives to the Frankfurt assembly and which denounced the pan-Slavism of the Prague congress. A minority report, submitted by the democratic leader Ruge and two colleagues, called for no action to be taken and for the protection of all nationalities. It was voted down by the assembly. In the meantime news arrived of civil war in Prague, and with it rumors of the "annihilation" of Germans by Czechs. Both the left and right in Frankfurt now called for prompt suppression of the Czech rebels by the Austrian troops under Windischgraetz. The news of the victory of the Austrian legitimists in Prague was welcomed with relief in Frankfurt. But the triumph in Prague was but a prelude to the royalist victory in Vienna in October and the triumphal progress of the counter-revolution.

The Polish question aroused even greater excitement. Ever since the partitions of Poland the cause of Polish nationalism had been the favorite cause of all European liberals and nationalists. The Frankfurt Vorparlament had passed a resolution calling for the reconstruction of a free Poland. Now the Frankfurt assembly was confronted with a clash between German and Polish nationalism. The Prussian government, despite the violent opposition of Polish leaders, proceeded to divide the Polish province of Posen and incorporate a large section of it into the Prussian state. The Poles and their radical German allies appealed to the Frankfurt assembly. A stirring debate on the question took place July 24–27 in St. Paul's Church. It was during this debate that Wilhelm Jordan broke with his comrades of the left to deliver one of the most chauvinistic speeches of the assembly. A pro-Polish policy, declared Jordan, is "a policy of weakness, fear and cowardice. It is high time for us at last to wake up from the dreaming self-oblivion in which we exerted ourselves for all kinds of nationalities while we ourselves lay in wretched enslavement and were trampled upon by the entire world. It is time to wake up to a policy of healthy national egotism." Ridiculing the claims of humanity and justice, Jordan, anticipating the *Realpolitik* of later days, proudly proclaimed that he was ready to admit without batting an eye that:

Our right is none other than the right of the stronger, the right of the conqueror. Yes, we have conquered. In the West we were conquered, in the East we had the great *malheur* to be the conquerors ourselves. . . . The German conquests in Poland were a natural necessity. The law of history is not like that of the legal code. It knows only the laws of nature, and one of these laws tells us that a people does not have the right to political independence merely by virtue of its mere existence. This comes only as a result of the force to assert itself as a state among other states.[23]

The democratic deputies, led by Robert Blum and Arnold Ruge, defended the rights of the Poles. Ruge vainly called for the assembly to issue a declaration in which Germany would recognize its obligation to help emancipate the Poles. His motion to support a reconstituted Poland was voted down. Blum's motion to delay action until after a commission had made a study of the question was likewise turned down. Instead the majority, whipped to a nationalistic fervor by the speech of Jordan, accepted a report giving its stamp of approval to the action of the Prussian government. The vote was 342 to 31. Here too the military power of the Prussian state was given its blessing by the assembly as in the case of Bohemia.

In the case of Schleswig-Holstein, the nationalist sentiment of the assembly had to yield before the political realities of Prussian policy. On March 21, 1848, King Frederick VII of Denmark proclaimed the incorporation of Schleswig-Holstein into the Danish kingdom. The Germans in these duchies revolted and called upon the diet of the Germanic Confederation for aid. Prussia and Hanover were thereupon empowered to come to the aid of the German rebels. Despite initial military victories over the Danish troops, Prussia withdrew in the face of the opposition of the other European powers and concluded an armistice with Denmark at Malmö on August 26. The action of Prussia was not only a blow to German national pride; it was also a severe jolt to the prestige of the assembly, since Prussian action in this matter was taken without reference to the existence either of the assembly or of its central executive. Resentment ran high throughout the country. The halls of the assembly rang with fervent pleas for patriotic action. But the assembly needed Prussia more than Prussia needed the assembly. After initially voting to resist the carrying out of the Malmö armistice, the assembly reversed itself on September 16 and by a vote of 257 to 236 decided to sustain the Prussian-Danish armistice. A wave of nationalist resentment resulted in serious outbreaks in Frankfurt and throughout the rest of Germany. It was during this crisis, too, that Struve decided to proclaim his republic in Baden. The troops of the central power were able, however, to overcome the unorganized and poorly led masses, and order was again restored. But the prestige of the assembly was badly shaken. Its dependence on Prussia became increasingly apparent and the trend to the right more marked than ever.

All these incidents served to bring out certain expansionist tendencies in the German national movement. Perhaps the most extreme expression of such pan-Germanism was the speech of Count Deym on October 26 in the debate on the constitution of the new Reich. Count Deym ridiculed the concern over constitutional forms. He had greater and more important problems for the assembly. It was the mission of the Germans to create "a Central European giant state" because the Germans are the élite class throughout Central Europe.

Our goal [declared Deym] is to establish a giant empire of seventy, and if possible, of eighty or one hundred million and to plant the standards of

Hermann in this Reich. Thus armed we shall stand against both East and West, against the Slavic and the Latin nations. We shall wrest the rule of the seas from England to become the greatest and mightiest nation upon this globe. This is Germany's future! In the face of this all the petty debates over the constitutional forms dwindle into insignificance.[24]

We have here a harking back to the imperialism of the Holy Roman Empire and a clear and unmistakable heralding of the pan-Germanism of the late nineteenth and twentieth centuries. But we must not over-exaggerate either the prevalence of these sentiments or the extent of their influence at the time. The democratic leaders in the assembly were cognizant of the dangers of this exaggerated nationalism and warned against it. Carl Vogt, scientist and democratic leader, declared in the assembly:

It seems strange to me, this preying upon territories, which appears to have taken the place of preying upon Frenchmen. . . . Yes, preying upon the French has developed into a general grabbing of territory. We grab in the north; we grab in the west; we grab in the east. Everywhere we seek to gobble up what they call the "German element," and in the end we shall ruin our stomach with all that.[25]

Arnold Ruge introduced a proposal to summon a congress of peoples for the purpose of bringing about general European disarmament. A union of France and Germany and a disarmed and peaceful Europe was the goal of these democratic leaders. The disdain and condescending "realism" with which these proposals were greeted was answered by Robert Blum. "It is easy," he declared, "to heap derision upon the slogan of the brotherhood of free peoples. I do not shun this derision in repeating the necessity for such brotherhood. I do not shun it because I know that I am paying service to an idea on which the future and happiness of Europe depends." [26] It is of course quite true that Ruge, Blum, and Vogt were not able to carry the majority either of the assembly or of the German masses with them. But it is as important to record the existence of this tradition in German national thinking as it is to high-light those aspects of German history which ultimately converged to create the aggressive and imperialist movement.[27]

On October 19 the assembly began its deliberations on a constitution for the new German Reich. The knotty problem of Austria immediately came to the fore. Here the clash between *Gross-deutsch* and *Klein-deutsch* was revealed in all its clarity. The former represented the desire to find a solution that would incorporate Austria, with its complex national problem, into a unified Germany; the latter aimed at the exclusion of Austria and the creation of an exclusively "German" national state. Droysen, Beseler, Dahlmann, and Waitz were the outspoken advocates of the *klein-deutsch* solution. "Germany," declared Droysen, "has been demoralized, has fallen into ruins and become powerless for three centuries because of Austria." "Austria's power," he said, "was conditioned by our weapons." "It is Austria's renown to have alienated one-third of the German people from its common fatherland." For these men Prussia represented the best in the German tradition and hence merited the leadership of a new and united Germany. Prussia, the land that had produced Luther, Frederick the Great, the classical German literature, and the leaders of the War of Liberation, "was destined to lead the new Germany."

Finally, on October 27, the paragraph of the constitution pertaining to the composition of the new German Reich was passed. It provided that no part of the German Reich was to be united with a non-German part into the same state. Where such a situation already existed (as, for example, in Austria) only a personal union of the two parts in the monarch was to be allowed. This action, of course, explicitly ruled out the incorporation of the Austrian Empire into the German national state.

In addition to the constitutional commission the assembly had set up a group of other commissions to plan national legislation for various phases of political and social life. There were commissions on international affairs, on naval affairs, on the army, on law and justice, on economic affairs, on church and education, on finances and on ministerial responsibility. Most of these commissions were unable to fulfill all or most of the tasks assigned to them. One of the most significant achievements of the assembly was the adoption of a Declaration of Fundamental Rights. It was obviously modeled after the French Declaration of Rights of Man and the American Declaration of Independence, and it represented the accumulated fruits of political liberalism of the previous half-century.[28] The Declaration of Fundamental Rights, passed on December 21, 1848, provided for freedom of movement for all within the Reich, for the freedom of person, of speech, assembly, press, and expression. It proclaimed liberty of religion and of conscience, the freedom of science and academic teaching. Education was declared to be subject to the authority of the state except for religious and clerical education. The rights of property were proclaimed as inviolable, and the independence of the judiciary was accepted as necessary for the freedom and welfare of the citizens.

The breach between the Frankfurt National Assembly and Austria, in the meantime, became wider and wider. The triumph of the counterrevolution in Vienna reached a climax with the arrest on November 8 of the two representatives of the assembly Blum and Froebel. These two democratic leaders had come to Vienna to help the liberal forces meet the growing reaction in Austria. Blum was executed in Vienna on November 9 on the charge of treason and became the martyr of the national cause. This action by the Austrian government was a frontal attack upon the authority of the assembly and an enormous blow to its prestige. It gave heart once more to the counter-revolutionary elements in Germany and gave the weak-kneed Frederick William of Prussia reason to ponder over his relations with the liberal assembly. In March, 1849, Austria adopted a constitution for a united empire. This precluded in any way the inclusion of Austria in the new German union. The *klein-deutsch* adherents now were able to point jubilantly to the rightness of their view. Welcker, formerly a leading spokesman for the inclusion of Austria, called for the immediate election of the King of Prussia as emperor. Beckerath exclaimed, "Waiting for Austria is the death of German unity."

On March 28, 1849, the assembly finally adopted a constitution for a united German Reich. At the head of the state was to be the "Emperor of the Germans," a hereditary monarch who was to be the supreme authority of the German union. His residence was to be wherever the seat of government was. He was given the right to dissolve the second chamber of the legislature and the right of a suspensive veto. The emperor was to have a ministry to govern with him, and every order of the sovereign was required to be countersigned by a minister. The parliament was to consist of two houses, one to represent the constituent states of the union and the other consisting of the representatives of the people. The former was to consist of 176 delegates, half of whom were to be appointed by the state governments and half by the state legislatures. Deputies were to serve for six years. They were to vote according to their own decisions and were not to be bound by government instructions. This chamber could not be dissolved. The structure of the second chamber was borrowed from the constitution of the United States. One representative for each 50,000 inhabitants was to be elected for a three-year term by secret, universal, and equal suffrage.

The finances of the new state were to be derived from the tariff duties and indirect taxes. If these did not suffice to meet the governmental obligations, then quota payments were to be made by each state according to its population. In special cases the legislature was given power to levy direct taxes. The budget, of course, was first to be presented to the lower house. A supreme *Reichsgericht,* patterned after the United States Supreme Court, was to decide on legal issues between the member states and between the government and parliament.

After the constitution was adopted by the Frankfurt assembly, it was submitted for approval to the various governments. Twenty-eight states declared their willingness to accept the constitution if it were amended to provide for an absolute veto by the emperor instead of a suspensive veto, open instead of secret elections, and the extension of the powers of the upper chamber. These changes, however, could not be carried in the assembly. Austria, Bavaria, and Hanover rejected the constitution completely.

The delegates at St. Paul's Church now proceeded to vote for emperor. Two-hundred and ninety votes were cast for the King of Prussia and 248 abstained. A deputation of thirty-two members, headed by Eduard Simson, its president, was dispatched to Berlin to offer the crown to Frederick William IV of Prussia. The Prussian king was bound to decline the offer by all the ideas he had entertained all these years. His ministers, however, had acted all along on the assumption that he would accept. The *Kreuz-zeitung,* Berlin organ of the Prussian Junkers, greeted the arrival of the deputation with the following words: "What, you bring an imperial crown? You are beggars! You have no money, no land, no law, no power, no people, no soldiers! You are bankrupt speculators in cast-off popular sovereignty. Do not give yourselves airs and be happy if you get free lodging in the hotel and are sent home with phrases just as you came here with phrases." The royal servants, obviously reflecting the spirit of their masters, abused the deputies in the palace. When the president of the assembly and head of the delegation, Simson, asked for a glass of water, he was curtly refused by one of the lackeys. At a reception given to the delegates the king thus addressed the Jewish member of the delegation, Gabriel Riesser, "Isn't it true, Herr Doktor, that you are also convinced that I cannot accept the constitution uncircumcised?" The delegation none the less waited hopefully for a favorable acceptance by the king. But none was forthcoming. On April 3, 1849, he declined the offer of the crown unless he were to receive the consent of the sovereigns of the local states. He would take it from princes and lawful sovereigns but not from peoples' representatives.

Consent by the sovereigns was not yet available. It had to wait for the might of Prussia and the diplomacy of Bismarck to bring that about. In 1849 the local rulers still clung hopefully to their sovereignty. Thus the climax of the work of the Frankfurt assembly came to nought, broken by the hostility of Austria, the indecision of the Prussian king, the jealousy of the local rulers, and the lack of vigorous and energetic will to unity by the deputies themselves. The deputation ruefully returned to Frankfurt to report on the failure of its mission. For a while the moderate constitutionalists in the assembly still looked to the possibility of negotiating an understanding with Prussia, but their hopes were in vain. Although twenty-eight of the German states had indicated their acceptance of the Reich constitution, and the lower house of the Prussian diet had also taken similar action, Frederick William ordered the Reich constitution rejected. On May 14 he also withdrew the Prussian deputies from the Frankfurt assembly. Austria had withdrawn its representatives on April 5. Although some of the deputies wavered at first in carrying out these instructions, the right and center groups yielded to the orders of their governments and left Frankfurt.

The die-hard democrats and republicans clung to the authority of the constitution and the assembly to the last. In their idealistic zeal they believed that an open appeal to the people to come to the support of the constitution would rally the masses to their side. Ludwig Uhland, the famous Swabian poet, drafted the "Appeal of the National Assembly to the German People," which was adopted on May 25. It called for the "active co-operation of the entire German people," and although it disclaimed any intention of inciting to civil war it declared that "we find it necessary in this iron age for the people to stand armed and trained to act against any overt measures against the Constitution." [29] A new central authority was set up and, finding the official climate in Frankfurt hostile, the assembly voted to move to the more favorably disposed Stuttgart. "If you allow yourselves to be conquered by Prussia," declared Ludwig Simon on May 17, "you preserve in Germany the peace of the grave and the order of the churchyard. If you rest on the support of the South German liberals you will then fashion the peace of liberty and the order of life." [30]

The noble band of republicans and democrats betook themselves to Stuttgart on May 30. There were the Saxon merchant Eisenstuck, who was the leading advocate of social legislation in the assembly; the radical Raveaux, the socialist Schlöffel, the active democratic leader Julius Fröbel, the scholar and rationalist Vogt, the poet Uhland, the witty and sad Friedrich Theodor Vischer, the passionate Ludwig Simon, and the last president of the assembly, Löwe-Calbe. "This assembly," said Vischer two days before its end, "has often appeared to me in these days like the venerable royal sage who wandered bareheaded and homeless in the stormy night, abandoned by his daughters who owed their crowns to him." [31] Not for long were they able to carry on in Stuttgart. When the "rump" parliament issued a call to the citizens of the states that had left the parliament to refuse to pay taxes, it was dispersed by the troops of the Württemberg government on June 18.

Uprisings in support of the assembly and the constitution took place in Saxony, Bavaria, the Palatinate, and in Baden. In the latter state in particular the democratic revolutionaries made a last desperate stand to save the revolution. Here a band of young idealistic democrats, which included such figures as Lorenz Brentano, Franz Sigel, Otto von Corvin, Karl Heinzen, Gottfried Kinkel, Carl Schurz, and many of the former followers of Hecker and Struve, set up a provisional government, called together a constituent assembly, and organized an army to protect "German liberty" against the counter-revolution. The veteran Polish leader of the uprising of 1831, Ludwik Mieroslawski, came to Baden to serve as commander in chief of the republican forces. But they were no match for the Prussian troops that had been dispatched against them. On July 23 the last stronghold of the radicals, the fortress of Rastatt, fell to the Prussians. The conquerors set up courts-martial that railroaded the leaders of the revolutionary army to their death and had their bodies thrown, without coffin or funeral service, into a big ditch. Many years later, in 1873, friends and relatives of the executed asked permission to set up a tombstone for those buried on this spot. The government of Baden raised no objection, but the government of Prussia exercised its veto over the project and thereby indicated how deep was the cleavage that still existed between the liberal forces of 1848 and those that triumphed later.

Thus did the revolution of 1848 and its assembly, on which the hopes of all Germany were pinned, come to its end. This marked the end of liberal nationalism in Germany. The assembly went out just as Donoso Cortes described it, "like a prostitute in a saloon," dashing for all time the hopes to achieve national unity on the foundations of the nineteenth century liberalism and constitutionalism.[32] "Thus," wrote Friedrich Engels, a year after the end of the assembly, "vanished the German Parliament, and with it the first and last creation of the Revolution. . . . Political liberalism, the rule of the bourgeoisie . . . is forever impossible in Germany."[33]

Engels's prediction regarding the prospects of German liberalism proved to be remarkably accurate. The defeat of 1848 meant the crushing of German liberalism. With the problem of national unity occupying the first concern of all the liberal elements in Germany, the means of attaining unity and the instrument responsible for achieving it were to become much more significant and be the object of greater attachment than concern for liberal constitutional and social institutions. If liberal democracy was not able to realize German unity, if the action of the people themselves was incapable of attaining this supreme goal of all Germans, then this meant that liberal democracy was a failure. And if unity could be achieved by might, by the action of the sword, by intrigue, diplomacy and war, then these instruments of political action justified themselves by their realization of the noble end. If the German bourgeoisie had fulfilled its historic task in 1848 as the French bourgeoisie had in 1789 and the English bourgeoisie a century before that, Bismarck would never have found the arena in which to play his role and he would have remained the Prussian Junker landowner that he was in 1847.

The most widespread and prevalent explanation for the failure of the Frankfurt assembly holds that it was due to too much talk, too much theorizing, and too many doctrinaires and professors among the delegates. This explanation has continued to be offered, especially by the opponents of nineteenth century liberalism who extolled forceful action as opposed to the mere talk of parliamentary bodies. This represents a widespread mistrust of the fundamentally rationalist foundations of constitutional and parliamentary government. There is much talk and much theorizing in all parliamentary countries. There was, it is true, much more of it in the German assembly. But so was there much talk in the revolutionary assemblies of 1789 and 1791 in France. The German failure was due to the enormous disparity between the political aspirations of the German liberals and the mass support and actual power and influence they commanded. Parliamentary activity was novel in Germany, and this made the initial task most difficult. But as Erich Brandenburg well points out, the chief reason for failure lay not in the assembly but in the situation of Germany. "The movement of 1848 came to ruin because of the power and self-assertion of the larger individual states, above all of the two great powers," that is, Austria and Prussia.

The victory of the counter-revolution was one over constitutional reform, over parliamentary and social-revolutionary democracy. The center elements were vanquished. A tiny radical minority remained to face a powerful, triumphant, and puffed-up authoritarianism. Politics became materialistic, authoritarian, and *Realpolitik*. The governments had to prepare themselves against any possible repetition of such revolutionary outbreaks, and they demanded discipline and trust from all. The master achievement of the counter-revolution was to diffuse among the German people the belief that they have no political talent and that they should leave politics to the few who know its ways better than they do.

The defeat of 1848–1849 proved tragically fatal to the cause of German liberalism in still another way. As in subsequent defeats, it resulted in depleting the ranks of the more militant and able political liberals by emigration. The wave of reaction after 1850 caused those who had fought for liberty or who yearned more intensely for liberty to seek refuge as political exiles. Some, like Mommsen, Richard Wagner, and Miquel, were to return chastened and reconciled to a nationalist but authoritarian Germany. Others like Herwegh, Heine, Marx, and Wilhelm Liebknecht were to remain exiles for the greater part of their lives. A large number of German political refugees came to the United States. Among these were Friedrich Hecker, Carl Schurz, Oswald Ottendörfer, Dr. Abraham Jacobi, Franz Sigel, F. A. Sorge, Karl Heinzen, Joseph Weydemeyer, Wilhelm Weitling, and thousands of unknown liberty-loving Germans who helped build a democratic society in the new world and who were the ancestors of men like Louis Brandeis or Wendell Willkie. Many of them fought in the Civil War in the battle against slavery and became prominent in the Republican party. Others became active in the American labor movement and helped build a socialist party in the United States. All these forces for democracy and social reform were lost for good to the German Reich.[34]

With all this it is also true that the revolution of 1848 had a positive significance in subsequent German history. It represented the first entry of the broad masses into politics, and whatever movements of political liberalism and radicalism developed in later years, they were nourished and fed by the experience, the memories, and the inspiration of 1848. Political Catholicism was initiated in the movement of 1848; the working classes developed a greater self-consciousness, and the *Communist Mani-*

festo of Marx and Engels became one of the basic documents of the proletarian movement. The Black, Red, and Gold of 1848 remained the banner of German political liberalism, even when it was not officially recognized as such. And when German liberalism was able once more to assert itself and take power, in 1918, it looked to 1848 for its ideals and traditions. The Weimar Republic of 1918–1930 picked up where the revolution of 1848 left off, and the post-Hitler Germany of today once again looks to 1848 as the German historical tradition upon which to create a new liberal régime in battered Germany.

CHAPTER VI

The Revolution from Above, 1849-1864

S'il n'y avait que des salauds dans le monde, le Réalisme serait aussi le Bon Sens, car le Réalisme est précisément le bon sens des salauds.

GEORGES BERNANOS

The collapse of the revolution of 1848–1849 left Germany in a confused and bewildered state. Above all, it left Austria and Prussia facing each other more ominously than ever before. Not that the time for a showdown had yet arrived. Prussia was still too weak, and Frederick William IV was hardly prepared to throw down the gauntlet to the Hapsburg Empire. But something had to be done to settle the status of the relation of the German states to one another, now that the old Germanic Confederation had been dissolved and the failure of the revolution of 1848 had produced no substitute. Frederick William IV was desirous of creating some sort of national unity, but he wanted an amicable arrangement with Austria. His chief minister at this time was the interesting figure Josef von Radowitz. Radowitz (1797–1853), converted to Catholicism at the age of thirteen, was far from the typical Prussian Junker. He dreamed of a harmonious working together of Protestant Prussia and Catholic Austria. Already in 1847 he had prepared a lengthy memorial on the need for reconstituting the old Bund. He incorporated the same ideas in his Memorial on Prussian Policy of June 12, 1849.[1]

Radowitz recognized the yearning for unity among all Germans. He pointed out that this required a unified executive strong enough to cope with external and internal dangers, and a unified system of law for all Germany. The conduct of foreign affairs and control of the army, he indicated, should be in the hands of a central executive. Austria could not become head of such a union because of the many non-German lands in its empire. Only Prussia could take the lead in creating this narrower union. But Prussia alone, declared Radowitz, could not maintain itself as a European power, hence a *Bundesstaat,* headed by Prussia, ought to be in perpetual union with Austria. Both states would pledge support and aid to each other for external and internal peace, and foreign relations would be carried on jointly by two representatives of each state.

This was the so-called Prussian Union Plan which the Prussian government presented to the other German states. What Radowitz and Frederick William IV wanted above all was to get Austria to recognize the right of Prussia to form a smaller Bund within a larger one. The larger Bund would be like the old Bund except that Prussia would share the praesidium with Austria. There would be no common German parliament but a sort of duumvirate of Prussia and Austria, which would dictate a common policy for all Germany. On May 26, 1849, a constitution drafted along these lines was adopted by Prussia, Hanover, and Saxony. The latter two states reserved the right to withdraw from the union if by the time elections were to be held Bavaria and Württemberg would not join. Most of the smaller states joined the Prussian union, and a national assembly was summoned to meet in Erfurt on March 20, 1850. Bavaria and Württemberg, however, refused to join, and Hanover and Saxony thereupon withdrew. The Erfurt parliament, therefore, turned out to be but a meeting of Prussia with the smaller German states. Prince Schwarzenberg, the Austrian chancellor and successor to Metternich, rejected the plan outright. His aim was to recreate the old Bund under Austrian domination, to keep Prussia out of the praesidium, and to keep the other four kingdoms tied to Austrian policy. He also pressed for the admission of Austria into the Zollverein. To counter the Prussian-inspired Erfurt meeting, Schwarzenberg summoned a meeting of the Diet of the Germanic Confederation at Frankfurt on May 10. On September 1 he officially proclaimed the renewal of the old Bund.

Two German unions were now in existence, and a conflict was not long in coming. Internal dissension in Hesse between the elector and his parliament was the pretext for an appeal for help by the ruler to the Frankfurt diet. Both unions claimed competence in the matter and both made ready to send troops. But Frederick William retreated before a showdown. Radowitz, distasteful to Austria, was dismissed, and the more yielding Manteufel was dispatched to Schwarzenberg at Olmütz, where, on November 29, 1850, he signed the Punctation of Olmütz. Prussia yielded on all points. Austria retained supremacy in German affairs, and the old order seemed to be back in the saddle for good. A conference of the German states, presided over by Schwarzenberg, convened in Dresden between December 23, 1850, and May 15, 1851; all plans for reform were abandoned and the old Bundestag was restored. Well could Metternich write in 1855:

All the efforts directed by the partisan spirit against the concept of the Bund and its legal form during the years 1848 and 1849 up to the present, have revealed themselves as empty aspirations contrary to the nature of things. The questions posed by the Austrian cabinet in 1813 were then and for all times the only ones theoretically possible, and there will never be any practical solution possible other than the one set down in the act establishing the Germanic Confederation.[2]

The renewed Bund resumed its old struggle against liberalism and nationalism. The German states vied with each other in striving to remove from the German constitutions what Frederick William IV called "the democratic filth of the year of shame." All the old feudal, absolutist, and clerical tendencies were revived, and the paramount influence of nobles and church was restored. The most marked reaction took place in Austria. There the liberal constitution of March 4, 1849, was rescinded, the diets were set aside, press restrictions were imposed, and all opposition was crushed. The national movements of the Slavs and the Hungarians were ruthlessly suppressed by the efficient minister of the interior, Alexander Bach. Schwarzenberg urged the same political course upon Prussia, and there too the reactionary elements came to the fore once again. The Prussian constitution of 1850 was not officially revoked, but the nobility was restored to power and clerical influence increased. A central police was created by the Bund to foster reaction. The central committee set up by the Bund to administer this policy was named jokingly by the delegates themselves the "Committee for Reaction." Its function was to see that no institutions developed in any of the member states that would threaten either the internal peace and order in the local states or the general security of the Bund.[3]

The policy of repression, however, could evoke neither popular enthusiasm nor support. Under the surface, and often above the surface, the reaction only stimulated hate and strengthened particularist sentiments. Even the Prussian Junker Bismarck, then a delegate to the diet at Frankfurt, saw the sham and unpopularity of the Bund. "Intercourse here," he wrote, "is at bottom nothing more than mutually distasteful espionage. All that people torment themselves about are trivialities, and these diplomats, with their pompous pettinesses, are already more ridiculous to me than the deputies of the [Prussian] second chamber in the consciousness of their dignity. No one, even the most malicious doubter of a democrat, can believe how much *charlatanerie* and pomposity is concealed in this diplomacy."[4] He predicted that Heinrich Heine's poem "O Bund, du Hund, du bist nicht gesund!" would soon become the most popular song in Germany. The cause of German unity and the hopes and aspirations of the more progressive circles in Germany now became tied up with the power of Prussia. And the power of Prussia, in turn, came to revolve around two historic figures, King William I and Bismarck.

The hopes of German nationalists were greatly stimulated by the accession to the throne of the new monarch, William I. In 1857 Frederick

Wiiliam had become so incapacitated that his brother William, then sixty years old, assumed the reins of government. He was officially designated as regent on October 7 of the following year. On January 2, 1861, Frederick William died and William ascended the throne. He revived the elaborate coronation ceremony which had been carried out in Königsberg in 1701 when the Electorate of Brandenburg had become the Kingdom of Prussia. On October 18, 1861, he was crowned also at Königsberg. This served to underscore the new position of Prussia in both Germany and Europe.

The outstanding characteristic of the new ruler was his Christian piety. Christianity was "the bread of his life, the comfort for his pains and the measuring rod for his actions." His guiding principle in life was, "Because I know I am powerless in God's hands I am powerful against all the world." He was not a great man but he had a clear and level head and good practical sense, in contrast to the mystical confusion of his predecessor. He had a strong sense of duty, was industrious, fearless and, once convinced of the rightness of his cause, ready to face anyone. Essentially William was deeply conservative and imbued with the idea of the divine character of his kingship. This he underscored in his coronation speech in Königsberg. Nevertheless, he wrote to King Max of Bavaria, "Where constitutions exist, they are to be carried out and not falsified by forced interpolations." [5] He did not like many of what he called the more liberal phases of the Prussian constitution, but he was determined to try to show the world that he could rule even with an "inconvenient constitution." Moreover, he disliked the circle of the *Kreuzzeitung,* the feudal conservative group led by Gerlach, Uhden, and Götze, who had oeen the close intimates of Frederick William IV. William looked outside this circle for his ministers. It was this fact above all which induced public opinion to believe that William had made a sharp break with the past and which led political writers to dub this the "New Era." On the national question William believed strongly in the mission of Prussia to unify Germany, but he did not think that he would live to see it realized. Such was the personality of the man around whom the hopes of nationalist circles in Germany, particularly in Prussia, were centered.[6]

Another factor which stimulated the revival of national sentiment in Germany was the progress of the movement for unity in Italy. Germany and Italy were the two great European nations aspiring to unity at the time, and there was much in common between them. Moreover, Austria was deeply involved in Italy. By the time William came to the helm, the activities of Mazzini, Garibaldi, and Cavour were beginning to bear fruit. The Austro-Sardinian War of 1859 in particular aroused tremendous interest and political tension in Germany. A complex of issues and sentiments of a political, religious, and cultural character were involved. Austria, it is true, was the great stumbling block in the path of the realization of German unity, but she was, after all, a sister state in the German Bund and German in culture and nationality. Italy, long the object of foreign aggression and alien rule, had always elicited the sympathy of adherents of the principle of nationality, and the heroic, romantic nationalism of Mazzini and Garibaldi had always evoked enthusiasm among European liberals and democrats. But papal hostility to the unification of Italy served to arouse Catholic opinion throughout Europe and rally Catholics to the support of Austria. Public opinion in Germany, therefore, divided along several lines.[7] There were many who, despite reservations regarding Austrian internal politics, still called for the support of Austria. As a German state, a member of the Bund, she should be helped by all Germans. South German opinion, especially Catholic opinion, leaned strongly in this direction. For many the arch-villain in the entire affair was Napoleon III, who was pictured as the enemy of Germany, the destroyer of peace, and the real threat to German unity. Had it been merely a contest between Austrian and Italian nationalism the sympathy of these circles might well have gone to the Italians. But, they argued, the defeat of Austria would leave Germany at the mercy of the combined influence of France and Russia, and Napoleon would proceed to attack Germany as soon as Austria was laid low. The battle of the Po, they said, was really the battle of the Rhine. This danger, they went on to point out, only made obvious the need for a strongly united Germany with a strong executive power to meet such a possible threat.

Only the radical Forty-eighters expressed open hostility to Austria and indicated their desire to see the defeat of the Hapsburgs by the Italian nationalists.* There were some who urged that Prussia utilize the embarrassment of Austria to take the lead in establishing a united Germany and to restore the constitution of 1849. The Prussian government, however, allowed itself to be swayed neither by the calls for aid to a sister German state nor by the anti-Austrian clamor from the other side. It adopted a policy of neutrality and refrained officially from taking any sides in the war.

---

* See Carl Vogt, *Studien zur gegenwärtigen Lage Europas* (Geneva, 1859), "Austria's defeat in Italy and the establishment of an independent Italy under the leadership of Sardinia are an absolute necessity"; Ferdinand Lassalle, *Der italienische Krieg und die Aufgabe Preussens* (Berlin, 1859), "Austria must be crushed, dismembered, destroyed, smashed . . . its ashes must be strewn to all the four winds!" Ludwig Bamberger, *Juchhe nach Italia* (Bern, 1859); Arnold Ruge, "Deutschland und Österreich," in *Das Jahrhundert*, i (1859), 211–214, "The hangmen of Italy are also our oppressors . . . German freedom means separation from Austria"; Karl Blind, *Kriegsgefahr! Deutsche National-Vertretung! Männer von Deutschland!* (Frankfurt a. M., 1859), "As friends of German freedom we earnestly wish for the day when Lombardy and Venetia, Hungary and Galicia will secure the political independence which they rightly deserve"; Heinrich Simon, *Don Quixote der Legitimität oder Deutschlands Befreier?* (Zurich, 1859).
The sage of the liberals, the historian Gervinus, also adopted a violent anti-Austrian policy, which conflicted with some of his younger disciples. See the interesting exchange of letters between Gervinus and Baumgarten, in J. Heyderhoff, ed. *Deutscher Liberalismus im Zeitalter Bismarcks*, i (Bonn, 1925), 27–39.

The tremendous influence of the Italian war is evident in the writings of Heinrich von Treitschke. This influential spokesman for German patriots pointed with envy to the example of the Italians, of whom he said, "The national goals of their struggle stand much clearer and more securely before their eyes." [8]

Whoever . . . has not lost his understanding of true human greatness, must gaze at this wonderful spectacle with utmost joy, how within fifty years a nation, sunk to the lowest moral depths, has raised itself to honorable unity and readiness to self-sacrifice and, out of the mere geographical expression of Italy, has become a political reality.[9]

The Germans, said Treitschke, should learn from the Italians, should emulate their self-sacrifice, their will power, "that persevering, almost nervous passion which, whether awake or in dreams, can think of only one thing: my country, my country, and always my fatherland." [10] Treitschke's masterful essay on Cavour, published in 1869,[11] not only fired the enthusiasm of his readers for the great national heroes of Italy, Cavour, and that "God-inspired prophet of his people," Garibaldi, but it did a great deal to influence German intellectuals to move away from exclusive admiration of poets and thinkers and to come to recognize that the political genius is worthy of as much glory as a Kant or Goethe. It set the stage and the tone for the subsequent cult of Bismarck, and Cavour was the model.

Whatever hesitation may have been evident in liberal opinion before and during the Italian war, there is no doubt that the defeat of Austria brought great satisfaction in the camp of the "little Germans." The Italian war, wrote the *Preussische Jahrbücher* in 1860, once for all prevented the triumph of reaction. The defeats of Magenta and Solferino, it said, will be recorded by history "among the events which protected Germany and Europe from great evil and which opened the gates to a better future." [12] To the objection that the triumph of France had brought danger to Germany, the writer replied that internal disruption was worse than foreign danger, and given the alternatives of being subject to a triumphant, reactionary Austria or facing the danger of a new war created by the victory of France, the latter was preferable. The defeat of Austria had demonstrated that "absolutism and hierarchism can no longer satisfy the needs of European nations; the future of our people, however, has lost its most dangerous enemy." [13]

A powerful wave of pro-Prussian and anti-Austrian sentiment developed, fed by journalists, literati, historians, and political scientists, economists, jurists, and politicians. The publicist Karl Bollmann called for "an armed reformer to lead us to the promised land of national unity and independence even if need be across the red sea of a general war." [14] The socialist Lassalle deplored the absence of a Frederick the Great, "who would have known that the moment had come finally to realize the German aspirations for unity." [15] Two periodicals in particular carried on an active pro-Prussian campaign. The *Grenzboten,* published in Leipzig by Gustav Freytag and Julian Schmidt, attained wide popularity in the moderately liberal circles throughout Germany. "For the question of liberty and national progress," it declared, "everything is to be expected from Prussia and nothing from Austria." [16] The *Preussische Jahrbücher,* founded by Rudolf Haym in January, 1858, came to be the most famous organ of "classical liberalism" of Prussian tendencies. In its pages Haym, the historians Max Duncker and Treitschke, the publicists Anton Springer and Theodor v. Bernhardi, and other leading publicists and scholars continued to urge upon German intellectuals to pin their national hopes upon Prussia. It aspired to represent the liberal-national point of view with the weapons of science, to be more German than Prussian, to place the greatest emphasis on the historical approach, and hence to follow the English more than the French liberal tradition. This journal continued to occupy a leading position in German public life down to the end of World War I. [17]

A very significant factor in molding national opinion during this period was the work of the great political historians. Max Duncker, Gustav Droysen, Heinrich von Sybel, and Heinrich von Treitschke not only helped mobilize national enthusiasm behind Prussia but did more perhaps than any other group to crystallize a theory of state and nation which became dominant in Germany all through the period of the Second Reich. These historians were greatly influenced by the political philosophy of Hegel. [18] Like Hegel, they adopted a middle position between extreme liberalism and extreme conservatism and were unalterably opposed to outright political democracy. From Hegel they took the conception of the state as a transpersonalistic national individuality and organism whose essence is *Macht.* Like Hegel, they saw in Prussia the genuine prototype of this concept. Their interest in history was not like that of Ranke, to discover what actually happened. History and the writing of history was for them part and parcel of the political battle, a tool with which to fire the patriotism of the reader and demolish the arguments of the political opponent. Droysen's voluminous *Geschichte der preussischen Politik* was intended not only to describe the course of Prussian politics but to provide a measuring rod for evaluating European and German history in terms of German nationalist values. The Hohenstaufen period, the era of the Great Elector and the age of Frederick the Great were the high-water marks of German history because these rulers, according to Droysen, had put themselves at the service of the German national idea. [19]

Already in 1849, in his *Preussen und die Grossmächte,* Droysen wrote the prophetic words, "The power or weakness of Germany determines the fate of Europe." In his political articles. addresses in the political assemblies of which he was a member, as well as in his historical works, he attacked Austria, glorified the Prussia of Frederick II, of Stein, Hardenberg, and Humboldt, and criticized the vacillatory attitude of Prussia, especially under "Horatio" Radowitz and "Hamlet" Frederick William IV.[20]

Heinrich von Sybel, like Droysen, studied the German past in order to forge weapons for the present. He ventured into the field of medieval German history in order to show that the ruin of Germany came as a result of the imperialistic non-German policies of the medieval emperors and that the Central European state formed by the union of Prussia and Austria was nothing but "a weak imitation of the old empire in the worst style . . . as little German as the rule of the Emperor Frederick II." [21]

Treitschke, in his letters and in a continuous flow of pamphlets and articles, hammered away at the notion that salvation for Germany was to come only from Prussia. It might be well to point out here that Treitschke as well as the other pro-Prussian historians of the time is not to be identified with the Junkers. The true bearers of nationalism in Germany at this time were the upper bourgeoisie and the National Liberals. There was infinitely more chauvinism to be found among them than in the old feudal Junker class. Treitschke called Prussian Junkerdom "the Achilles heel of the North," and applied the same epithet to the Ultramontanes of the South.[22] But "Prussia, with all its sins, had done all the truly great things that had been created in Germany since the Peace of Westphalia and it is itself the greatest political deed of our people." [23] The anti-German record of Austria and the selfish particularism of the local princes left only Prussia to carry out the mission of German unity. The hope for a popular movement to bring about German unity, declared Treitschke, is a romantic dream. The only way is "the step-by-step enlargement of Prussia. . . . While outside Prussia there is only a small minority earnestly desirous of ending the disunity of Germany, the Prussian government is being forced more and more by the command of self-preservation to extend its power." [24] As early as 1860 Treitschke wrote to Noth: "Not only a confederation of Austria and Prussia, but a federal state of monarchies is utter nonsense—a child can see that. There is only one salvation! One state, one monarchic Germany under the Hohenzollern dynasty. The driving out of the princely dynasties, annexation to Prussia —this is my program in short." [25] The influence of Garibaldi in Italy is patent. As for Austria, "our so-called German brethren," as Treitschke dubbed them, "there is only one way of reaching an understanding with them and that is by the sword." [26]

A great deal of the pro-Prussian and anti-Austrian sentiment was fostered not only by nationalist emotion but by deep anti-clerical and anti-Catholic feeling. The traditional alliance of the Hapsburg monarchy with the church, the universalist tradition of the empire, and the truly reactionary character of the Hapsburg rule elicited the hostility not only of the radical democrats and progressives, who looked with pleasure upon Austria's humiliation in the Italian war, but perhaps even more so of the bourgeois liberals and their followers. In a letter to his father in 1864, Treitschke tells of the Catholic attacks upon him in Freiburg, and adds: "It is becoming increasingly patent to me here that the opposition between Catholicism and Protestantism is unfortunately deeper than our well-meaning people believe. It is not a matter of differences regarding certain dogmas, but rather of the opposition between slavery and spiritual freedom." [27] This tension was to provide a fertile soil for the later *Kulturkampf* under Bismarck.

Vocal public opinion, however, was not exclusively pro-Prussian. It is true that none of the spokesmen in the other camps were as brilliant, and perhaps also not as gifted, certainly not as renowned, as the protagonists of Prussia. There were no historians and publicists to match Dahlmann, Duncker, Droysen, Sybel and Treitschke, and no publicists comparable to Haym, Freytag, Julian Schmidt, and Konstantin Rössler. But it is also true that, at least in part, their greater renown was due to the fact that the subsequent triumph of Prussia firmly impressed the stamp of success as well as the halo of glory upon its champions, and the historical writing of the Bismarck and post-Bismarck eras drowned into oblivion the other voices that were being heard at the time. Actually these voices are significant and interesting not only to complete the historical picture of Germany in the making but also for the way in which many of their ideas lived on to become resurrected and transfigured in subsequent political movements in Germany.

Another common error, made particularly by non-German historians, is to identify pro-Prussianism at this time with militarism and conservatism, and hence also to identify the opponents of Prussia with radicalism and progressivism. Both formulations are historically erroneous. The greatest support for Prussian leadership in Germany in the 1850's and 1860's came from liberals and progressives. True, there was a difference between German liberals at this time and the classical liberalism of Bentham, Mill, and Spencer.* It was more like a continental version of the Whiggism of Burke. It is also important to bear in mind that German liberalism underwent a significant transformation in content and outlook after 1871, with

---

* An excellent illustration of this difference is afforded by Treitschke's essay on liberty, written in 1861, which is really a discussion of John Stuart Mill's "Essay on Liberty." Treitschke in this essay still hails liberalism as the creator of all that was great in the nineteenth century, and calls the American Declaration of Independence, with its doctrine that all government must be based on the consent of the governed, the initiator of a new era in history. But while accepting Mill's desire for the highest degree of personal liberty, he rejects Mill's theory of the state as not giving sufficient recognition to the state as the source of the individual's creative energies as well as rights. See *Die Freiheit* (Leipzig, 1861), reprinted in his *Historische und politische Aufsätze*, vol. iii.

which we shall deal later. Nevertheless the overwhelming number of people in Germany who favored constitutionalism, parliamentary institutions, freedom of conscience, intellectual freedom, separation of church and state, progress, science, broad educational opportunities, and who were opposed to clericalism, absolutism, obscurantism, authoritarianism, and feudalism, were all ranged on the side of Prussia.

Even the most important spokesmen for the radical democrats, while objecting to the reactionary character of the existing régime in Prussia, nevertheless also pinned their hopes on Prussia.* Arnold Ruge, during the Italian war, wrote: "Prussia, with all its repugnant police barbarism, is the only salvation for Germany from Jesuits and reactionaries in politics." [28] In another pamphlet Ruge called Prussia "the sun in the German solar system." [29] He pointed out that the great task of the age was to combine German culture and intellectual freedom with political freedom. "This," he declared, "only Prussia is capable of realizing," even though he emphasized that it must be a democratic Prussia and not the then-existing Junker-led Prussia. [30] Later, during the Austro-Prussian War, Ruge described the Prussian war against Austria as "the war of unity against disunity, the war of the nation against the princes who had destroyed Germany and opposed its rebirth, the war of freedom against superstitious barbarism and against brainless and heartless separatists." [31] Even Ferdinand Lassalle, the great organizer of the German working class and the founder of democratic socialism in Germany, idealized Frederick the Great and looked to Prussia for leadership in the unification of Germany. [32]

The chief opponents of the pro-Prussian *klein-deutsch* parties were conservative and traditionalist. They were spokesmen for the small or middle-sized states, and more especially for Catholic opinion. The Prussian historians found their most vigorous adversary in the Hanoverian historian Onno Klopp.† In a series of historical works, especially on Frederick the Great, Klopp refuted the picture of the German past as depicted by Häusser, Sybel, and Droysen. [33] He bitterly attacked the policies of Frederick the Great and assailed the Prussia of his own day for

---

* This was pointed out most clearly at the time by the Bavarian Catholic publicist Edmund Jörg. Writing in 1865 on the opposition of the liberals to Bismarck at that time, he noted that their hostility was not due to their opposition to Bismarck's policies, since Prussian expansionism was also their own policy. What irked them was that this policy was being carried out by a conservative ministry and not by a liberal one. "King William," he wrote, "could at any moment change their anger into an enthusiastic pleasure by calling them to the helm." ("Deutscher Bürgerkrieg oder Vernunft?" in *Historisch-politische Blätter*, vol. lvi [1865], summarized in Rosenberg, ii, 846–847.)

J. F. Faber, a liberal proponent of the *gross-deutsch* program, was even more pointed in his attack upon the pro-Prussian liberals. Both the liberal-progressives and divine-right followers, he wrote, go back to the militaristic state of Frederick the Great. The only difference between the liberals and the conservatives in Prussia was that the former dreamed of expansion with French help, while the latter dreamed of expansion with Russian aid. One conceived of the best road to hegemony through democracy, the other through absolutism. See his "Confessionen eines Grossdeutschen," in *Deutsche Viertel-jahrschrift*, 1863, in Rosenberg, vol. ii, no. 84.

† Klopp became a Catholic in 1873.

continuing the policies of Frederick. The spirit of the Prussian monarchy. wrote Klopp, is opposed to and contradicts the German spirit. The Prussian spirit is that of "absolutism within and conquest without." [34] It brings only enslavement in its train. Prussia's aspiration is "not to become fully German but rather to make all the other states Prussian." [35]

Prussia, said Klopp, wants "all of Germany to don the Prussian uniform." "Out of every declaration by a Prussian foreign minister, out of every historical and political article by a Prussian professor, out of every Berlin newspaper of the Progressives as well as the reactionaries, there is manifest the single desire: to convert Germany into one unit by 'Berlinising' it." [36] Prussian policy, wrote Klopp, is like a weathervane that turns with every wind, now toward the East, now toward the West. "Prussian policy, directly or indirectly, bears chief responsibility for all the wars that have come upon us for the last 120 years." [37] The true German spirit, according to Klopp, is that of federation within and defense without. The preservation of the individuality and uniqueness of each German stock is what the German wants, and the union of the various German racial strains on this basis of mutual recognition and respect for one another is the only desirable union. The true German spirit, according to Klopp, is not expansionist in aspiration but only defensive. "Only the system of federation, and not a German centralized state, be it Austrian or Prussian, is historically justified." The goal of the *gross-deutsch* party, according to him, is that the needs for unity of the German nation be satisfied through the paths of law and peace and by firm adherence to existing ties. The maintenance of peace is the most important goal, and progress can come only through peace.[38] In contrast to Prussia, Austria is the protector of conservative interests, of the historically conditioned political entities and of the smaller and middle states. The dualism of Prussia and Austria can be bridged by a reform of the existing Bund and by an agreement between Prussia and Austria and between these two and the smaller states to secure German defense against any external foe. But such an agreement is possible only "by adherence to existing laws and the abandonment of every aspiration to conquest in Germany."

The greatest champion of anti-Prussian federalism was the political theorist Constantin Frantz (1817–1891). Born in Halberstadt, he became the most vigorous critic of the Bismarckian solution to the German problem and the philosopher of the "Central European" idea. Like Klopp, he believed that both Austria and Prussia must yield to a "higher" unity of a Central European federal union. He urged Prussia to give up its aspirations to the "chimera" of exclusive domination and to concentrate on the north and east, while Austria retained the south and west. The crucial point was to oust France and Russia from their dominance of the Continent, and this could be achieved only by a union of Austria and Prussia allied with other Germanic states. Austro-Prussian rivalry was to be neutralized only by a *Pangermanismus,* a general alliance of all the *Germanic* states, including England, the Netherlands, and Scandinavia. "Not the German principle," he wrote, "but the Germanic principle is a world power." [39] We find here a curious blend of pan-German expansionism with traditional universalism. In later writings Frantz hoped for the expansion of this Germanic Bund into a western European confederation, which would also include Belgium, Switzerland, Italy, and Spain. Universalism, held Frantz, is the "calling of the Germans," and he quotes with approval the saying of Gentz, "Europe has fallen because of Germany, and through Germany it will also rise up again." But most important of all, the union is to be carried out through the federalist principle, which is truly German in character, in contrast to the centralism of France. The German problem, therefore, can be solved only "with the princes and through the princes." "If we ever hope to become a great nation again," he wrote in 1861, "this can happen only by means of our principle, which expresses our true disposition, that is, by means of decentralization and then federation, since a decentralized nation can only have a federal unity." [40]

The history of Europe, according to Frantz, showed a gradual evolution from feudalism to liberalism and socialism to federalism. At the same time he was strongly opposed to constitutionalism, parliamentary government, separation of powers, political parties, and secularism. He was no follower of the conservative philosophers Haller and Stahl, but he wanted a Christian state in which power was to be exercised by the king with the traditional guarantees of justice, religious freedom, and intellectual freedom. There was also a marked antisemitic strain in his political thought. He considered the Jews to be one of the greatest hindrances to the development of federalism. The Semitic parasites, he said, have buried themselves in the organism of the Christian peoples like a tapeworm that undermines the body. Jews, therefore, should not have civic equality in the Christian state. [41]

A strong anti-Prussian and pro-Austrian campaign was waged by Catholic political spokesmen in South Germany. The *Historisch-politische Blätter für das katholische Deutschland,* founded by Joseph Görres in Munich, came to be the most vigorous and most able organ of political Catholicism. In 1852 Edmund Jörg, archivist and historian, pupil of Döllinger and influenced by the Görres circle, became editor of the paper. In its pages Jörg maintained a constant barrage against liberalism and Prussianism. Jörg stood for conservative legitimism as against revolution, for autonomy in the state, in society, and in the economy as against centralization and absolutism. Prussia, a bureaucratic and centralized *Militärstaat,* he declared, "only had a stomach for Germany, never a heart." It never was and never will be German, even if it swallows up the rest of Germany. Only "the emperor and the Empire can save Germany." He called for "conferences of princes" instead of "conferences of ministers" to solve the

German problem in the "spirit of conservative federalism." He too, like Klopp and Frantz, looked to a great Central European federation. But unlike Frantz, England, the inspirer of revolution, was for him the enemy as well as Russia. And he hoped for friendly relations with France. He developed a program for German penetration into the Balkans and the Near East that anticipated in many ways the subsequent German *Drang nach Osten*. Thus we observe the curious fact that it was precisely those elements opposed to militaristic Prussia who elaborated an ideology of Central European expansionism, which in this respect went far beyond the nationalism of the *klein-deutsch* followers. The subsequent pan-German movement is probably much more the heir of the anti-Prussian than of the pro-Prussian tradition in German history.

There were also other voices, voices of the smaller and middle states, advocates of a "Trias" idea, of setting up a union of the other German states in addition to Austria and Prussia. But these voices were drowned out in the battle between Austria and Prussia. As a Bavarian deputy (Dr. Edel) reported to the Chamber of Deputies on June 8, 1866: "The original *Stämme* of Germany, those that were the bearers of its destiny, with whom the best memories of the fatherland are tied up, the Bavarians, the Swabians, the Franconians and the Saxons, seem to have disappeared from the stage of history. One hears of Austria and Prussia, and only incidentally of the rest of Germany." [42]

The revival of the national movement after 1858 found expression not only in theoretical and publicist writings but also in an organizational way. Various groups of professionals and public figures in Germany came together and organized all-German associations. The Congress of German Economists, organized in 1858, carried on agitation for free trade, free customs, a unified system of coinage, co-operatives, and above all economic unity. It combined advocacy of free trade with political liberalism. In 1861 it organized the Deutscher Handelstag, a national chamber of commerce. Similarly, the German jurists founded an all-German association in 1860 to work for a unified legal system for all the states. The liberal members of the local diets organized in 1862 the Deutsche Abgeordnetentage for periodic gatherings of liberal deputies. The most influential and most active of these nationalist organizations, however, was the Deutscher Nationalverein.

The model for this political association was the Società Nazionale Italiana, which helped pave the way for Italian unification. The Nationalverein was the work largely of North German liberals, heirs to the "Erbkaiserliche" of 1848. On July 17, 1859, a conference of democratic leaders from Thuringia and Prussia convened in Eisenach, headed by Hermann Schulze-Delitzsch, one of the leading figures in the democratic movement of the time and the great champion of co-operatives. A conference of liberals of Hanover was also summoned by Rudolf von Bennigsen on

July 19, 1859. On August 14, 1859, there was a meeting of liberals from various German states in Eisenach. All these various groups were interested in reforming the constitution of the Bund and were advocates of Prussian leadership. It was out of these meetings that the Nationalverein emerged. It was officially constituted on September 15 and 16, 1859, in Frankfurt am Main. Among its most active leaders were Hermann Schulze-Delitzsch, Hans Viktor von Unruh, Franz Duncker, Rudolf von Bennigsen, and Johannes Miquel. The Hanoverian patrician and deputy Rudolf von Bennigsen was selected to be its head, and the able journalist Ludwig August von Rochau became editor of its organ the *Wochenschrift*.

The Nationalverein became the first political organization of Germany transcending the borders of the individual states and attempting to fuse all the liberals and democrats into one national party. Its general aim, as formulated in the *Wochenschrift* by Rochau, was "the concentration of all military and democratic power in one single hand, the restoration of a general representative assembly for the nation, alert protection of all true German interests against foreign nations . . . the supplanting of an illegal bureaucratic and police régime by a rationally constituted system of self-government in province, community, and association." [43] The Nationalverein, however, was not able to become a compact and solidified political pressure group owing to several factors. It included both radical democrats and moderate "constitutionalists," and it aimed to transcend the gulf between North Germans and South Germans.[44] For these reasons it had to straddle on such important issues as the validity of the constitution of 1849 and the Austrian question. Generally, however, it tended in the direction of the *klein-deutsch* program. Moreover, unlike its prototype, the Italian society, which maintained active and regular connections with Cavour and the government of Piedmont, the Nationalverein was forced to work for the most part in the face of opposition and restrictions imposed by the various governments of the German states. The leaders originally intended to set up their headquarters in Frankfurt, but the municipal authorities denied them permission to do so. It was only due to the friendly and sympathetic attitude of Grand Duke Ernst of Coburg that a home was found for the organization in Coburg, from which it was able to extend its operations. Many of the local states placed severe restrictions on the activities of the Nationalverein, and even Prussia was for a long time cool to its leaders. In November, 1865, Prussia issued an official declaration on the Nationalverein which declared:

The goals of the N.V. were never the goals of Prussia. Prussia has always rejected the leadership of Germany as the N.V. understands it because that would mean the end of Prussia. The N.V. wants a German *Bundesstaat* with Prussia at the head, but only on the basis of a purely democratic German constitution of the Reich. If Prussia were to take over the so-called leadership of Germany on these conditions it would have to subordinate to the will of the German parliament the foundation of its entire position of power hitherto, above all its strong monarchy and all the institutions on which the glorious development of our country rests. Prussia would cease being Prussia.[45]

The membership of the Nationalverein was drawn largely from the middle and upper bourgeoisie. It consisted of small businessmen, intellectuals, professionals, and government officials. But it also attracted important industrialists and financiers like Werner Siemens, Hermann Gruson, Georg Egestorff, Adalbert Delbrück, H. H. Meier (the founder of North German Lloyd), Theodor Molinari, and Count Henckel von Donnersmarck. In 1859 it had 5,000 members; by August, 1861, it had increased to 15,227, and it reached its peak in October, 1862, with 25,000. From then on it began to decline and in 1867 it had only 1,004 members. It was finally dissolved in June, 1868.

During the years of its activity the Nationalverein served as a leaven to stir the German liberals and middle classes to the support of Prussian leadership in the unification of Germany while it carried on at the same time a campaign to make Prussia a more liberal and more constitutional state. As Oncken, the biographer of Bennigsen, points out, however, German unity came not in response to the activity of the Nationalverein or other liberal movements, but "under the leadership of the strongest particularist force, through the historical instruments of power of the Prussian state. . . . The creation of the Reich in 1866 and 1870, therefore, is rather a fulfillment of Prussian history, of the great-power politics of Frederick . . . than the product of these newly awakened German national tendencies." [46] German unity came about largely through the work of William I and his chief minister Bismarck. And Bismarck came upon the scene as a result of one of the most crucial constitutional conflicts in German history, a conflict which had a more decisive influence on the complexion and character of German politics than perhaps any parliamentary event. The conflict arose out of the question of army reform in Prussia.[47]

The Prussian army in 1858 was based on the laws of September 3, 1814, and November 21, 1815, which had introduced the principle of universal military service into the country. In 1815 there were 11 million inhabitants in Prussia, from whom 40,788 recruits were taken annually. They served three years in the line regiments, two years in the reserve, and seven years in the first levy of the *Landwehr* and another seven years in the second levy. By the middle of the century the population of Prussia had increased to 18 million and the proportionate number of annual recruits should have been 65,000. For reasons of economy, however, the number of annual recruits was not increased beyond the early figure, so that in practice there was no such thing as universal military service. This also led to inequitable social consequences. Many older and married men were subject to mobilization in the *Landwehr* while some 24,000 young men remained free of any military duties. This situation was revealed most glaringly when Prussia mobilized all her military forces in 1859. King William thereupon decided to push through a thorough reform of the military. To help him in this task he appointed an efficient but extremely conservative Junker, Albrecht von Roon, as his minister of war.

Von Roon and the king were immediately confronted with the opposition of the lower house of the Prussian diet. The liberal majority in the diet opposed the three-year term of service and wanted it reduced to two years, and they were antagonistic to the vast expenditures that would be needed to realize the government program. There was a traditional anti-militarist sentiment among some Prussian liberals as well as the traditional economy-mindedness of *laissez faire* liberalism. Yet this sentiment was not really as powerful as is sometimes alleged. The liberal and progressive opposition fully appreciated the potential need for a striking force to help attain German unity. They were in favor of increasing the annual number of recruits to 63,000, and from the days before 1848 German liberals had been the most vociferous advocates of a Prussian navy. Similarly, both Bismarck and William might have accepted a compromise agreement had the issue been purely one of technical and military significance.[48] Actually, the roots of conflict were grounded in political issues. William, in particular, was haunted by the specter of the Berlin uprising of 1848. He did not trust the *Landwehr,* and came to look upon the regular army as the only loyal and secure protection of the crown against revolution. A strongly knit officer corps, with many non-commissioned officers and re-enlisted regulars, seemed to him to be the best protection against the aspirations of the people to freedom and self-government. The *Landwehr* was a "band of uncouth individuals" as contrasted with the line troops who formed a "disciplined army." The difference in political views between the king and the opposition was illustrated in William's reaction to the toast given by Schulze-Delitzsch at the Frankfurt annual festival of the rifle club on July 14, 1862. At this celebration Schulze-Delitzsch declared that German constitutional problems would not be solved "until the people's army in the armed nation stands behind parliament." "The ideas for which we stand," he proclaimed, "have a foundation and a future if we can look at you and see you behind us." William's comment on this was: "Here we have it, now it is clear what they want—it is to be a parliamentary army. But they will see whether the army belongs to me or to Schulze-Delitzsch." [49]

William wanted to keep the recruits three years so as to develop in them a feeling of deep attachment to the crown, and he wanted to increase the power and efficiency of the standing army at the expense of the militia. The opposition, however, considered the *Landwehr* to be an expression of a more popular and liberal régime. This is what basically pitted the liberals and progressives against the crown and the ministry.

On February 10, 1860, an army reform bill was presented to the Prussian lower house. It provided for the increase of the standing army by 39 infantry and 10 cavalry regiments, which would take care of all the young men eligible for military service and thus make compulsory service a fact. This increase required an additional appropriation of 9½ million taler. The parity between *Landwehr* and line regiments was to be abandoned, and the *Landwehr* was to be placed more immediately under the control of line officers but kept as far from the field army as possible.

Though the military commission of the Prussian lower house voted on April 30, 1860, to accept the government proposal to increase the number of annual recruits, it demanded the retention of the *Landwehr* in the field army and the reduction of the period of military service from three to two years. The ministry thereupon withdrew the bill, declaring that only the king had the right to determine the composition of the army and the chamber's only function was to vote the necessary funds. The ministry thereupon asked for an additional 9 million taler in the general budget, and this was granted by the chamber. These funds were used by the government to begin to carry out the army reform, even though no law authorizing it had been passed. The Landtag, in 1861, was still willing to grant the government increased general appropriations, although this time the majority vote was very close (151 to 148). New elections in December, 1861, brought in a majority for the liberals and progressives, and the new diet refused to pass either the government's proposed army reform or the increased general budget. The so-called Hagen motion, passed by 177 to 143, called upon the government to submit a detailed breakdown of the budget both for the past and for the future. This measure was the immediate cause for the dissolution of the diet and the call for new elections. The liberal Auerswald ministry resigned and the "New Era" came to a formal end.

The elections of May 6, 1862, brought a still greater triumph for the new Progressive party, which increased its representation from 109 to 135 deputies, and the left-center groups likewise increased their strength. The deadlock between government and the lower house continued, and the situation was so ominous that William was seriously considering laying down his crown and abdicating. What the Progressives really wanted was not to weaken the country militarily nor to cause the downfall of the ministry but rather to use this issue as a lever to extract from the government certain constitutional reforms, especially to decrease the powers of the upper house. Von Roon was disposed to make the two-year service concession to the parliamentary opposition, but William stood firm and refused to yield any of the powers of the crown to a parliament. Roon withdrew his compromise offer and declared open war on the lower house on September 23, 1862. He persuaded the king to call Count Otto von Bismarck-Schönhausen to deal with the impasse. On September 24, 1862, Bismarck was named chief minister, and he began the amazing career during which he not only resolved the constitutional conflict in his own inimitable way but also brought about the unification of Germany under Prussia and set his stamp upon German and world history for all time.

Count Otto von Bismarck was forty-seven years old when called to head the Prussian ministry.[50] He had previously served as Prussian representative to the Bund and in the foreign service in St. Petersburg and Paris. As a member of the Prussian diet in 1851 he had proudly proclaimed himself a Prussian Junker and assured his opponents that "we, on our part, shall bring honor and glory to the name of Junkerdom." [51] He was primarily a man of action, feeling, and will, a volcanic nature full of passionate drive. No one could equal him either in love or in hate. "I could not sleep the whole night," he once told his steward in the morning; "I hated throughout the whole night."

Carl Schurz, the ex-revolutionary of 1848 who had fled from Prussia and gone to the United States, where he rose to a high government position, has left us a memorable picture of Bismarck as he saw him in Berlin in 1868. Schurz described him as "tall, erect, broadshouldered, and on those Atlas shoulders that massive head which everybody knows from pictures—the whole figure making the impression of something colossal." [52] The exuberance and vitality of his personality were revealed most clearly when he talked. Schurz marveled at

the bubbling vivacity of his talk, now and then interspersed with French or English phrases; the lightning flashes of his wit scintillating around the subjects of his remarks and sometimes illuminating as with a searchlight a public character, or an event, or a situation; his laugh now contagiously genial, and then grimly sarcastic; the rapid transitions from jovial sportive humor to touching pathos; the evident pleasure taken by the narrator in his tale; the dashing, rattling rapidity with which that tale would at times rush on, and behind all that this tremendous personality—the picturesque embodiment of a power greater than any king's—a veritable Atlas carrying upon his shoulders the destinies of a great nation.[53]

Bismarck was a *"Herrschernatur"* who boasted that "if I have an enemy in my power, I must destroy him." "I want to make music," he said, "the way I like it or else nothing at all." From his subordinates he tolerated nothing but blind obedience. To Carl Schurz he said: "I am no democrat and cannot be one. I was born and raised as an aristocrat." His political *Weltanschauung* was made up of a combination of family pride, pride in his social class and Prussianism. His nationalism was not so much German as it was Prussian; of cultural nationalism he knew but little, and

German nationalism for him meant that the Germans were to be united and fashioned into a nation through the formation of a political state carried out by Prussia.

Bismarck had no feeling of sympathy with urban bourgeois life. "I feel best," he once said, "in greased boots, deep in the forest, where I hear nothing but the pecking and hammering of the woodpecker, far, far away from civilization." "I always yearned to be away from the larger cities and the stink of civilization. And every time I have to be there I only feel this all the stronger." His favorite verses in the Bible were verses 7–8 of the third Psalm:

> I am not afraid of thousands of people,
> That have set themselves against me round about.
> Arise, O Lord; save me, O my God:
> For Thou hast smitten all my enemies upon the cheek,
> Thou hast broken the teeth of the wicked.

His loyalty to his king, which characterized his entire public life, was deeply grounded in religious faith, although one often wondered how this tempestuous and imperious character could be loyal to anyone but himself. But his royalism was without doubt deeply felt, especially during the lifetime of William I. "I am first and foremost a royalist," he wrote; "everything else comes after that. I may call him names and, as a Junker, I can even conceive of rebelling against him. I take the king in my own way, I influence him, trust him, guide him, but he is the central point of all my thinking and all my action, the Archimedes point from which I will move the world." [54]

Bismarck's political program was simple. He held that every increase in the power of Prussia was for the good of Germany, every limitation of its independence and strength harmed Germany. From the start he was convinced that Austria would have to be defeated by force of arms, but the first essential was to establish Prussian hegemony over the north of Germany. Bismarck always considered domestic issues to be subordinate to questions of foreign policy, and his handling of internal issues can usually be interpreted in the light of Prussian foreign policy. A firm believer in the political philosophy of *Macht* as the decisive factor in all political questions, he always asked himself to what extent the state's power position in the world would be harmed or benefited by internal policies. In his conduct of diplomacy and foreign affairs he aimed so to influence the course of events as to bring about the crisis which suited his own plans while causing his opponents to seem to be in the wrong. He seemed at times to adhere to that school of political thought that considers it essential to accelerate the worsening of a situation so as to bring the situation to such a critical state that improvement would then be absolutely necessary.

William's call of Count Bismarck to the ministry was interpreted by public opinion as indicating his intention not to yield to the parliamentary opposition. The news of Bismarck's appointment was greeted with the comment, "Herr von Bismarck—here is the *coup d'état.*"

Bismarck tackled the constitutional struggle with full force and passion. Despite statements by some of his biographers that he was at first disposed to compromise, his first pronouncements to the diet left no doubt as to where he stood on the issue. His previous reputation as a rabid antidemocratic Junker could hardly make one believe that he was called to the ministry for any other purpose than to force the issue with the parliamentary opposition. In his first appearance before the Budget Commission on September 30, 1862, he made it clear that while the government "has always stretched out its hand for a settlement," he would never, "as long as he was in the government allow members to be named to the upper house who would be disposed to settle the conflict." To the claim of the opposition deputies that they were voicing the will of the people, he expressed the opinion that it is the duty of the deputies to enlighten and influence correctly the opinion of their constituents and not allow themselves to be influenced by them. "The position of Prussia in Germany," he declared, "will be determined not by its liberalism but by its power. Bavaria, Württemberg and Baden may indulge themselves in liberalism but no one will assign to them the role of Prussia; Prussia must concentrate its strength and hold it for the favorable moment, a moment which has already been missed several times. . . . Not through speeches and majority decisions are the great questions of the day decided—that was the great mistake of 1848 and 1849—but through iron and blood." *

Bismarck withdrew the proposed budget from consideration by the lower chamber and indicated that he would continue to carry on the finan-

---

* From the text in *Die politischen Reden des Fürsten Bismarck,* ed. Horst Kohl, 13 vols. (Stuttgart, 1892–1905), ii, 29–30. A letter by an observer of this session provides us with a most interesting description of the public reaction to Bismarck on his first appearance in the diet. The room was packed with curious spectators eager "to hear von Bismarck on Prussian constitutional law." At first there was "the surprising realization that hitherto we had not been accustomed to see Prussian ministers display so much spirit. Now something seemed to be effervescing. But when you applied your calm consideration to it all, it turned out to be not wine but at most soda. The longer the minister spoke . . . the sharper appeared the contrast between the serious and sober manner in which the Budget Commission had hitherto handled the affairs of state and this jabbering overadorned with foreign words. I am sorry there were no stenographers present to give the country an accurate version of this speech. Only one judgment would then be possible regarding the politician, Herr von Bismarck. In one breath he placed in question the most important right of parliamentary representation by the most audacious interpretation and then spoke of the necessity for mutual restraint in the handling of constitutional conflicts—vindicating rights of the crown that are not found in the constitution and then appealing to the deputies in most charming words: 'Trust us honest people, we are all children of one land!'

". . . Admitting that the conflict was paralyzing the powers of the government and then, without any positive proposal or indication how to remove this conflict, speaking of the great decisions made by 'blood and iron'! This hardly does anything to further the desired understanding" (Horst Kohl, *op. cit.,* ii, 37–38).

cial business of the state without a constitutional budget. The lower house passed a resolution declaring all such expenditures unconstitutional, but the resolution was rejected by the upper house. The diet was thereupon prorogued, and the liberal and Progressive deputies, returning to their constituencies, were received as heroes. Popular resentment against the government ran high even though the conservatives organized the Preussiche Volksverein to carry on a popular campaign for the support of the crown. The diet was reconvened on January 14, 1863, and on January 27 Bismarck elaborated the political theory on which he based his actions. In this speech to the lower house he developed what came to be called the theory of the "gap" (*Lücke*). Prussia, said Bismarck, was not like England, where the ministry is responsible to parliament. "We are ministers of His Majesty the King." According to the Prussian constitution, said Bismarck, all laws, including a budget, must be the product of the agreement of all three branches of the government—the crown, the upper house, and the lower house. "There is no provision in the constitution which tells us which of three must yield when the three fail to agree." This is the *"Lücke,"* or gap, in the constitution. It is idle, declared Bismarck, to speculate on what theories to follow when such an impasse is reached. "For me the necessity that the state exists is enough. . . . Necessity alone is the determining factor," and that calls for continued collection of taxes to finance all the necessary expenditures for state activities.

The Progressive majority, however, refused to follow Bismarck's reasoning or to yield to his combination of honeyed and harsh words. They adopted the resolution proposed by the liberal scientist-statesman Rudolf Virchow, censuring the government for breach of the constitution. Bismarck, on his side, commenced a war against the Progressives outside the halls of the diet. He brought pressure to bear upon government officials, judges, university professors, and the press to combat the liberal-Progressive opposition. On June 1, 1863, he issued an ordinance which imposed drastic restrictions upon the freedom of the press. The minister of the interior, on June 6, 1863, forbade all municipal councils from taking up any political questions and from meeting for the sake of drawing up memorials or addresses on the political situation. The government refused to confirm the appointment of Progressive municipal mayors and other officials. Public sentiment, however, was overwhelmingly against the government. On January 6, 1863, the leading Rhenish and Westphalian industrialists addressed a memorial to the king on the constitutional situation. "The basis of a constitutional monarchy," they said, "is law, and the law is violated if the government carries on its financial administration without a constitutionally established budget. We view with sorrow this deplorable conflict, aggravated all the more by the unconstitutional action of the Upper House, which is resulting in the disturbance of internal peace, the weakening of Prussian prestige in Europe and the threat to the respect for the crown among the people." [55] The eminent jurist Rudolf Gneist called upon Bismarck to respect the belief in a firm moral and legal order which, he said, is, in the last analysis, the determining factor in the history of a state. Von Sybel, subsequently to become the arch-apologist of Prussian hegemony, addressing Bismarck in the diet, said, "The ministers and the majority of this house speak different languages, they think along different thought patterns and act according to different rules of morality." Droysen wrote to Max Duncker, on October 19, 1863, that "this means an end to the Prussian state and to liberty." [56] The leader of the Progressives in the diet, Max Forckenbeck, declared that the rule of Bismarck means "governing without a budget, sabre rule internally and war externally. I consider him to be a minister most dangerous for the liberty and happiness of Prussia." [57] Even Crown Prince Frederick came out publicly against the repressive measures of Bismarck, and openly disassociated himself from these acts. In a speech delivered in Danzig, the crown prince declared on June 6, 1863: "I knew nothing of these ordinances. . . . I was away. I had no part in the counsels which led to them." [58] Those who gave such advice to his father the king he called "the most dangerous counsellors for Crown and Fatherland." [59]

Bismarck went his own way, however. He dissolved the diet again and ordered new elections for October 28, 1863. An even larger majority was now returned for the opposition groups. The government continued, however, to collect taxes and make all the governmental expenditures it deemed necessary. And nothing happened. True, a solitary figure like the democratic deputy Johann Jacoby vaguely suggested public refusal to pay taxes, but no one even dared to second the suggestion, and Jacoby was arrested and brought to trial for seditious utterances. A situation had developed which seems utterly impossible to one accustomed to Anglo-Saxon parliamentary institutions. Ferdinand Lassalle published a keen analysis of the constitutional conflict in which he attempted to show why a refusal on the part of the Prussian population to pay taxes that had not been voted by the diet would be ineffective. In this he drew a brilliant comparison between the situation in England and Prussia. In England, wrote Lassalle, if the tax collector were to come to demand taxes not voted by parliament he would be thrown out of the house by the citizen. If the citizen were arrested and brought to court, he would be freed by the court and sent home with praise for having resisted illegal force. If the tax collector were to come with troops, the citizen would mobilize his friends and neighbors to oppose force with force. A battle would ensue with possible loss of life. The tax collector would then be haled into court on the charge of murder, and his defense that he acted "on orders" would be rejected by the British court since he had been engaged in "an illegal act." He would be condemned to death. If the citizen and his friends had killed any soldiers, they would be released because they were resisting illegal force. "And because all the people know this would happen," wrote Lassalle, "everyone would refuse to pay the taxes—even those who are indifferent—in order not to be considered bad citizens." The government can do little since the Mutiny Act made the existence of the army dependent on annual grants from parliament.

In Prussia, Lassalle went on to say, it is different. If the Prussian citizen were to throw out the tax collector who came to collect taxes not approved by the diet he would be haled to court to receive a jail sentence for "resistance to lawful authority." If fighting and killing ensued, the soldiers would be protected from prosecution because they "obeyed orders," while the citizen who attempted to resist by force would be convicted and beheaded. "And because this is so and because from the start all the odds are against those who refuse to pay taxes, only a minority of most principled characters will refuse to pay, the government will feel confident of any action it undertakes and all the officials will be loyal to it." [60]

What would have happened if other matters had not intervened is hard to say. William, it is told, apparently considered the situation so serious that he would stand at his castle window, look down into the court, and say, "Down there in the courtyard of the castle they will set up a guillotine for me." But as has happened so often and so ominously in the history of Germany, foreign wars and nationalist issues entered the picture to cast their shadow upon the efforts of liberalism to make headway, and they were sufficient to bring about the defeat of liberalism. The years 1864–1866 and, later, 1871 saw three patriotic and nationalist wars. In the passion and enthusiasm engendered by the successes of Bismarck, sober and rational issues such as parliamentary government, ministerial responsibility, and constitutionalism were completely submerged and lost. The sparks of vigorous and healthy political opposition that seemed, for a while, to be animating German political life, and impelling it in the direction of responsible constitutional government, were snuffed out almost completely by the wave of nationalist sentiment that came with these wars. Bourgeois liberalism in Germany never again dared challenge the ultimate power of crown and sword.

The Wars of Bismarck

Triumphe sind wie Niederlagen
Wenn ihre Frucht besteht in Klagen
Im grenzenlosen Hass der Welt.

PLATEN

The Bismarckian Second Reich was the product of three wars: the Danish War of 1864, the Austro-Prussian War of 1866, and the Franco-Prussian War of 1871. A South German (not Prussian) historian, in his preface to a history of these three wars, written in 1889, calls them "the necessary condition for the establishment of a unified Germany," and goes on to say:

The German-Danish War tested the sharpness of the Prussian sword and the boldness and virtuosity of Prussian strategy; in the Austro-Prussian War the power of Prussian military power was measured against an equal partner; in the Franco-Prussian War the proof was demonstrated that the reorganization of the army by King William and the two war preludes had brought Germany's army to a peak of perfection which justified our chancellor in uttering the proud words: "We Germans fear only God, nothing else in the world." [1]

Each of these three wars laid the basis for the next one, and the last of the three helped pave the way for the world conflagration of 1914. The first war enabled Bismarck to consolidate his internal position in Prussia and to lay the groundwork for the defeat of his parliamentary opposition. The second war succeeded in ousting Austria once for all from the leadership of the Germanies and in consolidating Prussian hegemony in the north. The Franco-Prussian War succeeded in bringing the South German states under the aegis of the Prussian eagle, and it crushed all pretense to any solution to the problem of German unity other than through "blood and iron." [2]

Schleswig-Holstein was one of the European "sore spots" that plagued and baffled European diplomats for many centuries. It was Palmerston who said that only three men really understood the complexities of the

132

problem; one of them had died, another had gone crazy, and he himself, the third, had forgotten it all. The conflict involved the three provinces of Schleswig, Holstein, and Lauenburg. The latter two were ethnically entirely German, while the first was inhabited by a mixture of Germans and Danes. All three provinces were under the Danish crown, but Holstein and Lauenburg were also members of the Germanic Confederation. The growth of German national feeling in the nineteenth century produced an increased interest in these provinces as part of the German national organism. The geographic position of Denmark, however, also made it a matter of vital concern to the other great powers, particularly England, Russia, and Sweden. As a result of the intervention of the European powers, the London Protocol of May 8, 1852, was signed, which was designed to regulate the situation in this area. England, Russia, France, Sweden, Denmark, Austria, and Prussia all affixed their signatures to the protocol.

The London Protocol fixed the line of succession to the Danish throne of the childless King of Denmark, guaranteed the inseparability of the duchies, and established them in personal union with Denmark under the Danish king. The Danish nationalists, however, carried on active propaganda in and out of the duchies, advocating the incorporation of the three provinces into the Danish nationalist state. On March 30, 1863, Frederick VII of Denmark issued a proclamation which in substance amounted to the annexation of Schleswig and which also imposed a new charter on Holstein. The diet of the Germanic Confederation took up the question and urged that the duchies be set up as an independent state under the Duke of Augustenburg, the German claimant to these provinces, and then admitted into the Bund. This was, by and large, the position advocated also by German liberals. Liberal sentiment had always been stirred by the desire for the severance of Schleswig and Holstein from Denmark. Considerable agitation had developed during the sessions of the 1848 Frankfurt assembly over this question. The *Grenzboten,* one of the leading liberal organs in Saxony, had declared in 1863 that before German unity could be achieved, German unity would have to be demonstrated in a national question before the rest of the world, and the Schleswig-Holstein question offered such a possibility. "A successfully waged war for a specific German interest under Prussian political and military leadership, a war which, with respect to Schleswig, pursues those claims which Denmark's course of action has given us the rights to, is the solution of the German question." [3] German public opinion held that the London Protocol had been imposed by force by the European powers upon reactionary and weak Austria and Prussia. It was the liberals who, at this time, called for the repudiation of the international agreement by Prussia, while Bismarck declared in the diet that he would not be a party to such a breach of international obligations.

On November 16, 1863, Prince Christian of Glücksburg, in accordance with the London Protocol of 1852, succeeded to the Danish throne as Christian IX. Yielding to the clamor of Danish public opinion, he signed the new constitution of Denmark-Schleswig on November 18, 1863. This, in the eyes of the Germans, was equivalent to the annexation of Schleswig, the severance of the province from Holstein (in 1460 the two had been proclaimed as inseparable), and the loss of the province to Germany. A tremendous wave of national sentiment swept all over Germany in response to this act. Both the Nationalverein and its political opponent, the Reformverein, were at one on this issue. Mass meetings and demonstrations were held throughout the land calling for energetic action against Denmark. Similar motions and resolutions were passed by various diets of the local states. On December 2 the Prussian lower house passed a resolution, by 231 to 63 votes, calling for the repudiation of the London Protocol by Prussia.

Bismarck had his own plans, however. Much to the amazement and chagrin of his political opponents he chose to proceed on this issue hand in hand with Austria, the avowed enemy of German unity. On December 4 both governments, completely ignoring the Germanic Confederation, announced the conclusion of an agreement according to which they would act on the Schleswig-Holstein conflict only within the terms of the London Protocol. On January 16, 1864, Austria and Prussia dispatched an ultimatum to Denmark calling upon her to withdraw the constitution of November 18 within forty-eight hours, or face military action. Denmark, counting on aid from the European powers, rejected the Austro-Prussian ultimatum. Help, however, was not forthcoming. France refused to join England in supplying material aid to Denmark, and England hesitated to act alone. On February 1 the troops of Austria and Prussia crossed the Eider into Schleswig and overwhelmed the Danish troops. An attempt at mediation by the powers in London ended without result. The war was resumed again and continued to July 12. Denmark initiated direct negotiations with Austria and Prussia for an armistice and peace. A peace treaty was finally signed in Vienna on October 30, 1864. The claims of the Duke of Augustenburg were entirely discarded, and the duchies were turned over to Austria and Prussia. Their final disposal was made in the Gastein Treaty of August 14, 1865, between Austria and Prussia. According to this convention the Austrian and Prussian monarchs were to rule over the duchies jointly. The administration, however, was to be divided; Holstein, which bordered on Prussia, to be administered by Austria, and Schleswig by Prussia. Prussia was to have a military road and telegraph line through Holstein and also the command of Kiel, which was to be the port of the Bund. Both Schleswig and Holstein were to enter the Zollverein, and a canal was to be constructed from the North Sea to the Baltic. The small Duchy of Lauenburg was given outright to Prussia for a sum of 2½ million taler. As for the Prince of Augustenburg, the hopeful of the liberals, he was to be treated in the future only as a private citizen.[4]

Bismarck never considered this arrangement a permanent solution. He always thought that conflict would ensue between Austria and Prussia on the interpretation of the terms of the convention. The Italian diplomat Count Nigra tells the following regarding a conversation with Bismarck in Paris on November 3, 1865: "When Bismarck came to Paris in November 1865, on the way from Biarritz, he visited me and made no secret of the fact that the object of Prussian policy was the humiliation of Austria. He confessed openly to me that the Gastein convention can only gloss over the break between Austria and Prussia but not heal it. In joyous expectation he was already fixing the threads to the spool of the coming war. His king's love of peace will not be able to prevent war from coming for long." [5] To the query of Countess Hohenthal, wife of the Saxon ambassador, whether Bismarck really intended to attack Saxony and Austria, Bismarck replied, "Naturally, since the first day of my ministry I had no other intention." [6] The levity in the conversation and the surrounding circumstances of this conversation do not detract from the veracity and sincerity of this remark.

Bismarck himself did more than anyone else to disseminate the view that he had always believed that the "Gordian knot of German destiny was not to be untied by the gentle methods of dual policy but could only be cut by the sword." In his reminiscences he tells how, from his days as Prussian representative to the diet at Frankfurt, he had become convinced that war with Austria was inevitable. The idea of a conflict with Austria obsessed him so much that he actually dreamed of the battlefields of Bohemia. Bismarck himself told of a dream he had in the spring of 1863, in which he was "on a broad road leading down to the Bohemian plain; and everywhere there were Prussian troops and colors. I awoke strengthened and joyful." [7] Certainly from the moment he became prime minister he acted in keeping with this belief in the inevitability of a conflict with Austria. He immediately got in touch with the Hungarian exiles, chiefly Kiss and Count von Seherr-Toss. To the latter he said: "I want to secure for Prussia the position which is due her in Germany as a purely German state. . . . If we win, Hungary too will get her freedom. You may count on me." [8] Yet when the famous Austrian historian Heinrich Friedjung visited Bismarck on June 13, 1890, and asked him about his earlier Austrian policy, Bismarck declared that he had always wanted a firm alliance with Austria and would have welcomed a peaceful solution of the difficulties. When Friedjung reminded him of his dispatches from Frankfurt in which he had said that he believed war with Austria was inevitable, Bismarck replied:

In general, certainly, but not all the time, not in the day-to-day incidents of policy. It would be a misinterpretation of the spirit of politics to believe that a statesman can formulate a comprehensive plan and decide what he is going to do in one, two, or three years. Schleswig-Holstein was certainly worth a war, but you cannot pursue a plan blindly. You can only give a general indication of your aim. The statesman is like a man wandering in a forest who knows his general direction, but not the exact point at which he will emerge from the wood. It was difficult to avoid a war with Austria, but he who is responsible for the lives of millions will shrink from war until all other means have been exhausted. It has always been a weakness of the Germans to want all or nothing, but I was satisfied with any step which brought us nearer to German unification, and I should have welcomed any solution which cleared the way for the aggrandizement of Prussia and the unification of Germany without a war.

On reflecting further, however, Bismarck added to Friedjung, "Perhaps it was better that the affair should be settled by the sword, for the clock of German dualism has to be put right by a war once every hundred years." [9]

That Bismarck would have preferred to attain his objective of eliminating Austria from her position of German leadership without war is no doubt certain. What is open to more conjecture is whether he was willing to make any concession or take any steps which would have made war unnecessary. Certain it is that his entire policy, both foreign and domestic, from 1863 to 1866 was based on the plan for war with Austria, as was his policy after 1866 to win her back as a junior partner in a Central European alliance. Bismarck kept watching for a chance to put Austria in the wrong. And Austria, it must be admitted even by Friedjung, obliged him with numerous instances. The disposition of the duchies acquired from Denmark proved to be most convenient for this purpose. Before bringing a crisis actually to a head, however, Bismarck wished to solidify his position with respect to the other European powers and also do something about mobilizing more popular support at home.

In the foreign field Bismarck had already assured himself of the friendship of Russia by his sympathetic conduct during the Polish revolt of 1863. He now also sought to secure assurances of friendship from France and Italy. He carried on diplomatic conversations with Napoleon III at Biarritz, in which he made sure that he would not find France lined up against him in case of war with Austria. There was the delicate problem of securing some territorial compensation for Napoleon, who needed a diplomatic triumph abroad very badly for home consumption. But Bismarck maneuvered himself through this maze most adroitly. As for Italy, still the hereditary enemy of Austria and awaiting eagerly the moment to "liberate" Venetia, an alliance was concluded by Bismarck on April 8, 1866, whereby Italy pledged herself to join Prussia if war against Austria came within three months. The Italian alliance, when it became known in Austria, was hardly conducive to improving relations between Austria and Prussia. Bismarck also tried to secure Bavarian support but failed. As a matter of fact, when war with Austria did break out not a single German state lined up with Prussia.

At home Bismarck was still confronted with the opposition of the liberal and Progressive majority in the Prussian diet. While the success of Prussian arms in the Danish War had mollified some of the opposition, most of the liberal and democratic leaders still openly opposed the Bismarck ministry. In September, 1865, a meeting of democratic leaders was held in Darmstadt, and they declared: "There is nothing in between the enlarged Prussian unified state of Herr von Bismarck and the federated state of democracy. . . . Unity is not secure and it is valueless if it is not the product of liberty." [10] Bismarck apparently entertained no hopes of winning over the parliamentary leaders of the opposition without having to make too great constitutional concessions to parliamentary government.* What he did hope for was to wean away mass support from the liberals. Bismarck was too much of a traditional aristocrat to attach great weight to public opinion and public support. But living in mid-nineteenth century and witnessing the policies of Napoleon III as well as the Tory democracy of Disraeli, he also acquired a touch of "Caesarism," which led him to various moves toward gaining mass support. He told Carl Schurz in 1863 that he had toyed with the idea of proclaiming the constitution of the Frankfurt assembly of 1848–1849 but was only prevented from doing so by the opposition of the king. While this may have been said primarily to impress the old Forty-eighter, the mere suggestion of such an idea is indicative of that touch of Caesarism in Bismarck.

Now, however, Bismarck presented a plan to the Bundestag on April 9, 1866, which called for the summoning of a German parliament according to the electoral laws of 1849 on universal, equal, and secret ballot. The plan in itself was a tactical one. Bismarck knew that Austria would be unalterably opposed to such measures and thus would help bring on a direct conflict; [11] but he also really believed that universal suffrage would work to his advantage. He attributed the support of the liberals to the upper bourgeoisie, and their success to the three-class system in Prussia. Given universal suffrage he hoped that the clergy and landowners would be able to exercise their paternal influence over the peasants and win them

---

* On June 20, 1866, Bismarck had a talk with Unruh, one of the leaders of the liberal opposition. The war was already on. Bismarck was interested in finding out what the attitude of the liberals would be in the event of Prussian defeat. He expressed his fears for the existence of the Prussian state with the weak crown prince as the successor to the throne. Unruh assured Bismarck that no one except a few on the extreme left hoped for the defeat of Prussia, since Austria was looked upon as the arch-exponent of reaction, and that the triumph of Austria would only mean the extension of reaction throughout Germany. But Unruh pressed Bismarck for a return to the constitution and the recognition of the rights of the lower house on budgetary matters. It is interesting to note that he admitted to Bismarck that "even a Liberal ministry which had as its goal the union of Germany could not have avoided war with Austria" (Bismarck, *Gesammelte Werke*, vii, 128–131).

over to gain a conservative majority. The growth of the workers' movement also encouraged him at that time in this feeling. The chief object of attack by Ferdinand Lassalle, the rising leader of the working classes, was the liberals. Lassalle looked upon the liberals as the greatest enemies of the workers. This is what brought him to Bismarck and prompted several conferences between the two.[12] In any case Bismarck, the Prussian Junker and chief advocate of the doctrine of royal power by the grace of God, now also became the chief exponent of universal suffrage, and he felt sure that he had sufficient support at home to proceed with his plans against Austria.

Bismarck set about to exploit the mistakes of the Austrian cabinet. He passed on to the press reports of troop movements in Bohemia and encouraged exaggerated accounts of Austrian armaments. He accused Austria of encouraging the claims of the Duke of Augustenburg to Schleswig-Holstein and of conducting "seditious agitation" against Prussia. Moltke pressed his idea of an offensive war, but King William opposed it and ordered Bismarck to negotiate with Austria for disarmament. To this Austria agreed, and Bismarck's whole plan seemed on the verge of ruin. But false rumors of increased arming by Italy led Austria to disregard the plans for disarming and thus gave Prussia an excuse for further arming. Austria mobilized on April 27, and Prussia countered on May 3, 5, and 12.

Further excuse for conflict was provided by Austria's action in bringing the settlement of the Schleswig-Holstein controversy to the Bundestag on June 1, 1866. For Austria this was a way of getting the lesser states committed to her support in case of war. But Bismarck denounced this move as a breach of the Gastein convention. When Austria also decided to convene the Holstein diet to discuss the future status of the duchy, Bismarck declared this to be not an act of administration but an act of sovereign rule which, according to the Gastein treaty, belonged to both Austria and Prussia. He therefore proclaimed the Gastein treaty to be broken and ordered Prussian troops to march into Holstein. The Austrians retired in the face of the advance of Prussian arms. On June 11 Austria called upon all the armies of the Bund to act against Prussia, while Prussia at the same time declared that any vote for this plan would be tantamount to a declaration of war. Bismarck meanwhile presented to the states a new plan for reorganizing the Bund but he could not arouse any support for his proposals. On June 14 the diet took action on the crisis. The vote was not on the Austrian proposal but on a more moderate one by Bavaria to choose a commander for the forces of the Bund and to mobilize the forces of the smaller and medium-sized states. The Bavarian proposal was carried by a vote of 9 to 6, whereupon the Prussian delegate arose and declared that by virtue of this vote the Bund was dissolved and he called upon the other German states to follow Prussia into a new Bund. The war was officially on.

Hostilities lasted only three weeks. Even though the Italians were defeated, and for a brief moment it looked as if Napoleon's prognosis of a long-drawn-out war which would wear out both contestants would be correct, the decisive turn at the battle of Sadowa (Königgrätz) on July 3 brought the war to a speedy end. Austria was vanquished, and her smaller German satellites were now at the mercy of Prussia. Bismarck, however, displayed shrewd statesmanship and wise restraint in dealing with his German enemies. His main objective was achieved. He had established Prussian hegemony and eliminated Austria from her position of leadership in Germany. Now it was necessary to convert his former enemies into either dutiful vassal states or friendly allies. He treated Baden and Württemberg most leniently. They were to pay only an indemnity. No territory was taken from them. The Grand Duchy of Hesse, at first, was to be annexed to the North German Confederation that Bismarck was planning, but this was dropped and Hesse joined the confederation as an autonomous state. Bavaria had to make slight territorial adjustments and pay a war indemnity, but she was forced to sign a secret alliance with Prussia promising to aid Prussia in a war with France. Peace between Austria and Prussia was signed at Prague on August 23. "The dispute with Austria is decided," declared Bismarck; "now we have to win back the old friendship." According to the terms of the treaty, the old Germanic Confederation was dissolved; Austria was excluded from German affairs; Austria also renounced all her rights in Schleswig-Holstein; Hanover, the Electorate of Hesse, Nassau, and Frankfurt were annexed to Prussia, thus eliminating the corridor between the eastern and western provinces of Prussia; the territorial integrity of Austria was respected; and Austria was to recognize the union of North German states under Prussia, called the North German Confederation.

Prussia's success in the war and the ousting of Austria from German leadership brought most of Bismarck's enemies to his side. Prussian writers spoke of the war as a "revolution." The Prussian Junkers became the heroes of the day, and all the forces of old Prussia—the dynasty, the army, the nobility—now came to the fore. Once again the realization became acute that all the attempts of the people and its representatives to solve the national problem had failed again and again, while the Prussian dynastic state, with its army and its discipline, had solved it in a week. The dream of liberal nationalists for five decades—to free Germany from Austria—had been achieved by Bismarck through blood and iron. Gustav Mevissen, an old leader of the liberals in the Rhineland, wrote on the day the victorious Prussian troops returned to Berlin:

I cannot shake off the impression of the hour. I am no devotee of Mars; I feel more attached to the goddess of beauty and the mother of graces than to the powerful god of war, but the trophies of war exercise a magic charm even upon the child of peace. One's view is involuntarily chained and one's spirit goes along with the boundless rows of men who acclaim the god of the moment—success.[13]

Only the South German Catholic leaders and the socialists on the left continued to be critical. Wilhelm Liebknecht, the socialist, wrote on July 19, 1866, that the oppressor of yesterday had become the savior of today; right is now wrong and wrong right. "Blood," said Liebknecht, "seems to be a peculiar juice, for the angel of darkness becomes the angel of light before whom the people lie praying in the dust. The branding of the breach of the constitution is washed from his forehead and instead the glorious halo of fame shines from his head crowned by wreaths." [14] August Reichensperger, one of the founders of the Catholic Center party, entered the following in his diary on the day after the battle of Königgrätz: "It takes a great deal of effort to accommodate one's self to such decrees of the Lord and not to come around to the view that right exists only for the petty civic relationships, but that in the larger realm, force, intrigue, and deceit are called upon to prevail, and neither the means nor the end are subject to religious and moral principles." [15] Malinckrodt, another Catholic leader, put it much more succinctly. On July 7, 1866, his comment was, "The world stinks."

Prussia proceeded to consolidate its position in the north by creating the North German Confederation, consisting of twenty-two states and principalities in North and Central Germany. A Reichstag was convened on the basis of the universal suffrage law of 1849. The constitution of this confederation, largely the work of Bismarck himself, was the same as the one subsequently adopted for the larger German Reich after the War of 1870–1871, and we shall leave its analysis for later discussion.

Inside Prussia, Bismarck, aided by the popular enthusiasm for his success, was able to dispose of the constitutional conflict which had been pending ever since 1862. New elections for the diet were held on the day of the battle of Königgrätz. The returns showed a decided shift to the right in popular sentiment. The Conservatives returned 142 deputies, the Old Liberals 26, the Center 15, the Poles 21, the Left Center 65, and the Progressives 85. On August 11 the *Kölnische Zeitung* declared that the conflict over the army reform had been only a "misunderstanding." On August 25 the Prussian government, on its side, felt it could make some pretense of a concession, but at the same time it took pains to indicate that royal power was still absolute and supreme. King William, in his reply to the address of the newly elected lower house, claimed that the credit for the victories of the Prussian army was due to his army reform. He also indicated that as far as the budget was concerned he could have acted in no other way. "So I had to act and so will I always act whenever similar conditions are repeated." "But, gentlemen," he hastened to add, "they will never be repeated." [16]

Bismarck introduced an indemnity bill which was intended as a sort of compromise measure. According to this bill the chamber would approve the budgets of 1862–1864; the acts of the government during these years would not be considered illegal and would not be subject to prosecution; a budget of 154,000,000 taler would be voted for 1866 and the government was to produce a record of expenditures and receipts for 1866 in the following year. Most of the die-hard Progressives opposed this measure too, but some of them were won over to Bismarck's side and the Old Liberals favored it. Von Vincke, the Old Liberal leader, said, "The heavenly tribunal of success has cast its decision for the government." After a debate of several days the indemnity bill was passed by a vote of 230 to 75 (Poles, Catholics, and Progressives). On September 25 the lower house passed a vote of confidence in the conduct of foreign affairs by the government by a vote of 230 to 83. Thus was the constitutional struggle of German parliamentarianism concluded. True, the formal rights of parliament to initiate money bills seemed to have been accepted. But the shadow of 1862 hovered over the entire subsequent history of German parliamentary institutions. Were any similar situation ever to arise where parliament would refuse to give the government the credits it demanded, the ministry had the example of Bismarck to guide it. And the very awareness of this possibility served to make such a situation impossible. The memory of Bismarck's triumph was certainly a powerful factor in sapping the strength and vitality of German parliamentary life.

The final step in the creation of the Bismarckian Reich was the one which involved the reckoning with France in the war of 1870–1871. The problem of responsibility for the outbreak of this war has been hotly debated by pro-French and pro-German scholars. Many of the diplomatic documents have been published only recently, and much of the material is still unavailable.[17] But in the words of R. H. Lord, the most authoritative and objective student of this problem, "Unless one accepts the view that a Franco-Prussian war was under any circumstances inevitable, it is difficult not to accuse both governments in 1870 of criminally playing with fire."[18] Every student of European history, of course, is familiar with the line of continuity in French policy toward Germany from the days of Richelieu. It was a policy based on a mixture of real and manufactured fears of a strong and united Germany, and hence a policy of continuous opposition to the national unification of Germany. Napoleon III, as a public advocate of the principle of nationality, found it hard to reconcile the application of this principle to Germany and yet carry on the traditional policy of France. The results of the Austro-Prussian War, which ran counter to his expectations, and the skilful and adroit diplomacy of Bismarck forced him to modify his earlier position. In his speech from the throne on November 18, 1867, Napoleon said: "We must frankly accept the changes which have been introduced across the Rhine and let it be known that so long as our interests and our dignity are not threatened we shall not interfere with the changes which have been evoked by the wishes of the German nation." [19] But to Lord Clarendon, in 1868, Napoleon declared: "I can guarantee peace only as long as Bismarck respects the present status; if he draws the South German states into the North German Confederation, our guns will go off of themselves." [20]

Napoleon, moreover, was a would-be Caesar. Like all Caesars he was desperately in need of resounding triumphs in the foreign field. The fiasco of his adventure in Mexico only accentuated this need. He tried his hand at acquiring Luxemburg and was thwarted by Bismarck; he thought he had secured Bismarck's support for territorial compensation in Belgium, but there, too, Bismarck used the negotiations only to embarrass Napoleon before world opinion and thus bring the plan to nought. These frustrations, however, did not heighten the bellicose intents of the French government. On the other hand, they forced Napoleon as well as his ministers to become more reconciled to the situation in Germany. But it did serve to make French policy more jittery, more erratic, and more sensitive to diplomatic rebuffs and at the same time more eager to score at least a diplomatic if not a military triumph. Napoleon and his ministers, Ollivier and Gramont, would have preferred peace, but in the words of Lord: "It can scarcely be denied that the French ministers, by premature threats of war . . . by their unnecessary and imprudent demands on July 12, and in general by their too persistent efforts to achieve a complete and spectacular diplomatic victory, did much to bring on the conflict." [21] The recent study of French public opinion by M. Malcolm Carroll also reveals that contrary to the hitherto accepted opinion that Napoleon's ministers were forced into a declaration of war by the clamor of public opinion and parliamentary pressure, the press and parliamentary debates of the time show that public opinion in France was far from bellicose and that there were officials in the government of France who, although not guilty of plotting the war, were ready "to interpret the propaganda of a few newspapers as the expression of public opinion." [22]

Bismarck's statements on this subject are, according to Lord, "notoriously unreliable and misleading." Carl Schurz tells of a conversation with the Prussian historian Sybel. After one of his visits to Bismarck, Sybel asked Schurz what Bismarck had told him about the outbreak of the Franco-Prussian War. When Schurz recounted what Bismarck had said, "Sybel said with a smile: 'Well, Well! Bismarck has told that story so often that he must actually have come to believe it.'" [23] But a study of the various conversations reported with Bismarck from 1866 on show that war with France was uppermost in his mind. To Count Bethusy-Huc, a free conservative deputy, Bismarck predicted in March, 1867, that war would come in five years. [24] To Carl Schurz, the same year, he predicted war would come within two years. Like Hitler many years later, Bismarck passionately avowed his hatred of war when talking to foreign diplomats and newsmen. He told Schurz:

Do not believe that I love war. I have seen enough of war to abhor it profoundly. The terrible scenes I have witnessed, will never cease to haunt my mind. I shall never consent to a war that is avoidable, much less seek it. But this war with France will surely come. It will be clearly forced upon us by the French emperor. I see that clearly.[25]

Bismarck predicted too that this war would bring about German unity without Austria and the downfall of Napoleon. The real author of a war, once declared Montesquieu, is not the one who declares it but he who makes it necessary. We might also add, and he who thinks it necessary. For Bismarck, as for most German historians, these wars were somehow decreed by Fate; they lay "in the logic of history," and no one could work against these forces of nature and destiny. All the acts of Bismarck, according to Oncken, are justified in terms of national self-defense. Bismarck wrote in his *Reminiscences:*

In view of the attitude of France, our national sense of honor compelled us, in my opinion, to go to war, and if we did not act according to the demands of this feeling we should lose, when on the way to the completion of our national development, the entire impetus gained in 1866, while the German national feeling south of the Main, aroused by our military successes in 1866 and shown by the readiness of the Southern states to enter the alliances, would grow cold again.
I was convinced that the gulf which had been created in the course of history between the South and the North of the fatherland by a variety of dynastic and racial sentiments and modes of life, could not be more effectively bridged than by a common national war against the neighboring nation, our aggressor for centuries.[26]

The immediate cause of the war, as in the case of most of the major European wars, was not a matter arising from immediate relations between the two governments but from something more remote. In this case it had to do with the succession to the throne of Spain. In 1868 Queen Isabella of Spain was dethroned by a military coup, and the monarchist leaders looked for a candidate to the throne. Among those mentioned was Prince Leopold von Hohenzollern-Sigmaringen, a member of the Catholic Swabian branch of the Hohenzollern family, distantly related to the Prussian Hohenzollerns and as such subject to the authority of King William as the head of the family. All available evidence now proves beyond doubt that Bismarck was the chief promoter of this candidacy. This was revealed in the diaries of Carol of Rumania, published in 1894. Lord Acton, who was in intimate contact with many of the leading participants in the diplomacy of the period, in his essay on the origins of the war of 1870 declared that a well informed diplomat, now identified as Sir Robert Morier, wrote to him as follows: "From statements made to me confidentially I have obtained the certainty that the Hohenzollern candidature was deliberately arranged by Bismarck with a view of bringing on the collision with France in such a way as to make Germany to appear to be acting on the defensive." And in another statement by Acton, recently published, we find: "At Berlin Friday April 30 1897 at the Saxon legation Lerchenfeld [for many years Bavarian minister at Berlin] assured me that Bismarck arranged the Hohenzollern affair in order to bring on war. He had seen that the Luxemburg affair failed so he adopted the other plan." [27]

France warned Prussia on May 11, 1869, that this matter was for France "an interest of the first order." The specter of a revived empire of Charles V to threaten France on both sides of her borders loomed large. The French warning only seemed to confirm in Bismarck's mind the idea that this would provide a most convenient *casus belli*. Prince-Leopold at first refused the candidacy and then accepted on June 19, 1870. Even though all the negotiations had been secret the news did leak out. The Spanish authorities were forced to proclaim the decision officially on July 2, and the news reached Paris on Sunday, July 3. In France the effect was that of a bombshell. Prussia, however, blandly denied having any hand in the matter and maintained that both the Spaniards and the prince were free agents. On July 6 the following declaration, drafted by Gramont and adopted by the French Council of Ministers, was read to the Corps Législatif:

We do not believe that respect for the rights of a neighboring people obliges us to permit a foreign power, by placing one of its princes on the throne of Charles V, to disturb to our detriment the present equilibrium in Europe and to place the interests and the honor of France in peril. This eventuality, we firmly hope, will not be realized. To prevent it, we count both upon the wisdom of the German, and upon the friendship of the Spanish people. But if it should be otherwise, strong in your support, gentlemen, and in that of the nation, we should know how to do our duty without hesitation and without weakness.[28]

Benedetti, the French ambassador to Prussia, was instructed to see King William, who was then taking the cure at Ems. The king received Benedetti on July 9, and they had four interviews on this matter. William admitted that as head of the family he had previous knowledge of the affair. He could not order Leopold to renounce the candidacy now, but he indicated that he would not raise any objection if Leopold himself would turn it down. William had decided, as a matter of fact, to use his personal influence to induce Leopold to retract the candidacy in order to prevent war. On July 12 Leopold's retraction was announced by his father, and the excitement seemed to be over. But here the combination of French blundering and Bismarckian ingenuity fanned the dying embers into the flame of war. Gramont, eager to exploit the situation in order to achieve a diplomatic triumph, wired Benedetti the same evening to see the Prussian king and extract from him a promise that he would never again permit Leopold to renew his candidacy. By such "guarantees for the future" Gramont and Napoleon "were probably seeking only to end the affair in a way that would give them security against further surprises, and some kind of formal satisfaction from Prussia."

The events of the next day, July 13, at Ems and Berlin, have been called "one of the most dramatic and decisive turning points in German history," and they have been repeatedly described. Yet only with the recent publication of the diplomatic correspondence has a faithful presentation of what occurred become possible. Benedetti made an urgent plea for an early audience with the king, intimating what he was after. The king, thus put on his guard, decided to put off the interview for later in the day in order meanwhile to have a chance to consult with Count Eulenburg, Bismarck's emissary, who was due to arrive that morning. Benedetti, in quite unorthodox and impulsive fashion, set off to the *Kurgarten,* along the Lahn, and placed himself in the king's path as he was about to leave the park. William noticed the ambassador, approached him, and began to converse with him. This was precisely what the French ambassador wanted, of course. Benedetti, thereupon began to press the king for assurance that he would never again allow Leopold to become a candidate. Despite the king's firm but polite refusal to commit himself to such a pledge, Benedetti persisted. "Well, Sire," he finally said, "I can then write to my government that Your Majesty has consented to declare that you will never permit Prince Leopold to renew the candidacy in question?" We have a description of this scene from the pen of King William himself. "At these words," reported William, "I stepped back a few paces and said in a very earnest tone: 'It seems to me, Mr. Ambassador, that I have so clearly and plainly expressed myself to the effect that I could never make such a declaration, that I have nothing more to add.' Thereupon I lifted my hat and went on." [29] The king later decided that he had done all that was necessary to settle the matter, and informed the French ambassador that he considered the affair closed and would therefore not receive him again as previously scheduled. He also authorized Abeken, an official of the foreign office, to send to Bismarck an account of what had taken place, permitting him to inform the press and the Prussian embassies abroad of what had happened if he saw fit to do so.

Bismarck, in the meantime, had been deeply irritated and wounded by the course of the negotiations. He saw all his plans and intrigue apparently going to nought. He also was pained to learn of the personal conduct of foreign affairs by the king instead of through himself. On July 12 he had determined to proceed to Ems. Coming to Berlin, on his way, he found the report of Leopold's renunciation and decided not to go to Ems himself but to dispatch Eulenburg instead. He himself, he relates, had determined to resign. Bismarck has left us a memorable account of how he sat in gloom with Moltke and Roon commiserating with each other when Abeken's dispatch arrived with the king's account of the events at Ems. They were so despondent that they could not eat. Then, recounts Bismarck, an inspiration came to him. He saw glorious possibilities in the Ems dispatch just received. He asked Moltke as to the state of preparation of the Prussian army to meet a sudden risk of war. Moltke replied that if there was to be war he expected no advantage to Prussia by deferring its outbreak and that "he regarded a rapid outbreak as, on the whole, more favorable to us than delay." Bismarck thereupon proceeded to reduce the telegram to a brief message, without, however, adding or altering a word, and he read the text to his guests. "Now it has a different ring," commented Moltke; "it sounded before like a parley; now it is like a flourish in answer to a challenge." Moltke and Roon were all at once young and fresh as before, and recovered their appetite. They had their war.[30] In place of a lengthy and fairly matter-of-fact account, Bismarck, by skillful condensation, produced a terse and sharply worded text.[31] "If I not only publish this text . . . at once in the newspapers," said Bismarck, "but also transmit it by telegram to all our embassies, it will be known in Paris before midnight, and not only because of its contents but because of its mode of publication, it will have the effect of a red cloth upon the Gallic bull."

Bismarck's prognosis was perfect. The edited text was dispatched to all Prussian embassies and made public in the press. There was embitterment and fury in Paris, while in Berlin, on the other hand, according to Sybel, "the excited masses swayed to and fro; men embraced one another amid tears of joy and thunderous cheers for King William rent the air." On July 19 France declared war on Prussia.

In the light of all the evidence available now, we may conclude with Professor Lord that:

It is now agreed that, from 1866 on, Bismarck like most of those prominent in Prussian political and military circles, regarded a war with France as inevitable sooner or later, convinced as he was that France would not peaceably permit the union of South Germany with the North, which was at that time the great object of his policy. It is tolerably well agreed that he also regarded such a war as in itself desirable, believing that the South Germans were not likely to seek that union, at least for a long time to come, unless they were shaken out of their selfishness and apathy by a shock from outside, such as could best be furnished by a great common effort for a national cause, and by a great common victory over "that neighboring nation which was our age-long aggressor." It is clear that he shared Moltke's profound conviction that Germany would enter such a war with every chance of success. It is agreed that, wherever the idea of the Hohenzollern Candidacy may have originated, Bismarck took up the project and worked with all his might and main to put it through as a "political necessity, . . . " Finally, scarcely anyone will now deny that at least in the last stage of the crisis of July, 1870, at the time when he re-edited the Ems telegram, the Chancellor was working to provoke a war.[32]

Bismarck's hopes with regard to the South German states were soon realized. A wave of national sentiment swept through all Germany. Württemberg, Hesse, and Baden came to the aid of Prussia immediately. There were more hesitation and reservations in Bavaria. Immediately following the French declaration of war, the government of Bavaria, in keeping with its treaty obligations, asked for mobilization and war credits. The lower chamber referred the matter to a commission headed by the Catholic editor Jörg. The commission submitted a majority report (with a minority of three liberals) which declared that the conflict was not one of German national concern and hence concluded that Bavaria was not obligated to enter the war. They recommended the proclamation of armed neutrality. Then the aged Professor Sepp, one of the leaders of the Bavarian Patriotic party, arose and delivered a passionate speech in favor of the government's plea. He too, he declared, had been in favor of armed neutrality before. But after the French declaration of war everything was entirely different. "Yesterday one could still think of the pain of 1866; today the wrath against the foreigners has been aroused in all German men. We Bavarians did not participate in the battle of Leipzig but we do want to take part in the new national battle. . . . We too have a German heart and we adhere firmly to the words of the most German of the German princes: We wish to be Germans and remain Bavarians." [33] The final vote was 101 to 47 in favor of the government's request, and Bavaria too joined the war. All the German states were at last united in one great national enterprise. Bismarck's dream was realized, and the basis was laid for the unity of North and South Germany.

Bismarck assured himself of freedom from intervention by the other powers. Russia promised neutrality, and British neutrality was won through the publication of a facsimile of Benedetti's plan for the annexation of Belgium which Bismarck had carefully retained for use on just such an occasion. Fully confident of its power, with a highly trained, modern military machine and backed by a now united Germany, Prussia was able to overwhelm the armies of Napoleon in short shrift. Sedan fell on September 2, 1870, with a loss of 120,000 men, and Napoleon was taken prisoner. Strassburg fell on September 27 and Metz capitulated on October 27, with 173,000 French soldiers taken prisoner. Paris under the commune held out until January 28, 1871, and the war was officially settled by the Peace of Frankfurt, signed on May 10. According to the terms of the treaty, Prussia received all of Alsace except Belfort and the eastern part of Lorraine, including Metz. France was to pay an indemnity of 5 billion francs and German troops were to remain in northern France until the indemnity was paid. Final payment was made in 1873.

Amidst the triumphant din of Prussian victories, on the shattered ruins of the Napoleonic empire, in the very shadow of the hungry and embattled Jacobins of the Paris Commune, Bismarck officially proclaimed the new German Empire. In the Hall of Mirrors at Versailles, on January 18, 1871, William I was crowned German emperor, not by the representatives of a people's assembly, but at the hands of the princes of Germany and as a result of the fruits of "blood and iron."

A united and powerful Germany now emerged to take the place of France as the leading power of Europe. A humiliated, wounded, and resentful France draped the statue of Strassburg on the Place de la Concorde in black and impressed deeply in its memory the prophetic words uttered by Victor Hugo in the National Assembly at Bordeaux. The day would come, said Hugo, "when France would rise again invincible and take back not only Alsace and Lorraine but the Rhineland with Mayence and Cologne, and in return would give to Germany a republic, so freeing Germany from its emperors, as an equivalent for the dethronement of Napoleon." [34]

Within Germany the chief result of the war, apart from the creation of a new German Reich, was the realignment of political and social forces and the radical transformation in the character, content, and influence of German liberalism.

The nineteenth century had witnessed a flowering of liberal political thought in Germany as in the other countries of western Europe. True it did not have the same long history and the same firm foundation in economic and social relations as was the case in France and England. But out of the combination of Kantian ethics, natural law, French revolutionary ideas, the influence of English political ideas and institutions, and the carry-over of classical economic doctrines there had developed a German liberal tradition which likewise looked upon the development of the individual as the highest goal of society. It opposed all measures restricting the individual in his various relationships and those which stood in the way of the full realization of individual personality. Its supreme goal was a universal humanity based on world peace and equality of status for all peoples. It stood against the exercise of force in the state and accepted the major premises of economic liberalism as well. Furthermore, it was oriented toward the West European tradition. In the words of one of its leaders, Rudolf von Bennigsen, the theories and practices of the German liberals, both in the field of politics and in economics, "were nothing but the product of West European culture which had long been set down in France and in England in public institutions." [35] That is why German liberals, too, advocated the establishment of parliamentary institutions, constitutionalism, ministerial responsibility, and all the other institutions of government designed to make for personal freedom.

One of the unique aspects of German liberalism as contrasted with that of France and England, however, was the ominous intrusion of the question of national unity. For several decades the words *Freiheit* (liberty) and *Einheit* (unity) were the two words most often on the tongues and pens of liberal orators and writers. Both were the objectives of liberalism, and they were regarded as inseparable. The failure of 1848 shook the confidence of many in the possibility of achieving the two together, and the internal conflict within German liberalism between 1850 and 1871 was concerned with the question as to which of the two was to receive primacy. *Einheit* came gradually to overshadow *Freiheit,* and even when *Freiheit* was emphasized it was usually interpreted as national liberty opposed to the outside world rather than internal freedom and personal liberty. Even a radical like Arnold Ruge wrote in 1859, "German *Freiheit* means separation from Austria." [36]

After each of the three wars the change in emphasis became more evident and the patriotic clamor louder, until by 1871 the hosannas to *Einheit* completely overwhelmed the faint, weak voices that still dared hope for *Freiheit.*

The new direction of German liberalism became more marked after the Danish War of 1864. For some of the right-wing liberals the shift was not too difficult to make. For the historian Droysen who, in 1849, had written: "Not from liberty (*Freiheit*), not from national resolutions will the unity (*Einheit*) of Germany be created. It needs force (*Macht*) against the other powers to break the contradiction within it," [37] it was not too difficult to forgive Bismarck his breaches of law and justice. Writing to Sybel on June 12, 1864, Droysen said: "You know that I do not admire Herr von Bismarck very much, but the position of Prussia in Europe was for a very long time never as significant, as bold and possessed of the initiative as it is now." He reminded Sybel that he himself had always adhered to the principle that "the first interest of the state is *Macht.*" [38]

The former radical and leader of the Nationalverein, Johannes Miquel, in a speech at the general meeting of the Nationalverein in October, 1864, listed the successes of Bismarck and, while admitting that he was not favorably disposed to the ministry of Bismarck, declared that he was nevertheless forced to admit that all that Bismarck had done was in the best interests of Germany.[39] Miquel was to become one of Bismarck's ardent followers later on.

The *Preussische Jahrbücher,* organ of classical German liberalism, which in 1862 had still attacked Bismarck and declared his conflict with the liberal opposition to be basically "the struggle of the bourgeoisie against Junkerdom allied with absolutist tendencies," [40] revealed the new trend in August, 1864, when it wrote, "We do not want to minimize the successes achieved just because destiny decreed that the execution of our national program should fall into the hands of another party." [41] And by January, 1865, it proclaimed: "Our goal is national unity, or expressed in another way but still the same theory, it is the extension of the power of the Prussian state. It is quite immaterial to us which path leads us to this goal." [42]

The Nationalverein, of course, had been in the very thick of the battle against Bismarck during the constitutional conflict, and the editor of its publication, A. L. von Rochau, continued to attack Bismarck down to the eve of the Franco-Prussian War.[43] But the wider membership and the other leaders of the Nationalverein looked enviously upon the success of Prussia being carried out by other hands than theirs. An anonymous member, writing in the *Grenzboten* on the eve of the 1864 general meeting of the Nationalverein said: "What the Nationalverein needs is successes, practical successes. Respect in political life comes only with success and if the Nationalverein does not achieve any national triumph on its own it must support the triumphs of Bismarck, subordinate itself to them and make his triumph their own." [44]

Some, like the Prussian historian Sybel, plainly showed their distress and internal wavering. In a most interesting letter Sybel replied to Droysen's letter quoted above. He also had derived great satisfaction, he wrote, from the increased prestige of Prussia brought about by the success of the Danish war. Nevertheless he confesses that he cannot deny "that our authorities have consistently narrowed and endangered these results by the absence of a feeling for right, for consistency and for consequences." He cannot, therefore, continues Sybel, speak with such enthusiasm and hopefulness of the emergence of Prussia, and he calls upon Droysen to use his influence to attain parliamentary control of the budget in order to demonstrate that "you too recognize a limit beyond which right should not be sacrificed to might, a limit perhaps more elastic but nevertheless impregnable and absolutely firm." [45]

It was the triumph of 1866, however, that exercised the greatest influence on German liberals. Austria, the protector of reaction and the shield of clericalism, long denounced by all liberals and progressives, had now been ousted from Germany by Prussia. The dream of secular liberalism had been realized, even though by other hands. H. Baumgarten, a distinguished liberal historian and at the time professor of history at the Technische Hochschule in Karlsruhe, published a most significant article in the *Preussische Jahrbücher* of 1866. It was a public confession of classical liberalism and is at the same time one of the most important documents of the history of that period. Baumgarten has some revealing and brilliant things to say about the German liberals. He rightly criticized them for being too much concerned with "the realm of ideas," without looking down upon the world of reality. When they did engage in politics they carried over to this sphere the methods of science, which do not apply. "Science has done its work," wrote Baumgarten, "when it discovers truth and proclaims it. Politics only begins at this point. Science is all the greater when it is free of all motivations; a political policy, however, which does not take existing conditions into consideration is but a dream fantasy . . . We, however, concerned for such a long time with knowledge, came to place the greatest weight upon the formulation of theoretically correct sentences. . . . This discussion absorbed our best energies! and if we triumphed in debate, we were satisfied."

Baumgarten's retrospective evaluation of the constitutional struggle is especially interesting. In its analysis it resembles the position held by Lassalle, but it is radically different in its conclusions. Baumgarten admits the illegal position of the government but chides the liberals, not for having failed to wage their battle more effectively and more vigorously, but rather for not having recognized Bismarck's superior power and made terms with him. If, wrote Baumgarten, "the great majority of the electors of a great state repeatedly declare a régime to be unconstitutional and destructive of the state and at the same time they are satisfied to allow such declarations to remain without effect, then they do greater damage to public morality and to the healthy development of the state than if they were to resign themselves to come to a tolerable agreement with such a régime." In words that were not only historically true for his own time but for the generations after him, Baumgarten adds:

We have experienced innumerable times the unedifying spectacle of great assemblies, yes even the representatives of our highest political bodies, making vigorous demands and giving the impression that the nation would rise up against the rejection of such demands, and we then see them accept the complete absence of any results from this great act with an equanimity as if they had never expected anything different. . . . Only a demonstration that words will be followed by corresponding action gives worth to words in politics. Only the example of a leader who stands up for his conviction with all his personality and for whom "with *Gut* and *Blut*" is not merely rhetoric but something terribly serious, only such an example can fill a people with the energy to act before which no government can stand.

The corollary of all this for the liberal historian, continues Baumgarten, is not to call upon liberals to be more energetic, but rather the sad conclusion that energetic action is possible only by conservative government. And this the Prussia of Bismarck has demonstrated. "The struggle for Schleswig-Holstein has administered a serious blow to German liberalism, at the same time contributing a richly rewarding victory to the German nation." Bismarck has emerged triumphant and vindicated by his deeds. Consistency in politics, concludes Baumgarten, is foolish. The all-important thing is to realize your aims. The breach of right and law in the annexation of Schleswig-Holstein is nothing compared to the great achievement of having joined this province to Prussia. Liberals sighed so long for a man who would lead Prussia boldly forward. Now there was such a man and he has made tremendous advances. He wears quite a different appearance from that envisaged in liberal fantasy but his successes exceed the bounds of all the dreams of liberals. Liberals must, therefore, recognize that "complete liberty rests upon complete power." They must make peace with Bismarck and the Prussian governing classes and thus become themselves *"regierungsfähig."* [46]

The political correspondent of the *Preussische Jahrbücher* contributed from Berlin a hymn of praise to the new Prussia on February 4, 1867. As a result of the history of German disunity, he wrote, "if Germany is faced with the choice between *Einheit* or *Freiheit,* it must, in accordance with its history and its position unconditionally choose the former. . . . It must not retreat in terror before either the path of conquest or that of dictatorship and not even before the military dictatorship. It must willingly follow the despotic *Führer* who is able to secure for it the possessions of its members, its existence, its position of equality among nations and therewith its future." The writer denies that it is the task of parliament at this time to secure freedom for Germany. The primary task of parliament is the realization of the national idea. If the liberal idea can also be realized at the same time, well and good. But if this is impossible, "then the liberal idea must give way to the national idea . . . the realization of the national idea dare not be frustrated by the liberal idea." [47]

David Friedrich Strauss, the Swabian theologian who had created such a stir by his radical treatment of the life of Jesus, joined the chorus of praise. In the words of Franz Mehring, "he destroyed the mystery of Jesus Christ in order to proclaim the mystery of the Old Fritz and Old Wilhelm." [48] Strauss was attacked in the press in 1866 for having betrayed his early liberal anti-Prussian principles and for now singing hallelujahs to Bismarck. In a dialogue, "Prussia and Swabia," in the *Preussische Jahrbücher,* he defended himself against these assaults. To the charge that he supported the breach of law in the Schleswig-Holstein affair he replied that he identified law only with that "which helps the nation develop, become unified and strong and which elicits the respect of other nations." Whatever German state or statesman is able to bring the divided German peoples and states into a firmer unity has, according to Strauss, "also the right . . . to carry this out by force." Bismarck is, therefore, "one of the greatest statesmen that Germany ever had, and by a rare stroke of fate sent just at the time that he was needed most." [49]

The movement for liberty in Germany also suffered seriously from the fact that liberalism failed to enlist the support of two new political forces that should properly have been aligned with it—the Catholics and the proletariat. There was much in Catholic political theory, from Joseph Görres to Ketteler[50] and the Reichenspergers, that was common to political liberalism. The ideas of personal freedom, constitutional guarantees, anti-militarism and anti-Prussianism were characteristic of many of the leading Catholic thinkers in Germany as they were the possession of the liberals. But from both sides there was mutual distrust as well as serious differences of opinion on fundamentals. The nineteenth century liberals, heirs to eighteenth century rationalism, could see only medieval reaction in Catholicism as well as in traditional religion in general. Their faith in science, progress, and secular enlightenment blinded them to the deeply human and truly democratic elements implicit in traditional religion. Clericalism, personified primarily by Austria, was for them the arch-enemy. On the other hand, Catholic thought in Germany still looked with suspicion upon any and every idea that harked back to the French revolution, and Catholic spokesmen were all too ready to condone anything and everything for the sake of official clerical politics. Their attitude toward Austria, toward Poland, and toward Italy was too obviously influenced by official Catholic politics rather than by intrinsic values of human worth. It took over fifty years of political development on both sides to make possible the coalition of Catholic and non-Catholic liberalism in the Weimar Republic.

Similarly, the cause of liberalism was weakened by the severance of the proletarian democracy from the bourgeois democracy. Here, too, the combination which was so important in the early development of democracy in France and England failed to materialize in Germany. Serious differences arose from the outset.[51] The dogmatic laissez-faireism of nineteenth century economic liberals came up against a proletarian movement in which Marxism was dominant from the start. Then too many of the leaders of the Nationalverein and of the Progressive party were anxious that their cause should not be jeopardized by close association with the radical lower classes. True, a group of leaders in South Germany, like F. A. Lange, Leopold Sonnemann, Ludwig Büchner, and Ludwig Eckardt, felt that a free order could be brought about only by the union of the workers with the democratic elements of the bourgeoisie. But the truth of the matter must be stated that neither Marx and Engels nor Lassalle were really liberals. Lassalle's conception of *Macht* was not too far removed from that of Bismarck's and of the *Kreuzzeitung,* and the proletarian leaders chose to select the class struggle as their field of battle rather than the fight for personal freedom and human liberty. Thus the tragic division of the liberal opposition only served to play into the hands of the authoritarian groups and to leave only a weak and ineffectual group isolated from mass support to carry the chief burden of the cause of liberalism and democracy.

This minority refused to be blinded by the triumphs of Bismarck.

Ardent disciples of the cause of German unity, they nevertheless refused to surrender their hopes for *Freiheit*. "A national party," declared Hermann Schulze-Delitzsch in 1864, "can never be anything but a liberty-loving party; otherwise I contest its right to call itself national." What is the real meaning of the national idea? And his answer was: "It wants to guarantee in governmental forms those external conditions of the nation as a result of which it will be in the position to fashion its life according to its own needs. It is liberty which belongs here above all other things, with all nations and under all circumstances." [52]

Gervinus, the old liberal historian, wrote a "Memorial on the Peace" after the Franco-Prussian War, in which he called upon Prussia, now that it had laid low its enemy France, to give up the lands it had annexed within Germany and to transform the German Reich into a truly federalist state. All German history, wrote Gervinus, indicates that federalism is the most appropriate and most characteristic form of state for Germans. He warned that the triumph of 1866 had created a militaristic wave over Europe and that the North German Confederation was going the way of a militaristic unified state, and that the victory of 1870 was only intensifying this character. "After a half-century of desires, aspirations, and hopes to rid ourselves more and more of the soldierly institutions of former times and to see the impoverishing burdens of a standing army reduced if not completely eliminated, we now see the emergence of a permanent military power of such terrifying supremacy, the like of which has never even remotely been approached by the aggressive and conquering military powers of the past century." Gervinus warned that Germany was taking over the military position of France but that it would also from now on take over all the hate that France had previously inspired. The only way to overcome this justified mistrust, suggested Gervinus, is to transform Germany into a "true federal state," whose protector will not be an absolutist military dictator but a liberal and peaceful state that will take pride in inaugurating an era of peace and disarmament which will put an end to the "terrible burdens of militarism." [53]

Rudolf Virchow, one of the leading figures in modern medicine, early came to realize the interconnections of science, freedom, and social policy, and because of this he entered politics while carrying on, at the same time, his scientific work. He became one of the most vigorous champions of political liberalism in Germany and one of the most bitter opponents of Bismarckian policies. But in the land where science was so greatly revered, the political ideas of Virchow failed to take hold and to the end of his days he remained one of the leaders of an ineffectual opposition. To this day, while the contributions of Virchow to science, medicine, and public health are retained in public memory in Germany, his political liberalism is practically forgotten.

Perhaps the most interesting of the forgotten liberals of that period was

Johann Jacoby, a member of the Prussian diet from Königsberg. Jacoby was the only one who dared to urge that the people take action in their own hands during the constitutional struggle, indirectly suggesting that they refuse to pay taxes. For this he was arrested and sentenced to imprisonment. Jacoby refused to join in the shouts of triumph after the war of 1866. The war, he declared, was undertaken without the will of the people, and the victory was of no service to the cause of freedom but only to "the unlimited sovereignty and the absolutism of the war lords." In his speech to the diet on August 23, 1866, he said: "The judgment of the present about itself is not always unprejudiced; a later period will have to decide whether the days of Biarritz were more honorable for Prussia than the day of Olmütz." Enforced unity, he declared, "unity without *Freiheit* is a unity of slaves." [54] Commenting on the creation of the North German Confederation, Jacoby said on May 6, 1867: "Germany, united in political freedom, is the most secure guarantee for the peace of Europe; under Prussian military rule, on the other hand, Germany is a constant danger to its neighboring peoples, the beginning of an epoch of wars which threatens to throw us back to the sad days of the law of the club. May Prussia, may our German fatherland be preserved from such a calamity." [55] In these prophetic words the "unrealistic" political idealist perceived the true nature of the political situation better than all the hard-boiled and practical realists of his and later generations. Jacoby met not only with the opposition of the right; he also had to face the scorn of the left. For socialists his doctrine was nothing but the "petty-bourgeois ethics" of Kant. The gulf between ethical humanism and liberalism, derived from Kant, and socialist *Machtpolitik,* drawing its inspiration from Hegel, was too deep to be bridged, at least at that time.[56]

Apart from this small group, the great bulk of German liberals, from the larger manufacturing classes to the smaller merchants and intellectuals, established an alliance with the Prussian Junkers and militarists. They did not have to wage a struggle for their economic rights as did the bourgeois classes in England and France. Industrial and economic development was aided by the new German state; military security was provided by the army under the control of the crown. In return for this security and economic opportunity the German liberal bourgeoisie relinquished its fight for parliamentary and constitutional government until the time when the crown and the army were no longer able to provide these.[57]

CHAPTER VIII

Political and Social Currents, 1871-1914

Das deutsche Reich und der preussische Staat kann von einer Partei nicht regiert werden; dazu ist keine Partei stark genug und keine versöhnlich genug.

BISMARCK, 1882

1. THE CONSTITUTIONAL STRUCTURE OF THE SECOND REICH

The constitution of the Second Reich was not the work of a constitutional convention or a national assembly.[1] The German Reich came into being in the Hall of Mirrors in Versailles on January 18, 1871, as the product of a series of victorious wars, and the constitution as adopted was the handiwork of Bismarck.* A Reichstag deputation headed by Eduard Simson, who had also headed the deputation of 1849 to the King of Prussia, came to Versailles to bestow upon William the title of German emperor, but its members were refused an audience until after the consent of all the princes to the new constitution had arrived. It was amidst the pomp and ceremony of the military and princely aristocracy that William assumed the headship of the new Reich. The black, red, and gold colors of 1848 were discarded and instead the black and white colors of Prussia combined with the red of the Hansa were selected for the flag of the new Reich.

The constitution adopted for the new Reich consisted of the constitu-

---

* In August, 1866, Bismarck asked the historian Max Duncker to prepare a provisional draft for a constitution. At the same time the various Prussian ministries were requested to submit proposals regarding the constitutional provisions for their respective areas. For himself Bismarck took the political sections of the constitution. From these various suggestions and drafts Bismarck, on December 13, 1866, dictated the final draft to Lothar Bucher. The proposed constitution was discussed by the governments of the states entering the North German Confederation, but the Prussian representative practically forced the states to accept the draft with only minor modifications. Despite lengthy discussions and debates in the Reichstag of the North German Confederation and in the Prussian Landtag, here too Bismarck allowed only minor changes. The most important of these, the so-called Bennigsen amendment, which added the phrase that the chancellor is to "be responsible," hardly meant very much in view of the fact that the chancellor's position was entirely and exclusively dependent on the King of Prussia.

156

tion of the North German Confederation supplemented by treaties with the South German states of Baden, Hesse, Bavaria, and Württemberg. It was submitted to the newly elected Reichstag on March 21, 1871, adopted as submitted on April 14, and promulgated by Bismarck on April 20. Except for a few modifications, brought about more by usage and custom than by official action, this constitution governed the German Reich until 1917. Only seven votes were cast against its adoption in the Reichstag in 1871. The Progressives, who had voted against the constitution in 1867, now voted for it, in appreciation of the achievement of national unity.

The constitution was tailored to fit the personal relationship established between Bismarck and William I, and while the government was in the hands of these two it showed the least amount of strain. Basic constitutional questions such as federalism versus centralization, the problem of Prussia, ministerial responsibility, extension of democratic rights were all submerged as long as Bismarck remained at the helm. They became increasingly serious only after 1890, and finally caused the downfall of the Second Reich under the strain of war and military defeat in 1917–1918.

The state formed in 1871 was not a truly national state in the sense that the nation as a whole was the bearer of the political life of the country. What happened was that the old Prussian state was enlarged to include all the other entering states and the rule of the Prussian army and bureaucracy was extended to this larger domain. The written constitution of 1871 created the appearance of constitutionalism (*Scheinkonstitutionalismus,* Mommsen called it), but basically it was far from being such. The Bismarckian constitution contained elaborate provisions concerning matters on which most constitutions are silent, such as customs, commerce, railways, post and telegraph, and so on.* On the other hand it said nothing regarding individual rights, fundamental guarantees and abstract principles. The Centrist deputies attempted to amend the constitution to add a section on fundamental guarantees, desiring above all to guarantee the traditional rights of the Roman Catholic Church. A small group of South German liberals, headed by Leopold Sonnemann, publisher of the *Frankfurter Zeitung,* also introduced several such amendments. In the debate the Catholic deputy Reichensperger declared: "We have done a great deal since 1866, but only for unity. It is now time to think of the demands of the people for freedom." And Windthorst warned that "state absolutism leads directly to communism." These attempts were voted down overwhelmingly in the same way as Schulze-Delitzsch's amendments on fundamental rights had been voted down in 1867. National Lib-

---

* Constantin Frantz, in criticizing the constitution, pointed out that the new Reich was only a combination of the Prussian military state and the Zollverein and that the new constitution was concerned almost exclusively with matters pertaining to customs and trade (*Die Religion des National-liberalismus* [Leipzig, 1872]).

erals and Progressives refused to accept the clericals as champions of liberty, while Treitschke ridiculed the whole idea of fundamental rights as a reversion to the days of 1848–1849 when the Germans were still politically naïve and immature.[2]

Formally the new Reich was organized as a *Bundesstaat,* that is, something approximating a federal state. The independent states that became parties to this union did not lose their separate identity. In addition to Prussia there were the kingdoms of Bavaria, Saxony, and Württemberg; there were six grand-duchies, five duchies, seven principalities, three free cities, and the *Reichsland* of Alsace-Lorraine. Sovereignty was vested in the Reich government and not in the separate states. But the Reich had no administrative organs of its own except for the army, navy, foreign service, customs, post and telegraph, and later colonies. The entire internal administration of police, the judiciary, fiscal matters and education remained in the hands of the separate states. Up to 1913, for example, the total revenue of the Reich (4,121,000,000 marks) was exceeded by that of the state of Prussia (4,241,000,000 marks) and the Reich debt (4,897,000,000 marks) by the Prussian debt (9,902,000,000 marks). Nevertheless this was not a truly federal state, as we shall see, because of the very special and peculiar position of Prussia in the constitutional set-up.

The headship of the German Reich was vested in the King of Prussia and was hereditary in his house. There was considerable discussion regarding his title.[3] In the constitution of the North German Confederation there was no mention of the title "Kaiser." It was largely to win over the South Germans who still retained an emotional sympathy for the old empire that the title of "Kaiser" was selected. For many Germans, this was symbolic of the revival of the old medieval tradition of the empire. The subsequently famous Pastor Adolf Stöcker wrote in 1871. "The Holy Evangelical Reich of the German Nation is being completed . . . in this sense we recognize the mark of God's impress from 1517 to 1871." [4] Actually, the title meant nothing of the sort. Much more difficult was the question whether William was to be proclaimed "Emperor of Germany" or not. To use the title *Kaiser Deutschlands* would mean giving official sanction to the supremacy of the King of Prussia over the other kings in the Reich. To this the kings of Bavaria and Württemberg refused to agree, and William was proclaimed *Deutscher Kaiser,* or German Emperor, thus connecting the title with German nationality rather than with territorial sovereignty.

The emperor represented the Reich in all matters of foreign affairs and international law. He declared war and made peace, made alliances, received and accredited ambassadors, and appointed all the imperial officials from chancellor down. These he could also dismiss at will. The emperor was supreme commander of the army and the navy, and the oath of the military was taken to him personally. In internal matters his power derived largely from his position as King of Prussia. It was as King of Prussia that he or his minister presided over the Bundesrat or federal council, and in the Bundesrat he acted only through the agency of the Prussian government and not in behalf of the Reich. The emperor was vested with authority to convene and adjourn the two legislative bodies, and bills laid before the Reichstag from the Bundesrat were placed there in his name. Official publication of Reich laws was executed by him, although these also required the countersignature of the imperial chancellor. Scholarly jurists have often maintained that the emperor had no power to veto legislation. But Bismarck himself, in his important speeches of February 24, 1881, and January 24, 1882, pointed out that the emperor was the real and actual power in both Prussia and the Reich and that he could indirectly veto any legislation he desired by his control over the appointment and dismissal of the chancellor.

The legislative pattern of a federal state was set up with a bicameral legislature, the upper chamber or Bundesrat representing the states, and the Reichstag the people at large. But here too the constitutional façade is apparent to anyone who looks closely. The Bundesrat was not really an upper chamber. It was the bearer of sovereign power. In it, the remains of the old Bundestag, the sovereignty of the new Reich was vested. The Bundesrat, however, was really a camouflage for Prussian supremacy. For in this chamber the states were not represented equally, as in the case of the United States Senate, but according to their size and power. Of a total of 58 seats (after 1911 it was 61, with Alsace-Lorraine admitted) Prussia had 17 votes, Bavaria 6, Saxony 4, Württemberg 4, and the other states from 3 down to one vote each. The members were designated by their respective state governments and voted en bloc, as instructed by their governments. The imperial chancellor presided over the sessions of the Bundesrat, and no measure could become law without the vote of this house. On matters of army, navy, customs, and excise taxes the Prussian vote was decisive if cast in favor of maintaining existing institutions. Amendments to the constitution could be defeated by fourteen votes cast against them. This gave Prussia veto power over any changes in the constitution.

The Reichstag was the popular assembly elected by universal manhood suffrage of all citizens over twenty-five. Outwardly it had all the appearances of a genuine legislative body; actually, however, its powers were very circumscribed. There was no provision for redistribution of seats after 1867. Members of the Reichstag received no payment until 1906, when an amendment was passed which provided for an honorarium of 400 marks per month. The Reichstag had no say at all over foreign policy or the military. The most it could do was to refuse to pass the budget. But the memory of the constitutional conflict of 1862–1866 remained deeply impressed on all, as is indicated in the record of the Reichstag debates, which are full of constant allusions and references to this struggle. Ministers were responsible not to the Reichstag but to the emperor. The real government was divided between the Bundesrat and the government of Prussia. In the words of Hugo Preuss, the Reichstag was "a parliament without a government," condemned "to deliver monologues." [5] It is true that for a while Bismarck gave the appearance of wanting to rule with the help of a parliamentary majority and thus aroused the ire of the ultra-conservative *Kreuzzeitung*,[6] but he soon abandoned that hope and always declared himself opposed to the kind of parliamentary régime that was in use in France or England. It was only in the later years of the Reich, especially after the Bülow era, that the Reichstag began to exercise more decisive influence. Even then, however, it was still very limited in actual control of national affairs.

There was no cabinet in the German Reich. There was one minister, the Reich chancellor. He in turn appointed heads of departments of state, who were merely administrative officials responsible to the chancellor. There were repeated demands that Bismarck set up a Reich cabinet, but he stubbornly refused.* He hated, said Bismarck, to have to waste his time persuading his colleagues and all their friends and advisers that his policy was a wise one. The Reich chancellor was also the prime minister of Prussia, and his responsibility was solely to the emperor. The chancellor presided over the Bundesrat as the Austrian presidial envoy had done in the old Bund. An amendment to the constitution by Rudolf von Bennigsen (now Article 17) was adopted which made it necessary for the chancellor to countersign all measures approved by the emperor. This countersigning was, however, no act of sovereignty, since the chancellor occupied his position only at the pleasure of the emperor and King of Prussia. Most of the important duties were exercised by the chancellor not as the chief minister of the Reich but as the prime minister of Prussia. In 1872 Bismarck made an experiment in separating the two offices when he resigned as prime minister of Prussia and turned this post over to von Roon. But he soon concluded that this experiment was unsuccessful, and reverted to the previous arrangement. In his speech to the Reichstag of March 10, 1877 Bismarck said:

I am definitely convinced that the chief influence which I was permitted to exercise thus far has rested not in the imperial power but in the royal Prussian power. I made the experiment for some time of giving up my post as Prussian prime minister and thought that I would have enough power as imperial

---

* When the German Freisinnige Partei was formed they made the demand for the "organization of a responsible Reich ministry" a part of their party program. On April 5, 1884, the Bundesrat adopted a resolution directed against this demand. The resolution, drafted most probably by Bismarck, stated, "The setting up of responsible ministries in the German Reich is possible only at the cost of the rights exercised at present by the allied states in the Bundesrat and guaranteed to them by treaty." Cf. H. Triepel, *Unitarismus und Föderalismus im deutschen Reiche* (Tübingen, 1907), p. 98.

chancellor. I was completely mistaken. After a year I came back full of penitence and said: Either I go altogether or else once again be prime minister of Prussia . . . if you cut away the Prussian roots from me and make me only a Reich minister then I believe I will be no more influential than anyone else.[7]

Perhaps the most crucial constitutional problem since 1871 has been the relation of Prussia to the rest of the Reich.[8] It was present even in the deliberations of the National Assembly in 1848–1849, although before 1866 it was overshadowed by the Austro-Prussian problem. Actually, the tension between Prussia and the rest of the Reich was only a reflection of the tension between the newer industrial and commercial classes and the old but modernized feudal agrarian classes who dominated the Prussian scene. Prussia was much more than merely one of the territorial states that made up the unified German Reich. It was not a homogeneous state such as Bavaria and Württemberg or Baden. It had increased its size, population, and power by conquest and annexation. Silesia, Posen, the Rhineland annexations of the revolutionary period, and the larger annexations of 1866 brought into Prussia elements of the German population quite different in ethnic composition, religion, and temperament from the "original" Prussians. Some, like the Hanoverians, refused for a long time to recognize the forcible annexation of their state in 1866. Prussia thus was not *one* of the German *Länder* but, in the words of Gerhard Anschütz, a "complex of many German *Länder* melted into a unified state" and "the uncompleted German national state within the completed German national state." [9]

The men of '48 had wanted Prussia "to merge itself" into a greater Germany. Bismarck annexed the non-Prussian Germany to Prussia in order to create an enlarged Prussia. It is true that at least up to 1877 there are some indications in Bismarck's policies and speeches of a greater emphasis upon "Germanizing" rather than upon "Prussianizing." Yet Bismarck's basic loyalty always remained Prussian,[10] even though political exigencies often forced him into a broader German position. By means of his constitution Bismarck created an organic connection between Prussia and the Reich. The emperor was the King of Prussia, and the chancellor was also Prussian prime minister and Prussian foreign minister, and as such he was the head of the Prussian delegation to the Bundesrat and presiding officer of the upper chamber. The state secretaries of the Reich were also members of the Prussian state government. Prussia, although it needed the support of other states to make changes in the constitution, was the only state that could block changes in the Reich single-handed. Prussian hegemony has euphemistically been called the middle way between federalism and a centralized unitary state,[11] but there was nothing midway about the tight rein by means of which Prussia controlled the rest of the Reich. The laws of the Reich bear the stamp of Prussian influence, and Prussian law and administration were copied in other German states.

The Prussian army was the most obvious instrument of power and influence in the new Reich. Technically there was no such thing as a *German* army, a *German* general staff, or a *German* minister of war. The Prussian army law was extended to the entire Reich, and the army became one unified army but always under the immediate control of Prussia. One state after another transferred its military powers to Prussia, and only Bavaria, Saxony, and Württemberg retained independent military contingents. But the King of Prussia, as emperor, was in complete control of the army, and allegiance was sworn not to the constitution but to the emperor. Eugen Richter's dictum that "German army and German parliament were not to be separated" never became law in the Second Reich. The army was truly a *Gefolgschaft* of a *Führer*. The military, not subject to constitutional requirements, was thus removed completely from the realm of the civilian constitution. The army was "the core of the Prussian state"; "it was not, as was often said, 'a state within the state'; it was *the* state within the state." [12]

This Prussian soldier-state was recognized by most Germans as having been responsible for the unification of Germany. Political thought as well as political action throughout Germany, therefore, was deeply influenced by the Prussian crown, the Prussian general staff, and the Prussian army. "The German Reich," wrote Friedrich Meinecke, "was created with the forces of the old Prussian military monarchy. The forces of the national and liberal movement were also used by it but were not recognized as being primary. And the German Reich has for the most part been preserved by the same means through which it was established. All during this time it was the Prussian military state with all that goes with it—its royalist and aristocratic traditions and its favoring of those social classes that made up the core of the officer corps—that has remained the most firm pivot of internal policy and at the same time the citadel of the entire fortress." [13]

While the constitution of the Reich showed some traces of the influence of Western constitutionalism, especially with respect to the Reichstag and the universal suffrage by which it was elected, the constitution of Prussia remained the same one that had been proclaimed by the king in 1850. It retained its traditional feudal character and above all the three-class system of voting which elected the diet. For a short while Bismarck directed some attacks against the Prussian electoral system, but he soon gave this up. The Prussian diet became a source of great support for him, and served as a sort of upper house to the Reichstag. "Against the majority opposition in the Reichstag," says Meinecke, "the Prussian diet, conservative since the 1880's (since 1879 more precisely), grew to be a powerful bastion of support for the government. No German and

Prussian statesman could think of a reform of the three-class system as long as the great power and life-needs of the Reich—army, navy and colonies—were in danger of being rejected or mangled by the opposition parties." [14]

The organic connection thus established by Bismarck between the Reich and Prussia served to infuse Prussian power and political influence into the body politic of the Reich. While tension between Prussia and the Reich was suppressed during the greater part of the Second Reich, the conflict between federalism and centralization remained a serious constitutional problem for the entire period. The increase in power of the Reich, the increased military and naval demands, and the increased international obligations of the Reich all called for the extension of the competence of the Reich government. In 1873 a Reich railroad bureau was set up, in 1874 the Reichsbank was established, and in 1877 a Reichsgericht (Supreme Court). There was an increase in Reich administration and in the number of independent Reich authorities and agencies. Social legislation, when adopted, embraced the Reich as a whole, and in 1900 a uniform code of law came into being. The growing desire by Germany for "a place in the sun" was, above all, the driving force for greater centralization. At the same time, however, there were strong forces at work which were federalist in character. These included the various local state governments, the bureaucracies of the various states, the court nobility, and the influences of two political parties—the Conservatives and the Catholic Centrists. Whereas the parties of the left and center were for the most part in favor of increased state centralization, the Conservatives and the Centrists stood guard over the autonomy of the local states. For the former any centralizing tendency that would increase the power of the Reichstag was viewed as strengthening the democratic trend. The Catholics, opposed on general principles to state omnipotence, were especially interested in protecting the rights of the local states in order to ensure Catholic autonomy in areas where the Catholic population was in the majority.

All these tensions were held in check as long as the Prussian soldier-state provided the military protection and security for all the other classes and areas. When this was no longer the case, as in the defeat of 1918, the Prussian-German problem once more came to the fore as one of the basic constitutional questions for the new Weimar Republic.

2. POLITICAL PARTIES IN THE SECOND REICH

Political parties come into being only with the establishment of legislative assemblies in the government of a state. German political parties, therefore, may be said to have had their ultimate origin in the various groupings and factions in the National Assembly of 1848–1849, the first German parliament. Political parties of a local character had come into being in many of the local states even earlier. The "new era" in Prussia fostered the formation of more formal political parties in the Prussian diet. Generally speaking, however, all these earlier groupings were classified according to the loose categories of "conservative" and "liberal," and did not go beyond the borders of the separate states. Truly national parties in Germany did not begin to operate officially until the establishment of the North German Confederation in 1867 and the German Reich in 1871.

Viewing the political scene in the Second Reich from a realistic point of view, it must be said that political parties were relatively unimportant in Germany despite all the outward organizational and oratorical trappings which were displayed. Since true parliamentarianism was absent we cannot assign a too effective position to the parties. The Reichstag had no control of foreign affairs and no hold over the ministry. The control over the budget was the sole province in which the Reichstag could claim competence and legal power. *Weltanschauungen* rather than parties were the true rivals on the political battlefield, and individual personalities, groups, and personal contacts were actually more decisive in determining policy than all the debates and votes of the parties. The influence of groups like the Prussian Bund der Landwirte, or the Pan-German League or the churches, or of individuals like Albert Ballin, the close personal friend of William II, were of far more moment than the debates and the decisions of the political parties. The Reichstag was therefore primarily a debating society, and its chief significance lay in its claim of reflecting the prevailing sentiments of public opinion. The failure to reapportion the seats in the Reichstag, however, minimizes its importance even in this respect.

The weakness of the Reichstag allowed no room for the realization of great ambitions for strong personalities. This accounts for the fact that the level of party leaders in the German Reichstag was far below the caliber of political leaders in England or France and far below the quality of leadership in German economic and cultural life. Moreover, the older cleavage between conservatives and liberals did not result in the formation of a two-party system in Germany as in the Anglo-Saxon countries, but broke up into various splinter groups, after the tradition of France. However, even the larger groupings of "right" and "left" blocs, as in France, never developed in German parliamentary life. This multiplication of party groups only served to increase the feeling among Germans themselves that they were incapable of self-government and to elicit that scorn for party politics which was best expressed by Bismarck when he quoted Coriolanus and said, "Go, get you home, you fragments!"

Although after 1880 Bismarck turned hostile to all political parties, in the earlier days of the founding of the Reich he felt that his empire could best prosper by a coalition of the bourgeoisie with the Prussian ruling classes and he made the necessary concession to constitutionalism to provide for a Reichstag based on universal manhood suffrage, and hence the need for political parties. These parties show a certain amount of continuity from the beginnings of the all-Prussian diet in 1850 through the Weimar Republic. We shall begin our analysis from the extreme right and in each case attempt to point out the social composition of the party, its program and theories, its historical development, and its relative strength in German political life.[15]

The Conservatives were the party of "authority rather than majority." They were the ideological heirs of Haller and F. J. Stahl and the defenders of the interests of the Prussian landowning classes. The leading organizers of the party in its earlier period were Ernst von Gerlach, General Leopold von Gerlach, and Count von Voss. The newspaper *Kreuzzeitung* was for many years the mouthpiece and organ of the party.

The Conservatives represented the old feudal ideal of Prussian society. In contrast to revolution and progress they emphasized the process of slow growth, historically conditioned and organic in nature. True freedom was to be obtained only through limitations imposed upon the individual, who was the "subject" rather than the "citizen" of the state. In opposition to liberal and democratic political theory, they reaffirmed the organismic theory of the state as developed by the early nineteenth century romantic school with its emphasis on the monarchic principle, on corporate entities rather than individual citizens, as the political units of the state; on a positive affirmation of the virtues of *inequality,* and above all of the importance of military might for the endurance of the state. They always supported the military program of the government no matter what they thought of the other aspects of the program, and it was the Conservatives who, above all, propagated the fiction that Germany is surrounded by enemies and therefore in need of huge armaments.

The Conservatives also made "positive Christianity" a basic element of their program. "Our political ABC is the social and political principles of Christianity," said the Conservative program of 1859, and this was repeated in all subsequent declarations. They were not too detailed in specifying exactly what Christian ideals should be the basis of the state. That would have involved them in too many contradictions between Christian individual ethics and the political demands of *raison d'état* to disregard these moral principles. Bismarck once said: "If I would not lie I could not be foreign minister," but he was not denounced by the Conservatives for violating the Christian ideal of truth-telling. Nevertheless Conservatives agreed on the divine-right theory of kingship, on the protection of the Church by the state, on opposing civil marriage, and on an educational program controlled by the religious authorities. It was such principles that often found the Conservatives allied with the Catholic Center party, as in the *Kulturkampf.* Conservatives also adhered to an anti-Jewish policy. They declared themselves "opposed to the increasing and destructive Jewish influence in our national life"; they identified capitalist exploitation with Jewish influence and aimed above all to keep the Jews out of the officer corps, the bureaucracy, and the universities.

In the field of economics the Conservatives emphasized the supreme importance of agriculture. They were hostile to industrialization and mechanization, and many of their diatribes against the evils of capitalism could just as well have appeared in the socialist *Vorwärts* as in the conservative *Kreuzzeitung*. They wanted Germany to remain an agrarian state. In the 1840's and 1850's they were still predominantly free-trade. "Free trade," wrote the *Kreuzzeitung*, "is a consequence of the Christian religion." As late as 1875 the *Kreuzzeitung* still wrote: "The Conservative party and its press may be accused of having made many mistakes. But even its worst enemies will have to admit that it is free of the sin of protective tariffs or of straying at all into this economic era." [16] A change in the Conservative position on protection came in the late 1870's when increased competition on the world grain market reacted against the Prussian landowners. The party then became avowedly protectionist, presumably also as a "consequence of the Christian religion."

The outstanding feature of the Conservative program was its Prussianism. The party found its greatest strength in the old Prussian provinces of East and West Prussia, Pomerania, Mecklenburg, and Brandenburg. For the Conservatives Bismarck had been not only too liberal in allowing for universal suffrage but had also been too "nationalist" in having submerged Prussia too much into the Reich. They had also opposed his leniency to Austria in 1866, when he refused to annex Austrian territory. The theory of king "by grace of God," however, did not seem to suffer in their eyes when Bismarck deposed the "divinely ordained" King of Hanover and annexed his lands.

The Conservative party exercised political influence far out of keeping with its numbers. No matter what its parliamentary strength happened to be, it always remained the party closest to the throne and hence to the government. In elections it was able to swing the votes of the peasants. Under William II the Landlords' League became a great power in political life. From the Conservative ranks came most of the officers and generals of the army, the ministers and the highest officials in the state bureaucracy. After several splits in the ranks of the party, it was reconstituted in 1876 as the Deutsch-Konservativ Partei, and continued on as such until 1918.

The Free Conservatives, or Reichspartei, was an offshoot of the Conservative party. It was made up of the large landowners outside the old Prussian provinces, and the big industrialists and capitalists. It drew its chief strength from Silesia and the Rhineland. In political, religious, and economic views very similar to the Conservatives, it split with them on the Prussian issue. Proclaiming the slogan "Fatherland Above Party," they were ardent supporters of Bismarck. They accepted Bismarck's national solution as well as his form of constitutional government and thus became, together with the National Liberals, the backbone of Bismarck's support in the first sessions of the Reichstag. They also supplied the monarchy with many of its diplomats and high civil service functionaries. After 1878 they began to amalgamate with the old Conservatives and eventually became merged with them once again. From then on conservatism could be fittingly described, in the words of Naumann, as "the alliance of iron, coal and yarn with grain." [17]

Beginning in the 1880's the Conservatives made an attempt to become popular and to create a mass movement from the right. They tried to do what Disraeli had attempted in England, to attract the little people and make politics with them. Their organization of agrarian interests into the Bund der Landwirte was one such important attempt. Perhaps the most interesting attempt was its utilization of the Christian-Social movement of Adolf Stöcker. Stöcker (1835–1909), described by Heuss as "one of the most contradictory figures in German domestic politics," [18] and a product of the "new Pietism" of the era of Frederick William IV, became convinced of the need to combat socialism with a broad program of social reform. In an election leaflet of 1881 Stöcker declared: "I have emphasized that the social revolution has to be overcome by healthy social reform, built on a Christian foundation. . . . I do not want culture that is not Germanic and Christian. That's why I am fighting against Jewish supremacy." [19] Here we have the two major planks of Stöcker's program. He led the assault from the right on *laissez faire* economic liberalism, and identified capitalism and economic liberalism with Jews and Jewish domination. To further his political and social aims he organized in 1878 the Christian Social Workers' party. In 1881 the word "Workers' " was dropped from the title. Stöcker waged his political battles in behalf of Christian conservatism with all the methods developed by the left working-class movement. He organized mass meetings to take the place of hours of devotion, used the pamphlet instead of the tract, and became the most volatile, stormy, and controversial political agitator and demagogue of the Second Reich. In this agitation antisemitism was his most formidable weapon. In his combination of mass agitation, concern with social and economic reform, and antisemitism, Stöcker was one of the most important forerunners of the later National Socialist movement of Adolf Hitler. It is, therefore, no accident that Stöcker found his authoritative biographer in the official Nazi party historian Walter Frank. The pattern in which Stöcker and his antisemitism was embraced and utilized by the more respectable Conservatives in the 1880's and 1890's also offers an interesting preview of the alliance between the German nationalists and the Nazis in paving the way for Hitler's coming to power in 1933. Stöcker's period of greatest influence and prestige coincided with this alliance with the Conservatives. A former follower of Stöcker, Helmut von Gerlach, later wrote that antisemitism "made the greatest gain in prestige it could hope for when it became part of the Conservative party's program. Previously it had been represented only in various small splinter parties; now it became the legitimate property of one of the biggest parties, of the party nearest to the throne and holding the most important positions in the state. Antisemitism had come close to being accepted at the highest level of social respectability." [20]

The National Liberal party was the strongest party during the first period of the Second Reich. It was an outgrowth of the Nationalverein and was officially constituted in 1867 in a split from the Progressive party. The split came on the issue of support of Bismarck's constitution in the North German Reichstag. Lasker, Forckenbeck, von Unruh, Twesten, and others left the Fortschrittspartei and joined those "for whom History had spoken." The party was made up of bourgeoisie and professionals. It was the party of *Bildung und Besitz,* of education and property, and was largely non-Prussian and Protestant in composition. The National Liberals were the former members of the left and center who now recognized that Bismarck had been wiser than they. Although they still desired both *Freiheit* and *Einheit,* they were willing to make concessions all the way down the line for the sake of national unity and economic power. Their program emphasized "the further development of the Reich" and the "fight against particularism." They were the arch-champions of Reich centralization. In the south it was the Reich idea which drew for them their largest support; in the north it was their opposition to conservatism.[21] Thus the party had no real homogeneity. It included extreme nationalists like Treitschke and Miquel, as well as ardent advocates of the *Rechtstaat* like Rudolf von Gneist and Eduard Lasker.

Lasker (1829–1884) was the leader of the left wing of the party. A German Jew, Lasker became imbued with the ideas of 1789 and devoted his life to politics. With Windthorst he was the "smallest figure" in the Reichstag. He was clear-headed, a good speaker, and especially competent in fiscal matters. The general goals of his policy were: to retain the basic rights of freedom, to oppose the government, and to be sparing in government spending. He was thoroughly hated by Bismarck, who called him "the sickness of Germany." So great was the chancellor's hostility that when Lasker died while visiting the United States and the American House of Representatives sent a message of condolence to the Reichstag, Bismarck refused to transmit the message.

The right wing of the National Liberals was led by Rudolf von Bennigsen (1824–1902). Bennigsen, the former president of the Nationalverein, was a cool and calm parliamentarian, influenced greatly by English political ideas. He was an effective but not overpowering speaker, and lacked the dynamic power to hold the party together. Treitschke dubbed him "Hamlet-Bennigsen" because of his indecision.

The National Liberal party thus was not homogeneous nor consistent.

It supported Bismarck on broad policies but opposed him on smaller issues and thus could not be called a "governmental" party. It was on National Liberal support that Bismarck relied chiefly from 1871–1877. Strongly anti-clerical, it was Bismarck's main ally in the Kulturkampf. But the National Liberals broke with Bismarck in 1878 when Bismarck refused to admit two other liberals into his ministry along with Bennigsen. The passage of the tariff in 1879 marks the beginning of the decline of the National Liberals, and under Emperor William II they became less important. From the large representation of 155 deputies in the Reichstag in 1874 they declined to 99 in 1878 and then to 47 in 1881. After 1898 they were led by Ernst Bassermann (1854–1917), and became increasingly national and less liberal. As a party of bankers and industrialists they became the most active supporters of colonial expansion. Eugen Richter, leader of the Progressives, had once criticized the policies of Bennigsen and declared that his exclusive preoccupation with tactics would lead to the obliteration of the difference between liberal and conservative in the public mind. As far as the National Liberals were concerned, this is precisely what happened. The old party designation was hardly applicable to them any longer.

The left liberals or Progressives were constantly subject to splits and secessions in their ranks. Actually, they constituted the oldest of the Reichstag political parties. In June, 1861, the Fortschrittspartei was founded in Prussia under the leadership of Max von Forckenbeck, Freiherr von Hoverbeck, Hans Victor von Unruh, Hermann Schulze-Delitzsch, Theodor Mommsen, and Rudolf Virchow. It became the strongest party in the Prussian diet during the period of the constitutional struggle with Bismarck. The Fortschrittspartei lasted under this name until 1884. It then combined with a group of "secessionists" from the National Liberal party and took the name of Freisinnige Partei and under this name carried on until May, 1893. A split occurred and the left group took the name Freisinnige Volkspartei and the right wing Freisinnige Vereinigung. In 1910 the various left-liberal groups merged again to form the Fortschrittliche Volkspartei. After World War I it was reconstituted as the Democratic party.

The Progressives (we shall use this general name for these left-liberal groups) were the champions of the principles of 1789 and 1848. They were anxious to have Germany follow the "model of civilized nations" and become a full-fledged parliamentary state. They were *laissez faire* in their politics as well as in their economics. Anti-militarist, anti-protectionist, and anti-statist in general, they were also bitterly opposed to socialism and waged a constant duel with the leaders of the Social Democratic party. The Progressives derived most of their strength from the urban centers, from the commercial middle classes, from artisans, small merchants, lower officials, and intellectuals. Following the earlier founders, the **most** important parliamentary leader of the Progressives was Eugen Richter (1838–1906).[22] Together with Windthorst, Richter was the most obstinate opponent of Bismarck. Richter was pictured by Maximilian Harden as a "middle-sized burly man . . . in an ill-fitting coat with a pair of too short trousers, who had his figures and his quotations from former parliamentary speeches at his finger tips, and who shot arrow after arrow from the string of his bow up to the Federal Council's table,"[23] where Bismarck sat. Bismarck accused Richter of "always wanting the direct opposite of what the government wants." The chancellor usually left the Reichstag Chamber whenever Richter arose to speak. "It got on my nerves," he said. And there was in truth a good deal in Richter of just opposition "on principle." He spent the greater part of his life fighting against protective duties on foodstuffs, against imperialistic expansion, and against armaments. But he was equally opposed to state intervention in economic affairs and to a state system of social welfare. He was no doubt a most able and conscientious parliamentarian and a brilliant speaker. Even Bismarck (after his retirement) called him "the best speaker we ever had, highly educated and industrious, with unpleasant manners, but a man of character."[24] And the conservative leader Kardorff called him a "knotty oak."[25] But with all his ability and character there was an almost pedantic inflexibility in Richter's approach to political problems, and above all a certain dullness and lack of human appeal that did not allow his brand of liberalism to take hold of the larger masses. The Swabian writer F. T. Vischer rightly said of him, "From Richter's mouth there never yet has come forth an exalted, stirring or truly significant utterance regarding the state and the duties of the citizen."[26]

A new note in progressive politics was struck by the appearance of Friedrich Naumann (1860–1919), who emerged as the leader of the Progressives after Richter's death.[27] Naumann was a creative thinker and statesman. Influenced first by the Christian Social teachings of Wichern and Stöcker, then by Marxism, and finally by close association with a group of liberal and socially minded economists which included Max Weber, Gerhart Schulze-Gaevernitz, and Lujo Brentano, Naumann led German progressive liberalism away from dogmatic *laissez faire.* As early as 1890 Naumann began to preach the need of infusing social content into middle-class liberalism and creating a bridge to the working classes and the Social Democrats. In his *Demokratie und Kaisertum,* first published in 1900, he expressed the hope that genuine parliamentary institutions and social welfare could be combined with a revitalized and liberalized monarchy. But in the years approaching the outbreak of World War I, he, like many other liberal intellectuals, became increasingly exasperated with William II and his conduct and he looked with foreboding to an approaching catastrophe. After the war Naumann was one of the founders of the Democratic party and exercised a profound influence on such men as Hugo Preuss, Friedrich Meinecke, Walter Goetz, and Theodor Heuss.

Naumann's importance lies in the fact that he was one of the first to point out the profound discrepancy between the antiquated and agrarian character of German political institutions and the highly modern and new industrialism and technological developments. He called Germany "the industrial nation in the political garb of the agrarian state." [28] The modern German state, he said, is supported chiefly by the money of industry, "but governed by the sons of the feudal knights and by clerics." He showed that one-half of the income taxes of Prussia was derived from Berlin, Potsdam, Düsseldorf, Cologne, and Wiesbaden, but that these districts supplied only one-sixth of the representation in the Prussian diet. A change therefore, he wrote, must be made to "the English system" of monarchy and to a constitutional régime which would express the new industrialization of Germany. The basic ideas of liberalism must be retained but they must be infused with a "will to power" which liberalism after 1870 lacked, and liberalism must be adjusted to the new social conditions. Naumann was fully aware of the weakness of the liberal tradition in Germany. "Our history," he wrote, "does not contain one single and heroic battle for the convictions of the individual." [29] As long as it is a question of political institutions and economic organization the Germans adapt themselves to the most complicated forms of organization. But they remain weak when it comes to representing the sovereign rights of the individual against the world.[30]

Naumann pointed out that it was futile merely to work for a good constitution if the liberal spirit was not diffused among the people. This was the weakness of the older liberalism which spoke only of inherent eternal rights. There are no inherent rights, declared Naumann. "There are only rights that have been won by fighting for them. No human rights ever came into being without a struggle, and all such rights will collapse and be destroyed as soon as there is no longer a will to fight for them." [31] A liberal program, he declared, must demand an industrial constitution, free association, tariff treaties, the protection of labor, and a broad program of social security. Above all there must be a union of liberals with the socialist proletariat to restore the unity of all the progressive forces in the nation. And most of all there must be a revitalization of the citizenry and their leaders. "You are all politically weak!" he called out to the German citizens. "You are politically without ideas! You are good fathers and men of honor. You have a sense of duty to your occupations and to your children but not towards the state. . . . Your souls, in political matters, are the souls of slaves." And as for the intellectuals, they are most adept in "studying the programs of their own sickness. They are wise but without any will to power." [32] Naumann embarked on a far-flung program of political education and organization. The coming of the war, however, brought a halt to these activities, and he lived for only a short time after the emergence of the republic. His influence on the Weimar constitution and on political movements during the republic, however, was a profound and lasting one, and he has remained to this day one of the prophets of German liberalism.

In addition to these liberal groups there were also smaller progressive parties of South German liberals. Of these the most important were the so-called Sonnemann Liberals, or followers of Leopold Sonnemann, the founder and publisher of the most distinguished liberal newspaper in Germany, the *Frankfurter Zeitung*. There were also small groups of "irreconcilables" in the Reichstag who belonged to the opposition for national or dynastic reasons. These were the Guelphs of Hanover, who refused to recognize the annexation of Hanover by Prussia in 1866, and the Polish representatives from Posen and Silesia.

The two most important parties in Germany—important from the standpoint that they were representative of deeper and more significant currents in German social, economic, and political life than merely the Reichstag elections and Reichstag deliberations—were the Catholic Center party and the German Social Democratic party. These parties were more than political parties. Each of them represented an entire *Weltanschauung* regarding the future of society in all its ramifications. Their political aims were only a part of their general social scheme, which included morality, religion, culture, education, sports, and so on. None of the other political parties had their own dramatic societies, sport clubs, singing societies, fraternal organizations, and other cultural, social, and recreational organizations. But both the Centrists and the Socialists found it necessary to establish such associations. This was because of the fact that both Catholics and Socialists had this in common: they aspired to refashion the totality of society in keeping with a comprehensive and universal *Weltanschauung*. As such, therefore, they merit more extended treatment.

CHAPTER IX

The Catholic Tradition in Germany

In der Achtung, mit der Du, O Gott, mich achtest, ist meine Würde begründet. In Deiner Ehre ruht meine Ehre.

ROMANO GUARDINI

The organization of German Catholics as a political force was in part a phase of a widespread European movement of Catholic intellectuals and lay and clerical leaders who sought to meet the numerous challenges of modern political and social developments. In this movement Görres and Adam Müller, Ketteler and Kolping, the Reichensperger brothers and Windthorst take their places with De Bonald and De Maistre, Lacordaire and Montalembert and Comte de Mun. The organization of the German Center party, however, also took place in response to certain specific and unique features of German development.[1] Unlike most other European countries, which were either predominantly Protestant or Catholic, Germany, the home of the Protestant revolt, remained divided between the two faiths. With Austria included, Catholics and Protestants would have been about evenly divided. But after the exclusion of Austria, the Catholics in the new Reich became a minority, albeit a minority of such magnitude and concentration that it could not be dismissed merely as a "minority." German Catholics were concentrated especially in Bavaria in the south, in Silesia in the east, and in the Rhineland and Westphalia in the west. As a combined group they were a force that had to be reckoned with and one which came to play a decisive role in German politics.

Catholicism in the nineteenth century was confronted with the challenge of several serious and profound problems of modern development. The first of these was the tremendous increase in secularization. This process of transfer of allegiance and supreme interest from otherworldliness to the secular affairs of this world had begun far back in the Renaissance and had been deepened by the *Aufklärung* of the seventeenth and eighteenth centuries. But it was not until the nineteenth century with its mass revolutions, mass education, and mass propaganda that secularism engulfed the vast numbers of plain people in Europe. Catholicism, presuming as it did to be

173

an all-embracing and all-encompassing way of life which suffuses all phases of human activity with its influence,* refused to take a side seat as merely *one* aspect of modern man's life in an otherwise secular society. Nor could Catholicism adapt itself as easily to this challenge of secularism as did traditional Protestantism. Protestantism, by taking on the forms of national churches, was able to adapt many of its institutions, its ceremonial, and other phases of religious activity to the institutions of the state and to national customs and national practices. A Protestant could, therefore, more easily find expression for his religious heritage in the form of patriotic behavior, and the organized church could become a national state church. This was not as easy for the members of a universal and international Catholic church which, although making many concessions to national character and national tradition, could never allow its faith to become completely identified with national religion. In the case of a country like Germany, where Catholics were in a minority, there was even less room for such an outlet. German Catholicism, therefore, was especially insistent on retaining control over more than the merely church aspect of religion in order to carry on as a "civilization" and thus resist the great and ravaging inroads of secularism.

The triumph of etatism and the claims of the modern state to absolute sovereignty over the individual were another challenge that became particularly acute during the nineteenth century. The spread of the doctrine of popular sovereignty only intensified this political development. Roman Catholic doctrine, influenced by medieval political theory, was in its very essence anti-etatist. The revival of the doctrines of St. Thomas of Aquinas in the early part of the nineteenth century provided Catholic theorists with a body of thought directly antipathetic to the claims of the modern state. Catholic political theory, based on the natural-law doctrine of the Stoics and of Aquinas, asserted that earthly and temporal existence must also be ordered with respect to an otherworldly and supernatural goal. The state, therefore, is not sacrosanct and an end in itself but must be put at the service of the moral order. God, as the origin of all state power, imposes limitations upon state power. The power of the state, for example, must halt before the rights of human personality. Man is born a free and independent being with a dignity that dare not be debased. State power must likewise desist before the rights of private property and the rights of family because these are natural rights inherent in man and in human society. Every family, according to Catholic doctrine, has the natural right

---

* The Catholic writer Edgar Alexander, one of the best authorities on German Catholic social thought, writes: "Now we comprehend Catholicism as the gathering into one whole of all those manifestations of personal, social, national, and finally universal civilization which . . . creates the over-all 'civilization' characteristic of each historical epoch. . . . We may now approach the sociological problem of Catholicism as a manifestation of civilization." ("Church and Society in Germany," in *Church and Society: Catholic Social and Political Thought and Movements 1789–1950,* ed. Joseph N. Moody [New York, 1953], p. 333.)

to provide for and direct the education of its children in accordance with its own preferences. State education, therefore, must always accord with the will of the parents. Similarly, the church is independent of state power and it is the duty of the state to help the church exercise its rights within its own sphere.

Such are the limitations upon the authority of the state as enunciated by Catholic political theory. As for the rest, Catholics in each country are at liberty to have their own opinions. Even though God is the source of all political authority, the agency to exercise this authority is designated by the people. Hence Catholicism, in the last analysis, has been indifferent to the concrete form of government adopted in any particular country. The rules which it set up are elastic in character without practical bonds and hence adaptable to a variety of political régimes. This has made it possible for the Roman church to come to terms with all sorts of régimes if the guarantees to family, property, and church are accepted.*

The special conditions in Germany accentuated the Catholic opposition to statism. Wherever Catholics have made up the majority in a state there has always been the possibility of identifying state power with the dominant religion, and hence a close alliance between state and church was realized. The best instance of this was Spain. The minority status of Catholics in Germany, however, as in the case of England, made them much more acutely aware of the dangers of state tyranny and forced them into the camp of those who sought political guarantees against absolute state power. In this respect there is even a marked difference between political Catholicism in Bavaria and in the Rhineland. In the former, Catholics live in compact masses forming the overwhelming majority of the population. State authority in Bavaria, therefore, was closely allied with the church. Bavarian Catholics have, therefore, traditionally been more conservative. On the other hand the most liberal and progressive forces in the Catholic movement of Germany have come from the Rhineland and Westphalia. There, the proximity to western liberalism, the wider prevalence of industrialization, and the minority status of Catholics within a Protestant-dominated Prussia induced a more sympathetic understanding of the need of protection from the omnipotent state.

The anti-etatism of German Catholicism was further intensified by a strong anti-Prussian feeling in the areas annexed to Prussia and in the southern states after 1871. Temperamentally as well as religiously they felt a closer kinship to Catholic Austria than to Protestant Prussia. "We are always accustomed," wrote F. J. Buss in 1849, "and with us the Austrians, to let things go easy. In cultural life we also remain natural

---

* "History shows that Catholic and Christian inspiration can be realized in the largest variety of ethnic, economic, and social experiences. The Church knows that social and political régimes and the very forms of civilization are by definition changeable. The Church by definition is ready to live with all without tying her life to theirs" (From the Vatican newspaper *L'Osservatore Romano*, Jan. 18, 1950).

people. With the Prussian everything is artificial and pompous. He is always on parade and he is on active service even when in his sleeping robe. We are repelled by the eternal self-deification of the Prussians which we, in Baden, have experienced most recently." [2]

The development of modern nationalism was another serious challenge to Roman Catholicism. As already indicated above, Catholicism, intent on preserving its ecumenical and international character, found the new religion of national patriotism to be one of its most dangerous enemies. Here too Protestantism was able to adjust itself more readily and very often itself became one of the most active agents of national patriotism. But this very antagonism to extreme nationalism and the resultant suspicion regarding the patriotism of Catholics very often elicited an even more super-heated patriotism on the part of Catholic leaders who thus hoped to demonstrate their complete loyalty to the national state of which they were citizens. This ambivalence is responsible for the prominent role played by many Catholics in the nationalist movements as well as for the development of so-called "integralism" within the European Catholic movements. A good example of such exaggerated nationalism was the attitude of Bishop von Ketteler after the war of 1866. Ketteler, aiming to demonstrate the German patriotism of the Catholics which had been put into question by their attitude during the Austro-Prussian War, compensated for this by violent attacks upon France. Enough of imitation of French ideas, he declared. "Our political sentiments, our political concepts and views must once again become German. We must reconstruct our German political life upon German foundations; not according to the forms which were in vogue during the last centuries but according to the ideas which permeated the Germanic political life. The Germany of the past centuries was in many ways no longer Germany." Ketteler then proceeded to draw the distinction between German and French ideas of freedom, identifying the latter with everything that tyrannizes over the individual and the former with everything that is noble and beneficial to the rights of human personality.[3]

Catholics in the modern state, because of their resistance to etatism, have had to defend themselves against the frequent charge of being a "state within a state." One of the best refutations of this charge was made in the Frankfurt National Assembly by the distinguished Catholic historian Ignaz Döllinger. The occasion was a debate on a proposed amendment to the section of the constitution which dealt with the basic rights guaranteeing the autonomy of the churches. This autonomy, declared Döllinger, was not to be interpreted as asking for a position of a "state within a state." The clergy "wanted to be considered German citizens just like all others, subject to the same burdens, the same civic obligations, in so far as they are commensurate with their corporate status . . . and subject to the same laws. They desire no privileges, no special position, and no preferences." They do not want to stand outside the state, much less over and above the state. Döllinger then went on to make the significant statement regarding the difference between the church in medieval times and its role in the modern state. "Those earlier relationships of centuries long past in which, as a result of the integral connection of peoples of those ages and their entire consciousness and life with religion and the church, the church attained a partial superiority over the temporal powers —those relationships are irrevocably past. Whoever wants to see in the autonomous position of the churches the threatening danger of a return of the medieval supremacy of the church over the princes and peoples, must also be ready, with equal right, to see the revival of the feudal state as it existed in the eleventh century." [4]

Catholicism in Germany thus presented an interesting admixture of political liberalism and conservatism. The features described above, in so far as they challenged the omnipotence of the state and sought to protect individuals and groups from unnecessary interference by the state, were all in the direction of liberalism. Moreover, after a period of early opposition to liberal constitutionalism, Catholic political leaders came to realize that constitutionalism may be of service in providing legal protection to minority Catholic groups against the majority. Constitutionalism, with its demand for constitutional guarantees of fundamental rights, became as much a part of the political programs of German Catholics as it was of liberalism in all western European countries.

There were a number of significant and deeply rooted aspects of Catholic life, however, which were definitely conservative in character. Catholicism, in the first place, emphasizes tradition. As such its weight is cast for the old and the customary as against the novel and progressive. Traditionalism and conservatism are and always have been inextricably connected. The eternal values, the emphasis on absolutes in moral and religious life find resonant echo in Catholic teaching. Catholicism, moreover, has always emphasized authority. The hierarchical structure of its own church is authoritarian, and its doctrine of all political power emanating from God, while capable of revolutionary interpretation when power is abused, nevertheless generally tends to underscore the duty of the subject to submit to the authority of the ruler. The church has always considered itself to be a pillar of governmental authority, and in Germany it prided itself on the connection of "throne and altar."

German Catholicism, moreover, was historically bound up with the romantic movement. Early nineteenth century romanticism in its turn to medievalism, with its rediscovery of the Gothic and its development of medieval historiography, naturally found the center of the medieval scene occupied by the Catholic Church. Romantic idealization of the medieval meant also a deep attachment to the medieval church. This accounted for the wave of conversions to Roman Catholicism among the early German romanticists. Among these were Tieck, Friedrich Schlegel, Novalis, Wackenroder, Adam Müller, and others.* But German romanticism was essentially conservative in its politics. Romanticism was chiefly responsible for the development and spread in Germany of the conservative revolt against rationalism and for the elaboration of the organismic theory of the state. Catholic theorists likewise became the chief bearers of the essentially conservative organismic theory of the state. In this the influence of the English Protestant Burke was one of enormous significance. But Burke's doctrine was suffused with romantic emotionalism and irrationalism, and in the hands of Franz von Baader, Adam Müller, and Joseph Görres—all Catholic writers—it became the orthodox organismic theory of German conservatism.

Both Baader and Müller represented a violent reaction against the rationalist and individualist doctrines of classical and liberal economics.[5] Baader, the first German writer to use the term "proletariat" (in his *Ueber die Proletaire*, 1834), attacked big business, laid bare the shady sides of capitalism, and demanded "justice" for the workers. He was, in fact, the first to create a concept of "Christian socialism" and was also the real founder of Catholic social doctrine in Germany. Baader and Müller both rejected *laissez faire* capitalism and set up the ideal of the medieval corporate state (*Ständestaat*) as opposed to the modern liberal and constitutional state. But above all they emphasized the organic character of society and the inextricable relation between each individual and the national organism and the equally inextricable relation of each generation to the organic continuity of the generations that preceded it.

The most important single influence in the history of German Catholicism was Joseph Görres, erstwhile revolutionary and pro-French secessionist of the Rhineland who abandoned his early radicalism to become the champion of German nationalism and the founder of "political Catholicism." Called to Munich in 1827 as professor of history, Görres became the center of a circle of Catholic intellectuals and politicians which marked the beginnings of organized Catholic political action in Germany. His pamphlet *Athanasius* (1837), written in protest against the imprisonment of the Archbishop of Cologne who came into conflict with the Prussian state over the question of mixed marriages, was the great trumpet call for the political equality of Catholics and for the freedom of the Catholic Church. The *Historisch-politische Blätter für das katholische Deutschland*, founded in 1838 at the instigation of Görres, was both before and after his death, the most important organ of Catholic public opinion in Germany.[6]

Görres was not an original thinker. His theory of nationalism was but

---

* Edgar Alexander distinguishes Catholic political romanticism in Germany from the Catholic movement in France in that the German movement, "largely the work of converts," had no organic connection with the tradition of Catholic natural law. Alexander, therefore, holds Joseph von Eichendorff, whom he calls "the most Catholic of the romanticists," to be more genuinely representative of the Catholic tradition than Görres, Müller, and Schlegel.

an elaboration of Herder's, and his organismic, hierarchical, authoritarian, and anti-absolutist theory of the state was in all essentials identical with that of the leading conservatives of the period of reaction. But Görres clothed all these ideas with a concrete and symbolical expression, infused into them such a spirit of moralism and earnestness, and pursued them with such unbounded energy and ardor that he may justly be called the greatest of German publicists. For subsequent German Catholicism he became the model for the adjustment of traditional Catholicism with modern political and social conditions. The Görres Gesellschaft, founded in Bonn in 1876, became the most important agency for the development of Catholic scholarship in the social sciences.

German Catholicism thus bore within it tendencies of both a liberal and conservative character. The Catholic publicist F. J. Buss presented an admirable summary of Catholic politics, which while written in 1851 may be taken as a guide for the entire subsequent period. (1) Catholicism sincerely honors liberty and strives for it, but all liberty is limited by morality. (2) Catholicism honors order, not the order of a police state but one having its origins in the innermost essence of human society and formed after the divine pattern—an order consisting of the great natural institutions of family, church, the school, and the state. (3) Catholicism honors organic developments of public conditions. (4) Catholicism rejects revolutions. It does not make them but it accepts them as natural self-punishment for overweening tyranny. (5) Catholicism wants the free development and responsible participation of the citizens in the affairs of the state. (6) Catholicism is eager to further the peculiar and individual fashioning of public conditions and relationships; it favors the autonomy of corporate bodies and is opposed to enforced uniformity. (7) Catholicism stands for a universal outlook but also recognizes the validity of separate nations. (8) Catholicism strives for the simplification of public administration, the easing of state burdens, and the granting of the most feasible degree of liberty to the people.[7]

Political activity by Catholics stems in part from the integrated character of Catholicism as a way of life. It is this which provides a unified and integrated character to the Catholic point of view. Catholicism, especially in European countries, tends to embrace the entire life of its communicants just because it has resisted secularization so much more than did Protestantism. The Catholic leader of Württemberg, Dr. Hieber, wrote in 1902: "Certain definite and far-reaching consequences derive from the fundamental principles of Catholic dogma which serve to regulate worldly, civic and political matters. For the believing Catholic Christian there are a host of purely civic, political and social affairs which fall into the broad realm of religion which for Protestants do not belong to religion but to a completely free area. And this is the great difference between the Catholic and Protestant conception of things."[8] Christianity, for the Catholic, is a complex of definite precepts which are set up to regulate the entire life of man is all his relations to God, to himself, and to his fellows. Religion "is not to be laid aside like the hat and coat, cane and overcoat which one leaves when entering the room and puts them on again when going home. In one's chamber as everywhere, in relations of the princes to their subjects as well as in the affairs between nations, the eternal and immutable laws of religion are to be the norm and guide." [9]

The concrete political demands of German Catholicism in the nineteenth century revolved around three basic questions: (1) anti-centralization, (2) autonomy of the church, and (3) freedom for religious education. The Catholic parties remained the most outspoken and consistent supporters of the federalist structure of the state, and opposed further extension of the political powers of the Reich. Federalism allowed for a greater flexibility and especially for more influence in the predominantly Catholic states of the south. Religious organizations, they demanded, should remain independent of the state and autonomous. Opposition to civil marriage was the most crucial issue in this category. Equally important was the demand for Catholic schools and for the retention of educational control in the hands of the church. "We need Catholic schools," wrote the *Katholische Kirchenzeitung* in Aschaffenburg in 1832, "for the Catholic education of our children and descendants; we need them for the continued existence of our religion and our church in our fatherland." [10] The secular state could not be depended on to provide the proper kind of education. "This state is not our state," declared the Catholic organ, and hence the demand for freedom of education for the church.

Such was the range of concrete political demands by the Catholics ever since the beginning of the nineteenth century, and an analysis of all the major conflicts between the church and the state in modern Germany down to the present will reveal that these were the issues basically involved in one way or another.

Catholicism was also deeply interested in the social and economic issues arising out of modern industrialism, urbanization, and mechanization. Here too the German developments were part of a widespread European Social Catholic movement which began in the early part of the nineteenth century. This is not to say that Catholics were the only religious group to take a stand for the social and economic improvement of the working classes. The Christian socialism of Kingsley in England exercised a profound influence upon German Catholics. The Christian Social movement of Wichern and Stöcker in the German Protestant churches started about the same time as the Social Catholic movement, but it never was more than a minor movement in German Protestantism and never exercised the influence, both theoretical and practical, of Social Catholicism. [11]

Catholic social theorists, as Catholics, emerged as outspoken critics of *laissez faire* capitalism. Their dissatisfaction with capitalism had its roots in two factors: (1) the medievalism, which harked back to a pre-capitalist society; and (2) the ethical and spiritual character of their religion which revolted at the excesses of *laissez faire* industrialism. Here too the social and economic theories of St. Thomas Aquinas, which in turn were derived from Aristotle, were of primary importance.

Social Catholicism attacked economic liberalism because it failed to provide protection to industrial workers from capitalist exploitation. It was ideologically hostile to economic individualism because the motive of self-interest and the incentive of competition ran counter to Catholic religious belief, which espoused a social rather than an individual ethic. Society was a *corpus christi mysticum,* and the individual was not to be considered an isolated phenomenon. Moreover, the failure of capitalist society to take care of the spiritual aspects of life was, in the eyes of Social Catholics, one of the chief causes for the deterioration of the family and for the breakdown of religion.

German Social Catholicism owes its inception largely to the work of two individuals, Adolf Kolping (1813–1865) and Bishop Wilhelm Emanuel von Ketteler (1811–1877). Both came from the Rhineland, where they were able to observe the beginnings of German industrial development and its effects upon the lower classes. Kolping, the spiritual father of German Catholic youth organizations, was born in Cologne of poor parents and in 1845 became a priest in Elberfeld, in the Rhineland. He became especially interested in the lot of the apprentices and journeymen and began to think of ways and means to improve their economic condition. He saw that improved vocational instruction would give the workers a better chance in the new industrial economy. For this purpose he began to organize journeymen's associations. These associations were made up of unmarried journeymen eighteen to twenty-five years old. They elected a priest as president and he resided regularly in their center. The priest, as the spiritual leader of the guild, delivered lectures, and organized their educational program. The center of the work was vocational instruction. Subjects like shorthand, bookkeeping, and foreign languages were taught at these centers. The larger centers also taught designing and machine-shop techniques. Courses for masters were also organized. All this, in addition to the social and recreational activities, was designed to help the industrial worker improve his economic position. Traveling members were able to secure supper, lodging, and breakfast in the various branch centers which were organized. The larger guilds had their own buildings. The movement spread to all parts of Germany and also beyond the borders of Germany. By 1929 there were 1,901 such centers in Germany with 102,956 active members. The Socialist leader August Bebel tells in his autobiography how he came across these centers while tramping through the Palatinate in the 1850's:

It was at this time that I first became aware of the existence of the *Katholische Gesellenverein,* which had its own clubroom in Freiburg. After making sure that the club was open to non-Catholics, I became a member. As long as I lived in south Germany and Austria, I was a member of these Catholic unions, and I never had cause to regret it. There was no intolerance in respect of members of a different religious persuasion. The presidents were everywhere priests, and the members elected a senior member as their own representative. Lectures were given and classes held in various subjects—French for instance—so that these unions were to a certain extent educational institutions. In the reading room a number of papers and journals were available; although these were exclusively Catholic, I was glad to read them, for I was greatly interested in politics. The need for the society of decent young people was equally satisfied. These clubs derived a characteristic tone from the presence of the chaplains, who being young and full of animal spirits, were on their own side glad to meet with men of their own age. I have spent many a merry evening in the company of these young curates. To this day I have preserved my book of membership, having on its first page a picture of St. Joseph, the patron saint of the Union.[12]

The real founder of the German Social-Catholic movement was Bishop Wilhelm Emanuel von Ketteler, often known as the "fighting Bishop of Mainz." Ketteler's influence went far beyond the borders of Germany. Pope Leo XIII did not hesitate to call him his great predecessor, and Leo's famous encyclical *De Rerum Novarum,* issued in 1891, was based to a large extent on Ketteler's program. Unlike Kolping, Ketteler came from an old noble family of Westphalia. He met Görres in 1839 and was deeply influenced by this contact. He was ordained priest in 1844 and in 1850 became Bishop of Mainz. In 1848 he was elected to the National Assembly in Frankfurt. In the winter of 1848 he delivered in Frankfurt six sermons on "The Great Social Questions of the Present Day." In these he expounded the theories of St. Thomas on property and applied them to his own day.

The possessing and non-possessing classes [he declared] stand opposed to each other, the widespread pauperization grows from day to day, the right of property in the consciousness of the people is shattered and we see from time to time phenomena appearing like flames, which now here, now there break forth out of the earth—warnings of a great catastrophe that is coming. On the one hand we see a rigid clinging to the right of property and on the other hand an equally determined denial of all property rights and we desperately seek some mediation between these two extremes.[13]

The Catholic Church, asserted Ketteler, does not recognize the unlimited right to property. Property is given to man only to contribute to the general welfare. And the deep abyss which exists between the rich and the poor is due to this *laissez faire* attitude to property of economic liberalism. It is those who maintain this unlimited right to property, declared Ketteler, who have provided the partial truth in the slogan "Property is theft." They too, therefore, are responsible for the rise of communism, which is also a sin against nature. To heal the social evil, said Ketteler, "it is not enough that we provide a few poor people with more food and clothing and that we send our servants to the Poor Relief Committee with a few more dollars. That is but the smallest part of our task. We must straighten out the enormous gulf in society, the deeply rooted hostility between rich and poor. . . . We must seek out the poor and their poverty even to their most secret corners; we must study their conditions and the sources of their poverty and we must share with them their sufferings and their tears." [14]

The more constructive part of Ketteler's social program came as a result of his study of factory conditions in the Rhineland, the influence of Lassalle, and the works of French Social Catholics. In 1864 appeared his most important work on the social question, *Die Arbeiterfrage und das Christentum*. Here he affirms most emphatically that the social and economic conditions of the working classes must be of vital concern to Christian leaders. "Christ is not only the Saviour of the world in that He has brought salvation to our souls; He has also provided salvation for all other activities of man—civic, political and social. He is also particularly the Saviour of the working classes." And as a Catholic bishop, therefore, Ketteler said that he had "not only a right but a duty to pursue actively the affairs of the working class, to develop a point of view on the issues and to give public expression to this view according to circumstances." [15] Ketteler criticizes capitalism as the source of the physical, material, and moral deterioration of the working classes. He follows Lassalle in his acceptance of the iron law of wages, to which he attributes the workers' insecurity of existence, his inability to progress, and the general decay of the industrial working population. "A labor population immersed in all the miseries of a working life which has become dead to sensation is generally not responsive to the grace of Christendom as long as this is offered merely in the form of the usual pastoral ministration. Before we can deliberate how to Christianize these masses who have become savages, we ought to create institutions to humanize them."

Ketteler suggested a five-point program for dealing with the social problem. He urged (1) the establishment of institutions for those unable to work, (2) emphasis upon the Christian family and Christian marriage, (3) the dissemination of Christian teaching to provide the workers with Christian culture, (4) the organization and support of Christian trade-unions, and (5) the establishment of worker-producer co-operatives. Religion and morality, he declared, were not enough to solve the problems of the workers; hence his advocacy of trade-unions and co-operatives. Deep antipathy to the extension of state power led Ketteler at first to oppose the use of the state in any of the phases of this program. Like Kingsley in England, he at first hoped that the initial capital needed for the establishment of producers' co-operatives would be forthcoming from private benefactors. After 1869, however, his views changed on this score. He began to look more to state aid and state legislation to mitigate the evils of capitalism. This change was induced by the publication in 1867 of Alfred Roux's catalogue of social regulations of industry. From then on, despite Catholic hostility to etatism, he looked to the state for a broad program of social legislation to provide protection and economic security for the working classes.

While advocating such a broad program of social reform, Social Catholicism was emphatic in its repudiation of socialism and communism. Going back to Aristotle and Thomas Aquinas, it rejected communal ownership of property as being contrary to the law of nature. But even more basic was the essentially anti-Utopian foundation of Catholic belief. As against the Pelagian optimism of the socialists and their hopes for a society in which poverty and inequality would disappear completely, Catholic teaching, based on the doctrine of original sin, called attention to the fundamental sinfulness of man and hence the utter hopelessness of attaining a perfect society in the present world. As Pope Leo XIII proclaimed in his encyclical: "To suffer and to endure . . . is the lot of humanity; let men strive as they may, no strength and no artifice will ever succeed in banishing from human life the ills and troubles which beset it." This is the fundamental gulf which divides Catholic teaching from socialism.

Ketteler's last word on this subject was his unfinished essay *Kann ein Katholischer Arbeiter Mitglied der Sozialistischen Arbeiterpartei sein?* Ketteler divided the socialist demands into three groups. (1) The just demands were those pertaining to the organization of workers and the state protection of the workers against exploitation. (2) The partially just demands were those which aimed to raise the prestige of labor but by the wrong means. (3) The rejected demands pertained to the state ownership of the means of production. "I would rather," wrote Ketteler, "eat in peace the potatoes I grow and be clad in the skins of the animals I raise and be free than live in the slavery of the workers' state and be richly fed."

Out of these doctrines emerged the social program of the Catholic party. It was the Center party which in 1877 first proposed a program calling for (1) Sunday rest for workers; (2) the regulation of relations between masters and apprentices and the encouragement of corporative associations; (3) factory legislation; (4) child-labor laws; (5) regulation of women's labor; (6) the introduction of arbitration courts with representatives of the workers included; (7) the regulation of dining and drinking concessions in the factories.

Catholic industrialists' organizations as well as Catholic trade-unions were organized. In 1890 Windthorst took the initiative in establishing the Volksverein für das katholische Deutschland for the purpose of the dissemination and further elaboration of Catholic social doctrine and for the training of trade-union leaders, social workers, and teachers. It developed into a large mass organization of over 500,000 members, with 4,300 branch organizations and a large network of publications. A group of German Jesuits, including Theodor Meyer (1821–1913), Viktor Cathrein (1845–1931), and Heinrich Pesch (1854–1926), took the lead in further developing the ideas of Baader, Ketteler, and Pope Leo XIII. Their journal, *Stimmen aus Maria Laach* (after 1914 its name was changed to *Stimmen der Zeit*), established in 1869, became one of the most influential forces in the molding of Catholic social thought and social action. The entire social-legislation program of Bismarck and of the Wilhelmian epoch bears the imprint of Catholic influence. Count von Hertling, Dr. Ernst Lieber, and above all Franz Hitze (1851–1921), general secretary of the Association of Catholic Industrialists and Reichstag deputy from 1884 to 1918, were among the chief architects of the social legislation of the Second Reich.

The Catholic Center party was officially constituted on December 13, 1870. Its antecedents go back to the Görres group in Munich, the informal meetings of Catholic deputies in the 1848 National Assembly, and the Catholic faction in the Prussian diet. But the main impetus came from the effect of the Austro-Prussian War of 1866 and the exclusion of Catholic Austria from the Reich. Bennigsen, the leader of the National Liberals, began to speak of the "Protestant empire," and the avowed anti-clericalism of both the National Liberals and the Progressives alarmed the Catholics regarding their position in the new Reich and made them especially fearful of state control of education. On June 11, 1870, Peter Reichensperger published a call for the formation of a Catholic party in the *Kölnische Volkszeitung*. After several months' discussion the so-called Soest Program was adopted as the basis for an appeal to the voters in the elections to the Prussian diet. Headed by the caption "For Truth, Law and Liberty," the program called for the following: (1) the preservation of the independence and the rights of the church; (2) parity of all recognized religious denominations; (3) opposition to civil marriage; (4) confessional schools; (5) the creation of a *Bundesstaat,* with autonomy of the separate states; (6) the decentralization of administration; (7) reduction of expenditures and equal distribution of the tax burdens; (8) the harmonizing of the interests of capital with those of the landowners and of both of these with the interests of labor by means of the support of a sturdy middle class; (9) "freedom for all attempts to solve the social problem that do not deviate from the law, and legislative elimination of those evils

which threaten to bring about the moral and physical ruin of the work·
ers." [16] On the basis of this program about fifty Centrists were elected to
the Prussian diet. This group thereupon took in hand the elections to the
first Reichstag and on March 3, 1871, succeeded in polling 18.4 per cent
of the vote, electing 63 deputies and becoming the third largest party in
the Reichstag. They merged with the Guelphs under Windthorst and
established an alliance with the Bavarian Patriotic party and with the Poles.

While there had been considerable discussion and difference of opinion
within Catholic circles as to the advisability of creating a "confessional"
party, the epochal struggle between Bismarck and the German Catholics,
known in history under the name of the "Kulturkampf," * and the lessons
learned therefrom, left the question of the continued operation of the
party beyond any doubt whatsoever. It was here to stay, and it carried
on until its liquidation under Hitler in 1934.

On July 18, 1870, in the midst of the Franco-Prussian War, the dogma
of papal infallibility in questions of faith and morals was officially proclaimed from Rome. The German bishops had opposed the dogma before action was taken but submitted to the official pronouncement after
it was proclaimed. Only a small group of Catholics in Germany, led by the
venerable historian Ignaz Döllinger, refused to submit. Döllinger issued a
long statement on March 28, 1870, in which he declared that as "Christian, theologian, historian, and citizen" he could not accept this doctrine.[17]
The opponents of the papal dogma organized themselves as "Old Catholics" and laid claim to be the true heirs to Catholic property as well as
doctrine. In numbers the Old Catholics were very insignificant (52,000
in 1878), but they were convenient for the policy of Bismarck and the
government.

The proclamation of the dogma of papal infallibility was the occasion
for an onslaught against the Catholic church by the combined forces of
German liberalism and the government of Bismarck. The long-standing
anti-clericalism of both National Liberals and Progressives now burst
forth in all its fury. The dogma of papal infallibility followed close upon the
heels of the Pope's *Syllabus of Errors,* in which he condemned the "errors
of liberalism." The Kulturkampf thus became for the liberals a struggle
of modern liberal and scientific culture against medieval darkness. "Everything," declared a chronicler of the year 1873, "which European civilization has achieved since the end of the Middle Ages by bitter struggles and
at the cost of heavy sacrifices, everything which we consider to be the
most precious heritage from our fathers, . . . all this Rome declares to
be the work of the Devil, condemns it, considers it accursed, and attempts
with all the means at its disposal to destroy it, root and branch, and by

* The term "Kulturkampf" was first used by the Progressive deputy Virchow in a speech
in the Prussian diet on Jan. 17, 1873 (see *Stenographische Berichte des Abgeordnetenhauses,*
1872–1873, i, 631). The Progressives and liberals then used it in their election campaigns,
and the Catholics accepted the term in derision.

force to drive back the world once again into the ideas and, as far as possible, into the forms of the medieval period." [18]

In addition the liberals were desirous of asserting at this time the complete supremacy of the secular state over the church. They saw an opportunity to smash the new Centrist party and with it to deal a deathblow to all the vestiges of particularism of which the Catholic Centrists were the spearheads.

The motivations which led Bismarck into one of the few struggles he ever failed to win were not entirely of the same character as the above; neither are they too clear. It is true that Bismarck was hostile to the formation of the Center party and spoke of it as a "state within a state." He was likewise outraged by the alliance of the Centrists with the irreconcilable Guelphs of Hanover and their support of the Poles in Posen. The appearance of democratic elements within the Center party, as well as its social program, disturbed him. But probably the most important single motive was one related to foreign rather than to domestic policy. Bismarck was always swayed more by issues of international relations than by domestic politics. France at this time was still the traditional protector of the Roman Catholic church. On the other hand anti-clerical Italy and Greek Orthodox Tsarist Russia were not on good terms with the Vatican. By striking at the German Catholics and through them at the Vatican, Bismarck believed he could bring about the isolation of clerical France and the sealing of friendship with Russia and Italy.[19]

A violently anti-Catholic article in the *Kreuzzeitung* on June 19, 1871, led off the attack. The article was taken to be officially inspired by Bismarck. This was followed on July 8 by the abolition of the special division for Catholic affairs in the Prussian Ministry of Religious Affairs. The government indicated that it intended to throw its support to the Old Catholics. The minister of religious affairs, von Mühler, was replaced on January 22, 1872, by Adalbert Falk, a member of the Free Conservatives and a violent anti-clerical. Then Bismarck put through a law ordering the dissolution of the order of the Jesuits. Protestant hostility to the Jesuits is comparable to the continental attitude toward Freemasons. In both cases these groups are looked upon as the arch-fiends and Machiavellian master-intriguers in the other camp. The Jesuits were accused of having caused the Franco-Prussian War, and the proclamation of the dogma of papal infallibility was likewise regarded as their work. Acute resentment in government and liberal circles arose when the Pope refused to accept the anti-Jesuit Cardinal Prince Hohenlohe-Schillingsfürst as German minister to the Vatican. It was then that the law banishing the Jesuit order from the German Reich was passed. The Papacy replied to this action with a strong protest, and diplomatic relations were severed between the two powers.

On January 9, 1873, Minister Falk introduced a series of anti-Catholic laws intended to deal with the Catholic problem in a comprehensive and drastic fashion. These came to be known as the May Laws, having been promulgated in May of that year. This legislation took from the bishop much of his disciplinary power in the church; it placed the education of the clergy entirely under the supervision of the state; it facilitated secession from the church; and it brought ecclesiastical discipline under state control by providing for appeal to the ordinary secular courts of law. The Catholic bishops met at Fulda and proclaimed that "no Catholic Christian could acknowledge these laws or voluntarily obey them without the gravest violation of his faith." Partisan feeling and religious bigotry increased tremendously as a result of this struggle. But in the next elections for the Prussian diet the Centrists increased their representation from 63 to 91 deputies. Clergymen who refused to fall in line with the new legislation were persecuted and imprisoned. Among those who spent terms in jail were the Archbishop of Posen, the Archbishop of Cologne, and the Bishop of Treves.

Further anti-Catholic legislation was enacted in Prussia in 1874. Civil marriage was made compulsory in March, 1874. And when, as a result of the persecutions by the state, many church positions became vacant, the government proceeded to appoint Old Catholics to these posts. Further fuel was added to the fire by the attempted assassination of Bismarck on July 3, 1874. The German embassy to the Vatican was completely suspended in December, 1874, and on February 5, 1875, an encyclical by the Pope declared null and void all the Prussian laws which "contradict the divine institution of the church." This brought a storm of attack from the non-Catholic press which saw in the Pope's action proof of their charge that Catholic citizens do not consider themselves subject to the laws of the state as do the other citizens. The Prussian government continued with further legislation. All grants to the church were suspended in those sees in which the clergy did not obey the new laws. The provisions in the Prussian constitution granting autonomous self-government to the churches were repealed. All religious orders and congregations except those concerned with nursing the sick were ordered dissolved. These measures served only to increase the fighting spirit of the Catholic leaders and to bring them greater support from their followers. Orthodox Lutheran conservatives, fearful that this attack on traditional Catholicism would backfire against all traditional religion, threw their support to the Centrists. Bismarck himself began to see that he was losing the battle. He saw that the Center party was only being strengthened by the attack to which it was subjected. He too began to fear that this conflict might be inimical to Christianity in general. Coinciding with this came Bismarck's realization that his hope of building the National Liberals into a great governmental party had failed, and he turned more to his old friends the Conservatives. But above all his former reasons of foreign policy no longer held. The

France of the Third Republic was no longer the protector of the Catholic church but an anti-clerical state itself. The original aim to isolate France by an attack on the church was no longer valid, and Bismarck sought a way out of the conflict.

The opportunity came with the death of Pius IX in 1878 and the election of a new Pope, Leo XIII. On the same day on which he was named Pope, Leo XIII addressed a communication to the German emperor expressing the hope that peace could be re-established between the church and the German state. Negotiations were initiated through the Bavarian government, and mutual concessions were offered on each side. Prussia was to whittle down the Falk laws in practice and change them at a later date, while the Pope was to pledge the good behavior of the clergy and to accept the obligation of notifying the government in advance of all his clerical appointments. Bismarck gave way and receded from his previous stand. Falk was relieved of his post in 1879, and the ousted bishops were reinstated. The parishes were permitted to have their old priests back and churches were reopened. By 1881 all was peaceful again in the field of church and state, and legislation in 1887 brought the struggle officially to a close.

Out of this conflict emerged a more powerfully organized Center party than ever before. The Kulturkampf served to make Catholics in Germany realize even more the need for such a party. The Center party now became a mass party. A Catholic press developed, with the official organ *Germania,* established in 1871, and other important papers in the Rhineland and in the south.[20] Under the stress of the struggles of the Kulturkampf, and utilizing universal suffrage, freedom of the press, and assembly, it became a popular party using popular slogans. In the Reichstag elections of 1874 it increased its representation to 91 seats and polled 27.7 per cent of the vote.

The composition of the Center party followed ideological rather than social or class lines. A mixed assortment of peasants, workers, shopkeepers, intellectuals, Poles, Guelphs, and a sprinkling of Orthodox Lutherans made up the great bulk of the party electorate. Apart from religious and church problems the membership was hardly of the same political and social views. It was able to include on the one hand a figure like von Savigny, the last German ambassador to the *Bund* and the man whom Bismarck had originally selected for the post of Reich Chancellor in 1867, and at the other extreme a person like Dr. Joseph Krebs, who had stood with the radical Johann Jacoby in the constitutional conflict in Prussia. Its leaders in the first period were Savigny, Mallinckrodt (died in 1874), August and Peter Reichensperger, and Ludwig Windthorst. It was the latter who came to be the great parliamentary leader of the Centrist faction in the Reichstag and in the Prussian diet.

Ludwig Windthorst was born in 1812 in Hanover and remained the faithful servant of the Guelph ruling house, even after the annexation of Hanover in 1866. This, together with his Catholicism, made him a fierce opponent of Bismarck. Bismarck hated the Catholic Windthorst even more than he did the Jew Lasker. He once said: "Hate is just as great an incentive to life as love. My life is preserved and made pleasant by two things—my wife and Windthorst. One exists for love, the other for hate." [21] Bismarck's supporters called Windthorst "the evil genius of the German nation." He was a little man, with a big head and a colossal mouth. They called him *"die kleine Excellenz"* or *"der Kleine"* for short. Cool and deliberating, he was capable of arousing intense passion and hate. This contrast between the very calm Windthorst and the tempestuous outbursts of the Iron Chancellor only served to increase Bismarck's hate of Windthorst. In the debate of January 31, 1872, in the Prussian diet, Windthorst quipped at Bismarck on this point. "I have many faults," he said, "but certainly not the one of passion in debate. My pulse beat is 60 per minute in this house too, but I do not know if the prime minister can say the same for himself." [22]

Windthorst became one of the master political strategists in the Reichstag. Unlike the National Liberals, who would announce with great bravura their support of or opposition to government bills at the first reading and then yield one point after another—they came to be called *Fraktion Drehscheibe* or *Fraktion Windfahne*—Windthorst developed the strategy of being noncommittal at the first reading so that he could more easily maneuver his tactics before the third and final reading of a bill. Count von Hertling recounts in his memoirs the instructions he received from Windthorst when he served as party spokesman for the first reading of the anti-Socialist bill of 1880. Windthorst said to him: "You will speak in such a fashion that we might equally be able to vote either yes or no." "But your Excellency," retorted Hertling, "I can only speak in accordance with my convictions." To which Windthorst replied: "Bosh! you are not to hold a series of lectures; you are to deliver a political speech!" [23] These tactics earned for Windthorst the jealous animosity of other party leaders, who attacked him for his political bargaining (*Kuhhandel*). He was passionately absorbed in parliamentary politics, and his opponents often doubted the sincerity of his religious convictions, but no one ever questioned his personal honesty, integrity, and fearless courage.

After the end of the Kulturkampf it seemed as if the hostility between Bismarck and the Center party might be overcome. One of the chief factors in this situation was Bismarck's new commercial policy. The change from free trade to protection in 1879 lost Bismarck the support of the National Liberals. On the other hand this move was greeted favorably by the Centrists who represented large agrarian interests eager to have their farm products protected by tariff legislation. Other factors, too, tended to ease the tension between the Centrists and Bismarck. The German alliance with Catholic Austria on the one hand and the strong anti-clerical policies of republican France led the Center party to support Bismarck's foreign policy. Despite his earlier fears of the social demands of the Center party, Bismarck began to see that they were successfully weaning away many of the working classes from the more hated Socialist movement. Furthermore, it was no longer difficult to grant the chief demands of the Centrists. Bismarck did not plan any further extension of centralized controls, the church question was no longer a matter of controversy, reasonable concessions could be granted to the Catholic workers, and occasional government appointments could be bestowed upon Catholic political leaders. Bismarck thus was willing to co-operate with the Center party in the Reichstag. But a basic mistrust remained, and he took care never to be placed in the position of being dependent upon their support.

In a long discussion of the Center party in the Reichstag on December 3, 1884, Bismarck declared: "This party has a great deal which, in comparison with the other parties, greatly pleases me and is to my heart. It has very strong discipline and its structure is monarchical. . . . Many of its fundamental principles are completely sympathetic to me and I share in them. . . . But it has this danger for me: one cannot enter into relations with it without selling body and soul to its immanent spirit; one is taken with it completely and the moment always comes when the question arises: Will you fight now or will you continue to go along with me?" And he went on to say: "Besides, we are afraid of getting into a position in which, because of the displeasure of all the other parties, the support of the Center will be indispensable for us. For the center of gravity of the guidance which the Center party receives for its political attitude lies outside the German Reich." [24] On July 31, 1892, he declared: "I consider the Center as an enemy of the Reich in its tendency even if not in all its members. Among them are very many good honest Germans, but the main tendency is such that I would consider it to be a misfortune and a danger to the Reich if the government were to choose its leading advisers from the Center party and formulate its policy so as to please the Center. The Center can never be a lasting support." [25]

During the Wilhelmian epoch and also later the Center party came to achieve precisely the position which Bismarck said he feared. The greater the increase in the representation of the Social Democrats, the greater became the importance of the Center party as the holder of balance of power in the Reichstag. Between 1895 and 1906 the Center was the chief support of the imperial government, and after 1907 there was never a government majority without the Center. *"Katholisch ist Trumpf"* became the current saying in political circles, and it expressed the reality of the situation. For with its fairly stable representation of about 100 deputies and a well disciplined party organization, the Center party became the political arbiter of Germany. The chancellors Hohenlohe and Bülow always discussed the drafts of important new measures with the leaders of the Center party before going to the Reichstag. And during the last year of World War I the emperor found it necessary to entrust the post of chancellor to the Centrist leader Count von Hertling.

This does not mean that the Center party was an altogether homogeneous organization. Ideologically, its membership was united and ready to face any assault upon the freedom of the church. But on political matters there were some sharp divergences within the party. During the reign of William II the leadership of the party was essentially conservative. The party was in the hands of a group of Catholic civil servants who were really opposed to parliamentarianism and who adopted a die-hard attitude in support of the existing political situation in Germany. People like Spahn, Hertling, and Kopp, who were the chief party figures during the era before World War I, combined the basic principles of national conservatism with the belief that the German Reich, as then constituted, was the best possible one for German Catholics.*

On the other hand there was a left wing, led by the young Matthias Erzberger, which wanted to draw the party closer to the more progressive political groups. This coincided also with an increased tendency to convert the party into more than a confessional organization and to open wider its doors to members of other religious groups. On March 1, 1906, Julius Bachem published a very important article "We Must Get Out of the Tower." [26] Bachem argued that although the Center party had its origins in religious issues it was really not meant to be a religious party. Mallinckrodt had made the same point in the Reichstag on January 31, 1872. Bachem now called upon the Center party to co-operate with Protestant groups, and he even went so far as to suggest that the Center party throw its support wherever feasible to non-Catholics running for office. A heated discussion developed within Catholic circles on this question. Bachem and his so-called *Kölner Richtung* were attacked as advocating the supplanting of Catholic organizations by "super-confessional" and "general Christian" institutions. Here too the conflict between the democratic Catholic elements of the Rhineland and the narrower confessional conservatism in Bavaria came to the fore. Thus before 1914 a strong tendency was already developing to broaden the base of the party, to turn it more in the direction of liberal and democratic policy, and to co-operate toward these ends with other non-Catholic groups. Thus the basis was laid for the Centrist coalition with Socialist and other republican groups during the last years of World War I and especially during the entire period of the Weimar Republic.

---

* "The constitution of 1871 was a masterpiece. . . . On its foundations the German nation and with it the German Catholics enjoyed a long period of calm and peaceful external development such as they had never enjoyed since the days of Charlemagne" (Bachem, *op. cit.*, v, 108–109).

As one surveys the entire history of the Center party one cannot help concluding that basically it remained conservative, and in crucial decisions between conservative and liberal elements it tipped the scales in favor of the former. A passage in a pamphlet by the brothers Reichensperger to the Catholic voters in Prussia in 1861 illuminates this point. The Centrist faction, they wrote, has two aims, "the struggle for the rights of the Catholic church and a struggle for the preservation of the entire German fatherland." They preferred to disassociate themselves from the conservative *Kreuzzeitung* party, but when faced with the practical issue of the alternative of voting for liberals or feudals, where Catholics cannot hope for their own majority, then "better a compromise with the so-called feudals than with the liberals. It is better to have merely a decrease in liberty rather than complete slavery, better the rule of Protestantism than that of unbelief." [27] Here we have a key to consistent Catholic political action—a persistence of the identification of liberalism with atheism and disbelief and hence, in the last analysis, preference for an alliance with the right rather than with the left. This identification, it must be said, was not altogether without foundation. For liberals, too, failed to understand that in the last analysis the thing that matters most to Catholics is their religion and their church, and when it is a question of either/or, the alternative chosen is and must always be for that political force which seems to them to give greater freedom to Catholic belief. Virchow in his speech of January 17, 1873, put his finger on the crucial question. For, as he pointed out, in Catholicism, unlike Protestantism or Judaism, church hierarchy and church organization are inextricably connected with individual belief and dogma. Every conflict in modern times between the secular state and the Roman Catholic church is invariably linked to this problem. This liberals either could not or would not understand. "It is impossible for me," said Virchow, "to recognize the moral basis of any action if I do not understand it." And the calls from the benches of the Center party members to this were: "Materialism! Materialism!" [28]

CHAPTER X

The Socialist Tradition in Germany

Ich wandte mich und sahe an Alle die
Unrecht leiden unter der Sonne;
Und siehe da waren Thränen derer die
Unrecht litten, und hatten keinen Tröster;
Und die ihnen Unrecht täten, waren zu
mächtig dass sie keinen Tröster haben konnten.

Ecclesiastes

It used to be customary among writers on socialism, especially Marxist writers, to distinguish sharply between Marxian socialism and other social movements that designated themselves as "socialist." It was maintained that the "socialist" label properly and justly belongs only to the Marxian socialists and that its appropriation by other groups was only a demagogic maneuver. Since the advent of Italian fascism and German National Socialism on the one hand, and the concrete realization of a socialist society in the U.S.S.R. on the other hand, this sharp differentiation is no longer tenable. While we may not go as far as Hayek [1] in postulating an absolute and necessary development from Marxian socialism to the forms of absolute state dictatorship either of the fascist or of the communist variety, the events of the past two decades have made it clear that Marxian socialism, both in its historical development and in its concrete realization, cannot be segregated entirely from other forms of socialism. Even if such a sharp distinction could be made for Marx and Engels, it is certainly not valid for the wide following and organization which emerged from their teaching. The various other forms of socialism helped to create an environment favorable to the spread of the socialist movement, and the infiltration of diverse persons and groups into the Marxian socialist parties brought ideological influences that continued to persist. Just as the Marxian socialist background of Mussolini and other fascist and National Socialist leaders cannot be viewed as purely accidental, so the evolution of the Soviet dictatorship cannot be dismissed merely as a "corruption" or falsification of "true" Marxism.

194

Spengler's idealization of "Prussian Socialism" and his extolling of the "iron hand of Bebel," [2] as well as the "German Socialism" of Moeller van den Bruck and Sombart, not only bear an intimate relation to Hitler's National Socialism but must also be taken as part of the wide socialist tradition in Germany of which the German Social Democratic party was the most organized expression. The homage given to Fichte by Lassalle and by other Socialists, the relations of Lassalle and von Schweitzer to Bismarck, the close connection between Lassalle and Rodbertus, the entrance into the party of former members of Stöcker's Christian Socials and Naumann's National Socials (for example, P. Göhre), the subsequent deviations of Marxists like Paul Lensch, Johannes Plenge, and August Winnig [3]—all these facts point to a much more intimate connection between the German Social Democratic party and so-called conservative socialist currents than has usually been accepted.

Equally significant is the fact that the entire character of the history of the Prussian state was conducive to the development of a socialist movement. The background of state paternalism and of cameralism re-enforced by the influence of the economic theories of Fichte, Rodbertus, Lorenz von Stein, and others not only paved the way for the state socialism of the *Kathedersozialisten,* the Verein für Sozialpolitik, Stöcker, Naumann, and National Socialism, but also created a favorable climate for the beginnings of Marxian socialism. The word "socialist" never acquired the sinister connotation in Germany that it did in many other Western countries. Nevertheless, when all is said and done, if we accept Kautsky's definition of socialism as "the *democratic* organization of economic life," [4] as contrasted with Spengler's definition of socialism as being identical with "the principle of officialdom, in which each worker and entrepreneur assumes in the last analysis the character of officials instead of merchants," [5] then we must accept the Social Democratic party as the prime bearer of this tradition in modern German history.

The history of the Social Democratic party of Germany parallels in many ways the history of the Catholic Center party. Like the Center party, the Socialist party was more than a political party.[6] It too was the bearer of an entire *Weltanschauung* which looked to the complete reconstruction of the whole of society.* It too carried on not only political and economic activities but also developed a broad program of educational, recreational, artistic, and moral activities and institutions. Like the Cath-

---

* Paul Göhre, before he joined the Social Democratic party, and when he still was secretary of the Evangelical-Social Congress, worked for three months with the Socialist factory workers in Leipzig and published a most interesting account of his observations and experiences. The Social Democratic party, he writes, "also has as its goal and is at the same time successful in transforming the conventional education, the religious convictions and the moral character of the German workers. That is because the Social Democratic party of today is not only a new political party or a new economic system or both, but is at the same time a new '*Welt- und Lebensanschauung,*' the *Weltanschauung* of consistent materialism" (*Drei Monate Fabrikarbeiter,* Leipzig, 1891, p. 106).

olic Center party, and together with it, the Social Democrats were for a long time looked upon as *Reichsfeinde,* enemies of the state, and hence completely outside the pale of accepted society. Like the Centrists, the Socialists were the avowed enemies of liberalism and the liberal parties. And finally, like the Catholic Center party, the Social Democratic party went through the fire of persecution by Bismarck and of martyrdom only to emerge more militant, more aggressive, and more popular.

German Social Democracy as it finally evolved was the product of two currents of development. One emanated from within Germany and was embodied in the person of Lassalle; the other stemmed from the general Western socialist tradition of Marx and Engels. The inception of the party was due not to Marx and Engels but to Lassalle. The earlier socialist movement of the 1840's had been completely extinguished during the 1850's and the period of reaction. Marx, Engels, and their associates were exiles, and Marxist influence was practically non-existent in Germany until the 1870's and 1880's. The subsequent Marxist leader August Bebel, describing the period of 1860 in Leipzig, wrote: "Some of us, perhaps, may have read Weitling's writings on communism, but these were the exception. I don't remember any one at that time in Leipzig who was acquainted with the *Communist Manifesto* or with Marx and Engels' part in the revolutionary movement." [7] It was Lassalle who was the first decisive influence in the organization of a socialist party. It was Lassalle's speeches and writings which made the first converts to socialism. "Like most of us who then became Socialists," continues Bebel, "I went from Lassalle to Marx. Lassalle's writings were in our hands before we knew anything of Marx and Engels. My first pamphlet, *Our Times,* which appeared toward the close of 1869, clearly proves Lassalle's influence on my political development. It was only in prison that I found leisure to study Marx's first volume—*Capital.* . . . The *Communist Manifesto* and other writings became known to our party only late in the sixties and early seventies." [8]

The surge of economic development in the 1850's paved the way for increased activity of the working classes.[9] The textile and iron industries in Prussia, Bavaria, Saxony, and Baden showed a marked increase in production, and this was reflected in a growing self-consciousness of many workers. As in England, the workers were first taken under wing by the liberal groups. In Berlin, Frankfurt, Leipzig, Breslau, and other smaller centers, liberal leaders assisted in the formation of *Bildungsvereine,* or cultural associations for workers. These associations were designed to promote "the improvement of the moral and economic condition of the working classes." Activities were restricted to fraternal, cultural, and recreational affairs. Later, Schulze-Delitzsch and V. A. Huber initiated the movement for workers' co-operatives. In Prussia a state-wide federation of these associations was founded as far back as 1844. It published *Der Arbeiterfreund* in Berlin, with the co-operation of such liberal leaders as Rudolf Gneist, Huber, Jacobi, Schulze-Delitzsch, Guido Weiss, and others.[10] Political activity was taboo in these organizations. When the workers pressed for admission to the Nationalverein, the leaders of this political association refused to lower the membership dues or even to allow for monthly payment of the dues, in order that the workers be kept out. Schulze-Delitzsch tried to console them by urging the workers to consider themselves "honorary members" of the Nationalverein. Only in South Germany did liberals like Leopold Sonnemann and F. A. Lange [11] recognize the need for political action by the workers. But Sonnemann was strongly opposed to political activity by the workers alone. He wanted them to carry on their activities within his own Volkspartei. Sonnemann and his *Frankfurter Zeitung* worked actively against all attempts to organize independent political associations of workers in the Frankfurt area.[12]

It was from Leipzig that the first steps were taken to organize the workers.[13] Here a large Workers' Educational Association was active, and in 1862 the more radical members of the association organized a "Central Committee for the Convocation of a German Workers' Congress." Two of the leaders came to Berlin to invoke the aid of the Progressives. They asked the leaders of the Progressives and of the Nationalverein to endorse their demand for universal suffrage and to make it possible for the workers to enter the Nationalverein. Both demands were turned down by the liberal leaders. It was then that they turned to Ferdinand Lassalle, who accepted their call on March 1, 1863, and who with this action initiated the founding of the Social Democratic party of Germany.[14]

Ferdinand Lassalle was born in Breslau in 1825 as the son of a Jewish merchant. Both the larger milieu in which Lassalle was born and his own immediate family were more intensely Jewish than was the case with Marx. In his youth Lassalle even dreamed of becoming the heroic leader of the Jews. One of the early entries in his diary reads, "It was always my cherished idea to lead the Jews with weapons in their hands to make them independent." But his ardent Jewish nationalism did not last long. He soon came to resent the burdens and disabilities which his Jewish affiliation imposed upon him, and he often indulged in the kind of expression of self-hate which was characteristic of many German-Jewish intellectuals. He hated two things, he once declared, Jews and litterateurs—and he had the misfortune to be both. But there is no doubt that his resentment at the oppression of Jews had a great deal to do with making him a revolutionary. The youthful Maccabean who wanted to lead the chosen people to victory became the revolutionary who was to lead the proletarian masses to independence and liberty. Lassalle's turn to revolution emanated primarily from personal experience rather than from theoretical studies, as in the case of Marx and Engels. "Had I been born a prince or noble," he said, "I would have been an aristocrat with all my life and soul. But since I was born only a plain burgher's son, I became a democrat."

Young Lassalle refused to follow his father's advice to enter business. With the heroic flair and dramatic pathos which were so characteristic of Lassalle all through his life, he told his father that he had elected the battle for human rights as his career, "because God placed the voice in my chest, which calls me to battle, because God gave me the strength— I feel it—which makes me capable of doing battle! Because I can battle and suffer for a noble cause." Young Lassalle therefore proceeded to study philosophy and history, first at Breslau and then at the University of Berlin. In 1846 he went to Paris to work on manuscript materials related to his dissertation. Heinrich Heine, recommending him to Varnhagen von Ense, wrote the following interesting description of the young Lassalle:

Herr Lassalle, who brings you this letter, is a young man of most excellent intellectual talents with the most thorough erudition, the broadest knowledge, and the greatest keenness that I have ever met. He combines a very rich endowment for presentation with an energetic will, and with adroitness in action which simply amazes me. . . . Herr Lassalle is a true child of the new age, which will have nothing of that renunciation and humility which we in our day simulated more or less and on which we throve. This new generation wants to enjoy and to assert itself in a visible way. We old ones bent humbly before the unseen, snatched at shadow kisses and the scent of blue flowers, abstained and whined about it and we were perhaps yet happier than these stern gladiators who so proudly challenge death in battle.[15]

Lassalle's studies were interrupted by the interest he took in the case of a noble lady who was seeking a divorce from her husband. He took up the marital cause of the Countess von Hatzfeldt and threw himself into the legal battle in her behalf with all the energy and passion he was capable of until in 1854 he finally succeeded in freeing her from her husband. This case, though it earned him a great deal of notoriety, also brought him into contact with influential circles in German society. The battle against an antiquated legal system only intensified Lassalle's revolutionary zeal. He was jailed for six months in 1849 for revolutionary activity. From then on he threw in his lot with the radical movement. He came to Berlin in 1857 and was active as a radical journalist and pamphleteer. He attained some recognition for more ambitious scholarly works on Heraclitus and on legal philosophy. But through his political pamphlets and speeches he came to be one of the outstanding political leaders of modern Germany. As a result of this renown, the Leipzig workers asked him to help them organize a general workingmen's association. Lassalle saw the possibilities in the plan and asked them to invite him formally to express his views on the social question. To this invitation he replied with his most important social pronouncement—his *Offenes Antwort-Schreiben* of March 1, 1863—in which he laid the theoretical and practical foundations for the German Socialist party. In a letter to Moses Hess, six months later, Lassalle told of how he had decided to drop a systematic scholarly work on which he was working to take up this practical challenge. "A theoretical system of work," he wrote, "aims to advance science and fructify the spirit in thirty to fifty years. Here on the other hand was an opportunity for great, practical agitation which would permeate the entire nation. It was a question of suddenly, as if by a magic stroke, letting socialism appear as a political party."

On May 23, 1863, about 15 delegates convened in Leipzig to form Der Allgemeine Deutsche Arbeiterverein, the first political organization of the German working classes and the first parent of the German Social Democratic party. The organization did not grow very rapidly. Three months after its organization the total membership was only 900, and at the time of Lassalle's death it was 4,600. Lassalle's personal temperament was not fit for the long and patient struggle needed to build up a mass organization. He looked to becoming the leader of a mass movement, but the masses did not hasten to come forth. In so far as the actual mass organization was concerned, it was Schweitzer, the successor to Lassalle as head of the Workingmen's Association, who was chiefly responsible for the growth of the party. Nor did Lassalle live long enough to test his abilities as a mass organizer. He was fatally wounded in a duel over a lady on August 28, 1864, and died on August 31. He was buried in the Jewish cemetery in Breslau. The impress that Lassalle left on the socialist and labor movement in Germany was profound and lasting and, in the words of Karl Kautsky, "In so far as the origins of German Social-Democracy may be viewed as the work of a single individual, it was the creation of Ferdinand Lassalle."

Lassalle was not, like Marx, a builder of theoretical systems. Despite his oft-expressed desire to devote himself to scholarly work, and despite his publication of several respectable philosophical treatises, he was first and foremost a political leader. He wanted power for himself, and he told the workers that they were doomed unless they acquired political power. This is Lassalle's great historic achievement. He told the Leipzig workers that social legislation would not help them, that Schulze-Delitzsch's scheme for co-operatives would be of no avail to them, that the irresistible and ineluctable iron laws of wages (which he took over from Ricardo) would grind them down in the seesaw of capitalist exploitation unless they attained the power in the state to which they were entitled. "To you gentlemen," he said to the Leipzig workers, "the suffering classes, belongs the state, not to us the upper classes, for it is you who make up the state." [16]

The only way, declared Lassalle, whereby the discrepancy between workers and owners would disappear and the means for exploiting labor therefore be eliminated was for the workers themselves to become entrepreneurs. This they could do by setting up producers' associations in which they themselves would be the owners. But in order to organize such associations, capital outlay must be supplied by the state. "It is the task and duty of the state," said Lassalle, "to make this possible for you; to take in hand this great job of furthering and developing free individual associations of the working class and to make it its most sacred obligation to provide you with the means and possibilities for such organizations and associations of your own."

The only way to force the state to such action, declared Lassalle, is through direct universal suffrage. The achievement of universal suffrage, therefore, becomes the most important goal of the proletariat. And universal suffrage thus becomes not only the basic political principle of the working class but also the most elementary condition for social improvement. The defeat of 1848 had convinced Lassalle that the liberal bourgeoisie would never succeed in besting the absolutist and militaristic state. He now wanted to create alongside the existing parties of liberals and conservatives a third force, led by himself, which would find its source of strength in the masses and which would assume the task of carrying through far-reaching social and political reforms. "The universal suffrage of 89 to 96 per cent of the population, conceived as a question of the stomach (*Magenfrage*) and hence also diffused with stomach warmth (*Magenwärme*) throughout the entire national body—have no fears, gentlemen, there is no force that can resist this for very long."

It was this historic perception by Lassalle of organizing the workers politically that makes him the creator of the German Social Democratic party. In a letter to Rodbertus on April 30, 1863, Lassalle wrote, "Without universal suffrage, a practical instrument for the realization of our demands, we could be a philosophical school or a religious sect, but never a political party." [17] Marx, like Rodbertus, was also originally opposed to the emphasis on agitation for universal suffrage. Marx pointed to the use made of universal suffrage by Bonapartists in France and was afraid that action in behalf of universal suffrage would mean a loss of "revolutionary" spirit. Lassalle refused to admit of an antagonism between universal suffrage and revolution. To the workers of Frankfurt he once said, "Every time I say 'universal suffrage' you must take it to mean 'social revolution.' " [18]

Hermann Oncken, in his brilliant biography of Lassalle, has pointed out that Lassalle really represented the "extreme left wing" of the etatist tradition, born out of German historical conditions, which also produced Bismarck and Treitschke. And both Bismarck and Treitschke appreciated this side of Lassalle. Lassalle, unlike Marx, never really accepted the materialist philosophy of history. He was thoroughly imbued with the Hegelian theory of the state, and the state was the center of his thinking.[19] "It is the state," declared Lassalle in an address on April 12, 1862, "which has the function to realize the development of liberty, and the development of the human race to liberty." "The state is this unity of individuals in one moral whole, a unity which increases a millionfold the powers of all the individuals who make up this association. . . . The purpose of the state is, therefore, not that of protecting the personal freedom and property of the individual which, according to the bourgeoisie, the individual brings with him into the state. The purpose of the state is precisely to put the individual in a position, by this association, to attain such goals, and such a level of existence, which he could never achieve by himself; to make it possible for the people to arrive at a sum total of education, power, and freedom which would simply be impossible for them to achieve as individuals." [20] This was one of his chief points of attack against the liberals of his day. He derided their "night watchman" conception of the state, and in his address to the court in 1862 he allied himself with his judges "to protect the age-old vestal fires of all civilization, the state, against the [liberal] barbarians." [21]

Even as Bismarck, Lassalle was primarily interested in power. What to do with the "power" was secondary, and the possible contradiction between liberty and power hardly troubled him. It was this common understanding of the nature of political power which brought Bismarck and Lassalle together. The exact extent of their contacts and the content of their deliberations have long been a subject of controversy. Much of this controversy is now cleared away as a result of the discovery in 1928 of a bundle of letters exchanged between the two and published by Gustav Mayer.[22] But there never was any doubt of a restrained mutual admiration of these two for each other. Both looked upon the progressive liberals, in the midst of the constitutional struggle of the 1860's, as the chief enemy. In a speech in the Rhineland, Lassalle declared: "He [Bismarck] is a man; they [the liberals] are old women."

Wilhelm Liebknecht, in an unpublished letter to Marx cited by Gustav Mayer, describes a dinner he attended, given by Lassalle in Berlin to about twenty workers. At the end of the dinner Lassalle delivered a speech against the bourgeoisie. "That is our sole enemy," declared Lassalle, and, continues Liebknecht, "we were to vow to him to fight to life and death against this enemy and we were not to hesitate even to enter into an alliance with the monarchy against this foe." Liebknecht, the avowed enemy of the Prussian monarchy, sprang up from the table in a rage. Lassalle tried to calm him by assuring him that the crown was not an enemy of the working class, although it was also true that "without revolution there would be no salvation." This sympathetic attitude toward the power of the monarchy and even toward dictatorship is even more clearly expressed in a letter by Lassalle to Bismarck dated June 8, 1863. With this letter Lassalle had sent Bismarck the statutes of the newly organized Workingmen's Association in Leipzig, and he refers to the statutes as "the constitution of *my empire*." He then goes on to say:

From this miniature picture you will be able to see clearly how true it is that the working classes are instinctively inclined to dictatorship, if they can be fully convinced that this dictatorship is exercised in their interests; also how much they are inclined . . . despite their republican sympathies—or perhaps precisely because of these—to view the crown as the natural bearer of social dictatorship, in contrast to the egotism of the bourgeois society.[23]

Lassalle's ideas on the state, on monarchy, and on power were also a reflection of his own personal behavior. He was dictatorial in his personal relationships. He had a hankering for glamour and pomp and he was at all times full of pride and arrogance. The statutes of the General Workingmen's Association, which he wrote, gave him dictatorial power, and upon his death he left behind a Testament in which he named his own successor. According to Helene von Dönniges, the woman for whom Lassalle lost his life in a duel, he once told her:

Do I look as if I would be satisfied with any secondary place in the kingdom? . . . Do I look like a political martyr? . . . No! I will act and fight, but I will also enjoy the fruits of the combat, and will place on your brow that which, for the present, we will call your diadem.

Believe me, it would be a proud moment to be acclaimed "President" of a Republic, chosen by the people. To rest secure on the good-will of a nation, more securely than to be "King by the Grace of God" and to sit upon a rotten worm-eaten throne. . . . "Ferdinand, the chosen of the people," is a proud name, and if all goes well, it shall be mine.[24]

It was these personal characteristics as well as theoretical differences that made both Marx and Engels mistrustful of Lassalle. Engels never lost his deep antipathy to Lassalle. He spoke of him as a would-be "labor dictator." And Marx looked with scorn upon Lassalle's theoretical works, and said of him that "not only did he consider himself to be the greatest scholar, the most profound thinker, the most gifted investigator, etc., but in addition he was also Don Juan and the revolutionary Cardinal Richelieu." Perhaps the clearest and least bitter appraisal of Lassalle by Marx is found in a letter which he wrote to J. B. von Schweitzer a few years after the death of Lassalle:

After a slumber of fifteen years Lassalle aroused once more the labor movement in Germany, and this remains his immortal achievement. But he committed serious mistakes. He allowed himself to be dominated too much by the immediate circumstances. He made the minor point of departure—his opposition to a dwarf such as Schulze-Delitzsch—into the central point of his agitation—state help as opposed to self-help. In so doing he only took up again the slogan which Buchez, the leader or French Catholic socialism, used from 1843 on against the true labor movement in France. Much too intelligent to consider this slogan as anything more than a transitory *pis aller,* he could justify it only because of its (allegedly) immediate practicability. For this purpose he had to maintain its feasibility for the immediate future. The "state" thus became the Prussian state. Thus he was forced to make concessions to the Prussian crown, to the Prussian reaction (the feudal party) and even to the clericals. With Buchez's idea of state aid for associations he combined the Chartist call for universal suffrage. He did not see that conditions in Germany are different from those in England. He overlooked the lessons of the *bas empire* for universal suffrage. Furthermore, like everyone who declares that he has a panacea for the sufferings of the masses in his pocket, he from the start gave to his agitation the character of a religious sect. . . . Moreover, he denied, just because he was the founder of a sect, all the natural connections with the earlier movement. He fell into the error of Proudhon in seeking the real basis for his agitation not in the real elements of class movement but in trying to direct its course according to a particular doctrinaire prescription.[25]

Despite criticism on personal or theoretical counts there is no doubt that Lassalle stands out as the greatest single figure in the history of the German Social Democratic party. More than any other leader he made the social problem real and vivid to the broad German public; more than anyone else he made the German workers conscious of their historical role and taught them to organize themselves into an independent party.[26] And not only did he leave a direct impress upon succeeding generations of Socialist leaders but this for the very reason that Marx criticized him, namely, that he made concessions to immediate circumstances. The pattern of Lassalle's political thinking became a model for many German Social Democrats who, escaping from the more rigorous system of Marx and orthodox socialism, tried to adapt their Socialist theories to the more immediate exigencies of the particular situation.

Although Lassalle designated Bernhard Becker as his successor to head the General Workingmen's Association, Becker proved too weak and he was soon displaced by Johann Baptist von Schweitzer. Schweitzer came from a Catholic noble family of Italian-French extraction. He had received a Jesuit education and in his youth was close to the *Kreuzzeitung* circle in Berlin. Machiavelli's *The Prince* was of particular influence upon his thinking. After the defeat of Austria, Schweitzer became editor of the *Sozialdemokrat* in Berlin, and in 1867 he was named president of the Workingmen's Association. Schweitzer went even further than Lassalle in support of Bismarck and the Prussian state. He devoted five articles to Bismarck in 1867. In one of these he wrote, "Parliamentarianism means ineffectual talk while caesarism is at least bold initiative, at least overpowering action." [27] He posed the alternative of "Prussian bayonets or proletarian fists" but left room also for the combination of the two. Schweitzer was accused by Bebel and other Marxists of being an agent of Bismarck's. But both Franz Mehring and Gustav Mayer demonstrated to the satisfaction of all but Bebel that there was no real basis for this charge.[28] From an organizational point of view it was Schweitzer perhaps more than Lassalle who was the real creator of the Social Democratic party. But by this time a new socialist movement had arisen in South Germany which challenged the Lassalleans in the north and which eventually overshadowed Schweitzer and his followers.

While Lassalle and Schweitzer were active in Prussia and North Germany, another socialist current was being fashioned in South Germany under the leadership of August Bebel (1840–1913) and Wilhelm Liebknecht (1826–1900). Bebel, a wood turner by occupation, was a true child of the working classes.[29] Originally allied with the Progressives of South Germany, he was first attracted to socialism by the agitation of Lassalle and only later became a follower of Marx. Though Bebel was not a theorist, he possessed a great sense for practical detail. He developed into a powerful orator and parliamentarian and became the leader of the Socialists in the Reichstag until his death in 1913.

Wilhelm Liebknecht had taken part in the revolution of 1848 and fled to London, where he stayed until 1862.[30] There he became acquainted with Marx and Engels and began to consider himself a Marxist. He was not a consistent Marxist, however. A typical Forty-eighter, his democratic ideology often clashed with the Marxist conceptions of class struggle and revolutionary dictatorship. When he returned to Germany in 1862 he became allied with the Lassalle group. Both Bebel and Liebknecht were followers of Marx, however, and, more especially, both were deeply hostile to Bismarck and the Prussian state. Schweitzer's flirtations with Bismarck, therefore, induced them to disassociate themselves from the followers of Lassalle and they issued a call for the organization of a new socialist party. The invitation was issued on June 17, 1869, and the congress convened on August 7, 1869, in Eisenach. The new party was organized under the slogan of "Down with sectarianism, down with the leadership cult, down with the Jesuits who recognize our principle in words but betray it in deed." Thus was the Social Democratic Labor party constituted. Its members were known during those years as the "Eisenacher" or sometimes as the "Honest Ones," as distinguished from the Lassalleans. The party program, as adopted, called for the establishment of a free democratic state. It pledged itself to struggle for the abolition of all class domination and the attainment of full economic and political emancipation of the working classes. The influence of Lassalle was evident in the plank which urged "the abolition of the present method of production (the wage system) to assure, by means of co-operative labor, that every worker shall receive the full product of his work." It likewise declared that "political freedom is the indispensable basis for the economic emancipation of the working classes" and that the solution of the social question, therefore, "is only possible in a democratic state." On the other hand the Marxist influence was evident in the proclamation of the international character of the socialist movement and in the affiliation of the party with the Socialist International.

As the immediate and practical objectives of the party, the Eisenach program listed the following: (1) equal and direct universal manhood suffrage for all legislative bodies and payment of the deputies, (2) initiative and referendum, (3) the abolition of all privileges of class, property, birth, and creed, (4) the substitution of a national militia for standing armies, (5) separation of church and state and the secularization of the schools, (6) free compulsory education, (7) the independence of the judiciary and the introduction of the jury system, (8) the abolition of restrictions on the press and on the rights of association and combination, (9) legislation to establish a normal working day, to restrict female labor and abolish child labor, (10) the abolition of all indirect taxation and the introduction of a single direct progressive income tax and an inheritance tax, (11) state help and state credit for free producers' co-operatives.

For several years there was bitter rivalry and friction between the two Socialist parties. But the disappearance of Schweitzer from the political scene and, above all, the increased persecution of both groups by the police and the courts brought the two groups together. On May 22, 1875, a unification congress was convened in Gotha. The name taken by the unified party was the Socialist Labor Party of Germany, and a new program, known as the Gotha program, was adopted. The new program, following the pattern of the *Communist Manifesto* and of the Eisenach program, consisted of a theoretical part followed by a list of immediate practical demands. The first part showed an even stronger Lassallean influence than the Eisenach program. As unanimously adopted by the congress the Gotha program declared.

(1) Labor is the source of all wealth and all culture; and as labor of a generally useful type is only made possible by society, the whole product of labor is due to society, that is, to all its members, on condition that they recognize a general duty of labor, due by equal rights to each according to his rational needs.

In the present society the means of production are a monopoly of the capitalist class; the resulting dependence of the working classes is the cause of misery and servitude in all its forms.

In order that labor may be emancipated, the means of production must be transformed into the common property of society, and labor as a whole must be regulated on co-operative principles, and the product of labor applied to the commonweal in just division.

The emancipation of labor must be the work of the laboring classes, distinguished from which all other classes are but a mass of reactionary forces.

(2) Starting from these principles the Socialist Labor party of Germany aims by all legal means at the establishment of a free commonwealth and a Socialist society, the breaking of the iron law of wages by the abolition of the wage system, the extinction of every form of exploitation, and the removal of all social and political inequalities.

The Socialist Labor party of Germany, though working at first on a national scale, is conscious of the international character of the labor movement, and is resolved to assume all the duties which it imposes upon the workers in order to bring about in truth the fraternity of all human beings.

(3) The Socialist Labor party of Germany, in order to pave the way for the solution of the social question, demands the institution of socialistic productive co-operatives with state help under the democratic control of the people. These productive organizations, industrial and agricultural, are to be on such a scale that the socialistic organization of the whole of labor shall result therefrom.[31]

Then followed a list of demands for the democratization of the state and immediate social measures.

The Gotha program was severely criticized by both Marx and Engels for the concessions made to the Lassalleans. Marx devoted a pamphlet to a critique of the program,[32] which was not made public, however, until 1890. Engels in a letter to Bebel subjected the proposed draft to searching analysis. He criticized the lumping together of all classes other than the working classes into "one reactionary mass" and pointed, quite correctly, to the contradiction of collaboration with the "petty-bourgeois democratic *Frankfurter Zeitung*" and the Volkspartei. Similarly he pointed to the fact that of the political demands in the program, seven "directly and literally coincide with the program of the People's Party and petty-bourgeois democracy." Engels also criticized the weakened internationalist plank in the program, the acceptance of Lassalle's "antiquated" iron law of wages, the emphasis again on state-aid for co-operatives, and the Lassallean stress upon the institution of the state.[33] Engels predicted the union would not be a lasting one. But the united party was soon confronted with a more serious attack from without than from within.

After 1870 the dissatisfied voters in the Protestant areas thronged to the Socialist parties. In 1871, despite the anti-nationalist stand taken by Bebel and Liebknecht in the Franco-Prussian War, they still managed to receive 124,000 votes and to send two deputies to the Reichstag. In the elections of 1874 this increased to 352,000 votes and nine deputies. In 1877 the vote was increased by 40 per cent to 493,000, and 12 deputies were elected to the Reichstag. The chief strength of the party at this time was concentrated in Saxony, Thuringia, and Schleswig-Holstein. The amazing increase in the voting strength of the Socialists alarmed the government, and Bismarck began to seek legal means to suppress the movement. His earlier attempts met with failure. He was unable to secure international action against the Socialists and was equally unsuccessful in securing amendments to the press laws and penal code so as to be able to prosecute those who incited to acts of violence or attacked the institutions of property, family, and marriage. On May 11, 1878, a half-witted tinker of Leipzig, Hödel, made an attack upon the life of the emperor. This Bismarck immediately attributed to Socialist influence, and a new anti-Socialist measure was introduced. Again the government measure was voted down by 251 to 57 votes.

On June 2 of the same year, another attempt on the emperor's life was carried out by a Dr. Nobiling. In a manner reminiscent of Hitler's action at the Reichstag fire in 1933, Bismarck and the officially inspired press unleashed a violent assault upon the Socialists and charged them once again with having instigated the act of Nobiling. This time Bismarck also decided to dissolve the Reichstag and hold elections for a new Reichstag. He hoped to gain a conservative majority by exploiting the popular resentment against the Socialists. The elections did not turn out as he had hoped. The Conservatives and Reichspartei gained a few seats and the Socialists and Progressives lost a few seats, but the Centrists gained and the National Liberals still constituted the largest single party. At the new session, however, the National Liberals, satisfied with a few technical improvements in the law, joined with the Conservatives and Reichspartei and, by a vote of 221 to 149 (Progressives, Centrists, Socialists), the anti-Socialist legislation was passed on October 19, 1878. The *National-Liberale Korrespondenz* shed some tears at the forced change of front on the part of the liberals. "None of the men, who in the decisive moment cast their '*Ja*' into the balance, were free from a feeling of pain over the bitter fact that the law-makers of the young and aspiring German Reich were forced to take such an extraordinary step." But, said the liberal paper, it was made necessary by the struggle against the deadly enemy, socialism.[34]

The anti-Socialist law gave the Reich government the authority to suppress all independent labor organizations, all political and economic associations of the Socialists, all their newspapers, periodicals, and printing presses. The Socialists were forbidden to hold meetings and assemblies, and the government was given power to declare a state of siege wherever necessary in order to take action against them.

The anti-Socialist law was renewed at its expiration and again every two years until 1890. During this period many leaders of the party were arrested or exiled. Over 150 periodicals and 1,200 non-regular publications were suppressed by the police and over 1,500 persons arrested.[35]

The party organization was able to arrange its congresses outside Germany, and it transferred its chief party organ, *Der Sozialdemokrat,* first to Zurich and then to London. The immediate result of the legislation was a drop in the Socialist vote. In the elections of 1881 they got 312,000 votes as compared to 437,000 in 1878, but they sent 12 deputies to the Reichstag. By 1884, however, the increase set in once again and continued to climb despite the restrictive measures.

In 1890, after the coming to the throne of William II, there was a difference of opinion between the new emperor and Bismarck on the renewal of the anti-Socialist legislation, and Bismarck resigned. The Socialists were allowed to reconstitute themselves as a legal party once more, and a party congress was convened in Halle on October 12, 1890.

In 1891 the Socialists held their second party congress in Erfurt after the anti-Socialist legislation was allowed to lapse. The German Socialist party had by this time acquired a new theoretical leader in the person of Karl Kautsky, who took over the mantle of Engels and became the dean of orthodox Marxism. Originally a native of Bohemia, Kautsky came to Germany in 1882 and introduced theoretical Marxism into the German party. He started the publication of the scholarly *Die Neue Zeit* in 1883, and it became the leading and most authoritative expounder of Marxian socialism until its end in 1923. The program adopted by the party congress in 1891 was largely the work of Kautsky, and he published the official commentary to the program.[36]

The Erfurt program differed from the Gotha program in that it provided a different, now Marxist, foundation for its aims, in pointing a different path toward the goal of socialist development and in elaborating a more precise formulation of its social and political philosophy.

The Erfurt program followed the traditional division into theoretical and practical sections. The first was an orthodox Marxist analysis of political, economic, and social conditions. Whereas the Gotha program had derived its aims from law and philosophy, the Erfurt program was based on the class struggle. It is really only with the adoption of this program that Marxist theory came into its own in the German Socialist movement. With the adoption of this program the German Social Democratic party accepted the leading tenets of theoretical Marxism. It pictured the economic development of bourgeois society, the monopolistic developments which were bringing about the decline of the middle classes, and the increase in the elements depressed into the proletariat, thus emphasizing the contrast and widening the gulf between the exploiters and exploited, making the class struggle more bitter and dividing society into two hostile camps. The Erfurt program then proceeded to show the influence of recurring crises, pointing out that private property was no longer compatible with the full utilization of the forces of production. The socialization of economic life, therefore, means not only the liberation of the proletariat but of all the suffering people, and this liberation can be carried out only by the working classes of the entire world. The theoretical section was then followed by a list of practical and immediate political demands which were similar to the series of demands included in the previous programs. The demand for state-financed producers' associations, however, was dropped.

The activity initiated after the renewed legislation of the party resulted in the building up of an imposing party structure that became the model Socialist party of the entire International. The membership of the party grew from 384,327 in 1906 to 1,085,105 in 1914. The Socialist vote for the Reichstag and the number of deputies elected continued to increase until in 1912 it became the single largest party in the Reichstag, with 110 deputies.[37]

In addition the party in 1914 had 220 deputies in the various diets of the local states. It also built up a large network of party newspapers and party organs, capped by the Berlin *Vorwärts*. In 1914 the Social Democrats had 110 daily newspapers with a total circulation of 1,488,142. Their humorous magazine *Der wahre Jakob* had a circulation of 380,000. In addition, the Socialists organized clubs of bicycle riders, workers' sport clubs, singing societies, fraternal organizations, women's clubs, and youth groups and youth hostels. In all these varied non-political organizations the members participated as sharers in a common *Weltanschauung*. Intimate and close relations were also established with the free trade-unions.

The leader of the German Social Democratic party from the founding of the Second Reich to the eve of World War I was August Bebel. Bebel was, with Ferdinand Lassalle, the most towering figure in the history of German Social Democracy. Unlike Lassalle, however, he lived to a ripe old age, and his leadership of the party extended over a span of close to fifty years. And he was fortunate enough also to die before the outbreak of World War I and the ensuing crisis in international socialism and the split in the German party. Son of a non-commissioned officer in Silesia, Bebel was left an orphan at an early age. He became a wood turner and went through the experiences of a typical German worker. Thus while not literally a son of the proletariat, he was a "child of the people." His sense of popular feeling, his utter simplicity of personality, his complete and selfless identification with the party, his practical and organizational sense, and his oratorical ability all combined to make him the organizational head of the party and its leader in the Reichstag. His imprisonment on charges of treason gave him a halo of martyrdom which few German political leaders could boast of. He crossed swords with Bismarck, Caprivi and Bülow in the Reichstag and with Jaurès at the congresses of the Socialist International. And while his leadership of the strongest single party in the Reichstag never yielded any practical legislative victories, his command over the most disciplined and most respected Socialist party in the International helped to compensate for this sense of ineffectiveness by almost continuous triumphs over his opponents in the arena of international socialism. While Kautsky was the academic theoretician whose ponderous tomes were studied by the socialist intellectuals throughout the world and upon whom Bebel leaned for theoretical grounding, it was Bebel's *Die Frau und der Sozialismus* [38] that became the Bible of the German workers. Published first in 1879, it went through numerous editions, was translated into all European languages and became the standby and *vade mecum* for every Socialist home and for every Socialist agitator in Germany. In that respect we may say that Bebel's book, together with Lassalle's "Open Letter," did more to fashion the mentality of the German workers than the writings of Marx, Engels, Kautsky, or any other socialist authors.

Bebel was often accused of being a party dictator. The revisionist Vollmar once said to him: "I, I, I,—is that the language of equal to equal? Or is it not rather the language of a dictator?" And Bebel did rule the party with an iron hand. But unlike Lassalle or Schweitzer, who were motivated by dreams of personal glory, in the case of Bebel it was the impersonal and traditionally German sense of group discipline which he imposed upon the radical party. Bebel was not a consistent thinker. Like the party at large, he embodied within himself many contradictions. As Roberto Michels wrote, you could find in Bebel, as in the Bible, arguments for the most contradictory views. But with the magic of his personality and deep ethical and personal attachment to the working classes he was able, despite these contradictions and often precisely because of these contradictions, to hold the party firmly together. What the Swabians used to say of Uhland, the German workers, according to Mehring, said of Bebel: "Every word he ever spoke was right for us." [39]

The strength of the Socialist party came primarily from the large industrial centers—Berlin, Leipzig, Hamburg, Cologne, and Schleswig-Holstein, Saxony, Silesia, the Rhineland, and northern Bavaria. The bulk of its voting strength came from the industrial workers, with a small sprinkling of free-lance intellectuals and professionals. The Socialist attitude toward the trade-unions changed from an earlier attitude of skepticism to one of intimate co-operation. Earlier—and in the Erfurt program they are referred to as such—the trade-unions were looked upon as merely a "recruiting ground" for Socialist agitation. The trade-union preoccupation with immediate workers' demands was regarded as tending to cool the revolutionary ardor of the working classes for a social revolution. At the party congress of 1893 in Cologne, Bebel castigated the trade-union leaders for negotiating with the liberal parties and warned them that as the social legislation by the state increased, the field of activity of the trade-unions would become more restricted. But the pressure of circumstances forced the Socialists to enter into a closer liaison with the free trade-unions. Officially the principle became established that "Social Democracy and trade-unions are in every respect . . . entirely apart from each other." [40] But unofficially a working agreement was evolved between the two that operated well in normal times but was subject to severe strain in periods of political crisis.

German Socialists, like all other Marxian parties, paid very little attention to winning the peasantry. They looked upon the peasants as a backward, medieval element of the population that was impervious to Socialist agitation so long as traditional small holdings and older methods of farming continued. They hoped for the industrialization and mechanization of agriculture to alter the conservative mentality of the peasant, and they built their main strength upon the industrial worker. Revisionist writers, particularly Eduard David, called attention to the need of making an appeal to the peasant classes, but they made little headway against the orthodox majority.[41]

Characteristic of the period of Socialist activity before World War I was the deep gulf which existed between the Socialists and the rest of German society. Their gospel of revolution, their often sneering attitude toward intellectuals, especially academicians; their advanced views on marriage, the family, and the position of woman in society, their attack upon religion, and, above all, their internationalism and opposition to narrow patriotism and chauvinism, brought the Socialists into disrepute with the "respectable" elements of German society. To this the years of the anti-Socialist persecution added their mark. An almost unbridgeable chasm seemed to exist between the adherents of Socialism and the rest of society. Bülow in 1907 denounced the Socialists as enemies of society just as violently as Bismarck had done in 1878. In the session of February 25, 1907, Bülow called them "the party of hostility to Christianity," "the deadly enemy of the national state and bourgeois society," a party "born out of hate" and like an "Indian tribe on a war path." Socialist leaders, for the most part, did not care to bridge this gap. In theory, at least, they would have none of the capitalist society, capitalist state, or capitalist culture. An almost caste-like attitude was developed among the Socialist workers which bound fathers and sons to their party but which looked askance at all others. There were very few academic people attracted to the Socialist movement, and those that were recruited were usually unable to attain to full professorial rank. In the Reichstag the Socialists consistently opposed increased armaments, naval appropriations, and colonial expansion. This accounted for the anxious speculation as to what the Socialist attitude would be at the outbreak of the war in 1914 and the great feeling of relief and jubilation in bourgeois circles on August 4, 1914, when the Socialists joined all the others in voting for the war credits.[42] In theory, however, the Socialist leaders proclaimed their inflexible and unalterable hostility to the entire existing structure of society. At the Dresden party conference in 1903, Bebel declared, "I want to remain the deadly enemy of this bourgeois society and this political order in order to undermine it in its conditions of existence and, if I can, to eliminate it entirely."

Such an attitude also precluded any collaboration with other political parties in the Reichstag. When, after the elections of 1903, Eduard Bernstein proposed that the Socialists enter the praesidium of the Reichstag even though this would involve their participation in an official deputation to the emperor, he was bitterly denounced by the orthodox leaders of the party and his suggestion was officially rejected by the Dresden party congress. Similarly, the co-operation of the Bavarian Socialists under von Vollmar in the Bavarian diet with the bourgeois parties and of the Baden Socialists, under Ludwig Frank, brought severe condemnation from the party congresses. Not only were the German Socialist leaders able to establish the principle of non-co-operation with bourgeois parties for Germany but at the Amsterdam congress of the Socialist International in 1904 they succeeded in imposing their Dresden resolution upon the world socialist movement. This principle was adhered to by all Socialist parties until the outbreak of World War I.

Despite this apparent dominance of orthodox Marxism in the German party, a strong current of opposition began to develop in the 1890's, which assumed the name of "revisionism." The leading figure in this revisionist movement was Eduard Bernstein. First in a series of articles, then in collected book form, published in 1899 under the title of *Voraussetzungen des Sozialismus*,[43] Bernstein called for a radical review of some of the basic assumptions of orthodox Marxist theory in the light of historical developments which had taken place since Marx had set down his theories. Bernstein pointed to the gulf between Marxist theory and the economic and political realities. As opposed to the strict materialist interpretation of history, Bernstein emphasized ideological factors. He showed that Marx's prediction of increasing misery to the proletariat, his law of concentration and the predicted disappearance of the middle class and the imminent collapse of capitalist society were belied by actual conditions. "Social conditions," wrote Bernstein, "have not developed to such an acute opposition of things and classes as is depicted in the *Manifesto*. . . . The number of members of the possessing classes is today not smaller but larger. . . . The middle classes change their character but they do not disappear from the social scale." Bernstein, therefore, opposed the notion of an imminent collapse of the bourgeois economy and the suggestion that the policy and tactics of the Social Democratic party "be induced by the prospect of such an imminent, great, social catastrophe." Socialism, according to Bernstein, is a movement *toward* a co-operative scheme of production. "The movement," he declared, "means everything for me, and what is *usually* called 'the final aim of socialism' is nothing." Instead, therefore, of speculating on a great economic crash, the task of Social Democracy is "to organize the working classes politically and develop them as a democracy and to fight for all reforms in the state which are adapted to raise the working classes and transform the state in the direction of democracy."

"Unable to believe in finalities at all," wrote Bernstein, "I cannot believe in a final aim of socialism. But I strongly believe in the socialist movement, in the march forward of the working classes, who step by step must work out their emancipation by changing society from the domain of a commercial landholding oligarchy to a real democracy which in all its departments is guided by the interests of those who work and create." Bernstein was thus critical of the theoretical section of the Erfurt program. He wanted to bring the theoretical section into harmony with the practical demands and with the actual practical work of the party. He viewed the coming of socialism not as a result of a great and decisive political battle, but "as the result of a whole series of economic and political victories of the labor movement in the various areas of its activity." Socialism, according to Bernstein, would come not as the product of constantly increasing pressure, poverty, and humiliation of the workers, but as a result of the increased social influence of the workers and the improvements won by them in economic, political, and social fields. "Despite all the convulsions and changes of the reactionary forces," wrote Bernstein, "I nevertheless see the class struggle taking on more and more civilized forms. And it is precisely in this civilizing of the political and economic struggles that I see the best guarantee for the realization of socialism." [44]

Bernstein was joined in his revisionist position by a host of young and able Socialist writers, including Richard Calwer, Eduard David, Ludwig Frank, Albert Südekum, Max Schippel, Ludwig Quessel, Gerhard Hildebrand, Georg von Vollmar, and Karl Leuthner. The revisionist group established its organ *Der Sozialistische Akademiker* in 1895, which in 1897 became the *Sozialistische Monatshefte*. This journal carried on the polemical battle against the orthodox Marxism of Kautsky's *Die Neue Zeit*. In its pages Bernstein continued to "revise" the Marxist tenets of crises and class struggle; here Hans Müller and Max Maurenbrecher sought to develop a new synthesis between socialism and religion; here David and Vollmar advocated an agrarian program which would favor small peasant holdings instead of the large-scale farming advocated by the official party leaders; here, above all, Hildebrand, Schippel, Leuthner, and Quessel advocated a more "realistic" position with respect to patriotism, armaments, and colonialism. The developments in England and in the United States were seized upon by these writers to support the position that socialism could be reconciled with the positive acceptance of these aspects of German nationalism. The positive attitude toward the Prussian state by Lassalle and Schweitzer was now revived in the form of a neo-Lassallean current within the Social Democratic party.[45] "A nation with a world economy," declared Karl Leuthner, "is indissolubly tied to the external fate of its state. This truth, impressed upon the Germans by the example of England, shines forth clearer and clearer from the speeches of the German Social Democrats from party conference to party conference." [46] Max Schippel, therefore, called for a Socialist "military program of action," and Quessel for a "*Weltpolitik* without war." Quessel and Hildebrand advocated the acquisition of Portuguese colonies by Italy and Germany and urged, if necessary, seeking the help of Russia against the opposition of England and France.[47] Hildebrand was ousted from the party for nationalist utterances, but a large group within the party stood behind him.

A storm on the nationalist issue was caused by the speech of Gustav Noske in the Reichstag on April 25, 1907, in connection with the vote on the budget. In this speech Noske declared that the Socialists have always been scornful of the fantastic bourgeois illusion of disarmament. The existing economic conflicts, he asserted, are too powerful to make it possible for any nation to think of disarmament. Socialists look forward to an era of peace in the future, but for the present, said Noske, "the Prussian Minister of War should know that we have always demanded an armed nation." It is the duty of all, Socialists included, to see to it that "the German people not be pressed to the wall by any other nation. And if such an attempt is made then it is obvious that we will resist it with just as decisive action as any of the gentlemen seated on the right of the Chamber." While opposed to wars of conquest, Noske declared that the Social Democrats will always demand the military training of youth and look to the time when Germany "will have the best soldiers." He then quoted from Bebel's famous declaration that he himself would take a gun upon his shoulder to help defend Germany against a "real attack."

Noske's speech was warmly received by bourgeois and conservative circles. The *Berliner Tageblatt,* the *Frankfurter Zeitung,* and even the *Kreuzzeitung* expressed their pleasure with the speech. But he was widely attacked in his own party. The radical *Leipziger Volkszeitung* led the assault on Noske, and the whole issue was aired at the party congress at Essen in September, 1907. The Leipzig Socialist paper, in its editorial of April 29, 1907, pointed out that the distinction between offensive and defensive war was an empty one and that the Socialist attitude should be guided solely by the interests of the working classes. Noske was defended at the Essen congress by Bebel, who declared that while in some respects this "maiden speech" by Noske was not perfect it was "in general a good speech." Vollmar and Kurt Eisner also defended it as correct. When the same issue came up at the Stuttgart congress of the Socialist International in August of the same year, Vollmar declared: "It is not true that internationalism is anti-nationalism; it is not true that we have no father-land. . . . The love of humanity does not for one moment prevent us from being good Germans. . . . We do not share in the utopian aspiration that it is desirable for nations to cease to exist and that out of them be made one indiscriminate national brew." [48] Kautsky and the orthodox Marxists, however, decried the nationalist utterances of Noske. At the Essen congress Kautsky declared that it was a mistake to hold that in case of war "German Social Democracy would consider itself German first and as a proletarian party in the second place." [49]

Noske's defenders were correct in that the facts stated by him in his speech were in themselves not to be challenged nor were they at variance with even the orthodox Marxist position. But his critics, however, were quite right in pointing out that the whole tone of the speech and the circumstances under which it was delivered gave to it a decidedly nationalist tinge. A reading of the text of the speech within the context of the Reichstag proceedings reveals that Noske seemed to vie in patriotism with the other parties. Only at the end of his address did he venture a few mild words of criticism of the government's foreign policy. In the context of the tense world situation at the time and the Junker militarist ascendancy in Germany, the speech ran counter to the Socialist tradition. Small wonder that von Eisner, the Prussian war minister, immediately "accepted" the declaration. But the support that Noske got in his own party indicated the strength of the nationalist trend.[50]

All these revisionist manifestations were also coupled with a much more favorable attitude toward the bourgeois world than that of orthodox Marxism. In a significant article on "The Old and the New Liberalism," Ludwig Quessel, in 1911, attacked Bebel for conceiving of the Socialist party as opposed to the entire bourgeois world. Contrary to the predictions of Marx, declared Quessel, a new middle class has arisen which has nothing to do with the exploitation of the workers. This class could have been recruited for the Socialist party if not for the anti-Socialist legislation and the antagonization of these classes by the catastrophe theory of the Socialist program. They therefore joined the left-liberal parties. But an alliance between the Socialists and these liberals, he said, is most desirable and possible. "Although," wrote Quessel, "the interests of the new middle class and the workers do not coincide in all respects, they are nevertheless not so basically different as to prevent an agreement and a *modus vivendi.* They both have this in common that neither of them participates in the capitalist exploitation of producers and consumers." [51] At the Dresden congress of 1903 a resolution was adopted, by a vote of 288 to 11, which declared:

The Party congress condemns most decisively the revisionist attempts to alter our tactics, based on the class struggle, which we have triumphantly pursued hitherto, and in place of a policy designed to capture political power by the conquest of our opponents to pursue a policy of collaboration with the existing order.[52]

The vote, however, was not an accurate reflection of revisionist strength because many revisionists voted for the resolution, insisting that there were no revisionists such as described in the resolution.

Officially, therefore, the party remained opposed to revisionism. Actually however, in day-to-day activity it continued to carry on what amounted to a reformist policy. This discrepancy between revolutionary theory and reformist activity was one of the weakest points in the Socialist position up to World War I. In reality, the developments of the party organization, of a party bureaucracy, and of the greater part of the party activities all were reformist in character. Official proclamation of the "revolutionary" aims of socialism was reserved for ceremonial and ritual occasions, for party congress declarations, and at times for the Reichstag arena. These served only to antagonize other liberal elements in German society and thus to widen further the gulf that existed. Not being pursued consistently, the S.P.D. did not actually prepare the German Socialist masses for revolution when the favorable opportunity arrived, and it laid itself open to the scorn and ridicule of the non-German radicals on charges of hypocrisy and weakness. It was not until the Weimar period that this serious gap between theory and practice was more or less resolved.

The same sort of thing was true with respect to the problem of socialism and nationalism. That Socialists should love their country is just as natural as it is for others to do so, and only the chauvinists of other countries or the abstract and unrealistic Marxist theorists could criticize them for it. But the combination of Marxian internationalist theory with national-patriotic declarations was hardly one to elicit sympathetic understanding or avoid confusion. And Socialist nationalists not infrequently identified love of country with tacit if not open support of particular state policy.

In its weaknesses German Social Democracy showed some of the same characteristics of the general German trends. Like bourgeois liberalism, it too often combined high-sounding and bold pronouncements with weak and ineffectual action. And with the general Prussian emphasis on duty and discipline the German Social Democratic party became one of the most disciplined organizations in Germany and ruthlessly imposed its doctrinaire and dogmatic unity upon its membership. Naumann once called the German labor movement "the greatest voluntary militarism in the world." In the 1907 speech by Noske quoted above, the Socialist spokesman replied to the charge that the Socialists were attempting to undermine discipline in the army. "A more unjust charge against the Social Democrats," declared Noske, "is utterly inconceivable. I ask the Minister of War: Where in Germany, except for the army, is there a greater measure of discipline than in the German Social Democratic party and in the modern trade-unions?" [53] And while German Socialists undoubtedly carried the banner of "freedom" high during the entire history of the party, it is also true that they never attempted to inculcate the love of, and devotion to, liberty as an end sacred and desirable in itself. Freedom was always subordinated to the attainment of economic power and equality. "The worker has little interest," wrote Bebel, "in a state in which political liberty is merely the goal. What presses and drives him to achieve political liberty and equality is the prospect of also winning through them economic independence. What good is mere political liberty to him if he is hungry?" [54] The goal of Social Democracy, proclaimed Bebel, is not political liberty but "the attainment of economic equality." And these ideas were echoed by Kautsky in his commentary to the Erfurt program and by most other Socialist leaders. It was only after the challenge of the Communist dictatorship in the Soviet Union after World War I that Kautsky and other Marxian Socialists realized how weak their previous theoretical defense of political liberty had been.

Perhaps the most acute and most objective appraisal of the German Social Democratic party was made by Jean Jaurès in his historic oratorical duel with Bebel at the Amsterdam Congress of the Socialist International in 1904. Addressing Bebel and the German delegation, Jaurès said:

Certainly you are a great and admirable party which has given to international socialism not all its thinkers, as is sometimes said, but some of its most powerful and precise thinkers. . . . You are a great party, you are the future of Germany, one of the noblest and most glorious parties of civilized and thinking humanity.

But between your apparent political strength, as it is measured from year to year by the growing number of your votes and parliamentary seats, between that apparent force and the real force of influence and action there is a contrast which comes into view the more your election votes increase. Ah! yes, on the day after the June elections, which gave you three million votes, this flashed before all eyes: that you have an admirable machine for propaganda, for recruiting and enrolling, but that neither the traditions of your proletariat nor the mechanism of your constitution permit you to cast that apparent colossal force of three million votes into useful and real action of political life. Why? Because you still lack the two essential parts, the two essential means for action by the proletariat: you have neither revolutionary action nor parliamentary action. . . .

There is admirable devotion in the German proletariat. There is no historical revolutionary tradition. It did not conquer universal suffrage on the barricades: it received it from on high. . . .

You do not have any more of parliamentary strength. And even when you attain the majority in the Reichstag you are the only country where you cannot and socialism cannot become master even if it is in the majority. Your parliament is nothing but a demi-parliament. . . . You do not know yet, in practice, what road you shall take, whether you shall be revolutionary or parliamentary, how you will institute democracy in your country. . . .

You mask your powerlessness of action before your own proletariat and before the international proletariat by seeking refuge in the intransigeance of theoretical formulas which our eminent Comrade Kautsky shall continue to provide you with, up to vital exhaustion.[55]

Nevertheless it must be conceded that the German Social Democratic party, as the greatest organizer of the working masses, also developed the only compact and organized group in Germany which was politically mature and critical. German Social Democracy, apart from politics, was also a great educational agency in the fields of dramatic arts, in the temperance movement, in sports, and in the cause of woman's rights. Not so much by its political activity as by its influence in the labor and co-operative movements it succeeded in important ways in bettering the conditions of the working classes. It was the model Socialist party in the Socialist International, and it helped to make the term "socialism" popular and influential in Germany. And its strong discipline, while a weakness, nevertheless was responsible for holding the mass of its following true to its ideals. In the test of the years 1933–1945, the Socialist workers of Germany remained more steadfast in their opposition to the Nazi tyranny than any other single group or party in Germany. This was due in largest measure to the political education by the Social Democratic party.

CHAPTER XI

Social, Economic, and Intellectual Developments, 1870-1914

Mich drängt zu singen deutschen Geistes Kraft.

RICHARD DEHMEL

1. THE INDUSTRIAL REVOLUTION IN GERMANY

The most remarkable aspect of modern German history, and one of the most amazing chapters in the entire history of modern times, is the economic transformation which occurred in Germany during the last half of the nineteenth century.[1] In the course of about thirty years Germany experienced what England required over one hundred years to complete— the change from a backward and predominantly agrarian nation to a modern and highly efficient industrial and technological state. Only the economic developments in modern Japan might be considered comparable. Even the economic progress of the United States, spectacular as that was, was not as phenomenal as the economic revolution in Germany, for Germany did not have the vast natural resources and the large immigrant population with which the United States was blessed.

German economic development owed a great deal to British, French, and American influences. Foreign technical inventions, capital investments, examples of business and industrial organization, and various other facets of economic life all played an important role in the industrialization of Germany.[2] But all these foreign examples were studied and developed with typical German thoroughness and systematic exploitation to bring Germany to a point where she far outstripped France and challenged both England and the United States, first for economic and then for political supremacy. By 1913 Germany was the outstanding competitor of Britain and the United States in world trade, in banking, in insurance, and in shipping, and the German mark was the leading rival of the British pound.

During the period from 1870 to 1914 Germany was transformed from

219

a predominantly agrarian to a predominantly industrial state, from a people of "poets and thinkers" to a nation in which technological skill, financial and industrial organization, and material progress became the outstanding features of public life.* The chief characteristics of this period were an increase in population, widespread urbanization, increased well-being, and extension of world trade. It was not a period of pure and undisturbed economic prosperity. There were some mild and even some severe economic depressions—in 1873, in 1877, in 1900, and 1907–1908. But the general economic tendency during this period was decidedly upward. National income increased from 23,500,000,000 marks in 1896 to 43,500,000,000 in 1913, while per capita income increased from 450 marks in 1896 to 645 marks in 1913.[3] Simon Kusnetz, using a slightly higher estimate, gives the following comparative figures for national income for 1913.[4]

	TOTAL	PER CAPITA
U.S.A.	$35,723,000,000	$368
United Kingdom	$ 9,840,000,000	$250
Germany	$11,934,000,000	$178
France	$ 6,387,000,000	$161

The prelude to rapid economic development came in the 1850's, the "first *Gründerzeit*," when the first great flowering of corporate business in Germany was initiated. All sorts of banking establishments, industrial plants, mining and railroad companies were founded during this time, and a relatively wild speculative boom was set in motion. It was the first speculative period that Germany experienced, and it was during this time that modern capitalism became the basis for the German national economy.[5] After a crisis in the 1860's came the second great boom period, in the 1870's (the so-called *Gründerjahre*), following the Franco-Prussian War. Whereas between 1851 and 1870, 295 new corporations, or *Aktiengesellschaften* as they were known in German, were formed, with a capital of about 2,404 million marks, between 1870 and 1874 there were 857 new corporations formed, with a capital of 3,306 million marks.[6] A depression in 1873 and another one in 1877 were followed by a slow upturn to 1887 and a new wave of prosperity initiated by the development of the electrical industry after 1895. The depression of 1900–1901 was followed by another wave of prosperity up to the depression of 1907–1908, and then another great upswing to the outbreak of World War I.

---

* Exception may be taken to this chronological delimitation of the German industrial revolution in the same way that some historians have criticized the use of the term "industrial revolution" for England. Here too factual data may be mustered to show the existence of numerous instances of industrial development in Germany long before 1870 and even long before 1850. Such "antecedents" are readily available for practically every fact or event in history. A distinction must be drawn between individual instances and a dominant and widespread trend. Individual instances of industrial development are to be found in Germany before 1850; the number of instances begins to increase appreciably in the 1850's, but it is not until 1870–1900 that we have a veritable torrent of industrial development. Such a quickening of tempo of development may be appropriately designated as a "revolution."

As usual in the case of industrialization, there was a radical change in the population, both with respect to total numbers and with respect to distribution. At the opening of the nineteenth century the total population of the area equivalent to Bismarckian Germany was a little over 24 million. By 1914 it had risen to 67,790,000. In 1914, too, density of population was about 125 inhabitants per square kilometer. The change in the density of population is indicated by the following figures:[7]

	1800	1910
Silesia	48 per sq.km.	130 per sq.km.
Rhineland	70 " " "	264 " " "
Saxony	78 " " "	321 " " "

The period witnessed a rapid drift to the towns and cities and the development of the large urban centers of modern Germany. In 1820 Berlin had about 200,000 inhabitants; in 1910 it was the third largest city in Europe and the fifth largest city in the world, with a population of 2,071,907. The rapid development of the large industrial cities is indicated in the following table of population growth of the eight largest cities in Germany:[8]

POPULATION GROWTH OF EIGHT LARGEST GERMAN CITIES

City	1820	1870	1900	1910
Berlin	199,510	774,498	1,888,313	2,071,907
Breslau	78,930	207,997	428,517	517,367
Cologne	54,937	200,312	464,272	600,304
Essen	4,715	99,887	290,208	410,392
Frankfurt a. M.	41,458	126,095	314,026	414,576
Hamburg	127,985	308,446	721,744	953,103
Leipzig	37,375	177,818	519,726	644,644
Munich	62,290	440,886	659,392	665,266

The total population showed a very marked shift from rural to urban inhabitants. Whereas in 1861 the rural population was still 69.3 per cent of the total, by 1910 the relative position of urban to rural population had turned a complete cycle with the town dwellers outnumbering the rural inhabitants by 60 to 40 per cent:

CHANGES FROM RURAL TO URBAN POPULATION [9]

	Total	Per Cent of Rural	Per Cent of Urban *
1871	41,059,000	63.9	36.1
1880	45,234,000	58.6	41.4
1890	49,428,000	57.5	42.5
1900	56,367,000	45.6	54.4
1910	64,926,000	40.0	60.0

* Urban = population of 2,000 or more.

The changes in occupational distribution are revealed in the following table:

OCCUPATIONAL DISTRIBUTION (in per cent)

	1843 [10]	1882 [11]	1907 [11]
Agriculture and Forestry	60.84–61.34	42.3	34.0
Industry and Crafts	23.37	35.5	39.7
Commerce and Communications	1.95	8.4	13.7
Public and Private Services	4.5–5.0	5.8	6.8
Domestic Service	———	8.0	5.8

The progress in economic well-being was also reflected in emigration figures. During the middle of the nineteenth century millions of Germans left their homeland to find better opportunities elsewhere. Between 1881 and 1890, 1,342,000 emigrated; from 1890 to 1900 this number dropped to 528,000; from 1901 to 1910 there was a still sharper decline to 220,000, and in 1912 only 18,500 Germans left their fatherland.[12]

As a result of the rapid and extensive industrial development Germany ceased to be a food-exporting country and became a food-importing country. Agricultural progress was stimulated by technical and scientific developments which increased the yield and productivity of the land under cultivation. The production of sugar from beet roots was one of the most important developments in German agriculture after Liebig's discoveries in agricultural chemistry. But technical progress was not enough to enable agriculture to withstand the onslaught of industrialism. Appeals for government help came from the agrarian interests. With the advent of competition from the United States on the grain market, the landowning interests, formerly free traders, combined with the new industrial classes to force Bismarck to change German commercial policy to one of protection. In 1879 the first protective tariff was passed by the Reichstag. This, however, was also not sufficient to preserve the economic position of agriculture.

An extended and often bitter debate developed in political and economic circles in Germany on the question of the agrarian versus the industrial state. In 1897 Karl Oldenberg delivered his famous address "Deutschland als Industriestaat," in which he compared the national economy to a house of several floors with agriculture the street floor and industry the top floor. If industry, argued Oldenberg, develops beyond the capacities of the street floor then it must be supported by pillars resting on someone else's land. Such development, he declared, imperils the national independence of the state. A host of economists from Adolf Wagner to Pohle and Sering all called for a government policy which would protect and support agriculture and thus secure a balanced economy which would enhance the military security of the nation. Free-trade economists like Lujo Brentano and Dietzel supported industrialization.

A large sector of the German population remained on the farms. Holdings varied from small and middle-sized farms to the large holdings of the feudal nobles in East Prussia. German farmers continued to raise wheat and rye, livestock, fruit trees, hops for beer, grapes for wines, beet sugar, and tobacco. The drain of the rural population to the cities made for a dearth of seasonal and casual agricultural labor, which was taken care of by an influx of foreign farm labor from Austria-Hungary and Russia. Over 300,000 foreign laborers would come into Germany every summer. The large landed estates in the east were usually in heavy debt, and there was constant pressure upon the state for financial assist-ance. The Berlin *Post* described these estates as follows: [13]

There are estates, far from the larger towns, with good communication, which, conducted on the old economic methods, give little return, which are burdened with mortgages and other debts, and are unable to support adequately the numerous members of their old families. And these are families whose names appear often in the Prussian officers' list, are engraved in golden letters in the rolls of honor of Frederick the Great, and their preservation is a profound interest of the state, in that this military spirit of the best ages lives in them as a tradition, that imponderable quantity which cannot be attained or imitated at a moment's notice by others. How can these families, how can the landed proprietors in the east especially be helped?

This question continued to be asked down to the days of the *Osthilfe* in the Weimar period, and it never found a complete solution.

Apart from indebtedness, however, agriculture in Germany continued to need state aid, in the form of tariffs, subsidies, and loans, to keep it prosperous. The Bund der Landwirte, or Landlords' League, was the pres-sure agency established to further these needs. In 1907 it numbered 282,000 members from all over Germany. The Bund der Landwirte came to exercise a powerful influence in government circles. It was usually allied with the Conservative party, although the smaller farmers in Bavaria, Württemberg, and Baden usually voted Center. The solid bloc of farming interests was able to induce a governmental policy which fa-vored the landed interests and which thus kept Germany from going the way of England to almost complete industrialization.

All these measures to support agriculture, however, were not able to keep Germany self-sufficient. It had to depend on imports, especially of livestock and animal products. In 1912 Germany imported 200,000 cattle of all kinds, over $10,000,000 worth of beef, $5,000,000 worth of bacon, $5,000,000 worth of milk and cream, and $80,000,000 worth of butter, lard, and fats. Dependence on fats was greatest, and this proved to be one of the most vulnerable points in the German economy during both world wars. Altogether Germany depended for about 20 per cent of its agri-cultural needs on imports from abroad. These came mainly from Holland, Denmark, and the Danubian areas.

The last three decades of the nineteenth century witnessed the rapid onset of all the forces of modern industrialism and all the problems that usually come with it. Old industries like the textile industry were modernized and expanded; new industries, especially heavy industry, reached an unprecedented peak of development; financial and banking organization and expansion were adapted to the new needs, and government policies were modified accordingly. A rapid expansion of railway lines, waterways, and post and telegraph communication made possible the swift movement of raw materials and finished goods. In 1860 there were 11,026 kilometers of railroad tracks in Germany; in 1870 these were increased to 18,560; in 1890 to 41,818; in 1900 to 49,878; and in 1910 to 59,031 kilometers.[14] While private initiative was most active in the early period of railroad development, there was increased participation by the local states. Between 1879 and 1884 most of the Prussian roads were brought under state control. The other states in the Reich soon followed suit. Central Reich ownership of all the railroads, however, did not come until the Weimar period.

The most significant developments in the German economy took place in the coal and iron industries. J. M. Keynes was not far from the truth when he observed that "the German Empire was built more truly on coal and iron than on blood and iron." [15] The coal output in Germany rose from 29,398,000 metric tons in 1871 to 191,500,000 in 1913. During the same period the coal output of Britain increased from 118,000,000 metric tons to 292,000,000. The German figures do not include lignite or brown coal. The principal coal fields were those of the Ruhr, in Westphalia; the Saar basin, Upper and Lower Silesia, and Zwickau, in Saxony. In 1873 the Gelsenkirchener Bergwerks Aktiengesellschaft was formed in the Ruhr, and it became the most powerful coal syndicate in Europe. In 1913 it had 53,059 workers, 2,439 officials, and capital stock of 180,-000,000 marks.

The marriage of coal and iron produced the most powerful iron and steel industry in Europe. There were more iron-smelting, iron-working, and engineering firms started in Prussia between 1871 and 1874 than in all the previous years of the century. To the older Borsig locomotive works in Berlin-Tegel were now added the greatly expanded Krupp works in Essen,[16] carried on by Alfred Krupp (1812–1887), his son Friedrich Alfred Krupp (1854–1902), and the latter's son-in-law Gustav Krupp von Bohlen und Halbach (1870–1949); the huge Thyssen and Company works in Mühlheim in the Ruhr, established in 1871 by August Thyssen (1842–1926) and carried on by his son Fritz Thyssen (1873–1948).[17] In the Saar, Karl Freiherr von Stumm-Halberg (1836–1901) created a vast iron and steel empire over which he presided in autocratic, baronial fashion so that his companies were often referred to as "the Kingdom of Stumm" or "Saarabien." In Silesia Prince Guido Henckel von Donnersmarck (1830–1926) developed the coal and iron resources, then expanded his interests

:o the Rhineland and became, next to Krupp, the richest man in Germany. His private fortune was estimated in 1914 at 300 million gold marks.

The output of pig iron, a convenient gauge for the development of the iron and steel industry, rose from 1,564,000 metric tons in 1871 to 14,-794,000 metric tons in 1910. A comparison with the two other large iron and steel producing nations, the United Kingdom and the United States, is indicated in the following table: [18]

OUTPUT OF PIG IRON (in metric tons) 1871–1910

	GERMANY	U.S.A.	UNITED KINGDOM
1871	1,564,000	———	6,500,000
1880	2,729,038	3,896,554	7,800,266
1890	4,658,451	9,349,943	8,030,374
1900	8,520,390	14,009,624	9,052,107
1910	14,794,000	27,742,000	10,173,000

The development in England of the Thomas-Gilchrist open-hearth process for smelting ore, which for the first time rendered phosphoric iron ores completely available for the manufacture of steel, made possible the exploitation of the Lorraine iron mines which Germany had annexed from France in 1870, and from then on German iron and steel production forged ahead. By 1910 Germany outstripped the United Kingdom and was second only to the United States in the output of pig iron.

The increased output of iron and steel was reflected in the general expansion of industry in Germany and in increased specialization in iron and steel products, such as machines and tools, cutlery, and precision instruments. The greatest share of the products of heavy industry were used (1) to build up the railroad system, (2) to create one of the mightiest merchant fleets in the world, and (3) to develop the armaments industry.

With the advent of the age of discoveries in early modern times, in which Germany did not participate, Germany had lost the position of a mercantile nation which it had enjoyed in the late Middle Ages. Now in the nineteenth century the glories of the Old Hansa were revived by the Hamburg-Amerika Linie (HAPAG) and the North German Lloyd. The first of these was formed in 1847, but it was not until Albert Ballin (1857–1918), a Hamburg Jew, joined the firm in 1886 that its spectacular progress began.[19] From a fleet of 22 ocean steamers with a gross registered tonnage of 60,531 in 1886, Ballin developed the HAPAG fleet to 172 ocean steamers in 1913, with a gross registered tonnage of 1,028,762. Ballin made the HAPAG the foremost shipping company of Germany and of the world of his day. He introduced fast ocean liners and fitted them with new standards of traveling comfort. He expanded the lines not only to the United States but also to Latin America and the Far East. Despite the handicap of both Jewish and merchant origin, he became one of the close personal advisers of Wilhelm II. The degree of his influence has been greatly overrated, largely because his Jewish affiliation made it so unusual, and he failed to influence public policy in the cause closest to his heart—Anglo-German understanding—but there was nevertheless a high degree of personal intimacy which was as indicative of Ballin's great commercial attainments as it was of the Kaiser's absorbing preoccupation with navalism and *Weltpolitik*.

The other great shipping company was the North German Lloyd of Bremen, founded in 1857 by Hermann Heinrich Meier (1809–1898) and further developed under the administration of Director Lohmann. From Bremen and Hamburg now sailed a host of passenger and freight ships that by 1913 constituted the second mightiest merchant fleet in the world. From a fleet of 147 ships with 8,994 gross registered tons in 1870, the German merchant marine grew to number, in 1913, 2,098 ships with 4,380,000 gross registered tons.

Of even greater political as well as economic significance was the expansion of the armaments industry. From a small ironworks employing 140 men in 1846, the Krupp works of Essen grew into one of the mightiest munition plants, employing 68,300 workers in 1912. Alfred Krupp se-cured a practical monopoly for the supply of the Prussian army, and this gave him tremendous influence in the country. The growth of the German army helped increase the Krupp business, and the renown of Krupp artillery, established in the Franco-Prussian War, brought orders from all parts of the world. Krupp's had its agents all over the world, most of them being trained army officers or young noblemen. These helped their firm become one of the most notorious "merchants of death." But inside Germany the armaments industry was considered not only indispensable for political and national interests; it was also acclaimed as one of the mainstays of German economic prosperity. Even the liberal economist Gerhart von Schulze-Gaevernitz declared: "The German Reich is not oppressed by its armaments but is enabled through them to continue to make economic progress."

The automobile industry did not develop to large proportions in Germany until after World War I. But already before that time the firm of Adam Opel (1837–1895), of Rüsselheim, near Frankfurt am Main, was converting its plant from the manufacture of sewing machines and bicycles to that of automobiles. Gottlieb Daimler (1834–1900) in Stuttgart, and Carl Friedrich Benz (1844–1929) in Mannheim were laying the foundations for the subsequently famous Daimler-Benz auto works, and Robert Bosch (1861–1942), one of the unique figures among German industrialists, after a trip to the United States in 1884 returned to Stuttgart to become one of the largest producers of ignition and electrical parts for automobiles.[20] Altogether, however, there were only 64,000 automobiles in Germany in August, 1941.[21]

The German electrical industry was the product chiefly of the work of two men, Werner von Siemens (1816–1892) and Emil Rathenau (1838–1915). The former was one of the best examples of an engineer and inventor in business. He organized the firm of Siemens and Halske in Berlin in 1847 for telegraphic construction. But in 1866 he invented the electric dynamo, and Siemens and Halske became the leading company in the field of heavy current. Siemens introduced the first electric railway and soon began to cover Germany with an extensive network of trolley systems. Rathenau returned from the Paris Exposition of 1881 with the German patent rights for Edison's electric-light lamps.[22] At a party of leading business, industrial, social, and political figures in Berlin, Rathenau gave a spectacular demonstration of electric lighting by suddenly converting the fashionable candle-lit salon into a brilliantly illuminated room flooded with electric light. He created the German Edison Company in 1883 which later became the Allgemeine Elektrizitäts Gesellschaft, or AEG for short, the German parallel to the American General Electric Company, in the same way that Siemens and Halske may be compared to the American Western Electric Company.

During the period between 1890 and 1910 there was bitter rivalry between the two firms. The AEG was built on the spread of mass consumption and on the creation of mass demand for electric current and electric products. The Siemens firm retained more of the traditional artisan spirit. Siemens was strongly opposed to speculation. "We are not merchants," he once proudly declared. Until his death Siemens strongly resisted the corporate business form and outside control of his firm. His policy was to produce the best possible product, give it publicity, and wait for customers. Whereas the AEG was active chiefly in the competitive field, Siemens attained strong influence in government circles and secured monopolistic controls. In 1903 he acquired the firm of Schuckert and Company and constituted the Siemens-Schuckert Werke A.G., which competed with the AEG in the heavy-current field. To both the Siemens and Rathenau groups must be ascribed the rapid and extensive electrification of Germany, the construction of a wide network of electric railways and municipal and overland power transmission systems. In 1895 the electrical industry employed 26,000 people; in 1906 the number had risen to 107,000. The growth of this industry was a basic factor in creating the economic prosperity in Germany between 1890 and 1902. Moreover, Germany took the world lead in the utilization of electricity for all sorts of purposes. In 1913 Germany produced 34 per cent of the world's output of electrical products as compared to 29 per cent for the United States.

No branch of industry revealed such intimate connection with science as the chemical industries. The term "chemical industries" covers a wide and varied range of industrial activities. Germany was rich in salts and potash beds in Prussian Saxony, Thuringia, Hanover, and Alsace. The potash beds began to be worked in 1860. In 1889 about 1,000,000 tons of potash were mined; in 1899 this rose to 3,000,000 and by 1910 to 8,000,000.[23] In 1878 the total *world* output of sulphuric acid was about 1,000,000 tons, of which Germany produced 112,000 tons. In 1907 Germany alone produced 1,402,000 tons. Ammonia production rose from 84,000 tons in 1897 to 287,000 tons in 1907; potassium salts increased from 375,000 tons in 1871 to 9,607,000 tons in 1911. The number of people employed in these industries in 1885 was 78,000; in 1913 they numbered 282,000.

The most spectacular developments in chemical industries came in the fields of synthetic dyes, synthetic substitutes for rubber, oil, and nitrates, photographic supplies, and in new drugs and pharmaceuticals. Here science, industry, and national politics dovetailed beautifully to turn organic chemistry into a mammoth industry which came to affect every aspect of modern civilization and which also became a most powerful instrument of war. The story revolves largely around the utilization of by-products of coal. August Wilhelm von Hofmann, a pupil of Liebig, opened up this field of research in the 1850's. Hofmann taught for several years in England. Here one of his pupils, William Henry Perkin, succeeded in 1856 in producing the first synthetic dye. Hofmann returned to Germany with this discovery, and soon scores of new synthetic dyes were developed. The expansion of the textile industry created an increased demand for dyes, and the growth of the coal industry provided the increased amount of coal tar from which the synthetic dyes were made. England too used many dyes for her textile industry, but since she had access to natural dyes in her colonies she did not evince too great interest in the new technical developments. Germany, on the other hand, was forced to depend on synthetic dyes. "For Germany synthetics were the wealth of the Indies." Several chemical companies were formed, from which was to emerge later the renowned as well as notorious I. G. Farben works. Of these companies the most important were the chemical works started at Höchst, outside Frankfurt am Main, in 1863, the Badische Anilin und Sodafabrik at Ludwigshafen in 1865, the Elberfelder Farbenfabriken, the Bayer Company at Leverkusen, and the Agfa works in Berlin.[24]

Unlike the British and American chemical industries of the same period, German industry engaged the services of large numbers of trained scientists and engineers. In 1900 the six biggest German chemical firms employed over 650 trained scientists. At the same time the British chemical industry employed altogether no more than 30 to 40. Important scientific discoveries were thus made possible by German industry which of course also paid off well in dividends. Paul Ehrlich discovered salvarsan, for the treatment of syphilis, in an I. G. Farben laboratory near Frankfurt provided for him by the industry. The drug in this way became a monopoly of I. G. Farben and was withheld from the Western nations when World

War I broke out. Anesthetics were similarly developed by scientists in the service of the German chemical industry and likewise formed a monopoly. Another epoch-making discovery, which made it possible for Germany to hold out in the First World War as long as she did, was the synthetic ammonia process devised by Fritz Haber for producing ammonia from atmospheric nitrogen. Thereby the German military machine, deprived by the British blockade of the Chilean nitrates necessary for explosives, was able to manufacture its own nitrates at home. Professor Haber, a Jew, was rewarded by Hitler for this patriotic service by being removed in 1933 from all his academic posts, and he died in exile in 1934. The large-scale production of synthetic rubber and oil did not come until after World War I, and the final amalgamation of all these various companies into the vast I. G. Farben Trust did not materialize until 1925. But all the important scientific, economic, industrial, and political aspects were well established by the time World War I broke out.

The tremendous expansion of German industry brought about not only a great increase in domestic commerce and economic well-being but also a vast development of foreign trade. The trade-mark "Made in Germany," at first imposed by Great Britain to protect consumers against supposedly inferior competition, came to be a symbol of expert craftsmanship and high-grade quality. German exports were disseminated to all parts of the world. Imports increased as well as exports, as indicated in the following table: [25]

GERMAN FOREIGN TRADE (in marks)

	EXPORTS	IMPORTS
1872	2,492,000,000	3,465,000,000
1880	2,977,000,000	2,844,000,000
1890	3,410,000,000	4,273,000,000
1900	4,753,000,000	6,043,000,000
1910	7,475,000,000	8,934,000,000
1913	10,097,000,000	10,770,000,000

German capital was also exported abroad in the form of large investments in the Americas, the Near East, and Far East. German capital played a prominent role in the financing of railroad construction in the United States. In 1913 there were 30 billion marks of German capital investments abroad, while 5 billion marks of foreign capital were invested in Germany.

Germany thus went through a radical industrial revolution in less than thirty years. Old industries, like textiles, were modernized and expanded; new industries, new to Germany or new to the world at large, were organized and made Germany one of the most powerful economic nations of the world. How can this economic miracle be explained? We are confronted here with one of those baffling historical problems which allows for rational historical explanation only up to a certain point, and beyond that we must resort to speculative sociological or philosophical theories.

There is no doubt that even though considerable progress had been made before 1870, the political unification of Germany, first in the North German Confederation and then in the Second Reich, was a powerful stimulant to dynamic economic development. Political unity brought with it unified economic legislation in many fields, such as a unified system of weights and measures, a partially unified postal system (except for Bavaria and Württemberg), a new and unified currency system based on the gold standard, which was largely the work of the National Liberal leader Ludwig Bamberger, and the establishment of the central Reichsbank in 1875. All these measures created more stable and more favorable conditions for commercial and industrial activity.

The victory over France in 1871 brought certain economic advantages to Germany which made possible some of the spectacular economic developments. The indemnity of 5 billion francs collected from France was responsible for an immediate economic "boom," but it was also the cause of the "bust" of 1873–1874. Much more tangible and lasting advantages came from the annexation of Alsace-Lorraine. These provinces brought into the German Reich a highly developed textile industry and rich iron-ore deposits in Lorraine which, after the development of the Thomas-Gilchrist open-hearth process of smelting ore, were capable of being exploited to full advantage in combination with the rich coal fields of the Ruhr. The accession of the Alsatian potash deposits, when added to the potash deposits in Central Germany, gave to the German Reich a virtual monopoly of these products. Thus the military triumph of the new national state over the hitherto dominant political and industrial power on the Continent gave to Germany new resources and new wherewithal to proceed on a program of rapid industrialization.

One of the most important factors in stimulating German economic progress and making possible the expansion of industry and trade at such a rate of speed was the role of the German banks. The German banks, from the start, occupied a radically different position in the economy of the nation than did the banks in England or those in the early economic history of the United States.[26] It was most characteristic of the German banks that they were concerned not so much with "circulation credit" as with "production credit." The older private banks and banks of issue were not capable of meeting the new increased demand for capital for industrial development. The new banks thus became the active agents in promoting industry and trade and even themselves engaged in various industrial enterprises. Traditional and orthodox economic thinking looked askance at such developments. Albert Schäffle, one of the earliest economists in Germany, already in 1856 advocated the creation of "special economic organizations" to meet the needs for new capital, and warned

German public opinion "not to be terrified by the mere catchword 'crédit mobilier' like children by a bogey." [27]

Interestingly enough, it was the Crédit mobilier of the brothers Pereire in France, which in turn owed its origin to Saint-Simonian socialist propaganda, which was an important factor in encouraging the establishment of the earliest German banks for the financing of industry. The Darmstädter Bank was organized two years after the founding of the Crédit mobilier (1851), and the statutes for organization which it adopted were similar to those of the French bank. Abraham Oppenheimer, of Mannheim, one of the founders of the Crédit mobilier, was also one of the co-founders of the Darmstädter Bank, and Hess, one of the high officials of the Crédit mobilier, was one of the first directors of the Darmstädter Bank.

The modern German bank is a combination of commercial bank, investment bank, and investment trust, backed by a central bank. The new German banks participated immediately and directly in the establishment of industrial corporations. They provided a huge extension of credit facilities which allowed for an unending expansion of business enterprise. The banks participated directly in the management of industrial enterprises and most frequently delegated their own officers to the boards of directors of their industrial corporations. "The German credit bank," wrote Schulze-Gaevernitz, "allied with the active forces in industry itself, industrialized Germany." [28]

The most important German banks active in the development of the German economy were the A. Schaafhausensche Bankverein, established in Cologne in 1848; the Diskonto Gesellschaft, founded by the liberal statesman David Hansemann in 1851, but owing its enormous development to his son Adolf von Hansemann (1826–1903),* who for many years was the towering figure in the banking world; the Darmstädter Bank, established in 1853; the Berliner Handelsgesellschaft, established in 1856 but reorganized in 1883 and greatly expanded under the direction of the witty and elusive Jew Carl Fürstenberg who had acquired his financial training in the old firm of Gerson Bleichröder; the greatest of all these banks, the Deutsche Bank, founded in 1870 and developed under the direction of the phenomenal Georg von Siemens (1839–1901), cousin of the electrical wizard of Germany, Werner von Siemens, and aided by the Jewish banker Max Steinthal; † the Dresdner Bank, established in 1872, which attained its greatest glories under the leadership of Konsul Eugen Gutmann.‡ In Silesia the Schlesische Bankverein, established in 1856 in Breslau, carried out the same functions.

---

* In 1914 the Diskonto Gesellschaft took over the A. Schaafhausensche Bankverein.
† In 1929 the Deutsche Bank was merged with the Diskonto Gesellschaft to form the Deutsche Bank und Diskonto Gesellschaft under the presidency of Max Steinthal.
‡ In 1931 the Dresdner Bank took over the Darmstädter Bank.

The Diskonto Gesellschaft was originally founded as a traditional bank but in 1855–1856 it changed its constitution to become a "financing bank" after the pattern set by the Crédit mobilier and Darmstädter Bank. The latter in its first annual business report in 1853 stated: "By means of its eminent position and clear insight into the whole situation of German industry it is fitted to assist . . . in directing capital and the spirit of enterprise into the channels corresponding to the requirements of the moment. Its offices at home and abroad are intended to facilitate export and the thousand and one relations between German industry and the money market." [29] The Berliner Handelsgesellschaft, in its first circular in 1856, designated its fields of activity as "Banking, trade, and industrial enterprises of all sorts." Its operations extended "in particular to industrial and agricultural enterprises, mining, smelting, construction of canals, roads, and railroads, as well as to the establishment, amalgamating and consolidating of corporations and the floating of stocks and bonds for such enterprises." [30]

Some of the very large industrial enterprises, like Krupp and Thyssen, were at first independent of the financial influence of the banking interests. The chemical industry also was relatively independent of the banks. But even Thyssen and Krupp eventually came to establish very close relations with the banks. Most other industrial enterprises, large and small, owed their expansion to the support of these and smaller German banks. The Berliner Handelsgesellschaft and the Deutsche Bank were the chief financial backers of the electrical industry. Emil Rathenau, "the man with an idea but without money," found sympathetic ears in both Georg Siemens and Carl Fürstenberg; Max Steinthal and the Deutsche Bank helped support the firm of Gebrüder Mannesmann, and so it was with thousands of other German industrial concerns. Nor was this activity confined to domestic industry and trade. The German banks helped finance German exports and also participated in large-scale financing of industries abroad. Telegraph and railroads, mining, and scores of other industrial enterprises in Austria, Russia, Sweden, Italy, Africa, the Near East, Latin America, and the United States were actively financed by German banking interests. The Deutsche Bank, under Siemens, was particularly active in foreign industrial developments, coming to the aid of Henry Villard and the Northern Pacific in the United States, constructing the Anatolian Railroad in Asia Minor and entering the field of high international politics with its role in the construction of the Berlin-Baghdad Railroad.

The German banks also developed a wide network of branch banking and were thus a tremendous factor in making possible the rapid industrial and commercial expansion and also in impressing upon the German economy its special characteristics.

All the factors discussed thus far—technological and scientific progress, political unification, the fruits of victory, and the peculiar development of

German banking—provide an explanation for the incentives and the conditions under which the German economy was able to develop as it did. They do not explain, however, the inner drive, the capacity to make use of the conditions present, and above all the dynamic energy and systematic thoroughness with which all these conditions, favorable as they were, were exploited. To account for this, writers usually resort to such elusive and intangible conceptions as the "genius of the people," the inventive spirit, "characteristic" German thoroughness as well as "innate" German "ruthlessness." All these types of explanation, rooted in philosophical conceptions of the historical process, are as easy to dispose of by rational and scientific analysis as they are difficult to be replaced by more satisfactory substitutes. For in the last analysis the character and quality of the human material, whether that of the leader or of those led, is a factor which is perhaps more basic even for economic progress than the material and more concrete factors present. That is why the attempt by Thorstein Veblen to explain the industrial revolution in Germany in "matter-of-fact" sociological terms rather than by resorting to metaphysical concepts, open though it is to many minor criticisms, remains the most grandiose and at the same time the most satisfying explanation for the inner causes of Germany's phenomenal economic and industrial progress and its outstripping of the older industrial lead of both France and England.[31]

The prime cause for German economic development, according to Veblen, was not the inventive genius of the Germans but its very opposite, the capacity to borrow from others. Historically it is true that in the industrial field, as later in the military field, most of the spectacular developments in Germany were based upon the more thorough and efficient utilization of inventions first made in France, England, or the United States. But sociologically speaking, the borrower always has a great advantage over the original inventor. The borrower is not troubled by traditional inertia, by technological obsolescence, by capital investments in older technical plants, and so on. The borrower can take over, lock, stock, and barrel, the newest, the most efficient, and the best, and start building his industrial or business enterprise upon fresh foundations at the highest point of industrial progress and without the weight of the dead wood either of tradition or of previous installations that are neither so bad that they must be discarded at all costs nor so efficient as to be the best in the field.

The German captains of industry [writes Veblen] who came to take the discretionary management in the new era were fortunate enough not to have matriculated from the training school of a country town based on a retail business in speculative real estate and political jobbery managed under the rule of "prehension, division and silence." The country being at the same time in the main . . . not committed to antiquated sites and routes for its industrial plants; the men who exercised the discretion were free to choose, with an eye single to the mechanical expediency of locations for the pursuit of industry. Having no obsolescent equipment and no out-of-date trade connections to cloud the issue, they were also free to take over the processes of the new industry at their best and highest efficiency, rather than content themselves with compromises between the best equipment known and what used to be the best a few years or a few decades ago.[32]

2. INDUSTRIAL CONCENTRATION

The German economy exhibited a greatly accelerated development in the concentration of industry and banking. The trend toward huge enterprises, or *Riesenbetriebe,* as they were known in Germany, came soon after the general economic quickening. And this was followed by an enormous development of combinations of enterprises of various types, most of them generally subsumed under the title "cartel." German writers have benevolently referred to this development as an expression of the deeply rooted *"Genossenschaft"* or co-operative spirit of the German people as contrasted with Anglo-Saxon individualism. Non-German writers have pointed to it as the economic expression of Prussianism, pan-Germanism, and imperialist drive. The truth is that it was a combination of both, plus the more important fact that it was the same expression of dynamic rapidity of development in the *forms* of business organization as was present in the actual economic, technical, and industrial developments.

What is a cartel? There is no easy and universally acceptable definition. The very definition of a cartel usually involves value judgments regarding motivation and economic usefulness, which are subjects of controversy. Robert Liefmann, the outstanding German authority on cartels, defines a cartel as "an association based upon a contractual agreement between enterprises in the same field of business which, while retaining their legal independence, associate themselves with a view to exacting a monopolistic influence on the market." [33] He underscores the important point that cartels are "collective monopolies of entrepreneurs" only in their capacity as *sellers.* Perhaps more satisfying is the definition of Herbert von Beckerath, who calls cartels "associations of business enterprises in a particular branch of industry, remaining independent, for the purpose of the regulation of production and the market in the interest of the profit-earning capacity of the member firms." [34]

Cartels were of different types, depending on their primary purpose. There were cartels for the regulation of marketing conditions, cartels for the regulation of prices, cartels for the limitation of production or supply, district cartels which assigned to the members monopoly of particular areas, cartels for centralizing the entire domestic market in the given industry, and cartels for foreign trade. These types were not mutually exclusive. Cartels very often assumed several or all of these functions. And over and above these, German cartels later took the lead in establishing international cartels. Cartels were founded upon agreements which ran for a specified period of duration.

Economic historians have correctly pointed out that cartels existed as far back as the seventeenth and eighteenth centuries and that in several important aspects the economic activities of the modern cartel were paralleled in the guild activities of the Middle Ages. This does not alter the fact, nevertheless, that cartels were essentially a product of modern economic development and that Germany was the classic land of cartel organization. Here cartels developed with amazing rapidity in practically all branches of industry. Precise information regarding the inner workings of cartels and their exact number has always been hard to get at. The first study of German cartels was published in 1883 by F. Kleinwächter, a professor of economics in Czernowitz, Rumania.[35] Kleinwächter tells in the preface to his study that he had heard of the existence of cartels but he did not know to whom to address himself for information regarding them. He proceeded to write letters to many businessmen in Germany requesting data. He got sufficient material to publish his essay, but he adds, "For the most part the people involved in the cartels obviously keep information regarding them pretty secret." Sombart, writing thirty years later, lamented the fact that "all that is related to the institution of cartels is covered with an impenetrable veil," as if one were dealing with "secret gambling associations or gangs of counterfeiters."[36] Liefmann and Passow, writing in the 1920's, still complained about the paucity of precise data. Only after the German collapse of 1945 did a great deal of secret data regarding cartels fall into the hands of the Allied military authorities. But most of that is still either unavailable or in too confused a state to be used for research purposes.

The "official" defender of cartels, Emil Kirdorf, once stated that the institution of cartels arose "out of desperate need" and was developed only in order to overcome the influence of poor business conditions. Actually this was not so. As Sombart has shown, the greatest period of cartel formation came during the periods of greatest prosperity. In 1865 there were approximately 4 cartels, in 1875 about 8, in 1885 about 90, in 1890 about 210, and at the time of the government investigation of cartels in 1905 there were 366.[37] During the period of 1890–1905, the influence of American trusts was of paramount importance. Many German businessmen and industrialists traveled to the United States, were impressed with the development of trusts, and proceeded to organize cartels when they returned home.* Most economists, especially the German defenders of cartels, made a sharp distinction between cartels and trusts, and

---

* A very good example of this is the architect of the great I. G. Farbenindustrie, Carl Duisberg, who tells in his autobiography of his trip to the United States in 1903 and the effect of his study of American trusts. See *Meine Lebenserinnerungen* (Leipzig, 1933). See also the biographical article by A. Weiss in vol. iii of *Die grossen Deutschen*.

in terms of static definition there is indeed a difference. The legally protected secrecy surrounding German cartels also helped to provide German cartels with an aura of high-minded and solid respectability which American trusts could never enjoy in the rough-and-tumble trust-busting period of American history, and this circumspect attitude was retained by the German enterprises until the revelations after World War II. Perhaps the best example of such high-sounding adulation of the German as compared with the American industrial combine was delivered by Gustav Schmoller before the Verein für Sozialpolitik in 1905. Schmoller was the great intellectual entrepreneur of modern Germany. A man of extensive rather than profound learning, always to be found in positions of strategic importance in German academic and intellectual life, he often shocked his high-placed conservative friends by consorting with radicals and debating with them, but he always ended up with a fairly "respectable" position on all matters of moment. Schmoller delivered a long address on cartels before the Verein für Sozialpolitik. In the course of this address he made the following comparison between American trusts and German cartels:

> Trustification easily creates a system of robbery and deceit, but the proper kind of cartelization creates more or less a system of justice and equity. The founders of trusts are mainly moneymakers who are egotists and want to fill up their pocketbooks; the directors of the cartels are educators who wish to bring about the triumph of the wide interests of a branch of industry over the egotistic interests of the individual. The system of trusts makes use of brutal and ruthless men of violence who are for the most part devoid of the higher cultivation of spirit and sentiment, lacking in sympathetic and social feelings, and finding happiness only in business and in the making of money. . . . The cartel system is, like a co-operative or merchants' association, an important element in the education of commercial and technical officials who want to make money but who have also learned to put themselves in the service of general interests and to administer the property of others in a loyal and honorable fashion.[38]

Much more realistic was Friedrich Naumann's comparison of a cartel to a *Staatenbund* and a trust to a *Bundesstaat*. Naumann observed, however, that political scientists always have had great difficulty in distinguishing between the two because a *Staatenbund* if administered in energetic fashion may easily become indistinguishable from a *Bundesstaat*. So a cartel, while technically allowing for the independence and autonomy of the individual member enterprises, nevertheless, if administered in energetic fashion, may reduce this independence to such a nominal character as to make it entirely indistinguishable from a trust.[39]

The process of cartelization in Germany spread through most branches of German business and industry from the most benign and least criticized cartel, that of the German booksellers, to the large combines in coal, iron, steel, and chemicals. The largest number of cartels was found in coal, iron, and other metals, chemicals, textiles, and brickmaking. A typical example of a powerful cartel was the Rhenish-Westphalian coal syndicate. In 1913 it comprised 87 large mining enterprises; it controlled 50 per cent of the total coal production of Germany and 95 per cent of the production in the Ruhr. While each firm retained nominal independence, this was hardly evident to the outside world. All sales were made through the syndicate; the syndicate controlled the warehouses and the entire Rhine River transport of coal. Thus it was to all intents and purposes impossible for any coal producer to operate independently in the Rhineland. But the coal cartel was also in a position to exercise a decisive influence on other basic industries by the prices it set for coal. By manipulating coal prices it was able either to encourage or discourage speculative movements in almost all the industries which depended upon coal. The steel cartel was another typical example. It comprised 31 large firms, and the central office of the cartel had power vested in it to inspect the books of all member firms and it could even order new installations for new types of production to be introduced in individual plants. The chemical cartel did not officially come into being until after World War I, in 1925.

The development of huge economic and industrial units created a new class of public figures in Germany. The *Direktors* and *General Direktors*, the great managerial organizers and administrators, came to replace the old time factory owners and businessmen as the real powers in German economic and political life. They were "ministers of new industrial governments." The two most prominent examples of such industrial power in imperial Germany were Emil Kirdorf (1847–1938),[40] in the coal, iron, and steel industries, and Carl Duisberg (1861–1935), the architect of the I. G. Farben combine.

German public opinion, when it first became aware of the new institution of the cartel, was generally suspicious of it. To many it was an American importation, and there was much talk in the 1890's of the "American danger." The uneasiness was of sufficient intensity to bring about a government investigation of cartels which was carried out from November, 1902, to June, 1905.[41] The influential Verein für Sozialpolitik underscored the importance of the problem by devoting its session of September 27, 1905, to the "Relation Between Cartels and State." Emil Kirdorf was invited to this session to present his official analysis of cartels, and Gustav Schmoller opened the proceedings with the address referred to above. The German Jurists' Association also devoted some of its sessions to this problem. Despite heated discussions and mild criticisms Germany never experienced the vehement anti-trust movements found in Anglo-Saxon countries. When Friedrich Naumann described the emergence of the cartel as the economic equivalent of the development of the unified national state from the weakness and anarchy of *Kleinstaaterei*, he was giving expression to sentiments that found a very sympathetic chord in German public opinion. Most people came to view the cartels as a natural product of Germany's greatness and especially as a very useful instrument for building up German world trade, prosperity, and national prestige. Even the Social Democrats, uncertain in the beginning in their attitude toward the cartels, later contented themselves with either lumping the issue into their general condemnation of the capitalist system or else they expounded the theory that such concentration of industry was a welcome step toward the realization of socialism. Adolf Braun and Bruno Schoenlank, the first Socialist writers to deal with cartels, did not condemn the institution. At the party congress in 1894, Max Schippel introduced a resolution on cartels. The original draft of his resolution sounded like a paean of praise for the cartels, and it labeled all efforts to regulate them as "reactionary legislative attempts." In its modified form Schippel's resolution was less specific in spelling out the word "cartels," but it called every "advance in the concentration of capital" a "step toward the realization of socialism." [42] The revisionist Socialist Richard Calwer pointed with admiration to the coal cartel in the Rhineland as a beautiful example of economic planning, and spoke of the "progressive character" of cartel production.[43]

The debate on the comparative virtues and social dangers of cartels went on in Germany all during the pre-war years as it did in the United States, but whereas the debate in the United States was eventually fought out in the legislative halls of Congress and resulted in legislation outlawing trusts and all forms of combinations in restraint of trade the debates in Germany were restricted largely to the sessions of learned societies and the columns of learned journals. Liberal social reformers like Brentano, Naumann, and Max Weber called for state regulation of cartels; practically no one ventured to advocate their abolition; and concretely no legislative action was ever taken with respect to cartels until after World War I, under the Weimar Republic. Not only did the state not oppose the cartels but in many instances it encouraged or even enforced the formation of cartels, as in the compulsory cartel formed in the potash industry in 1910. For the ruling powers as well as for the majority of German public opinion the cartels made possible German *Weltmacht*, and hence they were socially beneficial.

3. THE STATE AND ECONOMIC AFFAIRS

The failure to regulate cartels during the Second Reich should not be taken as an expression of *laissez faire* policy. The tradition of *laissez faire* in German economic policy was very weak and, except for a brief heyday in the 1850's and 1860's, was soon overshadowed by much more vigorous governmental policy. Reference has already been made to the state nationalization of railroads in 1879. Even more of community control and regulation was displayed in the municipalities. Here electrical power plants, gas works, water works, traction companies, slaughterhouses, and other utilities were taken over by the municipal governments from private enterprise. Among liberals and socialists outside Germany these developments were frequently hailed as outstanding examples of social reform and municipal socialism.[44]

The state intervened in the economic life of Germany in many other ways. Government actually engaged in industrial and business enterprises as an entrepreneur. The local state took over business or industrial enterprises formerly owned by ruling nobles, as in the case of breweries in Munich, porcelain factories in Meissen and Berlin, and tobacco factories in Strassburg. More extensive still was state management in mining, forestry, and large-scale agriculture. "Imperial Germany had gradually become an economic system of mixed private and public ownership. In this era the foundations were already laid on which later the war economy, the experiments of the Republic, and finally the National Socialist system could be built." [45]

A radical change in German commercial policy was brought about in 1879. Up to that time the commercial policy of Prussia, of the Zollverein and of the German Reich had been free trade. Among economists and publicists Manchestrian economic theories were dominant, and in government circles the feudal agrarian interests all favored free trade in the first half of the century. Up to the 1870's Germany was still exporting more grain than it imported. In the ministry sat Rudolf von Delbrück, the leading protagonist of free trade. True, Friedrich List had preached the gospel of protection to build up Germany industry, but his views did not become popular in Germany until after the policy of protection was inaugurated. The writings of the American antagonist of Ricardian economics and the exponent of protection, Henry C. Carey, were translated and popularized in Germany by Eugen Dühring and K. Adler in the 1860's and 1870's.

The change from free trade to protection was not primarily the product of an ideological revolution. It came about because of a change in world economic conditions. In the late 1870's German agriculture for the first time was confronted with foreign competition on the world grain market. Imports of grain into Germany began to exceed exports. The interests of the landed classes, hitherto identical with free trade, now demanded protection. For the first time the economic demands of heavy industry in the west and of agriculture in the south and east were united. The Conservative leader von Wedell-Malchow declared, "Protection of iron and grain are equally indispensable for the welfare of the Fatherland." Bismarck rapidly switched from a free-trade protagonist to become an advocate of protection. Moreover, he saw in the tariff duties a new source of revenue for the Reich, which would make him independent of the financing by the separate states; he also saw the possibility of using the tariff as a weapon of foreign policy and he was pressed into action by the economic depression after 1873, when the industrialists clamored for heavy duties on manufactured goods. In 1876 Delbrück left the ministry, thus removing from office the leading champion of free trade. The Reichstag elections of 1878 brought a protectionist majority consisting of Conservatives, Centrists, and National Liberals. On December 15, 1878, came the first official declaration by the government for protection. The Reichstag passed the tariff law on June 12, 1879, by a vote of 217 to 117. The purpose of the tariff was not, as List had wanted, merely to support infant industries. It was an aggressive tariff designed to keep up the prices in the home market to the advantage of industry and agriculture and at the expense of the home consumer.[46]

The industrialization of Germany brought in its wake most of the social, moral, and cultural problems generally associated with the effects of the industrial revolution.[47] These included problems of health, fatigue, monotony, child and women labor, hours of labor, crowded conditions of urban industrial centers, housing, the disruption of the traditional family relationships, the effects of mass culture and the esthetic revolts engendered thereby. All these issues presented themselves in full force before German public opinion in very much the same way they had appeared in England. The reaction in Germany, however, was more immediate and more widespread than was the case in England, and very much more so than in the United States. Almost with the very inception of industrialism in Germany, Socialists, liberals, social reformers, and religious leaders began to point a warning finger at the deteriorating effects of the new industrial developments and to call for either private or governmental action to counteract the evils of industrialism. In 1855 the Prussian minister von der Heydt, after hearing a report from factory inspectors of Düsseldorf, Aachen, and Arnsberg of conditions in those cities, exclaimed, "If your reports are true, then I would rather that all of industry go to ruin." This was not the path chosen, however. To cope with most of these social problems, a highly developed system of social legislation was carried through, in which municipalities, local states, and the Reich participated and which made Germany not only the classic land of cartels but also the classic welfare state before World War I. A British admirer of this phase of German policy wrote in 1906: "At every turn German statesmen and philanthropists have endeavored . . . to ensure and to safeguard the conditions of physical efficiency, leaving as little as possible to chance, covering as far as may be the whole range of life and action, and doing it with the thoroughness and system which are characteristic of the German mind, and which . . . are the key to all Germany's progress in . . . practical and material concerns."[48]

The program of state social legislation met with relatively less resistance in Germany than in most other industrialized countries. Several factors contributed to smooth the path of German social legislation. In the first place the entire tradition of state cameralism and paternalism continued to exercise a profound influence on the rulers of Germany and their chief ministers. William I and William II both harked back to the example of Frederick II, who once prided himself on being "the king of the beggars," and both Bismarck and the chief architect of social legislation under William II, Count Posadowsky, were at all times fully conscious of this tradition. In his justification of the first measure of social legislation introduced in the Reichstag in 1881, Bismarck declared that the policy of the state must be one which "would cultivate the view also among the propertyless classes of the population, those who are the most numerous and the least educated, that the state is not only an institution of necessity but also one of welfare. By recognizable and direct advantages they must be led to look upon the state not as an agency devised solely for the protection of the better-situated classes of society but also as one serving their needs and interests." [49] Bismarck even went so far as to recognize the "right to employment" and the need for the state to help provide employment by a system of public works. "Is it not rooted in our entire moral relationships," he asked in his Reichstag speech of May 9, 1884, "that the individual who comes before his fellow citizens and says, 'I am physically fit, ready to work but can find no job,' is entitled to say, 'Give me a job!' and the state is obligated to provide a job for him?" [50] To von Bodelschwingh, Bismarck wrote in 1885, "No doubt the individual can do much good, but the social problem can only be solved by the state." [51]

Bismarck's social policy was also greatly influenced by the examples of the Caesarism of Napoleon III in France and by the Tory democracy of Disraeli in England. Bismarck referred frequently in his Reichstag speeches to what he had learned from his experiences in France. And in his speech of May 9, 1884, he referred specifically to Napoleon's success in securing the loyalty and allegiance of the peasantry by means of his social legislation. As for Disraeli, Tory democracy as an organized expression never gained the vogue in Germany that it did among the Conservative followers of Lord Beaconsfield in England, but the philosophy underlying the social reform aspirations of British conservatism was also shared by a large segment of the German conservative ruling classes. Bismarck himself looked up in great admiration to Disraeli. Despite the contrast between the arrogant Prussian aristocrat and the former commoner and Jew, there was in Bismarck's attitude toward Disraeli much of the prevailing German awe toward the achievements of the British empire. Personal relations between Bismarck and Disraeli became particularly close during the Berlin Congress of 1878, just before the inauguration of the Reich program of social legislation. We know from the testimony of both statesmen that they talked not only of foreign affairs but of all sorts of other matters and very definitely about social problems and socialism. The biographer of Disraeli, discussing that period, writes: "There can be no doubt of the strong impression the

Prime Minister made on the Chancellor. . . . To the Crown Princess Bismarck said that Beaconsfield fulfilled all his ideas of a great statesman. . . . Those who penetrated to Bismarck's cabinet in Berlin, in the times immediately following the Congress, found that Beaconsfield's was one of the three portraits there displayed. 'My Sovereign, my wife and my friend,' the Chancellor explained." [52]

Eight years later Bismarck, receiving Hucks Gibbs in Friedrichsruh, indicated that his admiration for Disraeli had not abated. "Bismarck," relates Gibbs, "spoke with reverence of Queen Victoria, with admiration and love of Beaconsfield. He told us that he has a picture of Beaconsfield in the library of each of his three homes." [53]

Disraeli's novels had circulated widely in Germany, especially in the cheap Tauchnitz edition, since 1844. Georg Brandes's life of Disraeli, first published serially in the *Deutsche Rundschau,* and then in book form in 1879, as well as numerous other articles in newspapers and reviews, all helped to popularize the social and political ideas of the Tory leader. There is no doubt that a large section of German conservative opinion found in Disraeli a model leader for coping with the social problem that was in keeping with their own class and political views. Like Disraeli, in his novel *Sybil,* they were disturbed by the development of "two nations; between whom there is no intercourse and no sympathy . . . The Rich and the Poor." What was common to all these conservative social reformers was the basic force of nationalism. To think that the degradation and debility brought about by the ills of industrialism had befallen Englishmen or Germans and that this would, in Disraeli's words, "place them lower than the Portuguese or the Poles, the serfs of Russia or the Lazzaroni of Naples," was more than they could accept. And so much lower did the poor fall that "they no longer believe in an innate difference between the governing and the governed classes of this country." Bismarck, like Disraeli, had this nationalist approach to the social problem and it was only re-enforced when the allegations were made by military and agrarian spokesmen that large numbers of the recruits drawn from the industrial population of Germany were unfit for military service.* Large sections of conservative public opinion were won over to the cause of state social legislation by this nationalist feeling.† When Adolf Wagner and Hans Delbrück pleaded the cause of the rights of labor and collective bargaining before the Verein für Sozialpolitik in 1897 in Cologne, their chief point was that labor peace was essential to the cause of national unity and

---

* This doctrine was propounded especially by the agricultural economist Max Sering. Subsequent studies based upon data gathered from Bavaria, and independent studies by Lujo Brentano disputed this claim for greater military efficiency for rural recruits. Cf. Dawson, *The Evolution of Modern Germany,* pp. 229–230.

† The close relationship between Bismarck's and Disraeli's social policies was already recognized by German writers of the day. Cf., e.g., "Earl of Beaconsfield, Bismarck und die soziale Frage," in *Allgemeines evangelisch-lutheranisches Kirchenblatt,* xiii (1880), 601–603.

national defense.[54] Nationalism in Germany, as throughout the world, was one of the chief driving forces behind state intervention in the problems created by the industrial revolution.

The churches in Germany likewise helped clear the way for the passage of social legislation in Germany. The social-Catholic movement of von Ketteler and the Center party, already described in a previous chapter, as well as the Protestant activities of Wichern, Stöcker, Naumann, Göhre, and others, all created a favorable climate for state intervention in the social problem.

A powerful stimulus to state intervention in the social problem came from a distinguished group of economists and university professors, who acquired the name *Kathedersozialisten,* or Socialists of the Chair. This group included both conservatives like Adolf Wagner and liberals like Lujo Brentano. What united them all was a revolt against the *laissez faire* economics hitherto dominant in academic circles. Here, too, the example of England was a powerful stimulus. What Friedrich Engels's study of the conditions of the working classes in England in 1844 was to the development of early Marxist theory, so were the writings of Adolf Held on the social question in England and more especially of Lujo Brentano on British trade-unions for the development of German liberal social reform. Brentano, in his studies on British trade-unions, developed the thesis that the Marxian analysis of labor conditions was correct so long as the workers remained unorganized, but he went on to show how the organization of the workers to a position where they could bargain collectively with the employers brought about a marked improvement in their condition. Brentano, until his death, for a period of over fifty years, remained the leading champion of liberal social reform in Germany.

In the early 1870's Brentano was joined by more conservative economists like Schmoller and Wagner in seeking to impress upon the newly founded Reich a policy of active interest in the improvement of the conditions of the working classes. On October 6 and 7, 1872, a group of 158 economists were invited by Schmoller and Wagner to convene at Eisenach for the purpose of "A Discussion of the Social Question." * Beside those already mentioned, the most prominent members were Bruno Hildebrand, Johannes Conrad, Wilhelm Roscher, Georg F. Knapp, Julius Eckardt, Adolf Held, Karl Knies, Konstantin Rössler, and Christian Lorenz Engel. Rudolf Gneist was elected president. Schmoller set the tone for the proceedings with his opening address. "We hope to find here," he declared, "a basis for the reform of our social relationships and to secure widespread acceptance of ideas which are to be found here and there but are not yet dominant in public opinion." [55] He pointed to the cleavage between the working and possessing classes not only in economic life but also "in

---

* The term "social question" in those years was a euphemistic way of referring to the "labor question."

morals, education, ideas, and ideals." "We are dissatisfied with our prevailing social conditions," he declared, and although opposed "to all socialist experiments," he continued, "we do not therefore favor giving up reform and the battle for improving conditions. . . . We will not, because of a doctrinaire principle, tolerate the miserable conditions and permit them to increase. We advocate moderate but firmly carried-out factory legislation; we demand that the so-called free-labor contract not be allowed actually to lead to the exploitation of the worker. . . . Our ideal is to include an ever increasing part of our people in the participation in the higher possessions of culture, in education, and in well-being." [56]

Out of these deliberations was born the most important association of social scientists in Germany, the Verein für Sozialpolitik, which was founded in 1873. The call for the first meeting proclaimed the dictum that state aid in social welfare was "not just a make-shift stop-gap or necessary evil but the realization of one of the highest tasks of our time and of our nation." The early ideal of this society was to stimulate practical social reform legislation. After 1878, however, it became a more purely academic association which brought together scholars, statesmen, and representatives of varying interests to debate important social issues and to publish learned studies on various social and economic questions. It continued to be sensitive, however, to newly emerging economic questions of a political and practical character, and both its deliberations and publications exercised a profound influence on social legislation down to its end in 1934, when it refused to be "co-ordinated" by the Nazi régime and preferred to end its long and honorable history rather than abandon its canons of free scientific inquiry. [57]

The emergence of the "Socialists of the Chair" was first greeted with derision and opposition by liberals, Socialists, and Conservatives. The term *Kathedersozialisten* had been coined earlier by the liberal journalist H. B. Oppenheim as a mock label for those who dared to doubt the "natural laws" of economics as expounded by the liberal school of Bastiat. From another side the nationalist historian Treitschke attacked Schmoller as a "furtherer of socialism." [58] Unlike the liberals, and notwithstanding his own National Liberal antecedents, Treitschke's opposition to social legislation stemmed not from a *laissez faire* conception of the position of the state. No one went further than he did in asserting the powers of the state. Treitschke's attack both upon Social Democrats and upon Socialists of the Chair emanated from his strong hierarchical conception of society. Despite his confession of "always having felt a deep respect for the homely virtues of the poor," [59] it was only the homely virtues that belonged to the poor, and these were the lowest in Treitschke's scale of values. The highest values of culture and politics, he maintained, are never intended for the masses. "The millions must plough and hammer and plane in order that the several thousand may carry on scientific research, paint and govern." "Only a minority is destined to enjoy completely the ideal possession of culture; the overwhelming majority works by the sweat of their brow," and since the occupation one is engaged in fashions one's cultural pattern then it follows that "whoever lives from coarse work day after day can seldom raise his thoughts above the circle of his personal interests." Such class stratification, according to Treitschke, is and should be more or less permanent. "The masses must for ever remain the masses," and "the poor man should know that his lament: why am I not rich? is not any more reasonable even by a hair's breadth than the lament why am I not the German crown-prince?" Social reform legislation motivated by the desire "to include an ever increasing part of our people to participate in the higher possessions of culture," said Treitschke, "is therefore contrary to nature and contrary to the best interests of the state." "It is the task of government to reduce and mitigate distress, but its abolition is neither possible nor desirable." [60] No social reform will ever bring greater blessings to the working classes than the old and simple admonition: pray and work.

Unlike Bismarck, who recognized the "piece of truth" in socialism and therefore favored a program of social legislation by the state, Treitschke remained adamant in his opposition to such action by the state. Those who have pointed to Treitschke as the arch-exponent of Prussianism should note that at least as far as the social problem was concerned there was this sharp divergence between Bismarck and Treitschke and that Bismarck's policy was the more deeply rooted Prussian tradition than was that of the historian. Nietzsche later developed his deep-seated antipathy to social reform legislation on the basis of an aristocratic estheticism. These views of Treitschke and Nietzsche, combined with a crude form of social Darwinism, became the ideological weapons of the spokesmen for heavy industry who continued down to World War I to oppose most social reform legislation and who condemned even such conservatives as Adolf Wagner as "allies of the Socialists."

Perhaps the most powerful factor behind the movement for social legislation sprang from the pressure created by the Social Democratic movement. The fear of socialism was very real and profound for both the ruling classes and the bourgeoisie. The reactionaries favored the method of ruthless and brutal suppression of socialism, without any concessions at all. The monarchy and Bismarck chose the paternalistic approach of trying to take the wind out of the sails of the Socialist propaganda and weaning away the masses from their rebel leaders to their fatherly ruler and protector. In his message from the throne on November 17, 1881, William I took pains to point out that "the healing of the social ills is not to be carried out by the repression of the Social Democratic excesses but is at the same time to be sought in the positive furthering of the welfare of the workers." [61] Catholic and Protestant leaders endeavored to win over the proletarians from their "atheistic and materialistic" leaders, and liberal social reformers were anxious to divest the Social Democrats of the "revolutionary" character of their program and show that the legitimate goals of the working classes could be achieved through piecemeal social reform legislation without involving the entire fabric of society in the cataclysm and chaos of violent revolution. All were spurred on, however, by the rapid rise and increase of the Socialist and labor movement.

The first measure of social insurance was introduced by Bismarck in 1881, providing for insurance against industrial accidents. The measure failed to pass the Reichstag because the Centrists opposed the bureaucratic administration provided for in the bill and Bismarck withdrew the bill. The first social insurance measure enacted was the Sickness Insurance Act of 1883, which set up an autonomous administration to which employers contributed two-thirds and employees one-third of the costs. The act was variously amended in 1885, 1886, 1892, and 1903. By 1913 there were $14\frac{1}{2}$ million persons thus insured. In 1884 came an accident insurance bill, further amended in 1885, 1886, 1887, and 1900, the costs of which were borne by the employers alone; in 1889 came a measure for old age and incapacity insurance, with payments contributed by employers, employees, and the Reich. German workers were thus the first to be protected against all these hazards of modern industrialism. If a worker or any member of his immediate family fell ill, the health insurance system provided the necessary medical treatment and hospitalization. If he became disabled, he received a pension, and after the age of sixty-five he was similarly eligible for pension. His dependents received an annuity if he died before the age of sixty-five.

These social-insurance measures were complemented by a thorough code of factory legislation regulating conditions of labor, an elaborate child labor law, passed in March, 1903, and an extensive system of labor exchanges to help unemployed workers secure jobs more easily. There was no state unemployment insurance until the Weimar Republic, but many cities followed the example of Cologne, which set up a municipal unemployment insurance system in 1894. Municipalities and private agencies also supplemented the state social legislation in such matters as housing, public works, the relief of migratory workers, and health. All these measures combined to make Germany the model for advanced social legislation before World War I. These measures also contributed greatly to cutting down emigration from Germany and to creating conditions favorable to the natural increase of population.

4. LABOR, CAPITAL, AND THE STATE

The development of trade-unions in Germany proceeded along much the same lines as in the rest of western Europe—the beginnings of workers' organizations among skilled workers such as book printers and cigar makers, the struggle for legal recognition of collective bargaining, the effects of large strikes, and the relationship established between trade-unions and political parties. All these factors were present in the progress of trade-unionism in Germany. Added to these were several elements not found in England or the United States.

The legal right for workers to organize was established by the law of 1869 of the North German Confederation. Three groups participated in the establishment of unions in Germany, the Socialists, the social Catholics and social Christians, and the liberals. Of these, the Socialists were by far the most active. But the anti-Socialist legislation of Bismarck seriously hampered the organizational work of the Socialists so that it was not until after 1890 that the rapid expansion of workers' organizations took place. The trade-unions organized by the Socialists were known as the Free Trade-Unions; the unions of the religious groups were called Christian Trade-Unions; and those organized by the Progressives were called the Hirsch-Duncker Unions, named after the two Progressive employers who were instrumental in setting them up. All three groups usually stood together on wage struggles and they had their representatives in the Reichstag in the respective parties with which they were allied. A series of great strikes was waged, especially among the Ruhr coal workers (1872, 1889), the steel workers (1905), the dock workers in Hamburg (1897), and the textile workers in Saxony (1903). While in several of these strikes the workers were not able to win their demands, the strikes did a great deal to arouse the German public to the acuteness of the labor question, to win support for labor among large sections of the bourgeoisie, and to build up the membership of the trade-unions. The following table indicates the growth of trade-union membership from 1891 to 1913.[62] The highest degree of organization was in the metal and construction industries.

MEMBERSHIP IN GERMAN TRADE UNIONS
1891–1913

	FREE TRADE-UNIONS			HIRSCH-DUNCKER UNIONS			CHRISTIAN TRADE-UNIONS	
	Assoc.	MEMBERSHIP		Assoc.	MEMBERSHIP		Assoc.	MEMBERSHIP	
Year		Total	Women		Total	Women		Total	Women
1891	62	278,000	——	18	66,000	——	—	——	——
1896	51	329,000	15,000	17	72,000	——	—	8,000	——
1900	58	680,000	23,000	20	92,000	——	23	79,000	——
1905	64	1,345,000	74,000	20	117,000	——	18	188,000	12,000
1910	53	2,017,000	162,000	23	123,000	——	22	295,000	22,000
1913	49	2,574,000	230,000	23	107,000	6,000	25	343,000	28,000

From the ranks of trade-union leaders came many of the more prominent parliamentarians of the subsequent Weimar period, such as Gustav Bauer, Hermann Müller, Robert Schmidt, Alexander Schlicke, Rudolf Wissell, August Winnig, Theodor Leipart, Adam Stegerwald, Treviranus, and others.[63]

The attitude of the employers toward workers' organizations varied all the way from the socialistic views of one of the most enlightened employers in Germany, Ernst Abbe, head of the Zeiss works in Jena, who turned over his entire plant to his workers, to the fierce opposition of the heavy industrialists like Stumm and Thyssen. The smaller and light industry owners on the whole came to recognize the value of collective bargaining and came to terms with the trade-unions. A progressive employer like Robert Bosch in Stuttgart became known for his exemplary relations with his workers.[64] It was in the heavy industries that fierce opposition to collective agreements continued almost down to World War I. Krupp declared that he intended to remain "master in his house" and would not deal with union leaders. And Baron von Stumm, the "King of the Saar," harking back to the words of Frederick William IV on constitutions, declared he would never allow any "artificial creations" to come between himself and his employees. He declared his unalterable opposition to all kinds of labor unions, condemning the Hirsch-Duncker Unions just as vigorously as those of the Socialists. He imposed an iron discipline on his workers to the extent of forbidding his workers to read the newspapers which he proscribed, on pain of losing their jobs. In the Prussian upper house in 1897 Stumm attacked the conservative monarchist Adolf Wagner, who had pleaded for capital-labor co-operation, "for making speeches against capital, property and employers." [65] Emil Kirdorf, the architect of the huge coal and steel cartels in the Rhineland, declared at the 1905 meeting of the Verein für Sozialpolitik that he too would not deal with any labor organizations because that would only lead to more unrest. He declared it to be the avowed purpose of all workers' organizations—and the Christian trade-unions were even worse than the Socialist unions—"to carry on a struggle for the purpose of the annihilation of the entire economic flowering of our industry." [66]

Employers early began to band together for purposes of common political activities.[67] In 1873 the iron manufacturers of the Rhineland founded the Centralverband deutscher Industrieller. They attracted industrialists from textiles, soda, sugar, hats, leather, paper, and other industries and reconstituted themselves on February 15, 1876. Under the active and skillful leadership of its secretary, H. A. Bueck, the association became very influential in government circles. It acted chiefly to secure protection for industry and to oppose social reform. They did not actively oppose the social legislation of Bismarck but they vehemently opposed anything that went beyond those measures. In fighting the child labor measures they declared, "It seems to be more reasonable to set children to work at pleasant jobs and let them make money, than to allow them to go idle and become wild." [68] The measure forbidding night work for women was assailed on the ground that it violated the principle of "liberty of the people to work whenever they want to." They accepted Treitschke's view of the inevitability of the worker remaining "uneducated and lacking in intelligence." In seeking to win sympathy for the owners who might become impoverished because of the workers' demands for higher wages, they once issued a popular pamphlet which declared, "It is indeed sad to remain poor all one's life, but to fall from a condition of well-being to one of poverty and cares of livelihood is a hell upon earth." [69]

This stubborn and ruthless attitude of the large industrialists called forth sharp criticism in the press and in academic circles. Max Weber, addressing the 1905 meeting of the Verein für Sozialpolitik devoted to the question of "Labor Relations in the Private Giant Industries," spoke of the general character of German policy, which gives the impression "that it seeks not so much power itself as, above all, the appearance of power, the passionate aspiration for power." And this also, continued Weber, "is in the blood of our employers," who rule over their industrial enterprises after the manner of a *paterfamilias*, demanding stern obedience of those under them.[70] Far-sighted thinkers like Brentano and Naumann saw at that time the need for some scheme to set up machinery to settle industrial disputes. Naumann, in a brilliant speech at the same conference, pointed out that the essence of the struggle between capital and labor was the conflict between monarchic-aristocratic control of industry versus democratic control, and he reminded his hearers that the age of individuals was over and the age of large collectives was at hand. It was in this vein that Lujo Brentano called for the corporate organization of all industries with representatives of labor and industry, and presided over by an impartial chairman to take care of all labor disputes. These trends of social thinking inspired the enlightened labor legislation subsequently adopted by the Weimar republic.

Despite strikes, tensions, and repeated business depressions, it must nevertheless be said that rapid industrialization, combined with social legislation and protective tariffs, all contributed to a general state of well-being. The narrow and crowded city streets gave way to wide avenues, boulevards, and allées; per capita income increased; the spread of electrification brought a host of new conveniences into the average German home, and even before World War I central heating, bathrooms, and kitchen improvements became more widespread, especially among the middle classes. Sugar consumption increased from an average of about 6 kilograms per capita in 1876 to 21.4 kilograms in 1913; cotton consumption increased from an average per capita consumption of about 2.84 kilograms in 1871 to 7.6 kilograms in 1913; and savings deposits rose from a total of about $1\frac{1}{2}$ billion marks in 1870 to about 20 billion marks in 1914.[71] Mass consumption of hitherto considered luxury items also was extended. Reservations were sometimes expressed regarding cultural and political conditions in the Wilhelmian Reich, but of one thing all were certain on the eve of World War I: Germany had entered upon a glorious stage of economic prosperity and comfort. Foreigners came to Germany and were impressed by the clean streets, by the scrubbed faces, by the shiny, gleaming tramways and railroads, by the newer experiments in housing and social planning, and by the general feeling of contentment that seemed to pervade all classes of the German population at that time.

The businessmen and the industrialists were happy in their alliance with the Junker feudalist and agrarian interests. They were on the whole satisfied to wield their power and influence in the economic field and to allow the traditional ruling class to carry on in the sphere of politics. Kirdorf, the head of the greatest cartel in pre-war Germany, declared before a session of the Verein für Sozialpolitik that men like him and his class had no political power. "We unfortunately have no say at all," he bewailed. And although his remarks were greeted with laughter by his hearers and later contradicted vehemently by Naumann, his words were on the whole true. During the reign of William I and Bismarck, the traditional disdain of the aristocracy for business and industry was almost universal. Under William II a change set in. William II had "two souls in his breast"; he was a romantic feudalist and at the same time displayed an active and genuine interest in the new technology and new industries. He visited factories, spoke to the workers and consorted with factory owners. In his reign German industrialists became more socially acceptable. But they never attained a leading place in the inner circles of the ruling oligarchy and never commanded wide popular respect and admiration. Despite all the new industrial and technological developments it was still the noblemen, the soldiers, and the artistic and cultural leaders who were held in the greatest social esteem. A liberal journalist writing on August Thyssen on the occasion of his seventieth birthday in 1912, bitterly lamented the fact that so little attention was paid on this occasion to the greatest industrialist and one of the richest men in Germany.[72] The public, he complained, has no interest in leading figures in the economic field.

What position did the captain of industry, financier and merchant prince occupy in German society? Some, like Werner Siemens, received the title of nobility and thus gained entree into the circles of the élite. But on the whole a wide gulf separated the ruling nobility and military circles from the business and industrial classes.[73] The latter created a sort of aristocracy of their own. They reveled in their titles of *Geheimrat, Kommerzienrat, Justizrat, Baurat,* and so on. They acquired university degrees, took pride in collecting libraries of finely bound books, especially art books, introduced better furnishings into the formerly drab bourgeois homes, spent a great deal of time and money in travel, and then basked in the glory of official Germany. Philanthropy was not developed among German rich men the way it was in England and the United States. Here the state was the great patron of the arts and sciences, and very little room was left for the possessors of private fortunes. There were exceptions in the newer technical fields, as in the case of the Technisch-Physikalischer Reichsanstalt, endowed by Werner Siemens, and the equally important Robert

Bosch Foundation for research in engineering, established by Bosch at the Technische Hochschule of Stuttgart. But apart from such rare exceptions they poured all their energy and talents into their businesses and upon their families. They ruled over their families with iron discipline and transferred the same psychological attitude to their business and industrial enterprises. The children were brought up to take over the dynasty when the head of the house relinquished the reins either because of old age or death. In most instances sons followed in the footsteps of the fathers. Only rarely, as in the case of Walther Rathenau, did the heir resist assuming the responsibilities and wealth imposed upon him. A few, like Albert Ballin, became intimates of the monarch. But while they exercised considerable power in economic matters their general influence never matched that of the military and the nobility. Ballin's complete failure to influence William to come to terms with England on the eve of World War I is testimony to the political ineffectiveness of the upper bourgeoisie.

5. INTELLECTUAL LIFE IN THE SECOND REICH

Intellectual and cultural activity in the Second Reich paralleled political and economic developments in many ways or else reacted against them.[74] The flowering of metaphysical idealist philosophy and romantic music and poetry during the first part of the nineteenth century gave way, especially between 1850 and 1870, to philosophical materialism, to a more sober realism in literature and art, and to a greater emphasis upon practical knowledge and technical education in the fields of scientific research. The combined influences of nineteenth century science, of the evolutionary theories of Darwin, and the realistic politics of the Bismarckian Reich served to encourage more practical and materialistic trends in art, in literature, in education, and in scholarship. Chief interest was now concentrated on man's environment. There was less speculation and more influence by the natural sciences. The aim and aspiration of the realist trends was to divert man's attention from "castles in the air" and to provide him with a richer and more powerful life based on the solid foundations of sense experience. Poetry, the characteristic expression of the age of Goethe and Schiller, of Hölderlin and Kleist, gave way to prose. Apart from Rainer Maria Rilke, the Germany of the Second Reich produced no outstanding poet of world renown, unless the philosophical outpourings of Nietzsche are also classed as poetry.

It was the age of the epigones, when creative imaginative thinking was replaced by painstaking, diligent, and systematic research produced by patient thoroughness and vast industry. This painstaking research was further stimulated by the enormous influence of the idea of "development" which continued on from the traditions of Herder and Hegel and which converted almost every domain of thought and research into a study of the "history" or "historical evolution" of the particular area of interest. It was this thoroughness of research that gained for German scholarship a supremacy in Europe that more than matched German political hegemony or the prized economic and technical status of the trade-mark "Made in Germany." In keeping with the general nineteenth century trend toward mass education, Germany, in perhaps a higher degree than any other country in the world, witnessed the spread of *Bildung,* of education and knowledge. Nowhere else did the prestige of a university education for even the average merchant or industrialist attain such a high degree of acceptance as in the Germany of the Second Reich, and nowhere else did such a profusion of Ph.D.'s blossom forth as from the German universities. The German equivalent to the French *citoyen* or to the British gentleman was to be a *gebildeter Mensch,* a person who had completed his *Abitur.* It is true that the content of *Bildung* showed a wide departure from the *Bildung* ideal of Wilhelm von Humboldt and the classical humanistic thought of his age. It was oriented more toward the practical mastery of nature and society than toward the cultivation of spirit or character.

The German universities and technical schools became not only the centers of learning but also the most active promoters of large collective enterprises in scholarship and research. Despite occasional lapses and breaches, and despite the fact that they were all state supported, the German universities retained a high degree of corporate autonomy; they jealously guarded the principle of *Lehrfreiheit* (academic freedom), and for the most part proceeded on the assumption that scientific research and scholarly investigation must be carried on independently of political or confessional bias or influence. German institutions of higher learning attracted students from all parts of the world, who were trained in the methods of German *Wissenschaft* and who returned to their respective homelands to emulate the German models. The historical seminars in France, the graduate schools in the United States, and the technical schools of Japan as well as similar trends elsewhere all bore the stamp "Made in Germany."

The wide diffusion of knowledge in Germany is apparent in the figures for German book production. In 1750 the number of books published in all the German states totaled 1,279; in 1850 the total rose to 9,053 books published; by 1890 the figure was 19,000. Popular cheap editions of books were disseminated among the masses in the Tauchnitz edition of works of foreign literature and more especially in the famous Reclam Universal Bibliothek which began its activity in 1867 with Goethe's *Faust* as its Number 1 publication and which soon became one of the chief vehicles of mass education in Germany.

Popular and adult education was furthered by the development of a large and influential daily press and popular and semi-learned periodicals.

The German newspaper, unlike the American, was conceived to be an educational agency. The most important newspapers never made any pretense at non-partisan collecting and presenting of news. Each newspaper was in effect a "party" paper intended to provide political education and guidance to its readers. The old liberal Berlin daily, the *Vossische Zeitung,* dating from the eighteenth century, was joined in the new Reich by the Ullstein papers in Berlin, the *Berliner Tageblatt,* the *Berliner Morgenpost* (which became the most widely circulated newspaper in Germany), and the most popular afternoon paper, the *B.Z. am Mittag,* which first appeared in 1904. In the south the *Frankfurter Zeitung,* established by the progressive leader Leopold Sonnemann in 1856, became the most internationally read German newspaper and one which came to command increasing respect if not influence in the field of foreign affairs. The conservative *Neue Preussische (Kreuz-) Zeitung* in Berlin and the nationalist *Kölnische Zeitung* were joined after 1870 by the *Tägliche Rundschau,* the *Deutsche Zeitung,* and the *Deutsche Tageszeitung* in Berlin and the *Hamburgische Korrespondent* and the *Hamburger Nachrichten* in the north. The most influential Catholic dailies were the *Germania* in Berlin and the *Kölnische Volkszeitung* and *Augsburger Postzeitung.* The *Vorwärts* in Berlin and the *Leipziger Volkszeitung* became the leading Social Democratic dailies. Editorial opinion, signed articles, literary and philosophical essays made up a large part of the contents of the German daily newspapers, and as such they served as disseminators of mass culture. Illustrated weeklies ranging from the popular Ullstein *Berliner Illustrierte Zeitung,* which attained a circulation of 1,800,000, to the more literary and esthetic illustrated monthlies like *Westermann's Illustrierte Monatshefte* and *Velhagen und Klasings Monatshefte,* contributed to visual and pictorial education. Typical bourgeois periodicals like the *Gartenlaube,* founded in 1853, and *Daheim,* founded in 1864, provided the cultural fare for the average German burgher; political journals like the *Grenzboten, Preussische Jahrbücher,* and the *Deutsche Rundschau* catered to the more serious conservative tastes, while the literary battles between conservatives and radicals were fought out in the columns of the *Kunstwart,* founded by Ferdinand Avenarius in 1887, and in the organ of the naturalists, the *Neue Rundschau,* also established in 1887.

It was in the field of the natural sciences above all that Germany attained its pre-eminence during the nineteenth century. In mathematics Karl Gustav Jakob Jacobi (1804–1851), with his pioneering work on elliptic functions and the theory of determinants, founded the first great school of mathematicians in modern Germany and revived the older tradition of Leibniz and Gauss. He was followed by Georg Friedrich Riemann (1826–1866), the originator of a non-Euclidian system of geometry, and Karl Weierstrass (1815–1897) and Georg Cantor (1845–1918). The pioneering work in chemistry carried out by Liebig in the first half of the century was followed by a distinguished group of German chemists, the most notable of whom were August Kekulé (1829–1896), Viktor Meyer (1848–1897), Emil Fischer (1852–1919), and Wilhelm Ostwald (1853–1932). In physics the earlier work of Robert Mayer (1814–1878), who first formulated the law of conservation of energy, and of Hermann Ludwig Helmholtz (1821–1894), who invented the ophthalmoscope and who did pioneering work in the field of acoustics, was followed by Gustav Robert Kirchhoff (1824–1887) and his work with the spectroscope; Heinrich Hertz (1857–1894), the discoverer of radio waves; Wilhelm Konrad Röntgen (1845–1923), the discoverer of X rays; and Max Planck (1858–1947), who formulated the quantum theory in 1900. In 1905 Albert Einstein (1879–1955), a native of Ulm, Bavaria, but then living in Switzerland, published his first papers on the theory of relativity. Einstein returned to Germany in 1913 but the growth of the antisemitic movement was to drive him out and in 1933 he settled in the United States.

In biology, Johannes Müller (1801–1858) created the science of comparative physiology, Mathias Schleiden (1804–1881) and Theodor Schwann (1810–1882) elaborated the cellular theory, and August Weismann (1834–1914), working in genetics, established the theory of the continuity of the germ plasm as well as the non-inheritance of acquired characters. In the related fields of medicine and public health, Robert Koch, (1843–1910), disciple of Pasteur, demonstrated the tuberculosis bacillus and the cholera vibrio and developed treatment for sleeping sickness; Paul Ehrlich (1854–1915) developed salvarsan for the treatment of syphilis, and Rudolf Virchow (1821–1902), apart from his role as political leader of the Progressives in the Reichstag, was one of the leading pathologists of his time and was active in the development of modern methods of public health. Wilhelm Wundt (1832–1920) established the first experimental psychological laboratory in Leipzig in 1875, and Moritz Lazarus (1824–1903) and Heymann Steinthal (1823–1899) laid the foundations for the scientific study of group psychology. Just as Alexander von Humboldt had served as the great popularizer of the achievements of science in the first half of the century, so at the close of the nineteenth century Ernst Haeckel and Wilhelm Ostwald brought the fruits of modern science to a wide reading public in Germany. Haeckel also was the chief advocate of Darwinism in Germany and was chiefly responsible for its acceptance there. Both he and Ostwald went beyond the bounds of pure research to advocate the acceptance of a general materialistic philosophy of life based on the results of natural science. Haeckel's *Die Welträtsel,* first published in 1899, passed through many editions and was translated into numerous European languages. His rejection of a personal God, immortality of the soul, and free will made Haeckel a storm center of German intellectual life at the turn of the century. With Ostwald, Haeckel founded the Monistenbund in 1906 to propagate these views.

The enormous expansion of the natural sciences in Germany did not necessarily mean the widespread acceptance of naturalistic or positivist philosophies of life. Materialism enjoyed only a brief period of general popularity in Germany during the years between 1850 and 1880. Carl Vogt (1817–1895) and his most popular book *Köhlerglaube und Wissenschaft,* published in 1854; Jacob Moleschott (1822–1893) and his *Kreislauf des Lebens,* published in 1852; and above all Ludwig Büchner (1824–1899) and his *Kraft und Stoff,* published in 1855, were the most active propagandists of scientific materialism. They carried on the older tradition of Feuerbach and paved the way for Haeckel's and Ostwald's Monist movement. Büchner's *Kraft und Stoff* in particular became the Bible of German materialism with its gospel of the immortality of matter and its denial of the creation of the world. Atheism was a concomitant aspect of this movement, but not social and political radicalism. It was only in Marxist materialism that the fusion of political radicalism and scientific materialism was effected. Nor did this movement leave as deep an impress on German culture and scholarship as was the case in France and England. There were no figures in Germany comparable to Comte, Mill, or Spencer. Positivism in philosophy and in scientific research found adherents in academic circles, but they were outnumbered and overwhelmed by the revival of metaphysical movements oriented on a "return to Kant" or a "return to Hegel." And natural scientists themselves for the most part allied themselves with the stand taken by Emil Du Bois-Reymond, who in 1872 delivered a famous lecture to German scientists and doctors in Leipzig, "On the Limits of the Knowledge of Nature," in which he confessed the limitations of natural science and ended with an *ignorabimus* in the face of the riddle of nature.

Second only to the developments in the natural sciences was the flowering in the Second Reich of the historical and social sciences. Historicism, having its roots in the romantic movement, and the towering figure of Leopold von Ranke (1795–1886) loomed high in the German historiography of the nineteenth century. Bridging the whole course of modern Germany from the Napoleonic wars well into the Bismarckian Reich, Ranke represented the fusion of the historical concepts of romanticism with the critical methodology of classical scholars like F. A. Wolff, Gottfried Hermann, and Barthold Niebuhr. Ranke and the students that emerged from his seminar set the model for the critical study of archive materials and other historical sources. Rejecting the pragmatic conception of history of the Enlightenment and its idea of progress, Ranke was skeptical of abstract concepts and sought to apprehend the "living forces" in history, which he found in the unique and the individual. "Every epoch stands in immediate relationship with God," wrote Ranke, "and its value rests not upon what results from it, but rather in its own existence, in its own self." The object of the historian, therefore, was to describe *"wie es eigentlich gewesen,"* that is, what actually happened. The historian must experience joy in individual phenomena in the same way that one picks flowers without thinking of the classification of Linnaeus. Ranke nevertheless retained sufficient of the influence of the Enlightenment to recognize the universal ties connecting the various nations of the world which are an expression of the mysterious and unfathomable laws emanating from a Divine Being. Ranke never allowed his universality to be completely overwhelmed by the flood of German nationalism. In addition to his elaborate work on the German Reformation and on Prussian history, he also directed his attention to the fields of English and Gallo-Romanic history and crowned his long, scholarly career with a *Weltgeschichte* which was to show his concept of the unity of history. He commenced this universal history when he was eighty-five years old, and managed to complete seven volumes, which carry the story down to 1453.

Ranke's concern was primarily with the history of the political state, and the disciples that followed him—Giesebrecht, Waitz, Sybel, Dahlmann, and Droysen—identified historical writing almost exclusively with political history. His successors, too, carried historical relativism to a more extreme phase of development, identified themselves more completely with the cause of German nationalism, and helped to diffuse the Hegelian concept of the *Machtstaat.* Treitschke's *Deutsche Geschichte,* in particular, exemplified this departure from the more Olympian reserve, the political quietism, and more universal outlook of Ranke.

Critical historical research, however, branched out into all areas and periods to make German historical scholarship the paragon for historians all over the world. Theodor Mommsen (1817–1903), in his work in ancient history and philology, sought "to bring down the ancients from the fantastic pedestal on which they appear into the real world." His narrative accounts of the Roman world, the host of his contributions to all phases of constitutional, political, and economic aspects of Roman history, and his initiation of the huge project of a critical edition of the texts of the entire corpus of Latin writers won him universal renown and immortal fame. His work in ancient history was carried on by Eduard Meyer (1855–1930) and Ulrich von Wilamowitz-Moellendorff (1848–1931). German scholars also came to occupy a leading place in the development of biblical higher criticism and Semitic studies. Julius Wellhausen (1844–1918) in his *Prolegomena zur Geschichte Israels* (1878) and his *Israelitische und jüdische Geschichte* (1894) laid bare the fragmentary development of the Bible and prophetic Judaism from primitive forms and earned for himself the title of the "Darwin of biblical criticism." Wellhausen stands with William Robertson Smith, Kuenen, Vatke, and de

Wette as the giants of biblical studies. In the same way Friedrich Delitzsch (1850–1922), with his work in the deciphering of Assyrian and Sumerian and with his archaeological work in the Near East, ranks as one of the foremost orientalists of modern times. Practically all ranking Assyriologists of other countries were trained in his seminar. German higher criticism also supplied fuel to popular antisemitism. Orientalists like Paul de Lagarde and Delitzsch argued that the creative ideas found in ancient Judaism were nothing but borrowings from Babylonian and Sumerian cultures and thus supported the antisemitic theory of the "parasitic" character of the Jews.

Catholic historical scholarship bore fruit in the masterful studies on the Reformation by Ignaz Döllinger (1799–1890), in the voluminous account of Germany on the eve of the Reformation by Johannes Janssen (1829–1891), and in the magnificent history of the popes by Ludwig von Pastor (1854–1928).

Economic history, under the influence of Wilhelm Roscher and Friedrich List, showed active progress after 1870. August Meitzen (1822–1910) and his studies of the village community, the numerous monographs on German towns and industries by Gustav Schmoller (1838–1917), the studies of German agrarian conditions by Georg Friedrich Knapp (1842–1926), the investigation of the industrial revolution in England by Adolf Held (1844–1880), the studies of English guilds by Lujo Brentano (1844–1931), the works on medieval German towns by Georg von Below (1858–1927), the wide range of historical-sociological studies by Max Weber (1864–1920) (from the economic ideas of the peoples of the ancient Orient, to the effects of the Protestant Revolt on modern capitalism, to field studies in modern technological unemployment), and the epoch-making history of modern capitalism by Werner Sombart (1863–1941) represent but the high-water marks of economic historical writing in Germany. In this field the influence of Marxian socialism was particularly evident.

The turning away from the more exclusively political history of Ranke was also evidenced in the work of Karl Lamprecht (1856–1915). Lamprecht attempted to write history on the basis of general psychological laws. History, he held, must be more than a description of events; it must be an explanation of change. History, therefore, is the study not of individuals but of "social-psychic" factors and of collective personalities, and the unity of history is derived from the total unity of society. *Kulturgeschichte* rather than political history was cultivated by Lamprecht and his disciples in Leipzig. In this respect, although from quite a different set of values, Lamprecht's influence, like that of the Swiss historian Jakob Burckhardt, was to initiate a departure from the Rankian school of political history with its exclusive concern with the state. Lamprecht's writings aroused considerable controversy among academic historians, but his method never succeeded in gaining wide currency nor in establishing a lasting school of historical writing.

A much more significant influence in changing the character of German historiography and other social sciences came from the development of the theories of *Geisteswissenschaften*. The term *Geisteswissenschaften* was first used as the German equivalent for John Stuart Mill's "mental and moral sciences," but soon acquired quite another connotation. Eventually it marked a radical reaction to the positivist approach in the social sciences. The theory of *Geisteswissenschaften* owes its development and influence to the work of the "southwestern" school of philosophy of Wilhelm Windelband and Heinrich Rickert and above all to the profound and penetrating thought of Wilhelm Dilthey (1822–1911). Windelband and Rickert, revolting against the trend of applying the methodology of the natural sciences to the study of man and society, set up the sharp distinction between the nomothetic character of the natural sciences and the ideographic character of history. The former aspire to and are capable of establishing general laws that are mechanical, rational, and predictable. History deals with the individual and the unique and is concerned only with particular facts.

Wilhelm Dilthey, following the lines laid down by Windelband and Rickert, valued most the "individual," the subconscious and irrational forces that fashioned the living reality of man. He had just as little use for the abstract metaphysics of Kant and Hegel as for the mechanical and automatic character of materialism and positivism. He was not interested in "social control" but in recapturing the spiritual and cultural possessions of man, and he attacked both empiricism and speculative idealism. The modern road to truth, held Dilthey, is through history. We ascertain "what man is only through history." Man does not have a nature, he has a history; and universal history is the highest teacher of mankind. Dilthey's conception of *Geisteswissenschaften,* therefore, was a sort of "cultural anthropology" or a general science of man which would discover human nature as revealed in man's experience of the great cultural areas of the human spirit, in philosophy, literature, art, and religion. This historical experience, said Dilthey, is not to be recaptured by mere descriptive or explanatory techniques. The spiritual traditions of the past must be relived and re-experienced by the true historian. The historian does not explain (*Erklären*), he seeks to understand (*Verstehen*), and true understanding comes only through inner sympathy (*Einfühlung*) and spiritual and conscious experience (*Erlebnis*). Dilthey provided the theoretical formulation of his concept of the *Geisteswissenschaften* in his *Einleitung in die Geisteswissenschaften* and other essays; but he also demonstrated concretely the methods he advocated in a series of masterful studies in intellectual history dealing with the periods of the Renaissance and Enlightenment and in studies of Lessing, Goethe, Novalis, Hölderlin, Hegel, and Schleiermacher.

From these concepts of the individualizing character of the *Geisteswissenschaften*, and the need for *Erlebnis, Verstehen*, and *Einfühlung*, emerged the sociology of Max Weber with his concept of "ideal types," the *Geistesgeschichte* of Ernst Troeltsch, Max Weber, and Friedrich Meinecke with its trend to go beyond political history to the history of ideas and the history of the human spirit, and the almost mystical *"verstehende"* economics of Werner Sombart. History and the historical approach came to dominate almost all the social sciences. Economics, following the trend set by Friedrich List and Wilhelm Roscher, was dominated in Germany primarily by the historical school of economics, which rejected the speculative and theorizing economics of the English classical school as well as those of the newer Austrian school, and which in becoming more historical became more nationalist and more social reformist, leading to the great influence in Germany of the so-called "Socialists of the Chair."

In sociology too, while the positivist influence of Comte and Mill gave rise to empirical studies, the more fruitful German sociology, as found in the works of Ferdinand Tönnies, Georg Simmel, Paul Barth, Max Weber, Alfred Weber, and Alfred Vierkandt, was in the area of historical sociology and cultural anthropology. It was in keeping with this trend that social scientists studied the "spirit" of modern capitalism, with Troeltsch and Max Weber finding it related historically to the influence of Calvinist and Lutheran ethics, while Sombart identified it with the rationalist spirit of the Jews. In the same way Max Weber and his disciples studied the changing intellectual climate of the modern age with its loss of magic (*Entzauberung*), its barrenness of spiritual content, its depersonalization, its matter of factness, and the loss of the earlier charismatic character of political and social leadership. It is here that the trends in the social sciences begin to converge toward the general neo-romantic reaction in Germany at the close of the nineteenth century and the quest for new spiritual forces to combat the mechanization and depersonalization of modern industrial and urban society.

Historicism was thus a peculiarly German development which had a continuous tradition in German thought from Leibniz, through Herder and Goethe, to the early romanticists and to Dilthey, Troeltsch, and Meinecke. Nowhere else did it result in such a rich and varied flowering of imaginative and creative studies of the spiritual history of man. But in its deviation from the generalizing, rationalist, and universalist traditions of the Stoic, Christian, and modern natural-law doctrines and movements, in its stress not only upon the idea of development, but above all on the supreme importance of the "individualizing" rather than the "generalizing" character of human and social forces, it also contributed to the intellectual and spiritual isolation of Germany and German thought. "Everything," writes Friedrich Meinecke, "is an individuality, according to its own laws, everything has its own right to existence, everything is relative, everything flows—give me the place to stand. How can we get out of this 'anarchy of values'? How can we proceed from historicism once again to a doctrine of values?" [75] Older metaphysical and theological speculation found its answer in the belief in a universal and general divine basis from which all individualities emanate. Modern historicism, as Meinecke points out, in so far as it aspires to be scientific and hence free of metaphysical or theological foundation, has nothing to offer that is certain and tangible and, above all, universally valid for all man's highest values in life. The most it can do is to tell man "to comprehend the meaning of the individual living entities in which they exist and to serve them resignedly in order to carry them further to the highest possible individual realization. Its metaphysical universal solace is reserved only for the select spirits of highest cultural attainment." [76]

German belles-lettres in the Second Reich were likewise the work of epigones. The great epoch of German literature as world literature had ended with Goethe. German literature of the second half of the nineteenth century was almost exclusively for home consumption, and very few if any of the German authors of this period attained the stature of either the classical German period or of the novelists, poets, and dramatists of nineteenth century England, France, Russia, or Scandinavia. Besides, some of the most original German creative writers during this period were either Swiss, like Gottfried Keller, Conrad Ferdinand Meyer, and Carl Spitteler, or Austrian, like Hermann Bahr, Artur Schnitzler, and Hugo von Hofmannsthal.

German literature between 1850 and 1914 went through the whole gamut of schools and styles of world literature found in the classifications of literary historians—realism and "consistent realism," naturalism and "pseudo-naturalism," expressionism and decadence, symbolism and impressionism, neo-romanticism and neo-classicism. It was subject to influences at home that derived from scientific determinism and the influence of Darwin and Haeckel, from the pessimism of Schopenhauer and the militant naturalism of Nietzsche, from bourgeois nationalism and proletarian socialism. It also drank deeply from the influence of foreign authors —especially Scandinavians like Ibsen and Strindberg, the Russian novelists Tolstoy and Dostoievsky and the French naturalist school of Zola.

The realist trend in mid-nineteenth century was initiated by Berthold Auerbach (1812–1882), whose *Schwarzwälder Dorfsgeschichten,* depicting life in the villages of the Black Forest, harked back to the influence of Young Germany and liberalism and combined the older humanistic tradition with poetic sympathy for the life of the simple folk. Auerbach was, with Uhland, the most popular author for the generation between 1848 and 1870. German realism reached its highest peak of creative development in the dramatic works of Friedrich Hebbel (1813–1863). Hebbel's *Judith* marked a new epoch in German drama. The wave of national patriotism and race consciousness that swept the country during and immediately following the Franco-Prussian War brought a vogue of historical fiction or fictionalized history, as in Gustav Freytag's *Bilder aus der deutschen Vergangenheit,* which came to adorn almost every good National Liberal home; Felix Dahn's glorification of the primitive Teutons; and a decade later the historical plays and novels of Ernst von Wildenbruch (1845–1909).

Most expressive of the spirit of bourgeois realism of the late nineteenth century were the novels and tales of Gustav Freytag, Theodor Storm, Wilhelm Raabe, and Theodor Fontane. Freytag (1816–1895) extolled the virtues and made himself the champion of the German bourgeoisie. His *Die Journalisten* dealt with the life of the bourgeois journalists; *Soll und Haben* was concerned with the merchant class; and *Die verlorene Handschrift* turned attention to the learned classes. In these works as in his political journalism, Freytag depicted the bourgeoisie as the mainstay of the national state and as the bearer of all progress, culture, and civilization.

Wilhelm Raabe (1831–1910) became the favorite author of the academic classes of the late nineteenth century. His more than thirty large novels were full of what the nineteenth century called *Bildungsbesitz,* the spiritual property of the "cultural classes." He had gone to the first meeting of the Nationalverein and described it in his novel *Gutmanns Reisen,* and he recognized the success of Bismarck's new Reich. But his essential ideals harked back to pre-Bismarck Germany. Raabe and Theodor Storm (1817–1888) idealized the towns and villages of their grandfathers. Their work shows a modest and quiet spirit of resignation, which indicated a flight from the dynamic world around them, and their realism is tinged with an optimistic faith in human power to overcome pain and suffering. Raabe came to be revered by the cultural bourgeoisie as the embodiment of the "conscience of Germany."

Social realism came to characterize the late works of Theodor Fontane (1819–1898), a journalist who at the age of sixty discovered the deadening automatism of the Prussian system, stripped himself of his Prussian influence, and began writing social novels of the big city. The political ideology of the radical democrats of 1848 and of the Progressives of the constitutional conflict in Prussia found expression in Friedrich Spielhagen (1829–1911). His series of long and disjointed novels depict the entire range of German social and political developments from 1848 to 1900.

He attacked the militarism of the new Reich and continued to plead for humanitarian and democratic ideals to be achieved through disciplined action (*In Reih und Glied*—By all for all).

German naturalism was inspired by the influence of Ibsen (who lived in Munich from 1875–1892), Björnson, and Strindberg, Zola, Dostoievsky, and Tolstoy. It echoed the effects of positivist science and often stood close to Socialism. Following Nietzsche it revolted against conventional religion and morality. In 1889 the *Freie Bühne* was established in Berlin under the direction of Otto Brahm and began to perform the first works of Gerhart Hauptmann (1862–1946). Hauptmann's first play, *Vor Sonnenaufgang,* created a storm with its depiction of humanity in the raw, and a physician in the audience threw a pair of forceps onto the stage in heated rage. Scientific determinism dominated his treatment of characters. Instead of "heroes" there was "tragic guilt" with tender pity for humanity. With *Die Weber* (1892), the first play to handle mass psychology successfully, Hauptmann achieved European fame and also was soon taken over as their hero by the Socialist workers. The poet Richard Dehmel (1863–1920) was likewise loosely associated with the Socialist movement, and his "Der Arbeitsmann" became one of the official anthems of the Social Democratic party.

Naturalism gave way to the decadence and eroticism of the *fin de siècle,* and to the forerunner of expressionism, Frank Wedekind (1864–1916), and to the new currents of symbolism, impressionism, and neo-classicism. Rainer Maria Rilke (1875–1926), the greatest lyric poet of Wilhelmian Germany, represented the "lament of the individual in an alien and hostile world." Thomas Mann (1875–1955), in his great novel *Buddenbrooks* (1901), which depicted the decay of a merchant family in his native Lübeck, initiated a series of novels and short stories in which the dominant theme is the conflict between the artist and bourgeois society and in which degeneration is presented as the necessary fruit of culture. Hermann Hesse (1877–1962), Jakob Wassermann (1873–1934), and Heinrich Mann (1871–1950) began their literary work in this era although the full fruition of their talents and full recognition of their genius did not come until after World War I. Stefan George (1868–1933) issued the first number of his *Blätter für die Kunst* in 1892, but he too did not attain wider recognition and influence until the era of the Weimar Republic.

German painting and sculpture even more than belles-lettres failed to achieve a position of pre-eminence in European culture. In the main the plastic arts in Germany also followed the various currents of expression of general European painting and sculpture. The realism of Adolf Menzel (1815–1905), Franz Lenbach (1836–1904), and Anselm Feuerbach (1829–1880) succeeded the earlier romantic school. The portraits of Prussian rulers by Menzel, the depiction of historical scenes by Feuerbach, and the realistic portraits by Lenbach all were expressive of the new

German nationalism, and Adolf Menzel's "Eisenwalzwerk" in 1875 was the first important artistic representation of the new industrial age. The German impressionist school of painting showed not only the influence of the French impressionists but also the profound impact of the Dutch school of Anton Mauve and Josef Israels. German impressionism found its leading exponents in Fritz von Uhde (1848–1911), Max Liebermann (1847–1935), Wilhelm Leibl (1844–1900), and Wilhelm Trübner (1851–1917). With Lovis Corinth (1858–1925) and Max Slevogt (1868–1932) came the transition to naturalism, and with Emil Nolde (1867–1956) to expressionism. Max Klinger (1857–1920) and Adolf Hildebrand (1847–1921) were the most prominent sculptors of the epoch. In addition, the federal government, the local states, and municipalities covered the country with a great number of new massive public buildings and patriotic and national monuments. The architecture of the period only accentuated all the more the heaviness of most German plastic art during this period, and for that reason art connoisseurs both in and outside Germany preferred the art of neighboring France to that of Germany.

The great German musical tradition of Bach, Beethoven, Schubert, Schumann, and Mendelssohn was carried high in the second half of the nineteenth century by Johannes Brahms (1833–1897). Brahms was born in Hamburg but lived the greater part of his mature musical life in Vienna. Yet by personal contact and by his creative imagination he was the heir to the early nineteenth century German composers. In his four symphonies, his concertos for piano and for violin, and in his rich collection of chamber works he was the symphonist who carried on the tradition of Beethoven; in his romantic piano works he was the heir to Schumann and Mendelssohn; and in his vocal compositions he takes his place beside Schubert and Schumann as a master of the German *Lied*. Like Beethoven, Brahms combined romanticism with universality, discipline, tradition, and regard for form. He combated the extreme subjectivism and formlessness of the later romanticists. In the words of Paul Henry Lang he was "the Lord Keeper of the seal of classic heritage in whom all threads united once more before they were lost in chaos." Of smaller stature but in the same tradition were the symphonists Max Reger (1873–1916), Joachim Raff (1822–1882), and Max Bruch (1838–1920), and the song writers Robert Franz (1815–1892), Adolf Jensen (1837–1879), and Carl Loewe (1796–1869). Engelbert Humperdinck (1854–1921) attained international fame with his children's opera *Hänsel und Gretel,* while Richard Strauss (1864–1949), as the heir of Brahms and Wagner, exhibited both the virtuosity and the decadence of the turn from the nineteenth to the twentieth century.

Subjectivism in music attained its highest expression first in Franz Liszt (1811–1886) and then in Richard Wagner (1813–1883). Liszt was born in Hungary of an Austro-German mother and Hungarian father, but after a dazzling career as a piano virtuoso he settled down in Weimar, Germany, in 1848 and became identified with the cause of German music until his death in Bayreuth in 1886. There he became one of the valiant champions of Wagner and there too he achieved recognition for himself as a new force in musical composition. His early work was devoted chiefly to the creation of romantic piano music, but he then turned his attention to the sonorities of the orchestra. Liszt in Germany, like Berlioz in France, broke down the traditional symphonic form and the dominance of absolute music. In his symphonic poems Liszt became one of the first great exponents of program music. Evaluation of his musical achievements varies from enthusiastic adulation to the censure of Eduard Hanslick, who found his music "contrived," "artificially distilled," and "banal in both its pathos and its sentiment." Perhaps a more objective evaluation is that of Paul Lang, who writes of Liszt, "He may become noisy, bombastic, even border on vulgarity, but he always remains essentially musical."

No musician in the entire history of world music has ever been as much of a storm center as was Richard Wagner. For Wagner was not content merely with writing music. He entered politics as a young man and was forced to flee from Dresden in 1849 for participating in barricade street fighting. He took over the racial theories of Comte de Gobineau and became one of the chief propagandists for Nordic racialism. With his essay on "Judaism in Music" he made himself the spearhead of the antisemitic movement, even though he depended on a number of Jews for support and for help in staging his dramatic operas and even though there is strong evidence to substantiate the charge, first made by Friedrich Nietzsche, that Wagner was himself the son of a Jewish father, Ludwig Geyer, the actor who married Wagner's mother after Wagner was born. Wagner entered the realm of musical controversy with his essays on esthetics and musical form, and made a bid for poetic and literary recognition as the author of the poetic texts for his own operas. On top of all these areas of conflict, Wagner's personal and professional life gave constant cause for contention. This resulted from his arrogant and boundless egotism, his flair for theatrical and melodramatic showmanship, and his unbridled eroticism and passion. Zealous idol worshipers were ranged against violent detractors. Amidst all these strands of personal involvements it is not too easy to isolate Wagner's genuine influences in the realm of musical creation from the polemical bypaths and crooked ways into which Wagner so frequently strayed.

Wagner's earlier operas, *Rienzi* (1840), *The Flying Dutchman* (1841, performed 1843), *Tannhäuser* (1845), and *Lohengrin* (1848), were essentially a continuation of the operatic tradition of Gluck, Weber, and Beethoven's *Fidelio*. It is only after *Lohengrin* that Wagner developed his theory of the "music of the future," which was to be realized in the *Gesamtkunstwerk,* the music drama that was to be a synthesis of all the arts. This theory Wagner attempted to realize in his cycle of the *Ring of the*

Nibelungen, Tristan und Isolde, Die Meistersinger, and in his last opera
Parsifal. Music, held Wagner, was not the "end" of drama, nor was it to
be only the "means"; poetry and music together are to grow organically
out of the needs of the dramatic situation and other arts are to join with
music and poetry to effect the *Gesamtkunstwerk.* The form and quality of
the musical expression are to be determined by the poem, and the melody
is to be molded to the text. The orchestra, like the ancient Greek chorus,
is to express what speech cannot do, the inner meaning and feeling of the
action of the characters on the stage. Wagner also developed the idea of
the *"leitmotiv,"* which played an enormous part in his musical construction and which created its unity. Melody, with Wagner, was revolutionized.
Not only was it compounded of the various *"leitmotivs,"* but it did not
exist as a musical factor in itself as formerly but was determined by the
text. The vocal lines were interwoven with the voices of the orchestra (now
vastly enlarged in size and significance) to form an overall musical fabric
the like of which had never before been heard.

Wagner also dreamed of making art into a religious cult. With the establishment of the Festspielhaus in Bayreuth in 1876, which was made possible by the help of King Ludwig II of Bavaria, and which became a mecca
for Wagnerites from all corners of the world, Wagner hoped to make art
a religion and the theater its temple.

Wagner's grandiose system of the music drama, with all its literary
eloquence and all its philosophic and esthetic embellishments, was essentially a failure. Not only did Wagner not have any successors who carried
on his operatic tradition but even in his own operatic works his musical
and esthetic theories broke down. The most creative and most enduring
elements in Wagner's operas are the orchestral pieces. Wagner is basically
a symphonist, not a dramatic composer. The poetry, the acting, the vocal
parts can all be omitted without detracting very much from the effectiveness of the orchestral music. It is in this manner that Wagnerian music
has found its way into the repertory of all modern symphony orchestras.
The poetic lines are often weak or meaningless rhetoric, and the vocal
parts, especially when Wagner uses his "speech song," painfully long and
tedious bellowing and shouting. It is only the orchestra, with Wagner's
mastery of modern instrumentation and his genius for inventive harmonic
creations and tone color, that gives the whole its intensity, its feeling, and
its expressiveness.

The nature and character of Wagner's music itself, however, became
and still remains a subject of violent and profound controversy. In his
own lifetime the controversy took on the form of a bitter war between
Wagnerites and Brahmsians. Others posed the contrast between Wagner
and Verdi as the antipodes of operatic creation. For the "perfect Wag-
nerite," his music was intoxicating and overpowering, dazzling, erotic, and
above all new. In a world of "unending yearning" he brought to life

characters like Tannhäuser, Lohengrin, Hans Sachs, Tristan, Siegfried, and Parsifal, who were taken to be expressions of the "strong and noble man." In the Wagnerian opera, writes Ernest Newman, "the new expressive, half-poetic power of Beethoven's music finds its further logical development." His critics, on the other hand, pointed to just these qualities of intoxicating sensuousness and eroticism as being responsible for the poisoning of the intellectual and artistic climate. The pessimism of Schopenhauer and his stress upon pure will and pure passion, the influence of the unbridled passion of Schlegel's *Lucinde,* his cult of the night and of the ideal of self-destruction, his constant reveling in the ecstatic, are all combined to create the most extreme form of erotic and individualistic romanticism. It led Max Nordau to brand Wagner as "the last mushroom on the dunghill of romanticism." The noisiness, the often bombastic and inflated character of the scoring, the dramatic pathos that frequently bordered on melodramatic bathos, and the endlessness of his music not only in actual time but in the very inner character of the music, repelled many Germans and non-Germans alike. Langbehn, *Der Rembrandt Deutsche,* pointed to *"Innigkeit"* (quiet inwardness) as the basic German characteristic, and found precisely this quality lacking in Wagner. He called attention to the absence in Wagner of the inner security of a Shakespeare, to "the stupefying and intoxicating elements so characteristic of the Wagnerian art but which are so specifically un-German." The general tone of Wagner's music, admits Thomas Mann, "is heavy, pessimistic, laden with sluggish yearning, broken in rhythm; it seems to be wrestling up out of the darkness and confusion to redemption in the beautiful." It is this sluggish heaviness which led the painter Lenbach to say, "Your music—dear me, it is a kind of freight truck to the kingdom of Heaven." It is the same quality which leads Romain Rolland's Jean Christophe to speak of Wagner's "massive sentimentality and its glowing boredom," and of "the huxtering chivalry, the hypocritical mummery . . . the incarnation of cold and selfish virtue admiring itself and most patiently self-satisfied."

Wagner's music does not speak with reverence and religious conviction as does Bach's; it does not swell up with human tenderness and sympathy as does Mozart's; it does not stir one to nobility of soul or to moral revolution as does Beethoven's; it does not offer the immediate appeal of song and melody as does Schubert's; it overwhelms you and overpowers you—if you allow yourself to be overpowered—and makes you drunk and carried away in one endless swoon of sensuous expressiveness. This is both the grandeur and the weakness of Wagnerian music.

The Viennese music critic and leading anti-Wagnerite of the time, Eduard Hanslick, pointed to the complete absence of human qualities in Wagner's *Nibelungen.* Gods, giants and dwarfs dominate the scene and their motives are deceit, prevarication, violence, animal sensuality, even ecstatic incest. "Not a single ray of noble, moral feeling," wrote Hanslick, "penetrated this suffocating mist." Yet even Hanslick was forced to admit that whenever Wagner appeared there was immediate stimulation, and that despite all strictures upon him Wagner stood at the head of the moving forces of modern art. "He shook the opera and all its associated theoretical and practical questions from a comfortable state of repose bordering on stagnation." He was fought and attacked but he could never be denied. Music was never the same again because of him.

That Wagner was a herald of Nazism is a charge that has frequently been made even by respectable musicologists like Paul Henry Lang. It is a charge, however, that does not lend itself to solid substantiation. True, Wagner's Teuton paganism, his revolt against bourgeois morality, his racial antisemitism, his hostility to liberalism and democracy, all made him most palatable to later Nazi leaders. Racialists from Houston Stewart Chamberlain to Alfred Rosenberg and Hitler placed Wagner in their pantheon of Teuton gods. But these are all extra-musical factors and are, if anything, of secondary importance as compared to the clusters of sound that combine to form Wagner's music. To translate clusters of sound into words and political ideas or political ideas into clusters of sound is a process still fraught with grave intellectual hazards. Such a slippery path may be taken by those who indulge in metaphysical speculation or whose intellectual outpourings are largely the product of subjective and imaginative feeling. It is not the way of the sober historian of ideas.

The tremendous influence of Richard Wagner both inside and outside Germany was only matched by the influence of the philosophy of Friedrich Nietzsche (1844–1900), onetime friend and admirer of Wagner, and later his bitter enemy. It is interesting to note that the two Germans of this period whose genius was most widely recognized were both leaders of the radical revolt against all the accepted values and traditions of Western civilization.

Nietzsche ran counter to all the accepted marks of a German philosopher. German philosophy had always been systematic, and its representatives had always aspired to produce metaphysical systems. Apart from Nietzsche, German academic philosophy, after freeing itself from the dominance of realist positivism and empiricism on the one hand and theistic spiritualized Hegelianism on the other, proceeded under the banner of "back to Kant." Beginning with the work of Friedrich Albert Lange (1828–1875) at the University of Marburg, Otto Liebmann (1840–1912), Hermann Cohen (1842–1918), and Paul Natorp (1845–1924) sought to salvage the ethical idealism in Kant and find place for it within the framework of modern natural science. A little later Edmund Husserl (1859–1938) initiated the school of phenomenology which attempted by means of a new a priori science derived not from psychological experience, as was Kantian subjectivism, but from phenomenological intuition and experience, to establish a new logic which would serve as the basis for the explanation of all sciences of reality.

Nietzsche was no academic philosopher, and it took quite a while before he received any attention from the academic schools of philosophy. Nor was he systematic. Most of his philosophic works read more like prose poems and rhapsodic effusions, often even wildly incoherent. Like Wagner's music, Nietzsche casts a spell over his readers. He bewitches and intoxicates them. His influence is always one of dazzling fascination. As in the case of Wagner too, this was his strength as well as his weakness.

Nietzsche's place in modern thought is even more a matter of controversy than Wagner's, even though Nietzsche dealt with words and not with sound clusters. Much of the confusion is due to the deliberate fabrication of a Nietzsche legend and a distorted picture of the philosopher, first by his sister, who took over the physical care of her illustrious brother when he suffered a mental and nervous collapse and who supervised the publication of Nietzsche's writings to suit the image she had decided to create. The George Kreis subsequently further distorted the picture by deliberately using Nietzsche's biography and writings to develop their own doctrine of contradictions. But Nietzsche himself also contributed to his reputation for incoherence. In his hostility to rationalist and methodical science he did not hesitate to express his scorn for systematic explanation and logical consistency. "Why? Thou askest Why?" says Zarathustra. "I am not of those who may be asked after their Why."

The Nietzsche problem, aggravated particularly with the advent of Nazism and the appropriation by the Nazis of a good deal of Nietzschean ideas and phrases, comes down essentially to this: How can one resolve the contradiction between Nietzsche the good European, the enemy of national chauvinism, the arch-opponent of antisemitism, the severe critic of his fellow Germans (particularly after the creation of the Bismarckian Reich), with the all too frequent occurrence in Nietzsche's writings of exaltation of the blond beast and heroic barbarians, of his ideal of "will to power," and of his complete assault upon all the values and moral virtues of the accumulated traditions of Western civilization? The humanist defenders of Nietzsche point out that Nietzsche was really not interested in providing a new set of values for the future. "I am no man, I am dynamite," he proclaims in his *Ecce Homo,* but he also hastens to add that the last thing he will do is to "improve" mankind. He will not set up any new "idols" (his word for "ideals"). His job is to overthrow them. Nietzsche's historic significance in calling for a transvaluation of all values was his painful quest for philosophical truth and his boldness in daring to challenge and question both his own assumptions and the very assumptions on which all Western culture was based. Philosophy as Nietzsche understood it was "to seek out everything alien and questionable, everything which hitherto has been banned by morality." Zarathustra's admonition to his disciples is not that of a founder of a new school of values or ideals.

> I now go alone, my disciples! Ye also now go away and alone! So will I have it.
>
> Depart from me and be on your guard against Zarathustra! Better yet: be ashamed of him. He may have deceived you.
>
> A man of knowledge must not only love his enemies, he must be capable of hating his friends. . . .
>
> You revere me. But suppose your veneration should collapse some day? Take care that a statue does not fell you!
>
> You say you believe in Zarathustra? But of what value is Zarathustra! You are my believers, but of what value are all believers!
>
> You have not yet sought out yourselves; then you found me. That is what all believers do; that is why all belief means so little.
>
> I therefore call upon you to lose me and find yourselves; only when you have all denied me will I return again to you!

After the German victory of 1870 there was a widespread feeling among the German bourgeoisie and intellectuals that this military victory also meant the triumph of German culture over French culture. Nietzsche warned of the dangers of this cultural arrogance. The elements that made for German victory—military power and discipline—he pointed out, have nothing to do with culture. And he set for himself the task of throwing the powerfully illuminating light of all his keen sarcasm upon the smug self-satisfaction and complacency prevailing in Germany. He condemned the state as the arch-enemy of art, religion, philosophy, and all esthetic values. He combated uncreative smugness, intellectual snobbery, the superficiality of mass culture, and philistine morality. His attack upon Christianity was essentially an attack upon the hypocrisy and insincerity of the Christianity of his day, upon those who "mouth the word righteousness like venomous spittle." Above all, he hated the petty, little man, who out of a sense of guilt and bad conscience becomes the resentful and envious underminer of all that is free and healthy, of all that is full of sunshine and of the optimistic will to live. It is from the bad conscience, from the soil of self-contempt and the will for self-torture that hypocritical religion emanates. This is the hidden source of the ascetic ideal, which is the ideal of "discontented, arrogant, and repulsive creatures, who never got rid of a deep disgust of themselves, of the world, of all life, and did themselves as much hurt as possible out of pleasure in hurting." Nietzsche's call for "good air! good air!" is echoed in Oswald Alving's cry "The sun! The sun!" in Ibsen's *Ghosts*. His call away from those who are filled with the "great nausea with man" and from those who proclaim that "It is a shame to be happy," is the call of Havelock Ellis, G. B. Shaw, Georg Brandes, and

Daniel Halévy. It was this assault upon all the sham and all the stuffiness in modern society that made Nietzsche the inspired prophet of the new youth in Europe at the close of the nineteenth century.

When all this is said and done, however, the fact remains that Nietzsche and the movements that derived from his teachings bear the historic responsibility for helping to create the intellectual climate from which anti-intellectualism, moral relativism, the very nihilism that he struggled to combat, and many other seeds of totalitarianism emanated. His rejection of reason and science, his ridicule of moral virtue, his use of words that lent themselves to abuse, like "will to power," "blond beast," "superman"; and above all his assault upon Judaism, Christianity, and democracy as variations of the same "slave morality" that succeeded in supplanting the original "master morality" by stratagem, hoax, and slippery cunning —all these contributed not only to undermine the ethical, political, and intellectual foundations of European society but also provided ideological tools that could easily be adapted and used by resentful racialists, militarists, and totalitarians for their own ends.

Had Nietzsche lived on to the era of the Third Reich, he would undoubtedly have been one of the first to land in a Nazi concentration camp. And despite the heralding by his sister of Adolf Hitler as the "true son of Zarathustra" and the appropriation of Nietzsche by Alfred Baümler and Alfred Rosenberg to become a prophet of Nazism, there can be no stronger condemnation of the Nazi agitator than that expressed in Nietzsche's *Genealogy of Morals,* the agitator that is "a hollow head . . . heavy with the echo of the great void . . . that nearly always speaks hoarse . . . that speaks aggressively" as opposed to the spirit who is sure of himself, who "speaks softly, seeks secrecy, and lets himself be awaited." But Nietzsche, like Hegel, and like all "dynamic" philosophers must bear the responsibility for having set upon the sea of German and European culture a lot of ideas and phrases which allowed themselves to be vulgarized and distorted. Léon Brunschvig has summed up this responsibility of Nietzsche in these words:

Nietzscheism has been subjected to the same test as Hegelianism. And no doubt here and there philosophical themes have served especially as pretexts to cover up a new offensive on the part of barbarism. But the fact that they have been utilized, the manner in which they have been utilized, have a significance which must not be overlooked. Is it not the criterion of a philosophy which may be called rational without reserve and equivocation, that it should remain incorruptibly faithful to itself? On the other hand, the systems which begin by accepting contradictions, reserving the right to add that they are capable of surmounting them or of "living" them, lodge their enemy in their midst. Their punishment is that their antithesis still resembles them; and that is what happened to Nietzsche.[77]

Nietzsche's critique of the accepted canons of morality and culture was but one, albeit the most brilliant, instance of a current of dissatisfaction with the intellectual climate of Bismarckian Germany. There were some few who rediscovered the anarchical work of Max Stirner, *The Ego and His Own,* and embraced Stirner's assault upon democracy as not compatible with genuine liberty. A few liberals followed the great historian Mommsen when he said: "Have a care lest in this country, which has once been a power in arms and a power in intelligence, the intelligence should vanish and nothing but the pure military state should remain." A very few even took this warning of Mommsen's seriously enough to organize, within the militarist Second Reich, a German branch of the world peace movement. In 1892 Alfred Fried organized the Deutsche Friedensgesellschaft, and the Austrian peace leader Bertha Suttner found many readers in Germany for her peace novel *Die Waffen nieder.*

Most of the so-called *Kulturkritik,* a criticism of the intellectual climate of the Second Reich, came from the right, from those who still could not or would not adjust themselves to the mechanization, industrialization, and urbanization of German society. In many of these currents of thought we find the seeds of subsequent totalitarianism. Julius Langbehn (1851–1907) attained wide popularity with his book *Rembrandt als Erzieher,* first published in 1890. This semi-esthetic and semi-academic volume was a jeremiad on the decline of German culture accompanied by increased specialization, by the absence of epoch-making individuals, by the disciplinization and automatization of intellectual life by the Prussian "commando" spirit, by the drying up of spontaneous creative imagination through the effect of history and science and of the professors, who, declared Langbehn, had become "the general entrepreneurs of German culture" and hence "the German national disease." The "devil of the Germans," according to Langbehn was "plebeianism," which expressed itself in "art as brutalism, in science as specialization, in politics as democracy, in culture as doctrinairism, in humanity as pharisaism."

Similar laments were echoed by the orientalist Paul de Lagarde (1827–1891), who called for the elimination of all Semitic and Roman elements in German culture and a return to the "pure" Germanic culture and German national religion of the *Urzeit.* An even more volatile racialist doctrine was propagated by the German followers of Gobineau. These included Richard Wagner and his son-in-law, the renegade Englishman, Houston Stewart Chamberlain, who in his *Foundations of the 19th Century* sought to prove that all the great cultural figures of history were of Aryan racial stock, and who found his strongest propagandist in the person of Emperor William II. A Gobineau Society and museum were founded by Ludwig Schemann.

Most of these currents of *Kulturkritik* merged at the end of the nineteenth century to foster a revived neo-romanticism combining the traits of anti-rationalism and anti-intellectualism in a reaction against science, materialism, and conventional morality. The proponents of this movement sought a way out of the soulless mechanization of modern mass society and mass culture in a return to the romanticist concept of an organic society, by an exaggerated faith in tradition and even in the mystical notion of "blood." In such widely divergent critics as Lagarde and Walther Rathenau, the plaint against mechanization went hand in hand with that against "de-Germanization." In the pre-war days, when all such movements were merely movements of protest of a small intellectual minority, the political shadings and complexions of the participants were not too clearly defined, and often liberals, Socialists, and militant nationalists of the right were found together in intellectual and spiritual brotherhood.

Neither formal religion nor the intellectualism of modern science provided spiritual satisfaction and emotional security any longer. "The most profound error of the social thought of our day," wrote Walther Rathenau, "is found in the belief that one can demand of scientific knowledge impulses to will and ideal goals. Understanding will never be able to tell us what to believe, what to hope for, what to live for, and what to offer up sacrifices for. Instinct and feeling, illumination and intuitive vision—these are the things that lead us into the realm of forces that determine the meaning of our existence." [78] Rathenau's *Zur Kritik der Zeit,* Lagarde's *Deutsche Schriften,* Langbehn's *Rembrandt,* Nietzsche's *Ecce Homo,* the erotic expressionism of Wedekind and Dehmel, the aristocratic neoclassicism of Stefan George—all joined to sow the seeds of a radical revolt against the rational-bourgeois civilization of ninteenth century Germany, and especially against those elements which Germany shared with other Western countries.

This cultural and social revolt came to a head in the German youth movement of the first decade of the twentieth century. Youth groups of different political and cultural persuasions and of different economic strata, but all aspiring to find a way out of the meshes of the mechanized modern life, organized themselves first in 1896 as the *Wanderbund,* and then in 1900 as the *Wandervogel.* They sought liberation by contact with nature and hoped to find refuge from "atomistic individualism" in new forms of group loyalties, in a revolt against "bourgeois" ethics and sex mores, and in new forms and types of leadership. In their restless hiking and camping they gave expression to the romantic spirit of *Wandern* in contrast to modern *Verkehr;* in their *Scharen* and *Bünde* they contrasted organic *Gemeinschaft* with artificial *Gesellschaft.* If one asks, wrote Hans Blüher, what it is that the German youth rise up against most profoundly and "what is the human type that we oppose continuously and which is entirely unbearable in our vicinity—then we must answer—the bourgeois type." [79] Bourgeois here means not a social or economic class but the entire complex of traditional spiritual values. The high-water mark of the Youth Movement was reached in the meeting on the Hoher Meissner, near Kassel, in 1913. Soon, however, the movement split up into various groups and the coming of the war in 1914 took a grave toll of both leadership and following. Out of the experiences and traditions of the Youth Movement, however, came much of the idealism, the intellectual groping, the quest for new forms of social and political life and also the mental confusion, the moral anarchy, and the political authoritarianism which blossomed forth in the Weimar Republic.

All these negative currents were but tiny ripples upon the huge and vast sea of optimism that engulfed the German Reich before the outbreak of World War I. William II railed against these *Schwarzseher,* or prophets of doom, who refused to bow down and to worship the idol of success personified by the mighty image of wealth and power which Germany had· become by 1914. And the majority of the German people gloried with their emperor in the proud achievements of the German Reich.

CHAPTER XII

Wilhelmian Germany, 1888-1914

Wer soll Herrscher sein? Der Bescheidenste.
LANGBEHN

1. THE HUNDRED DAYS OF FREDERICK III

On March 9, 1888, at 8:30 A.M., the old Emperor William I breathed his last. He had lived to the ripe old age of ninety-one. The evening edition of the *Frankfurter Zeitung* wrote, "High politics throughout the world stands still for a moment to mourn for Kaiser William." The reflections on the progress of Germany in the historic thirty years during which he occupied the throne as King of Prussia and then as German emperor, as well as the anxieties regarding the future of European peace occasioned by his death, all underscored the mighty and central position that Germany had come to occupy among the powers of Europe.

William I was succeeded by his son Frederick III, the most tragic figure of the Hohenzollern dynasty.[1] Aged fifty-seven, Frederick was already a dying man when he ascended the throne. He had developed cancer of the throat in 1887, and by the time he became emperor he was no longer able to speak but had to communicate his wishes by written message. A tall, manly figure, a veteran of the Austrian and Franco-Prussian wars, he struggled valiantly until his death to cope with the ravaging onset of the dreadful disease. He was to reign for only ninety-nine days. On June 15 he passed away, the second German emperor to die within the year.

Frederick III was the great hope of German liberals. Married to the oldest daughter of Queen Victoria of England, he became familiar with British parliamentary institutions through his travels in England. He was greatly impressed with English constitutional government and became critical of Prussianism as practiced by Bismarck. His wife, Victoria, strengthened these tendencies in him, and exercised a great deal of influence over him up to his death. As crown prince, Frederick had on several occasions indicated his objections to Bismarck's strong-arm methods and the disregard of parliament and public opinion. Mention has already

274

been made above of his Danzig speech during the Prussian constitutional conflict. Among his circle of advisers and intimates were many of the leaders of the German Progressive party. An entry in his diary during the Franco-Prussian War reads, "Our chief thought is how, after the hard-earned peace, to carry on the development of Germany in a progressive manner." [2] His entry for New Year's Day, 1870, reads as follows: "I maintain even today that Germany could have 'conquered morally,' without blood and iron, and become united, free and powerful. . . . It will be our noble but immensely difficult task in the future to free the dear German fatherland from the unfounded suspicions with which the world looks upon it today. We must show that our newly acquired power is not a danger but a boon to humanity." [3]

Frederick's first royal proclamation, addressed "To My People," was greeted with enthusiasm and high hopes by liberal public opinion. The liberal *Nation,* edited by Theodor Barth, in its editorial of March 17, 1888, wrote, "What the liberals yearned for and hoped for was a humane prince who would show himself to be amenable to progressive ideas." The democratic *Frankfurter Zeitung* heralded the dawn of a new liberal era The emperor's proclamation, it wrote, "arouses the happy promise of a constitutional régime which will show understanding for and keep step with the demands of a cultural life and free us from the terrible nightmare of the fear of egotistical and intolerant reaction." [4]

Bismarck expressed his official pleasure with the new emperor despite his liberal background. But difficulties soon arose. Relations with the empress were strained, and Bismarck tried to isolate the royal pair and prevent access to them by the Progressive leaders. The emperor and empress were able to maintain contact with the liberal leader Ludwig Bamberger only by secret emissaries and by the use of coded messages.[5] One of the first issues to arise between the new emperor and the chancellor concerned the emperor's desire to bestow royal decorations on his liberal friends Virchow, Forckenbeck, Simson, Siemens, Gneist, Mommsen, Stauffenberg, and others. Bismarck strenuously opposed the emperor's plan, and succeeded in curtailing the list to Forckenbeck and Virchow and, in the case of the latter, to indicate that he was being honored only for his medical and scientific (and not for his political) services.

The only firm action of a liberal nature taken by Frederick III was that of forcing the ouster of Robert von Puttkamer from the Prussian ministry. Puttkamer, who had been named Prussian Interior Minister in 1881, had become popularly identified as the most rabid enemy of the democratic and liberal elements. The "System Puttkamer" was responsible for the hounding of the Socialists during the period of the anti-Socialist legislation and for the ruthless suppression of all political and social aspirations of the working classes. Above all, Puttkamer used his police powers to attempt to sway and influence voting in the national elections. It was because of this latter activity that Frederick ordered Puttkamer to be relieved of his post, to the great joy of the Progressive elements.

What the course of German (and world) history would have been had Frederick lived on is one of the controversial and problematic questions in German history. German liberal historians have often indicated their belief that the entire course of internal and external policy would have been turned into new liberal and pacific directions had Frederick reigned long enough to put his liberal stamp on German affairs. Yet many others have cast doubts concerning the genuineness of the liberalism of Frederick. Hans Delbrück, historian and editor of the *Preussische Jahrbücher,* held that Frederick, while somewhat more progressive and tolerant than the groups which customarily surround a prince and a king, remained basically the Prussian officer. One of the most recent students of this period holds that Frederick, while more humane and liberal than either his predecessor or his sucessor, nevertheless was not a liberal in a truly concrete way. "His thoughts . . . betray the dilemma of a mind which places supreme importance on authority and prestige and yet would like to be considered progressive." [6] Whatever might have happened had he lived on, it nevertheless remains true that he became a symbol and rallying point for German liberals and Progressives, particularly after his death. Karl Schrader, Progressive deputy, wrote: "A better future, evolving from the people, must be based on him, and we must make it possible by keeping him alive in the mind of the nation." [7] Bismarck, on the other hand, declared that the legend that Frederick was a liberal was dangerous for the whole dynasty, and must be destroyed. Of the two, Bismarck was the more successful. The stormy events of the Wilhelmian epoch soon effaced completely the tragic and problematic figure of Frederick from the picture. The "Hundred Days" of his reign remain but a minor episode in the annals of German history and an insignificant interlude between the "heroic" epoch of William I and the "stormy" era of William II.

2. THE AGE OF BISMARCK COMES TO AN END

Frederick III's son and successor, William II (1888–1918), was both temperamentally and politically a sharp contrast to his father.[8] William came to the throne as a young man of twenty-nine. His early English education had given way to training in the Prussian guard. Relations with both his parents, but especially with his mother, had been strained and often bitter. A deformity of his left arm was in part responsible for the fact that his mother cared for him less than for any of her other children, and this physical handicap was no doubt an important psychological factor in developing in the young prince an inner uncertainty and insecurity which he most frequently covered up with a blustering arrogance. Under the mask of the proud emperor there was an essentially sensitive, insecure, timid, and nervous individual who was always self-conscious and whose every act and motion was deliberately intended to overcome this inner weakness. Walther Rathenau described him as being "without scarcely one unconscious moment . . . unconscious only of the struggle with himself; a nature unconsciously directed against itself." [9] His "preoccupation with his ego," wrote Rathenau, "was never overcome." But he possessed an interesting and colorful personality which cast its spell over all he met. Even August Bebel, the Socialist leader, said of him, "He is every inch a man." He was charming and full of good will and amiability in personal relations, and he was a brilliant talker, if not a good listener. Of unusual grasp of mind and powers of assimilation, he cultivated a wide sphere of intellectual interests ranging from art and music to the latest developments in science and technology. He was above all a gifted speaker. With his "particularly sharp, resounding delivery," every speech of his was a "momentary outpouring." He usually spoke without notes, and he let himself go with a torrential outpouring of phrases born of momentary impulse. When he began to speak it was never quite certain where he would end, and this spontaneous exuberance and impulsive speech-making were more often than not the cause of worry to his ministers and anxiety for foreign world opinion. There was thus in William II, despite these intellectual gifts, very much of the irresponsibility of the dilettante. A profound observer like Rathenau complained of his "dilettante foreign policy, romantic conservative internal policy and bombastic and empty cultural policy."

An important key to William's personality was the wide range of dual and internal conflicts to which he was subjected. There were his mother versus Bismarck, Prussia versus England, Potsdam versus Hamburg, absolutism versus liberalism, tradition versus modernism, and in the last years of his reign Bethmann-Hollweg versus Ludendorff. Most significant for the understanding of William II was the fact that he personified a mixture of feudalistic romanticism and the most modern ideas, especially of science and technology. He was predisposed to mystical and spiritualistic ideas and movements (after the manner of his granduncle Frederick William IV) and at the same time was the first Hohenzollern ruler to befriend big industrialists and actively support the most up-to-date technological advances. In this respect William was the royal symbol of Germany as a whole. For, as pointed out above, it was this combination of the most advanced technology with archaic, feudalistic romanticism in the political and social field that created the "German problem" in the modern world. And in this respect too William II was a modest but real forerunner of "William III," or Adolf Hitler.

As Bismarck pointed out, William II inherited from his earlier Hohenzollern ancestors the love of display and official pageantry, including Frederick William I's predilection for tall officers. "Every day is a masquerade ball for the monarch," wrote his confidant Eulenburg. He ordered thirty-seven changes of uniform for his guard during the first sixteen years of his reign. This was not only a result of his love of pageantry but also an expression of deep personal vanity. "Don't for a moment imagine," said his mother, "that my son does anything from any motive but vanity." His happiest moments were those when he was encircled by enthusiastic sycophants brimming over with nothing but praise and adulation for him. And he was constantly surrounded by such flatterers. Their motto was, "He must have sunlight only," and they isolated the monarch from anything but pleasant and optimistic news. Court nobility and Junkers, members of the plutocratic bourgeoisie, rich Hanseatic citizens, and wealthy Americans made up this coterie of the emperor's adulators.

Extremely nervous and unstable and even unbalanced at times, the young emperor was continually on the go. The Berlin *Vossische Zeitung* in August, 1894, estimated that during the preceding year William had been traveling 199 days. The witty Berliners dubbed him the *Reisekaiser* (traveling kaiser) in contrast to William I, the *Greisekaiser* (old kaiser) or *Weisekaiser* (wise kaiser). His was not only physical restlessness but also mental instability. Bismarck complained in 1890: "The bad part of it is his [William's] wild flights of thoughts. There is never any calm deliberateness, but rather spontaneous utterances of subjective inspiration without any consideration for the caution demanded by his high station."

William II's Calvinistic tutor, Georg Ernst Hinzpeter, had implanted in him a pharisaic note. He was most certain that he was ordained by God to lead his people to great deeds. "Our Lord God," he once said, "would not have taken such great pains with our German fatherland and people if He did not have still greater things in store for us." His belief in his divine election and calling was almost naïve in the simplicity of his acceptance. He considered himself the elect of God, sure to find the right way for his people.

This acceptance of the "divine calling" was the basis for William's thoroughly absolutistic view of his royal powers. He was violently opposed to constitutionalism and to the political parties. At a public meeting in 1891 he declared, "There is only one master in the Reich and that is I, and I shall tolerate no other." To a group of young recruits he said, "When your emperor commands you to do so you must shoot at your fathers and mothers." In the guest book at Munich he inserted the inscription, *Suprema lex regis voluntas est*. After twenty years of rule he once proudly admitted that he had never read the constitution and was unacquainted with it. The Reichstag deputies he dubbed "sheep's heads" or "night watchmen," and he refused to have any personal contact with the party leaders of the Reichstag. "If Windthorst ever comes to the palace," he said, "I would have him collared by a subaltern and three men and thrown out." He gloried in the fact that he never read newspapers and was completely indifferent to what "these sheep's heads" were writing.

"The soldiers and the army, and not the decisions of parliaments," he declared, "forged the German Reich."

Characteristically enough, therefore, the first public proclamation by the new emperor was not "To My People" (as his father had done), but "To My Army." "We belong together," he proclaimed, "I and the army. We are born for each other and we shall stand indissolubly together no matter whether God's will brings peace or storm." This display of militarist mentality only confirmed the fears of liberals in Germany, among whom he was already known as "the bellicose young master." Theodor Barth's *Nation* and the *Frankfurter Zeitung* greeted the accession of the new monarch with forebodings as to his militarism and absolutism. Foreign public opinion was likewise filled with concern for the future. In 1894 Ludwig Quidde, a liberal, pacifist journalist and historian, published a book which he called *Caligula, eine Studie über römischen Cäsarenwahnsinn.* This was a most adroit and brilliant attack upon William II, but so skillfully and carefully did the author confine himself to historical truths about the ancient Roman emperor Caligula that government authorities found it embarrassing to prosecute the author without being themselves forced publicly to draw the comparison between Caligula and William.

An apt and amazingly prophetic analysis of William II was made by the wise Portuguese diplomat Eça de Queiroz, in 1891, after only three years of rule:

In him as in Hamlet [wrote the Portuguese consul-general], there exist the germs of various men, and we cannot foresee which of them will prevail, or whether, when one has finally developed, he will amaze us by his greatness or by his triviality.

In this Sovereign what a variety of incarnations of Royalty! One day he is a Soldier-King, rigid, stiff in helmet and cuirass, occupied with nothing but reviews and maneuvers, placing the change of guard over all the business of the State, regarding the drill-sergeant as the fundamental unity of the nation, putting barrack discipline above every moral and natural law, and concentrating the glory of Germany in the mechanical precision with which his recruits march. Suddenly he strips off the uniform and dons the workman's overalls; he is the Reform King attending only to questions of capital and wages, eagerly convoking social congresses . . . and determined to go down in history embracing the proletariat as a brother whom he has set free.

Then all unaware he becomes the King by Divine Right, haughtily resting his Gothic sceptre on the backs of his people . . . subjecting the highest law to the will of the King, and, convinced of his infallibility, driving over the frontiers all who do not devotedly believe in him.

[Then he becomes the] Courtier-King, worldly, pompous, thinking only of the brilliancy and sumptuosity of etiquette. . . . The world smiles and presto! he becomes the Modern King, the Nineteenth Century King, treating the past as bigoted, . . . determined to construct by the aid of Parliamentarism the largest amount of material and industrial civilization, regarding the factory as the supreme temple, dreaming of Germany as worked entirely by electricity. . . .

Some say he is merely a youth ardently thirsting for newspaper fame. . . . Others aver that there is in him nothing but an overbalanced fancy, carried madly along by the impulses of a morbid imagination which, for the very reason that he is an almost omnipotent Emperor, he is allowed to exhibit without restraint. Others again see in him simply a Hohenzollern in whom are summed up and in whom flourish with immense parade all the qualities of Caesarism, mysticism, sergeantism, red tape-ism and dogmatism, which have alternately characterized the successive kings of the most lucky race of petty lords of Brandenburg. . . .

It is my opinion, however, that he is nothing but a dilettante of activities— I mean a man strongly enamoured of activity, comprehending and feeling with unusual intensity the infinite delight it offers, and desiring, therefore, to experience and enjoy it in every form permissible in our civilization. . . .

This is what makes the German emperor so prodigiously interesting a figure; in him we have among us in this philosophical century, a man, a mortal, who, more than any other expert, prophet or saint, lays claim and appears to be the ally and intimate friend of God. The world has never seen, since the days of Moses on Sinai, such intimacy, such an alliance between the creature and the Creator. . . .

To him nothing is impossible for he commands two million soldiers and a people who seek liberty only in the regions of philosophy, ethics and exegesis and who, when their Emperor orders them to march, silently obey. . . .

William II runs the awful danger of being cast down the Gemoniae. He boldly takes upon 'himself responsibilities which in all nations are divided among various bodies of the state—he alone judges, he alone executes, because to him alone (not to his Ministers, to his council or his Parliament) God, the God of the Hohenzollerns, imparts His transcendental inspiration. He must therefore be infallible and invincible. At the first disaster—whether it be inflicted by his burghers or by his people in the streets of Berlin, or by allied armies on the plains of Europe—Germany will at once conclude that his much-vaunted alliance with God was the trick of a wily despot.

Then there will not be stones enough from Lorraine to Pomerania to stone this counterfeit Moses.[10]

Such was the person of the ruler who in 1888 inherited not only the Kingdom of Prussia and the leadership of the German Reich but also with them the Iron Chancellor, Prince Otto von Bismarck, then seventy-three years old, who had guided the destinies of Prussia and Germany for twenty-seven years. A clash between these two strong-willed and authoritarian personalities was inevitable. Contemporary political observers expected it to come and were not surprised when it did. William, as crown prince, had been an enthusiastic admirer of Bismarck,* but, as the

---

* "I revered and idolized him. . . ." he writes in his *Memoirs*. "Bismarck was the idol in my temple, whom I worshipped" (*The Kaiser's Memoirs*, New York, 1922, p. 1).

chancellor had himself predicted, the young man was going to be his own chancellor when he became the ruler.

Bismarck's dismissal did not come until two years after William's accession to the throne. The circumstances and motives involved were many and complex, and a large literature has accumulated on the subject with many diverse interpretations. Each of the chief participants has left his version of the story: William II in the form of a long letter to Emperor Francis Joseph of Austria-Hungary written on April 3–5, 1890, but not intended to be published until after his death, and Bismarck in the third volume of his *Reminiscences,* also not to be published until after William's death. The downfall of the monarchy in 1918 provided the grounds for the publication of both these documents even though William was still alive.[11]

There were several questions of governmental policy on which serious difference of opinion developed between the young emperor and the old chancellor. While Bismarck had been the architect of the extensive social-legislation measures inaugurated in 1881, he had by now become convinced that no future action in this field was necessary. Moreover, his hopes that the social legislation would take the wind out of the sails of the Socialist movement had failed to materialize, and the Socialists continued to increase their hold on the working population of the Reich. William, on the other hand, had developed an active interest in the social question. From his early tutor, Hinzpeter, he had acquired a deep and lasting concern with the social problem. Hinzpeter had likened the solution of the social question to the Protestant Reformation, and had often declared that this would become the "second confirmation" of the supremacy of the German idea. William had also fallen under the spell of the Christian Social movement of Adolf Stöcker. He was, therefore, eager to extend the earlier body of social legislation and bring about legislative enactment of compulsory Sunday rest and control and limitation of hours and conditions of labor for women and children. A sharp disagreement between emperor and chancellor developed on this issue.

Another issue, closely related to the former, revolved around the renewal of the anti-Socialist legislation, which came up in 1890. Bismarck, thoroughly disillusioned with the attempt to win over the working population by peaceful means, was set on suppressing the Socialists with even greater violence than before. In the new anti-Socialist law which he prepared for the Reichstag, he introduced an article (Article 24) which would empower municipal authorities to deport all Social Democratic leaders from the towns and drive them into the country villages. Bismarck hoped in this way to provoke the Socialists into acts of violent resistance and thus provide him with the excuse for smashing them ruthlessly. This proposal, however, met with the opposition of most of the Reichstag party leaders. Even the Conservatives, fearing that the deportees from the

towns would spread socialism in the rural areas, declared themselves opposed to the bill in this form. William II likewise looked with disfavor upon
this measure. Not that he was any more tolerant of the Socialists than Bismarck. But his personal vanity led him to believe that he could win the
workers to him by peaceful means. To the ministers in a Crown Council
he declared that he was determined "to be *le roi des gueux* [the king of
the beggars]; the workers shall learn that I care for their welfare." He was
not going to start his reign with bloody suppression and violent assaults
upon the workers. The Socialist law was, as a result, voted down by the
Reichstag and the period of legality for the party renewed.

While there were also differences between Bismarck and William on
questions of foreign policy, notably on relations with Austria and Russia,
these did not play any role in bringing about Bismarck's dismissal as is
sometimes alleged. The major issues in this area came to a head after
March 17, 1890, the date of Bismarck's resignation.

The actual resignation of Bismarck came as a result of a minor matter
pertaining to the relation of the emperor and his ministers. Bismarck,
who with age and ill health had grown even more authoritarian and
suspicious than he had always been, sought to prevent political influence
other than his own from being brought to bear on the kaiser. He therefore dug out of the archives a royal order of September 8, 1852, by
Frederick William IV, according to which all ministers, except the minister of war, were obliged to consult with the prime minister before they
could discuss important matters with the king. William resented this
limitation of free access of his ministers, and he repeatedly asked Bismarck
to have the order repealed. On March 17 William sent General von
Hahncke to Bismarck bearing an ultimatum either to draw up the repeal
of the order of 1852 or to submit his resignation. Bismarck thereupon
resigned and the emperor accepted it forthwith.

It is quite obvious that these differences, while serious in themselves,
were not of such gravity that they could not have been ironed out had the
desire to work together been present with both parties. They were not in
themselves more than pretexts for the final break. Basically there was
something more complex and more serious. Hans Delbrück, who was well
informed and close to governmental circles, advanced the thesis that the
break came because William refused to go along with Bismarck's plan
of a *coup d'état*. According to Delbrück, "Bismarck no longer had a program that could be carried out." Bismarck, writes Delbrück, had never
really had a stable majority in the Reichstag. He always manipulated
various combinations. The growth of the Socialist party and of the Progressives increased the permanent opposition to him, and by 1890 he did not
see his way to rule as in the past. Bismarck then conceived the idea of
bringing about a change in the constitution because he was no longer
able to juggle the Reichstag majorities. His plan, according to Delbrück,

was to bring on a conflict with the Reichstag, provoke riots by the opposition, which then would have to be put down by force. The kaiser would lay down the imperial crown, then reconvene the princes and establish a new Reich with a restricted suffrage and open ballot. Delbrück quotes a letter from von Helldorff, the leader of the Conservative party, in which the Reichstag leader relates that Prince Bismarck "told him in all earnestness that he wanted to devote his last years to making good the greatest mistake of his life, which was the creation of equal universal suffrage." [12] This course of action William II refused to accept, and this, according to Delbrück, was the real cause for Bismarck's dismissal.

While this thesis is appealing in that it provides a concrete cause for the dismissal of the Iron Chancellor, and while there is no evidence to contradict Delbrück, it must also be admitted that existing evidence in support of the thesis is meager and inadequate. We must fall back on the less tangible but more real factor of the irrepressible conflict between an old man who had become accustomed to have his own way and run the show for thirty years and a headstrong young ruler equally bent on being master and not to be put in the shade by anyone else. Intrigue of court personnel only aggravated the situation. When Count Waldersee said within earshot of the new emperor that Frederick the Great would never have become "the Great" if, upon coming to the throne, he had found a minister of the importance and position of power of a Bismarck, it must have made a deep impression on the young ruler, who was more than eager to be another Frederick II. William was too vain and too young to be willing to knuckle down to the old chancellor, and Bismarck had become too old and too rigid to be able to adapt himself to the new ways and the new demands of the young ruler. Francis Joseph was right when he wrote to William, "Prince Bismarck and Metternich both had the misfortune to be unable to find the exit from the stage, and to remain too long."

Although the news of Bismarck's resignation caused widespread comment and some excitement in political circles, the interesting thing is that few were surprised, many (especially in liberal circles) expressed a sense of relief, and no one raised a voice or a finger to demand the continuance of Bismarck in office. The *Vossische Zeitung,* on March 18, 1890, wrote as follows:

Much as the emperor may venerate the great statesman, he has himself too pronounced an individuality to be able to subordinate himself to the chancellor's guidance. Today the crisis is upon us and—a sign of the times, and also a sign of the loyalty of the chancellor's party—not a finger has been lifted, not a pen taken up, so far as individuals and journals in an independent position are concerned, to advocate Prince Bismarck's continuance in office. The Iron Chancellor had lost his sureness of touch, he had begun to vacillate, while the will of the youthful and energetic ruler was coming more and more strongly into play. . . . On one side stood the chancellor, child of the pre-1848 days, brought up in the system of Metternich; on the other the emperor who has imbibed the spirit of the days since the uplifting years of the war! [13]

Prince Otto von Bismarck retired to his estate at Friedrichsruh, supposedly to pass his closing years as a Prussian landowner. But the old chancellor smarted under his defeat. He not only resented his own dismissal but was bitterly grieved in having his hopes for a "Bismarck dynasty" dashed to pieces. He had carefully trained his son Herbert in the arts of politics and diplomacy and had looked forward fondly to establishing him as his successor in the chancellery. Resentment together with an incapacity to resign himself to a place outside the public view combined to induce the old man to keep his iron in the political fire at long range. He traveled, made speeches, gave interviews, published his memoirs, and inspired political writers to keep up a barrage of criticism of the "new course" of the monarch and his new chancellor. The *Hamburger Nachrichten* in particular came to be known as Bismarck's mouthpiece. The activities of Bismarck and his friends had all the earmarks of a concerted effort to arouse popular enthusiasm for him, and thus embarrass the emperor and force him to oust Caprivi, Bismarck's successor, and then recall Bismarck. These efforts were not successful, however, despite popular recognition of the achievements of Bismarck in unifying Germany. It is significant to note that a motion in the Reichstag on March 23, 1895, to send good wishes to the former chancellor on the occasion of his eightieth birthday failed to pass the house by a vote of 163 to 146. The real Bismarck cult developed only after his death.

Bismarck was a great master of politics, but he was not a political educator, and, apart from his hopes for a Bismarck dynasty, he did nothing to educate the German people or any segment of the German nation to political leadership. That is why he reaped the fruit he sowed. In 1890 he complained to a reporter that all the political parties looked upon him only as "the man of the past and not of the future." To which the *Frankfurter Zeitung* wrote: "He himself reared the type that now rewards him with ingratitude and he himself bred the absence of principles. He himself put the stamp of 'patriotic' virtue upon characterless cowardice which yielded, without any will of its own, and which shouted its praises upon success." [14] That is why Bismarck also left behind him a political vacuum bordering almost on chaos. There was no political élite or politically trained aristocracy. And among the people only the following of the Center party and the Social Democratic party had developed something of a political tradition—both, however, hostile toward the work of Bismarck. The old bourgeois parties had been "denatured and demoralized" by Bismarck. Max Weber, writing in the *Frankfurter Zeitung* in the summer of 1917, summarized the legacy of Bismarck as follows:

Bismarck left behind him as his political heritage a nation without any political education, far below the level which, in this respect, it had reached twenty years earlier. Above all, he left behind a nation without any political will, accustomed to allow the great statesman at its head to look after its policy for it. Moreover, as a consequence of his misuse of the monarchy as a cover for his own interests in the struggle of political parties, he left a nation accustomed to submit, under the label of constitutional monarchy, to anything which was decided for it, without criticizing the political qualifications of those who now occupied Bismarck's empty place and who with incredible ingenuousness now took the reins of power into their hands.[15]

3. BISMARCK'S SUCCESSORS

The period between the dismissal of Bismarck and the close of World War I (1890–1918) is usually referred to as the "Wilhelmian Epoch." [16] It was the monarch and not the chancellors that set the tone and the pattern for this era. All the glitter, all the brilliance of material prosperity together with the militarism, navalism, and inner insecurity which characterized Germany as a whole during this period was a reflection as well as a product of the dynamic personality of the emperor. It was the "new course" as set by William. No longer did the office of Reich chancellor occupy the central position it had under Bismarck. The absolutism of the emperor, the caliber of the men selected to hold the post of chancellor, as well as the growing complexity of public affairs, all tended to reduce the significance of the chief minister. On the one hand major decisions were made by the emperor himself, and on the other hand the influence and power of the various ministries in the cabinet increased considerably over what they had been under Bismarck. The range of problems for the chancellor's office had increased greatly, and the holders of the office were not of the caliber of Bismarck. The result was a sort of unofficial splitting up of many of the chancellor's functions.

Four men occupied successively between 1890 and 1914 the post left vacant by Bismarck: General Leo von Caprivi from 1890 to 1894, Prince Chlodwig zu Hohenlohe-Schillingsfürst from 1894 to 1900, Prince Bernhard von Bülow from 1900 to 1909, and Theobald von Bethmann-Hollweg from 1909 to 1917. The person selected as Bismarck's immediate successor, General Caprivi, was a Prussian army officer and former head of the admiralty. By contrast with Bismarck he was hailed as a "progressive." Theodor Barth wrote of him that "he combined the best traits of a Prussian officer and Prussian bureaucrat. His high sense of duty did not allow him to become the tool of special interests. During his four years as chancellor he was first unconsciously and then consciously an exponent of the democratic idea." [17] It was under Caprivi that the anti-Socialist law was dropped, the period of military service lowered from three to two years, a more conciliatory policy adopted toward the Poles, tariff duties lowered, and a progressive income tax introduced in Prussia. These were all measures that found favor in the eyes of the liberals and roused the ire of the Junkers. The progressive income-tax law was largely the work of Johannes Miquel, who became Prussian minister of finance in June, 1890. The outstanding achievement of the Caprivi era was the negotiation of commercial treaties with Austria, Italy, Belgium, Switzerland, Rumania, and Russia and the consequent lowering of German tariffs. These were intended to stimulate German industrial exports in agrarian countries, and compensation was necessary in the form of a reduction of German grain duties. Though this made Caprivi more popular among the liberals, it also made him the target for the ruling clique of Prussian landowners who finally forced him out in 1894.

Hohenlohe-Schillingsfürst, who succeeded Caprivi, also enjoyed some good will among the liberals. He was a Bavarian, and had a creditable record as governor of Alsace-Lorraine. But he was more diplomat than statesman, and, as Maximilian Harden remarked, his motto was, "One must always wear a good black coat and always hold one's mouth." [18] Above all, he was too old to exercise anything more than nominal power.

Bernhard von Bülow was more cultured and more suave than his predecessors. He was far from profound, but he knew his way around, had a great command of language, and above all he had the capacity to win people. A flatterer of the emperor, he was *un homme des expédients*. He administered his office like a grand seigneur, without much sense for detail. He had great skill in political maneuvering and was adept at improvisation to avoid conflicts. He was possessed of ready wit and was a master of the phrase. These helped him on more than one occasion to extricate himself from embarrassing situations. But despite his charm and *esprit* he was never able to convey to his hearers in the Reichstag or to diplomats at home and abroad any sense of weight or of compelling conviction. Most of his talents and energy were concentrated on problems of foreign policy. At home his motto was "Beware of internal crises." The most important domestic question for him was the fight against the Socialists. The agrarian Conservatives who first ridiculed him and called him "little statesman" were soon won over by his pro-agrarian tariff policies, and they sang his praises as "our best chancellor." Bülow thus became the inventor and manager of the bloc system of parties in the Reichstag. His goal was to prevent further democratization by deepening the cleavage between the bourgeois parties and the Socialists. After the elections of 1907 he created a combination of Conservatives, National Liberals, and Progressives, known as the "Bülow bloc," which commanded a majority in the Reichstag and which held together until June 24, 1909, when the Conservatives left the bloc to help defeat a government bill for inheritance taxes. Bülow thereupon resigned as chancellor.

Bülow's apparent dependence on a Reichstag majority and his policy of avoiding conflicts with the Reichstag made it appear as if Germany was developing a sort of parliamentary government with the cabinet responsible to the Reichstag majority. Actually, this was anything but the case. Two incidents served to underscore the basically absolutist and militarist character of the German government, which had not changed from what it had been as created by Bismarck. The first of these incidents was the *Daily Telegraph* interview by the emperor in 1908 and the other the Saverne (Zabern) incident in 1913.

On October 28, 1908, the London *Daily Telegraph* published an interview with the emperor in which William made some startling pronouncements on foreign policy. He declared that he was a friend of England but that he was in a minority in his country and that German public opinion was hostile to England. His naval policy, he explained, was directed not against England but against Japan. He also made claim to having sent a military plan to England during the Boer War which was later used by Lord Roberts. These tactless and undisguised indiscretions by the chief of a state astounded all. Such conduct stirred up a wave of indignation abroad and a storm of protest and consternation in Germany. The political parties, the press, all raised their voices in protest against the "personal rule" of the emperor. Maximilian Harden, the brilliant editor of *Die Zukunft,* who did more than any other single individual to undermine the prestige of William II in the country, devoted a series of articles to the incident in which he described the storm let loose against the emperor.[19] "Personal government, absolutism, impulsive action, romantic politics, duty of responsible advisers, all these old themes were heard once again; only this time the orchestra was much larger and it played *fortissimo.*" Even the executive committee of the Conservative party issued a public statement calling upon the emperor "to act with greater reserve" in the future. The emperor continued on his travels during the storm as if nothing had happened. He did explain, however, that the text of the interview had been approved before publication by the Foreign Office. Interpellations in the Reichstag forced the admission from Chancellor Bülow that he had given his permission to publish the interview without taking the trouble to read the text. This was indicative of the slipshod character of Bülow's administration, but it did not minimize the degree of indiscretion demonstrated by the emperor.

The storm against the "personal government" of the emperor brought forth repeated calls from the liberals for constitutional reform and parliamentary control of foreign affairs. Max Weber, writing to Friedrich Naumann at the time, said: "The political structure is to blame. . . . A dilettante has the threads of policy in his hands." The *Berliner Tageblatt* wrote: "How is this possible? Here is a people of over 60 million, a nation that has reached the heights by its own powers, a nation of the highest intelligence, and yet the fate of the chancellor and, on his fall, the choice of his successor are dependent upon the will of one single individual. Such a condition is unbearable for a self-conscious nation." [20]

All this political excitement, nevertheless, brought forth no change whatsoever in the absolutist and militarist control of the government. Rightly could the liberal sociologist Ferdinand Tönnies bemoan the fact and point once more to the political immaturity of the German people. Never had there been a more favorable situation for peaceful constitutional reform. Not only the necessity but the opportune moment for action was present. There was universal indignation and unanimity of opinion on the effects of the emperor's behavior. Now was the opportunity to establish solid, responsible government. But nothing was done about it, and the Conservatives and Centrists in the Reichstag, without whom no majority could be formed, were content with their verbal expressions of protest. "If the events which led up to the Reichstag session of November 10, 1908," wrote Tönnies, "will not have any great internal political consequences and effects, then this will provide the proof of the unfortunate political immaturity of the German people." [21]

Another test of the real seat of political authority in the Wilhelmian Reich was provided by the incident in the small village of Saverne (Zabern) in Alsace in the latter part of 1913. In this village was stationed the 99th infantry regiment under the command of Colonel von Reuter. There had been considerable tension in Alsace between the French and the Germans and between the native civilians and the imperial troops. A young lieutenant, von Forstner, addressing new recruits on October 28, 1913, told them that they were to try to stay out of trouble with civilians but that if attacked they were to use their weapons. Then he is alleged to have added the sentence, "If in doing so you stab a *'Wackes'* you will get 10 marks from me." The word *Wackes* originally meant "rowdy," but it had come to be used as a slanderous designation by the Germans for "Alsatian." News of this incitement against the Alsatians spread throughout the area, and resentment increased and incidents multiplied. On November 28 Colonel von Reuter had 28 civilians picked up on the street and held in custody. This assumption of police powers over civilians by the military raised a furor not only in Alsace but throughout Germany. There were heated debates in the Reichstag on December 3 and 4, and Socialists, Progressives, National Liberals, and Centrists attacked the role of the military. The Prussian minister of war, von Falkenhayn, delivered a brutal defense of the military, and Chancellor von Bethmann-Hollweg backed him up. This defense of the officer corps only further infuriated the Reichstag deputies. A vote of no confidence in the position of the chancellor on the Zabern affair was passed by a majority of 293 to 55. Only the Conservatives and the Reichspartei stood by the government. But this action by the majority of the people's representatives was of no consequence other than as an oral expression of indignation. For the emperor, the chancellor, and the military authorities this was a matter of the defense of the prestige of the army and an underlining of its position of supreme authority in the Reich. A court-martial in Strassburg on January 10, 1914, cleared Reuter completely, declaring that the civilian police had failed to keep order and that Reuter's action was therefore justified. Reuter was rewarded with an imperial decoration. Thus once more was seen the camouflage character of German parliamentary institutions, and the source of real power was revealed to be where Bismarck had originally placed it—in the throne and in the army. "In Prussia," wrote Wickham Steed in the *London Times* of January 12, 1914, "the army is supreme and, through Prussia, the army rules Germany. This is the first lesson of the trial for those who lightly imagine the German Empire to be even as other states." [22]

Bülow's resignation as chancellor on July 14, 1909, seemed to be due to his failure to command a majority in the Reichstag. Actually, this was not the case. The emperor let him go because he resented his behavior in the *Daily Telegraph* interview affair. Bülow was succeeded by Theobald von Bethmann-Hollweg, the chancellor who was destined to lead Germany to war in 1914. Bethmann-Hollweg was a combination of the typical Prussian bureaucrat and schoolmaster. "He always had the chalk in his hand," wrote Theodor Wolff. He was a serious and earnest person with a high sense of duty but with little imagination or dynamism, and he had no experience in foreign affairs. With the heritage left to him by Bülow and with the doings of William and his intimate advisers, Bethmann was not the best equipped statesman to deal with the world crisis confronting him in 1914.

The constitutional structure of the German Reich under William thus remained substantially the same as it had been under Bismarck. The federal structure with the dominance of Prussia allowed for the continued existence of the local dynasties in the other German states and for a certain amount of local and individual expression. Bavaria, with its strong Roman Catholic concentration, retained the greatest amount of local sovereignty, particularly in the field of education and in the development of its own military units. Saxony was the most industrialized of the states, and in Leipzig and Chemnitz a strong Socialist movement was developed. Württemberg, under King Karl and then under its William II, saw the development of a strong liberal movement which found political expression in the Volkspartei. There, as in Baden, the revisionist wing of the Social Democratic party and the left wing of the Catholic Center party were the more dominant elements, making it possible for the two political parties to co-operate frequently. While Prussia continued to be governed by its three class systems of suffrage, these and other local states introduced universal suffrage, and Württemberg also had proportional representation.

Demands for constitutional reform of the Reich and of Prussia con-tinued to be pressed by Socialists and Progressives—demands for the abolition of the three-class system in Prussia, for the introduction of ministerial responsibility, and for democratic control of foreign policy. In conservative and moderate circles the continued growth of the Socialist movement and of the Social Democratic party was the most serious cause for alarm. In Progressive circles, however, the desire for co-operation with the Socialists became more pronounced. Theodor Barth in 1903 wrote that no matter what one personally thought of the Social Democratic party, one could not overlook the fact that it was gathering around its banner an increasing part of the German population. "The most important task for German statesmen today is, therefore, to bring back Social Democracy into the circle of the other political parties and to make the valuable national energies which are found in this party serve an enlightened national policy." [23] Without a political *modus vivendi* between liberals and the Social Democrats, continued Barth, "liberalism remains impotent against the reactionary forces. Liberal politics in Germany, as in all countries with a highly developed industry, can only be carried on with the aid of the class of wage workers. This is the alpha and omega of all political knowledge."

In his *Liberalismus und Sozialdemokratie,* Barth, one of the early liberal opponents of socialism, carried his conversion to *social* democracy still further and thus made it possible for his group to unite with the followers of Friedrich Naumann. Barth's *Nation,* Friedrich Naumann's *Hilfe* and *Patria, März,* established in Munich in 1907 by Ludwig Thoma, Hermann Hesse, Albert Langer, and Kurt Aram, and later edited by Theodor Heuss; the Berlin literary and political monthly *Die Neue Rundschau;* and Germany's best dailies, the *Frankfurter Zeitung,* the *Berliner Tageblatt,* and the *Vossische Zeitung,* continued to give expression to the democratic forces in the era of William II. But these forces continued to be limited in number as well as in strength. Their following included but a thin layer of intellectual opinion. And even the majority of intellectuals continued to turn their backs on political life. The absence of any chance for a career in politics for gifted persons, the individualism of the intellectuals, the cult of "pure" esthetics, and the enchanting magic of the new aristocratic gospel of Zarathustra which enveloped the younger generation of intellectuals, all contributed to let the call of democratic liberals go unheeded.[24]

Minor concessions were made by the government. Legislation was passed in 1911 converting Alsace-Lorraine from an imperial domain to a separate state; payment of members of the Reichstag was introduced in May, 1906, giving each member 400 marks per month, a free pass on all German railroads, and providing for a deduction of 20 marks for each day absent from Reichstag sessions. The greatest concessions were made in the field of social legislation. Protection was extended to large groups of workers not hitherto covered by the earlier social legislation, and new avenues opened in factory inspection, child and women's labor, and employment statistics and improvement of labor conditions in the government-operated enterprises. William II, following the instruction he derived from Hinzpeter, was more than any of his predecessors the "social emperor."

The dominant feeling in Germany under William II was one of pride in its political and industrial achievements and optimism for the future. In 1913 the twenty-fifth anniversary of William's accession to the throne was celebrated with a chorus of glowing praise, flattery, and rhapsodic eloquence by historians, economists, sociologists, philosophers, technicians, and journalists, the like of which had never been heaped on any other German emperor. There were some in Germany who were not deluded by the external brilliance of material prosperity and military prowess. Paul de Lagarde and Friedrich Nietzsche, on the right, gave expression to the doubts as to the real strength and lasting character of the German glory— doubts that were to sow the seeds of a later nationalist resurgence. On the left, Samuel Saenger, the wise and urbane political writer of the *Neue Rundschau,* bemoaned the fact that "the German of today [1908] has become grossly sensual, materialist and almost completely an empty-headed specialist. . . . Gradually he has become hard and realistic and distrustful of every activity which does not immediately yield an increase in economic power." [25] Walther Rathenau, the son of a rich industrialist but more at home in philosophy and esthetics than in the electrical business, warned of the hollowness and sham of Wilhelmian prosperity.

I see shadows rising wherever I turn [wrote Rathenau in 1911]. I see them in the evening when I walk through the noisy streets of Berlin; when I perceive the insolence of our wealth gone mad; when I listen to and discern the emptiness of big-sounding words. . . .

An age is not without care just because the lieutenant beams and the attaché is full of hope.[26]

Such voices, however, were confined to a tiny minority of German public opinion. They were denounced by the kaiser as *Schwarzseher,* or somber pessimists.

4. THE NEW COURSE—*WELTPOLITIK*

German energies and attention were focused chiefly on the field of foreign policy during this era. Here the "new course" charted by William II was one of *Weltpolitik.* The role of the dominant continental power in Europe was no longer enough for Germany. It aspired to the "place in the sun" of world politics. This meant above all a colonial empire, a giant navy, and a commanding role in world affairs. To this field we must now direct our attention.[27]

The discussion of German foreign policy in the Wilhelmian epoch inevitably revolves around the climax of this policy, that is, the outbreak of World War I and the problem of German responsibility for the war. The story of German and European diplomacy as the background of the war has been studied and analyzed in greatest detail, and it is not intended to recapitulate this story here. The overthrow of the ruling dynasties in Russia, Austria-Hungary, and Germany in 1918 resulted in making available to students and writers the records of the foreign offices which under normal conditions would have been delayed more than fifty years for study. These in turn made it necessary for the French and British governments to publish extensive collections of documents on their respective foreign policies. These, together with hundreds of volumes of memoirs, recollections, reminiscences, confessions, and self-justifications by participants, provided historians with a wealth of material hitherto undreamed of by writers on recent and contemporary history.

Yet important as these materials are, it is illusory to think that they can provide the definite and conclusive answer to the problem of the origins of the war and to the assessment of responsibility. The real designs and deeper motivations of statesmen and governments seldom if ever appear in these state papers. "The really vital things, the motives," wrote the diplomat Friedrich Rosen, "are much more concealed than clearly presented in the political documents, and the personalities appear to the reader in the way in which they themselves seek to present themselves." There are so many different points of view usually present that it is easy to make any sort of case out of the welter of documents. Most important, however, is the fact that the purely diplomatic approach to the study of foreign policy fails to take into consideration the all-important factor of the "spirit" of the national policy. The forces of historical tradition, public opinion, national ideals and education and all those factors that make up the "mind" and the "will" of a people and its leaders are perhaps more revealing and more pertinent than the sequence of foreign-office telegrams and the unraveling of the maze of diplomatic documents.

It was through the effects of foreign policy that the glittering brilliance of the Wilhelmian Reich came to tragic and ruinous catastrophe. But foreign policy and domestic policy were closely linked. The spirit of home affairs breathed its spirit into that of external policy, and vice versa. The assessment of responsibility leads one into the whole philosophical problem of historical causation. Historians often assume the tragic, exalted, and nobly classic approach of viewing the destinies of men and nations as being guided by powerful but unknown and mysterious forces that determine the ultimate course of human affairs. The acts of individuals, great and powerful as they may seem to their contemporaries, are viewed as but the ineffectual and frustrating attempts of puny mortals to grapple with problems beyond their ken and beyond their control. Such a view has the added enchantment in that it lays claim to calm detachment, impartial objectivity, and noble serenity. Yet unless one accepts the theological interpretation of history and identifies these forces with the active guidance of a Supreme Being, the end result is to be left with a Great Unknown as to the ultimate source of these so-called great forces. Such a view, of course, relieves the historian from social responsibility and the mortal danger of committing himself to any particular cause or opinion. It is the view of the present writer that great and transcendent forces do indeed operate in the historical process but that these forces are in themselves the product of the wills, the desires, the passions, as well as the intelligences, of men of all kinds. The composite of all these wills and desires is what creates historical tradition, and historical tradition exercises an enormous influence on the wills and desires of every new generation of men. Historical tradition, however, is not static and rigid. It is constantly being modified, sometimes more and sometimes less, by every succeeding generation. And the modifications are made by individuals or groups of individuals acting upon or reacting to the product of the forces of historical tradition and other forces. That is why ultimate understanding of historical events must take into consideration the long-range factors of history and tradition as well as the wills and desires of individuals. Both interact with each other to determine the course of human affairs. Thus an explanation of German foreign policy leading to World War I involves the consideration of the deep-seated and rooted historical traditions of German politics and of German mentality as well as the influence exercised by the men in positions of leadership with authority to act.

Let us first dispose of certain obvious fallacies and erroneous assertions regarding the origins of World War I. In the first place no one deliberately planned or willed the war. It was not as simple as all that. Even the most aggressive and most militant individuals or groups in all countries would have preferred to realize their goals without a war. As for Germany, there is no shred of evidence to indicate that either William II or any of his ministers deliberately planned and plotted the war. That does not eliminate their responsibility, but responsibility was of a much more complex nature. No more tenable are the over-simplified assertions that particular individual philosophers or thinkers, like Nietzsche or Treitschke, are to be held responsible. Treitschke, as we shall see later, plays an important role in the picture and Nietzsche a very small one, but here too the problem is much more complex. Even less valid is the frequent assertion that the war was the work of the Prussian Junkers. As seen earlier, and as we shall observe later, there was frequently more violent German nationalism among the industrial classes of western Germany than among the agrarian Junkers. The circumscribed Prussianism of the Junker often took exception to the pan-Germanist expansionism and navalism of the industrial groups. It is also naïve to believe that war-mongering and nationalist aggression were limited to one country alone—Germany. There were dangerous elements in almost all nations of the world. There were Déroulède's chauvinist followers in France, ruthless imperialists in England, and saber-rattling militarists in the United States. Nor was Tsarist Russia the torch-bearer of liberalism, humanitarianism, and democratic internationalism. But when all that is said and done, the fact still remains that of all the nations involved, Germany must bear the major share of the responsibility for having allowed a local dispute in the Balkans to flare up into a world conflagration that not only resulted in greater destruction and dislocation than that produced by any previous wars but one that so completely ravaged and disorganized the world that it laid the basis for the even greater catastrophe of World War II and for all the still unpredictable and unknown results which that war brought on.

We learned a great deal about the origins of World War I from those of World War II. World War II saw the bankruptcy of the widespread economic interpretation of war as the product of rival economic imperialisms and of the equal share of complicity by international groups of bankers, industrialists, or munitions makers. The kind of reasoning which pervaded the Nye Senate Investigating Committee in the United States and which gave such powerful support to the thesis of equal complicity and which did much to bolster the pro-German version of the origin of World War I was proved to be shallow and superficial by the events of World War II. The kind of thing which would-be objective historians had grown accustomed to labeling as products of Allied, especially British, propaganda, and which were utterly fantastic and unreal to their minds, suddenly became very real and concrete. Atrocities, dreams of world conquest, pan-Germanism, romantic absolutism, and fanatical militarism could no longer be dismissed as brain children of British intelligence officers and paid propagandists. Hitler and the Nazis revealed all these and other things in such realistic and unadorned fashion that even the most skeptical had to accept their reality. And we came to see that World War I was the dress rehearsal for World War II, that Hitler and the Nazis brought to the surface in a tremendously magnified form the same forces that operated to bring on World War I.

From the experience of the coming of World War II we also learned to realize that because there never is one side that is all black while another is all white, it does not mean that we cannot tell which is right and which is wrong. There is always *some* justice and *some* right even on the most aggressive side. The devil is the devil precisely because he is a fallen *angel,* and his blandishments would not be so alluring nor his malevolence so enormous were he not to make use of just grievances or appeal frequently to the better instincts of man. Evil is dangerous only when it is mixed with good, for undiluted evil stands so clearly exposed that it is summarily rejected. And we learned also from World War II not to dispose as lightly as did the "sophisticated" generation following World War I of moral judgments and ethical values as mere window dressing and hypocrisy. The hard-boiled, so-called "realistic" approach to foreign policy was recognized to be so characteristic of fascist and Nazi conduct that we came to see, as Wickham Steed had seen long before, that "no shrewd calculation of interests, no canny avoidance of moral responsibilities, avails to replace a sane ideal in the management of foreign affairs."

There were differences, especially in degree, between the handling of foreign affairs in the various periods of modern German history. The basic, underlying difference between German foreign policy under Bismarck and that under William II was that Bismarck's policy was limited, circumscribed, and intelligible, and therefore essentially peaceful in character. After the victory of 1870 Bismarck realized that the new German Reich needed a long era of peace. He therefore was satisfied to contain German energy within the European continent. Even the Balkans were not considered by him to be a direct field of German interest. He sought to maintain the security of the Reich by an elaborate system of alliances. The core of his policy was the Triple Alliance with Austria and Italy, and Bismarck always stressed the defensive character of this alliance. Through the Three Emperors' League and the Reinsurance Treaty he maintained friendly ties with Russia. France was to be isolated in Europe, and Bismarck sought to get Austria and Russia to come to an agreement on the Balkans. For Germany he desired no additional territory either in the southeast or in the Baltic area. He had as little interest in the German Balts as he did in the Germans in Austria. He always sought to maintain good relations with England, and considered peace with that country to be more valuable for Germany than either the acquisition of a colonial empire or the building of a large navy. German support was given to the expansion of other powers in Asia and Africa in order to divert them from Europe or else to create tension between them and have them look with more favor to Germany. His prime purpose was to establish Germany as the arbiter of Europe, and he well-nigh succeeded in realizing this. But he had no ambitions to become the *arbiter mundi,* as William later did. And this was the profound difference. Bismarck had concrete and tangible "interests." A policy based only on "prestige" or "power" was denounced by him in a speech in the Reichstag of February 6, 1888, as completely unrealistic. Bismarck had little sympathy for pan-German aspirations, and his attitude toward colonies during most of the years he was in office was one of extreme reserve.

It is true that some of Bismarck's commitments contradicted each other, as for example the Reinsurance Treaty with Russia and the ties to Austria, Rumania, and Italy, and his system of alliance, therefore, depended too much on his own personality and on his own individual skill in juggling the conflicting commitments. His loyalty as an ally was also not to be taken without reservations. Moreover it is open to speculation whether or not the peaceful character of German foreign policy between 1871 and 1890 was not due merely to the fact that Germany required a pause after unification and that its expansionist character would have come later under any circumstances. Be that as it may, the fact remains that, except for the scare of 1875, so long as Bismarck remained in the Wilhelmstrasse there was no fear or alarm in the capitals of Europe, of war by Germany.

The advent of William II to the helm brought about a sharp break with Bismarck's policy. "The course remains the same," declared William II, but at the very same time he said, "Full steam ahead." His contemporaries soon recognized that he was pursuing a "new course." This "new course" is best expressed in one word, *Weltpolitik,* or world policy. The aspiration to advance from a continental to a world power and the concomitant policies of colonialism and navalism marked the turning away from the foreign policy of Bismarck. "The entire political situation of Germany," wrote the *Frankfurter Zeitung* on January 26, 1896, "is going through a far-reaching transformation. Rarely has active agitation in so important a question been carried on in so superficial a manner as is now being done by numerous circles in arousing a certain national chauvinism for the inauguration of a world policy. . . . Germany is chiefly a continental power. Its strength on land has given it its undisputed position as a world power. . . . The desire for a world policy for Germany is in no way in keeping with the strengthening of Germany's position; it rather puts in question the peaceful intentions of the German Reich and creates new imponderables on the political scene." [28]

William and his new ministers, however, went "full steam ahead" on the new course of *Weltpolitik.* Bismarck's policy, declared Bülow "must be transcended." In his first Reichstag speech Bülow declared: "We do not desire to put anyone else in the shade, but we want our place in the sun." Foreign countries, said Bülow, were benefiting from the emigration of thousands of good German citizens who were leaving Germany because there was no room for them. Germany therefore needed a colonial empire and a navy to protect it. "The sea," continued Bülow, "has become a factor of more importance in our national life than ever before in our history. . . . It has become a vital nerve which we must not allow to be severed if we do not wish to be transformed from a rising and youthfully vigorous people into a decaying and aging one." [29] It was necessary for Germany, according to Bülow, to be strong at sea, "so that we might be free to protect our overseas interests, independently of the influence and the choice of other sea powers. Our vigorous national development, mainly in the industrial sphere, forced us to cross the ocean. For the sake of our interests as well as of our honor and dignity, we were obliged to see that we won for our international policy the same independence that we had secured for our European policy." [30]

This new course of German policy was the product of several factors. It represented a trend of natural growth in power of a nation that had consolidated its strength and position on the Continent and was seeking to find new outlets for its nationalist and expansionist energies. It was also the result of the rapid industrial development of Germany in which Germany, like other imperialist nations, sought new sources for raw materials, new outlets for export of its industrial products, and new avenues for capital investment. But there was also a goodly mixture of a sort of romantic universalism which was a product of the neo-romanticism of the last decades of the nineteenth century and which looked back to the universal German Empire of the medieval era. This, too, represented a profound departure from the Bismarckian mentality. Bismarck was anything but a romanticist, and he had no use for these wild and fantastic dreams of political romanticism. He was a champion of the old order based on the idea of the monarchical state, and he was not attracted either by the "larger Germany" ideals of the ardent nationalists or by the world aspirations of the romantic imperialists. In this respect his position with regard to expansionist and dynamic politics was parallel to that of Metternich in the earlier part of the century.

The beginnings of German colonial penetration into Africa were made in the period between 1840 and 1860 by commercial houses in the Hanse towns. Missionaries also played their part. The economist Roscher had published a series of articles in 1847–1848 on colonial problems for Germany, particularly as related to emigration. Later Treitschke advocated the acquisition of colonies by Germany because he believed that Germany was doomed to be only a second-rate power without colonies. In 1879 the former inspector of the Rhenish missionary association, Friedrich Fabri, published a small volume which aroused considerable attention. It was called *Bedarf Deutschland der Colonien?* Fabri advocated the establishment of colonies to take care of surplus population and to receive deported undesirables, but above all for the "ethical" reason that colonies would "provide the nation with new tasks." [31]

Bismarck was originally opposed to any kind of governmental colonial policy. He rejected repeated projects for the acquisition by Germany of colonial areas. "As long as I am chancellor of the Reich," he declared in 1881, "we shall not carry on any colonial policy. We have a fleet that cannot sail and we do not need any vulnerable spots in other parts of the world which will fall as booty to the French as soon as war breaks out." [32] In July, 1883, he wrote, "Far from increasing the power of a state, colonies give the forces of the state a more one-sided direction toward the external world which might heighten the halo of its power for a while but not permanently." [33] Writing to the Bremen merchant F. A. Lüderitz,

Bismarck said he hesitated "to embark upon colonization without adequate preparation and a definite impulse from the nation itself." He also pointed out that the international situation was not opportune. By 1884 the international situation had improved and a great wave of colonial propaganda had created the "definite impulse from the nation." The *Kolonialverein,* founded in 1882 in Frankfurt am Main under the presidency of Prince Hermann zu Hohenlohe-Langenburg, and the Gesellschaft für Deutsche Kolonisation, founded by Karl Peters in Berlin in 1884, became the most active agents in promoting a campaign for an energetic colonial policy. In 1887 the two organizations combined under the name of the Deutsche Kolonialgesellschaft. Lüderitz in West Africa and Karl Peters in East Africa were the most active propagandists for colonialism.

April 24, 1884, was celebrated in Germany as the "birthday" of German colonial policy. On that day Bismarck proclaimed German protection over the area of Southwest Africa exploited by Lüderitz. In July of the same year a German protectorate over the Cameroons coast was proclaimed by Gustav Nachtigall, and in the following year German protectorates were proclaimed over East Africa and Zanzibar. Thus Germany had made a substantial beginning toward a colonial empire under Bismarck. Bismarck's colonial policy, however, was that "German colonization was to come only *after* and not before the German merchant." "We do not want to go there and occupy territory in the hope that the merchant will follow." He was also opposed to the setting up of a colonial administration with garrisons and colonial officials. This he considered too costly. He wanted Germany to follow the pattern of the early East India Company and have the commercial interests bear the cost of administration.

With the new course under William a much more aggressive colonial policy was inaugurated. German penetration was extended to the Far East, to the South Seas, to the Near and Middle East and to North Africa. The older form of commercial company was replaced by outright exercise of German sovereignty over the areas annexed, and a modern and efficient Colonial Office was set up as a special government bureau.

The motivations for colonialism were varied. The business and industrial groups sought to further their interests by exploiting these new areas. Theoretical exponents of colonialism, like Hans Delbrück, who carried on extensive agitation for a German colonial empire, were impressed by the national prestige (not the economic advantages) achieved by England as a result of her empire. "What was and is valid for England is also valid for us." [34] In cruder form this was a vague sort of "me too" attitude. Germany, coming upon the scene later than the other colonial empires, was eager to grab at anything in order that her prestige among world powers should not be lessened. "We wished," writes the National Liberal historian Erich Brandenburg, "in a general sort of way not to be left out, and whenever others were getting something, to secure a bit for ourselves." [35]

As in the case of other imperialist nations the argument for German colonies was often dressed up in more pompous and grandiose terms. "Germany needed colonies," wrote the nationalist historian Adalbert Wahl, "as much as her daily bread." Not so much for economic reasons but "in order to provide a field of activity for the German people overflowing with the spirit of enterprise and energy and to help create a new and less commonplace type of German." A growing and energetic nation, wrote Wahl, "must not be hemmed in," and colonization was the only outlet for this energy.[36] Young Stresemann in 1907 called the colonies "also a piece of the German soul."

By 1914 the German colonial empire covered 1,027,000 square miles with a population of about 12 million colored peoples and 24,389 whites. Hopes for German emigration to these colonies remained unrealized, as was the case with most imperialistic ventures (German emigration, in so far as it continued, went predominantly to the United States and to Latin America). By 1912 there was a total investment of 505 million marks in these colonies. Exports from the colonies included cotton, rubber, hemp, oil products, timber, coffee, cocoa, copper, and diamonds.[37]

The acquisition of colonies and the expansion of German foreign commerce provided the impetus behind the drive for an expanded navy program. William II was from the start imbued with the desire for a large navy. The first intimation of far-reaching naval expansion came in a speech by the kaiser on January 18, 1896, when he proclaimed the fact that "the German Reich has become a *Weltreich.*" On June 17, 1897, Admiral von Tirpitz became state secretary for naval affairs, and the kaiser secured the man that was to transform Germany's "baby fleet," which in 1897 occupied seventh place among the great powers of the world, to the mighty German fleet which came well-nigh to challenge the British supremacy of the seas. Tirpitz it was who not only worked out the technical plans for the great naval program but also combined with his great skill and energetic determination a keen sense of the value of propaganda. He exploited systematically all the arts of propaganda for his cause among political leaders, in the press and among the people. The traditional background for popular support was not lacking. The old seafaring tradition of the German Hanse could be played upon to call up the romantic aura of the past. Liberal opinion could be reminded of the strong desire for a German fleet found among the democrats of the 1840's. Tirpitz's sympathy for the industrial and commercial classes was indicated by his repeated demands for a "commercial" general staff which was to consist not only of soldiers but also of industrialists.

The emperor set the tone in numerous speeches for the naval propaganda. Statements like "A strong fleet is a matter of desperate need for us" or "Imperial power means sea power" (*Reichsgewalt bedeutet Seegewalt*) were echoed throughout the country. At the kaiser's personal request the work of the American Admiral Mahan on the influence of sea power was translated into German, and exercised an enormous influence in building up enthusiasm for a big navy. The most effective instrument created by Tirpitz to put his program across with the public was the Flottenverein, which he organized in 1898. By 1908 it had more than a million members throughout Germany, and its official organ had a circulation of over 370,000. More technical and scientific aspects of navalism were treated in the yearbook *Nauticus,* published in Berlin, which was of considerable importance. Here too, as in the case of colonies, Tirpitz found his most ardent supporters not among the Prussian agrarians but among the industrial and commercial classes and the professors. The agrarians, as a matter of fact, frequently identified navalism with industry, and Friedrich Naumann, in 1898, went so far as to set up the slogan of "Fleet versus reaction."

The first naval-expansion bill was passed by the Reichstag in 1898. Official assurances designated the measure as purely defensive and peaceful in intent. There was no intention, it was declared, to challenge any other nation's naval power. But the fears of liberals were aroused by the constitutional aspect of the naval bill which set the naval budget for a period of seven years and thus deprived the Reichstag of any effective control of the expenditures. The measure was nevertheless passed by a large majority, despite the opposition of Progressives, Socialists, Poles, and Guelphs, and a minority of Centrists. By 1899, however, came the request for further expansion and the statement that the provisions of the naval bill of 1898 were no longer adequate to meet needs. Further expansion was approved in 1906, 1907, and 1908. Fears as to the aggressive character of the German program increased both in liberal circles within Germany and abroad, especially in England, as Tirpitz expanded his program of construction of heavy battleships. German rivalry of England became acute as a result of Britain's introduction of the dreadnought in 1906. Germany followed the British model immediately. Her position as a "newcomer" gave her distinct advantages. She did not have as large a fleet of old vessels to discard as did England and she could therefore concentrate a larger part of her building program upon the heavier type. Thus by introducing this innovation Great Britain reduced the advantage that it had previously held over the German navy.

The theory elaborated to defend the German naval program was that of the so-called "standard of risk." The German fleet, while not necessarily the strongest in the world, was to be so strong that even for the most powerful naval power an assault by sea would not be without grave danger and risk. This would prevent aggression by even the strongest sea power, and the fleet would thus constitute a guarantee for the maintenance of peace. Tirpitz and his naval program thus came to represent one of the major factors in German foreign policy, especially with respect to relations with England. His naval program was chiefly responsible for arousing the fears of German aggression. "To be the greatest land power on the continent and at the same time to possess the greatest fleet in the world was impossible," reflected von Kühlmann after the war.[38] And he adds, "Many years of political work in England before the war left me with the conviction that the rapidly increasing construction of a German war fleet was the ultimate motive that ranged England on the side of our enemies." [39]

Friction with England on naval armaments was but one of the areas of discord between Germany and the other powers. Territorial rivalries between England and Germany in Africa also marred the friendly relations of the two powers from time to time. Alsace-Lorraine and disputes over Morocco gave Franco-German relations the jitters every so often. The rival ambitions of Russia and Germany's ally, Austria-Hungary, in the Balkans were cause for alarm on many occasions. And the Berlin-Baghdad railway, spearheaded by the initiative of the Deutsche Bank, inspired fears of aggression among all the powers. Yet the fact remains that all these and other issues were eventually settled by mutual agreements, and adjustments were made. Even the difficult Berlin-Baghdad railway problem was settled by an Anglo-German agreement of June 14, 1914, just a few weeks before the assassination of Archduke Francis Ferdinand. This indicates clearly that wherever there were definite and clearly defined points at issue they were capable of peaceful adjustment. Yet war did come after all! Why? Because behind all the specific claims and counter-claims there was the "spirit" of German foreign policy which was in the ultimate sense undefinable and insatiable.

That there was justice in many of the German demands has never been denied. But as Bernadotte Schmitt put it nicely:

A policy of naval expansion, the development of an African empire, commercial and financial penetration of the Near East could each be justified. But to pursue all three courses at the same time was the worst possible policy, for it kept alive the distrust and suspicion of the Entente powers, convinced them of the dangerous reality of German militarism and made them more anxious than ever to act together.[40]

German foreign policy prided itself on being "realistic." Anglo-Saxon expressions of concern for "international morality" were sneered at as pious frauds and expressions of hypocrisy. The notion of "interests" and supremacy of interests dominated German thinking. The Machiavellian tradition of the supremacy of power and force over ethical and moral principles was so deeply ingrained in German leaders that they could not understand nor were they willing to admit the sincerity of expressions of good will and desires for concessions on the part of other governments. "We did not realize then," writes Sir Edward Grey, "how inveterate and deep-rooted at Berlin was the habit of attributing a sinister and concerted motive to any proposal from another Government." [41] The abrupt, rough, and brusque manner of even the most pacific of German diplomats was also a permanent characteristic of the "spirit" of German foreign policy. And yet it always came as a surprise to German travelers and observers that there was so much "fear" of Germany abroad. In 1905 the French journal *Le Courrier Européen* conducted an inquiry into the attitude of Europeans toward Germany as a world power. Hans Delbrück, writing of this in his *Preussische Jahrbücher,* confessed that he never realized that hostility toward Germany was as great as indicated in this survey.[42] Above all, there was the complete unintelligibility of German foreign policy. No one was able to figure out what was really wanted. And this was so because German desires were pervaded by the romantic dreams of world rule. German policy, writes Brandenburg, caused irritation among other powers, and they "suspected Germany of concealing deep-laid and dangerous schemes which seemed all the more formidable because no one could say in what they consisted or what their ultimate limits might be." Brandenburg rejects this interpretation and describes German policy merely as "planless, petty and uncertain." And so it would seem if rational considerations of a finite character are the only factors considered. But in the same way in which Brandenburg gives us a large volume on German foreign policy without once mentioning the pan-Germans, he is also completely incapable of understanding the irrational factors operating in the world of German foreign politics.

In the 1890's wide distribution was given to a print of an Amazon defending herself against a crowd of assailants and bearing the legend, "People of Europe, Unite and Preserve Your Holiest Possessions," signed "William II." This was an expression of the new curious combination of power politics and a neo-romantic revival of medieval German universalism. The tradition of the old medieval universal empire of Frederick Barbarossa and all the mystery of the Kyffhäuser legend gained widespread currency during the latter years of the nineteenth century. The conflict between nationalism and universalism had not completely died out in Germany. Now that the "little German" solution had created the German Reich and it had become powerful, a sort of diseased and psychopathic kind of universalism was created out of a synthesis with nationalism to bring forth the dream of a united world, but a world under German hegemony. This was the unintelligible but very real factor in German foreign policy which did not emerge with full clarity until it was magnified many more times over by Hitler and the Nazis.

German foreign policy under William was not only full of contradictions but it was also never quite clear who really determined foreign policy. It is a mistaken notion that authoritarian and absolute government necessarily means unified and efficient control and administration. While William II was the absolute ruler and constitutionally the sole arbiter of both military and foreign policy, he was subject to various and conflicting influences and pressures. Three men were crucial figures in the foreign office during William's reign. These were Friedrich von Holstein, Count Philipp von Eulenburg, and Alfred von Kiderlen-Wächter.

The mysterious figure of Holstein, the *éminence grise,* was the only one to remain over from the days of Bismarck. But his hostility to Bismarck and his fears for the return of Bismarck to the foreign office made him anything but a follower of the Bismarckian policy. Until he resigned in 1905 Holstein played a commanding position in the determination of foreign policy. Yet such was the constitutional system of Germany that his importance was wholly unknown to the public, for he was responsible neither to the public nor to the kaiser, and it was not until the post-war revelations that his true significance emerged. Leading a secluded and solitary life, brooding upon a lasting inner resentment at having been used as a spy by Bismarck in the early days of his diplomatic career, he developed, as compensation for the absence of the social glamour and public prestige of diplomacy, a passion for work and for intrigue. He held all the threads both of policy and of personnel in his hands, and he exercised a commanding influence over Bülow. Not having direct access to the kaiser, he established contacts with him through the kaiser's intimate, Count Philipp von Eulenburg, who acted as his intermediary. Holstein's policy, as pursued by Bülow, involved a deliberate zigzag between England and the Dual Alliance. He believed that any final choice by Germany between the two would make her lose the advantages of her central position. In the words of Brandenburg, "For nearly a decade they pursued this policy of tacking, of two irons in the fire, 'balance and counter-balance,' a 'zigzag course,' without ever clearly envisaging the dangers inseparable from it."

The place of Kiderlen-Wächter in the direction of German foreign policy is a subject of keen controversy. Unlike his friend Holstein, who has been assailed by all writers, Kiderlen has found ardent supporters as well as bitter critics. In the Foreign Office he was considered a man of superior ability. Called to the office of foreign secretary by Bethmann-Hollweg in 1908, he played a leading role until his death in 1912. For his admirers he was the "second Bismarck," and the only outstanding statesman after the Iron Chancellor. Cambon once declared that all the European cabinets had become accustomed to ask, "What does Kiderlen think of it?" And Jäckh, his personal friend and biographer, laments, "He came too late and departed too soon." On the other hand the military and naval leaders were extremely antagonistic to him. Tirpitz saw in Kiderlen the greatest enemy of his naval plans, and Eulenburg tells of the general hostility of this whole crowd to the "malicious but wise Kiderlen . . . because he is too 'clever' and too 'superior' for them with his Swabian keen-edged humor and his knowledge." [43]

Kiderlen's handling of relations with Russia during the Bosnian crisis and especially his part in the Agadir crisis have been criticized severely, especially by Brandenburg and Paul Nathan. There is no doubt that Kiderlen, even if imbued with a genuine desire for peace, very often aggravated affairs by his ruthless manner, which he learned from Bismarck and Holstein, and by his belief that he could accomplish everything by beating his fist on the table. But he was actuated by a real and sincere desire to come to terms with England. He personally would have yielded to England on the naval question, but here the influence of Tirpitz was too powerful and the kaiser swung the balance against him. "I am an opponent of Tirpitz," he said, "because I am afraid his policies will bring us to war with England." Take Ionescu, the Rumanian diplomat and friend of Kiderlen's, records an interesting and moving conversation he had with Kiderlen in 1910 on this matter. He asked Kiderlen:

"What are you after with all these armaments carried to the extreme? I understand them so long as it was a question of achieving a position of second rank among the naval powers. What more do you want now? To be both the greatest military power and the greatest naval power? But that would be world domination and that can never be realized. Others like France and Spain have attempted the same and have gone down to defeat. You are too wise not to know that England will never allow itself to be surpassed before it is completely broken. . . . You are rushing directly into war with England. You know well that this is no joke. But granted even that you win, how long can this last? You will arouse a world coalition against you. . . ."

To which Kiderlen replied bitterly: "I wanted to accomplish this limitation that you speak of but I was unable to do so. All that you tell me. I too said, perhaps with less eloquence. I told it to Tirpitz, who was sitting in my place and I sat where you are sitting."

"And?"

"I was unable to convince him."

"But the kaiser?"

"He placed himself on the side of Tirpitz." [44]

This too was the tragedy of Bethmann-Hollweg. He was not able to steer his course between the political demands made upon him as a statesman and German patriot on the one hand and the moral revulsion which these very demands aroused in him as an ethical individual. Like Kiderlen-Wächter, he was in favor óf an agreement with England but he too found Tirpitz too strong for him.* The last years before the war

* "As you know, Sir Edward Goschen and von Jagow worked long and in perfect harmony to bring about a complete agreement on all outstanding differences or questions between the British and German governments, and had wonderfully and almost miraculously

were marked by a continual struggle between Tirpitz and the chancellor on political questions. This struggle was the key to the outbreak of the war. Tirpitz constantly proclaimed that "we must protect our world trade." This trade could have been protected without rivalry with England. England did not seek to destroy German trade, and it went out of its way to try to come to terms with Germany. But Tirpitz's orientation, unlike that of Bethmann and Kiderlen, was eastern rather than western. He wanted to frighten England with a powerful fleet and thereby make Germany desirable as an ally to Russia and Japan. He was not able to carry out his schemes for alliance, but by his naval program and his opposition to the Foreign Office he was able to prevent Bethmann from coming to terms with England. "The fact is," wrote Sir Edward Grey, "that in dealing with Chancellors and Secretaries for Foreign Affairs at Berlin, we could make no progress, because we were not dealing with the men who really directed German policy." Now something that he had suspected long before "came to the front and took more definite and ugly shape. There were forces other than Bethmann-Hollweg in the seat of authority in Germany. He was not master of .the situation; in negotiating with him we were not negotiating with a principal." The last and decisive word was with some military or naval person. "Yet," adds Grey, "Bethmann was the only authority with whom we could negotiate at all." [45]

Yet such was the spirit of German politics that Bethmann was forced to carry out a policy which he did not will and then to act as its spokesman. That his conscience was troubled by this conflict was evident in his speech to the Reichstag on August 4, 1914, in which he defended the German violation of Belgian neutrality. "This is a breach of international law," he declared. "The wrong—I speak openly—the wrong we thereby commit we will try to make good as soon as our military aims have been attained." It was a wrong, however, justified by the higher demands of necessity, and "necessity knows no law." In February, 1915, Bethmann revealed to Theodor Wolff, the editor of the *Berliner Tageblatt,* the qualms of conscience that persisted even during the height of the war. "When one comes to the question of the responsibility for this war," he said, "we must candidly admit that we have our share of it. To say that I am oppressed by this thought would be to say too little—the thought never leaves me. I live in it." [46] This was not only Bethmann's tragedy. It was the tragedy of the entire civilian population of Germany who accepted the final word of the militarist *Realpolitiker* without murmur or

---

succeeded. It was at their last meeting, when the document of understanding had received its last touches that von Jagow exclaimed: 'Now if only the Kaiser will remain long enough away and not suddenly return, we shall have secured the peace of the world.' But the terrible thing happened, the Kaiser suddenly returned, and Germany did not sign the agreement. I know that in this respect the Kaiser and the Junkers or the Pan-Germans are responsible for having plunged this devastation upon the world." De Fiori, Bavarian agent, to George Davis Herron in July, 1918 (from R. H. Lutz, *The Fall of the German Empire,* 2 vols., Stanford, 1932, i, 564).

protest. Only after the war was over and lost could they say with Bernhard Guttmann of the *Frankfurter Zeitung:* "This man was our own destiny in every sense. And when we read about him and the complete bankruptcy of his policy we want to say: *nostra culpa, nostra maxima culpa.*" [47]

The position of the kaiser in the entire situation was even more difficult to understand. His own ambivalent attitude was in a sense indicative of a general national ambivalence. Expressions of desire for peace and vehement denials of desire for world supremacy are plentiful in both his public utterances and in the archive materials. That in the final hours he recoiled from the idea of war is also quite evident. But German foreign policy was constantly disturbed by his sudden and impulsive interference. And his public speeches, instead of allaying the fears of Germany's neighbors, more often served to spread alarm. His constant references to a "place in the sun," to the "mailed fist" and "glistening coat of mail" were not conducive to a peaceful frame of mind. Nor did he impress Herbert Asquith with his peaceful intentions when he said to him, "There is no balance of power in Europe but me—me and my twenty-five corps." [48] His message to German soldiers dispatched to quell the Boxer Rebellion in China on July 27, 1900, in which he advised them to take the ancient Huns under Attila as their model, gave more than desirable ammunition to Allied propaganda during the war. The ambivalence of his attitude is perhaps best indicated in the comments he wrote on an article on the international situation written by J. A. Spender for the *Westminster Gazette* and sent to the kaiser by Albert Ballin. William's comment was, "Quite good except for the ridiculous insinuation that we are aspiring after the hegemony in Central Europe." This was an apparent repudiation of the idea of European hegemony. But, William goes on to say, "We simply *are* Central Europe and it is quite natural. . . ." [49]

The Portuguese diplomat quoted earlier, and the kaiser's uncle, Edward VII of England, provide two of the most important keys to the understanding of William's role in the coming of World War I—his deep-seated desire to experience war and his basic cowardice when confronted with it. The Portuguese diplomat, Eca de Queiroz, writing in 1891, said:

A splendid and insatiable desire to enjoy and experience every form of activity, under the sovereign conviction that God warrants and promotes the ultimate success of his every undertaking, explains, I think, the conduct of the mysterious Emperor. Now did he rule an Empire at the other side of Asia, or did he not possess in the Julius Tower at Spandau a war treasure for the mobilization of two million soldiers, or were he hedged round by a public opinion as active and coercive as that of England, William II would be merely like many other Emperors in history. . . . But being unfortunately in the heart of the workshop of Europe, with hundreds of disciplined legions, with a people formed of citizens disciplined and obedient as soldiers, William II is the most dangerous of Sovereigns, for in his dilettantism he has still to experience the most seductive form of activity a King can know—war and its glories.

It may indeed happen that one day Europe will take to the roar of clashing armies, only because in the soul of this great dilettante the burning desire to "know war," to enjoy war, was stronger than reason, counsel, or pity for his subjects. . . .[50]

Edward VII, who knew his nephew intimately, wrote thus of William II:

Through his unbelievable vanity my nephew succumbs to all the syco-phancies of the nationalists that surround him and who are always assuring him that he is the greatest sovereign in the world and that he must assert the supremacy of Germany over the world. . . . But since his cowardice is even greater than his vanity he will tremble before these flatterers, when, under pressure of the general staff, they will call upon him to draw the dagger. He will not have the courage to bring them to reason and will pitifully submit to them. He will release the forces of war not as a result of his own initiative, not in warlike *élan* but—out of weakness.[51]

The account of the kaiser's signing of the orders for German mobiliza-tion on August 1, 1914, provided a remarkable fulfillment of Edward's prophetic prediction. As he laid down his pen, William said to the generals surrounding him, "Gentlemen, you will live to rue the day when you made me do this!" [52]

Final decisions in the realm of foreign affairs rested entirely in the hands of the emperor. There was no parliamentary control, except as it pertained to the budget; the general press was rigorously controlled on matters of foreign policy and there was very little critical discussion. As a result there was no check on any of the forces operating around the emperor by the cross-play of discussion and informed public opinion. Public opinion played no role in the shaping of German foreign policy and in the making of vital decisions. Once decisions were made, public opinion came into play only as an object of government propaganda. The German historian Brandenburg, commenting on the German opposition to the peace plans of the Hague conferences, makes the interesting ob-servation that although all the great powers found the Tsar's proposal extremely troublesome, yet "the majority of the Great Powers had to take into consideration the pacific tendencies in their own countries, and were therefore very cautious in their attitude. German statesmen were differently placed, because in Germany there were few adherents of these ideas, and the opinion of the outside world seemed to them a very secondary matter."

The crucial point then was this fact that "in Germany there were few adherents of these ideas." Sir Edward Grey recognized this too when he wrote: "There was not in Germany a dread of war or a repugnance to war strong enough to create a determined will to peace. If German opinion did not desire war, it was at least content to leave the conduct of affairs in the hands of the Emperor and the powers behind the throne, whoever they might be." When war came, while all the peoples of the warring powers rallied to their flags in support of their governments, in no other country but Germany was the declaration of war greeted with such enthusiasm and with such festive jubilation. "Who were those," wrote Walther Rathenau in 1921, "who cheered jubilantly on August 1, 1914? It was almost everybody. Who were those who waved the flag twice a week, who drank a toast to the sinking of the Lusitania, who agreed to the submarine warfare and who made light of every declaration of war? There were many good Socialists among them. These are not reproaches, but recollections. Recollections of how deeply rooted was the monarchical-militarist consciousness among the masses." [53] This deeply rooted spirit was a product of an older German historical tradition refreshed anew by the teachings of a new and more virulent nationalism that came to the fore at the close of the nineteenth century.

The Socialist leader Wilhelm Liebknecht once said to Wickham Steed:

> If you want to understand Germany you must grasp the fact that Germany, particularly Prussia, is an inverted pyramid. Its apex, firmly embedded in the ground, is the spike on the top of the Prussian soldiers' helmet. Everything rests on that. One day, unless people are very careful, it will topple over, smashing itself and much else in the process. If you can get to understand how the pyramid became inverted you will begin to know something about Germany.[54]

The supremacy of the soldier, the peculiar attitude toward war and peace and the Hegelian view of the state as "power" rather than "welfare," all contributed to form a climate which, as Grey said, if not ready to take the initiative toward war was willing to follow once the warriors made it.

This tradition was of course not new in Wilhelmian Germany, but it received powerful re-enforcement during this era from the work of the great historian Heinrich von Treitschke. It is naïve to say that Treitschke was the cause of World War I. But it is equally naïve and uninformed to close one's eyes to the tremendous influence on the German mind of Treitschke's historical and political writings. It was Treitschke who made popular Hegel's concept of the state as power and that this power had to be embodied in a well organized army. It was Treitschke who proclaimed the dictum that "war must be conceived as an institution ordained of God," that war was to be declared for even the most trivial insult to the state, that "those who proposed the foolish notion of a universal peace show their ignorance of the international life of the Aryan race" and that "the establishment of an international court of arbitration is incompatible with the nature of the state." Is it any wonder then that whereas public opinion in almost all countries of the world was cordial to the idea of the Hague Peace Conference, public opinion in Germany ranged from mild skepticism to outright indignation, and that William II, who had attended Treitschke's lectures on politics, declared: "I consented to all this nonsense only in order that the Tsar be not discredited before Europe. In practice, however, I shall rely on and call upon only God and my sharp sword! And I sh . . upon all their decisions." [55]

Nietzsche's name has often been coupled with that of Treitschke's. This is a crude misinterpretation of Nietzsche's thought. Moreover Nietzsche's influence did not really assert itself until much later. His part in shaping the *Weltanschauung* of the generation of National Socialism was greater than his influence on the leaders of the first decade of the twentieth century. Nietzsche, in those days, was still unacceptable in most respectable circles, and he was the philosopher primarily of the revolting youth. But vulgarization of Nietzsche's thought had already begun. A book by General Friedrich von Bernhardi entitled *Deutschland und der nächste Krieg,* which was published in 1911 and by 1913 had reached its sixth edition, represented one such vulgarization of Nietzsche's philosophy. It expressed, on the one hand, the mood of German opinion and at the same time helped to carry the Treitschke tradition further. Bernhardi was an influential military writer, and his pronouncements, therefore, carried great weight. He too, like Treitschke, considered the desire for peace not only hopeless and Utopian but "immoral and inhuman." War, wrote Bernhardi, "is not only a necessary element in the life of people, but also an indispensable factor in culture, indeed the highest expression of the strength and life of truly cultured peoples." He called for the final reckoning with France so that "it would never be able again to stand in our way." For the Germans there was only one alternative, "World Power or Destruction." Strong, sound, and flourishing peoples, declared Bernhardi, increase in population and need constant expansion of their frontiers, in order to accommodate the surplus population. But since the earth is colonized almost everywhere, new land can be won only at the expense of those already in possession of these lands, that is, by conquest. War and conquest, therefore, emanate from the law of necessity.*

A new form of militant nationalism which developed at the close of the century combined the older form with antisemitism and the new racial dogma popularized by Houston Stewart Chamberlain. This found its characteristic expression in the Alldeutsche Verband, or Pan-German League.[56] This organization was founded in 1891. Its first president was

---

* The incapacity of German leaders to comprehend the effect of such thinking upon foreigners was illustrated by the attempt of Dr. Dernburg, who was sent to the United States in 1914 to direct German propaganda, to interpret Bernhardi to the Americans in terms of democracy. The New York *World* wrote on September 20, 1914, that it may seem "plain enough to Dr. Dernburg, but we doubt if it could ever be made plain to the American mind." (Cf. Louis L. Snyder, *From Bismarck to Hitler.* Williamsport, Pa., 1935, p. 72.)

the colonial explorer and propagandist Karl Peters. The militant activity of the league, however, set in with the election of Dr. Ernst Hasse of Leipzig as its president in 1893. Hasse remained at the helm of the Pan-German movement until 1907. He was succeeded by the even more militant and aggressive nationalist Dr. Heinrich Class, who also exercised much greater influence than his predecessor. The Pan-German program consisted of two main parts: (1) the union of all Germans in the world into one huge pan-German state with a huge Central Germany as its core, and (2) the claim to world rule by this enlarged Germany. Pan-German writers usually included under German territory also the Netherlands, Belgium, Luxemburg, parts of Switzerland, Hungary, Poland, Rumania, an enlarged Serbia and, of course, Austria. The Pan-German League carried on intensive and influential propaganda in leading industrial and government circles and developed a wide network of organizations among the Germans abroad in all parts of the world. Its influence is not to be measured in terms of its membership only. It acted as a sort of general staff for the various other nationalist organizations like the Navy League, the Army League, the Colonial Society, the Jung Deutschland Bund, and others. But even more significant was the intimate contacts it had with leading government circles. Among its leaders were key military and industrial figures, bureaucrats, members of the Reichstag, and university professors. Bassermann and Stresemann, leaders of the National Liberal party; Kardorff, the founder of the Central Union of German Industrialists; the antisemitic Prussian leader Liebermann von Sonnenberg, and Count Udo von Stolberg-Wernigerode, president of East Prussia, were some of the more distinguished of its members. Class established intimate relations with Tirpitz and with the Foreign Office, with von Oldenburg-Januschau and the Bund der Landwirte, with nationalist academicians like Dietrich Schäfer, and with Emil Kirdorf, the head of Germany's largest cartel. Important newspapers like the *Tägliche Rundschau, Deutsche Tageszeitung, Deutsche Zeitung, Leipziger Neueste Nachrichten,* and the *Rheinisch-Westfälische Zeitung* followed the Pan-German "line."

The Pan-German League was ridiculed by the progressive circles in Germany, and its true importance was barely recognized.* This attitude was assimilated by many non-German historians as well, who treated it as merely the "lunatic fringe" of German nationalism. But Kurt Eisner, the Bavarian Socialist, provided an accurate evaluation of the Pan-Germans in *Die Neue Zeit* in 1914:

---

* A good example of the German liberal's incapacity to grasp the significance of pan-Germanism is found in Theodor Wolff's *The Eve of 1914,* pp. 321–330. In the same way German liberals placidly ignored the National Socialist movement until a few months before they seized power. The Conservative Hans Delbrück, on the other hand, declared the Pan-Germans to be a graver danger to their country than the Socialists. But he added that he merely deplored their methods. He was not opposed to their objectives. See *Preussische Jahrbücher,* cliv (1913), 573.

Who in Germany exercises the decisive influence upon the course of foreign policy? For a quarter of a century none but the Pan-Germans. They have attained a greater influence on the direction of policy than even the powerful associations of landlords and capitalists. In the course of this time they have achieved more than all the political parties and all the parliamentary groups in Germany put together. . . . From the first naval measure to the last army bill, all the armaments plans originated in the circles of the Pan-Germans. They were the shock troops. . . .

Behind the program of the Pan-German League and its manifold branches and daughter associations stand the Bund der Landwirte, the Zentralverband der Industriellen and other employers associations, a part of the finance capital interests, especially the shipping interests, and finally—and that is the peculiar feature of this association—an executive of former generals and admirals. In addition they are equipped with a staff of "intellectuals" spread widely all over.

This evaluation is quoted by Dr. Class, the head of the league, as an accurate appraisal of its work.[57]

Sir Valentine Chirol, London *Times* correspondent in Berlin in 1892, tells of a conversation he once had with Bebel concerning Treitschke's lectures on politics and his glorification of war. During the course of the conversation, writes Chirol, a battalian of Prussian guards—the Alexander Regiment—marched past them. Bebel said to Chirol: "Look at those fellows! Ninety per cent Berliners and eighty per cent Social Democrats! But if there was trouble, they would shoot me or anyone down at the word of command from above," and he pointed to the Royal Schloss. "The whole nation," he continued, "is still drunk with military glory and there is nothing to be done until some great disaster has sobered us."[58]

Bebel's words were prophetic. His own Socialist party was swept along in the popular enthusiasm for the war and joined in voting for the war credits on August 4, 1914. True, many were sincerely convinced that they were fighting a defensive war against the brutal Russian bear. But in the main it was the deep-rooted traditions of which Rathenau reminisced, traditions inculcated by education, customs, and public life, which revealed their lasting effects. A note of warning of uncanny presagement was penned by a contributor to the Berlin *Morgenpost,* Dr. Arthur Bernstein, following the declaration of war upon France:

In a few days no one will any longer be able to speak the truth, not to say write it. Therefore, in this last moment: the warmongers are miscalculating. In the first place, there is no Triple Alliance. Italy will not go along, at least not with us, and if it does it will join the side of the Entente. Secondly, England will not remain neutral but will stand with France. England will also not tolerate a German march through Belgium, which since 1907 is generally known as the plan of strategy. But if England fights against us, then the entire English world, particularly America, will come out against us. Most probably the entire world. For England is respected all over, even though not loved, and this much can unfortunately not be said of us. Thirdly, Japan will not attack Russia, more likely it will attack us. . . . Fifthly, Austria-Hungary is militarily hardly a match for the Serbs and Rumanians. Economically it can hunger through 3–5 years. It can give us nothing. . . . Whether we can be the victors at the end of this most terrible war the world will have seen, is questionable. But even if we win the war, we will win nothing. . . . Germany is waging this war for nothing in the same way in which it has entered the war for nothing. One million corpses, two million cripples and 50 billions of debts will be the balance of this "fresh and happy" war. Nothing more.[59]

No one was able to read this marvelous prognosis at the time. Military censorship prevented its publication. But even if it had appeared there would have been few, very few Germans, who would have heeded its sober call to reason.

CHAPTER XIII

War and Collapse, 1914-1918

Weh! Weh, sie ist zerstört, die schöne Welt.

GOETHE

1. THE BURGFRIEDEN

Walther Rathenau was standing with Prince von Bülow in the Hotel Adlon one day in the autumn of 1914 looking out upon the falling leaves on the wide Unter den Linden. Pointing toward the Brandenburg Gate, Rathenau said to the Prince:

Can a monarch of such arresting personality, so charming and human a man, so utterly inadequate as a ruler, as is the Emperor William II—with an impossible chancellor like Bethmann and a frivolous chief of staff like Falkenhayn,—ever expect a triumphal return through that arch? If he gets it, history will have no meaning.[1]

There were very, very few Germans in 1914 that sensed the forebodings of doom as did Rathenau on that day.[2] As the Austro-Serbian duel developed into a European conflict, all of Germany, except for a tiny pacifist minority, stood united behind the imperial government. The entire nation greeted the declaration of war with enthusiasm and exaltation.[3] "When it comes to war," declared William II on August 1, "all parties cease and we are all brothers." The Pan-Germans, of course, outdid all others in their expressions of patriotic exaltation, and they did not hesitate to indicate openly their intense satisfaction that the negotiations with England "had gone down the drain." But men of all parties and professions were equally engulfed in this tremendous wave of national enthusiasm. "This war," wrote Max Weber to Ferdinand Tönnies on October 15, 1914, "with all its ghastliness is nevertheless grand and wonderful. It is worth experiencing." [4]

The parties in the Reichstag established a political truce known as the *Burgfrieden*. All traditional party differences were submerged for the duration of the war, and united support was given to the government to

313

prosecute the war. By this action the Reichstag abdicated its powers to the military for the period of the war. It approved the war credits requested by the government and then dispersed. While such action had been expected of all the bourgeois parties, there had been considerable speculation as to what the Social Democratic party would do. Traditionally the Socialist representatives in the Reichstag had always voted against every government budget because it contained appropriations for military purposes. The question was, What would they do in this hour of crisis? But the Socialists were engulfed by the same patriotic storm that swept the entire country. They justified their position by centering all their hostility at first upon reactionary and absolutist tsarist Russia, which they branded as Germany's enemy Number One and as a threat to world civilization. At the party caucus only 14 out of the 92 members present voted against approval of the war credits in the Reichstag. Carrying out the traditional party discipline of voting in the Reichstag as a solid block, all the Socialists, including Karl Liebknecht, cast their votes on August 4 for the war credits. Hugo Haase, the Socialist spokesman in the Reichstag, despite his own personal reservations, read the statement of the party in the Reichstag, in which he declared:

We stand today before the brutal fact of war and the terrible threat of enemy invasion. The decision to be made is not whether to take sides for or against the war but rather on the means necessary for the defense of our country. . . . Our heartiest best wishes go out to our brethren, irrespective of party affiliations, who are called to the colors. . . . Much if not all would be lost to our people and its future independence in the event of a victory of Russian despotism. . . . We therefore shall act in accordance with what we have always emphasized: We shall not abandon the fatherland in its hour of danger. . . . We condemn . . . every path of annexation. We demand that as soon as our goal of security is achieved and our opponents are disposed to make peace the war be brought to an end and a peace be concluded which will secure friendship with our neighbors. . . . Guided by these fundamentals, we approve the requested credits.

The same position was reaffirmed by Haase in the name of his party on December 2, 1914. This display of national unity by those hitherto regarded as "enemies of the Reich" discharged a wave of patriotic enthusiasm throughout the country that came to be called the "spirit of August 4." That part of the mobilization plan of the general staff which called for the arrest of all the Socialist leaders was not carried out. The ban on Socialist literature in military installations was lifted on September 2, 1914, and the *Vorwärts* now was sold at all railway bookstalls. The trade unions on their side called off all strikes. Ludwig Frank, one of the ablest of the South German Socialist leaders, then forty years old and a Jew, enlisted in the army "in order that the attitude of his party on August 4 not be interpreted as false enthusiasm and mere lip-service." He fell in action a month later.

A propaganda campaign of national hate soon was let loose in Germany as it was in all the other warring nations.[5] Post cards appeared on the newsstands with slogans like *"Jeder Schuss ein Russ," "Jeder Stoss ein Franzos," "Jeder Tritt ein Britt,"* and *"Jeder Klaps ein Japs."* Leading literary and scholarly figures contributed their talents to the war of hate. Whereas the Socialists concentrated their fire upon tsarist Russia, the bourgeois intellectuals and scholars joined in a torrent of abuse of England that reached its apex in Ernst Lissauer's "Hymn of Hate":

> Hate by water and hate by land;
> Hate of heart and hate of the hand;
> We love as one and hate as one;
> We have but one foe alone—England.

Venerable scholars like Adolf von Harnack, Wilamowitz-Moellendorff, Otto Gierke, and Werner Sombart joined with the renegade Englishman Houston Stewart Chamberlain in this chorus of Anglophobia. "Our *Kultur*," wrote the theologian Harnack, "has been entrusted to three nations—ourselves, the Americans and the English. I veil my head in shame —only two are left." England, wrote the great classical scholar Wilamowitz, is "the prime mover, the evil spirit which has conjured up this war from hell, the spirit of evil and the spirit of hypocrisy." And the eminent exponent of the *Rechtstaat*, Gierke, wrote: "Storm on with thy Slav and Gallic accomplices, thou low-minded nation. Thou shalt never falsify the judgment of God, perfidious Albion." Some accepted the charges of German militarism and reveled and exulted in them. The economist and historian of capitalism Werner Sombart wrote *Händler und Helden*, in which he interpreted the war as a struggle between the trader and the hero, between the materialist, rationalist, and matter-of-fact mentality of English merchant civilization and the militant, spirited, warrior mentality of the German hero. "That is why," wrote Sombart, "for us, who are imbued with militarism, the war is holy, yes the most sacred thing on earth." [6] The Catholic philosopher Max Scheler, in his essay "Ueber Gesinnungs- und Zweckmilitarismus," similarly did not attempt to refute the charge of German militarism but rather gloried in it. Scheler took great pains to distinguish between German militarism, which he described as an expression of "German ethos" and as a "work of art," and the militarism of Germany's enemies, which he said was merely a "utilitarian" instrument to meet the enemy.[7]

A group of ninety-three of the most distinguished German intellectuals, men of science, and artists issued a manifesto in which they offered a reply to the charge that Germany had violated Belgian neutrality and provoked the war. "It would have been suicide on our part," declared the manifesto, "not to have been beforehand in Belgium." They denied all charges of German atrocities and violations of international law and exuberantly proclaimed that "the German army and the German people are one." Among the signers were Alois Brandl, Lujo Brentano, Richard Dehmel, Adolf Deissmann, Paul Ehrlich, Rudolf Eucken, Heinrich Finke, Emil Fischer, Ludwig Fulda, Fritz Haber, Ernst Haeckel, Adolf von Harnack, Gerhart Hauptmann, Engelbert Humperdinck, Max Klinger, Paul Laband, Karl Lamprecht, Philipp Lenard, Max Liebermann, Franz von Liszt, Eduard Meyer, Friedrich Naumann, Max Planck, Max Reinhardt, Alois Riehl, Wilhelm Röntgen, Gustav Schmoller, Reinhold Seeberg, Martin Spahn, Hermann Sudermann, Hans Thoma, Wilhelm Trübner, Karl Vossler, Siegfried Wagner, Felix von Weingartner, Ulrich von Wilamowitz-Moellendorff, Wilhelm Windelband, and Wilhelm Wundt—a truly impressive list of some of the greatest figures in world literature, music, painting, philosophy, science, and academic life. All political parties were represented, as were Catholics, Protestants, and Jews.

Anti-war sentiment in Germany was, in the beginning, confined to a tiny group of revolutionaries, centering around Karl Liebknecht and Rosa Luxemburg, a few pacifist writers like Herman Hesse,[8] and a group of pacifist professors who later formed the Bund Neues Vaterland in 1915 to work for a compromise peace. The latter group counted among its members the student of English literature Professor Ernst Sieper of the University of Munich, the historian Ludwig Quidde, author of *Caligula;* the students of international law Professors Walter Schucking and Hans Wehberg; the militant opponents of Prussian militarism Friedrich Wilhelm Foerster and Georg Friedrich Nicolai, and the then still relatively unknown Albert Einstein. A courageous and militant lone wolf in the field of pacifist journalism was Helmuth von Gerlach, who established the newspaper *Die Welt am Montag* for the purpose of subjecting German foreign policy to sober and critical analysis and who initiated the struggle for peace which was later to be continued by Carl von Ossietzky. The voices of these pacifists, however, were drowned in the general outburst of patriotism and in the exuberance over the brilliant victories of the German armies in the early stages of the war. It was only the failure of German arms to bring the war to a speedy finish and the ensuing tensions and weariness occasioned by a long-drawn-out war that finally won over larger groups in the population to the cause of peace. In August, 1914, most Germans believed that the war would be over by Christmas of the same year. The significance of the battle of the Marne in preventing a decisive victory for Germany was little understood, and public opinion was poorly informed as to what was really happening at the front. It took a long time before the true nature of the military situation stood revealed in all its stark realities.

At the outbreak of the war the younger von Moltke was chief of staff of the German army. He was a man of weak nerves and never felt equal to his post. He committed the strategic blunder of departing from the Schlieffen Plan, which not only called for a decisive victory in the west in six weeks but also for a strategic retreat from Alsace-Lorraine. Moltke transferred a large army to Lorraine in order to prevent the invasion of German territory. The battle of the Marne on September 5–12 dashed the possibilities of the quick decision which the Schlieffen Plan called for. On September 14, 1914, Moltke was succeeded by Erich von Falkenhayn, who was not much of an improvement, and it was not until two years later that the brilliant team of Hindenburg and Ludendorff was brought in from the eastern front to take command of the still triumphant but already greatly weakened German forces. All the hopes of both military and political leaders had been pinned upon a war of short duration. The sense of national duty and obligation was sufficiently powerful among the German masses to hold them in line even when the prospects for a speedy victory began to dim. But the enthusiasm of the early days began to wear thin and the national unity of August 4 began to show serious signs of cracking.

The prolongation of the war saw the emergence of the military Supreme Command as the *de facto* dictator of Germany up to the close of the war. The team of Hindenburg and Ludendorff, first catapulted into fame and into the confidence of the country by their dazzling military triumphs on the eastern front, forced the emperor to relieve General von Falkenhayn of his position as chief of staff on August 29, 1916. Ludendorff is reported to have gone to the emperor and told him that if Falkenhayn was not deprived of his leadership the army would become demoralized in a few months. William was forced to yield to the dictate of the two generals, and he named Hindenburg as chief of staff and Ludendorff as first general quartermaster. This team, with Hindenburg supplying the character, dignity, and tradition, and Ludendorff the dynamic energy and driving force, now took into its hands not only the direction of the military affairs but also the actual control of all major political decisions. The emperor receded completely into the background. Despite his constitutional position as the chief of state and supreme war lord he was incapable of asserting his leadership in either capacity. He established his headquarters in the field, but his sycophantic servants and ministers fed him only with rose-colored news. The Centrist leader Erzberger tells that before his first audience with the emperor on March 1, 1915, after Erzberger's return from Rome, an adjutant came to him and said, "You will report only good news to His Majesty, will you not?" [9]

Albert Ballin, friend and intimate of the emperor, tried repeatedly to gain the emperor's ear and enlighten him on the real situation, but he failed. He found the emperor living in a "fool's paradise" and his intimate circle convinced that William would break down completely if allowed to see things as they really were. The result was that William came to be disregarded almost entirely by the real makers of policy. Marginalia by the emperor on dispatches of the period reveal that William was often not able to get even a hearing with the Supreme Command. Edgar Jaffé, a German economist who went to Switzerland to establish peace feelers with Allied representatives, told the American George D. Herron: "Kaiser William now figures only in the world of Germany's enemies. In Germany herself he has been completely set aside or rather swept aside as an incompetent fool. In Germany no one ever speaks of him. He has politically ceased to exist. He is not even formally consulted in Berlin." [10]

The real ruler in Germany during the greater part of the war years was Ludendorff, the ruthless, stubborn, and dynamic member of the Supreme Command. Ludendorff was not content with guiding the military conduct of the war. He intervened in all vital aspects of civilian rule. He took a hand in labor policies, food questions, raw-material problems, and he made and unmade ministers. It was Ludendorff who forced the resignation of Bethmann-Hollweg as he did of Foreign Secretary von Kühlmann. Though a disciple of Clausewitz, he failed to grasp Clausewitz's real meaning on the relation between the political and the military. He refused to understand that war is merely the instrument and the means with which to achieve a political aim and that, therefore, it is absurd to subordinate the political leader to the military point of view. That he was a brilliant strategist, dynamic organizer, and indefatigable administrator is beyond dispute. But it is more than probable, as Hans Delbrück pointed out, that he was impelled by a super ego and stubborn willfulness that made him incapable of objective evaluation of a situation apart from his own role in it and apart from his own will. Ludendorff rejected emphatically the idea of subordination to the civil government and instead was able to force the political leaders to bend to his will. There was no political figure of stature to pit his will against that of the Supreme Command. Germany, as Lloyd George remarked, had no Clemenceau, Gambetta, or Pitt.

When Bethmann-Hollweg was forced out by Ludendorff in 1917, he was succeeded by a mediocre Prussian bureaucrat Michaelis, who had attracted some attention by his activity as Prussian food administrator. Michaelis was in turn followed as chancellor by the Bavarian Hertling who had an almost childish trust in the Supreme Command. All the hopes of German victory were centered on the Supreme Command, and so long as they seemed to be able to triumph, very few were disposed to challenge either their prestige or their authority. Only after the war was over did German political leaders dare to reveal the true situation. "For four years," declared Erzberger in the Reichstag on July 25, 1919, "Germany had practically no political government but a military dictatorship. This we can openly declare now." [11]

The Reichstag Commission that investigated the causes after the war of the German collapse brought in the following majority report on the activity of the Supreme Command, which is a fair evaluation of the situation:

The Supreme Command always acted under the full conviction that they were serving the welfare of the entire country. It accorded with their military views that, as long as it appeared at all feasible, they voiced the idea of a militarily advantageous and, afterward, at least a bearable peace. . . . The government relied upon the judgment of the Supreme Command till the latter themselves acknowledged the impossibility of victory. It had at its disposal no personality capable of opposing the will of the Supreme Command.[12]

Under a parliamentary régime the agency that could have challenged the power of the Supreme Command would have been the Reichstag. This the Reichstag failed to do. Even the final triumph of the civilian government over the military, just on the eve of collapse, was carefully "arranged" by the Supreme Command. The Reichstag's failure to meet the situation is the main thesis developed by Dr. Bredt in his long and detailed report on the internal government of Germany which he submitted to the Reichstag Inquiry Commission.[13] The *Burgfrieden* of August 4, 1914, united all the parties of the Reichstag behind the government in the prosecution of the war. This *Burgfrieden* lasted up to the passage of the peace resolution by the Reichstag in 1917. Reichstag party leaders were taken to the front, were shown around by the military leaders, and were at times received by the emperor. But even when they were aware of the discrepancies between the optimistic claims and hopes of the Supreme Command and the graver aspects of the real situation they did nothing or very little either to improve the situation or to enlighten public opinion.*

On May 25, 1916, the Independent Socialist deputy Wilhelm Dittmann delivered a speech in the Reichstag in which he called upon the parliamentary body to "be hard" and assert its power by voting an end to the state of siege and demanding the restoration to the people of their constitutional rights. "Arbitrary power and anarchy," declared Dittmann, "reign in the country. The laws are torn up as spider webs, and force rules instead of law." Addressing his fellow deputies Dittmann said:

You will not be able to say in the future: "We are not responsible for all this!" No, my dear sirs, the people will have the right to make you, the representatives of the people, responsible for the internal conditions in the land. The Reichstag has the obligation to force the restoration of conditions of law with all the

---

* Ernst Troeltsch tells how Karl Helfferich made one of the keenest attacks upon the Supreme Command's plan of unrestricted submarine warfare and then voted for it enthusiastically in the Reichstag commission. Asked how this was possible, Helfferich replied: "This is the heaviest *sacrificium intellectus* that I have ever made" (Troeltsch, *Spektator-Briefe* [Tübingen 1924], p. 3).

parliamentary means at its disposal. . . . Is the capitulation of the civilian legal and constitutional state before the military dictatorship of imperialism complete? Has parliament abdicated before it? Has it become a fig leaf for it?[14]

Only the combined Socialist groups voted for the resolution of the Independent Socialists to end the state of siege and restore the power of the civilian government.

The Reichstag parties wanted Bethmann-Hollweg removed in 1917, but the actual removal of the chancellor came only because of the threat by Hindenburg and Ludendorff to resign if he were not removed.

Michaelis was appointed without consultation with the party leaders of the Reichstag. It was not until the end of 1917, with the appointment of von Hertling, that Reichstag leaders came to play more than a nominal role in the government. The supreme assertion of political independence by the Reichstag was its passage of the famous Reichstag peace resolution in 1917, but as we shall soon see the resolution was nullified by subsequent action.

The Reichstag parties during the war consisted of a Right made up of the Conservatives and Free Conservatives; a Left, consisting of the Majority and Independent Socialists; and a Center, made up of the National Liberals, who almost always tended toward the Right, and the Progressives who leaned toward the Left. The Center party, as was the case frequently in German politics, was the key to final decisions, but, as Dr. Bredt points out, it did not adhere to a firm and fixed policy. It went with the Right to support unrestricted submarine warfare, then turned Left to support the peace resolution, then Right again to support the Supreme Command at Brest Litovsk. "There were only two parties," concludes Dr. Bredt, "which, I recognize, maintained a consistent policy. These were first the Conservatives, who did not deviate the slightest from their line, and secondly the Social Democrats, who also pursued their path consistently. But neither the Conservatives nor the Social Democrats had reliable allies, for the center of the Reichstag seesawed back and forth. When the fortunes of war went bad they approved a peace resolution. When things at the front improved they once more turned to the Right." [15]

Dr. Bredt's charges against the Reichstag, as well as Dittmann's plea during the war, were, of course, predicated on an assumption that the Reichstag was constitutionally a governing body. This was not the case even during normal peacetime conditions. The Reichstag, therefore, was neither by its tradition nor by its legal status in a position to assert itself against the dictatorship of the Supreme Command. Its deliberations and expressions of opinion are important and interesting primarily as manifestations of the state of public opinion. The real and final source of power lay in the hands of the Supreme Command, and Ludendorff, in particular, displayed no hesitancy in taking it and using it.

The Supreme Command instituted a rigorous censorship and clamped down on all news items that would have raised doubts as to ultimate German victory. The military leaders, however, showed little understanding for propaganda and psychological warfare. Practically all the daily reports spoke only of victories. Defeats were either suppressed entirely or so reported that only a few experts could grasp the true situation. The most glaring instance of this was the complete suppression in Germany of the true effect of the battle of the Marne in 1914. All that the Supreme Command allowed the German public to know about this crucial battle was the following:

On the western front, operations regarding which it is not yet possible to publish details have led to a new battle, which is going favorably. All the unfavorable reports being spread by the enemy through various means are false.[16]

The famous economist Lujo Brentano tells how doubly grieved he was when he came to Florence, Italy, at the end of September, 1914. Here he learned for the first time about the true character of this decisive battle, and when he returned to Munich four weeks later and assumed that by that time all his colleagues knew all about it he was treated as one who had fallen an easy prey to enemy propaganda. Even the highest circles in civilian life were fed with a continuous string of glowing reports of victory, of promises of enormous gains for Germany as a result of the war, and were subjected to a complete blackout on all indications of any serious concern. Expression of sympathy for the hungry and suffering German people was banned by the military censorship. All descriptions of want of food or clothing or other physical suffering were forbidden. The official motto was, "No one can beat us!"

Such a manipulation of public opinion bred a dangerous state of confidence that was not justified by the facts. Some began to wonder why the war was lasting so long if there was such a continuous procession of triumphs. The interesting thing is that more did not begin to wonder sooner. And when collapse finally did come it found the German people completely unprepared for it and dazed by the news of total defeat after they had been led all the time to believe that total victory was well in hand. Von Heydebrand, the leader of the Conservative party, ran up and down and shouted, "We have been deceived and cheated," when the news of the request for an armistice came to him.

2. THE WAR ECONOMY

Economically, politically, and psychologically Germany was not in a position to wage a long-drawn-out war. Historically, German arms had always won decisive victories in brilliant and rapid action. The wars of

Frederick the Great, the Six Weeks' War in 1866, the rapid victory in 1870, all had conditioned the German people to look to a quick decision in 1914. When it did not come war weariness began to set in and sap the endurance and vitality of the nation.

Germany was at a distinct disadvantage, from an economic point of view, in carrying on a protracted war. She was dependent on imports of food, fats, and oils and strategic chemicals such as nitrates to fill many of her vital needs. Manpower shortages also began to loom ominously in the picture, and eventually proved to be the Achilles heel of the German war machine. That she was able to hold out as long as she did was an indication of the national discipline, the scientific ingenuity, and the marvelous organizing capacity which the war elicited from the people and its leaders. Laboratory technicians and scientists initiated the saga of *Ersatz* (substitute) materials to take the place of supplies not available to the German war economy. The nitrogen fixation process perfected by Professor Fritz Haber of Berlin made possible the manufacture of explosives in Germany without the importation of nitrates from Chile. Synthetic ammonia was perfected, and cellulose was developed as a substitute for cotton in the manufacture of explosives. The most important factor, however, was the organization of the entire economy of the country by the military to serve the ends of the war machine—the so-called *Kriegswirtschaft,* or war economy. From a relatively free economy in 1914, Germany emerged in 1918 with a thoroughly militarized economy of state socialism in which government controls and regulation covered all phases of economic life.[17] An agency for feeding the nation in wartime (*Kriegsernährungsamt*) was set up that established price controls and regulated consumption. K bread (war bread) had to be made of flour mixed with *Ersatz* materials, such as turnips and potatoes. Two meatless days were decreed, a system of rationing was initiated, and bread cards were introduced on January 25, 1915.

The most far-reaching phase of *Kriegswirtschaft* was concerned with the provisions for raw materials and the establishment of the *Kriegsrohstoff-abteilung* (KRA). It was Walther Rathenau who was chiefly responsible for the setting up of this agency. Rathenau later recounted the dramatic story of this phase of German war history.[18] Three days after England declared war on Germany, he says, "he could no longer stand the agony," and went to the war office to find out what had been done to assure an adequate supply of raw materials. On August 9 he was called by von Falkenhayn and put in charge of the KRA. He discovered that "few of the materials needed for the army were available in quantities sufficient for a year . . . in most cases they were considerably less." Rathenau decided on a threefold program of (1) regulation, (2) synthetic manufacture, and (3) substitute products. He started with a staff of five men and four rooms, and for the first six months "no one had any idea what we were trying to do." By December the KRA occupied sixty rooms; Rathenau introduced a policy of sequestration (*Beschlagnahmen*), and set up mixed government and privately owned companies to administer the sequestrated raw materials and to act as trustees for the government. In the spring of 1915 Rathenau was able to report to the minister of war: "As far as essentials are concerned our supplies are sufficient; the outcome of the war is not threatened by a lack of raw materials."

Rathenau was himself conscious of the enormous significance of this new type of economic organization, not only for the prosecution of the war but for its effects on subsequent social and economic organization. "In its methods," he described the set-up, "it is closely akin to communism and yet it departs essentially from the prophecies and demands resulting from radical theories." As for the future he predicted: "Our methods will leave their impress on future times." Not only did other governments follow this model in both World War I and World War II, but it is safe to say that a great deal of the theorizing and many of the concrete proposals for "economic planning" which came to the fore after World War I throughout the Western World, and in which German economists and social theorists played a leading role, had their ultimate origins in the system of *Kriegswirtschaft* initiated by Rathenau. It is of course needless to point out how much the Nazi economic system learned from this experience.

As a complement to the measures for the regulation of production and consumption came the regulation of the labor supply by means of the so-called Hindenburg program, or the National Service Law (*Vaterländischer Hilfsdienst*) adopted on December 5, 1916. The chief architect of this program was Karl Helfferich, aided by General Wilhelm Groener of the War Office and by leaders of the trade-unions. The Hindenburg program was in effect an alliance between the military leaders and the trade-unions to put into operation a system of forced labor for the adult population to meet the needs of the military authorities for more soldiers and at the same time also increase the production of war materials. Through this program the economic life of the country was completely militarized. Every male between the ages of seventeen and sixty who was not in military service was to be regarded as a member of the auxiliary services and under the authority of the minister of war. A system of compulsory arbitration of labor disputes was set up, and local workers' committees were established in the factories to help put the law into effect and thus regulate industry.[19]

3. PUBLIC OPINION, THE PARTIES, AND WAR AIMS

All of these economic measures, however, were insufficient to bring quick victory. Food shortages, aggravated by the British blockade, began to be keenly felt, political tensions began to appear despite the official *Burgfrieden,* and war weariness was definitely apparent by 1916. As all these difficulties increased, the question "What are we fighting for?" came to occupy more and more attention. What were the war aims of Germany? No one really had asked the question in 1914. People with different points of view took for granted that the government's war aims were identical with their own aims. By the end of 1916, however, opinion began to sharpen and crystallize.

Broadly speaking German public opinion was divided into three uneven groups. On the one hand stood those who viewed the war as purely defensive for Germany and its allies and who looked for very little or nothing from the outcome except a return to the *status quo ante*. On the whole those in this group considered Russian tsarism as the main enemy and as the chief culprit in dragging Germany into the war. On the other extreme were those who openly espoused imperialism, either in a milder or in a more aggressive form. With a glorified philosophy of history as its conceptual grounding, it posited the thesis that every great nation has its day in history. The day of England and France was over and the "day of the Germans" was nigh, the day of "world supremacy of the German spirit, of German labor, and of German culture." It was the duty of present-day Germany, according to this view, to provide not only for the current needs of its population but also to look forward at least another century to the time when the German state would have to accommodate 200 million Germans. Imperialist expansion, therefore, was a historic necessity for the fatherland, and England, for this reason, was the main enemy.[20] Between these two extreme positions were those whose war aims shifted and varied in accordance with the turns of the fortunes of war. When the military situation showed improvement, annexationist sentiment was strongest; when the news from the front was not so promising, the stakes were lowered. Count Schulenburg, in his testimony before the Reichstag Inquiry Commission, tells how in the early part of 1918, after the initial successes of the German offensive, a group of Socialist deputies visited the Supreme Command headquarters. Under the influence of the military victories they said: "Yes, we do not take the peace resolution so literally any more. Our goals are extended somewhat higher again." [21]

Annexationist war aims were espoused by the Pan-Germans, by the associations of industrialists, by the Prussian agrarians, by the Supreme Command, and in the Reichstag by all the political parties except the Socialists.[22] The Socialist leader Scheidemann tells of a meeting of William II with party leaders during the war during which the monarch said, "When we have defeated this lot, I shall start the second Punic War and the British will get an eye opener." [23]

On December 2, 1914, the Centrist Reichstag deputy Spahn presented a statement to the Reichstag in behalf of all the parties except the Socialists, which gave veiled expression to a demand for indemnities to pay for the "enormous sacrifices" made by Germany. On March 10, 1915, Spahn again declared in behalf of all the non-Socialist parties that peace will have to provide Germany with greater security than before. And on December 9, 1915, Spahn likewise presented a declaration in behalf of all the non-Socialist parties which called for a peace which "would make secure for Germany the entire range of its military, economic, financial and political interests and all means thereto, including the acquisition of territories necessary for them." The Progressive leader Naumann proposed on October 10, 1914, that Belgium be divided among France, Luxemburg, Holland, and Germany. Erzberger, in September, 1914, wanted not only the annexation of Longwy and Brie, but also German domination of Belgium and the French coast to Boulogne. Bassermann, the leader of the National Liberals, proclaimed the principle, "Where a drop of German blood has flowed there we remain," and this was re-echoed by his followers throughout the land. Stegerwald, the leader of the Christian trade-unions, as late as April, 1918, declared in Essen, "If we are in the position to be able to achieve a peace by force (*Machtfrieden*), then we are by all means for a *Machtfrieden*." Stresemann asked the Conservative leader Count Westarp in July, 1917, "If you could have peace today on the basis of the *status quo,* would you accept it?" Westarp replied, "No." [24] German victory by arms, he declared, would have to impose a peace that would lessen the chances for a repetition of the attack upon Germany. Oldenburg-Januschau, in a speech before the Bund der Landwirte on February 18, 1918, attacked the policies of Bethmann-Hollweg and said that in order to preserve peace in the future, "We need different frontiers and greater independence." Bethmann's statement regarding the "wrong done to Belgium" he branded as "one that no rain would wash away," and he made the frank avowal that "this war is a war for world domination, and hard though it may be to wage, it must be fought out to victory, and the victory must be exploited." [25]

The future of Belgium was the key question in the whole discussion of war aims. Dietrich Schäfer, a prominent nationalist historian, became one of the most vociferous spokesmen for the Pan-German League on this issue. "We must retain military, political and economic control of Belgium," he wrote, "in order to prevent its resources and its geographical location from being used by our enemies against us. Whoever . . . views the entire situation, cannot come to anything but the conviction that a peace which will take us back to the status of before the war . . . is synonymous with permanent and serious jeopardy to our Reich and to our people." A powerful German fleet combined with the possession of the Belgian coast land, said Schäfer, is necessary to make England fear Germany. Only a person of limited mentality could look forward to the harmonious settlement of differences after the war when there would be "neither conquerors nor conquered." After this war the enemies of Germany, wrote Schäfer, would continue as before to try to keep Germany down. "Against this, only force is of avail. Whoever teaches that Germany can assert itself among the nations in any other way than by the accretion of its force, sins against his fatherland." [26]

The annexationist point of view of the Pan-Germans was identical with that of the Supreme Command. "If Germany makes peace without a profit," declared Ludendorff to Count Czernin in February, 1918, "it has lost the war." [27] On September 15, 1917, Hindenburg wrote to the chancellor that giving up the Flemish coast would be "a heavy blow" to the navy and to "extensive patriotic circles," unless there are other compensations such as naval bases in and outside the German colonies. He urged the occupation of Belgium for several years after the war, in order to ensure its economic affiliation with Germany, and the retention of Liége for an indefinite period. On December 15, 1917, Hindenburg again wrote to the chancellor as follows:

Belgium will continue to exist and will be taken under German military control until it is ripe politically and economically for a defensive and offensive alliance with Germany. . . . Nevertheless, for reasons of military strategy, Liége and the Flemish coast, including Bruges, will remain permanently in Germany's possession (or on 99 years' lease). The cession of this territory is an imperative condition for peace with England.[28]

These demands were justified on the grounds of the need for security. But, as Hans Delbrück pointed out before the Reichstag Inquiry Commission, all annexations are made to ensure security; and, said Delbrück: "A nation that wants to secure so much security for itself that the other nations will not be able to attack it, such a nation rules the world, and the great nations will not allow themselves to be ruled by *one* nation. There can be no such thing as world domination by *one* nation. The world rightly rises up against that." [29]

The civilian government leaders never went as far as the Pan-Germans in their public utterances. Privately they often expressed their horror at the ravings of the Pan-Germans. Scheidemann tells of a conference with Bethmann-Hollweg on March 9, 1915, in which the chancellor said: "The aims demanded by the Pan-Germans are senseless. I have no intention of realizing them." But he then went on to speak of "very close economic relations with Belgium and perhaps a military treaty," together with territorial adjustments in the Vosges and Belfort.[30] These could be termed mild annexationism, and the Socialist leaders raised no objections to such a formulation. Meinecke tells of a similar conversation with von Kühlmann in which the foreign secretary also lashed out against the annexationists and contented himself with the "modest" war aims of a line at the Maas River on the west and at the Narew River on the east.[31] But no matter what differences existed between the civil government and the Supreme Command, policy in the last analysis was dictated by Ludendorff and Hindenburg. The war aims of these military leaders were identical with those of the Pan-Germans. Until July 15, 1918, they believed they could bring victory and with it the annexationist fruits of victory. The ministers, the parliamentary leaders, the press and public opinion were confident that their military leaders would deliver such a victory, and the war was therefore prolonged until all hopes of a rational peace were shattered.

The chief opposition to annexationist war aims was centered in the Social Democratic party. Here too, however, there were divergent currents which eventually led to serious splits in the hitherto solid organization of the party. The outbreak of the war overwhelmed the German Socialists as it did all the other parties of the Socialist International. In the first years of the war, however, most of the German Socialists were able to rationalize their support of the war and even find "socialist" justification for it in the writings of Marx and Engels by pointing to the dangers of absolutist tsarist Russia. "Once again," said Kautsky's *Die Neue Zeit* on August 28, 1914, "we have the old wicked opponent to the development of liberty in Europe, tsarism." The most popular party slogans were "The Fight Is Against Russia," and "Down with Tsarism!"

Not all the Socialist deputies agreed with the sentiments expressed in the official party statement presented by Haase on August 4, 1914. Fourteen party deputies had voted at the caucus against the approval of the war credits. Included in this minority was also Haase himself. But party discipline was still very powerful in the Socialist group. All the Social Democratic deputies, including Karl Liebknecht, voted for the war credits in the Reichstag, and Haase himself carried out the burdensome obligation to read the party statement even though it was contrary to his own convictions.* Karl Kautsky, the theoretical pontiff of Marxian Socialism, was sure that the war would not last more than a few months. He ruled out the alternative of working for the defeat of one's own country, and concluded, on October 2, 1914, that "the problem reduces itself to the question whether one's attitude toward the war be one of passionate enthusiasm or one of reserve." [32]

Among the Socialist supporters of the war there were several variations of opinion. The majority continued to the end to view the war as a defensive war imposed upon Germany against its will, and its war aims, therefore, called for no compensations of any significant character to be won by Germany. The party leaders Ebert, Scheidemann, and David were the chief spokesmen for this point of view, and the term "Scheidemann peace" came to be used to denote a peace without annexations. Alsace-Lorraine and the German colonies were considered by these Socialists to

---

* One Socialist deputy, Fritz Kunert, went out of the hall on Aug. 4 when the vote was being taken and returned again after the vote. No one noticed this incident at the time, but a year and a half later Kunert divulged the fact and explained that he could not bring himself to vote one pfennig for war nor did he dare at that time to commit a breach of party discipline. (See K. Haenisch, *Die deutsche Sozialdemokratie in und nach dem Weltkriege,* 4th ed. [Berlin, 1919], p. 25.)

be legitimate possessions of the German Reich and hence to be retained by Germany. They sometimes distinguished between "rectifications" of boundaries, which they found acceptable, and "annexations." They believed, and led their followers to believe, that Bethmann-Hollweg shared their own views regarding annexations, and hence continued to give him their support. It is interesting to read the speech by Scheidemann in the Reichstag on April 6, 1916, in which he interpreted the statement on peace aims just made by the chancellor as being identical with those of the Social Democratic party—this right after Stresemann and Westarp had found support in the same statement for the annexationist demands of the National Liberals and the Conservatives. Scheidemann inveighed against those who considered the boundaries between states to be so sacred that they would not allow a single stone to be moved. As for the German campaign to wean away the Flemings from the Walloons in Belgium, he declared: "If we are able by treaty to secure for the Flemings the possibility to develop their own culture on the basis of their own language, I ask: Is this violence?" [33]

At the party conference of September 21–23, 1916, the resolution introduced by Eduard David to continue the policy of August 4 was passed by a vote of 251 out of 451 delegates. The resolution declared:

This war continues to be a defensive war for Germany. . . . The Social Democratic party is determined as hitherto to hold out in the defense of our country until our opponents are prepared to conclude a peace which will make secure for Germany its political independence, its territorial integrity and freedom of economic development. It opposes the claims and demands of those who wish to give to the war the character of a war of conquest.[34]

It was a phrase like "freedom of economic development," however, which, as Haase pointed out, lent itself easily to annexationist interpretation. And such interpretations multiplied or decreased within the party, depending on the course of the war at the front. By and large, however, it must be affirmed that the party leaders adhered consistently to a policy of a negotiated peace, a peace without victors or vanquished, and a peace which rejected the war aims of the other bourgeois parties.

The position of the Majority Socialists during the war has been subject to severe criticism from many quarters. The violent and vituperative attacks by Lenin on the German Socialists have left a lasting mark on subsequent historical writing. But while there may be logic in the position of Lenin, who threw *all* national loyalties to the winds and took his stand outright on the platform of class warfare, it is another thing for bourgeois historians of non-German countries to criticize the German Socialists for exhibiting love of country and not being loyal to the doctrine of class warfare. Even their opposition to annexations and imperialism has been "exposed" and censured because this opposition was allegedly based not upon adherence to an intrinsic idea but was "opportunist" and "pragmatic" and conceived only because annexationism "was harmful to German interests."[35]

The position of the Majority Socialists was a truly difficult and tragic one. "It has not been easy for Social Democrats," declared Ebert on April 5, 1916, "to defend the ruling system while we are defending our country. We were highly dissatisfied with the economic conditions and stood in sharp opposition to the political conditions in the Reich." But the belief that Germany was in mortal danger from tsarist Russia led most of the German Socialists to feel that they were not only defending their country but also fighting the greatest force against liberty in Europe.* The really serious charge that can be leveled against the Social Democratic party is that they did not recognize soon enough the imperialistic aspirations of the ruling powers of Germany and that when they did come to see them they reacted only feebly to the danger. Eduard David, in the early years of the war, demanded of his Socialist party colleagues to have "the courage to remain silent" on the question of war aims.[36]

Within the party of the Majority Socialists there was one group that was avowedly socialist-imperialist in its aspirations. The more vociferous exponents of this faction were Paul Lensch, Konrad Haenisch, Wilhelm Kolb, Wolfgang Heine, Ernst Heilmann, Albert Südekum, and Ludwig Quessel. This group harked back to the nationalist tradition of Lassalle and Schweitzer and to the pro-militarist and colonial agitators in the party before the war.† For these Socialists the war served to make clear once for all, and beyond all doubt, that the working classes were deeply attached to their fatherland. For the first time the Socialist workers could, without hesitation and without apologies, join their fellow Germans in the singing of "Deutschland über alles." This, wrote Haenisch, was something which could not be understood by "foreigners" like Rosa Luxemburg,

---

* The Socialist leader Eduard David in a speech to the Reichstag Commission of Inquiry on this subject on May 10, 1926, declared that open attack upon the Supreme Command during the war "would have meant a revolution during the war. . . . The front would have been broken. But we could not do that because the higher restraint in the interests of our native land imposed restrictions upon us. The majority were aware and constantly reiterated that the Reichstag must not make itself to blame in any way for the defeat of our country. Otherwise the parliamentary system and everything else would have been done for if we had made ourselves to blame for the defeat. We dared do nothing that helped the enemy. That was the real final restraint" (Lutz, *Causes of the German Collapse*, pp. 244–245). Walter Schücking, the pacifist leader, commenting on Dr. David's speech, said: "The detailed account by the deputy Dr. David revealed to me for the first time the full tragedy of the position of the S.P.D. in this last phase of the war. These men saw clearly: with the present political leadership we shall be hurled into the abyss. Yet they could not take the only action possible; namely, to go over to a policy of violent opposition or to passive resistance. It was out of patriotism that they could not do this because they said to themselves: then everything will go under, for if we stage the general strike and tell the soldiers not to fight any more then the enemy will derive an enormous advantage out of this. . . . This was a hopeless condition to be in, and the S.P.D. adopted in this situation a position dictated by their love of their fatherland!" (*Die Ursachen* . . . , vii, 269.)

† See Chap. X.

Karl Radek, and Anton Pannekoek. Wilhelm Kolb elaborated the view he held before 1914 and published his *Die Sozialdemokratie am Scheidewege* (Karlsruhe, 1915), in which he attempted to show that the war was altering the entire traditional policy of the Socialist party. The Social Democrats were now no longer set off from the other parties. They were *regierungsfähig,* and should continue to be so even after the war. "The act of August 4," wrote Kolb, "was the last decisive step of the Social Democratic party in the path of development from a sect to a party." [37] Important too was the attempt to interpret the nationalist war as an enormous step in the direction of the socialist revolution. The war, said these Socialist patriots, finally resulted in the creation of a true people's army in place of the old feudal army. The *Kriegswirtschaft* measures were "milestones on the path to socialism" that proved beyond doubt the superiority of a socialist economy over capitalism. England, said Lensch and Haenisch, represents backward capitalism as against the forward-looking and progressive economic forces embodied in Germany, with the most organized economy and most organized Socialist proletariat. The war will therefore realize Marx's predictions, and England, the backbone of reactionary capitalism, will be dethroned and replaced by revolutionary Germany. A German victory will, therefore, also aid both the British working classes and international socialism. Running through the statements of these writers is a definite undercurrent of scoffing at the outmoded and old-fashioned ideals of democracy and peace and an identification of national military force with revolutionary struggle.

Paul Lensch, writing in the *Hamburger Echo,* gave clear expression to this point of view: "The most terrible catastrophe burst upon us and only confirmed what the Marxist school had maintained before the war on the role of force and economics in social development. In place of the peaceful idyl of the Philistines now came the world revolution, only it was more grandiose, more all-embracing and more explosive than the radicals ever could dream of." Many of these old radicals, declared Lensch, had now become "most gentle Heinrichs" who "tremble before any act of force." Now that the revolution is here, these radicals suddenly become so scrupulous that "no little stone in Europe dare be moved and no treaty, however outworn it may be, dare be broken." Scoffing at the radicals who "lament the violation of law," Lensch cried out: "It was a symbolic act that the world revolution began on the German side with willful insurrection, the tearing up of Belgian neutrality." [38] This was indubitably one of the currents from which subsequent German National Socialism was to draw its sustenance and provide the basis for mass support of the Nazis among the working classes.*

* In the foreword to the 4th edition of his *Die deutsche Sozialdemokratie in und nach dem Weltkriege,* published after the revolution in 1919, Konrad Haenisch affirms his continued adherence to the thesis of the book and writes as follows: "In the end the ideas of

The rift in the Socialist party began to come to a head when it was observed that the war was not being waged primarily against Russian tsarism. For a few, the fact that the Supreme Command, in the initial stages of the war, threw its main force not against Russia but against the West was an eye opener. By December 2, 1914, the number of opponents to the war credits rose from 14 to 17 at the party caucus. But only Liebknecht voted against the war credits in the Reichstag. In March, 1915, he was joined by Otto Rühle. By this time the opposition in the party caucus rose to 24. After Italy joined the Allies against Germany the opponents of the war in the Social Democratic party became more vocal. On June 9, 1915, the opposition issued a pamphlet, "An die Genossen," which called upon the party leadership to renounce the *Burgfrieden* and "inaugurate the Socialist battle in behalf of peace." This was followed by a declaration, "Das Gebot der Stunde," signed by Eduard Bernstein, Karl Kautsky, and Hugo Haase, and published first in the *Leipziger Volkszeitung*. The three veteran Socialist leaders pointed to the many signs of a German war of conquest and raised the question whether the Social Democrats should vote for new military appropriations. At the party caucus in August, 1915, the opposition to the war numbered 36, and at the vote in the Reichstag 29 Socialist deputies left the hall during the vote. Karl Kautsky issued what amounted to a call for a party split in two articles which he published in the *Neue Zeit* on October 29 and November 5, 1915, in which he urged the minority to act as an independent unit in the Reichstag vote.[39] As a result, in the Reichstag session of December 21, 1915, twenty Socialist deputies recorded their opposition to the war credits, and Fritz Geyer read an explanatory statement in their behalf to the Reichstag. Eighteen members, led by Haase, officially left the party and constituted themselves first as a separate faction under the name of *Sozialdemokratische Arbeitervereinigung* and later as the Independent Social Democratic party.[40]

The division in the Social Democratic party cut across the old lines between orthodox Marxists and revisionists. The two chief opponents in the old party fight, Bernstein and Kautsky, were at one on the war issue. Similarly, former radical and orthodox Marxists such as Wendel, Cunow, and Lensch joined with revisionists like Winnig, David, and Südekum to support the war. What brought the opposition together was not the particular brand of Marxian socialism they believed in but certain psychological and ethical attitudes toward war, nationalism, and the common ideals of Western democracy. The Independent Socialists recognized the nature of German militarist expansionism, and they looked with horror

1914 as personified in Germany will *yet* . . . triumph over the ideas of 1789 which today seem to be victorious because of the military and political successes of the western powers. The future belongs neither to western democracy, outmoded both in its essence and in its form, nor to the sombre aberrations of eastern Bolshevism, but to the *organizing socialism of Germany*" (p. 7).

at a breach between the German exponents of peace and democratic ideals and France and England, the sources of these ideals. In the declaration of July 13, 1918, Geyer, in behalf of the Independent Socialists, affirmed:

> The war was never a war of defense. It was and is a war of conquest with imperialistic objectives. The imperial government covers up and favors the drives of the annexationists. . . . Upon Russia and Rumania they forced a peace of violation. . . . Peoples, whose liberation had been promised in big words, are being enslaved and exploited. The right to self-determination is . . . being mocked. . . . The reputation of the German Reich, the confidence in the sincerity of the promises made by the government is being destroyed. . . . A state of siege and censorship gags the free world and deceives us regarding the true attitudes of the people. . . . We reject the credits. . . . Down with the war! [41]

The Independent Socialists established relations with anti-war Socialists in other countries, sending representatives to the Zimmerwald peace conference of September 8–15, 1915. They looked forward to re-establishing the influence of the Socialist International to work for a peace of understanding. A left wing of the party, led by Ledebour, emphasized more revolutionary action and become the chief advocate of the political strike as a weapon of peace.

Besides the Independent Socialists there were two other Socialist groups that were both revolutionary and anti-war. Karl Liebknecht, Rosa Luxemburg, Franz Mehring, and Leo Jogiches formed what was known as the Internationale group. They published one issue of a magazine under this name on April 1, 1915, and it was immediately confiscated by the police. Out of this group came the later Spartakusbund and the Communist party. Another group, known as the Internationale Sozialisten Deutschlands, was led by Karl Radek and Julian Borchardt and followed closely the political line formulated by Lenin in Switzerland. Both of these groups emphasized the need for world revolution, but the Luxemburg group wished to realize their aims through the election of people's representatives, while the others thought only in terms of mass action. From Rosa Luxemburg came a most penetrating analysis of the position of the German Socialists on the war, which she issued under the pen name of Junius. Unlike Lenin, who subjected the Junius pamphlet to bitter attack [42] and who threw overboard all sense of responsibility to nation and country in favor of the interests of the world proletariat and world revolution, Rosa Luxemburg made her plea for opposition to the war precisely because it was against the true interests of the nation. "Yes, the Social-Democrats," she wrote in the Junius pamphlet,

> are pledged to defend their country in a great historical crisis. And therein a burden of guilt lies on the Social Democrat group in the Reichstag. . . .

In the hour of greatest need they deserted their country. For the chief duty to the country at that time was to demonstrate the true background of this imperialist war; to tear asunder the tissue of patriotic and diplomatic lies in which this attack against the fatherland was veiled: to indicate clearly that victory or defeat were equally fateful for the German nation in this war; . . . to proclaim the immediate necessity for arming the nation, and for giving people the chance to decide for peace or war; to demand with the utmost firmness the permanent session of the representatives of the people for the duration of the war, so as to assume that the government should be vigilantly supervised by the representatives of the people, and they in turn by the people themselves; to demand the immediate abolition of all political inequalities; since none but a free people can effectively defend their native land; finally, to substitute for the imperialist program of the war which is designed for the preservation of Austria and Turkey and means a reaction in Europe and in Germany, the old truly nationalist program of the patriots and democrats in 1848, the program of Marx, Engels, Lassalle, whose solution is a great united German Republic. This was the banner which should have been borne before the country, and which should have been truly national, truly liberal, and in accord with the best tradition of Germany as with international class policy of the proletariat.[43]

The outbreak of the Russian revolution in March, 1917, provided a mighty impetus to the peace movement within Germany. To all who had argued that Germany had been forced to defend herself against the danger of tsarist Russia it could now be shown that Russia was no longer a danger either to European freedom or to Germany. The war lost most of its meaning in these circles. The Russian revolution was an important factor in influencing the formation of the Independent Socialist party, but it also pushed the Majority Socialists to action. The Majority Socialists in turn, were able to win over a considerable number of Centrist deputies to their view of the war and war aims, and out of this alliance emerged the most independent action taken by the Reichstag during the war, the passage of the famous Reichstag peace resolution of July, 1917.

On July 6 the Centrist leader Matthias Erzberger, having just returned from a tour of the eastern front, presented to the Reichstag main commission a very pessimistic picture of the military situation. He pointed out especially that the high hopes of the admiralty that the prosecution of unrestricted submarine warfare would bring England "to her knees" and would force her to sue for peace in six months were not being realized. The optimism engendered by the official and naval circles, reported Erzberger, was not in keeping with the true situation, and the time had come to return to the "defensive war" position of August 4. Erzberger's speech was a terrific shock to the Reichstag deputies, who now for the first time became aware of how ill informed they had been on the true conditions. No one had ever before brought out the naked and brutal reality as he did. A majority of the Reichstag parties now united in support of a resolution which would reaffirm the peaceful aims of Germany in the war. On July 19, 1917, the full session of the Reichstag adopted the following resolution:

As on August 4, 1914, the German people, on the threshold of the fourth year of the war, stand behind the words of the speech from the throne: "We are not driven by a desire for conquest!" Germany took up arms only for the defense of its freedom and independence and for the preservation of its territorial integrity.

The Reichstag strives for a peace of understanding and lasting reconciliation of nations. Such a peace is not in keeping with forcible annexations of territory or forcible measures of political, economic or financial character.

The Reichstag also rejects all plans which would result in economic isolation and hostility among nations after the war. The freedom of the seas must be made secure. Only economic peace will prepare the ground for the friendly living together of nations.

The Reichstag will actively support the creation of international judicial organizations.

So long as the enemy governments will not agree to such a peace, so long as they threaten Germany and its allies with annexations and violence, the German people will stand together as one, hold out unshakably and fight on until the right to life and development is made secure for it and its allies.

The German people is invincible in its unity. The Reichstag is at one in this with the men who are protecting the fatherland with heroic courage. The everlasting thanks of the entire nation is theirs.

This resolution was not only approved by the majority of the Reichstag but also received the blessing of the Supreme Command [44] and the approval of the new Chancellor Michaelis. The sincerity of the support that came from these quarters, however, is open to serious question. Michaelis gave his approval to the resolution in his speech to the Reichstag on July 19, and the report of the Reichstag proceedings shows a great deal of applause for the speech from the left and center. The majority parties thought the chancellor was at one with them. They did not notice that Michaelis had appended to his acceptance of the resolution the significant phrase "as I understand it" and, as he wrote to Crown Prince William on July 25, 1917: "By means of my interpretation of it [the Reichstag resolution] I robbed it of its greatest dangers. We can make any kind of peace we want with this resolution." [45]

The Supreme Command, despite assurances to the leaders of the Reichstag majority that they had no objections to the peace resolution, inspired the organization of the Vaterlandspartei, a mass party designed to combat the Reichstag peace resolution. The chief organizer of this party was the subsequently notorious Wolfgang Kapp, and Admiral von Tirpitz became its official head. Over one and a quarter million dues-paying members were enrolled in this organization, the chief support coming from the Conservatives and National Liberals.*

4. PEACE WITH THE BOLSHEVIKS

The complete dominance of the Supreme Command over the civil government and over the mentality of party leaders was best revealed in the relations with the new Bolshevik government in Russia. Within several weeks after they seized power the Russian Bolsheviks made an offer of an armistice and peace to Germany and its allies. Negotiations commenced at Brest Litovsk, in German-occupied Poland, on January 4, 1918. The civilian representatives, led by von Kühlmann, while in formal control of the negotiations, were plainly dominated by the representative of the Supreme Command, General Max Hoffmann, who in no uncertain terms let Trotsky and his colleagues know that they were the vanquished and would have to accept a dictated peace.† When on February 10 Trotsky left the negotiations and declared the war to be ended without the signing of a peace, Hoffman ordered the resumption of hostilities and the advance of the German armies deeper into Russia. It was the stubborn insistence of Lenin, against the objections of the majority of the Bolshevik Central Committee, that brought the Russians back to Brest Litovsk on February 28, with final acceptance of the dictated treaty on March 3.[46]

The Treaty of Brest Litovsk indicated unmistakably how strong pan-German sentiment was in the government and in public opinion. By its terms Germany secured control from the Narva on the Arctic to the Caucasus and the Black Sea. A spurious use of the principle of self-determination placed German power in the entire Baltic area, the Ukraine, and the Caucasus, and brought more of the Russian Empire under German domination than the Nazis were later to conquer during their deepest penetration. By this treaty Russia lost one-fourth of its territory, 44 per cent of its population, 27 per cent of its income, 80 per cent of its sugar factories, 73 per cent of its iron, and 75 per cent of its coal. "Never in the history of the world," declared the German parliamentarian Bredt to the Reichstag Inquiry Commission, "has there been an instance of greater annexationist politics than the Peace of Brest Litovsk." And yet this peace,

---

* As a counter-movement to the Vaterlandspartei the liberal elements under the leadership of Ernst Troeltsch, Heinrich Herkner, and Friedrich Meinecke organized the Volksbund für Freiheit und Vaterland to support the domestic and foreign policies of Bethmann-Hollweg. This organization likewise received the blessings of Ludendorff. According to Professor Walter Schücking, however, Troeltsch and other leaders ceased their public support of a peace without annexations when the early offensive of 1918 seemed to be successful. (Cf. *Untersuchungsausschuss*, i, 447.) On the history of the Vaterlandspartei, see Karl Wortmann, *Geschichte der deutschen Vaterlandspartei 1917–1918* (Halle, 1926); see also *Die Ursachen* . . . , vol. xii, pt. 1.

† Leon Trotsky relates how in replying to one of Hoffmann's attacks he mentioned the German government, whereupon "Hoffmann interrupted me in a voice that was hoarse with anger: 'I do not represent the German government here, but the German High Command'" (*My Life*, New York, 1930, p. 374).

coming almost immediately following the adoption of the Reichstag peace resolution which had rejected an annexationist peace, was accepted with glee by all the Reichstag parties except the Socialists. Stresemann, of the National Liberals, hailed the treaty and "the advance of the unbroken military might of Germany which has brought us peace in the east." A new wave of optimistic hope on the possibility of a peace by German victory spread through the country. Hertling declared the Reichstag peace resolution to be out of date. Erzberger, the leading architect of the Reichstag peace resolution, now believed that the collapse of Russia made German victory possible. "We warmly welcome the peace in the east with Russia," he declared in the Reichstag, "for it is completely within the framework of the resolution that we formulated." And when this statement was greeted with laughter from the left, he reiterated: "Completely within the framework of our decisions—only wait, only wait! It costs nothing to laugh." [47] Scheidemann was the only one in the Reichstag debates who reminded the deputies of the resolution of July 19. When it came to a vote only the Independent Socialists voted against the treaty.* Scheidemann, in behalf of the Majority Socialists, read a declaration in which he denounced the treaty as a violation of true "self-determination"; since it did bring peace, however, he declared that the Socialists would not oppose it but only abstain. "The layman," writes Bredt, "stands amazed and the scholar wonders how it was possible for the Reichstag to approve the Peace of Brest Litovsk after it had passed the peace resolution. We stand before a riddle." And by this treaty, comments Bredt, "Germany placed itself in the light of a power addicted to annexations and violence, and destroyed thereby the last remnant of confidence from enemy and neutral countries abroad." [48] If one desires to know what sort of peace would have taken the place of the Treaty of Versailles if Germany had won the war, let him study the provisions of the peace with the Russian Bolsheviks.†

The Treaty of Brest Litovsk is extremely interesting in throwing light on subsequent Russo-German relations. On the Russian side both opposition and support of the treaty among the Bolsheviks were intimately bound up with the hopes for a workers' revolution in Germany. The so-called "patriotic" opposition among the Bolsheviks realized as well as Lenin did that the Russian army was no longer in a position to fight. But they

---

* On Oct. 23, 1918, Haase declared in the Reichstag: "This peace resolution surely should once for all be buried. . . . How this resolution is to be understood can be determined only by its application, and it received its application in the peace treaties of Brest Litovsk and Bucharest. . . . No one today affirms that these peace treaties were not treaties of force" (Lutz, ii, 389).

† "What the Supreme Command considered to be an acceptable peace in the east, we have seen in the treaty of Brest Litovsk. In the event of victory the peace in the west by the Supreme Command would have been of the same kind. It would have been a dictated peace just like the one we concluded at Brest Litovsk" (Dr. Ludwig Quessel before the Reichstag Inquiry Commission, i, 405).

were sure that the imperialist world war had brought about the impending collapse of the capitalist structure of the West and that the German proletariat would follow immediately the example of the Russian, set up a communist state, and join with the Russian soviet state. All that was necessary, therefore, was for the Russians to hold out and fight on a bit longer until the contagion of revolution was kindled in Germany.

Lenin opposed the continuation of the war and forced his fellow Bolsheviks to sign the oppressive treaty, but he too was sure that the German revolution would not be too long in coming. Lenin had always been an admirer of the progressive industrialist development of Germany and of the great Socialist party built up in that country. When the news came to him that the German Social Democrats had voted for the war credits on August 4, 1914, he refused to believe that the report was true. Marxists had always considered Germany to be the logical place for the first Socialist society. "If it were necessary for us to go under," said Lenin to Trotsky, "to assure the success of the German revolution, we should have to do it. The German revolution is vastly more important than ours." [49] In his long speech to the Communist-party conference of March 7, 1918, Lenin reiterated that "it is an absolute truth that we will go under without the German revolution." [50] And "Liebknecht will rescue us from this," and bring to the Russian Bolsheviks "such a magnificent organization" that the Russians will be able to take over the highly developed instruments of revolution with the same advantageous effects as when they took over "the completed Marxian doctrine of western Europe." [51] The question was, however, when will this German revolution come? Lenin was a bit more realistic than his colleagues. He was afraid that it might not be just around the corner. "That there will be a Socialist revolution in Europe," wrote Lenin on January 20, 1918, "there is no doubt. All our hopes in the final triumph of socialism are based on this certainty, which is in the nature of a scientific prediction. . . . But it would be a mistake for the Socialist government in Russia to formulate its policy on the supposition that within the next six months (or thereabouts) there will be a European, to be more specific a German socialist revolution." [52] But on February 23 of the same year he said: "The German revolution is not yet ripe. It will take *months*." [53] In any case Lenin was certain, in his "scientific prediction," that within a relatively short period there would be a German revolution that would then proceed to free the Russian Bolsheviks from the yoke of the treaty of force.

From the very start Lenin undertook to vie with the German Supreme Command as to who would outsmart whom in the game of military might versus revolutionary propaganda. His acceptance of the offer by Ludendorff to proceed from Switzerland to Russia in a sealed train by way of Germany was part of this strategy. In the Central Executive Council of the Soviets he was asked on February 23, 1918, whether the Treaty of Brest

Litovsk would not prevent the Bolsheviks from carrying on their propaganda in Germany. Lenin replied: "The Central Executive signs the peace, the Council of Commissars signs the peace, but not the Central Committee of the party. For the behavior of the latter the Soviet government is not responsible." [54] As soon as diplomatic relations were established, Russian agents immediately became active in Germany. Adolf Joffe, the first Soviet ambassador to Germany, boasted of having supplied "money for the German revolution" and was forced to leave Berlin at the request of the German government. Karl Radek, Zinoviev, and a host of lesser known Bolshevik figures played an active role in the founding of the German Communist party, all of which is a later story.

On the German side there were optimistic hopes of another character. Quite apart from the feeling of exultation in the triumph of German arms and the prospects of filling the German larders from the Ukrainian granary, there was a revival of the Eastern orientation of German policy. Among conservative nationalists like Otto Hoetzsch, among liberals like Georg Bernhard, and among the Socialists gathered around the *Sozialistische Monatshefte* a trend developed which advocated an alliance between Germany and Russia against England. The Socialist leader Eduard David said to General Hoffmann, while on a visit to the eastern front: "Think of the chances offered by a real understanding with Russia *after* the war! Naumann's idea of Central Europe is nothing but a collection of petty states and no real world economic area. But Central Europe with Russia as far as the Pacific and Indian Oceans—that is a world economic area. That is a war aim which ought to be pursued." [55] Even before the outbreak of the Russian revolution Georg Bernhard, editorial writer of the Berlin *Vossische Zeitung,* had written:

From a purely economic point of view there are hardly two states that complement each other so splendidly as Germany and Russia. If we assume that Russia will have to reform itself after the war, then where will there be a better market for most of the articles of our industrial productivity than in Russia? Here chances of infinite dimensions beckon to us for many decades to come. Here there is by nature no economic rivalry. England, on the other hand, will always look with jealous eyes not so much on the development of German industry as on the continued development of German trade. Whoever, therefore, believes that the economic foundations of the life of a people are not entirely without influence on the relations between nations can therefore not believe that there will be greater areas of friction in the future between Germany and Russia than between Germany and England.[56]

The revisionist *Sozialistische Monatshefte* had been particularly active in advocating an eventual alliance between Germany and Russia as complementing each other in the economic sphere. When the tsarist régime fell, the pressure along these lines increased greatly. Max Cohn predicted a constellation of power after the war with an Anglo-American alliance on the one hand and all of continental Europe, including Russia, on the other. "For Germany," wrote Cohn, "two roads were open. One led to England, the other to Russia." The war, he declared, has revealed the need of a pro-Russian orientation "as a condition for a continental alliance against England." [57] Only rarely, wrote the Socialist-imperialist Max Schippel, do two states complement each other so beautifully as do "the predominantly agrarian Russian and the industrial capitalistic and more highly developed Germany." [58] The Treaty of Brest Litovsk was denounced in these Socialist circles as annexationist and as harmful for the development of this working alliance between Germany and Russia. But the tradition of such Russo-German co-operation continued to hold fascination for many circles in Germany and showed its effects in both the Weimar epoch and during the Nazi régime.*

5. COLLAPSE IN THE WEST

The German military decision on the eastern front proved to be inadequate to bring victory also in the west. Food shipments from the Ukraine were far below the expectations of the Supreme Command, and distress among the German civilian population because of food shortages continued to mount. The effects of the unrestricted submarine warfare, on the other hand, not only did not paralyze Britain, as expected, but brought the United States into the war against Germany to more than offset Russia's defection. Economic distress, profiteering, the privileged position of the upper classes—all contributed to widen the gulf between the aristocracy and the lower classes, between those who lived better and the poor working classes. In the army and navy there was resentment among the rank and file against the system that provided better food for the officers. Moreover German commitments in the Ukraine and the Caucasus failed to free as large a number of troops from the east to the west as had been expected. All these elements began to be reflected in the mood of both the soldiers at the front and of the civilian population at home. Letters from the front began to reveal increasing bitterness. The public began to pay less attention to the war bulletins. Mothers displayed increasing resentment at the undernourishment of their children. Among the poorer classes, especially in the large cities, the misery became very acute. The misery was so great, reported Scheidemann, "that it is like asking a complete riddle when one asks one's self: What does north Berlin live on and how does east Berlin exist?" [59]

---

* "It is the destiny of Germany to regain its independence in the struggle against Europe. Germany can only be rewon if it collaborates with the Russian-Asiatic spearhead against Europe. . . . The moment one hundred million Russian fanatics are joined by eighty million German fanatics, the old order will fall apart like a house of cards" (Ernst Niekisch in *Entscheidung* [Berlin, 1930], quoted in Melvin J. Lasky, "Inside Soviet Germany," in the *New Leader*, April 16. 1951).

Dissatisfaction among the sailors, influenced by the activities of the Independent Socialists, showed itself in a mutiny on June 6, 1917, by the crew of the *Prince Regent Leopold,* who went on a hunger strike. Their action was followed by similar strikes on other ships. The leaders of the sailors were condemned to death and shot on September 5, 1917.

Finally, opposition to the continuance of the war began to be displayed by organized labor. The news of a wave of successful strikes in Austria directed against the German annexationism at Brest Litovsk resulted, in January, 1918, in the first big outbreak of political strikes in Germany. On January 28, 400,000 workers in Berlin went out on strike, demanding a peace without annexation, the democratization of the government, the abolition of martial law, and the repeal of the National Service Law. Both the Majority Socialists leaders and the Independents joined the strike committee. The movement spread to most of the larger industrial cities of Germany and embraced over a million workers. It was a tremendous mass protest against the military dictatorship and against Ludendorff himself. But there was as yet neither the all-out revolutionary will nor the power to stand up against the Supreme Command. Ludendorff was able to suppress the movement with ruthless action, and the leaders were forced to call off the strike on February 3. This too was a sign for the Russian negotiators at Brest Litovsk that they could not as yet depend on immediate help from the German proletariat, and they agreed to accept the dictated Peace of Brest Litovsk.

The military leaders now decided to stake all on a new great offensive in the west, which was initiated on March 21, 1918, by an advance from Saint-Quentin. For a while it seemed as if the plans of the Supreme Command would be carried to a successful realization. When Foreign Secretary von Kühlmann declared in the Reichstag on June 21, 1918, "In view of the vast dimensions of this coalition war . . . an absolute end can scarcely be expected through a purely military decision, without . . . an exchange of views and without any diplomatic negotiations," he was violently denounced by the leaders of all the parties except the Independent Socialists, and Hindenburg and Ludendorff forced the emperor to oust him from office. But the establishment of a unified Allied command under Foch and the re-enforcement of the Allied armies by large numbers of American troops broke the back of the German drive and the last hopes of a German victory were shattered.

According to the testimony of von Hintze before the Reichstag Commission, Ludendorff was still certain of beating the Allies in the middle of July, 1918. On August 13 he was no longer sure of it.[60] At the Crown Council on August 14, 1918, "The Chief of the General Staff of the Army in the field so far defined the military situation as to say that we can no longer hope to break down the fighting spirit of our enemies by military action, and that we must set as the object of our campaign that of gradually wearing down the enemy's fighting spirit by a strategic defensive." [61] The failure of the German offensive coincided with the collapse of Germany's allies, first Turkey, then Bulgaria, and finally Austria-Hungary. On September 27 Ludendorff was unable to assure the government that there would not be a collapse in the west, and he determined that a change of government was necessary, that parliamentary reforms should be instituted, and that the time had come to sue for an immediate armistice.*

On October 2 Baron von dem Bussche, representing the Supreme Command, appeared before the Reichstag party leaders. He indicated to them that the collapse of the Bulgarian front had radically changed the military situation for the worse. "The Supreme Army Command," he told the leaders, "has had to come to the extremely painful determination that according to all human calculation, there exists no longer any prospect of compelling the enemy to plead for peace." The appearance of large numbers of enemy tanks coupled with the huge superiority of Allied reserves, declared the baron, have created a situation in which "we can carry on the struggle for an appreciable time yet and can cause severe losses to the enemy; we can, however, no longer win." These events, continued Bussche, "have caused the General Field Marshal and General Ludendorff to arrive at the determination to propose to His Majesty the emperor that an attempt be made to put an end to the struggle in order to save the German people and their allies from making further sacrifices." The situation was so critical in nature that "no time must be lost. Every twenty-four hours can impair the situation." [62] The request for an armistice was to be coupled with the democratization of the internal régime, in order thereby to secure better peace terms. Thus a "revolution from above" was imposed upon the Reich by the Supreme Command.

Pressure for internal reforms had mounted since the beginning of the war. Haase had demanded in the Reichstag on March 10, 1915, that "the amount of political rights should be equal to the amount of duties." Baron von Richthofen, of the National Liberals, had advocated parliamentary reform at the beginning of 1916, although the leadership of his party was still opposed to it. Moderate intellectuals of the group around Meinecke, Troeltsch, Max Weber, Hans Delbrück, not to mention Friedrich Naumann, began to press for reforms, particularly the suffrage reform in Prussia. They had arrived at the conviction that it was not possible to wage war with the full utilization of universal conscription unless the masses were allowed to share in the political affairs of the state.

---

* The only important document between Aug. 8 and Sept. 28 is the report on the Spa Crown Council of Aug. 13–14. According to this report Chancellor Hertling appeared and inquired as to the situation. The minutes then continue as follows: "The Field Marshal hopes that he will be able to remain on the defensive on French soil and thus be able to secure a beautiful peace." Ludendorff, however, changed the word "hopes" (*hofft*) to "declares that" (*führt aus*). (Cf. Reichstag Inquiry, i, 412.)

The pressure of the military reverses, however, was the determining factor in influencing the swing toward reforms among rightist circles. So long as the Prussian military aristocracy was able to keep Germany powerful, the alliance between soldier and civilian, on which the Bismarckian Reich rested, was able to be maintained. As soon, however, as the soldier state was no longer able to provide the military protection expected from it, the civilian bourgeoisie broke away and began to clamor for parliamentary reform. It reverted to the bourgeois position of the liberals of 1866. Stresemann, who succeeded Bassermann as the leader of the National Liberals, declared in the Reichstag, on March 29, 1917, that "a new era demands its new rights" and "that the time has come to begin a reorganization of affairs in Germany and the federal states." The experiences of the war have shown, he said, that a parliamentary system was far more stable than previously imagined. General Groener, of the Supreme Command, also arrived at the recognition that reforms were needed, and he held a long conversation with the industrialist Hugo Stinnes to induce him to influence Ludendorff to support reforms.

On September 28 the Supreme Command requested that a government resting on a broader base be formed. Prince Max of Baden, one of the more liberal members of the South German aristocracy, was named chancellor, and took over his office with an open avowal that his government was to be based on the support of the majority of the Reichstag. Representatives of the Majority Socialists, Progressives, and Centrists were taken into his cabinet. Ebert fought vehemently against those of his Socialist colleagues who had no desire to serve as "liquidators for the Hohenzollerns" to induce them to enter the government for the sake of the "fatherland." And Prince Max declared to the Reichstag on October 5, 1918, "I am convinced . . . that when peace comes a government cannot again be formed which does not find its support in the Reichstag and does not include leading men from it." [63]

The new government proceeded immediately to oust General Ludendorff from his post, and General Groener was named to succeed him. Hindenburg remained untouchable. A series of measures amending the imperial constitution was passed by the Reichstag between October 2 and 26, and signed by the emperor on October 28. Reichstag approval was now required for a declaration of war and for the making of peace, and the chancellor was made responsible to the Reichstag. Democratization of the federal states was to follow after the pattern of the reform of the Reich. Germany was thus converted into a constitutional monarchy. Friedrich Naumann delivered a "funeral oration" on the Bismarckian Reich, declaring it to be no longer feasible. The *Vorwärts* wrote editorially: "Without flourish of trumpets, without honors and warm tributes, like a culprit sentenced to death on a knacker's cart, and under the contemptible shouts of the masses, someone was carried yesterday to the grave in the Reichstag: the bankrupt Junker régime, the smashed system of Prussian-German feudalism." [64] But the new government was not to carry on for long. Its main purpose was to bring peace. And the Supreme Command kept pressing that no time be lost and that hostilities must cease. Prince Max and his ministers were not of the opinion that the best interests of Germany would be served by an immediate request for an armistice. They believed that in the event Germany was not offered acceptable peace terms there was still a possibility of continuing the war. It was the Supreme Command rather than the civil leaders that had given up hope of further German resistance and that demanded that the government ask for an armistice. The chancellor used all the means at his command to avoid making this move. The Supreme Command, however, insisted that all would be lost if an armistice were not requested at once. Finally Prince Max declared he would not take this step unless he received a written request to this effect from Hindenburg and Ludendorff. On October 3 came a letter signed by Hindenburg:

The Supreme Command continues to hold to its demand expressed on Sept. 29 of this year that a request for an armistice should be sent to our enemies immediately. As a result of the collapse on the Macedonian front, the consequent weakening of the reserves on the western front, and the impossibility of making good the very severe losses which we have suffered in the last few days, there is, as far as it is humanly possible to judge, no future chance of forcing a peace on the enemy. . . . The situation becomes daily more critical, and the Supreme Command may be forced to take very grave decisions. The circumstances call for a cessation of hostilities in order to spare the German nation and its allies needless sacrifices. Each day that is lost costs the lives of thousands of brave soldiers.[65]

This was followed immediately by Prince Max of Baden's peace note to President Wilson on the night of October 3–4. Negotiations continued for another few weeks until on November 11, after the emperor had been forced to abdicate, the German armistice delegation, headed by Erzberger, was forced to sign the armistice terms dictated by Marshal Foch at Compiègne. Germany was not only to evacuate all territories occupied on the western front but also to renounce the treaties of Brest Litovsk and Bucharest and to withdraw all German troops in the east to the borders of the German Reich. Thus the Bolshevists in Russia were relieved of their oppressive treaty by the military victory of the Allies and were left free to reconquer the Ukraine and the Caucasus and bring these territories once again under Russian rule.

The German request for an armistice came as a stunning shock to German public opinion. German armies apparently stood victorious on enemy territory on all fronts, and not one foot of German territory had been occupied by the enemy. Most people believed to the end that Germany's strength was unshaken. True, physical exhaustion was widespread among the lower classes, and the collapse of Bulgaria and Austria-Hungary created in Bavaria a jittery feeling of expected enemy invasion from the south. But so accustomed had the German people become to the optimistic reports of the Supreme Command and so conditioned had they become to the certainty of German victory that it was hard for them to reconcile their desire for peace with the recognition of the brutal realities of German defeat. Among some, and particularly among the more liberal elements, the democratization of German political institutions called forth the hope of a new people's war with a *levée en masse* to fight against a dictated peace by the Allies. The *Vorwärts,* in its issue of September 28, called for continued national defense under the new parliamentary government. The most impressive plea came from Walther Rathenau, the subsequent foreign minister of "fulfillment" who was later to be shot down by a nationalist assassin. On October 7 Rathenau published an article in the *Vossische Zeitung* entitled "A Dark Day." He wrote:

> The premature request for an armistice was a mistake. The enemies should have been made to see that the new spirit of the state and the nation also strengthens the spirit and the will power of the fighters. . . . The country is not broken, its means are unexhausted, and her people are unweary. . . . A beginning must be made with national defense, the rousing of the people; a Ministry of Defense must be created. . . . This Ministry . . . appeals to the nation in the language of truth, pure and simple. . . . We do not want war, but peace. However, not a peace of submission.[66]

Rathenau was supported publicly by the poet Richard Dehmel. But otherwise his appeal fell on deaf ears. "Enough have died," wrote Käthe Kollwitz; "no one should fall again."

Rightist circles, immediately after the conclusion of the war, developed the legend of the "stab in the back" (*Dolchstoss*). According to this theory German arms had remained invincible and Germany would never have been conquered by its external enemies. The collapse of Germany, this theory held, was due to the treacherous and deceitful action on the home front by the radical, pacifist, and revolutionary movements which administered the "stab in the back" to the brave army, which was not expecting attack from that quarter. The origin of this "stab in the back" theory is attributed to the British General Maurice, head of the British Armistice Commission, but he has denied this.[67] Whatever its origins, it fitted neatly into the introspective, romanticist, soul-searching character of a good deal of the conservative German tradition, which sought explanations for German weakness in the *Zerrissenheit* of the German national body. At the same time this theory provided an explanation for German defeat that did not have to admit of the inferiority of German arms and of German courage. Defeat by craftiness, cunning, and treachery, foɪ some reason or other, appears to be more honorable to this type of mentality than defeat by arms.

The Reichstag Inquiry Commission, after the war, went into the *Dolchstoss* legend very thoroughly. Its *rapporteur,* Dr. Ludwig Herz, presented a most detailed analysis of the origin and validity of the theory, and found no basis for it whatsoever. "The whole problem of the history of the war is beclouded," declared the conservative historian Delbrück, "if our final defeat is attributed to treachery in the German nation, in the navy and the army. . . . The attempt to explain our defeat by the stab in the back is not only a distortion of the truth . . . but stupid propaganda." [68]

The German nationalist leader Kardorff declared in Berlin in 1919:

> The war was lost as a result of serious and great military blunders, especially at the beginning of the war. . . . They did not tell us the truth. . . . The slogan of the stab in the back of the front by the home front is not true. . . . Furthermore we lost the war because we falsely evaluated our allies. . . . We overestimated our own strength and underestimated that of our enemies. . . . We were blind to the dangers that threatened us.[69]

The truth and reality of Germany military defeat was a bitter pill to swallow for a people that had been educated to look upon the soldier as the highest ideal in society. The rancor of defeat and the image of the "stab in the back" were therefore to play a profound role in the politics and in the mentality of the post-war generation.

The position of the emperor had become extremely problematic in the midst of all these developments. His importance was emphasized more outside Germany than within the country. On October 23 President Wilson called upon Germany to rid itself of its "monarchial autocrats" or face the alternative of complete surrender. The feeling that Germany would secure better peace terms if the emperor was no longer at the helm raised the problem of William's abdication. The overthrow of the monarchy in Bulgaria and Austria and the proclamation of republics in Poland and Czechoslovakia further added to republican sentiment in Germany. There was talk of the new "republican encirclement" of Germany. Pressure by the radical left forced the Majority Socialists to come to grips with the issue. On October 31 the *Vorwärts* published an editorial "What Will the Kaiser Do?" in which it merely raised the question as to what William was going to do and "when he will do it." [70] On November 3 the *Vorwärts* returned again to the problem, writing, "It is more popular at the present time to profess loyalty to the monarchical principle than allegiance to the monarch as a person." Hostility toward the person of William was at this time stronger among the Conservatives than among the Socialists. Prince Max, writing to his cousin the Grand Duke of Baden on October 15, 1918, said: "The Conservatives talk openly of the emperor's abdication. Thank God that I have in the Social Democrats men on my side in whose loyalty I can rely completely. With their help, I hope I shall be able to save the emperor." [71] Most of the Majority Socialist leaders were desirous of retaining the constitutional monarchy and only wanted to get rid of the two most unpopular members of the Hohenzollern dynasty, William and his eldest son Crown Prince William. On October 30 Scheidemann delivered a letter to the chancellor in which he demanded that the kaiser be asked to abdicate. The chancellor begged him to withdraw the letter, which he did, but the continued pressure of the radical elements among the Spartacists and the Independents forced the Socialists to press their demand.

On November 1, Dr. Drews, the Prussian minister of the interior, arrived at Spa and was the first one to broach the question of abdication to William. He was met by an indignant refusal by the emperor, supported by Hindenburg and Groener. At that time General Groener would have liked to see William seek his death in the front lines of his army. "He should go to the front not to review troops or to confer decorations but to look for death. He should go to some trench which was under the full blast of war. If he were killed it would be the finest death possible." [72]

On November 7 the Socialist members of the government presented an ultimatum to the chancellor demanding that the emperor abdicate or else they would withdraw from the government. Prince Max by this time had also become fully convinced that the kaiser's abdication was necessary to prevent civil war and to preserve the monarchy. Groener and Hindenburg had likewise come to realize that the emperor no longer had the support of the army. On November 9 the fateful conference took place at Spa. Groener told the emperor, "The army will march home in peace and order under its leaders and commanding general, but not under the command of Your Majesty, for it no longer stands behind Your Majesty." Hindenburg sadly confirmed the accuracy of Groener's analysis. The emperor demurred. He would resign as German emperor but not as King of Prussia. The telephone lines from Berlin were feverishly demanding the official announcement of abdication, indicating that delay of minutes was fraught with grave consequences. When confronted with William's dilatory indecision, Prince Max took the matter into his own hands and confronted William with a *fait accompli*. "I found myself confronted," wrote Prince Max later, "by the alternative either to wait and do nothing, or to act upon my own responsibility." Without authority from the emperor, the chancellor, at noon on November 9, issued the following statement through the Wolff Press Agency:

The emperor and the king has decided to renounce the throne. The imperial chancellor will remain in office until the questions connected with the abdication of the emperor, the renunciation of the throne of Germany and of Prussia by the Crown Prince and the setting up of a regency have been settled.[73]

Crushed by the realization that he had been abandoned by his ministers, by his once glorious army and by the navy, in which he had taken such pride, the former war lord left secretly for Doorn, Holland, to spend the rest of his days as a lonely exile. In the seat of the former mighty ruler now sat the former saddle maker Fritz Ebert, who succeeded Prince Max as chancellor. "I commend the German Reich to your loving care," said Prince Max to Ebert as he turned over to him the reins of government. "For that Reich," replied Ebert, "I have lost two sons." Ebert thereupon proceeded to form a new government of Majority Socialists and Independent Socialists. From the balcony of the Reichstag building Philipp Scheidemann, without waiting for the convocation of a National Assembly, proclaimed the formation of the German Republic. Thus the fateful twin relationship of military defeat and the establishment of the Weimar Republic came into being on November 9, 1918.

The news of the request for an armistice hit the soldiers at the front like a bombshell. An army chaplain has left us a moving description of the effect of the news.

It was [wrote Chaplain Raymund Dreeling] as if a terrific natural catastrophe was approaching. The internal tension reached such a height that it required only a relieving irritant to cause its discharge. This external impulse soon came. When the Supreme Command and the government . . . decided to . . . make an offer of peace and ask for armistice terms, the tension which had been maintained for so long was finally relaxed with full force; all breathed freely once more . . . as if they had awakened from a nightmare. . . . Let us neither see nor hear anything more of the war; anything is better than this murder and destruction. . . .

What the average fighting man wanted and imperatively demanded was that an end and a final end should be put to the war and then peace and nothing but peace. . . . No power in the world could have induced the average soldier at the front to take part in fighting that was to last still longer. . . .[74]

Slowly the men began trudging back home from the scenes of their military triumphs and spectacular successes, dazed by defeat and stunned by the new situation.

Along the road, step upon step, in their faded, dirty uniforms tramp the grey columns. The unshaved faces beneath the helmets are haggard, wasted with hunger and long peril, pinched and dwindled to the lines drawn by terror and courage and death. They trudge along in silence; silently, as they have now marched over so many a road, . . . without many words, so too now they trudge along this road back home into peace. Without many words.

Old men with beards and slim lads scarce twenty years of age, comrades without difference. Beside them their lieutenants, little more than children, yet the leaders of many a night raid. And behind them, the army of slain. Thus they tramp onward, step by step, sick, half-starving, without ammunition, in the companies, with eyes that still fail to comprehend it: escaped out of that underworld, on the road back into life.[75]

For many the experiences of the war and the effects of the war served as a sober warning that what they had formerly accepted as the goals and aims of society were no longer valid. They felt that they had been duped by the rulers of Wilhelmian Germany.

They told us [says Ludwig in Remarque's *The Road Back*] it was for the Father-land, and meant the schemes of annexations of a greedy industry. They told us it was for Honor, and meant the quarrels and the will to power of a handful of ambitious diplomats and princes. . . . They stuffed out the word Patriotism with all the twaddle of their fine phrases, with their desire for glory, their will to power, their false romanticism, their stupidity, their greed of business, and then paraded it before us as a shining ideal! And we thought they were sounding a bugle summoning us to a new, a more strenuous, a larger life.[76]

Among those who reacted in this way came the resolve never again to allow such destruction to take place. Remarque, Hermann Hesse, René Schickele, Arnold Zweig, and other writers represented this pacifist reac-tion to the experience of the war, a reaction which was shared by a large section of the younger post-war generation. Scholars like Ernst Troeltsch, Friedrich Meinecke, and Max Weber began to question the validity of the political premises on which they had based their own previous adherence to and support of the monarchic and militarist Germany. Troeltsch found that Germany had never embraced the idea of natural law, and Meinecke shifted his interests from the fusion of *Geist* and *Macht* to the inherent dangers and evil potentialities of the idea of *Staatsraison*.

Hermann Hesse's message for Germany in December, 1918, was not to go back to the idyllic ways of the period of "poets and thinkers," for "it cannot become a child again." But Germany can derive energy and strength, he said, from reflecting upon itself, its origins, its period of grand development and its decline. It must "go into itself," after the manner of the pious. "And within itself, in its innermost self, it will find undisturbed its own essential nature. This nature will not seek to escape its destiny, but accept it with affirmation in order to begin anew out of the redis-covery the best and innermost part of its being." [77]

The thing for us to do, wrote Hesse, "is to go down like men or to continue to live on like men. Not, however, to whimper like children. . . . Our goal is not to become once again great and rich and powerful as rapidly as possible and have once again ships and armies. . . . Our goal is not a childish illusion. Have we not seen what comes of ships and armies, of power and wrath? Is all that forgotten?" [78]

This mood of chastened and reverent self-criticism was not, however, the only reaction among thinking Germans, even though for many years it was the one most familiar to foreigners. There was also a large section of German public opinion which refused to give up the heroic tradition of German arms. The war and its experiences only intensified the glorification of the warrior hero. Ernst Jünger is a good illustration of this type of mentality, the exact counterpart to Hermann Hesse.

War [wrote Jünger], father of all things, is also our father. It has hammered us, chiseled us and hardened us into what we are. And always, as long as the swirling wheel of life revolves within us, this war will be the axis around which it will swirl. It has reared us for battle and we shall remain fighters as long as we live. . . . Under the skin of all cultural and technical progress we remain naked and raw like the men of the forest and of the steppe. . . . That is the new man, the pioneer of the storm, the choice product of central Europe. . . . This war is not the end but the new ascendancy of force. . . . New forms will be filled with blood, and might will be seized with the hard fist.[79]

Behind all the social, economic, and political tribulations of the next fourteen years of German history it was the basic conflict between these two reactions to the experiences of the war and to the lesson of German defeat that determined the fundamental and basic lines of German development. The forces that molded the Weimar Republic were those which on the whole took the message of Hesse and Remarque to heart. For a while it seemed as if they were ascendant.

CHAPTER XIV

The Revolution of 1918-1919

Denn wer leugnet es wohl,
dass hoch sich das Herz ihm erhoben,
Ihm die freiere Brust mit
reineren Pulsen geschlagen,
Als sich der erste Glanz der neuen Sonne heranhob,
Als man hörte von Rechte der Menschen, dass allen gemein sei,
Von der begeisternden Freiheit und von der löblichen Gleichheit.

GOETHE, *Hermann und Dorothea*

1. THE NOVEMBER REVOLUTION

The so-called November revolution in Germany came like an unwanted child. Those who wanted it had very little or nothing to do with its success, and those who became the repositories of revolutionary power were forced into such a position almost entirely against their will and against their desires. Two days before the abdication of the kaiser, Max Weber delivered a speech in Munich in which he declared that "the German revolutionists should not be deluded in believing that they can overturn the old system in Germany overnight." There were, as we shall see, very few revolutionists in Germany who thought they could or who actually desired to overthrow the old system overnight. The French revolution of 1789, the Russian revolution of 1917, and to some extent the German revolution of 1848 had been preceded by periods of intellectual and revolutionary ferment which sowed seeds of discontent, developed a revolutionary leadership, and crystallized a certain amount of political thinking. No such tradition antedated the German revolution of 1918. While the official program of the Social Democratic party rendered homage to a set of "revolutionary principles," the whole notion of "revolution" was but a formal phrase for the overwhelming majority of Socialist leaders and followers. The events of November surprised and overwhelmed the Social Democrats as much as it did all the other elements of German society.[1]

The German revolution was, as most political writers of the time pointed out, a "collapse" rather than a revolution. The military front collapsed,

350

the soldiers and sailors were in no position to carry on, and the war weariness of the civilian population reached a point of climax when the German people for the first time realized that a military debacle had occurred at the very time they had been led to believe that they were on the road to victory. "Everything," wrote Scheidemann, "collapsed in woeful impotence after the telegram [of Ludendorff]. The emperor departed from the country, and the government asked the Social Democrats to take over." The old authority broke down and the Social Democratic leaders were the "official liquidators." In the chaotic situation that ensued, the leaders of the Majority Socialists, in order to retain their hold on the masses, "adopted" the revolution, which they did not want, as their own baby. Through tragic irony, Fate forced upon the Social Democrats a succession of measures hardly in keeping with their traditional policies, such as the armed suppression of the Spartacists, the preservation of bourgeois society, and the recreation of an army.

The negative character of the revolution is perhaps best exhibited in the fact that it found no echo among the poets and writers of the time. There was no Rouget de L'Isle to provide it with a German "Marseillaise"; nor was there a Freiligrath or a Young German movement as in 1848. It was "the first and only completely songless revolution in world history." The poet Richard Dehmel, horrified by the development of party strife, sang of German unity in the nationalist *Deutsche Tageszeitung*.[2] Rainer Maria Rilke, never before seriously concerned with political affairs, was too thoroughly disillusioned at the absence of a real change of heart in German society to wax enthusiastic about the revolution.[*] Gerhart Hauptmann first and Thomas Mann later became the "writers laureate" of the Weimar Republic, but neither of them was himself inspired in a creative way by the revolution or in turn attempted by his artistic creation to inspire the German people with zeal for the revolution.

[*] Rilke wrote on Feb. 2, 1923:
For me, as I see things and live through them, perforce in my own way, there is no doubt that it is Germany who is arresting the progress of the world, because she does not know herself. The many-sided and broad nature of my make-up allows me the necessary perspective to see this. Germany in 1918, in the hour of collapse, could have shaken and put to shame the whole world by an act of honesty and repentance, by a visible and determined renunciation of her spurious prosperity—in short by a humility which would have been of the very essence of her character and dignity and which would have forestalled all the humiliations that could be imposed on her from without. It was then—so I hoped for a time—that this long-lost trait of humility, so inherent in the charm of Dürer's drawings, would once again have appeared in the strangely one-sided and docile countenance of Germany. Perhaps there were a few who felt this, who desired and believed in such a conversion—but now we begin to perceive that it never took place, and we are already reaping the harvest. . . . Germany neglected to re-establish her purest and highest standards, which were based on the most ancient traditions. Hers was not a complete conversion and change of heart; she did not acquire that dignity which springs from the deepest humility; she was concerned only with salvation in a superficial, hasty, distrustful, and grasping sense; she wanted to do something and get away with it, rather than to follow her innermost call, which was to endure, to overcome and to be ready for her own miracle. She wanted to persist, and not to alter" (from *Briefe an eine junge Frau*, English translation by E. M. Butler *Rainer Maria Rilke* [Cambridge, 1941], pp. 43ff.).

Much of the polemics that went on in German political circles during the first years of the Weimar Republic revolved around the question whether the revolution was "made" or "just happened." Left-wing Independent Socialists, like Emil Barth, Richard Müller, and Georg Ledebour, arrogated to themselves the credit for having engineered the revolutionary overturn; [3] Majority Socialists and bourgeois writers, on the other hand, insisted that revolutions are "never made" but just occur as a result of revolutionary situations. The very fact of a polemic of this nature underscores the absence of a genuinely revolutionary sentiment in the country. And the overwhelming majority of political writers and leaders, including those who were the bearers of the new "revolutionary" power, passionately and vehemently refused to admit paternity of the new republic. The revolution of 1918 in Germany never produced any "sons" or "daughters" of the German revolution. Except for the first few months, and in limited circles at that, it was no feather in one's political cap to have had anything to do with its initiation.*

The chronological proximity of the German revolution of 1918 to the Russian revolution of 1917 gave occasion to political writers and historians to indulge in comparison of the two. Most of the criticism of the German revolution that is found in this literature stems from the fact that it did not follow the pattern of the Leninist revolution in Russia. The vogue of Marxist interpretation during the 1920's and 1930's, particularly when it came to pointing out the negative aspects of capitalist society, further extended this line of historical interpretation. Actually, it is more accurate to compare the situation of Germany in 1918 to that of France in 1871 rather than to that of Russia in 1917. In both the France of 1871 and the Germany of 1918 there were a military debacle, a complete political and moral bankruptcy of the dynasty, absence of any widespread enthusiasm for the republic, an overwhelming conservative majority pitted against a small radical opposition, and above all the crystallization of a set of republican institutions, not out of positive republican activity, but rather out of the negative situation created by division in monarchist circles. What drove Thiers to reconcile himself to the Third Republic in France in 1871 was the same consideration which brought both bourgeoisie and Socialists to the republic in Germany in 1918. The republic was that form of government which divided the factions least. There was, however, a great difference between France and Germany. The longer endurance of the Third Republic and the greater vitality of the republican spirit in

* Some exceptions to this state of mind were found among small democratic circles of intellectuals in South and Southwest Germany, especially those centered around the *Frankfurter Zeitung*. These persons really envisioned at first the dawn of a new day in Germany with the final victory of Western democratic ideas. An "Association of 1918" was founded in Dec., 1918, in Frankfurt am Main. Among Jews in Germany, too, who were freed by the republic from all the social and political disabilities under which they lived in monarchist Germany, there was also, particularly in the early years, a note of genuine republican exuberance and enthusiasm.

France were due to the fact that republican supporters in France had a powerful and vital revolutionary tradition on which to lean, something entirely lacking for the republican leaders of Germany. The great tragedy for Germany was not that it did not have a Lenin or Trotsky to provide it with revolutionary leadership, but that it had no Gambetta, no Clemenceau, no Zola, no Jaurès, to infuse it with republican élan and with passionate zeal for democratic institutions.

There were three main focal points of revolutionary action in November, 1918: Kiel in the north, Munich in the south, and the capital, Berlin. In all three the underlying factor behind the unrest was a desire for peace, driven to a heightened pitch of urgency by the sudden realization, after the request for an armistice had become known, that further fighting was useless and wasteful, and stimulated by the realization that a change in government would secure better peace terms for Germany from the Entente. President Wilson's demand that the kaiser abdicate was a powerful factor in turning the country against William, particularly after the war lord had led his country to nothing but chaos and defeat. The mood was not necessarily against the institution of monarchy. It was directed at first exclusively against the persons of the kaiser and the crown prince, both of whom had been active at the front. Had the kaiser not delayed making up his mind to abdicate in the critical first week of November, it may well be that the monarchy would have remained. For several weeks before November 9 a process of democratization had been going on in the federal states and in the central government. The *Frankfurter Zeitung* ran two columns regularly every day during the first week in November—one headed "The New Germany," which listed the advances in democratic government adopted in the various local states, and the other under the caption "The Kaiser Question," which detailed the latest news on the emperor's abdication.* It was this interaction between the desire for peace and the notion that the position of the emperor was impeding the peace negotiations that was either directly or indirectly beneath the agitation which led to the proclamation of the republic on November 9. "The 9th of November," wrote Scheidemann, "was the logical conclusion of a lost war, of unmatched privation and of loathing of the war mongers. . . . It was the protest against the continuation of an utterly hopeless slaughter. . . . It was the day on which it was just impossible to carry on any longer." [4]

A certain amount of revolutionary agitation had no doubt been carried on, especially during the last two years of the war. The chief center of this agitation was the left wing of the Independent Socialist party, led by Georg Ledebour, Emil Barth, Ernst Däumig, and the subsequently inde-

---

* The role of the *Frankfurter Zeitung* in bringing about the abdication of the kaiser still requires careful study. Both Socialist and monarchist circles at the time credited this paper with having brought about the crisis in the "Kaiser Question."

pendent Spartacist group of Karl Liebknecht, Rosa Luxemburg, and Leo Jogiches. Neither the Majority Socialists nor the Haase group in the U.S.D.P. participated in "preparations for the revolution." Ledebour, in a speech before the Workers' and Soldiers' Council on December 17, 1918, and in his testimony in his trial of May and June, 1919, described in detail these "preparations." Already in 1916, according to Ledebour, he and his followers were planning to "accelerate the revolution," convinced that only a complete break with the past would be able to solve Germany's troubles. A sort of revolutionary committee was organized at that time. Both at the Stockholm and the Zimmerwald conferences of anti-war Socialists, Ledebour pressed for mass general strikes to bring the war to a revolutionary end. Even the Bolsheviks, according to Ledebour, opposed him at first, and he adds, "This proves that we were not imitators of the Bolsheviks in our revolutionary aspirations." Propaganda by illegal literature was carried on in the army and especially among the sailors. The munitions strike of January, 1918, was intended to be one of the acts that would "stir up the masses," but the Majority Socialists "took over" the strike and steered it away from its revolutionary goal. After that strike the conviction grew in these left-wing circles that if trouble started again "we should not be content with a strike but should take to arms." On October 5 the U.S.D.P. issued a proclamation calling for a "socialist republic" as part of a world-wide change. A committee of "revolutionary shop stewards" was formed, headed by Barth, Müller, Däumig, Eckert, Wegmann, and Neuendorf, which also began to collect arms.* On November 2, 1918, this revolutionary committee held a meeting, attended also by Karl Liebknecht. They had as yet no knowledge of the unrest developing among the sailors in Kiel. Ledebour and his followers urged that a mass strike and demonstration be called for November 4. He claimed that they could rely on 75,000 workers to follow their call. Haase and Dittmann opposed "striking the first blow," and by a vote of 22 to 19 action was postponed to November 6. The plan for revolt, says Ledebour, was revealed to the government by spies, and they could not go through with their action as originally planned. Däumig and other leaders were arrested on November 8, and the "revolutionary shop stewards" decided to strike on the 9th. "The difference between the 5th and 9th of November," explained Ledebour, is that "in the meantime the Social Democrats, the ministers, the secretaries of state and the brand-new imperial chancellor, Ebert, could prepare for the situation. . . . The revolution had finally to be victorious without them." [5]

The Russian revolution of 1917 was also a factor in stimulating these revolutionary preparations. The example of the Bolsheviks and their suc-

---

* This committee stood in close contact with the executive committee of the Independent Socialists, and at the end of October they also invited officially the leaders of the Spartakus Bund to participate in their deliberations.

cess in Russia provided a model for the German radicals. Moreover, the institution of Councils of Workers and Soldiers in all the major cities of Germany in the early days of the revolution followed a pattern set by the Russian soviets. Just as real, although more difficult to assess tangibly, was the financial assistance given to these revolutionary circles by the Bolshevik government and the influence of Russian agents and party workers in these circles.

The revolutionary circles as described by Ledebour, Barth, and Richard Müller were no doubt active and their revolutionary preparations had some influence. Nevertheless it seems quite evident that the actual revolutionary events transpired outside the area of influence of these circles, and when the overturn actually occurred it surprised the Independent Socialists and Spartacists as much as it did the other parties. It was not in Berlin that the revolution was started, but in Kiel first and in Munich after that. And in both places the "revolutionary preparations" of the Berlin committee played no role whatsoever. What existed in Germany was a revolutionary situation, in the sense that there was a widespread mood of despair brought on by the military collapse, a considerable amount of apprehension regarding Bavarian separatism after Austria-Hungary laid down its arms, and hence a high degree of *Revolutionsfurcht*.[6] Because of this "fear of revolution" came the belated democratic reforms by the imperial government of Prince Max. These were insufficient and too late. The situation in the country was such that all that was needed was a revolutionary "incident" to set the whole structure toppling over. Such an incident was provided by the sailors' revolt in Kiel.

The revolt of the sailors at Wilhelmshaven and Kiel began on October 30, when a report circulated that the German fleet had been assembled to make a dash at the British fleet in the North Sea as a last heroic stand.[7] The morale of the sailors was already quite low by this time. The monotony of their routine aboard ship, the strong feeling against the officers engendered by the open and inordinate disparity in food rations between officers and crew, and the harsh discipline still maintained made them amenable to the general anti-war propaganda being carried on by the Independent Socialists.* Now that armistice negotiations were under way, this order for a naval offensive seemed a useless gesture intended only "to satisfy the pride of a fanatic" and a serious threat to the successful conclusion of the negotiations with President Wilson. Moreover, the men be-

---

* That there was a more intimate connection between the U.S.D.P. and the movement among the sailors is also the conclusion arrived at by the Reichstag Inquiry Commission. It is also noteworthy that the news of the sailors' revolts received either no attention at all or very little in the bourgeois newspapers until Nov. 7 or 8. The Berlin *Vorwärts* carried a small notice of the Kiel disturbances on Nov. 5 on the inside page but nothing else until Nov. 10. On the other hand the U.S.D.P. *Leipziger Volkszeitung* carried a full story of the Kiel revolt on its first page on Nov. 5, under the full-page headline "Workers' Blood Has Flowed!" On the following day its front-page headline was "The Revolution Is on the March," with further details of the events in the north.

lieved that these orders had been issued without the knowledge of the new government. The authoritarian discipline hitherto maintained in the German military machine could no longer hold. The men passed resolutions declaring that they would fight to the finish if attacked but would not sail beyond Heligoland to take the offensive. The officers countered with the arrest of some of the sailors, and a mass demonstration of the men on November 3 was fired on, resulting in eight dead and twenty-nine wounded. The news of this incident engendered a wave of excitement throughout the north coastal area and among radical circles elsewhere. The Kiel workers seized the opportunity on November 4 to create a Workers' and Soldiers' Council and to defy the existing authorities. The situation became so serious that the Berlin government dispatched the democratic leader Haussmann and then the Majority Socialist Gustav Noske to Kiel to keep the movement under control. Hugo Haase, the leader of the U.S.D.P., also arrived on the scene.

The sailors' revolt was not conceived by the men as the beginning of a revolution. The demands formulated by the Workers' and Soldiers' Council were of a limited character. They demanded the release of all political prisoners, freedom of press and speech, abolition of censorship, better conditions for the men, and a promise that no orders were to be issued to the fleet to make a suicide offensive.* The council in turn guaranteed the respect of private property. Noske recounts that when he arrived in Kiel a soldier jumped on the running board of his car and shouted, "Long live freedom," but the crowd laughed at him without any feeling that a revolution had begun.[8] Noske also found no evidence of a directed revolt or of planned leadership. It was the impulsive act of a tense, embittered, and peace-yearning population. Noske was able to come to terms with the Workers' and Soldiers' Council and he was named governor of the province by its members. The very fact that Noske, whose political record as a right-wing Majority Socialist was well known, was able to come to terms with the sailors and workers and be accepted by them as governor of Kiel is conclusive proof that the revolt in Kiel did not come about as a result of a well planned revolutionary program of the left-wing Independents or Spartacists.

The situation in the country, however, was so tense that the spark ignited in Kiel soon spread from one city to another. The movement spread to Lübeck, then to Hamburg, to Bremen, Hanover, Magdeburg, Braunschweig, Oldenburg, Schwerin, Rostock, Cologne, Dresden, and Leipzig. The Majority Socialist *Schleswig-Holsteinsche Volkszeitung* wrote

---

* The quite naïve and purely spontaneous character of the sailors' revolt is illustrated by some of the demands they set up. Thus, almost all of the 13 demands of the council at Wilhelmshaven had to do with questions of discipline and relations between officers and men. Amusing is point No. 9, which demands that the salutation *Herr Kapitän* should be obligatory for the men only at the beginning of the conversation. From then on the men could address their officer with the usual salutation *Sie*. (Cf. *Die Ursachen . . .*, x, 293.)

on November 5: "The revolution is on the march! What happened in Kiel will spread throughout Germany." But it added, "What the workers and soldiers want is not chaos, but a new order; not anarchy, but the social republic." Everywhere the same pattern was present: the formation of a Soldiers' and Workers' Council that took over the local authority. In some cases the council was controlled by Majority Socialists, in other cases by Independents and in a few instances by Spartacists still working within the Independent Socialist party. In numerous instances there was a genuine attempt to make this the occasion for the re-establishment of the unity of the Socialist movement. In Lübeck the council issued a proclamation to the people on November 5, in which it said: "Our goal is an immediate armistice and peace. We ask the people to maintain the utmost calm. Nothing will be undertaken by us to change industrial conditions so that we can keep the economic life going. Everything will be carried on in the old way." [9] In Hamburg the Independent leader Dittman addressed a large meeting on November 5 in which he called for the abdication of the emperor. The streets were full of sailors, and officers were forced to remove their insignia as a symbol of equality. The Majority Socialist paper *Hamburger Echo* was taken over by the Spartacists, and its name was changed to *Die Rote Fahne;* it was edited by Paul Fröhlich. It denounced the "formal democracy" of the Berlin government and called for a socialist republic, world revolution, and unity with the Soviet government in Russia.

The sailors' revolts may thus be technically regarded as instigating revolution. But they had no such aim in the beginning. It was only in the course of developments that this movement began to take on a more definitely revolutionary character and became integrated with the revolutionary movements in Munich and Berlin, which first started quite independently of the events in Kiel.

Events of more clearly defined political objectives, and also of more momentous consequences, took place in Bavaria. The capitulation of Austria-Hungary to the Entente had left Bavaria exposed to possible invasion by the enemy. This was a prospect that seemed utterly frightening to a population that had until most recently known only of German triumphs far away on enemy soil. The movement for peace gathered momentum there and brought with it a marked resurgence of Bavarian separatist feeling.* In such a situation, the Independent Socialist party, the party officially associated with opposition to the war, was looked to for leadership and action. A minority party a few days before, it became the spearhead of the revolution in Munich, and its quixotic leader, Kurt

---

* "We must make an end to the fraud," was the way in which popular sentiment in Bavaria was expressed, when referring to the war. The peasants, in particular, irked as they were already by the stringent economic measures of the central government in Berlin, yearned for peace.

Eisner, was catapulted into prominence as the head of the new Bavarian Republic.

On November 4 a large meeting of workers, called by the Bavarian Majority Socialists and the trade-unions, passed a resolution calling for the unity of the Socialist parties, and established a joint commission with equal membership from both parties "to unite the entire strength of the proletariat in the struggle against the common enemy, capitalism and reaction." Both Eisner and the leader of the Majority Socialists, Erhard Auer, spoke at this meeting. Auer warned against Bavarian separatism and listed four questions most crucial for Germany at the time: (1) the abdication of the emperor, (2) the oath of loyalty by the army to the constitution, (3) the rejection of the call of the extreme nationalists for a last-ditch stand, and (4) the elimination of the reactionary elements from the administration, especially in Prussia.

A mass public demonstration was called for Thursday, November 7, at 3:00 P.M., on the Theresienwiese in Munich, of all workers except those engaged in transport and communications. The demonstration was carried out by thousands of Munich workers in orderly and disciplined fashion. Placards called for "Bread and Peace," "Peace and the Eight-Hour Day," international understanding, and the removal of the dynasty. The representatives of the Majority Socialists emphasized in their speeches to the crowd that they were not calling for strikes or revolution; they wanted to secure only the development of a "people's state." Most of the Munich inhabitants, including the demonstrators, went home unaware of any impending revolutionary events. But in the early morning hours of the 8th Kurt Eisner and the Independents seized the initiative. They organized a "Constituent Soldiers', Workers', and Peasants' Council" which in turn proclaimed the establishment of a Bavarian Democratic and Social Republic headed by Kurt Eisner. The inhabitants of Munich, deprived of their newspapers on the 7th because of the mass demonstration, picked up their morning newspapers of the 8th confronted with the proclamation by the Council of Workers, Soldiers, and Peasants, Kurt Eisner, Chairman. Eisner was keen enough to sense that in Bavaria he needed the support of the peasantry, and he included peasant leaders in the council and issued a special proclamation "To the Farming Population of Bavaria" as one of his first acts. To the Council of Soldiers and Workers Eisner declared: "It was with a strategy of surprise that we unhinged the old Bavaria. Two days ago no one would have considered such a thing possible and today no one can conceive it to be possible that those institutions of yesterday which today seem to us to be of the hoary past, will ever be able to be reconstituted. Bavaria became a free state yesterday and it will remain a free state." [10] A cabinet consisting of Majority and Independent Socialists was formed, and liberal pacifists like Professor Edgar Jaffé, Ludwig Quidde, and Friedrich Wilhelm Foerster were also called into service. Masses of people milled around in the streets, military trucks dashed through the streets, and there were a few instances of pillaging, but by 9:00 P.M. the *Münchner Neueste Nachrichten* reported that there was "peace and order everywhere."

In the proclamation of November 8 the new provisional government of Bavaria promised peace, a constitutional convention, the security of property and person, the maintenance of order, and the retention of the government officials in their positions. "In this time of senseless and wild murder," it announced, "we declare our abhorrence of all shedding of blood." On November 15 the government submitted a more detailed program, which won kind words even from the conservative and monarchist *Münchner Neueste Nachrichten*. It called for a "United States of Germany," including German Austria, the convening of a constituent assembly from Bavaria, the democratization of the country, the equal and free status of all religious denominations, and the transfer of the educational system to the state. In the economic field the government reaffirmed its Socialist beliefs but declared "that it seems impossible for us to transfer industry into the possession of the community at a time when the productive forces of the country are almost exhausted. It is impossible to socialize when there is hardly anything to socialize." [11]

The man who led the Bavarian revolt is one of the most controversial figures of the revolution. Kurt Eisner was born in Berlin in 1867, the son of a Jewish merchant.[12] As a student of Hermann Cohen in Marburg he became deeply imbued with Kantian ethics, and even when he became a member of the Social Democratic party it was the ethical aspect in socialism that meant most to him. From 1898 to 1905 Eisner served as editor of the Berlin *Vorwärts*. He came to Munich in 1910, and worked as a free-lance writer and contributor to the Socialist *Münchner Post*. At first a supporter of the Majority Socialist position on the war, he soon became convinced that it was a mistake, joined the U.S.D.P., and was jailed in January, 1918, for agitating among the workers to strike. He remained in prison until October 14, 1918, when he was released under the pressure of political events, and he resumed his role as leader of the Independent Socialists.

In the eyes of his political opponents Eisner was an unrealistic and fantastic dreamer, more the litterateur than the political leader. "We all," wrote the Berlin *Vorwärts* on December 2, 1918, "wish you [Eisner] all the luck in the world and we recognize your real abilities. No one, however, . . . has any confidence in your political judgment." His opponents among the bourgeois groups were even more violent. They looked upon him as a "half-comic street figure," an east-European Jew who spoke with a Berlin jargon, who was vain, theatrical, a demagogic orator who once in power was ready to use any means at his disposal to stay in power and who, after he had become prime minister, had lost all traces of his

earlier idealism. But perhaps Haase was more correct when he said at
Eisner's funeral, "They cursed you and called you a visionary, those who
imagined themselves to be *Realpolitiker,* when you with your bold spirit
were far ahead of us all." And Gustav Landauer, on the same occasion,
eulogized his friend and colleague: "Kurt Eisner, the Jew, was a prophet
who struggled against the pusillanimity of mankind because he had faith
in mankind. He was a prophet because he was a friend of the poor and the
downtrodden, because he was a poet and a fearless herald of truth, a
Schwärmer, and at the same time a tireless student of reality." [13]

The events in Bavaria were of momentous significance for the progress
of the revolution in the rest of Germany. This was not a local revolt of
soldiers and sailors. As the *Frankfurter Zeitung* wrote in its leading article
in the evening edition of November 8: "The German revolution is developing with frantic speed. What yesterday, from a political standpoint,
was an almost indifferent soldiers' movement in North Germany, has
overnight in Munich become a political revolution." Eisner's action in
Munich pushed the Socialist leaders in Berlin to more urgent and immediate action, and his proclamation of a republic in Bavaria set at rest the
fears in North German republican circles that a "monarchist" Bavaria
would secede from the German Reich if a republic were proclaimed. The
joint action by Majority and Independent Socialists in Bavaria also provided both the impetus and the pattern for unified action by both Socialist
groups in other parts of the country.

In Berlin, in the meantime, two questions had come to the forefront—
the armistice negotiations and the question of the abdication of William II.
Both issues were tied together. Public opinion as well as government
circles had been led to believe that the Entente would agree to an armistice
and indeed to better terms for such an armistice if the ruling powers of
Willhelmian Germany were eliminated from positions of responsibility.
The interrelation between these two questions became the foundation for
the policy of the Majority Socialists who came to occupy the key position as
events progressed. Two of the Majority Socialist leaders, Philipp Scheidemann and Gustav Bauer, had joined the cabinet of Prince Max of Baden
when the process of reforming the constitution began. On November 2
Scheidemann delivered a letter to Prince Max in which he asked for the
abdication of the emperor. The following day the Socialist party organ
in Berlin carried a front-page leading article, "Before Weighty Decisions,"
in which it kept the demand for the kaiser's abdication within the bounds
of reasoned argument and urged upon its followers the need for unity,
for discipline and patience, and above all the all-important need to
prevent civil war. But changes must come, it declared. "The great transformation in the midst of which we find ourselves cannot be halted; it
can only be directed into orderly channels."

On November 4 the executive committee of the Majority Socialists warned the workers of Berlin not to give heed to those agitating for a strike and urged them to remain on their jobs. The Socialist cabinet members Bauer and Scheidemann joined with their bourgeois colleagues on November 5, in signing a proclamation to the populace in which the promise was made that Germany would be transformed into a *Volksstaat* which would outdistance all other states in respect to political freedom and progress. The following day the party executive once more called for unity and discipline and for political changes that would not, however, result in "Russian conditions." Behind the scenes the party leaders, pressed by events but also by the agitation from the radical left, were increasing their pressure upon the government of Prince Max. On November 6 the party executive drew up a list of political demands, and the next day Ebert and Scheidemann presented an ultimatum to Prince Max in which they demanded (1) freedom of assembly, (2) the relaxation of military and police regulations, (3) the abdication of the kaiser and the crown prince by noon of November 8, (4) greater representation of the S.P.D. in the cabinet, and (5) changes in the Prussian cabinet in line with the majority parties in the Reichstag. "Not terror, but freedom!" wrote the *Vorwärts,* "Not dictatorship but democracy! Not callous experimentation on the living body of society, but a planned construction of a new socialist economic order based upon scientific knowledge and practical experience. This is the course which is being steered by our party ship." All the demands of the Socialists were accepted by the imperial government, but the kaiser still hesitated and refused to agree to abdication. The Socialist leaders prolonged their ultimatum to the 9th of November. As they explained in the *Vorwärts* of November 9, the postponement was designed to allow the armistice negotiations to be completed without the interjection of any acts that would delay bringing peace to the country.

The Independent Socialists and Spartacists, as described above, were going on with their preparations. The meetings of the U.S.D.P. were forbidden by the Berlin police "in contact with the Supreme Command and the government" for fear "they might lead to incidents like those in Kiel and Hamburg." [14] Däumig and Barth were arrested, and the revolutionary shop stewards committee made preparations for revolutionary action to protest these arrests.

By the evening of November 8 there was still no news from the kaiser's headquarters. The Socialist ministers and under-secretaries thereupon resigned, leaving Prince Max to carry on. A meeting of the S.P.D. representatives in the Greater Berlin trade-union council was called for the morning of November 9th at 8:00 A.M., and a twelve-man action committee was set up to carry out a general strike in Berlin if the emperor's abdication was not forthcoming. The order was issued by the S.P.D. for a general strike for the morning of the 9th and for a mass demonstration by the workers in the streets. A Workers' and Soldiers' Council was formed, and the regiments of troops stationed in Berlin were won over largely through the indefatigable agitation of Otto Wels. Only after that did the government issue the order not to shoot on the populace.

In the morning of November 9 Ebert, Scheidemann, and Otto Braun and two other colleagues presented themselves to Prince Max. They notified him that the troops had joined the Socialists and that a new and democratic government was to be set up. Von Payer, the vice chancellor, asked Ebert whether he wanted to take over power "on the basis of the constitution" or in behalf of the Workers' and Soldiers' Council. Ebert answered, "On the basis of the constitution." [15] Although no definite word had as yet been received from the kaiser, Prince Max anticipated his action and announced through the Wolff Telegraphic Agency at about twelve o'clock noon the intention of the kaiser and crown prince to abdicate both as German emperor and as King of Prussia.* Prince Max turned over his office to Ebert, and the latter, signing himself as "Reich Chancellor," issued the following proclamation:

Fellow Citizens:

Prince Max of Baden, Reich chancellor up to now, with the consent of all the state secretaries, has turned over to me the task of carrying on the affairs of the Reich chancellor. I have in mind to form a government by consent of the parties and will give a public report on this shortly.

The new government will be a people's government. Its goal will be to bring peace to the German people as soon as possible, and to establish firmly the freedom which it has achieved.

Fellow Citizens: I ask you all for your support in the heavy tasks that await us. You know how seriously the war has threatened the sustenance of the people, the first basic condition for political life.

The political revolution should not interfere with the feeding of the population.

It must remain the first duty of all, both in the city and on the farms, not to hinder but rather to further the production of food supplies and their transportation to the cities.

The want of food supplies means plunder and looting and suffering for all. The poorest will suffer most, the industrial workers will be hit hardest.

Whoever uses force to seize food supplies or other consumer needs or interferes with the means of transportation necessary for their distribution, sins heavily against the entire community.

Fellow Citizens! I implore you most urgently to leave the streets and maintain calm and order!

Ebert's initial proclamation is of the utmost importance in throwing light on his conception of the changes in Germany. In the first place it

* William's actual official abdication did not come until Nov. 28, 1918, from Amerongen in Holland.

indicates that he was interested in maintaining legal continuity from the previous government. Hence his designation of himself as "Reich Chancellor" and the first sentence in which he indicates that there is a continuity from Prince Max to him. It also shows that Ebert conceived the major victory of the revolution to have been achieved by the transfer of power to him and his colleagues and the groundwork thus laid for a democratic national assembly. It was not a question of acquiring freedom or furthering liberties but rather of establishing more firmly the freedom already attained. Finally, and most important of all, it was peace and the food problem that were in the forefront of his mind. He knew that the revolution had come about because the people were suffering privation owing to a war which they no longer felt capable of continuing. The passionate and intensive concern with "peace and order" was not merely an expression of "German discipline"; it was based on the human and political feeling that the new order would only be able to endure if it satisfied the physical and material wants of the people.

Ebert had no idea of establishing a republic at this time, even though he had always been a republican himself. He most likely thought of a constitutional monarchy. In any case he believed that the final decision on the form of government should be made by a democratically elected constitutional assembly. That is one of the reasons why Prince Max was not hesitant in turning over the government to him. "My confidence in Ebert stood firm," he wrote later. "The man was determined to fight the revolution tooth and nail." Ebert, continues Prince Max, "is the only possible chancellor. I said to myself: The revolution is on the eve of success; we can't smash it, but perhaps we can throttle it. . . . If Ebert is introduced to me as the tribune of the people, then we shall have a republic; if it's Liebknecht, Bolshevism; but if the abdicating Kaiser appoints Ebert chancellor, there is a faint hope still for the monarchy." [16]

Events on the streets of Berlin and throughout the Reich were pushing the Majority Socialist leaders beyond the limits they themselves had set. The proclamation of the Bavarian Republic by Eisner, and the agitation of the left Independents and Spartacists for a Socialist republic forced the Majority Socialists to proclaim a republic even before a constitutional assembly had made the decision. A mass demonstration of Berlin workers swarmed before the Reichstag building, and the Majority leader Scheidemann went out on the balcony to address them at 2:00 P.M. Intent on counteracting Liebknecht's proclamation of a Socialist republic, Scheidemann concluded his harangue by shouting: "Workers, Soldiers, the German people has triumphed all along the line. A large part of the garrison has joined us. The Hohenzollerns have abdicated. Long live the great German Republic!" When Scheidemann came in from the balcony he found Ebert horrified and "livid with wrath" at what he had done. "He banged his fist on the table," writes Scheidemann, "and yelled at me:

'Is it true?' On my replying it was not only true but a matter of course, he made a scene which passed my understanding. 'You have no right to proclaim the republic. What becomes of Germany—whether she becomes a republic or something else—a constituent assembly must decide.' " [17]

On leaving Prince Max, Ebert and his friends had come upon Oskar Cohn, Dittmann, and Ewald Vogtherr, members of the Independent Socialist party. Ebert made an offer to the U.S.D.P. to share the government responsibility with the Majority Socialists and he was most generous in his offer. Despite the far larger representation of the Majority Socialists in the Reichstag, Ebert's offer provided for parity between the two parties in the cabinet. There was also no attempt by him to dictate the selection of U.S.D.P. representatives. When Oskar Cohn asked him what he thought of Liebknecht joining the government, Ebert replied: "Please, bring us Karl Liebknecht, he will be agreeable to us. We do not make the formation of the government dependent on questions of personalities." [18]

At the meeting of the Independents there was a sharp division of opinion on whether or not to accept the offer of the Majority Socialists. Ledebour, Liebknecht, Richard Müller, and the left wing wanted no truck with the "government Socialists," who were identified with August 4, 1914. Liebknecht insisted that "all executive, all legislative and all judicial powers be in the hands of the Workers' and Soldiers' Councils." * The majority of party leaders, however, after considerable exchange of conditions and counter-conditions with the Majority Socialists, agreed on November 10 to share the ministries with the latter. Haase, Dittmann, and Barth, representing the U.S.D.P., joined with Ebert, Scheidemann, and Landsberg to form the first revolutionary government.† The Independents made their participation conditional upon the acceptance of three main points: (1) that the ministers in the cabinet be only Socialists, (2) that all political power be vested in the hands of the Workers' and Soldiers' Councils, and (3) that the constituent assembly be delayed until the revolution was consolidated. These stipulations were accepted by the Majority Socialist leaders, who were also eager to achieve unity in the Socialist movement. The new government was constituted as a Council of People's Representatives with Ebert and Haase as equal co-chairmen. On the same day that it was formed, Hindenburg and the army swore an oath of allegiance to the new government. In its first proclamation to the people the new Council of People's Representatives, making known that

---

* Eduard Bernstein relates that when he heard Liebknecht set forth these demands the thought flashed through his mind: "He will bring us the counter-revolution!" (*Die deutsche Revolution*, p. 34).

† In a letter to his son, dated Nov. 26, 1918, Haase indicated that the Independents apparently considered taking power by themselves. "I would have seized the government myself with my friends," he wrote, "had not the soldiers insisted almost unanimously that we share power with Ebert, and because if we took power without Ebert a considerable portion of the bourgeois technicians would have carried on sabotage" (Ernst Haase, *Hugo Haase, Sein Leben und Wirken*, Berlin, n.d., p. 173).

its "leadership is entirely Socialist," declared that it "sets for itself the task of realizing the Socialist program." The next few days saw the abdication of all the other dynastic rulers in the local states and the establishment of revolutionary governments throughout the land. On November 10, too, the new government accepted the armistice terms dictated by Marshal Foch, and on the following day the armistice was signed at Compiègne, bringing World War I to a close and thus achieving what was for most Germans the main goal of the revolution.

The revolution in Berlin was carried out with relatively little violence and bloodshed. Fifteen persons lost their lives on November 9, and they were given a public funeral on November 20. Otherwise there was little or no opposition or bloodshed. The Wolff Telegraphic Agency correspondent reported from Berlin on November 9: "Here the revolution achieved a brilliant and almost bloodless triumph." The *Frankfurter Zeitung* correspondent reported on the next day: "A glorious feeling of liberty and brotherliness has taken hold of the entire nation. . . . This is the liberty yearned for by the nation." Theodor Wolff wrote in the *Berliner Tageblatt* on November 10, 1918:

The greatest of all revolutions has, like a suddenly onrushing storm, overturned the imperial régime, with all that belongs to it both above and below. It may be called the greatest of all revolutions because never before has such a strongly built Bastille with such solid walls surrounding it been captured in one attack. . . . Yesterday morning, at least in Berlin, everything was still there; yesterday afternoon nothing of all that existed any longer.[19]

Ernst Troeltsch, the noted historian and religious philosopher, has left us a more sober and more realistic description of those November days in Berlin in his *Spektator Briefe,* which he contributed to the *Kunstwart:*

In the evening [of November 9] the newspapers arrived and reported the triumph of the revolution in Berlin as well as the sailors' revolts in Kiel and Wilhelmshaven. The next Sunday morning, after a night of suspense, the picture became clear from the morning papers: the Kaiser in Holland, the revolution triumphant in most of the centers, the local princes in the process of abdicating! No one dead for Kaiser and Reich! The civil servants in the service of the new government! The continued validity of all obligations guaranteed and no rush on the banks!

Sunday November 10 was a wonderful autumn day. The citizens went as usual in droves to walk in the Grunewald. No elegant toilette, only *Bürger,* many obviously and consciously clad in simple garb. Everything somewhat subdued, like people whose destiny is being decided somewhere far off in the distance but who nevertheless are reassured and at ease that things went off as well as they did. Street cars and subways are running as usual, a guarantee that everything was in order for the immediate needs—and food supplies. On all faces there was written: salaries are being paid.[20]

2. THE SOURCE OF POLITICAL POWER: SOVIETS VERSUS PROVISIONAL GOVERNMENT

One of the first questions to confront the new government related to the source of its political power. By what right did it rule and from whom did it derive its prerogatives? [21] We have seen that Ebert's first conception was to carry on by the continuity of the constitution and the powers vested in the imperial chancellor. His first proclamations, therefore, bore the designation *Reichskanzler*. But the triumph of the revolution both in Berlin and throughout the country was accompanied by, if not caused by, the establishment of Workers' and Soldiers' Councils. These councils took over executive authority in many of the cities in Germany as the monarchical institutions collapsed, or, in most instances, they were set up alongside the existing governmental authorities. A sort of dual government was thus created, very much like the situation in Russia in 1917 and 1918.

Soldiers' and Workers' Councils sprang up in spontaneous fashion throughout Germany in the November days of the revolution.* They grew out of demonstrations, mass meetings and calls by workers' organizations. In the case of the soldiers they were set up in opposition to the officers' corps. The model of the Russian soviets was definitely a factor of tremendous influence, which set the example for the revolutionary elements in Germany. But just as in Russia, it must not be forgotten, the *origin* and *establishment* of soviets are not to be identified with the Bolsheviks, so too the German councils, in their first stages, were not identified with only one wing of the Socialist movement. As a matter of fact, 95 per cent of the soldiers' councils threw their support to the Majority Socialists, and Liebknecht and Rosa Luxemburg had so little influence in these circles that they were not able to secure election to the first Soldiers' and Workers' Congress in Berlin. A special ideology, however, began to

---

* From the dispatches to the Berlin *Vorwärts* for Nov. 9 and 10: "A Workers' and Soldiers' Council was formed consisting of equal representation of both Socialist parties and of representations of the soldiers." *Nov. 7, Oldenburg:* "A Soldiers' Council was formed." *Nov. 7, Hanover:* "The Provisional Workers' and Soldiers' Council has issued a call for a meeting." *Nov. 6, Wilhelmshaven:* "Wilhelmshaven is under the rule of the Soldiers' Council." *Nov. 7, Bremen:* "All important communication centers are occupied by representatives of the Workers and Soldiers." *Nov. 8, Schwerin:* "At one P.M. today the Grand Duke and the ministry received representatives of the Workers' and Soldiers' Council." *Nov. 8, Cologne:* "The Workers' and Soldiers' Council has taken over control over all soldiers." *Nov. 8, Nürnberg:* "The city is since Friday 9:30 P.M. completely in the hands of the Workers' and Soldiers' Council." *Nov. 9, Düsseldorf:* "Here too a Workers' and Soldiers' Council was formed yesterday." *Nov. 9, Barmen:* "In Elberfeld-Barmen a Workers' and Soldiers' Council was formed, which is regulating general business." *Nov. 9, Essen:* "In the whole industrial area from Dortmund to Duisburg the railroad stations are occupied by members of the Workers' and Soldiers' Council." *Nov. 9, Coblenz:* "The entire administration placed itself at the disposal of the Workers' and Soldiers' Council." *Nov. 9, Mannheim:* "A Workers' and Soldiers' Council was formed here and it has occupied the Commandatur and the railroad stations." *Nov. 9, Bayreuth:* "A Workers' and Soldiers' Council was established. All the soldiers joined." The image of the progress of the revolution is at this time without doubt the establishment of Workers' and Soldiers' Councils.

be formulated as to the relative importance of the councils for the government of Germany. The Independent Socialists, in particular, placed great stress on the political power of the councils and made it a condition for their partnership with the Majority Socialists.

Elections were held in all Berlin factories and garrisons on the morning of November 10, and the elected councils convened at 5:00 P.M. on the same day in the Zirkus Busch "to name the provisional government." The motion by Emil Barth to approve the composition of the new Council of People's Representatives was passed by an overwhelming majority, and an Executive Council of the Socialist German Republic (*Vollzugsrat*) consisting of twenty-eight members was elected to carry on the business of the larger council. Both Socialist parties had equal representation, and two chairmen were named, Richard Müller and Captain von Beerfelde. The latter was replaced a few days later by Brutus Molkenbuhr.

Negotiations began almost immediately between the Vollzugsrat and the ministers to define clearly the competence of the two bodies. On November 17 Dr. Landsberg told newsmen that "there is no longer a Reich chancellor but only a collegium of six equal members. Ebert is the chairman and Haase is vice chairman. We have our authority from the Executive Commission of the Workers' and Soldiers' Councils. The latter is the real bearer of power." [22] On November 22 the Vollzugsrat and the cabinet issued a joint statement defining the respective relationships. The official text (which amended the original draft by the Vollzugsrat) stated:

The revolution has created a new state law. For the first period of transition the new juridical situation finds its expression in the following agreement between the Vollzugsrat of the Workers' and Soldiers' Council of Greater Berlin and the Council of People's Representatives.

1. Political power rests in the hands of the Workers' and Soldiers' Councils of the German Socialist Republic. Its task is to protect and further develop the achievements of the revolution as well as to suppress the counter-revolution.

2. Until an assembly of delegates of the Workers' and Soldiers' Council has elected an Executive Council of the German republic, the Berlin Vollzugsrat exercises the functions of the Workers' and Soldiers' Councils of Greater Berlin.

3. The confirmation of the Council of People's Representatives by the Workers' and Soldiers' Council of Greater Berlin signifies the transfer of the executive powers of the republic.

4. The appointment and recall of members of the cabinet of the republic and—up to the final regulation of the relations between the local states— also of Prussia is to be carried out by the central Executive Council, which also possesses the right of control.

5. The Vollzugsrat is to be consulted before the cabinet appoints the technical secretaries of state.

As soon as possible an all-Reich assembly of delegates of the Workers' and Soldiers' Councils is to be convened.[23]

It is significant to note that the organ of the Berlin U.S.D.P., the *Freiheit,* carried the story of this agreement as a front-page lead under the big caption, "Sovereignty of the Workers' and Soldiers' Councils," whereas most of the other newspapers either ignored it entirely or published it on an inside page. It indicates the close identification of the Independent Socialists with the idea of the councils. That Ebert, however, also interpreted the agreement in the same way is clear from his statement to the conference of representatives of the federal states on November 25. "In place of the monarchy, the socialist-republican form of state has been established, in which the People's Representatives exercise the executive functions, while political power rests in the hands of the workers and soldiers." [24] When the presiding officer of the old Reichstag, Konstantin Fehrenbach, tried on two occasions to reconvene the Reichstag, Ebert declared that the Reichstag no longer possessed competence. The Vollzugsrat was regarded as the substitute for the Reichstag.

Calls for election to the all-Reich assembly of councils were issued on November 23, and the First Congress of German Soviets convened in Berlin from December 16 to 21. There were 500 delegates, of whom 300 were supporters of the Majority Socialists, 100 of the U.S.D.P., 35 bourgeois, and 65 undetermined. The Majority Socialists had made a determined effort to elect their representatives, and they had both a superior party machinery and the support of the trade-union apparatus. But it is also true that the Majority Socialists undoubtedly had undisputed mastery over the greater majority of the organized workers at the time.

The question of ultimate source of political authority was further clarified. A majority of the Congress passed a resolution delegating its power to the ministers until the National Assembly convened. A Central Council (Zentralrat) of the Congress was set up to carry on the work of the councils and, at the insistence of Ebert, the Congress refused to empower this Central Council to intervene at any time in the acts of the government. Ebert was willing to allow the Central Council a certain over-all right to withdraw its support from the ministry and thus effect a change in policy, but he stubbornly refused to allow his council of ministers to be hampered by continuous interference. This position received the support of the majority of the delegates, and because of this the Independent Socialists refused to name candidates for the Central Council, with the result that the elected committee consisted exclusively of Majority Socialists. This made the eventual elimination of the Workers' and Soldiers' Councils much simpler. On December 21 the Berlin Vollzugsrat transferred its national functions to the Central Council elected by the Congress. The date for the elections to the National Assembly was set for January 19, 1919, and the Assembly convened in Weimar on February 6. A second congress of the Workers' and Soldiers' Councils was held on April 8–14, 1919, but by that time its role as a political power had been completely eliminated. In the words of Dr. Bredt, "The general congress of the Soviets was responsible for the salvation of bourgeois Germany." It rebuked the radicals and turned over its power to the Council of People's Representatives and to the National Assembly.[25]

The ideological conflict over the power of the Workers' and Soldiers' Councils, however, continued to agitate political circles during the first two years of the revolution and was one of the issues over which the various proletarian parties came to be divided.[26] The chief advocates of the council idea came from the Spartacists and the Left Independents. For them it was more than a political idea or an institution. "All power to the Soviets," the call with which Lenin and Trotsky magnetized their following in Russia, was echoed in Germany by both the Spartacists and the Left Independents, and both groups conceived this to be identical with the "dictatorship of the proletariat." Their almost mystical devotion to the idea of the councils revealed too their basic and deep mistrust of parliamentary democracy and parliamentary institutions. The Majority Socialists were willing to recognize the usefulness of the councils as a transitional stage to a stable democratic régime, and they used the councils as such. But they were committed to the establishment of a democratic republic based upon Western representative institutions.*

Among the Independents, however, two important elements entered into their insistence on the political power of the councils. In the first place they identified democratic institutions with "bourgeois capitalism" and were mistrustful of "bourgeois democracy" as they were of "bourgeois capitalism." Secondly, however, they were keenly aware of the political backwardness of the German people and knew only too well that no radical transformation from the old order would be possible by means of a democratic majority decision. "I insist," declared Däumig to the Congress of Workers' and Soldiers' Councils on December 19, 1918,

that salvation will come not by the slavish imitation of the old democratic principle but by the new democratic principle of the soviet system. The Ger-

---

* There was a body of opinion in the Majority Socialist party that actively propagated the utilization of the council idea as an economic complement to political democracy. This group was centered mainly around the *Sozialistische Monatshefte,* and Hugo Sinzheimer and Max Cohn were its leading advocates. They rejected the whole notion of party or class dictatorship, but pointed to the limitations of democratic forms and to the grave dangers of tension between the political system and social conditions. They argued, therefore, that political democracy required complementary social and economic institutions with parliament as the organ of political democracy and the councils as the agencies of economic democracy. How the two were to be integrated was the subject of differences between Cohn and the majority of the party. This trend of thinking left its mark on the economic provisions of the Weimar Constitution. Cf. Hugo Sinzheimer, *Das Rätesystem* (Frankfurt, 1919), and Max Cohn, "Der Rätegedanke im ersten Revolutionsjahr," in *Sozialistische Monatshefte,* liii (1919), 1043–1055, and "Was wird aus dem Rätegedanken?" in *Die neue Rundschau,* xxxi (1919), 657–670.

man proletariat is too good to sink to the stage of the Western democracies. The German people, with its servility, must be shaken out of its lethargy. That you cannot do if you press a ballot into their hands every few years and say to them: Now go home, the parliamentarians will take care of things. This can happen only when, by means of the soviet system, you have the workers always on the bridle-rein, when the people are actively participating in the fashioning of its destiny.[27]

In his speech before the Leipzig party conference of the U.S.D.P. on March 4 and 5, 1919, Däumig again dealt at length with the problem of soviets. He heaped scorn and abuse on the "old democracy" of the bourgeoisie. Socialism, he maintained, cannot be achieved with the "old democracy," and he had no patience to wait a long time "until Reformism fully develops its goals." Socialism can be achieved only by the "dictatorship of the proletariat," and that, for Däumig, was equivalent to the idea of the soviet system. It is in the sharpest opposition to the parliamentary system and is the only means whereby to combine legislative and executive powers, parliament with administration. When criticized for not having a clear idea of how the soviet system was to be organized, Däumig answered, with almost Nietzschean arrogance:

According to my opinion you misunderstand the soviet system thoroughly [if you make this point], for it is not merely a means, but also the goal of the revolution, *i.e.,* the soviet system can never be presented in a completely finished form as far as its structure and form of organization is concerned. It will be completely transformed with the progress and development of the revolution. . . . I cannot give a systematic presentation of a revolutionary institution, in a revolutionary epoch, which is growing up from the mother soil of the revolution.[28]

For the Spartacists, as for the Independent Socialists, the councils or soviets were to be a useful instrument only when and if they themselves were able to control a majority in them and use them against the government. Councils elected on the basis of genuine democratic balloting and resulting in majorities not in line with their policies would have met the same end they did in Bolshevik Russia. This the Majority Socialist Scheidemann clearly recognized when he replied to Däumig at the first Congress of the Workers' and Soldiers' Councils. After admitting the usefulness of the councils in the transitory stage of the revolution, Scheidemann went on to say:

They come in from the street and hold placards under our noses saying: All Power to the Workers' and Soldiers' Councils! At the same time, however, they let you understand: If you do not do what we want, we will kick you out. . . . They can only represent a force as long as they are in the possession of the majority of machine guns. What is Russia's present would then become a certain future for Germany. . . . We need bread, peace and work. . . . The Councils can bring us neither bread nor peace. They will create civil war for us.[29]

Scheidemann's analysis proved to be most accurate. The most serious disturbance that agitated Germany during the first year of the new régime came from the left rather than from the right. The swift collapse of German might on the battlefield and the pitiful breakdown of the monarchy as a result left the conservative circles of Germany completely stunned at first. The fact of the revolution was accepted completely by the bourgeois groups. The monarchist newspapers dropped their royalist slogans from their mastheads. The *Kreuzzeitung* removed its slogan "With God for King and Fatherland," and the *Deutsche Tageszeitung* took off its "For Kaiser and Reich." They paid a tearful farewell to the monarchist tradition and to the Hohenzollerns and expressed hopes that the new ruling groups would bring Germany to an honorable peace and not set up a one-sided party state. There was not a single instance of an attempt to resist the revolution for the sake of the emperor. A determined stand against the revolution by one officers' corps might well have deflected the entire course of events, but no such group was to be found to die "for Emperor and Reich." The military were definitely convinced that any attempt by army leaders to oppose the revolution would not be carried out by the rank and file.

The Supreme Command under Hindenburg and General Groener proclaimed their loyalty to the new government, and this served to keep the officers' corps and the entire monarchist group in check. The futility of resistance to the revolution at the time was no doubt a large factor. But the behavior of the military in the early days of the revolution also illustrates the fact that much more important for them than fealty to the monarchy was the preservation of the officers' corps and the army as the potential instruments of a renewed and revived nationalist Germany. To prevent the armies of the Entente from marching into Germany and finding a pretext for destroying completely the German military structure was their most crucial goal. To achieve this meant accepting, at least for the time, the fact of the revolution, and arranging a *modus operandi* with the new régime. "As long as the Field Marshal and I are at the head of the Supreme Command," declared General Groener to Ebert, "I can give you the binding assurance: 'We have not the slightest thought of counter-revolution.' " [30]

The bourgeois conservative parties began to adjust themselves to the new situation. The word "people" or "people's" came to be used as a symbol of acceptance of the new order. The Conservatives reformed themselves as the Deutschnationale Volkspartei; the National Liberals became the People's party; and the Centrists for a while reconstituted themselves as the Christian Democratic People's party. The associations of big industrialists hastened to enter into an agreement on November 15, 1918, with the trade-unions granting the right of collective bargaining to the trade-unions and agreeing to the long-standing demand of workers for the eight-hour day. The pact, promulgated by both the government and the Berlin Vollzugsrat was acclaimed in all labor circles as the end of the era of the "Master in House" ideology of Stumm-Hallberg and Kirdorf.

It is quite likely that monarchist and conservative circles decided to bide their time and wait for an opportune time for a comeback later. Be that as it may, however, during the first crucial year of the revolution the most serious and fateful divisions were not between the right and the left, but within the ranks of the very groups that were identified with the cause of the revolution—the socialist and workers' movement. The revolutionary government was confronted with overwhelming problems—the making of peace, demobilization, the providing of food while the blockade was still in effect, the maintenance of order, the organization of police power, socialization, the convocation of a national constituent assembly, and a host of lesser problems of immediate consequence. On almost all of these questions, the working classes and their leaders, the groups to whom the people looked for direction and guidance, found themselves hopelessly divided and set against each other. At a time when the success of the revolution demanded vigorous, forceful, and united action by all the supporters of the revolution, Germany, defeated in war, humbled in peace, its pride grieved by loss of prestige, hungry and disorganized, was in the hands of a government that was beset by enemies from within its own social and economic classes and paralyzed by division in its own ranks.

3. PROLETARIAN DIVISION

The German labor and Socialist groups, at the outbreak of the revolution, fell into three main groups—the Spartacists, the Independent Socialists (U.S.D.P.), and the Majority Socialists. Between the latter and the first two was the deep gulf of the policy of August 4, 1914, and the attitude toward the war. Much of the difficulty among the Socialist groups stemmed either from the continued persistence of the ideas of 1914 or as a result of the memories of the past. In his address to the 1919 Socialist Party Congress of Weimar, the first after the war, Eduard Bernstein, one of the first Independent Socialist leaders to seek his way back into the parent party, was hooted and booed by the delegates when he tried to present an objective analysis of Germany's foreign relations. While Bernstein himself proclaimed that "for me the 3rd and 4th of August 1914 was the blackest day of my life," his hearers responded with such nationalist expressions and interruptions that the otherwise serene Bernstein was led to exclaim: "You are still captives of your vote of August 4. Get out of this tower, become free at last in this matter too." [31]

The Majority Socialists were never able to free themselves from this association with the pro-war policy. Politically and psychologically they could not bring themselves to admit that their policy of the *Burgfrieden* had been a mistake. And the deep and profound nationalism which prompted their stand on August 4, 1914, remained equally strong in 1918–1919. It never occurred to them that a complete break with the past was either desirable or feasible. It was not only that they were reformist Socialists and opposed to violent revolution because of possible bloodshed and chaos. It was that both the strength and the continuity of national tradition were matters of profound conviction for them. It was not utilitarian or pragmatic design when Scheidemann referred to Marshal von Hindenburg as a man "before whom the entire nation can have only the greatest reverence," [32] or when Albert Grzesinski, the Majority Socialist chairman of the Workers' and Soldiers' Council in Kassel received Hindenburg as a hero, declaring, "Hindenburg belongs to the German people and the German army." [33] Despite the long anti-militarist tradition of the party, the Majority Socialists could never get themselves to eliminate the glories of German arms from the memory of their nationalist past.

The Majority Socialists and Spartacists represented the extreme poles of the working-class movement. For the former there was this deep attachment to the national past and to the national cause of Germany; for the Spartacists the primary allegiance was to the world revolution and to the international proletariat. The Majority Socialists were sincerely devoted to the cause of democratic and parliamentary institutions; the Spartacists had no use for political democracy or for "bourgeois" parliaments. The Majority Socialists rejected any and all forms of dictatorship, including the dictatorship of the proletariat; the Spartacists preached the gospel of dictatorship, even if it meant rule by a political minority. The Majority Socialists retained a horror of violence and bloodshed and a sense of the dignity of the individual; the Spartacists were so inspired by zeal for their revolutionary goal that they were not deterred by the hesitancies prompted by bourgeois ethics or humanitarian considerations, and they halted before neither violence nor bloodshed. The Majority Socialists, at that early date, clearly saw what was going on in Bolshevik Russia and recognized the calamitous threat to liberty, democratic institutions, and human rights created by the Soviet régime; the Spartacists reveled in the achievements of the Leninist experiment and paraded the Bolshevik system as their model for Germany and the rest of the world.

If by revolution is meant a swift, violent, and radical transformation of society, in the fashion of the Bolshevik revolution of 1917, then it is no doubt true that the Majority Socialists wanted to have none of it. "If the Kaiser does not abdicate," Ebert is reported by Scheidemann to have said to Prince Max, "social revolution must come. But I don't want it. I hate it like sin." [34] The Socialist defenders of Ebert, however, are correct in pointing out that if Ebert actually said these words it was Bolshevism that he had in mind. He hated revolution in the sense of bloody civil war. But he wanted a forward program of social development based on the democratic belief that the people should determine their own destiny.[35] The older, experienced practical men of the party and of the trade-unions looked with scorn upon the "new upstarts, the heaven-stormers, who only see goals and no paths," who are intent on bringing on socialism no matter what chaotic conditions resulted. "Socialism," wrote Friedrich Stampfer in the *Vorwärts*, "is organization. Disorganization is the worst enemy of socialism." [36] The purpose of the revolution, declared Ebert at a Socialist rally on December 1, is not dictatorship but "Germany liberty," and that means liberty for all irrespective of class. But the most immediate tasks were those of providing food for the populace and strengthening the democratic system. The revisionist and reformist tradition in the party was now dominant. To the Spartacist call for complete socialization of industry the Majority Socialists replied: "The only thing that counts is the today and tomorrow. And today and tomorrow we need bread and work and elimination of disease." [37]

It was this heavy sense of responsibility for the immediate welfare of the German population that hung over the deliberations and actions of the Majority Socialists. They did not want the revolution, and it was thrown into their laps by the bourgeois groups and they had to carry on as best they could.* The first party congress after the revolution was held in June, 1919, in Weimar. As one studies the record of the proceedings one is amazed to note the complete absence of any trace of satisfaction or exhilaration. A sense of gloom over the national defeat was far more in evidence than any joy in the triumph of the revolution. Scheidemann, holding forth on the "Tasks of the Social Democratic Party in the German Republic," complained that "when the historical autumn storm of 1918 swept away the old crews, they seized upon us because no one else was available to steer the course." Noske lamented the fact that "it was our misfortune to have taken over the government . . . at a moment when millions of people could not be fed." And Otto Wels completed the dark picture when he said: "For weeks we find ourselves in the most difficult period of our history. Dark and heavy is the burden of the past and blacker still is the omen of the future. Our destiny is no longer determined by ourselves; it rests in the hands of the victorious imperialism of the Western powers." [38] These were men who approached their tasks with a high sense of moral responsibility but certainly without either the necessary spirit of confidence or the joy of revolutionary triumph. Friedrich Meinecke relates that he asked Foreign

---

* The S.P.D. deputy Schulz said before the Weimar National Assembly on March 27, 1919: "We Social Democrats did not want the revolution. We would have preferred that the path of freedom be created for the German people without the violent acts of the revolution. (Hear! Hear! from the S.P.D.)" (*Die National Versammlung*, iii, 12.)

Secretary Solf on November 18, 1918, "Did not Ebert and Scheidemann experience a secret pleasure on this day [Nov. 9] at the outbreak of the revolution?" "Oh, no," answered Solf, "not at all. They were seized with deathly fear." *

In between the Majority Socialists and the Spartacists stood the Independent Socialists (U.S.D.P.). They were by no means a unified and homogeneous party. What united them primarily was their past record of opposition to the war, their recognition of the German designs of aggression, and their designation of German militarism as enemy Number One. But in their attitude toward the immediate problems confronting Germany in 1918–1919 there was a wide divergence of opinion between a right wing, led by Haase, Kautsky, Hilferding, and Dittmann, and the left wing under the leadership of Ledebour, Däumig, Barth, and Müller. The U.S.D.P. illustrates most acutely the quandary as to what to do with democratic controls in a revolutionary situation, among a people who are antidemocratic or, to say the least, non-democratic. The Spartacists on the left did not give a hoot for democracy and democratic rights. They could, therefore, carry on an opportunistic policy with prattle about "true democracy" while not worrying too much how it would work. The Majority Socialists were formal advocates of democratic institutions but were not as acutely sensitive to the persistence among the masses of the nationalist militarist tradition and its threat to democracy. The August 4 tradition was still omnipresent in their own midst. The Independent Socialists (or at least all except the left wing) wanted a democratic Germany, but they saw only too clearly that the German mentality had not been altered radically as a result of the revolution and they therefore wished to delay the introduction of parliamentary institutions until the masses had become more democratized. This is perhaps the key to the reason why the U.S.D.P. was so often most sound in its analysis of a situation from the standpoint of logic and why it proved to be so weak and ineffectual politically. This is also the reason why the Independent Socialists were opposed to an early convocation of the National Assembly and were more enthusiastic supporters of the Workers' Councils.

When we came to power on the 9th of November [declared Hilferding], Germany was constituted as a soviet republic and we of the U.S.D.P. represented the point of view at that time that there should be no election for the

---

* Meinecke, *Erlebtes*, p. 259. A more extreme characterization of the Majority Socialist leaders is given by Emil Barth. "These people lacked any kind of revolutionary defiance, any kind of will driven either by love or hate. Neither by love of the masses, the hungry, groaning proletariat . . . nor of hate for the exploiters, the robbers and the tyrants did they do anything that would be dangerous for themselves. . . . Whoever does not possess this defiance, forged out of love and hate, will in revolutionary times never act as a dynamic influence but rather as a confusing, deterring, disintegrating and destructive influence, because he will always lack the will to power and hence to act" (Barth, *Aus der Werkstatt der deutschen Revolution*, p. 58).

National Assembly but that we maintain a dictatorship of the proletariat by means of the political representation of Workers' Councils until . . . the bourgeoisie had been driven out of its most important positions of power.

A dictatorship of the proletariat was necessary

because in Germany the character of historical development has made a period of dictatorship of the proletariat an unavoidable necessity. . . . It is impossible to secure a firm footing with democratic means in a country which has been so reactionary as was Germany and where the reactionary mentality, the belief in the supremacy of force, is so deeply engraved in the minds of the citizens.[39]

Gustav Landauer, Bavarian "anarchistic socialist," wrote in *Die Republik* on January 21, 1919:

Only a few people rejected the German war from the beginning and recognized that it was what its instigators designated it to be from the start: a German war. This war had such military, political and economic consequences that a large number of soldiers, a not insignificant number of workers and women were brought into a revolutionary mood. The few determined individuals carried through the revolution with vehement energy, their determination derived from the fact that they bore the future, socialism, within themselves, that they wanted not only not to tolerate things any longer but to be creative. Those that helped them constituted a minority among the German people; all others need a long and thorough enlightenment and education in truly democratic institutions. Of this minority many were lost to the revolution on the day after the revolution. . . . Before the revolution they were soldiers plagued beyond endurance; in the revolution they were death-defying rebels; on the day of victory they were soldiers who had acquired salvation; the day following they were timorous and anxious *Bürger*.

Hugo Haase, respected by his political opponents as well as by his followers as a man of indisputable integrity and of statesmanlike qualities, retained his adherence to the Marxist goal of world revolution and world socialism.[40] Like left-wing Social Democrats throughout the world at that time, he viewed the Bolshevik revolution in Russia as a positive step forward toward the goal of international socialism. But he, like Hilferding, Kautsky, and Dittmann, was repelled morally by the brutality and terror of the Russian régime. These Independent Socialists were not opposed to a dictatorship per se, but they wanted a dictatorship resting not upon a minority, as in the case of Russia, but upon the will of the majority of the people. The Independent Socialists were objective and honest enough to admit that the great bulk of the German workers were in the ranks of the Majority Socialists. All that the Independents could do under the circumstances, therefore, was to pursue a program of educational propaganda in order to develop revolutionary clarity and revolutionary energy among the masses and to hope thereby to win them over to their side eventually. The U.S.D.P., declared Crispien, wants a soviet system based on the free will of the masses and not on a militarily disciplined obedience, as in Russia. "By dictatorship of the proletariat," he maintained, "we understand . . . not the setting up of a reign of terror, but the exercise of political power by a working class led by scientifically schooled Socialists with a considered and conscious planning and organization and imbued with the highest form of socialist ethics." [41]

It is the ethical moment above all that divided the Haase-Hilferding faction of the Independent Socialists from the Spartacists and from their own left-wing faction. "The rejection of morality," declared Hilferding, "is not Marx but Bismarck." [42] It was the ethical revulsion against the terror of the Bolsheviks and their disdain for human life and personality that made communism so abhorrent to this group of the U.S.D.P.

For a while the U.S.D.P. leaders conceived of themselves as a possible bridge between the Majority Socialists and the more radical groups. People like Eduard Bernstein, Hilferding, Ströbel, and Eisner tried desperately to restore the unity of the Socialist movement.[43] But the U.S.D.P. only disintegrated, torn as it was by factional division. A left wing, led by Ledebour, Barth, Däumig, Richard Müller, and Wilhelm Herzog, came to be identified more and more with the Spartacists and the followers of the newly founded Third International. As indicated above, they scorned the institutions of parliamentary democracy and were too impatient to wait for the evolutionary development of Socialism. The issue which brought the factional division to a head was the question of whether or not the U.S.D.P. should become affiliated with the Moscow Third International. A commission headed by Crispien, Dittmann, and Däumig was dispatched to Moscow to negotiate the terms of affiliation. The delegates reported back to the party congress in September, 1920, and a special party conference was convened in Halle on October 12, 1920, to take final action on the matter. Here the spokesmen for both sides hurled arguments and invectives at each other, the climax being reached in the memorable oratorical duel between Zinoviev, who came from Moscow to plead the cause of the Comintern, and Rudolf Hilferding.

Hilferding pointed out the profound cleavage between the tactics of the Communists and the traditional policies of European Marxian socialism, but warned especially that the parties affiliated with the Third International would lose all their autonomy and independence and that the policies of the International would be determined not by the interests of the world movement but would be dictated by the needs and interests of the Russian Bolsheviks. Hilferding's masterful presentation proved ineffectual, however, against the demagogic oratory of Zinoviev and against the infiltration and dividing tactics already used successfully by the Communists. The conditions of the Comintern were accepted by a vote of 236

to 156. The minority, to avoid incidents, marched out of the hall to reconvene in another place, while Zinoviev stood on the platform watching
with a sinister and gloating smile of triumph the fruition of his policy
of fomenting the disintegration of the working-class movement.[44]

4. INSURRECTION ON THE LEFT

The Spartacist group had been formed in March, 1916, and it continued to work within the framework of the U.S.D.P. during the last two
years of the war. On December 14, 1918, it published its revolutionary
program whereby it set itself apart from the U.S.D.P., and on December
29 to January 1 the organization meetings of the Communist party of
Germany were held and the Spartacists formally seceded from the Independent Socialist party.

The leaders of the Spartacists were Karl Liebknecht and Rosa Luxemburg. Liebknecht, the son of the revered founder of the Social Democratic
party, Wilhelm Liebknecht, became identified in the public eye with the
fight against militarism and as the martyr for this cause. Not beloved in his
own circles, he was possessed of great egotism, which was enormously
inflated after he had been released from prison and hailed by cheering
crowds as the martyred victim of Prussian militarism. But he was lacking
in a sense of responsibility, and his intimate colleagues, well aware of
this, had little faith in his political judgment.

Rosa Luxemburg, a Polish Jewess who had played a prominent role
in the Polish Socialist movement before she came to Germany, was an
intellectual giant compared to Liebknecht. But as Bernstein points out,
"There stood before her eyes and lived in her soul an abstract conception
of a proletariat that hardly corresponded to the real proletariat." [45] There
has been an attempt recently, especially by dissidents from the orthodox
Communist party, to re-evaluate Rosa Luxemburg and to set her off
from Lenin and the Russian Bolsheviks. Her essay on the Russian revolution, it is true, indicates a wavering feeling regarding the course of events
under Lenin. And it is also true that she had greater intellectual acumen,
a higher sense of personal integrity, and more political maturity than the
band of youngsters who made up the bulk of the Spartacist group. But the
basic lines of Spartacist policy, which were to be so fateful for the subsequent political situation in Germany, were laid down by her and bear
the stamp of her personality and her ideas. A week after the outbreak of
the revolution she wrote an article for *Die Rote Fahne* on "A Week of
Revolution." Although the Hohenzollerns had been laid low, she declared,
this was not of momentous consequence. For it was not the monarchy or
the Hohenzollerns who were the real enemies and who had brought on
the war. The monarchy was "like every bourgeois government, merely
the business agent for the ruling classes." The real enemy was the im-
perialist-capitalist bourgeoisie. There could be no real revolution before

it was eliminated, and "the future of the German revolution is anchored in the world revolution of the proletariat."

The Spartacists savagely attacked the Independents for entering into a partnership with the Majority Socialists. "Our first duty," declared Rosa Luxemburg before a Berlin meeting of the U.S.D.P., "is to destroy every bridge to the present government." The formal equality of democracy, she went on to say, "is nothing but lies and falsehoods so long as the economic power of capital still exists. . . . Socialism does not mean getting together in a parliament and deciding on laws. For us socialism means the smashing of the ruling classes with all the brutality that the proletariat is able to develop in its struggle." [46] She further elaborated her conception of proletarian brutality in the *Rote Fahne* of December 14, 1918:

It is not when the wage slave and the capitalist, the agricultural proletarian and the Junker sit in sham equality to engage in parliamentary debates on their vital issues, that you have democracy; democracy that is not a swindle is to be found only when the million-headed proletarian masses seize the entire power of the state with their hardened fists in order, like the God Thor, to shatter the heads of the ruling classes with their hammer.[47]

At the founding conference of the German Communist party Rosa Luxemburg delivered a long speech on "Our Program and the Political Situation." In it she called for a return to the Marxian doctrines of 1848 and a revision of the Socialist program which had existed up to August 4, 1914. Kautsky and the other party leaders, she said, had developed a parliamentary kind of Socialism which was a degeneration of Marxist theory. "The immediate task of the proletariat is none other than . . . to realize Socialism and to eradicate capitalism root and branch." [48] This, she maintained against the majority of the delegates, cannot be carried out unless you have the masses behind you, including the peasantry. The masses must be educated and revolutionized to know what their duties are. But "the way to educate the masses to power is by letting them exercise power." And this is best achieved by strikes and civil war. The socialist revolution, she maintained, will come with a wave of strikes. Political strikes will become the central point of the revolution and put political action into a secondary role. "Civil war," she had written on November 20, "which they try to avoid with anxious care, does not allow itself to be eliminated. For civil war is only another name for class struggle, and the idea that you can introduce socialism without class struggle and by parliamentary majority decisions is a ludicrous petty-bourgeois illusion." [49]

The Spartacist tactics and plan of action were, therefore, to undermine the existing government by all means possible, including armed insurrection. There was a division of opinion between Liebknecht and Luxemburg on the one hand, and the majority of the Spartacist following on the other, on the question of advisability of participating in the elections to the National Assembly. The party leaders urged participation because, they held, the tribune of the assembly could be utilized as a vehicle for revolutionary propaganda, but they were overruled by a vote of 62 to 32. But both factions agreed that "the chief action is to be on the streets" and not in the parliaments. The Ebert government was to be harassed and undermined at every step, and all means, including armed insurrection, were to be used to bring about its downfall. A Spartacist manifesto of December, 1918, proclaimed:

The rule of the working class is to be realized only through the path of an armed workers' revolution. The Communists are its vanguard. . . . The National Assembly that is being prepared by the present government will become an organ of the counter-revolutionists to crush the workers' revolution. All means must be used to prevent it from coming into being.[50]

With a naïve belief that the process of history was working for them and that speedy world revolution was soon to be realized, the Spartacists began a policy of strikes, riots, street fighting, insurrections, which made the danger from the left the severest and most critical problem for the new revolutionary régime. This policy and tactics, incidentally, became the model for the strategy of the mass counter-revolution that later came from the right. The Spartacist tactics of revolt was a policy of catastrophe which drove the Majority Socialists into the arms of the reactionary militarists, which confused and divided the progressive elements of the population, which prevented the consolidation of democratic rule in republican Germany, and which contributed considerably to the brutalization of German political life.*

The Spartacists represented at the time but a tiny fraction of the German workers. The great masses of the working population of the Reich were divided between the two other Socialist parties, with the Majority Socialists counting the largest following. But the Spartacists could always count on two things: (1) in a period of distress and want they could count on support from large elements of those disaffected at the time, and (2) they could always count on considerable support from the Independent Socialists. The U.S.D.P. in a sense bears the historical responsibility for making possible the growth and development of the Spartacists into the large Communist party of Germany. Had the Independents joined with the Majority Socialists to form one united party and had both groups car-

---

* "There are radicals now," wrote Ernst Toller in prison in 1921, "who, for the sake of a phrase, sacrifice the blood of the workers as they did in the April days in Munich, when they called on them to fight on the barricades, a fight that had no sense and no prospect of success, because 'bloody defeat' helps the proletariat to reach maturity and because 'to negotiate' is treason" (E. Toller, *Letters from Prison* [London, 1936], p. 97).

ried out a decisive social and political policy, then one may safely say that the Spartacists would never have amounted to more than a tiny political faction. The ambiguous role of the U.S.D.P., and its constant attacks upon the government of the Majority Socialists, created an atmosphere favorable for the tactics of the Spartacists even in circles that were not Communist. Both the Spartacist policy of civil war and the Independents' equivocal position are revealed in the lamentable record of political strikes and armed insurrections that beset Germany between December, 1918, and June, 1919.

The disturbances, strikes, or insurrections, as the case may be, involved in some instances legitimate grievances by sailors, soldiers, or workers. In almost all cases a large share of the violence was caused by undisciplined and irresponsible elements. Nor did the Majority Socialists do all they could to reassure the disaffected elements or the country at large of either resolute intention to carry out a plan of social and economic reform or of their complete break with the forces of the old order. But, with all that, it was the Spartacists who carried on agitation of the wildest character and favored a spirit of civil war, and it was the large elements of Independents and even bourgeois progressives who seemed to be engaged in rivalry with the Spartacists as to who was more revolutionary, and who gave them support in the cause of either world revolution or of social progress, who were chiefly to blame for the virtual civil war that began with the outbreak in Berlin on December 6 and continued throughout the Reich for the succeeding six months. Involved to a degree which cannot be established clearly and definitely, but the reality of which is indisputable, were also the support and help which came both from Bolshevik agents and from the Russian treasury.

Friday, December 6, 1918, was the first of the "bloody days of the revolution." A minor action by rightist soldiers led to a counter mass demonstration by Spartacists, and ensuing excitement and bloodshed resulted in 16 dead and 12 seriously injured. A much more serious and violent outbreak occurred on December 23 and 24 when the sailors of the Volksmarine Division carried out a *Putsch,* occupied the Marstall and Schloss in the capital as well as the *Vorwärts* building, and held the Socialist commandant of Berlin, Otto Wels, as prisoner. This action led to several days of bloody fighting between the radicals and the government troops, caused death and serious injury to scores of persons and was the immediate cause for the resignation of the three Independent Socialist ministers from the government.[51] Haase, Dittmann, and Barth were replaced by the Majority Socialists Noske and Rudolf Wissel, and the period of joint Socialist rule came to an end.

The tension between the Independent Socialist ministers and the Majority Socialists in the cabinet had been one of long standing. Their resignation from the cabinet on December 29th, for the alleged reason that they could not go along with the rest of the cabinet in sanctioning the "blood bath" of December 23–24, was only the climax of long-standing conflict. Haase and Barth have written that they were on the point of resigning on several occasions before this. The chief source of trouble revolved around the actions of the Majority Socialists in vesting too much confidence in the old military leaders and in the attempt made by the government to retain some of the old military divisions to fight against the Poles in the east and in the Baltic area against the Bolsheviks. The real trouble, however, was that the three U.S.D.P. ministers could never count on whole-hearted support for a policy of Socialist coalition within their own party. They were being continuously pressed to radical policies by the increased activities of Liebknecht and his followers, by the echo which these activities found in the left wing of the U.S.D.P., and by the continuous call for a break with the "traitors to the revolution" and the "blood hounds." * The resulting resignation of the Independent Socialist ministers was a serious blow to the revolution in that it weakened the new republic before the outside world by removing from power the very elements that stood for a complete break with imperial Germany. Internally it helped to increase the mistrust of the government by the more radical elements. It was, as Bernstein calls it, "a fatal capitulation before Spartacus." †

The Spartacist uprising in January, 1919, has aptly been termed by Rudolf Hilferding the "Battle of the Marne" of the German revolution. It was more violent than any of the previous incidents, and also revealed more clearly than the others the patent political designs of the Spartacists.[52] The ostensible cause of trouble in this instance revolved around the ouster of Emil Eichhorn, the police president of Berlin and a left-wing Independent. On January 3, the U.S.D.P. ministers in the Prussian government resigned from the cabinet, following the lead of their colleagues in the Reich cabinet. Eichhorn, anxious to retain hold of the key position as head of the police force in the capital, refused to leave his post. Called upon by Paul Hirsch, the Prussian minister of interior, to explain his obstructionist tactics or resign, Eichhorn declared that he had received

---

* Hugo Haase, after his resignation, gave vent to his resentment against the members of his own party who harassed the Independents in the cabinet, in the *Freiheit* of Jan. 1, 1919, in a piece called "Die erste Phase der Revolution." He also expressed the belief that had the U.S.D.P. not refused to share membership in the Central Council of the Workers' and Soldiers' Council with the Majority Socialists, it would have been the Majority Socialist ministers who would have been forced to resign and the Independents could then have carried on the government alone. They would have removed the old military leaders, carried out complete demobilization, initiated a program of socialization, and carried out a foreign policy in the spirit of international Socialism.

† The resignation of the U.S.D.P. ministers has often been described as having been cleverly maneuvered by Ebert. This view was strengthened by the testimony of General Groener at the *Dolchstoss* trial when he described the manipulations of Ebert as uncommonly clever. This testimony of Groener was later disputed when Scheidemann took the stand in the same trial. (Cf. *Der Dolchstossprozess in München* [Munich, G. Birk, ed. 1925], pp. 223–224, 247.)

his power from the revolution and would hold on to it in the interests of revolution. He was thereupon summarily dismissed by the Prussian government on January 4. This action aroused the heated passions of the left groups. The revolutionary shop stewards, the Berlin U.S.D.P., and the newly organized Communist party joined in a manifesto on January 5 which called the Berlin masses to a monster demonstration in the Siegesalee for that afternoon.

The official Communist party policy adopted at the time did not consider this to be the opportune time to overthrow the government. But at the meeting of the revolutionary shop stewards several reports were presented which claimed that strong military support was available for the radicals. Liebknecht and Wilhelm Pieck thereupon came out for the overthrow of the Ebert-Scheidemann government. The majority voted to take up the struggle against the government until it was overthrown. A revolutionary committee of fifty-three was named, headed by Liebknecht, Ledebour, and Paul Scholze, and manifestoes were printed which proclaimed the overthrow of the government and the establishment of a new revolutionary government headed by the above three. The various newspaper buildings, including the *Vorwärts* building and other public buildings, were occupied by the insurgents. A general strike was proclaimed for January 6. The Majority Socialists countered with a call to their followers to a mass demonstration in the Wilhelmstrasse. Two rival mass demonstrations were thus going on simultaneously. From one side came the cries: "Down with Scheidemann! Down with Ebert! Long live the World Revolution!" The others shouted: "Down with Liebknecht! Down with Spartacus! Long live Democracy! Long live Socialism!" The Central Council of the Workers' and Soldiers' Councils called on all the councils to support the government, and the Executive of the Berlin Workers' Council voted 12 to 2 to support the ouster of Eichhorn. The moderate elements in the U.S.D.P. worked frantically to stop the fighting and restore unity, but to no avail.

The government demanded the full evacuation of all the occupied buildings, but the rebels stubbornly refused to give up the *Vorwärts* building. This was a challenge which no government, aiming not only to achieve stability at home but also engaged in delicate negotiations abroad, could afford to let go unanswered. The insurrection of the radicals had to be met with all the force the government could organize. What forces were there, however, that the government could muster? The tragedy of the German revolution lay in the fact that when the democratic elements of the revolution required the necessary force and power to give stability to their rule, they found no such source of military power among their own worker supporters. The pacifist and anti-militarist tradition of the Socialist movement stood in the way of creating a strong republican military force to protect the new régime. After the resignation of the Independent Socialists from the cabinet, the three Majority Socialist ministers published the following plea to their supporters: "If you burden us with responsibility you must do more: You must create power for us! There can be no government without power! Without power we cannot carry out your mandate! . . . Do you want the German Socialist Republic? . . . Then help us create a people's force for the government that will be able to protect its dignity, its freedom of decision and its activity against assaults and putsches. . . . A government . . . that cannot assert itself has also no right to existence." [53]

The response from the followers of the Majority Socialists and from the democratic bourgeoisie was weak and ineffectual. When military force was needed, the Majority Socialist government had to seek allies among the militarist circles of the old officer caste and the old army. The government decided to entrust Noske with the obligation to restore order. Noske, fully aware of the ominous character of his task, declared: "Someone must become the bloodhound! I cannot evade the responsibility." He became governor general of Berlin, and established his headquarters in Dahlem, a suburb of Berlin. He secured the co-operation of several old-régime generals—von Lüttwitz, von Wissel, von Roeder, von Maercker, Max Hoffmann, and von Held—and recruited and drilled several thousand soldiers and officers. On the night of January 10 he marched on the center of the city. The buildings held by the rebels were stormed in several days of bitter fighting. The troops that rallied to the government were full of bitterness and scorn for the rebels and did not bother too often to discriminate between the different political tendencies. Indiscriminate shooting, brutality, and terrorization were practiced upon the prisoners. Even Karl Kautsky was arrested and held for several hours by a band of soldiers on the charge that he had once been in contact with Rosa Luxemburg. By January 13 the Communist revolt was completely suppressed. Ledebour and several other leaders of the rebels were arrested. Though Liebknecht and Rosa Luxemburg were able to hide out for several days, they were apprehended on the 15th of January. Liebknecht was shot "while trying to escape," and Luxemburg was brutally beaten down and her body thrown into the Landwehrkanal, from which it was not recovered until May 31.

The *Manchester Guardian*'s correspondent in Berlin thus described the situation in Berlin on the 15th of January 1919:

The formidable military machine, which seemed to be crushed for ever, has risen again with astounding rapidity. Prussian officers are stalking the streets of Berlin, soldiers marching, shouting and shooting at their command. Indeed Ebert and Scheidemann very likely got more than they bargained for. Already there are signs that the newly-risen military system is disposed to take the law into its own hands and it remains to be seen how long it will be content to remain the instrument of the present government. The coalition between

Government, Socialists, the middle classes, Pan-Germans, and militarists is for the moment perfect, and Germany is now under the control of the same elements which applauded and carried on the war. They have crushed, or are in a fair way of crushing, the political sections which combatted the German war party for years. It is a fact which will scarcely fail to affect Germany's international position at the present juncture. At the same time there is no reason at all to believe that the Government's military victory will make for internal peace, order and stability. Everything points to the contrary.

Events of the next months were to prove that this prognostication was in most respects true.

The election to the National Assembly and the convocation of the Assembly on February 6 were the signals for a new wave of strikes and disorders. The Spartacists and left Independents, bitterly hostile to the idea of a National Assembly in the first place and aroused all the more by the anti-radical complexion of the elected membership of the Assembly, were determined to prevent its work from being completed. The stabilization of the country into a democratic republic would mean an end to their dream of a proletarian dictatorship in Germany and world revolution at large. Under the slogan of "All Power to the Soviets" instead of to the Assembly, a widespread series of strikes was fomented by Spartacists in all the industrial regions in Germany. In Baden, Württemberg, Leipzig, Halle, and Braunschweig, in the Ruhr, in Magdeburg, Munich, Berlin, and Hamburg, there were outbreaks of street fighting and attempts to proclaim soviet republics.

The Communist daily in Berlin, the *Rote Fahne,* on February 27, carried a full front headline "The Wave of Strikes in Central Germany"; the following day came the big lead story on "The Increased Flood of Strikes," which proclaimed: "The National Assembly declares war on the power of the Councils; the general strike declares war on the National Assembly." On March 1 the *Rote Fahne* put forth the slogan: "Ebert-Scheidemann or Revolution! Victory or Death!" and the following day it proclaimed "The Second Revolution," which was to be fought out not in the halls of parliaments but in the factories. It coupled this with a savage attack on the U.S.D.P. for its wavering, and thus goaded on the leftist elements in the U.S.D.P. to more radical action.

The purely political character of this strike movement was revealed in the strike call issued to the workers of Berlin on March 3 by the combined Communist agencies of the general party and of the Berlin organization. The proletariat, it stated, must complete the work of the revolution, and the general strike is the weapon with which to administer the final blow to the mortally wounded capitalists. "The revolution can only advance over the graves of the Majority Social Democrats." "Down with Ebert, Scheidemann, Noske! Down with the Traitors! Down with the National Assembly! All Power to the Workers' Soviets!" The specific demands put forth were: (1) the election of workers' councils to take over control of all factories, (2) the removal of the *Soldateska* and the transfer of police power to the soviets, (3) the dissolution of the officers' groups and the creation of a Red Guard, (4) the liberation of all political prisoners and the setting up of a revolutionary tribunal which was to bring to trial all the war criminals, including Ebert, Scheidemann, and Noske, and (5) immediate peace with Russia and resumption of diplomatic relations.

These political demands in a modified form (for example, the elimination of the names of Ebert, Scheidemann, and Noske from the list of war criminals) were adopted by the Executive Council of the Workers' and Soldiers' Council of Greater Berlin and made the basis for a call for a general strike by all the workers of Berlin. The Majority Socialist representatives either voted against the strike or abstained, but when the strike call was issued they found themselves forced to join the strike committees. Such a state of tension had been created, and so marked was the "rivalry of radicalism," that all the labor leaders in Berlin were terrorized into joining the strike. It was only when the strike committee decided to shut down all water, light, and power in the city, bringing serious danger to the health and life of all the people in the city, that the Majority Socialist trade-union leaders resigned from the strike committee. For five days Berlin was in the throes of anarchy, wild disorder, street battles, and a complete paralysis of normal economic activity. There were exaggerated rumors of brutal treatment of prisoners, particularly in Lichtenberg, which led Noske to proclaim a state of siege and martial law. Negotiations were carried on between the more moderate elements among the strike leaders and the National Assembly in Weimar, but it was Noske's military formations that decided the issue here as in January. By March 8 the strike leaders saw that further fighting was useless and they capitulated and called off the strike. The radical Spartacists, however, continued to battle the government troops, and fighting went on for several more days. It was not until March 17 that martial law was lifted. About 1,200 persons had lost their lives in the fighting, and another tragic victory was chalked up for the Majority Socialists.[54]

5. CIVIL WAR IN BAVARIA

Events in Bavaria took an even more tragic and crucial turn. The elections to the Bavarian Landtag on January 12 and February 2 had resulted in the decisive defeat of Kurt Eisner and his Independent Socialist party. The Bavarian voters returned 66 deputies for the Bavarian Volkspartei, 9 for the Nationalists, 16 for the Peasant League, 25 for the Bavarian Democratic party, 61 for the Majority Socialists, and only 3 for the governing U.S.D.P. There was speculation as to what Kurt Eisner would do. His political opponents, accusing him of vain ambition to cling to power at all costs, believed that he would not turn over the government to the new majority but would establish himself as political dictator. A statement later published by his colleagues Jaffè and Frauendorfer, however, declared that Eisner, at a cabinet meeting on February 20, had announced his intention to submit the government's resignation to the Landtag, and the convening of the Landtag was announced for February 21.

What Eisner's intentions were may also be gathered from several speeches he made to the Workers' and Soldiers' Council during these weeks. As a convinced adherent of political democracy he felt bound to lay down his office to the newly elected Landtag. But he intended, no doubt, to use the Workers' and Soldiers' Council as the vehicle whereby to continue to exercise influence over the course of events and with which to force the new government to carry out social and economic reform. The councils, he declared on January 14, must be the instrumentalities to force through the nationalization of industry. He declared his intention to resist any decrease in the power of the councils. "I stand and fall," he told the Executive Committee of the Bavarian Workers' and Soldiers' Councils on January 15, "with the maintenance or abolition of the Councils." And in the last public speech he delivered, on February 20, he indicated clearly that he entertained no ideas of violent insurrection. "We have shown thus far in Bavaria, that we have secured the revolution by reason and calm and determination. There shall not be any civil war here. But in the same way there shall not be any counter-revolution."

The bourgeois majority [he continued] shall now carry on a bourgeois policy. We shall see if it is capable of governing. At the same time, however, the councils should do their work and build the new democracy. Then perhaps the new spirit will also come to Bavaria. I yearn for the time when the Socialists, irrespective of what faction they belong to, will finally cease governing and once more become the opposition. . . . Tomorrow the Landtag begins, tomorrow also the activity of the councils shall begin anew and then we shall see where the palpitations of a society doomed to death are to be found.[55]

On the 21st of February, at about 9:30 A.M., as he was about to set out for the session of the Landtag, Kurt Eisner was shot down by Count Arco, a young student who was infused with all the reactionary venom that had been let loose against the radical prime minister. The Landtag members were thrown into consternation by this political murder, and an anarchical situation was further created by the attempted assassination of Erhard Auer, the Majority Socialist leader, in the hall of the Landtag by a follower of Eisner's. There was no question now of carrying on the sessions of the Landtag. Anarchy and street fighting set in. A coalition cabinet was later formed under the head of Johannes Hoffmann, Majority

Socialist, but at the advice of the Berlin government it withdrew to Nürnberg in northern Bavaria.

In Munich two radical groups vied with each other for control. The first, led by a group of Independent Socialists, young littérateurs who, with fanatical idealism, were resolved to remake the world into a paradise of perfect justice and equality, who were theoretically quite ready to use force to accomplish their ends, but who did not understand the political realities of the distribution of force and who, with their ethical and esthetic sensibilities, actually shrank from the use of force when confronted with a concrete situation which demanded it. Ernst Toller, by that time already recognized as one of the most talented poets and playwrights, described by Professor Weber as "a man of absolute purity of motives, combined with an uncommon sense of unreality and lack of knowledge of political and economic realities, a man whom only God's wrath could have turned to politics"; Gustav Landauer, a philosophical anarchist and an independent and unique ethical thinker; Erich Mühsam, a young poet and playwright who left the Communists to join this group; Ernst Niekisch, an unstable Majority Socialist who subsequently went through the gamut of National Bolshevist, National Socialist, and anti-Nazi—these were the men who decided to carry on the work of Kurt Eisner and who, on April 7, proclaimed the Soviet Republic of Bavaria. The newly created Hungarian Soviet Republic acted as a spur to this movement. Now the world revolution was really on the march, and not restricted merely to Russia. The Bavarian Soviet Republic proclaimed its solidarity with the Russian and Hungarian soviets and voiced its determined opposition to the Ebert-Scheidemann government.

The official Communist party in Bavaria, however, had no use for the revolutionary idealists of the U.S.D.P. Led by hardened Spartacists Max Levien, the Russian Jew Eugen Leviné, and the sailor Rudolf Eglhofer, the Bavarian K.P.D. proclaimed its own soviet government on April 9. Bavaria thus had three rival governments.

The Hoffmann government, as was the case in Berlin, was forced to call upon nationalist officers from both outside and inside Bavaria in order to assert its sovereignty. The Freikorps, headed by Ritter von Epp, and federal troops marched into Munich to restore order. Savage fighting raged for several days. The story of the brutalities committed by both sides during this civil war is one of the saddest pages in German history before the advent of the Nazis. Indiscriminate shooting of hostages and civilians, brutal treatment of prisoners, summary executions, and other forms of violence fill the authentic records of the events of these weeks. Between April 30 and May 8, according to official figures, 557 persons were killed. The government troops asserted their mastery over the city of Munich. Levien and Leviné were condemned to death, Gustav Landauer was brutally beaten to death, and Ernst Toller and other leaders were sentenced to long prison terms.[56]

The civil war in Bavaria had fatal consequences for the subsequent history of the German Republic. The defeat of the radicals turned the young and more irresponsible circles in Munich towards the nationalist camp. Munich, the center of Bohemian littérateurs and radicals under the monarchy, became the breeding ground of all sorts of Bohemian nationalists and militaristic adventurers. The relatively large number of Jews among the leaders of the soviet republics gave, not justification, but a rationalized basis for otherwise latent antisemitic feeling. Out of this combination came the first beginnings of the National Socialist movement. And the political terror practiced during this period in Bavaria was a paradigm and a rehearsal for the atrocities committed later by the Nazis.*

The suppression of the insurrections in Bavaria, as well as in the rest of the Reich, by the alliance between the Majority Socialists and the old military groups has given rise to one of the most controversial problems in the story of the German revolution. The history of this alliance goes back to the working agreement between Ebert and General Groener, on November 9, 1918. The aim of this alliance, in the words of General Groener, "was to combat the revolution without reservation, to re-establish a lawful government, to lend this government armed support and to convene a National Assembly as soon as possible." General Groener, and other officers and military men who have presented their versions of this alliance, have always exhibited great glee in describing the dependence of the Socialists on the old officer caste, and they have no doubt exaggerated the character of the agreement.†

Ebert's aim was not "to combat the revolution" but to combat Bolshe-

---

* The brutalization of German political life at this time is one of the curiously unexplainable aspects of the German revolution. Where did such brutality come from to a people who had a reputation for discipline and order and whose history lacked any such manifestations since the time of the Peasants' War? How were such cruel and unrestrained outbursts of political passion possible in a country described by Heine as a *"fromme Kinderstube und keine römische Mördergrube?"* The brutalization of life and the breakdown of ethical and moral standards brought about by the World War undoubtedly played its role. The influence of Communist terror was already a factor. But neither of these reasons seems altogether satisfying. A detailed psychological and historical investigation of this problem would be of the greatest importance.

† Together with the testimony of General Groener at the *Dolchstoss* trial, the following extract from General Maercker has frequently been used by the radical opponents of Ebert and Noske: "On April 1 [1919] the People's Representatives, Ebert and Noske, came at my request to the camp in Zossen to address the troops. They were pleasantly surprised to see once again 'real soldiers.' When they saw the troops move in from all sides with beating of drums and in smart, disciplined formation, Noske leaned over to Ebert, slapped him on the shoulders and said: 'You may feel reassured, everything will turn out all right again.'" Maercker adds the comment: "A sign of the pressure under which the government found itself at the time" (*Vom Kaiserheer zur Reichswehr*, p. 64). Count zu Eulenburg also testified that General von Wrisberg had told him that Ebert called him on Dec. 25-26, 1918, and begged him: "For God's sake send us officers, or else we are lost" (*Die Ursachen . . .* , v, 200).

vism.* But in pursuing this aim Ebert and Noske came to rely heavily
on the old-line soldiers. There had always been a direct secret telephone
connection between the chancellor's office and the office of the Supreme
Command. When Ebert moved into the chancellery he used this line to
confer with Groener every evening. Whether this meant, as Volkmann
describes it, that "Ebert took off the iron mask he carried all day, opened
up to Groener and received from him encouragement and comfort," [57]
and, as Emil Barth describes him, that he came back to the cabinet meetings more cocky and self-assured after these secret conversations, is difficult to establish. The private line was most convenient to Ebert and his
colleagues on December 23, when they were locked up by the revolt of
the sailors and this was the only way in which Ebert was able to summon help for the government.

Be that as it may, Ebert and Noske came to rely for the support of the
government upon the monarchist soldiers and officers who were interested
not in saving the republic but in preserving a military framework on
which to create a revived military machine in the future. The chaotic
conditions in the east and in the Baltic, where Polish and German nationalism confronted each other and where the armed struggle against
Bolshevist troops was carried on, led also to the organization of various
types of military formations. These volunteer corps, or *Freikorps,* became
the centers for military adventurers, reactionary officers, chauvinist nationalists, and designing generals who laid their plans for a future comeback. Organized to protect the revolution against insurrection from the
left, they became the spearheads of the counter-revolution and the sources
from which came eventually the gravediggers of the Weimar Republic.[58]
Ebert, Noske, and the Majority Socialists certainly did not have this ultimate objective in mind. Nor did they realize the brutalities and terroristic
acts committed by many of these officers. They were horrified by the
brutal murder of Liebknecht and Luxemburg and by the assassination of
Eisner. They publicly branded these incidents as "acts of lynch justice"
which "disgrace the German people" and "to be morally condemned by
everyone, no matter on what side he may be." Noske frankly admitted
that his government troops had been guilty of excesses. Nor can it be said
that Noske exulted in his sense of military power. Every act of repression
that he ordered was forced upon him by a putschist or insurrectionary act
of the Spartacists. He spurned all overtures made to him from various
channels to become "the man of the hour" and make himself military

---

* The interpretation of Ebert and Noske propagated by official Communist literature
has unfortunately been assimilated by too many bourgeois academic historians. Thus Clark
calls Ebert "the sabotager-in-chief of the revolution," and speaks of the murder of
Liebknecht and Luxemburg as "a murder which to their shame the government condoned" (*The Fall of the German Republic,* pp. 47–53). Knight-Patterson writes: "Noske
was determined to drown the revolution in blood," and "He and Ebert were the principal grave diggers of the Revolution" (*Germany, from Defeat to Conquest,* p. 230).
Such statements are over-simplifications of complex problems and are untrue.

dictator.[59] What he did was always carried out on instructions from and with the consent of the government.

The Majority Socialists, however, were still so much the "prisoners of August 4" that they were not sufficiently sensitive to the grave dangers of an alliance with the militarists. Their national patriotism was so embedded in their consciousness that it led them to place far too great trust in the old generals, and not only to use them for the necessary purposes of the government but also to give them credit for purer motives and higher ideals than they merited. It was this unrealistic appraisal of the continued *esprit de corps* of the officer caste that led the Socialists to turn over the murderers of Liebknecht and Luxemburg to be tried by their own fellow officers and as a result to get off with light sentences and then be aided to escape. Similar incidents occurred with the murderers of Gustav Landauer and other radicals. This only caused further intensification of the mistrust of the new government by anti-militarist circles at home and by public opinion abroad.

CHAPTER XV

The Weimar National Assembly

*Eine Republik zu bauen aus den Materialen einer niedergerissenen
Monarchie, ist freilich ein schweres Problem. Es geht nicht, ohne
bis erst jeder Stein anders gehauen ist, und dazu gehört Zeit.*

GEORG CHRISTOPH LICHTENBERG

The hopes of the majority of the German people to achieve political stability were pinned on the convocation of the National Assembly. The promise to convene such an assembly had been made on the first day of the revolution. There were, however, serious differences of opinion as to when it should be called together. Conservative and bourgeois liberal circles kept reminding the revolutionary government of its promise to leave all final decisions on form of government to a national constituent assembly, and they pressed for its immediate convocation.

The Majority Socialists favored an early convening of the constituent assembly. Several motivations entered into their thinking. Some Socialists argued that early elections would still be under the impact of the events of the revolution and that therefore the reactionary parties would still be discredited and the Socialists would ride into a majority on the crest of the revolutionary wave of November. There was also an uneasy wariness of responsibility which weighed on the Majority Socialists. They had no zest for political power or leadership and they wanted a representation of the people to free them from this sole responsibility for the welfare of the state. Above all, however, there was the long-standing, almost stubborn and dogmatic faith in the "will of the people" and in majority rule, which led them to press for an early poll of the people's will in order to guide them in making the final decisions on the basic problems confronting the country.

The Independent Socialists, on the other hand, advocated postponement of the elections until there was greater certainty that the revolution had actually triumphed and that public sentiment had been adequately conditioned toward the full acceptance of the revolution. Kurt Eisner expressed the sentiments of this group when he declared: "I am opposed to

392

a too early convocation of the National Assembly. . . . We need time before the National Assembly is called to enlighten the people because they have been misled for so many years." [1] Richard Müller declared on November 16: "We want not a bourgeois republic but a proletarian republic. . . . The political instruments of power are today in the hands of the workers and soldiers. They must not give up this power. Were we to convene the National Assembly at this time that would mean a death sentence to the Workers' and Soldiers' Councils. . . . We must assert our power, and if impossible in any other way, then with force. Whoever wants the National Assembly forces a struggle upon us. . . . The National Assembly is the road to the rule of the bourgeoisie, is the road to battle; the road to the National Assembly will go over my dead body." [2]

Under pressure from the Majority Socialists, the Congress of Soldiers' and Workers' Councils set the date for elections to the Assembly for January 19, 1919. All Germans over twenty years of age were eligible to vote, and for the first time German women were to participate on equal terms with the males. A total of 423 deputies was to be elected *—one deputy for every 150,000 persons—and proportional representation was adopted for the various parties.

Most of the old political parties were reconstituted under new names. Only the Majority Socialists and the Independent Socialists continued under their original labels. The Conservatives and Free Conservatives reconstituted themselves on November 24, 1918, as the Deutschnationale Volkspartei. At the first party conference, von Kardorff, the Conservative leader, proclaimed the party as "a new party" which rejects "all responsibility for the past." He declared that the new party will co-operate with whatever form of government will provide "stability, law and order," but he expressed the hope that the hour would come again when the German people would turn to the monarchical principle. *Weltpolitik* was specifically given up, and a recognition of the pressure for social and economic reform was indicated by the declaration that they would "agree to the socialization of the big industries if productive capacity would not suffer thereby." The revolution, however, was denounced as the "greatest crime" perpetrated against the German people. In their election campaign the Deutschnationale Volkspartei placed chief emphasis on racialism (*Volkstum*), on orthodox Christian teaching, private property, and equality for Germany in foreign relations.[3]

The old National Liberal party was reorganized on November 23 as the Deutsche Volkspartei. It proclaimed its adherence to "democratic, universal, equal and secret suffrage for both sexes," but carefully avoided committing itself to the ideal of a republic. Insistence on economic indi-

---

* This number includes two deputies elected by the soldiers on the eastern front, both Social Democrats, and does not include the 12 deputies provided by the Assembly for Alsace-Lorraine.

vidualism and free enterprise and on a nationalist policy at home and abroad were the chief lines of their election campaign.

The most progressive of the bourgeois parties was the newly formed German Democratic party, organized on November 20, 1918. It was constituted chiefly of the old Progressives, joined by a small group of the left wing of the National Liberals and by a large contingent of liberal intellectuals and persons from the academic world whose monarchist loyalties had been shaken by the events of 1914–1918. It was the party most committed to the ideals of a democratic republic, and it made its appeal largely to those in Germany who were truly democratic and socially minded but who rejected all notions of a class party, as represented by the two Socialist parties. These circles wanted a democratic republic and a "state of social justice." The peculiar combination of political democracy, of a modified *laissez faire* to allow for a wide program of social legislation, and of deep-seated nationalism, which characterized the later thinking of Friedrich Naumann, was integrated into the program of the Democratic party.[4]

The old Catholic Center party changed its name for a short while to the Christliche Volkspartei and then reverted to its older designation. It centered its election campaign upon attacks on the Social Democrats as a class party and as a threat to the educational and social interests of the Catholic population. The attitude of its leaders toward the revolution was perhaps most accurately stated by Deputy Gröber in the National Assembly on February 13, 1919. Gröber declared that the members of his party could not recognize the revolution as being either an inner necessity or as favorable to the development of political conditions in Germany. The reforms of Prince Max of Baden, he held, had achieved all that was required, and a republic was not essential for the guarantee of democratic rights. Nevertheless the Centrists, after all that had taken place, would take their stand on the basis of the existing facts and recognize the full consequences of the situation. They conceded that the democratic republic was "the only possible vehicle with which to get out of the chaos of the revolution."

The two Socialist parties carried on their election campaigns in the light of the differences that had developed between them as described above. The Communists, against the counsel of both Rosa Luxemburg and Karl Liebknecht, decided to boycott the elections to the National Assembly.

The elections took place on January 19 without incident. Out of 36 million eligible voters, over 30 million, or 83 per cent, went to the polls. The result of the balloting was a blow to the Socialist aspirations of the two parties that had taken the lead in the revolution. The bourgeois parties received a majority of the votes cast, and the period of exclusive Socialist control of affairs came to an end. The official election results were as follows·

Nationalists	3,121,500 votes	44 deputies
People's party	1,345,600 "	19 "
Centrists (including Bavaria)	5,980,200 "	91 "
Majority Socialists	11,509,100 "	165 "
U.S.D.P.	2,317,300 "	22 "
Democratic party	5,641,800 "	75 "
Miscellaneous	484,800 "	7 "

The National Assembly was convened at 3:15 P.M. on February 6 in Weimar with what Georg Bernhard called a *"Thron Rede"* by Friedrich Ebert.[5] Weimar had been selected as the place of meeting, and not Berlin, because Berlin, as the center of the Prussian state, was the symbol of Prussian hegemony. *"Los von Berlin"* was a cry that resounded throughout many parts of southern and western Germany at that time. Weimar, as the home of the classical humanistic tradition of Goethe and Schiller, seemed to be a fit place to set a new tone for republican Germany. A more important reason, however, was that Berlin was a center of radical insurrection. In Weimar, protected by the divisions of General Maercker, the Assembly would not run the risk of being subjected to violent intrusion by militant soldiers, sailors, and workers.

In composition the Weimar Assembly differed profoundly from the Paulskirche Assembly of 1848. This was not an assembly of the cultural and scientific notables of the land as had been the case in 1848. Only one poet, Wilhelm Vershofen, was a member. With a tradition of political parties since 1867, the Weimar Assembly was made up chiefly of party leaders, and party and trade-union functionaries. In cultural and intellectual breadth it was far below the level of the Paulskirche, but it more than made up for this in political maturity, experience, and efficiency.[6]

Three main tasks confronted the 423 deputies of the National Assembly: (1) the creation of a "legal" government, (2) the making of peace, and (3) the writing of a constitution for the new republic.

The Central Council of Workers' and Soldiers' Councils, the repository of political power emanating from the revolution, turned over its powers to the National Assembly. The Assembly first proceeded to designate a chief of state. Friedrich Ebert, by a vote of 277 out of 379 present, was elected to the post of Reich President. His office as head of the cabinet was then left vacant, and a new prime minister had to be named. The cabinet, if it were to rest on the confidence of the majority of the Assembly, could no longer be exclusively of Social Democrats. The Majority Socialists had to form a coalition with the other parties. On February 5 the Majority Socialists, despite the bitter feelings that had developed since December 29, addressed an invitation to the Independent Socialists to join with them to form a government on the condition that they accept parliamentary democracy and give up any idea of a *coup d'état*. This offer was rejected by the U.S.D.P. The Majority Socialists were thereupon forced to find allies in the Centrist and Democratic parties.[7] A coalition cabinet was formed by Philipp Scheidemann in which half the ministers were members of his party and the other half representatives of the two other parties. It was the coalition of these forces that became the mainstay of the Weimar Republic.

The armistice terms and the terms of the subsequent peace treaty aroused widespread reaction in Germany, ranging from stupefaction on the left to bitter nationalist resentment on the center and right. Even the Independents and pacifists, who had opposed the imperial war policy, were overwhelmed by the severity of the terms and the even more severe manner in which the terms were imposed. There had been a widespread feeling that the change of régime in Germany would elicit from the Entente a favorable attitude toward the defeated nation and that Germany would be received as a penitent partner in the new world community. Unfortunately the rest of the world, France in particular, could not be relieved of its apprehensions and was not sufficiently impressed by the changes in the régime. The persistence of nationalist and militarist evidences in Germany was only too apparent to an outside observer. But the Allies, on their side, made it doubly difficult for the anti-militarist and democratic forces in Germany to make headway. The continued occupation of German territory, the retention of German war prisoners, the rampant nationalist and militaristic behavior of the Poles in the east, and above all the continued maintenance of the naval blockade, which caused widespread and needless suffering and want, were the principal sources of resentment which united almost all the factions of Germany into an elemental popular wave of indignation against the *Gewaltfrieden.*

This unity of national sentiment was demonstrated with passionate vehemence in the session of the National Assembly on May 12, which was transferred from Weimar to Berlin. Prime Minister Scheidemann opened the proceedings with a savage attack on the treaty as a "terrible and murderous *Hexenhammer.*" One party leader after another, including Haase for the Independents, arose to add his denunciation, and the pacifist Professor Quidde, claiming for himself the special moral right to reject the treaty, concluded his address with the words, "No, and a second time, No, and a third time, No!" The president of the Reichstag, Fehrenbach, summed up the session's proceedings in the following words.

The course of today's proceedings is great comfort in these trying times. It is a powerful, united solid demonstration of the entire representation of the German people against the violent peace treaty that they wish to dictate to us. One can hardly speak of different shades, of different moods; no, the mood of all the speakers was equally ardent! This peace we cannot accept.

The session was brought to a close with all the members rising to sing "Deutschland über alles"!

The responsible political leaders, however, were confronted with the hard reality of either accepting the treaty as presented to the German delegation in Versailles or else facing a resumption of the war and invasion of Germany by Allied troops. The Allied powers refused to make any significant concessions to the German pleas and, after several extensions of time, set June 23 as the final date for the Germans to make their decision. Count Brockdorff-Rantzau, the foreign minister and chief of the German delegation, was against acceptance, as was Scheidemann, the head of the government. The Nationalists and the People's party obviously were for rejection. The Democratic party was solidly for rejection too. The Independents, while agreeing that the treaty was severe and unjust, cautioned against a wave of militaristic nationalism that would be set in motion by rejection, that resistance would be futile anyway, and that the only hope for Germany rested with the progress of the world revolution and the eventual liberation of Germany with the help of the Socialist parties in the Entente countries. The Centrists and Majority Socialists were divided on the issue. Erzberger, the Centrist representative on the peace delegation, was for acceptance, as were the Socialist ministers David and Noske. Scheidemann, whose passionate German nationalism reached fervent proportions during this time, declared he could not head a government which would put its signature to such a treaty. In the cabinet 6 ministers were for acceptance of the treaty and 8 for rejection. The cabinet, therefore, submitted its resignation during the night of June 19. Ebert too wished to resign, but was induced by his colleagues to remain in his post. The party caucus of the Majority Socialists, however, decided to vote for acceptance of the treaty. The influence of General Groener at this juncture was decisive. Groener declared to Ebert:

Not as first General Quartermaster, but as a German, who views clearly the total situation, I consider it my duty in this hour . . . to give you the following counsel:
The resumption of the struggle, despite transitory initial success in the east, is in the end result without any prospect of success. The peace treaty with the conditions imposed by the enemy must therefore be signed.[8]

In the Center party there were great indecision and wavering. The appearance of General Groener at the party caucus to assure deputies that the officers would remain at their posts even if the treaty were accepted was decisive in swinging the majority of the Center deputies to acceptance of the treaty. A new coalition cabinet, headed by the Majority Socialist Gustav Bauer, was formed, and it presented its recommendation to the Assembly for acceptance of the treaty just four hours before the expiration of the Allied deadline. "We cannot assume the responsibility," declared Bauer, "of a new war, even if we had the weapons. We are without arms. Without arms, however, does not mean without honor." The vote on the motion: "The National Assembly agrees to the signing of the peace treaty" was 237 for, 138 against, and 5 abstentions. A number of deputies who could not get themselves to vote for the treaty but who did not wish to vote against the position adopted by their parties absented themselves from the session. Representatives of both the Democratic party and the People's party made declarations in which they affirmed their faith in the national loyalty of the deputies who voted for acceptance even though their own parties had rejected the treaty. The Majority Socialist Hermann Müller and the Centrist Dr. Johannes Bell accepted the fateful mission of proceeding to Versailles to sign the treaty in behalf of Germany. The treaty was signed on June 28 and officially ratified by the National Assembly on July 9 by a vote of 209 to 116. The rightist newspapers appeared on June 28 with a black band of mourning on the front page. The pan-German *Deutsche Zeitung* published the following statement on its front page on June 28:

Vengeance! German nation! Today in the Hall of Mirrors of Versailles the disgraceful treaty is being signed. Do not forget it! In the place where, in the glorious year of 1871, the German empire in all its glory had its origin, today German honor is being carried to its grave. Do not forget it! The German people will, with unceasing labor, press forward to reconquer the place among the nations to which it is entitled. Then will come vengeance for the shame of 1919.[9]

The *Vorwärts* wrote: "We do not dream of a bloody revenge like the pan-German fools . . . but we hope and have unshakeable confidence in the triumph of right." The moderate bourgeois press counseled sober acceptance of the hard realities and a slow process of regeneration of Germany and international understanding. "What shall we Germans do on this black day of our history?" wrote the *Kölnische Zeitung* on June 29. "To complain and continue to complain, as it is no doubt human in such an hour? To make accusations, as unfortunately it seems natural to many in our Fatherland now and to search for those guilty in the collapse of the Reich? Or in hard recognition of the facts, irrespective of how they came about, to meet the new times with the most tenacious will to life, for us, for Germany? To us it seems that the latter is the only possible and worthy path." The *Frankfurter Zeitung* in the issue of June 30 wrote editorially: "Germany sees all this with bitter resentment, but we allow it to take place because we must. But we have firm faith in the final judgment of the tribunal of humanity [*Weltgericht*]. This triumph is too cheap, this superiority of the victors too ostentatious and this condemnation of the vanquished too unscrupulous for us Germans not to feel clearly today: it must not and it cannot remain so. We have only one concern; we ask ourselves daily: What is the right way for the German people to awake to a new and vigorous life out of the tribulations of this peace of violence and . . . out of the lethargy of our defeat?"

The question of "to accept or reject" the treaty was definitely decided. From now on the problem took on a new dress, "To fulfill or not fulfill," and in this formulation continued to agitate German political life for the next decade. The deep nationalist resentment around the treaty discussion, however, left a profound mark on the German mentality. The vow not to forget came from all sides. "We vow, today," said the spokesmen for the Majority Socialists, "that we shall never abandon our compatriots who have been torn from us. . . . Unbreakable is the bond which ties us to the Germans in Bohemia, Moravia, and Silesia, in Tyrol, Carinthia, and Styria. In all of us lives the hope that all Germans . . . will soon be united. . . . We protest against the taking away of our colonies. . . . We shall not rest in our zealous task to create . . . the power . . . to renounce this treaty." [10] From now on, too, in the eyes of very many Germans the acceptance of the treaty came to be identified exclusively with the November revolution and the Weimar Constitution. It is from this situation that emerged the slogans of "November criminals," "*Dolchstoss,*" "*Diktat* of Versailles," and the like, which right-nationalist circles were able to hurl with such effectiveness against the political leaders of Weimar.

The National Assembly also proceeded to draft a permanent constitution for the new state.[11] On November 15, 1918, the People's Representatives called Hugo Preuss, an academic authority on constitutional law and a member of the newly founded Democratic party, to become secretary of state of the interior with the chief task of drafting a constitution. The Weimar Constitution, as adopted, is largely due to the work of Preuss. But his original draft was modified considerably by the Constitutional Commission appointed by the Assembly and by the Assembly itself. Preuss's first draft was founded on two basic principles: (1) that of a democratic and parliamentary republic and (2) that of a centralized state (*Einheitsstaat*). The first of these principles remained unchanged; the second, however, met with considerable opposition from the South German states and was therefore modified. Preuss also had no interest in social and economic questions, and he did not include any such provisions in his draft. The pressure of the Socialist deputies, as well as the effect of the insurrections by Spartacists and left Independents, forced the Assembly to incorporate a section into the constitution dealing with economic and labor questions.

The deliberations on the constitution commenced on February 24, and the final draft was passed on July 31, 1919, by a vote of 262 to 75. It came into effect on August 14, 1919.

The Weimar Constitution is a unique document—unique in comparison with the German constitutions of 1849 and 1871 and unique also in comparison with the written constitutions of other nations. It paid obeisance to the older tradition of "fundamental rights," but unlike the German

constitution of 1849 the section on *Grundrechte* was not made the
ideological foundation for the constitution but rather was integrated into
a total relationship with community life, religion, education, and economic
life. The section on "economic life" revealed especially the imprint of
twentieth century social and economic developments. The political
thought underlying the constitution was made up of three basic principles:
the clear conception of the Reich as a state entity, the unitary doctrine,
and the democratic idea.[12] Unlike the constitution of Bismarck, the new
Reich was not a composite of *Länder* or of *Fürsten* but was the entity of
the united nation. Unlike all previous German constitutions, it created a
more centralized and unified state. And it was not a *Kaiserstaat* but a
Volksstaat, a state based on the sovereignty of the people. This constitution was not granted to the German people by the gift of a gracious
monarch. It was the work of the people's representatives. The preamble
of the constitution reads:

> The German people, united in all their branches, inspired by the determina-
> tion to renew and strengthen its Reich in liberty and justice, to preserve
> peace both at home and abroad, and to foster social progress, have adopted the
> following constitution.

The democratic foundations of the constitution were further indicated
in the first article. "The German Reich is a republic. Political authority
derives from the people."

The old problem of *Bundesstaat, Staatenbund,* or *Einheitsstaat,* which
fills the pages of German constitutional history since the beginning of the
nineteenth century, became manifest again in 1919. Preuss was a firm adherent of a centralized and unified state, and his first draft called for
such provisions in the constitution. But the vigorous opposition that
came from Bavaria, Baden, and Württemberg caused the Assembly to
modify the draft by Preuss and to effect a compromise. Most of the local
states were allowed to remain and to retain a good measure of control
over local affairs. But all states were bound by the constitution to be republics with universal suffrage and proportional representation, and the competence of the central government far exceeded the powers of the Reich
government under the monarchy. The military forces were now organized
as an arm of the central government, control over means of communications was vested in the central government, and the Reich now had its
own finances instead of being dependent on the contributions of the local
states. The representation of the separate states as found in the old
Bundesrat was retained in the setting up of a federal council called the
Reichsrat, in which each state had at least one vote and the larger states
had one vote for each million inhabitants (but no state could have more
than two-fifths of all the votes); but the *Reichsrat's* powers were almost
nil. All it had was a suspensory veto on legislation.

The problem of Prussia and the Reich also aroused considerable discussion.[13] Preuss's original draft called for the breaking up of Prussia into several states. Professor Walter Schucking declared in the National Assembly: "Up to 1867 Prussia was against the Reich; from 1867 to 1918 Prussia was above the Reich; the Reich must hereafter be above Prussia." [14] But the final draft left Prussian territorial integrity intact. The special rights of Prussia, of course, were gone. The central position of the Prussian king as the emperor, his appointment of the chancellor, the control of the army and the key position in the Bundesrat—all these powers were eliminated with the adoption of the republican constitution. But Prussia continued to have a preponderant influence by virtue of its size. It numbered four-sevenths of the entire population of the country.

The breaking up of the Austro-Hungarian Empire and the revolution which brought a Socialist government to power there also revived the old *Gross-Deutschland* movement. From both the Austrian and the German sides it was taken for granted that what was impossible in 1848–1849 would now become realized, and an Austria consisting now exclusively of Germans would take its place with the other German *Stämme* in one unified democratic state. The Austrian revolutionary Provisional Assembly had on November 12 declared itself to be a part of the German Republic and had asked the German government to take the necessary action to make this effective. For some unexplained reason the Ebert-Haase government failed to take formal action on the matter. It is open to speculation what the Allied reaction would have been in November, 1918, to a *fait accompli* of a spontaneous union of Austria and Germany. By the following year it was too late. The Austrian government sent Ludo Moritz Hartmann, a distinguished historian, as its emissary to Germany. Professor Hartmann participated in the preparatory work of the National Assembly as well as in the subsequent deliberations. Ebert, in his opening address, declared, "German-Austria must be united with its motherland for all times," and these sentiments were echoed by one speaker after another. Article 61 of the final draft of the constitution read:

German-Austria after its union with the German Reich will receive the right of participation in the Reichsrat with the number of votes corresponding to its population. Until that time the representatives of German-Austria have a deliberative voice.

This article, however, remained a dead letter. On September 2, 1919, the Allied Supreme Council forced the government to strike this article from the constitution as constituting a violation of the boundaries set by the Treaty of Versailles.

The form of government laid down for Germany by the National Assembly was a republic. But the Assembly rejected the name "German Republic" and adopted instead the designation "German Reich." The use of the latter term was defended in the Assembly by Hugo Preuss in the following words:

The word, the thought, the principle of the "Reich" has for us Germans such deeply rooted emotional values that I believe we cannot assume the responsibility of giving up this name. Tradition of centuries, the entire yearning of a divided German people for national unity are bound up with the name "Reich," and we would wound the feelings of wide circles without reason and to no purpose if we gave up this designation.[15]

This indicates the profound desire of the majority of the Assembly to look upon the new régime as a continuation of the tradition of older Germany and not as a sharp break with the past. The Majority Socialists and the Democrats looked to the tradition of 1848, and Ebert in his opening address pointed out that the 9th of November takes up where the 18th of March, 1848, had left off. The parties of the right wished to resume the continuity of tradition of the Hohenzollern monarchy.

The problem of national colors also aroused deep-seated national feeling. On one side were those who wanted the black, red, and gold colors, to resuscitate the tradition of 1848 and also to make it easier for Austria to come in under these colors. On the other side were those who refused to give up the glories associated with the colors black, white, and red of the Bismarckian Reich. A compromise was finally arrived at whereby the national colors were declared to be black, red, and gold, while the merchant flag was to be black, white, and red with the national colors in the upper inside corner.

The political institutions adopted were derived from the parliamentary institutions of the Western European countries and from the structure of the American state. A bicameral legislature was set up consisting of a Reichstag, elected by secret, direct, universal suffrage with proportional representation, and a *Reichsrat,* as the council representing the local states. It was the Reichstag, however, which was the supreme expression of the popular will and the sovereign legislative power. The executive office was vested in a president, elected by popular vote for a term of seven years. His powers were conceived to be more like those of the president of France than of the American presidency. Article 48, which later came to play so crucial a role in the political crisis of the republic, was not intended to put in the hands of the president the powers later used by von Hindenburg. The president was given the power, in the event of sudden disturbances which threaten public safety and order, to restore order by decree and to suspend temporarily the fundamental rights guaranteed by the constitution. These measures, however, were to be rescinded at the demand of the Reichstag. A Supreme Court for the Reich was established after the model of the United States Supreme Court.

The second part of the constitution provided for the guarantee of the fundamental rights of the individual—equality before the law, personal liberties, freedom of movement and freedom of expression—liberty of belief and conscience, separation of church and state, and state supervision of the educational system. A section on economic life was added at the insistence of those who looked to the new republic to blaze a new trail in the realm of social and economic legislation.[16]

The Weimar Assembly brought peace to the country and supplied the nation with a constitution. But the mood in the country was far from stable and satisfied. The Spartacists and left-wing Independents, intent on a Soviet republic instead of a parliamentary democracy, gave vent to their dissatisfaction in the wave of strikes and insurrections described above. But even the more moderate elements of both Socialist parties became more and more disillusioned. True, the eight-hour day had been attained, constitutional right to collective bargaining and rights of labor were guaranteed, and democratic political rights were established throughout the country. But there had been high hopes for more. A Socialization Commission set up by the revolutionary government had aroused hopes that there would be far-reaching changes in the social and economic structure and that the power of the large industrialist combinations as well as of the large feudal landowners would be broken. This commission, however, met with stubborn resistance on the part of the old civil service bureaucracy and received no support from the government. On April 9, 1919, the Socialization Commission, headed by Karl Kautsky, submitted its resignation to the government. In their letter of resignation the members wrote:

We dispute . . . the moral right of a democratic government to deprive the German people of the foundations for an independent position with the antiquated methods of a narrow-minded bureaucracy that believes it incorporates within itself the sum of all wisdom.[17]

Everywhere the Socialist critics saw evidences of the old order still in positions of power and influence—in the civil service, in the judiciary, and especially in the military. "One year," declared Crispien at the U.S.D.P. party congress in Leipzig, "after the November 1918 in which the powers of the past were overthrown, the old forces are again the powers of the present."[18] The revolution had not realized what it had promised. Corroboration for this view was found in the reports of foreign observers, and this in turn served to disturb and discourage this school of Socialists.

The hope [wrote Haase in April, 1919] that the transition from monarchy to republic would win sympathy for Germany abroad has proved to be mistaken. There is no faith in the inner transformation of the German people.
The representatives of the large foreign newspapers, who have lived many

years in Germany before the war and who have now returned here, are unani-- mous in their view that nothing has substantially changed here. They have often summarized their observations in the statement that the officer caste has never made such a great show of themselves as now and that the military spirit has never been revealed in so unpleasant a fashion as at present.[19]

As for the German bourgeoisie, the earlier fears that had driven them into hiding or else into opportunistic support of the Majority Socialists or the Democrats began to ease. They refused to meet the Majority Socialists halfway or to attach themselves wholeheartedly to the republic and to democracy. They now went into opposition at any cost and began to blame all their ills on the Jews. High prices, inflation, the disorder and the dirt of the masses, the din of party campaigning, and the revulsion at walls plastered with election placards, the widespread relaxation of morals and disciplined behavior unloosed by the revolution after four years of tense war conditions, the ever present real and unreal fears of Bolshevism—all these jarred the political and social sensibilities of the hitherto staid and disciplined bourgeoisie. They came to look upon the revolution as the incarnation of danger to all the values they cherished and which they associated with the benevolent paternalism of the Hohenzollerns.

The group of liberal intellectuals who arrived at a rational acceptance of the republic but without the emotional attachment they had hitherto felt for the old régime also were far from satisfied with the progress of events. Von Payer, the leader of the Democratic party, noting the absence of a "festive mood" in the Weimar Assembly as contrasted with the Assembly of 1848, told his fellow deputies on April 10: "The psychical regeneration of the entire people and the spiritual ennobling of the whole people, which so many hoped for and wished would be effected by the revolution—these, alas, have not ensued." [20] The inner weakness of this circle which could have become the political élite of the new Germany is perhaps best expressed in the diary of Friedrich Meinecke. "There among the Right," he wrote, "is will without wisdom; among us there is wisdom, without will, without those men of strong will that we now need. The old deficiency of German liberalism." [21]

A year after the outbreak of the revolution general disillusionment sets in and the yearning for the good old days begins. The militarist and reac- tionary circles, emboldened by the reliance which the republican govern- ment was forced to place on them, begin to assert themselves again. The centers of reaction come to be found in the Deutschnationale Volkspartei, in the People's party, in the organized officers' groups, in the newly estab- lished Reichswehr, among the old officials, and in the urban academic circles. The university students were especially reactionary at this time. Two ideas began to dominate the counter-revolutionary circles. One was antisemitism, which came to blame the Jews for the German collapse, and the other the *Dolchstoss,* or the legend of the invincible and undefeated German army that was brought to ruin only by a traitorous stab in the back from the home front. "If ever anybody should affirm," declared General von Scheuch to a group of homecoming soldiers on December 12, 1918, "that the German army was beaten in this war, history will call it a lie. Let the consciousness of having returned home undefeated never be taken from you!" [22]

Antisemitic manifestations had begun to appear almost from the outbreak of the revolution in the form of anti-Jewish inscriptions on walls, antisemitic leaflets and outbursts of physical violence against persons who seemed to be Jews. Antisemitism was not new in Germany, and it always comes to the surface in periods of political and social crisis. The reasons usually given for it are really not explanations. They merely indicate the irritants that bring to the surface the antisemitic sentiments already present. In 1918–1919 such irritants were to be found in the presence of larger numbers of eastern Jews who had come into Germany during the war, the relatively large representation of Jews among the parties of the revolution, especially in the Bavarian revolutions, and also the instances of Jewish war profiteers that stood out from amidst the much larger number of non-Jewish profiteers. Even in Socialist circles there were expressions of antisemitic resentment against the undue proportion of Jewish leaders.* The situation became so ominous that it was taken up by the Berlin Vollzugsrat, and an appeal to the populace was issued on December 14, 1918, warning against the dangers of pogroms in Germany such as had occurred in Lemberg and other parts of Poland at that time.[23] On July 26, 1919, Haase called the attention of the National Assembly to the increased antisemitic activities in the Reich. He pointed to the activities of organizations like the Ausschuss für Volksaufklärung, the Deutsche Erneuerungsgemeinde, the Deutschvölkische Bund, and the Reichshammerverband, that distribute leaflets in the military barracks and in the railroad stations calling upon the people to destroy the Jews and "to kill all those who have risen up against the divine order." [24] Noske, in replying to Haase, was forced to admit the truth of these charges. He declared that these manifestations were "of extraordinary danger" but that it was most difficult to uncover the sources of agitation. He was doing all he could to eliminate this pest from the armed forces, he said.[25]

Antisemitism combined with militarism came to be the twin poles of the German counter-revolution. Spengler and Moeller van den Bruck be-

---

* The most prominent incident of this character was the appeal "To the German People" signed by Strobel, a Majority Socialist member of the Executive Council of the Workers' and Soldiers' Council, and Hall-Halsen, published in the reactionary *Deutsche Tageszeitung* of December 13, 1918. The authors call upon the German people to realize that they are a people of 70 million Aryans who are being ruled by 60,000 Jews who think "they alone have the claim to intelligence." They point to the fact that 80 per cent of the leaders in the government are Jews, that 99 per cent of the Jews are capitalists, and are, therefore, the supreme enemy of Socialist Democracy. This statement was denounced by the Berlin Vollzugsrat, and Strobel was divested of all his official posts.

gan to provide the "respectable" bourgeois and aristocratic circles with the ideological arsenal with which to combat the revolution. Artur Dinter, Alfred Rosenberg, Anton Drexler, aided by Sudeten Germans like Rudolf Jung, and later with the added prestige and appeal of the racialist movement of Erich and Mathilde Ludendorff, laid the groundwork for the "proletarian" variant from which emerged the National Socialism of Adolf Hitler.

The nationalist counter-movement to the revolution was intensified by the violent upsurge against the terms of the Versailles Treaty. There was revived talk of a combination of defeated Germany with outcast Russia to fight against the imperialism of the West. In proletarian circles this took the form of National Bolshevism.[26] In the Communist movement as well as in right nationalist circles there was talk of such fusion. This was the time when Karl Radek sent out feelers to Moeller van den Bruck for both Germans and Russians to battle against the Treaty of Versailles. Count von Reventlow, at the time the Bolshevik army marched on Warsaw, tried desperately to win over German political leaders to a policy of military and political co-operation between Soviet Russia and Germany. Both Communists and extreme nationalists paid homage to the idealism present among their opponents and expressed the feeling that they had much more in common with each other than with Social Democrats or Democrats. Even the nationalists of the more orthodox variety publicly expressed the possibility of such an alliance coming into being. Professor Eltzbacher, a member of the German Nationalist party, writing in the *Tag* of April 2, 1919, said: "If the Entente do not come to their senses at the twelfth hour, then the future of the German people can be saved only by Bolshevism." [27] Professor Hans Delbrück wrote in the *Preussische Jahrbücher* of April, 1919, that while he abhorred Bolshevism and while reason would dictate a policy of co-operating with the West,

Yet vengeance, hate and the delusions of the Entente threaten to drive us into a path which contradicts all reason and yet appears to be unavoidable. . . . If the Entente will dare to impose conditions upon us which will mean economic and national death for us, then we shall have no other reply but: Very well! then at least you shall go down to the abyss with us.

Here again we have an instance of a continuing pro-Russian orientation which was to bear fruit in the Rapallo agreements made several years later.

The events of the years of war and revolution had also not failed to leave their mark on some of the military circles. The conception of a possible alliance between the military and the workers to replace or to supplement the old union of the military with the bourgeoisie came to occupy the thoughts of younger officers and generals. August 4, 1914, had convinced the military of the fact that the Socialist working masses were not anti-national. The collapse of the monarchy made them realize the power of the working classes. There now developed the idea that if one could bring about a combination of the soldiers and the workers under the authority and discipline of the officers, the cause of German nationalism would be invincible. Out of this trend of thinking came the ideas of Kapp and Lüttwitz, of the young major and later "social general" Schleicher, of Reventlow and the National Socialists, and probably too of Moeller van den Bruck, Spengler, and later Ernst Jünger.

The military and industrialist leaders now felt sufficiently confident to make their first open bid to oust the new government. The old ruling classes, cowed at first by the onset of the revolution, now made confident by the reliance placed upon them by the republic to suppress the insurrections on the left and infuriated by the acceptance of the Versailles Treaty, made the first of a series of attempts to recapture their old positions of power, in the Kapp Putsch of 1920.[28]

As Scheidemann declared in the National Assembly on March 18, "Whoever had not deliberately closed his eyes and ears was able to see coming what we have experienced in the course of the last few days with disgust and anger." The coming storm from the right was headed for an outbreak. Noske, after the acceptance of the Versailles Treaty, tried to calm the officers, but there was a new tone of mistrust apparent. General von Lüttwitz, whom Noske had publicly praised for his loyalty only a few months before in the National Assembly, told Noske with icy frigidness that after what had happened the officer corps had completely lost its confidence in the government. A plot began to be hatched for the overthrow of the government, the chief instigators of which were the intimate of Ludendorff, Colonel Bauer; a retired officer, Major Pabst; the commanding general of Berlin, General Walther von Lüttwitz; and Dr. Wolfgang Kapp of Königsberg, who had been one of the founders of the Vaterlandspartei.

The ringleaders looked for a strong man. They even pleaded with Noske to become the dictator. Major Pabst came to Noske for confidential talks and begged him to take power. He told him that a military dictatorship would be able to endure only if it could rest on the support of a section of the working classes. "It would be a calamity, Herr Minister," said Pabst to Noske, "if the national wave would not find you on the side of the officers." Noske spurned all such suggestions and warned Pabst, as he had warned General Lüttwitz, that the government would brook no interference by the military in politics and that if they pursued a policy of force it would lead to the destruction of the Reich. Pabst and Lüttwitz continued their scheming however. With Colonel Bauer, Kapp, and a journalist named Schnitzler, they organized a National Union to carry on preparations. General von Lüttwitz made efforts to win over influential officers in the army. General von Maercker refused to support the move unless they found a person to head the new government who was more distinguished than Kapp and unless the Majority Socialists and above all Noske would participate in the government.

The immediate cause for the *Putsch* was the order issued by Noske, in pursuance of the demands of the Inter-Allied Military Control Commission, to disband by March 10 the two marine brigades stationed in Döberitz, near Berlin, under the general command of Captain Ehrhardt, notorious Freikorps leader. General von Lüttwitz declared that he would never allow such crack troops to be dissolved. Noske, aware that something was brewing, removed the two divisions from Lüttwitz's command. Lüttwitz now felt that the time had come to act. At a meeting with Ebert and Noske on March 10 Lüttwitz submitted a series of political demands to the government, calling for a strong government and demanding that the marine division remain under his command. Ebert and Noske once again told him sharply that he must not interfere in political matters. Admiral von Trotha was sent by Noske to warn Ehrhardt against rash action and to report back to the cabinet. Trotha returned to report that all was quiet. It later turned out that he himself was one of the plotters. On the night of March 11, 5,000 members of the brigade under Captain Ehrhardt marched through the Brandenburg Gate to occupy Berlin.

The cabinet was hastily convened. "This night," cried Ebert, "means the bankruptcy of my activities and of my confidence in the officer corps." He asked the Reichswehr leaders if they would carry out orders to resist the uprising. Only two officers, General Reinhardt and Major von Gilsa, gave their assurances of such loyalty to the government. For all other officers the crucial question was not the protection of the government but the preservation at all costs of the unity of the officer corps. Under no conditions should officers fire upon fellow officers, said General von Seeckt to Noske. "Obviously there can be no talk of letting Reichswehr fight against Reichswehr. Do you have the intention, Herr Reich Minister, to allow a battle to take place at the Brandenburg Gate between troops that a year and a half ago were fighting shoulder to shoulder against the enemy?" Deeply wounded by this failure of the military, Ebert and the cabinet decided to move to Dresden and to leave the vice chancellor, Schiffer, to deal with the insurgents in Berlin.

The Ehrhardt brigade occupied all government buildings and proclaimed the old government deposed, the National Assembly dissolved, the Weimar Constitution null and void, and a new government headed by Dr. Kapp and General von Lüttwitz in power. The military leaders in Berlin and in eastern Germany declared their adherence to the Kapp government. In western and southern Germany the military proclaimed their loyalty to the Ebert government. In Silesia and in Pomerania the military and bourgeois groups also declared for Kapp. Even those officers, however, who declared themselves for the legal government were only passive supporters. They refused to take any active measures against the rebels. Some, like General von Seeckt, simply returned to their homes and remained out of the public eye.

The collapse of the Kapp Putsch came about as a result of weakness, indecision, and division in the rightist circles and in the insurgent régime, and as a result of the loyal adherence of a large section of the civil service to the Weimar government. Most of all it was due, however, to the overwhelming effectiveness of the resistance of the Berlin workers. Before they left Berlin the Socialist members of the cabinet issued a proclamation to the workers of Berlin for a general strike. The call was supported by the democratic trade-unions. The strike was 100 per cent effective. Railroads, newspapers, communications and all industrial activity was halted and the life of the city was completely paralyzed. It was the last demonstration of the unity of the German working classes in the Weimar period, and it was most effective. After five days of attempted rule under these conditions Kapp gave up and resigned. Lüttwitz was also induced to resign. They burned their papers and fled from Berlin. General von Seeckt was appointed to succeed von Lüttwitz as chief of the Reichswehr.

The National Assembly convened in Stuttgart on March 18 and devoted the session to a discussion of the Kapp Putsch. Scheidemann delivered a bitter attack on the parties of the right and a veiled attack on Noske for having allowed the spread of counter-revolutionary elements in the Reichswehr. The trade-union leaders also demanded the ouster of Noske. Karl Legien proposed the formation of a labor government supported by both Socialist parties and the free trade-unions and Christian trade-unions, but the Independents once again spurned the offer for unity. Ebert, much against his desire, was forced to accept Noske's resignation on March 22, and a new government was formed five days later under the Majority Socialist Hermann Müller.

The Kapp Putsch, regarded by some writers as merely a ludicrous fizzle, was really much more serious and significant. The attack upon the republic from the left had been suppressed. Danger from those sources still continued. But from now on the serious and grave danger was from the right. Kapp and his fellow intriguers had been forced to flee. But the officer corps and the Reichswehr were the victors. General von Seeckt, noncommittal during the *Putsch,* chiefly concerned with the preservation of the structure of the old army, was now made head of the Reichswehr. The officers who took part in the revolt were allowed to escape or else soon amnestied. "The Kapp Putsch and its aftermath were the first step in making the Reichswehr a state within a state."

In Bavaria the Kapp Putsch resulted in the ousting of the Hoffmann government and the coming to power of von Kahr and a rightist coalition government, which provided the setting for the revolt of Hitler and Ludendorff in 1923. The counter-revolution was to make this one more unsuccessful bid for control and then finally succeed ten years later. The Kapp Putsch, the Hitler Putsch of 1923, the wave of political assassinations of republican leaders—all are the prelude to January 30, 1933. And in the elections to the first Reichstag on June 6, the swing to the right was clearly apparent. The revolution had spent its force, and the next ten years would be a story of continuous struggle against the onset from the right and the final overthrow of the system established by the November revolution.

CHAPTER XVI

Republican Politics, 1920-1930

It may be said: Better a Zero than a Nero. Unfortunately the
course of history has shown that behind a Zero lurks always a
future Nero.

THEODOR LESSING

Ever since 1933 the Weimar Republic has too often been treated
merely as a prelude to the Nazi epoch or as an interlude between imperial and Hitlerite Germany.[1] Any stand on this question is intimately
related to one's interpretation of the course of German history. Viewed
in terms of length of duration, the fourteen years of the Weimar Republic
represent but a brief episode in a political history basically at variance
with the trends current during these years. From the standpoint of those
who hope for a future liberal and democratic Germany and who seek to
find support for their hope in the historical past, it is Weimar Germany,
as the heir to the liberal tradition of 1848 which, while inundated by the
holocaust of Nazi revolution in 1933, nevertheless provides the basis for
the future development of a democratic Germany. If such a democratic
Germany is to succeed it must learn from the mistakes of Weimar, but it
must also build upon its ideological foundations. Whatever be its ultimate
place in the long-range perspective of German history, Weimar Germany
none the less deserves proper evaluation in its own right and in terms of
its own accomplishments.

The fundamental fact in the history of the Weimar Republic is one that
has beset and plagued every other liberal movement in German history—
a basic weakness of the forces of liberalism, weakness in numbers as
well as in ideological conviction. In addition it was beset by a combination of domestic and world problems that proved too complex and too
overwhelming for the liberal democratic forces.

It has now become a truism to describe the Weimar régime as a "republic without republicans." The Weimar Constitution was effected by a
coalition of Social Democrats, Catholic Center party, and the bourgeois
democrats who were organized at first as the Democratic party. After

411

the elections of 1920 the Socialists never enjoyed a majority in the Reichstag by themselves. The legend of the "Socialist" republic was invented by the nationalist opponents of the régime, and while it served their political purposes most conveniently it was hardly in keeping with the facts.[2] As a matter of fact the Catholic Center party occupied more of a key position in the politics of the republic than did the Socialists or any other party.

The Catholic Center party, during the republic as before 1918, was not a homogeneous party on any issue but religious affiliation and religious interests. Even the formal unity of the pre-war Center party was broken by the defection of the Bavarian Catholics. The latter found it not to their liking to consort with the Social Democrats as did their co-religionists in the north, and they formed their own Bavarian People's party, which acted independently on many crucial issues. In the national Center party there was also divergence of political orientation. The left wing, led at first by Matthias Erzberger and then by Dr. Joseph Wirth, co-operated wholeheartedly with the republican Socialists and Democrats and was fully dedicated to the democratic ideal. The left wing of the Center party, however, aroused greater mistrust among the other elements in its own party than in the other parties. Dr. Martin Spahn, conservative Centrist leader under the empire, expressed his satisfaction that the leadership of the republic had come into the hands of the Socialist Ebert rather than those of the "unpredictable" and "erratic" Erzberger of his own party. Wirth enjoyed the support of his own party only as long as conditions on the national and international scene favored democracy. When the conservative and nationalist elements in Germany began to reassert themselves and threaten the democratic foundations of the republic, Wirth first found himself forced to resign from the Centrist faction; and later, even when he rejoined his Centrist colleagues, his influence became negligible and leadership passed to the right wing under Monsignor Ludwig Kaas and Heinrich Brüning.

The German Democratic party started out with a galaxy of notables and intellectuals hardly matched by any of the other parties and with a fanfare of political liberalism that attracted several million voters to its banner. Its mass following, however, soon was dissipated under the impact of political and economic crisis and of nationalist agitation on the right. Its two ablest leaders, Max Weber and Friedrich Naumann, died soon after the revolution. As for the others, one by one they left the standard of political democracy to end, as in the case of Dr. Hjalmar Schacht, one of the founders of the Democratic party, as one of the gravediggers of the republic, and as a godfather of the Hitler régime, or, as in the case of Willy Hellpach, Democratic party candidate for the presidency, as a warm supporter of the Hitler régime after it was once established.

The German People's party, anti-republican and monarchist at the start, performed the extraordinary feat of projecting its leader, Dr. Gustav Stresemann, to become not only one of the few great statesmen of the republic but also one who accepted the republic as the best possible régime under the circumstances. Despite Stresemann's own deep inner attachment to the monarchy and to the old order, despite his sympathy for the "cry of German youth for the romantic ideal," there are abundant evidences of Stresemann's sober recognition of the practical necessity to work for the republic. Stresemann, however, never enjoyed the full confidence of his own party. It is a poignant element of personal tragedy in the political biography of this statesman that to the very last moments of his life his most taxing and most exasperating conflicts were with the members and leaders of his own party.

The Social Democratic party had originally assumed the largest measure of initiative and responsibility for the establishment of the republic, and throughout the fourteen years' duration of the republic it was the recipient of most of the wounds and scars inflicted by opponents of the republic on both the left and the right. It was not prepared for rule, however, either by tradition or by the composition of its leadership. The major interests of its party functionaries had been concentrated on workers' problems and Socialist theory. Never had it been so acutely conscious of the imminence of Socialist rule as to make plans for the day it would be called to power. Beset in the first years of the revolution by fatal division in the working classes, it could not muster the necessary cohesive strength to pursue a vigorous policy of thoroughly democratizing the country. It rightly sensed the dangers and perils of Bolshevism, and due recognition must be given to the Social Democrats of Germany for having saved not only Germany but all of Europe from the very real threat of Communist world revolution that hovered over Europe in the first years of the republic. But in so doing the Socialists were paralyzed in the effort to establish republican institutions on a firm foundation. Their alliance with the imperial military leaders permitted the old forces of reaction to find a secure haven in the Reichswehr and to make of the Reichswehr a "state within a state," strong enough and sufficiently autonomous to undermine and eventually to overthrow the democratic republic.

When Socialists finally succeeded in 1924 in creating a Republican defense organization, the Reichsbanner, it was already far too late for it to be a match for the firmly entrenched military formations of the right. The civil service and judiciary likewise were left untouched, and remained in their composition pretty much the same as they had been under the imperial Prussian eagle. The Socialists could indeed pride themselves on having exhibited a generous and decent respect for the independence of both these governmental agencies, and in the Kapp Putsch the civil servants on the whole remained loyal to the republican government. But revolutionary transformations call for revolutionary transfer of power. The best that can be said for the record of most of the German civil servants is that they considered themselves to be technicians ready to carry out the orders of any government that happened to exercise authority. Such was the case, for example, of one of the highest civil servants, Dr. Otto Meissner, who was first appointed state secretary to the Socialist President Ebert, but who continued to exercise the same functions and duties with equal loyalty and faithfulness under Field Marshal von Hindenburg and under Reichsführer Adolf Hitler.

As for the German judiciary their record for judicial independence was not even that good. The story of the treatment of political crimes by German courts under the republic is one of the most shameful chapters in the history of that epoch. German judges throughout displayed an extraordinary degree of leniency to the host of political assassins that came from the nationalist right and a high degree of judicial severity for cases emanating from the left. This flagrant and unconcealed hostility displayed by the judiciary to the republic was a significant and dramatic factor in undermining the political authority of the democratic régime. Neither the Socialists nor their bourgeois allies did anything to cleanse the judiciary from these elements.[3]

Perhaps the most serious charge against the Socialists and their bourgeois allies is that they failed to effect any significant changes in education. True, the educational problem was rendered complex by the fact that it was subject to the various jurisdictions of local state governments and because there were serious differences with the Catholic Center party on the role of the church in this area. It is likewise true that there were some new appointments to professorial rank in the universities of individuals previously barred because of religion or politics. But the essential control of administration of both lower and higher education remained in the hands of those who had nothing but contempt for the republic and who therefore made no effort to effect any changes in curriculum to prepare the German youth for "republican citizenship." Not a single school text in Weimar Germany presented the true story of German defeat in 1918. German geography texts still inculcated in the minds of the young the definition that "Germany was a country surrounded on all sides by enemies." The result was that the high schools and universities became focal centers for the rightist nationalist movements, and the personnel of the German teaching body became a fruitful recruiting center for Stahlhelm and National Socialist functionaries and leaders.

To all this, the German Socialists countered merely with a few feeble efforts at progressive education, like the famous Karl Marx Schule in Berlin. But they failed to reach the large masses of even their own following. And the legends of "November criminals" and *Dolchstoss* were actively propagated by the educational agencies of the republic without interference by public officials.

All the charges of weakness by the Social Democrats are more obviously pertinent to the first four years of the republic. They are partially condoned by the fact that the Socialist working classes were divided not only into Socialists and Communists but also, until September 24, 1922, into Majority and Independent Socialists. After 1924, however, the Socialists pursued on the whole the only policy they could carry on under the circumstances. False too are the charges often leveled against them of graft, corruption, and extravagance. There were a few instances of Socialist association with political corruption, as in the Barmat and Sklarek scandals. These were, however, isolated cases and rare exceptions. To the end of its days the leadership and party apparatus of the S.P.D. remained personally incorruptible and honorable. The Nazi slogans of *"System"* and *"Bonzen,"* like all their other slogans, were combinations of lies, slander, and half-truths.

What the S.P.D. did fail to develop was sufficient imagination and sufficiently modern propaganda techniques to cope with the new mass agitation of both Communists and Nazis. Their very decency and strict adherence to their traditional tactics, which were a source of pride to the party leaders and which were able to retain the steadfast and loyal adherence of the main core of older and middle-aged membership, were inadequate and a source of ineffectual weakness in the efforts to win over the new proletarianized and pauperized masses attracted to the extreme left and extreme right. Only in the papers of the *Sozialistische Monatshefte* does one find a new and fresh note in the Socialist movement that departs from the rigid and dogmatic orthodoxy of the S.P.D. tradition. Around the person especially of Carlo Mierendorff was gathered a group of younger, able, and energetic Socialists who called for a modernization of the party apparatus. But Mierendorff came upon the scene only in the last two years of the republic, too late to be more than a flash of genius shining across the Socialist horizon, and then to be brought to a martyr's death under the Nazis.

Gustav Mayer, illustrious historian of the Socialist and labor movement, who could hardly be accused of hostility either from the right or from the left, has left us in his posthumous memoirs a scathing but on the whole accurate evaluation of the leadership of the S.P.D. "I admit," writes Mayer,

that there was scarcely a single figure in the entire leadership cadre of the S.P.D. who, measured by a strict standard, aroused within me any profound ethical respect and admiration. Petty bourgeois pedantry was combined in many of them with egotism and ambitious place-hunting.

Mayer tells how Landsberg, the Socialist member of the first republican government, boasted of the fact that he read Treitschke's history to his wife every evening, and how Scheidemann boasted that he never read any book at all.

These new statesmen [continues Mayer], appeared to me to be more or less all little people who saw themselves placed before great tasks which could only have been tackled by unusual personalities and by means of unusual methods.

The majority of them, says Mayer, were

narrow-minded upstarts, musty petty bourgeois without beliefs, without genuine ideals, without moral courage and without an adequate sense of responsibility. . . . The individual policies that Hermann Müller, Scheidemann, Ebert, and so forth, attempted to carry out were often correct, certainly more so than what the demagogic cliques on the right proposed, but the smallness of their moral and intellectual frame made them completely unfruitful.[4]

The opponents of the republic found their political focal points in the right wing of the People's party and in the German Nationalist party on the Right and in the Communist party on the Left. The German Nationalists emerged from their initial stupefaction caused by the events of 1918–1919 and formed the major opposition party to the republic in the Reichstag. Their strength, however, was enormously greater than their political party representation by virtue of their close affiliation and cooperation with powerful economic groups, with the Stahlhelm, with leading personalities of the old régime, and with their on-and-off alliances with the racialist and National Socialist groups. Eventually it was the machinations of the leader of the Nationalist party, Alfred Hugenberg, that were responsible for the Harzburg Front of 1931 and the revived Harzburg Front that culminated in the formation of the Hitler cabinet in January, 1933.

Communist party policies in Germany were both as simple and as deviously complex as Communist policies everywhere else in the world. Changes in party line and shifts in party leadership came frequently and without warning—enough to baffle intelligent and rational political observers. The simplifying element, however, rested in the fact that all these tergiversations were dictated entirely and exclusively by the policy of the U.S.S.R. The German Communist party developed into the most numerous and powerful Communist party outside the Soviet Union. But it was plagued by constant vacillation, factional disputes, and purges of leadership that were primarily related not to events in Germany but rather to events and needs of the Soviet Union. No party in Germany gathered around its standard more will to sacrifice and more capacity for courage and endurance and desire for revolutionary change. It was all corrupted and destroyed, however, by rigid and bureaucratic direction from Moscow that eliminated one by one all leaders suspected of independence of judgment and will. By 1925 the party was safely in the hands of Ernst Thälmann, a completely submissive tool of Moscow. Ruthless pressure by the Stalinist machine was imposed on German party functionaries, and the German party apparatus was converted first into a political tool of the Soviet foreign office and then into a vast network of espionage for the political and military agencies of the U.S.S.R.

In its political propaganda and parliamentary activity the German Communist party vied with the parties of the right in making its appeal to the nationalist sentiment in the country and in exploiting nationalist slogans. They toyed first with National Bolshevism,[5] raved against the Treaty of Versailles, promised to liberate Germany from the "chains of Versailles," and were even ready to accept Albert Leo Schlageter, Nazi martyr, into the pantheon of proletarian heroes. Nor did the German Communists desist from using antisemitism as a tool of propaganda. On numerous occasions, in the Reichstag, in the Prussian diet, and in economic conflicts, they co-operated with the Nazis in undermining the republic. During the entire history of the Weimar Republic the chief butt of Communist agitation was not the reactionary parties of the right but the fellow proletarians of the Social Democratic party. It was most essential, Stalin told the *Rote Fahne* on February 5, 1925, for the German Communist party to represent the majority of the working class and it was, therefore, the prime task of German Communists to smash the Social Democratic party and to reduce it to an insignificant minority. "Without such pre-conditions the proletarian dictatorship is unthinkable. . . . If there are within the working class two rival parties of equal strength then the lasting and firm triumph of the revolution, even under the most favorable conditions, is impossible."

The height of nationalist agitation by the German Communists was reached in the "Program Declaration of the K.P.D. for National and Social Liberation of the German People" issued by the Central Committee on August 24, 1930. In opposition to the "National Socialist demagogy" the Communists proclaimed that they would "tear up the predatory Versailles 'peace treaty' and the Young Plan, which enslaves Germany, and annul all international debts and reparations payments imposed by the capitalists on the working population of Germany." They promised also the aid of the Soviet Union to help "disarmed and isolated Germany" to achieve not only "social liberation" but also "national liberation." "Only the hammer of the proletarian dictatorship," they proclaimed, "can smash the chains of the Young Plan and of national oppression." They called upon the followers of the "traitorous S.P.D." to break with the "party of the Versailles Peace Treaty, of the Young Plan and of the enslavement of the working masses of Germany." [6]

A truly fatal political act by the German Communist party was their behavior in the elections of 1925 for a successor to President Ebert. The parties of the right named Karl Jarres as their candidate, and he received 10½ million votes; the Socialist candidate Otto Braun got 8 million votes; the Centrist Wilhelm Marx secured 4 million votes; the Communist Thälmann got a little less than 2 million votes; and General Ludendorff received about 300,000 votes. Since no candidate received a majority of the votes cast it was necessary to have a run-off election. All the republican groups thereupon joined their forces on the candidacy of Wilhelm Marx, while the anti-republican elements hauled General von Hindenburg out of retirement and made him the standard-bearer of the enemies of the republic. It was quite obvious that the legendary figure of Hindenburg would draw many votes away from the Center party, while Marx would not be able to win over any of those who had voted for Jarres. The vote would obviously be very close. The Communists were confronted with the issue of whether to help strengthen the republic or contribute to its downfall. They chose to follow the latter course. They renominated Thälmann, drew the same number of votes as in the first vote, and in this way made possible the election of Hindenburg. In the final count Marx received 13,751,615 votes, Hindenburg got 14,655,766, and Thälmann 1,931,151. Had the almost two million Communist votes gone to Marx, Hindenburg would never have become president and the entire course of German and world history might have been directed into different channels.

The Communist cry of "social fascism," directed primarily at the Social Democrats, did more than anything else to confound the naïve and unsophisticated German workers and to sharpen the division within the labor and proletarian classes. When the slogan of "social fascism" gave way to that of a "united front" policy, it was a call for a united front from below rather than from above. This was equivalent to an appeal to the masses of Social Democratic workers to repudiate their own leaders and come over to the Communist side. Such an appeal was one that could hardly be taken as a sincere effort to bring about harmony in the German working classes. Finally, when the danger of the collapse of the republic and the triumph of Nazism was at the very door, the Communist leadership developed the fantastic and fateful doctrine of the "inevitability of fascism": that according to the law of historical necessity it was inevitable that Hitlerism first triumph so that it could then be exposed in its futile efforts to save Germany and thus lead eventually to the realization by the working classes that Communism is the only true solution to their problems. Hitlerism, thus discredited, would then crumble and be replaced by a Communist dictatorship of the proletariat.*

* H. R. Knickerbocker tells how he asked a German Communist in January, 1932: "Why can't you six million oppose Hitler by force?" The reply came: "The Soviet Union is not ready for a German revolution. We think if Hitler comes in he will run the country down so fast that by next autumn we can take power" (*The German Crisis*, New York, 1932, p. 46).

It is difficult to assume that Communist leaders really believed in such nonsense. It is more likely that this was but an attempt at a rationalization of Soviet foreign policy. The Soviet Union, fully engaged at the time in the rapid industrialization of the five-year plans, was dependent on Germany for technical supplies, personnel, and raw materials. A revolutionary upheaval in Germany was the last thing the U.S.S.R. desired at that time. At the same time, however, it was necessary to maintain the revolutionary *élan* of the party followers. Hence these gyrations of party line from one unbelievable theory to another. Communist leadership thus succeeded in effectively splitting the working-class movement and at the same time completely neutralizing the revolutionary spirit among the workers. After 1923 there never was any real danger of a Communist coup in Germany. The specter of the Bolshevist danger was conjured up only by the imagination of the right. Informed and intelligent observers knew that despite the swell of Communist votes the real peril to the republic now came from the right. And in both the Kremlin and among nationalist circles of the German right there were strong tendencies for a German-Russian alliance that would present a powerful challenge to the "plutocratic" powers of the West.

Between June 6, 1920, and March 5, 1933, there were eight general elections for the Reichstag, and between February 13, 1919, and January 28, 1933, there were 21 Reich cabinets. The very first Reichstag election already showed a decline in republican sentiment from that displayed by the electorate in the elections to the National Assembly. The democratic parties managed to muster sufficient strength to carry on the government without the aid of rightist deputies up to November, 1922. Until that time the Weimar coalition of Social Democrats, Center party, and Democratic party retained the reins of government. From 1923 to 1930 the democratic coalition was compelled to join forces with the rightist People's party of Stresemann. The elections of September 14, 1930, which brought into the Reichstag 107 deputies of the National Socialist party, brought parliamentary government in Germany to a crisis from which it never recovered. Failure to attain a parliamentary majority ushered in the Brüning era of rule by the right wing of the Center party, by the grace not of parliament but of the Reich president. This lasted from March 29, 1930, to May 30, 1932. From May 31, 1932, to January 28, 1933, the von Papen and Schleicher cabinets, which were entirely and officially presidial cabinets, attempted to carry on without the Reichstag. During the entire period between 1919 and May, 1932, there was not a single cabinet without Centrist participation. During the early years of the republic it was the left wing of the Center party under Dr. Wirth; in the later years it was the right wing of Marx, Kaas, and Brüning.

The Weimar Republic was beset from the start by baffling and overwhelming problems of a constitutional, political, and economic character.

The constitution, as finally adopted, was hailed as the most modern and most democratic in the world, but it allowed serious difficulties in the functioning of the parliamentary system. The federal structure of government, proportional representation, the retention of the Prussian state in its inordinate size and influence, the political inexperience of the German masses—all combined not only to make for difficulties in functioning but also to discredit the democratic and parliamentary system. Proportional representation in the Reichstag made for a high degree of inflexibility. Unlike the parliamentary system of France, which also functioned with more than two parties, there was no possibility for deputies in the German Reichstag to shift their votes from their party group. This made the attainment of a parliamentary majority a most difficult task. On a smaller scale the same problem was present in the diets of the local states. The existence of numerous splinter parties, multiplied by the total number of states, made for constant political crises. This, combined with the fact that a substantial segment of the parliamentary representation was from the start hostile to the republic and to republican institutions, tended to undermine in a people little experienced in the ways of democracy the attachment to and respect for the republic. Millions of Germans were confirmed once again in the belief made current by the failure of the revolution of 1848 that Germans are by nature not fit for democratic rule and that only authoritarian discipline is capable of holding the nation together.

The Socialist and laboring classes who looked to the new state for some imaginative and radical social program were soon disillusioned in their hopes. The cry for socialization and for the break-up of the larger latifundia in East Prussia received but scant attention even by the early Socialist cabinets. Lip service was paid to this demand by the setting up of a Socialization Commission and by the provisions in the Weimar Constitution for a Reich economic council. But no energetic action was taken along any of these lines, and large elements of the laboring population turned away because of this from the moderate Socialists to the radical Communists.

The most difficult problem for the republic was the liquidation of the war. From the outset the Weimar Republic began with the handicap that it was associated in people's minds with the Versailles Treaty. "Our republic is based not on the Weimar Constitution but on the Peace of Versailles" was a view often expressed, especially in nationalist circles. The republican governments, moreover, did little or nothing to disassociate themselves from the defeat in the war. Instead of making a clean break with the foreign policy of the imperial régime and attempting to enlighten the people regarding the responsibility of their former rulers for both the war and defeat, the republican leaders vied with each other in nationalist declarations on war guilt, reparations, and the "chains of Versailles." In not a single school text of republican Germany were there any readings to indicate the responsibility of General Ludendorff and the General Staff for the acceptance of the armistice terms. This only furthered the widespread acceptance of the nationalist propaganda of the "stab in the back" and of the "November criminals." The foreign policy of the republic, instead of trying to forge a new path for itself, revealed a uniform pattern of nationalist goals and aspirations.

CHAPTER XVII

Republican Foreign Policy

*Wir Deutsche ziehen uns gar zu leicht auf Schicksal und Tragik
zurück.*

ERNST ROBERT CURTIUS

In a letter to a friend dated November 14, 1918, Walther Rathenau
wrote:

The events appear to me in the form of the following picture: It is necessary
to climb a steep cliff. We had ascended up to an appreciable height; then
appeared the deep cleft which stood in the way of further ascent. Now we must
descend to the valley in order to begin anew and with difficulty the ascent up
the road which, this time, however, will lead to the top.[1]

We may use this image of Rathenau's to describe the goals of German
foreign policy after the defeat of 1918. In terms of aspirations and ends
there were, apart from the Communists, no appreciable differences among
the various parties and groups in Weimar Germany.[2] All felt that they
had been tricked by President Wilson into laying down their arms by the
promise of generous treatment in accordance with the Fourteen Points
and that this promise had been brutally violated by the final treaty. They
expected, after they had substituted a republican form of government for
the old monarchy, to be received with open arms and as an equal partner.
Instead they found a world that refused to believe that any radical change
of heart had really occurred in Germany and which, therefore, refused to
negotiate a peace with the German delegates but insisted on "imposing"
what the Germans later loved to call the *"Diktat"* of Versailles.

German spokesmen were able to seize on all the inconsistencies in
Allied policy and to dwell on the fact that for the most part these inconsistencies worked specifically to the disadvantage of Germany. Territorial
adjustments were carried out by the peacemakers on the principle of national self-determination, but Germans in Austria, the Sudetenland, and
the Tyrol were denied the exercise of this right. The war was proclaimed

422

to be the war to end all wars with resulting universal disarmament, but while Germany was completely disarmed its neighbors stubbornly refused to follow suit. Imperialistic domination over colonial areas was to be replaced by enlightened international regulation known as the system of mandates, but only the colonies of Germany and its ally, Turkey, were to be graced by this beneficence, while the victorious nations still wielded imperialistic power over their own foreign possessions. A new world order was to be established to create a family of nations, but Germany was excluded from membership as a "pariah" nation. While there was a great deal of Allied talk of good will and universalism, the Germans could say "Amen" to J. M. Keynes's pronouncement that "never in the lifetime of men now living has the universal element in the soul of man burnt so dimly."

The Treaty of Versailles has been subjected to harsh and acrid criticism not only by Germans but also by historians and political writers in Allied countries. From a general world point of view it is difficult to see how the peacemakers, laboring under the tensions and pulls of so numerous and varied a concatenation of national interests and demands, could have done very much better than they did. By and large the treaty managed to carry out certain broad principles of international regulation even though it had to make numerous concessions to national self-interest. Certainly by comparison with the Treaty of Brest Litovsk, which the Germans imposed on Bolshevik Russia, it was a model of fairness and generosity. It merits neither the designation "Draconian" nor "Carthaginian." The perspective from the specific German national point of view, however, is another story. For Germans the treaty was harsh and drastic, and they were all at one in the determination that it be subjected to radical revision.

The depth of German rejection of the treaty can only be understood in terms of the almost universal certainty of Germans that they would win the war and of the enormous discrepancy, therefore, between the kind of treaty such a victory would have brought and the treaty born of German defeat. German moderates agreed fully with the extremists in attributing German defeat to a purely accidental and unique configuration of circumstances, and they too looked for the eventual disunity among the Allies that would undo the German defeat. The goal of German foreign policy, to borrow Rathenau's figure, became the ascent once more to the top of the mountain. In this goal there was unity among all parties. The only difference between the moderates and the extremists was as to means. The moderates were resigned to the process of slow ascent from the bottom of the valley. The radical nationalists, impatient of such slow progress in regaining national glory, were ready to risk the hazardous adventure of jumping across the wide cleft. Ultimate objectives, however, of Socialists as well as of conservative nationalists, were the same: to convert Germany from the "object" of policy of the Entente to that of active and free determination of its own policy, to nullify the Versailles Treaty, to rectify the eastern borders, to regain its lost colonies, to end Allied occupation and reparations, to regain its military power, and to be restored once again to a position as one of the great powers, if not *the* great power, of Europe. Differences there were as to methods and tempo of attaining these goals, and these differences cannot be dismissed as trivial or insignificant. But ultimate objectives were on the whole uniform. Therein lies the main reason why, when Hitler later took the radical path to these ends, there were some misgivings among the other Germans as to method but no real opposition of a profound nature to his ultimate objectives.

Foreign observers joined with German pacifists and idealistic visionaries in what amounted to a Utopian dream of a radical transformation of German national character and a complete reorientation of national policy. They demanded of the Germans that they return to the life of pure spirit as found in the era of classical humanism and abandon once for all the pleasures and prerogatives of a great political power. In the words of Wickham Steed, the German leaders should have established the new republic on the "firm resolve . . . to have done with the past, to accept even the military conditions of the Versailles Treaty as a blessing in disguise, and to set their minds and their hands to the task of making Germany a center of attraction to all men and peoples of goodwill in a Europe deliberately warless." In other words, in a world in which political and military power was still regarded as the sole measure of a nation's prestige and greatness, and while Germany's neighbors, even little Poland, reveled in playing the role of "great powers," foreign opinion expected a people, as steeped in the authoritarian and militarist tradition as were the Germans, to become the "messiah" of Europe and to take the lead in the spiritual conversion of the rest of humanity. This was truly a noble dream, and like many another noble dream would have been most effective in maintaining the stability of both Germany and Europe if it were capable of realization. But it was too much to expect of any nation, particularly of Germany. And it took on a "pharisaic" note when such a formulation of a noble dream for Germany emanated from loyal citizens of states which were at the very same time striving to expand their own political and military power.

For the average German, irrespective of political party, and reconciled though he might have become to the restoration of Alsace-Lorraine to France and Eupen and Malmédy to Belgium, the Treaty of Versailles was an "instrument of subjugation." It had turned over German territory and German population in the east to Poland, a nation traditionally regarded by Germans as beneath contempt; it created the "impossible" Polish corridor which divided the German Reich in two and cut off the "hallowed" soil of East Prussia from the rest of the Reich. Measured in terms of the resources of Germany before the war, the treaty meant the loss of 13 per cent of its territory, 10 per cent of its population, 100 per cent of its colonial domain, about 15 per cent of its arable land, 74.5 per cent of its iron ore, 26 per cent of its hard coal assets, 68 per cent of its zinc, 17 per cent of its potato yield, 16 per cent of its rye, and 13 per cent of its wheat. To top all that, the Treaty of Versailles meant the complete demilitarization of Germany and the military occupation by the Allied powers of 6 per cent of its remaining domain.

These grievances took on a general European character when Germans could point out, with the support of Allied writers like J. M. Keynes, that before 1914 Germany had been the center around which the European economic system had been built, that by virtue of its geographical location Germany was destined to play a leading role in the reconstruction of Europe, and that "on the prosperity and enterprise of Germany the prosperity and enterprise of the rest of the continent mainly depended." German political leaders, aware of the strength of this argument, made abundant use of it in their negotiations with Allied statesmen. This argument, together with the plea that Germany constituted the most stalwart dam against the flood of Bolshevism, proved to be most effective in winning support for Germany in Allied countries. "Today," Rathenau told Stephen Bonsal, "economically, Germany is dying, and the gangrened corpse that will result, I tell you again ᛫ . . . will infect the entire world." And Dresel, the head of the American Commission in Berlin, reported to Secretary of State Colby on his conversation with Ebert, and wired: "Like everyone else with whom I have talked here lately (they all say the same thing as if by clock-work), he enlarged on the Bolshevist danger, and argues for the retention of a sufficient army to keep down Communist uprisings." [3]

The foreign suspicions and fears of a revived Germany which were still active in the first year after the war soon evaporated and were lost completely in the divergences of policy that developed among the victorious Allies. Bolshevist Russia, of course, was no longer an ally but a "pariah" nation like Germany, a fact which resulted in the development of a secret community of interest between the two powers and in a maze of mysterious negotiations and arrangements that led from the Rapallo Treaty of 1922 to the Nazi-Soviet Pact of 1939.

The United States, repudiating the work of its President and rejecting both the Treaty of Versailles and the League of Nations, made its own separate peace with Germany without, in the words of President Wilson, "exacting from the German government any action by way of setting right the infinite wrongs which it did to the peoples whom it attacked, and whom we professed it our purpose to assist when we entered the War." By 1922 the British ambassador in Berlin was able to note in his diary that "American businessmen here are pro-German, going as far as to doubt

Germany's responsibility for the war." The years between 1922 and 1933 saw a tremendous efflorescence of pro-German sentiment in the United States. American relief agencies worked actively in the years immediately following the war to bring aid to the poor and suffering in Germany. American bankers and investors later pumped huge sums of American capital into the country to help in the process of reconstruction. American governmental opinion as well as the American press and general public opinion openly showed their sympathy for Germany as opposed to the policy of France.

Great Britain, beset by economic and financial dislocation and the beginnings of the dissolution of its traditional empire, was likewise more than satisfied to resume its own peculiar form of insular isolationism. The "normalcy" of America's Harding and Coolidge era was matched by the "tranquillity" of Bonar Law and the "complacency" of Stanley Baldwin, while the moralistic, pacifist, and pro-German sympathies of American progressives and radicals were more than evenly matched by the Oxford Union devotees and by Laborite leaders like Ramsay MacDonald, Philip Snowden, and George Lansbury. Lloyd George himself soon chose to forget the slogans of his "khaki campaign," when he promised that Germany was to be made to pay the cost of the war, and when he advocated "squeezing the German lemon till the pips squeaked." Instead the slogan for most Englishmen became the gentlemanly maxim of "forgive and forget."

British policy on the Versailles Treaty was revisionist almost from the start. Now that Germany's attempt at hegemony of Europe had been defeated it was important to prevent France from assuming this position. British objectives favored a rapid recovery of Germany as essential for the creation of a "new temper in Europe." The British ambassador in Berlin, Viscount D'Abernon, whose wit, urbanity, and charm of manner lent an undeserved air of political sagacity to his reputation, from the start became the center of revisionism. Whereas French diplomats after 1918 sought contact with German pacifists and democrats, D'Abernon established his contacts with the Right. His entry in his diary in December, 1921, read, "England and the United States were the two countries to which the Germans looked with some degree of hope."

France, at the close of the war, was more exhausted and disrupted than any of the other participants. With a low birth rate, a population depleted by dead and wounded, its most flourishing regions ravaged by invasion and destruction, with the war of 1870 as well as of 1914 still fresh in its memory, it was left alone clutching at the Versailles Treaty as its sole source of security and protection against a more populous, more industrialized, more dynamic, and more aggressive neighbor. Having given up its demand for the left bank of the Rhine in return for a guarantee treaty by the United States and Britain, it found itself abandoned by the defection of the United States and the widening rift with Britain and was thrown back upon the letter of the treaty as its sole protection. To the demands of Lloyd George for a "just peace" Clemenceau had replied, "In view of the German mentality, it is not sure that justice is conceived by the Germans as it is conceived by the Allies." Nevertheless he asserted his will over that of Marshal Foch and gave up the demand for the left bank of the Rhine; he accepted Wilson's League and he too agreed that German disarmament was to be but a prelude to general disarmament.

All these concessions by France were made on the strength of the promise of the security treaty with the United States and Britain. Left puzzled and abandoned by the rejection of the treaty, France, especially under Poincaré, pursued a policy of dogged and legalistic adherence to the terms of the Versailles Treaty. For most Frenchmen such a course meant the sole defense against the potentially still dangerous *Boche;* to Britons and Americans it seemed to be aggressively militaristic and imperialistic, while for Germans it served to validate the nationalist slogans against the "hereditary enemy." Other causes of indignation against France were her use of French African troops in the occupation of the Rhineland, a fact which intensified the already existing Nordic racialism current in Germany, and the varying degrees of encouragement given by French political and military officials to "separatist" tendencies in the Rhineland and in Bavaria. Much of this "separatism" was not so much anti-German as anti-Prussian. It was motivated by the desire not to sever political affiliation with the German state but rather to become free from political control by the oversized state of Prussia. For purposes of foreign consumption, however, all these movements were branded by German spokesmen as acts of treason.

Enforcement of the Versailles Treaty was to be ensured by the occupation of the Rhineland by Allied troops and by continued inspection of the demilitarization of Germany by an Inter-Allied Military Control Commission. The Rhineland occupation area was divided into three zones: the first zone, at Cologne, was to be held for five years; the second zone, at Coblenz, was to be occupied for ten years; and the third zone, at Mainz, was to be held for fifteen years. These terms were carried out by the Allies. The first zone was evacuated from December 1, 1925, to January 31, 1926; the second zone was cleared by November 30, 1929; the third zone was evacuated ahead of schedule, the last Allied soldier leaving Germany on June 30, 1930.

The reparations problem was the issue which occupied the first place on the international scene and which dragged on for the longest period of time. Claims for reparations aroused the highest hopes in Allied countries, stirred up the most furious resentment among Germans, and presented the most complex interlocking of political and economic problems. It was not until the passions of war had worn off that the problem could be taken out of the heat of international and domestic political squabbling and be treated within the framework of rational economic potentialities. By the time the reparations problem was terminated, however, the fuse of German nationalist resentment was just about ready to explode.

During the first year and a half of the republic, German foreign policy was characterized by petulant nationalist sabotage of Allied policies and demands. On May 10, 1921, however, the new coalition government under the Centrist leader Dr. Joseph Wirth brought this phase to a close and initiated the policy of "fulfillment." This was the policy which, except for the interlude of the Cuno government and the Ruhr occupation, was taken up again by Marx and Stresemann in 1923. It was a policy which owed a great deal to the support of the Centrist party, but it aroused such violent opposition in extreme nationalist circles as to bring about the assassination first of Erzberger, then of Rathenau, and had much to do with sending Stresemann prematurely to his grave.

Joseph Wirth, a former mathematics professor in Baden, became the leader of the militantly republican wing of the Catholic Center party. A brilliant orator and a convinced democrat, he was more radical than most of his party. He called in Walther Rathenau to be, first, minister of reconstruction and then foreign minister in his cabinet. Wirth and Rathenau, both positively committed to the republic, were of the opinion that Germany was unable to improve its position by open resistance to the demands of the Entente. They argued that the best way to convince Germany's former enemies that their demands were utterly impossible was to demonstrate by faithful attempts to carry them out how incapable they were of realization. Wirth and Rathenau were anxious above all to take the entire problem of reparations out of the realm of political passion and heated controversy and bring it where it belonged, into the area of economics, where cold, hard facts could replace super-charged emotion, nationalist pathos, and political slogans, and where, as Wirth said, "one must drink the clear and oft-bitter waters of truth." Their program called for patience, for understanding, reconstruction, and reconciliation. It was necessary to yield to the Allied demands, declared Wirth in Essen on June 19, 1921, in order to preserve German freedom and unity and the economic freedom to be able to carry on. "Behind us," he told his hearers, "are seven years of war, of sorrow and need." Ahead of the German people, he declared, are thirty years of painful work and effort to attain once again a position of well-being and an ordered state.

Germany, according to Rathenau and Wirth, was morally committed to make good the economic damage caused to the industrial areas of Belgium and northern France. With this aim in view Rathenau initiated discussions with Louis Loucheur, French minister of economics, leading to the Wiesbaden agreement of October 6–7, 1921, whereby German deliveries in kind were to be substituted for gold payments in order to speed the material reconstruction of the ravaged areas of France. This agreement came to nought chiefly because of the opposition of French industrialists, who found that such an arrangement would abolish a source of great profits for them.

Wirth and Rathenau also emphasized that Germany was honor bound to make every effort to carry out the pledges made inviolate by the signatures of German delegates. In one of his great speeches to the Reichstag on July 7, 1921, Rathenau declared:

We Germans are obligated by our signature, by the honor of our name that we have placed under the treaties. We will fulfill and we will go to the limit of our ability in order to preserve the honor of our name, which stands affixed to the treaties, and we recognize their binding character even though they do not express our wishes.[4]

This, held Wirth and Rathenau, did not mean that they could not persist in their efforts to convince the Allies that these demands were beyond the powers of Germany. Nor did it mean that they could not hope for eventual recognition by the Allied leaders of the reasonableness of their arguments. Rathenau placed his hopes on Article 234 of the Versailles Treaty, which allowed for re-examination from time to time of Germany's capacity to pay, and eventually on the sympathetic ear of the more reasonable elements in Allied countries. "I am convinced," Rathenau told the Reichstag on June 1, 1921, "that the world is not made up 100 per cent of chauvinists, nor does it consist only of 150 million enemies; it contains also a large number of objective-minded people. The millions of eyes of such people turn to Germany and inquire: What will Germany do? Will it lead a life of reconciliation and fulfillment or not? Not enslavement; none of us want that; but it is in keeping with the dignity of a debtor to pay." [5]

The Reichstag approved the policy enunciated by Wirth and Rathenau and accepted the London ultimatum of the Allies on reparations payments. Nationalist opposition, however, soared in vehemence of expression and violence of action. The fact that the leaders in this policy were a Catholic and a Jew provided added fuel to the virulence of the agitation. It became especially bitter and venomous against the Jew, Rathenau. An antisemitic wave of the most extreme violence was set in motion. "Knallt ab den Juden Rathenau, die gottverdammte Judensau," was echoed up and down the country. On June 23, 1922, Karl Helfferich, one of the leaders of the German nationalists, delivered a violent and provocative attack on Rathenau in the Reichstag. The following day Rathenau was assassinated as he was leaving his home in his open car to go to his ministry. The assassins came from a group of youthful nationalists. Rathenau's death caused widespread consternation abroad and bitter resentment among republican elements at home. Otto Flake, liberal publicist and author, wrote in the *Weltbühne*:

A people that has no political temperament has no right to political existence. It only stands in the way of the rest of the world. . . . If the government does not get rid of the militarists then France and its spokesman Poincaré stand justified. . . . There is a straight line from the Saverne affair to the assassination of Rathenau.[6]

A law for the protection of the republic was passed by the Reichstag in deference to the resentment in democratic circles. Perhaps a better gauge of the reaction of German public opinion to this deed, however, was seen in the way in which the assassins were dealt with. One of the group, Kern, had been shot while being pursued; another, Fischer, committed suicide. Ernst Werner Techow, the third of the major criminals, was tried and sentenced to fifteen years' imprisonment but was pardoned after serving seven years. Ten other participants got off with light sentences, and one of them, Ernst von Salomon, a gifted novelist, achieved success with his best selling novel *Die Geächteten,* in which he reveled in his account of the nationalist circles responsible for the murder. Von Salomon duplicated the same sort of comeback after World War II. Kern and Fischer were later honored by the Third Reich and entombed in a special grave.[7]

Nationalist agitation against Rathenau was augmented by the even wider resentment engendered by the plebiscite in Upper Silesia and the subsequent decision of the League of Nations to award part of this area to Poland. In the meantime economic inflation spread with the alarming fall of the mark until it reached astronomical proportions. At the same time the advent to power of the Right in France, under the stubbornly legalistic Poincaré, brought Franco-German relations to a serious crisis. In January, 1923, the majority of the Allied Reparations Commission declared Germany to be in default in its deliveries of timber and coal. Acting on this pretext French and Belgian troops were ordered to march into the Ruhr to enforce the terms of the treaty. It was not, of course, the matter of the 2,000,000 telegraph poles or the specific number of tons of coal that were at stake. This default, and it was a default, merely brought to a head the long-smoldering problem of reparations. The French government had come to the conclusion that German ill will was unalterable and that the methods of procedure used by Germany against France in 1871 were the only methods to be applied. The Germans believed that the French were out to ruin them, and the French believed that the Germans were out to cheat them. France, by this action, hoped to embarrass the German government and create in Germany "a will to pay." England refused to go along in this action, although it also refrained from official opposition. Unofficially, however, public opinion both in England and in the United States condemned the French action as an expression of aggressive militarism and imperialism.

German public opinion was only united all the more in an orgy of nationalistic frenzy. Except for a tiny group of pacifists and anti-militarists like Friedrich W. Foerster and the circle around the *Welt am Montag*, leaders of all political parties united in a chorus of vehement national emotion. Passive resistance in the Ruhr was organized and subsidized by the Berlin government and emissaries were sent into the Ruhr to direct the resistance against the French. A flood of propaganda was let loose, both in Germany and throughout the world, charging the French with carrying out a policy of terror, brutality, rape, destruction, abuse of justice, sadism, and willful creation of starvation and disease. Accounts of the so-called "national passive resistance" have been greatly exaggerated. Much that was touted about in nationalist propaganda was not carried out into effective action. The coal-mine owners of the Ruhr resisted demands for a general strike and allowed the mines to be operated and coal deliveries to be collected by the French. Violent nationalist propaganda, however, was waged by the two countries against each other. Hatred for the "hereditary enemy" reached a higher peak than it ever did during the war years, and the scars caused by the tension of the Ruhr occupation left their mark on both France and Germany for many years to follow.

The financial strain of subsidizing the resistance policy in the Ruhr became too burdensome, however, and the feeling grew that some way of coming to terms with France was essential. The conservative big-business cabinet of Cuno, which was the second cabinet to rule without the support of the Socialists and which guided the republic through the Ruhr crisis, was forced to resign. It was replaced by a wide coalition cabinet ranging from Socialists to People's party, bringing to the helm Gustav Stresemann, one of the outstanding statesmen of the Weimar period, who was to resume the threads of foreign policy left off by Wirth and Rathenau and who was to bring to Germany and to Europe the period of greatest stability and international good will enjoyed after the war.

Gustav Stresemann, with Erzberger and Rathenau, was the only political figure of first rank brought forth by Weimar Germany. A son of a Berlin innkeeper, he always retained a healthy sense of humor and a strong dose of self-irony. He always remained the Berlin *"Junger"* and never lost his sense of perspective. Before the war he had succeeded Bassermann as the leader of the National Liberals and during the war he had been an ardent monarchist and annexationist. To the end of his days he retained a strong attachment to the former crown prince and kept many vestiges of his pan-German antecedents. He differed from his party colleagues, however, in that he had healthy common sense and never entered into arguments with facts, but respected them. He learned the lessons of the war, and his sense of practical reality usually won out over the more romantic political dreams of pan-Germanism which still remained part of him, particularly on "literary" and "philosophical" occasions. "I wanted," he wrote to Kahl in 1929, "to be the bridge between the old and the new Germany."

Stresemann recognized the need for a practical *modus vivendi* with the republic, despite his preference for monarchy, and he brought this same good practical sense to the field of foreign relations. First called to head the cabinet on August 13, 1923, he gave way to the Centrist leader Wilhelm Marx on November 28 and to Hans Luther and Hermann Müller subsequently. But up to the time of his death on October 3, 1929, he held the threads of foreign policy in his hands. It was during these years that the reparations problem found its solution first in the Dawes Plan, then in the Young Plan. It was Stresemann who inaugurated an era of good feeling with France by the negotiation of the Locarno Pact. Germany once more assumed a leading role in European and world affairs with its admission to membership in the League of Nations in September, 1926, and to a place in the Council of the League. It marked its participation in the movement for world peace by becoming a signatory, in February, 1929, to the Kellogg-Briand Pact.

On September 24, 1923, the Stresemann cabinet decided to abandon the policy of passive resistance in the Ruhr, and a proclamation to that effect was issued on the 26th. The Allies were similarly notified of this intention. The coming to power of Herriot and Briand in France and of Ramsay MacDonald and the Labour party in Britain helped to create an atmosphere of international good-will which gave rise to widespread optimism that looked to the final liquidation of the tensions and problems still left by the war. An intimate and friendly relationship was established between Stresemann and Briand such as had never existed between spokesmen of the two traditional enemies. This bore practical fruit in the Locarno treaties and in Germany's admission to the League.

In a letter to the former crown prince on September 7, 1925, Stresemann outlined his conception of the main goals of German foreign policy. It was necessary, he wrote, to bring about a solution of the reparations problem in a way that was bearable for Germany, and thus give Germany the necessary peace and security that was a prerequisite for Germany's "renewal of strength." It was necessary to secure a correction of the eastern frontiers, regaining for Germany Danzig, the Polish Corridor, and Upper Silesia. In the background, declared Stresemann, was the ultimate *Anschluss* with Austria. Moreover, Germany was to become the protector of the 12 million *Auslandsdeutsche,* or German minority population, living outside the boundaries of the Reich. A security pact with France, he admitted, means giving up Alsace-Lorraine, but this, he wrote, is of no practical importance since there was no chance of a war with France. Stresemann projected his view to the future and predicted that the reparations payments under the Dawes Plan would become unbearable by 1927 and that it would be necessary to demand a new conference at that time. Membership in the League would provide Germany with the arena for becoming the spokesman for all Germans abroad as well as with the place to press all other German demands. The most important task, he told the prince, was to free German territory from foreign occupation and to use British opposition to French hegemony to further the German cause. "Therefore," wrote Stresemann, "German policy in this respect will have to be, as Metternich said of Austria after 1809, *zu finassieren* and to avoid major decisions."

This letter by Stresemann, published only after his death, gave rise to serious controversy as to his sincerity in his dealings with Briand. The crux of the matter hinges on the translation of the word *finassieren*. It is a word borrowed from the French and not frequently used in German. The French word *finesser* means "to act with subterfuge," and the opponents of Stresemann use this to prove that his entire policy was intended as a cover-up for Germany to recoup its armed strength and, by lulling France into a false sense of security, prepare the ground for an eventual assault on both eastern and western fronts. Stresemann's supporters, on the other hand, deny these charges of duplicity. They claim that the German usage of this word is much more harmless than is its French original and that Stresemann may perhaps have tried to win favor for his policies in nationalist opposition circles by posing as a bit of a Machiavellian, but that actually he had no stronger desire than to bring peace to Europe and that there is no reason to doubt his integrity and sincerity in this wish. This latter position is, on the whole, borne out by the total record of Stresemann both in his official acts and in his collected writings. On the other hand his choice of the word *finassieren* is embarrassing, especially since he links it to the use made of it by Metternich after 1809.

Three issues of foreign policy continued to agitate German public opinion even after Locarno. They were the problem of armaments, the eastern border of Germany, and the relation of Germany to German-speaking populations outside the borders of the German Reich.

The Treaty of Versailles provided for the complete disarmament and demilitarization of Germany. A small army of 100,000 was to take the place of the imperial military machine; the General Staff was to be abolished, and the production of war weapons and war potential was limited as to size, number, and form. The reduced Reichswehr was to be confined purely to police functions of defense. In addition Germany was forbidden to institute compulsory military service and had to dispose of all submarines, large capital ships, tanks, naval and military aircraft, and to demolish all fortifications. The Rhineland, moreover, was to be completely demilitarized. An Inter-Allied Commission of Control was set up to see to it that these disarmament provisions of the treaty were carried out. On July 22, 1927, the Conference of Ambassadors notified the League Council that the disarmament sections of the Treaty of Versailles had been carried out to their satisfaction.

The disarmament of Germany was, according to the treaty, to be the preliminary for general European disarmament and was so indicated in the letter handed by Clemenceau to Count Brockdorff-Rantzau on June 16, 1919. The efforts to realize this goal of universal disarmament represent a tragic record of diplomatic wrangling and international futility. The Germans pressed upon the Allied powers to fulfill the promise of general disarmament or else allow for German equality of arms. The cry for German "equality," measured in terms of armaments, became the chief slogan of German republican foreign policy. France countered this seemingly just plea with the argument that it could not disarm until it was guaranteed full security not only by a Locarno pact on the Franco-German border but on all outstanding issues of German foreign policy. England, under MacDonald and Baldwin, on the other hand, pursued a wavering policy. Weimar Germany made the same mistake that William's imperial Germany had made; it counted on a permament and effective split between England and France to the benefit of Germany. Like imperial Germany, it too lost its gamble and failed to see that when a really serious crisis arose England would have to stand with France.

At the same time German authorities and German public opinion were intent from the first days of the republic on rebuilding the old German army. The German army organization, beaten in 1918, was never really destroyed. Its reconstruction began the day following the signing of peace. Max Weber, leading social scientist and one of the founders of the Democratic party, said in 1920, "I have no political plans except to concentrate all my intellectual strength on one problem: how to get once more for Germany a great General Staff." [8] General von Seeckt wrote at the end of 1918 that Germany must become *"bundnisfähig."* But it could never be so without arms. He said to Count Brockdorff-Rantzau at Versailles in 1919:

Since we Germans were summoned to Versailles and the allies did not come to Berlin, we can easily play down at home the extent of our military defeat. We should be grateful to the allies for this oversight. Thanks to it, we'll be able one day to resume and conclude this war. I'll make it my business to see that we shall then be in a position to make up once and for all for all our present misfortunes. In the final battle we shall be the victors.[9]

General Groener, writing to Seeckt on November 18, 1919, wished him health so that his work would provide the firm foundations "not only for the renewal of a small professional army" but for "the position of power of our fatherland in the future." [10] The Treaty of Versailles was in this respect a boon for the German military. It forced the Germans to scrap entirely their old and in many respects outmoded weapons and organization and to reconstruct an army that was to be built in accordance with the most progressive and most modern canons of efficiency and might. While France remained armed but saddled with the "technological obsolescence" of the old army, the German leaders were able to make use of the latest developments in mechanized warfare and air power.

The story of the secret German rearmament was one of the most delicate and touchy subjects during the Weimar period. Socialists and pacifists in Germany who attempted to bring the facts to light were silenced by judicial and political pressure. Foreign writers like Wickham Steed, and the *Manchester Guardian,* brought some of the facts out into the open. The charge has been made, however, by General Morgan, British member of the Allied Control Commission from 1918 to 1920, that the price paid to Stresemann for Locarno was silence on the question of German rearmament.[11]

The full story of this phase of German policy still remains to be told as to detail. But the larger lines were fully evident even by 1928 or 1929. The former German military leaders under General von Seeckt made it their first and foremost purpose to retain intact the officer caste as an autonomous arm of the state, completely independent of civilian authority. The old General Staff was also kept intact under the new name of Truppenamt, with headquarters in the Potsdam Reich Archives. The Reichswehr was converted by General von Seeckt into a vast officers' training school. He adopted the system of short-term volunteer training groups as cadres of expansion to increase the number of potential officers and men. The Reichswehr revived Scharnhorst's so-called "Krimper System" of 1807, whereby men were trained as soldiers in short-term labor companies. Full use was made by the legal Reichswehr of all sorts of "illegal formations"—the free corps, sport clubs, home guards, Stahlhelm and nationalist formations. Special agreements were made with the police as in the Gessler-Severing agreement of 1927.[12]

Seeckt's conception of the Reichswehr was that of "a small professional army whose technical requirements could be mass produced in case of need." For this he established close relations between the army and industry and called upon the industrial leaders to help finance the program of secret rearmament. Articles 168 and 169 of the Treaty of Versailles, which called for the elimination of the industrial capacity to make war, were never enforced. The Germans made the plea that they needed their industries to maintain their "capacity to pay." In this way the huge chemical and iron and steel plants carried on and made possible German rearmament. Seeckt's training program was for "offensive operations" and not merely for the maintenance of order, and he made the basis for his training "the men, armament and equipment of the army of a great, modern, military power and not merely the German army of 100,000 men."

The Reichswehr founded a corporation known as the Gesellschaft zur Förderung gewerblicher Unternehmungen [GEFU], for the manufacture of poison gas and aircraft. Allowed by the Allies to retain civil aviation,

Germany became the leading power in this field and created a civilian air force that could easily be converted to uses of war. The Reichswehr also retained control of merchant shipping and strategic bridges, and developed a wide network of propaganda agencies. A great deal of the secret rearmament was carried on outside the borders of the Reich. The Dornier Airplane Company was moved from Friedrichshafen across Lake Constance to Switzerland; the Rohrbach plant went to Denmark; Heinkel and Junkers plants were set up in Sweden and Russia; Fokker returned to Holland; Captain Canaris and Captain Lohmann worked with submarines in shipyards in Spain.

The most intriguing chapter in the story of German rearmament is the co-operation in this field between the Reichswehr and the Soviet Union. It is usually alleged that General von Seeckt belonged to the so-called "eastern" orientation. Carl Severing rightly points out, however, that Seeckt would have gone east or west in order to attain his goal of restoring the German army to its pre-war position. The political isolation of the U.S.S.R. offered the Reichswehr the opportunities it needed along these lines. Secret relations were established between German military leaders and the Bolsheviks from the earliest days of the republic. Karl Radek, jailed by the German Socialist authorities in Berlin, received visits regularly in his cell from German officers. In 1923 a secret agreement was effected between the Reichswehr and the U.S.S.R. for the production of aircraft and poison gas on Russian soil. New weapons and new techniques were tested out on Russian territory, and armaments manufactured in Russia were secretly shipped to Germany. Exchange of military information between the Reichswehr and the Red army was certainly carried out, although the extent of this still remains to be cleared up.

The magnitude of all these armament activities was apparent in the Reichswehr budget. As the Socialist leaders pointed out, the official budget of the Reichswehr in 1924 was 450,000,000 marks; in 1927 it was 700,000,000 marks, and in 1928 it was 726,000,000 marks. By contrast, the budget in 1914 for combined army and navy of 879,846 men was 1,824,513,795 marks. Figuring an increase in the cost of living of 60 per cent, it meant that in 1914 the cost per man was 3,300 marks, while in 1928 it was 6,300 marks. In May, 1925, the German League for the Rights of Man published a *White Book* on secret rearmament pointing out that the Reichswehr was planning an army of 35 divisions. The accuracy of this information is attested by the fact that in March, 1935, the German military machine, coming out into the open under the Nazis, revealed an army of 35 divisions. Sporadic protests against this program by Socialist deputies in the Reichstag were hushed up in the secret Foreign Affairs and Military commissions of the Reichstag. Writers like Carl von Ossietzky, Berthold Jakob, Carl Mertens, Walter Kreiser, O. Lehmann-Russbueldt and Professor Ludwig Quidde, who struggled valiantly to bring this information before the public, were howled down as traitors, imprisoned, or met by stony silence from almost the entire German press.[13]

The pressure for rearmament emanated from a multiplicity of causes. The long and deeply ingrained military tradition of Germany undoubtedly chafed under the limitations imposed on it by the Allied victors and sought to restore to Germany what was considered to be the true mark of German glory. For many, the disarmament of Germany in a world that continued to remain armed wounded their national pride and sense of equality. But for many too the main point was the eventual rectification of the terms of the Versailles Treaty and especially those pertaining to the eastern borders of Germany. Germans were hypnotized by the Polish question and saw no way out except by eventual military action. A powerful military machine was necessary to restore to Germany its lost territories in the east and make it once again the leading power in that area. While a Locarno on the western borders was conceivable, there was never any suggestion of a similar arrangement for the east. Here the eventual decision was to be by force of arms.

At a demonstration of 40,000 uniformed members of the Stahlhelm in 1931, the leader of the veterans, Franz Seldte, declared:

Today your grey front stands in the Ostmark and only fifty kilometers divide you from the frontier of the country [i.e., Poland] from which threats and cries of hatred have been assailing our ears for twelve years, whose politicians and officials cannot do enough to oppress and vex our fellow nationals, who have been placed in their power by the arbitrary fixing of frontiers at Versailles. We at this place assert that no measure of internal or foreign policy calculated to bring aid and re-enforcement to the oppressed Ostmark in its distress is possible except through a strong national government in the Reich, as well as in Prussia. . . . Stahlhelm comrades, there lies the German east, there lies Germany's destiny.[14]

This point of view, not always overtly expressed, was none the less the consensus of the leaders of all the major political groups in Germany. And this dangerous situation was not mollified or improved by the saber-rattling colonels who ruled Poland. It was here, therefore, logically that World War II was to find its point of origin.

Closely allied with the eastern question was the relation of Germany to other German-speaking areas. *Anschluss* with Austria became a major objective of German foreign policy from the first days of the Weimar Republic.[15] Socialists joined with bourgeois democrats and conservatives in clamoring for such union. France, however, remained adamant in its opposition. French political leaders were fearful that the union of Austria and Germany would open the way for German penetration into Czechoslovakia and Poland. These fears proved to be only too well founded when the Nazis used precisely this strategic advance following 1938. But under the Weimar Republic even liberal and pacifist groups in both Austria and Germany considered *Anschluss* not only desirable but inevitable. Stresemann had written in his letter to the crown prince that "in the background stands the union with German Austria." In his conversation in Paris with Poincaré in 1928 Stresemann admitted to the French prime minister that any positive attempt to carry out the idea at that time would be "condemned to futility." But he went on to paint a highly exalted and romanticized picture of what Austria and Vienna meant to Reich Germans and how the Austria of Mozart and Schubert represented the "lost soul" of old Germany in an otherwise "Americanized" Germany. "After all," said Stresemann to Poincaré, "we have lived under one empire for centuries" and "we have a strong feeling for Austria." [16] Paul Löbe, the Socialist President of the Reichstag, was for many years the head of the Oesterreichisch-deutscher Volksbund. But whereas the Socialist supporters of *Anschluss* desisted from pushing the problem to the fore for fear of bringing on an international crisis, the more nationalist groups carried on active agitation in behalf of this cause. In March, 1931, after secret negotiations between Dr. Julius Curtius, Brüning's foreign minister, and the Austrian pan-German Vice Chancellor Schober, announcement was made of a customs union between the two countries. This action stirred a storm of resentment in France and Britain, and under pressure both Austria and Germany backed down and withdrew their agreement. This served as tangible evidence, however, of the existence of strong nationalist feelings of pan-Germanism in both states.

The espousal of the cause of German minorities in other countries likewise served to fan excitable and deeply sentimental nationalist emotions among all Germans. The terms *Grenz* and *Auslandsdeutsche,* referring to German-speaking populations in border areas and as minorities in non-German states, came to be widely used, and these populations received increasing attention from Germans. Theorists of nationalism like Max H. Boehm pointed out that nationals in such areas represent the most vulnerable danger spots of a nationality. Here the struggle for nationalism is an omnipresent and daily recurring phenomenon. These, therefore, are the centers of the most ardent nationalism.

Before World War I the cause of "Germanism" abroad was mainly cultivated by the Pan-German League and scattered groups in Austria-Hungary and Germany. Neither the German nor the Austro-Hungarian governments devoted too much attention to the problem. The break-up of the Austro-Hungarian Empire and the defeat of Germany placed the general problem of national minorities and minority protection on the world agenda, but it made Germans peculiarly conscious of the problem. Some Germans, confronted with the loss of the war and with the loss of power in the world, fell back on the eighteenth century concept of nationality as developed by Herder. They elaborated the distinction between *Staatsnation* and *Kulturnation,* between the political nationalism of the national state and cultural nationalism which is independent of, and over and above, the political boundaries of a state.

The national pride of the Germans, wounded by the loss of the war and the loss of territory, could be fed by the image of a vast cultural organism of German-speaking populations scattered over all parts of the globe, united by ties of common culture and language, and representing a glorious cultural tradition. Reich Germans looked across their own borders and saw German-speaking peoples in Austria, in the South Tyrol, Poland, Czechoslovakia, Rumania, Yugoslavia, Alsace, Denmark, Belgium, Luxemburg, the Baltic states, Hungary, and Switzerland. Some even looked farther, to the Volga Germans in the U.S.S.R. and to the millions of German emigrants in South Africa, South America, and the United States. A curious fusion of old pan-Germanism and non-political or cultural nationalism was effected which conceived, as Stresemann said, of some 30 million Germans of "German blood" outside the borders of the Reich and of some 12 million Germans "torn from the Reich," who looked to the German Reich to protect their interests and who needed to be stimulated to retain and perpetuate their *"Deutschtum."*

"Volkstum" became a popular designation for the national content of this kind of grouping as distinguished from state and nation. Various organizations already existing were expanded, and new ones formed to defend the interests of these border and *Auslandsdeutsche.* The Verein für das Deutschtum im Ausland and the Deutscher Schutzbund were the most active of these organizations. Special institutes, some independent and others attached to universities, were established to provide the apparatus of scientific research and study of these problems. Writers like Max Hildebert Boehm, Karl von Loesch, Wilhelm Stapel, Hermann Ullmann, Karl von Hugelmann, and Karl Haushofer within Germany were aided by institutes in Austria and by minority Germans abroad.

The establishment of the system of minority rights by the Versailles Treaty and the setting up of the League of Nations Minority Commission provided the legal framework for carrying on all these activities. Scientific research, actions in defense of German culture, legal and political action in behalf of German minorities, festivals of German life and culture, youth groups, guided tours, action in plebiscites, publication of books, journals, pamphlets, and calendars—these were among the chief functions carried out by and in behalf of the German minorities. One of the main reasons advanced by Stresemann for Germany joining the League of Nations was to provide him with a forum for the defense of German minorities. He declared that it was "one of the chief tasks of German policy to further the cultural autonomy of the Germans in foreign countries." The Germans abroad, he declared in a speech to the press on *Kulturpolitik* on December 13, 1925, have been placed, as a result of the new order in Europe, in a new and important relation to the total German *Volkstum*. Everywhere in Europe *Deutschtum* is engaged in a bitter struggle for the maintenance of its culture, and the defense of *Deutschtum* is definitely part of the work of the foreign office. "The smallest [German] school in a South American forest," he announced, "is a significant cultural act." From the day Germany was admitted to the League of Nations until Hitler left it, German activity there revolved chiefly around two issues—armaments and minorities. And it made little difference as to whether the German spokesman was Stresemann, the Socialist Hermann Müller, or the Centrist Brüning. Eventually the minority issue broke out from the relatively harmless bounds of cultural demands to become the central issue of the Sudeten crisis in 1938 and of the war with Poland in 1939. And most of the German *cultural* associations and groups outside the borders of the Reich proved to be political fifth columns that paved the way for the forcible creation of the Greater Germany of the Nazis.[17]

For many Germans in the Weimar Republic the regaining of the lost overseas colonies was also an active and vital goal of foreign policy. Colonial leagues kept alive the memory of Germany's colonial empire throughout these years. In many cities and towns public squares were adorned with tombstones dedicated to the lost colonies, and maintained with proper nationalist care by draped flags, wreaths, and periodic pilgrimages and speeches. Others, however, looked to Russia and the east as the proper field for German expansion. This brings us to the important problem of German-Russian relations which has baffled and puzzled historians, politicians, and statesmen all during these years and which still remains one of the "unknown factors" in the alignment of forces between east and west.

German-Russian relations during the Weimar epoch were carried on under the impact of a number of interacting and often contradictory influences.[18] First there was the relationship between the German Communist party on the one hand and the Comintern and world policy of the Soviet Union on the other. This relationship operated more openly and more powerfully in the first years of the republic when the role of Germany in a world Communist revolution occupied first place in the strategy of world revolution of Lenin. The collapse of the German Communist uprisings in 1923 brought this phase to a decline. Second, there was the identity of feeling shared in by both Bolshevik Russia and defeated Germany as the "outcast" and "rejected" nations of Europe, the latter by virtue of its role in World War I, the former by having espoused the threatening and "poisonous" doctrine of Bolshevism. Third, there was the historical background of German foreign policy which harked back to the days of Bismarck and the Reinsurance Treaty with Russia which was intended to protect Germany from a war on two fronts. Many Germans attributed a great measure of responsibility for the loss of World War I by Germany to the abandonment of this pro-Russian oriented policy by William II and his political advisers. Fourth, there was the geographic position of Germany in the heart of Europe, resting squarely between Russia and the Western democracies and forced by its very position to find a way to overcome the dilemma of this location. Fifth, there was the economic factor which pointed to the natural alliance of interests between the highly industrialized Germany and agrarian and backward Russia, and the long record of Russia and the east as the large export market for German manufactured goods. Finally there was the development of an intellectual current in Germany which found greater spiritual kinship with the land of Tolstoy and Dostoievsky than with the "shallow optimism" and "decadent" culture of the West. Literary figures like Moeller van den Bruck and Thomas Mann helped build up a cult of intellectual affinity between Russia and Germany that came to permeate not only academic and scholarly circles but also the political and military groups of the right. Moeller was the first to provide a complete German translation of Dostoievsky and even suggested that perhaps the Russians were the "Aryan *Urvolk*." But he also argued that when Bolshevism moved against India it really meant England, and when it pressed against Poland it meant France. "It means our enemies," wrote Moeller. "And that unites Russian and German socialism." [19]

Thomas Mann, in the early years of the republic, contrasting the profound and "tremendously genuine nationalism" of a Tolstoy or Dostoievsky with the shallow notions of liberalism and progress of the West, called upon Russia and Germany to learn to know each other better so that "they might go hand in hand together in the future." [20]

There was, thus, a strong pro-Russian orientation among generals and officers who saw there a field for German rearmament, among industrial and economic leaders who looked to the revival of the pre-war economic penetration of Russia by Germany, among the new group of geo-politicians of the school of Karl Haushofer who dreamed of the establishment of a Eurasian bloc from the Rhine to the Amur and the Yangtze to oppose the Anglo-Saxon "sea-ruling world-power," among diplomats who saw in Russia the ally against France, among intellectuals who combined Nietzsche, Dostoievsky, and Bolshevism to conjure up a picture of "German socialism" and "conservative revolution" that would bring about the true revolutionary *élan* of Germany in place of the abortive and feckless revolution of 1918, and among the several million German Communists for whom the idea of a German-Soviet alliance was the cornerstone of their entire program.

We know very much more about the inner secrets of German-Russian relations from the German side than from that of the Russians. From the Russians have come no materials other than the veiled references thrown up in the various trials of opposition leaders in the U.S.S.R. While there is as yet no sufficiently reliable data with which to separate fact from fiction and trumped-up charges in these fantastic trials, it is safe to assume that Soviet leaders from Lenin and Trotsky down through Stalin also had strong feelings for close Russo-German relations and that the statement made by Krestinsky before the court in 1938 was in conformity with the truth when he said:

Trotsky argued that our line in foreign policy coincided with that of Germany at that period, that Germany was in a state of ruin after the war, and that in any event, in view of the existence of revenge sentiments in Germany with regard to France, England and Poland, a clash between Germany and the Soviet Union, or Soviet Russia at that time, in the near future was out of the question, and that therefore we could agree to this deal without actually committing a grave crime.[21]

A variety of influences and factors, therefore, operated during these years to bring Russia and Germany together. Often these influences were in contradiction to one another. Certainly apart from the Communists none of the German groups looked toward the triumph of Communism in Germany. But an identity of interest and aspiration united these sides, and at the same time there was no doubt a Machiavellian confidence on the part of both Russians and Germans that each would outsmart the other, secure what was to their own national interest, and then be able either to swallow up the partner or else at least keep him at bay. In the same way that Soviet leaders, no doubt, kept the hope of ultimate world revolution in the back of their minds, there is also no doubt that at least among some of the German military and political leaders there was the dream of ultimate domination of Russia by the "superior" Germany.

Negotiations between Weimar Germany and the Soviet Union began as early as 1920. But the first concrete result of these negotiations was the Treaty of Rapallo in 1922, which fell like a bombshell on the foreign offices of Europe. German and Bolshevik representatives at the Genoa Conference, kept at a distance and ignored by the victorious Allied leaders, turned the tables on their opponents by announcing the signing of the treaty. Walther Rathenau, the German foreign minister, had long been an adherent of an alliance with Russia. In January, 1920, he wrote to a friend that "we must enter into an economic relationship with Russia" and he founded at that time a "Commission for the Study of Russian Affairs." Writing to Professor Hoffmann regarding this commission, Rathenau declared:

I am in complete agreement with you as to the necessity of finding some common ground between Russia and ourselves. . . . It is my hope that the labors of the Commission will bring about the first and decisive rapprochement in the economic sphere, to be followed, let us hope, by a corresponding rapprochement in the political sphere.[22]

Baron Ago von Maltzan, a disciple of Kiderlen-Wächter, who was secretary of state to the Foreign Office, was the real architect of Rapallo. He carried on all the preliminary negotiations with Chicherin and worked out all the details. Seeckt, who had already carried on extensive negotiations himself with Radek, Krassin, and Chicherin on Reichswehr expansion and who had dispatched several of his staff officers for consultation in Russia, was kept closely informed of the negotiations by Chancellor Wirth. Seeckt was interested in close ties with Russia not only for military but also for political reasons. Writing to Wirth in 1922, Seeckt indicated that he had no hopes for cordial relations with France and that he counted on a cleavage between England and France. An active Russian policy, therefore, was essential. Above all, wrote Seeckt, the existence of Poland was unbearable and irreconcilable with the living needs of Germany. But Poland was even more unbearable for Russia. Poland, he wrote, "must disappear and will disappear through its own internal weakness and through Russia—with our help." Germany's hopes for regaining her position as a world power could succeed only by "a firm union with Great Russia." The basis of understanding between the two, declared Seeckt, should be the boundaries of 1914 of Germany and Russia.[23]

The Rapallo Treaty was formally signed on April 16, 1922. It provided for the resumption of full diplomatic relations between the two countries, and in return for Germany's giving up all claims for nationalized property of Germans in Russia, the U.S.S.R. abandoned all claims to German reparations. No longer were these two weakened and dependent nations isolated and at the mercy of the Western powers. The potential of their combined economic, military, and political power was sufficient to set off a scare in the Western camp that has persisted to this day. In Germany the signing of the treaty was received with jubilation by both left and right. "The 'yes' we gave to the Russians in Genoa," wrote Moeller van den Bruck, "is a 'no' to the West." The monarchist *Tägliche Rundschau* hailed it as a "decision of world historical importance," and the democratic press called it the end of Germany's international isolation. Rudolf Hilferding, the Socialist member of the German delegation to Genoa, told the Paris *Temps* that "the co-operation between Russia and Germany is an economic necessity" and the only way for Germany to fulfill its reparations obligations to France. Chancellor Wirth, returning to Berlin, announced jubilantly that the treaty had "broken through the circle of '*Schuldknechtschaft*' " that threatened Germany. Only the pacifist *Weltbühne* dared to be critical. In the issue of April 27, 1922, it wrote:

At a moment when after four years of war and three of post-war confusion, the European powers have assembled in order to take common counsel as to their future, Germany—apart from Russia the one country utterly dependent on the help of others—commits this escapade and isolates herself voluntarily, excludes herself from the conference table, rises in opposition to all other powers . . . and falls again under the suspicion that she is the disturber of peace in Europe.

German home opinion was hardly aware of the secret military negotiations that were going on at the same time, and they looked upon Rapallo as purely political and economic in character; but in Moscow Leon Trotsky, on May Day, 1922, hailed the new Red army that was the "finely sharpened sword" that would hurl back the enemies of the Soviet Union "supported by the treaty with Germany." Radek, at the Fourth Congress of the Comintern in 1922, proclaimed the mutual necessity of Germany and Russia for each other and that the existence of Germany was of the utmost necessity to Russia "as a counter-weight to the preponderance of the Allies."

Despite incidents between the German government and diplomatic representatives of the U.S.S.R. in Germany, the spirit of Rapallo continued to characterize Russo-German relations. When Stresemann began the negotiations of the Locarno Pact with France and England, there was considerable nervousness in Moscow. This was allayed immediately by the signing of a Russo-German commercial treaty on October 12, 1925, a few days before the Locarno Treaty was initialed, and by a political treaty of friendship on April 24, 1926. The new treaty was received with enthusiasm in Germany as a continuation of the Rapallo Treaty and as a legitimate extension of Bismarck's Reinsurance Treaty with Russia. The Center, People's party, Democrats, and Social Democrats accepted it as a necessary complement to the Locarno Pact; Professor Hoetzsch, the spokesman for the Nationalists, called it the necessary act to restore the balance toward Russian orientation; and Count Reventlow, the racialist spokesman, reaffirmed his stand that "Germany's future is only in the east" and that Germany was not to be a "bridge between east and west." Only the tiny faction of dissident Communists, led by Karl Korsch, that had split off from the K.P.D., voted against the treaty. Actually, Germany was playing off the Allies against Soviet Russia while Russia was doing the same for the Allies and Germany. German political and military leaders were using their geographical and strategic position in Europe to gain whatever they could for Germany.

This policy was indeed successful in making Germany count once again in the world of international politics and in making her *"bündnisfähig."* It provided both the material and diplomatic conditions for eventual German rearmament, and in this way paved the way for the Nazi-Soviet Pact of 1939. This is not to say that there were no significant differences between the foreign policy of Rathenau, Stresemann, and Brüning and the subsequent policies of Ribbentrop and Hitler, and that the aggressive moves which brought about World War II flowed inevitably from the line of policy laid down during the pre-Hitler era. It does mean, however, that the Weimar political leaders, bent only on the supreme goal of "liberating" Germany from the "shackles of Versailles," failed to realize that any foreign policy that would not result in allaying the ever present and understandably jittery fears of France would continue to preserve within Central Europe all the potentialities of war and conflict. Even while the last vestiges of occupation and reparations were being obliterated by the world crisis, the Hoover moratorium of 1931, and the Lausanne conference of 1932, the Socialist Hermann Müller and the Centrists Wirth and Brüning continued to feed the flames of violent nationalism by both act and public pronouncement. The tragic irony of it all is that just when all the outstanding issues that had created bitterness between Germany and the Allied powers were being brought to a satisfactory solution with the evacuation of the Rhineland, with the acceptance of Germany as a member of the Council of the League of Nations, and with the end of reparations, the flame of violent nationalism and aggressive expansionism was just ready to burst forth into the satanic cataclysm of Nazi rule in 1933.

The statesmen of the Weimar Republic did not learn the lesson of the defeat of 1918. They did not realize that a policy of "isolation" for Germany was impossible even when it had allies like Austria and Italy. And a policy of playing off East against West was also tantamount to "isolation." The Weimar Republic might possibly have saved itself and Europe if it had acted boldly in liquidating the foreign policy of the empire and taken the courageous step toward a continental democratic European policy based on Franco-German understanding. An imaginative leader like Carlo Mierendorff pointed out in 1932 that not only was Germany in peril but that the entire world was in peril, that large empires had been fashioned in the Anglo-Saxon world, the U.S.S.R., and the Far East while in Europe the numerous political states were devouring each other in the name of national honor and national liberty, and that the only solution lay in the pacification of Europe and its organization into a free and democratic "world state." The Nazi slogan of "Down with Versailles," wrote Mierendorff, must be countered with the slogan of "Transcending Versailles by Europe." Mierendorff's words, however, found little echo even in his own party. Centrists and Socialists vied with Nazis in their appeals to the nationalist anti-French and anti-Polish sentiments.

CHAPTER XVIII

Economic Life in Weimar Germany

Was wir halten, ist nicht mehr zu halten
Und am Ende bleibt uns nichts als Weinen.

FRANZ WERFEL

German economic life during the Weimar Republic went through three distinct stages: (1) the period of inflation, 1918–1923; (2) the period of prosperity and boom, 1923–1929; and (3) the period of economic crisis, 1929–1932.[1] The first period was dominated by the fantastic course of currency inflation. The German mark which had stood at 4.2 per dollar before the war and at 8.9 in 1919, after the conclusion of hostilities, continued to decline steadily for the next three years. In the middle of 1922 the decline began to assume fantastic and astronomical proportions. By November, 1923, the German mark reached the dizzy figure of 4,200,-000,000 to the dollar. Those were mad days in Germany. The daily dollar quotation took the place of the weather as the standard subject of conversation. The American dollar became the measure of value in Germany, and prices were adjusted to the dollar rather than to the mark. The situation developed with such speed that paper mills and printing presses could not keep pace with the need for supplies of paper money. Over 300 paper mills and 2,000 printing establishments worked on 24-hour shifts to supply the Reichsbank with the needed bank notes.

The mark lost all value and a wild scramble ensued for real goods of all kinds. Barter replaced the use of money for large sections of the population. Fabulous fortunes were built up in the course of weeks and months. The Reichsbank stimulated the inflationary trend by extending credit at relatively low rates of interest to businessmen, who then hastily bought up goods and real property at terrific profits. Hugo Stinnes emerged out of this period as the most vivid example of such accumulated wealth. A descendant of a prosperous Rhineland merchant family, and an important figure in German industry before the war, Stinnes took advantage of the inflation period to build up the most spectacular fortune

446

and the most amazing vertical trust in post-war Germany. From iron and steel he branched out into shipping, transportation, lumber, hotels, paper, newspapers, and politics. He was the supreme example of the German post-war tycoon who took advantage of any and every opportunity to build up his fortune and his personal power. Many German industrialists and merchants took Stinnes as their model.

The inflation left havoc and distress among the workers and especially among the middle classes. Soaring prices far outdistanced increases in wages, and there were resulting strikes and unemployment. Workers had to pay the equivalent of nine to ten hours of work for a pound of margarine, several days' work for a pound of butter, six weeks' pay for a pair of boots, and twenty weeks' pay for a suit of clothes. The most disastrous effects of inflation, however, were felt by the urban middle classes, especially fixed income groups and those living on savings and pensions. These classes suffered economic and psychic damage that left permanent injuries to the social body of Weimar Germany. As Stresemann declared on June 29, 1927, "The intellectual and productive middle class, which was traditionally the backbone of the country, has been paid for the utter sacrifice of itself to the state during the war by being deprived of all its property and by being proletarianized."

The mad days of inflation brought economic ruin, a loosening of morals and social ties, a wave of political and social malcontent and cynicism, and a class of proletarianized burghers who became the happy recruiting ground for all the nationalistic and racialist movements that came to undermine the republic. Who and what was responsible for this inflation?

The economic dislocation brought about all over the world by four years of war had left its mark also on Germany, even though Germany itself suffered no physical damage by war. But the territorial changes and the dislocation of world markets were bound to affect seriously a country as highly industrialized as was Germany. Germany had always depended to a considerable extent on food imports, which were paid for by export of manufactured goods. The disruption of the iron and steel industries, of the potash and textile industries, and of transportation caused a serious deterioration of the German balance of payments. Dominating the entire picture, however, during these years was the problem of reparations demanded by the Allied powers of Germany for damage caused during the war.

The reparations problem became intertwined with a variety of moral and political aspects. It was tied to the problem of war guilt and was made the object of political football in rivalries between political factions and parties in Allied countries. It became entangled in the mesh of inter-Allied war debts to the United States and thus was brought into the arena of American party politics and the battle between isolationists and internationalists. Only gradually, and after most of the damage had been done, did both Allied and German political leaders come to realize that irrespective of moral and political considerations the problem of transfers of huge payments from one nation to another over long periods of years in a highly unstable and disrupted world economy is an extremely delicate one and hardly capable of being carried out without serious economic dislocation.

Allied reparation policy immediately following the conclusion of the war made the serious error of not realizing that what the world needed most was stability and a feeling of security, in order to bring about economic recovery. The Allied powers began by stretching the concept of reparations to cover the demand that Germany pay for the entire costs of the war instead of merely for damage done. They then continued to keep the problem in a continuous state of agitation and nervous hysteria by refusing to set either a total bill for Germany to pay or a definite time limit of responsibility. From the German side, even with the Wirth-Rathenau policy of fulfillment, came more than casual and accidental symptoms of unwillingness to pay. The increased pressure by the Allies on Germany in 1922–1923, culminating in the Ruhr invasion, was the most immediate cause of the German inflation. And the end of inflation came with the negotiations that culminated in the first reparations settlement under the Dawes Plan. Political events, therefore, represented the chief cause of the inflationary crisis. It must be added, however, that the German government, together with banking and industrial leaders, must also bear a large share of the responsibility for this catastrophe.

Neither the imperial government of the kaiser nor the post-war republican governments attempted to meet the huge obligations incurred during the war by taxation. Instead they resorted to internal loans. During the period of 1919–1923 the amount of receipts coming into the Reich treasury averaged only about 25 per cent of the expenditures. Huge sums were spent by the government to finance passive resistance in the Ruhr. But industrial and financial leaders like Helfferich, Havenstein, and Stinnes maintained a determined opposition to any system of direct taxation to pay for the mounting needs of government expenditures. In the endeavor to keep itself alive and to meet the reparations payments, the German government resorted to borrowing and to the printing presses. As a result Germany emerged from the inflationary crisis with almost its entire internal national debt wiped clean. In January, 1919, the internal debt was 170,000 million marks; after stabilization in 1924 it was only 1,958 million marks. At the same time Britain was left with an internal debt of 7,500,-000,000 pounds and France with that of 6,400,000,000 pounds.

Proof of government responsibility for the inflation is further adduced by the fact that stabilization came just when the government decided to act. In November, 1923, the German cabinet decided to abandon passive resistance in the Ruhr and to come to terms with France on reparations.

A new *Rentenmark* was introduced on November 15, 1923. It was officially denominated in gold but actually was without a gold basis and not convertible. The new mark was nominally issued against a mortgage on all the land and real estate in Germany. Actually, however, currency stabilization was effected by the fact that public confidence resulted in the acceptance of the new mark. Public confidence was restored by the balancing of the Reich budget and by the political stability ushered in by the Dawes Plan negotiations on reparations.

Under the terms of the Dawes Plan, which Germany accepted and signed on August 30, 1924, Germany pledged to make annual payments starting at $250,000,000 and rising gradually over a four-year period to $625,000,000. Future payments were to vary according to the index of German prosperity, and foreign credits were to be extended to speed German recovery. Neither a final total nor a final date was set at this time. This was not done until the adoption of the Young Plan in 1929, when a final settlement equivalent to $28,800,000,000 was set to be paid out in a period of fifty-nine years. An International Bank of Settlements was established to handle the delicate and complex problem of transfer of payments. The entire reparations problem came to a final end at the Lausanne conference in June, 1932, when, under the impact of the world depression, the decision was made to set aside the Young Plan payments entirely.

The total amount of reparations paid by Germany for the period prior to 1924 is still a subject of dispute, depending on different methods of computation. The Allied Reparations Commission admitted to 10,426,-000,000 gold marks while the German government claimed it had paid 42,059,000,000 gold marks. The best impartial estimate, made by Keynes and the Institute of Economics, is that of 26,000,000,000 gold marks ($6,-200,000,000). Between September 1, 1924, and June 30, 1931, Germany's reparations payments totaled 11 billion gold marks, or $2,600,000,000. Between 1924 and 1930, however, Germany's reparations payments were made possible by the pumping of foreign loans into Germany, chiefly from the United States. A total of 25 billion marks made its way into Germany, a sum which more than made up for the reparation payments made by Germany. During these years American money thus made a complete cycle—to Germany in the form of loans, from Germany to the reparations creditors, and from them back to the United States as payments on Allied war debts.

Beginning in 1924 and lasting to 1929, Germany went through a period of rapid economic recovery and prosperity which James W. Angell has called "one of the most spectacular recoveries in the world's entire economic history." Within six years after what appeared to be a complete economic collapse, Germany rose like the fabled phoenix to become once again one of the great industrial nations of the world. The basic indus-

tries, iron and steel, coal, textiles, chemicals, electrical supplies, and precision and optical instruments, all came up to or went beyond the 1913
level of production and profit. Real income and standard of living for
the great majority of the population was restored to the prosperous level
of 1913. The estimate for German national income for 1928 was placed
at close to 18 billion dollars as compared to 12 billion dollars in 1913.
Per capita income rose from $178 to $279. The combined fleets of the
Hamburg American Line and the North German Lloyd once again challenged Britain for supremacy of merchant shipping, and the Lufthansa,
taking advantage of the permission granted by the Versailles Treaty for
retaining civil aviation, came to occupy the leading position in the development of this new means of transport. The automobile industry, while
never reaching the level of American production, nevertheless came to
occupy the first place among continental powers, and this was furthered by
the planning and building of new and improved automobile roads. Municipalities erected magnificent public buildings, opera houses and theaters,
public baths and large modern housing projects. Germany once again
came to lead all other European countries in the development of the
"modern" way of life, fashioned by modern technology.

The prosperity ushered in by the reparations settlement is attributed
in large measure to the amazing capacity of German industry and labor to
concentrate its energies on recovery. It speaks highly for German technological and economic genius. It was, however, also the product of two
significant trends—one external and the other internal. During these years
the German economy was primed by means of an enormous flow of foreign
capital, chiefly from the United States, in the form of short-term loans,
long-term loans, and sales of German securities abroad. A great deal of
this capital went to German municipalities to help finance public works
and display of municipal munificence. Much also went into the financing
of German industry.

During the same years, too, Germany took over with a vengeance not
only American capital but also American methods of scientific management of industry and efficiency. It was the era of the "rationalization of
industry." New and more scientific methods of production were introduced; greater standardization of patterns and specifications and new and
improved methods of accounting and advertising were brought into existing economic and business organization, and the full and efficient application of scientific research to business and technology was realized. Moreover, the older tendency of industrial combination, evident already in the
trusts and cartels of the empire, now reached a new peak of development.
The number of cartels, both internal and international, increased enormously. This trend of industrial combination served to acquire for Germany a rapidly expanding share of world trade. The Siemens Konzern in
the electrical industry, Hapag in shipping, the Wiking Konzern in cement,

and above all the Vereinigte Stahlwerke A.G. in steel and the I.G. Farben in chemicals and dyes were the chief examples of this concentration of industry.

The huge steel trust, formed in 1926 under the chairmanship of Dr. Albert Vögler, linked together the various enterprises and interests of Thyssen, Stinnes, Phoenix A.G., and Otto Wolff. Of even greater and at times more sinister significance was the I.G. Farben trust, which came into being in 1925 under the aegis of Carl Duisberg, who was later succeeded by Dr. Carl Bosch and Dr. Hermann Schmitz as heads of this giant octopus of industry. Besides dyestuffs, I.G. Farben had giant interests in nitrogen fertilizers, acids, pharmaceuticals, photographic chemicals and film, artificial silk, motor spirits, lubricating oils, perfumes, varnishes, tanning materials, plastics, and sundry other enterprises. Its strategic economic, political, and military power lay in its thoroughgoing utilization of modern science to find substitutes for critical raw materials. By 1928 Germany dominated the world production of nitrates, of which German synthetic nitrates occupied the leading place. Under the direction of Dr. Carl Bosch, I.G. Farben developed the process of hydrogenation of coal for the making of synthetic oil as well as for the making of synthetic rubber. Its control of strategic patents in these areas of industry led to wide and still unraveled international connections with oil and chemical industries in the United States like Du Pont and Standard Oil, and in Britain with Imperial Chemicals Ltd. and Royal Dutch Shell. I.G. became a giant empire that built up political connections with the various political parties, had its own intelligence service, and established close and intimate ties with the German General Staff. The full-scale character of I.G. Farben operations became more readily apparent during the period of Nazi rule and during World War II, but the full story still remains to be unraveled from the maze of captured documents in the hands of Allied governments after the close of World War II.

The concentration of industry during the Weimar Republic was paralleled at the same time by the increased organization of labor and its heightened economic and legal recognition. The Weimar Constitution had placed labor "under the special protection of the Reich." Article 163 guaranteed to every German citizen "the opportunity to earn his living by productive labor"; Article 159 guaranteed the right of combination; and Article 165 gave the workers the right to participate in the shaping and determination of conditions of labor. The trade-unions were given legal recognition as the spokesmen for the workers, and the collective contract negotiated by the union was given legal primacy over individual contracts. In addition an elaborate and unified system of district and federal labor courts, capped by a supreme Reich labor tribunal, was set up in 1927 to adjudicate labor disputes. The number of industrial disputes in Germany had reached an all-time high in 1922 with 4,785 disputes, involving

1,823,921 employees, and resulting in 27,733,833 lost working days. In 1929 there were only 435 disputes, involving 179,667 workers, and resulting in the loss of 4,254,877 working days. The number of disputes dropped still further in the succeeding years, but these came in the slump years and hence cannot be attributed exclusively to the legal economic system in operation.

Trade-union membership had climbed to an all-time high of 9 million in 1923 during the unusual conditions of inflation, but in 1929 the total union membership was 5,748,000, of which the Free Trade Unions, now organized into the Allgemeiner Deutscher Gewerksbund, constituted the overwhelming majority. The eight-hour working day was guaranteed by the constitution and, despite some legal deviations from this brought about by economic and political pressures, it remained the capstone of labor policy during the entire Weimar epoch. The average real wages of workers were about 6 per cent higher in 1928 than in 1913. The already highly developed system of social security was further strengthened with new provisions for unemployment payments.

The picture thus created in Weimar Germany was one in which highly concentrated employer organizations confronted highly organized associations of labor, with the state in the position of ultimate arbiter and mediator. This system worked smoothly during the time of economic prosperity and boom. When the economic depression set in, however, this dependence upon the state resulted in a more acute struggle for the control of the state apparatus. More specifically, the increase in unemployment involved increased costs for social insurance and other social services. For these costs to be met it was necessary to introduce a program of increased taxation. This was the program proposed by the Socialist minister Hilferding in 1929. He met with the united opposition of the president of the Reichsbank and the other parties, and he was forced to resign in December, 1929.

The very factors which made for economic prosperity between 1924 and 1929 were also chiefly responsible for the collapse of the German economy beginning in 1929–1930. The rationalization movement, bringing about a large measure of technological displacement, was responsible for the development of large-scale unemployment. The dependence on foreign capital made Germany immediately sensitive to the effects of the "Great Depression" in the United States. A great deal of German capital was dependent on short-term foreign credits. In November, 1928, Dr. Stresemann had the foresight to declare:

I must ask you always to remember that during the past years we have been living on borrowed money. If a crisis were to arise and the Americans were to call in their short-term loans we should be faced with bankruptcy.

This is precisely what happened. The Wall Street crash in 1929 affected these areas immediately. Unemployment rose sharply from 1,368,000 in 1929 to 3,144,000 in 1930, and this was immediately reflected in the elections of September, 1930, when 107 National Socialists were elected to the Reichstag. These elections increased the panic among foreign creditors. The collapse of the Austrian Creditanstalt in May, 1931, was followed in July by the crash of the great German Darmstädter und Nationalbank (Danat). Foreign trade tumbled, exchange and currency restrictions were instituted, unemployment continued to mount to 5,668,000 in 1931 and 6,014,000 in 1932, and Germany was now joined to the rest of the world in the throes of severe economic crisis and depression. As early as 1925 the government had initiated a public works program to take up the slack in employment. The cabinets of Brüning, Papen, and Schleicher increased this activity to help ease the crisis. A voluntary labor service of twenty months for young people was instituted in 1931, from which was to develop Hitler's subsequent compulsory Labor Service (*Arbeitsdienst*). Economic crisis now combined with international tension and nationalist agitation to set the stage for totalitarian dictatorship as the way out of the crisis. The government headed by the Socialist Müller was forced out in March, 1930. It was the last parliamentary government of Weimar Germany. The Brüning cabinet that followed it was able to carry on only by the use of dictatorial emergency measures based on Article 48 of the constitution. It introduced many new controls of economic life, thus preparing the country for the regimented economy that was to come after 1933.

Intellectual Life in Weimar Germany

Ich beschreibe was kommt, was nicht mehr anders kommen kann: die Heraufkunft des Nihilismus.

NIETZSCHE

In the realm of intellectual and cultural life there was hardly time for the Weimar Republic to develop a pattern of its own. It was, culturally speaking, however, one of the most dynamic periods in German history.[1] It was a period of social crisis in which there was a high degree of instability and widespread acceptance of moral, esthetic, and intellectual relativism. But there was a release of a vast amount of cultural and spiritual energy that manifested itself in practically every phase of literature, art, philosophy, and academic scholarship. Germany now recovered its position of intellectual eminence even more rapidly than it achieved economic recovery. During the first years following the end of the war Germany fairly seethed with new and experimental movements. Berlin and Munich soon came to rival Paris as the cultural meccas for artists, literati, and scholars. The expressionist drama, the modern dance, non-objective art, atonal music, functional architecture, and progressive education flourished in Weimar Germany and attracted devotees from all parts of the world. In the eyes of many these movements came to be identified with the political régime of republican Germany. But there was vastly more to Weimar culture than these new and experimental movements, and much of this energy was ultimately to realize itself in the very destruction of the republican régime.

In painting and sculpture the older pre-war figures of Max Liebermann, Lovis Corinth, and Max Slevogt were joined by the more modernist creations of Oskar Kokoschka, Paul Klee, and Karl Hofer, while Käthe Kollwitz made herself the idol of republican Germany by her humane and sympathetic delineation of the poor and the suffering. The Bauhaus of Dessau blazed the way for a new architecture, functional in character and modern in design. To the older composers of international repute, Richard Strauss and Hans Pfitzner, was added the genius of Paul Hinde-

454

mith. The elder Max Planck was now joined by Albert Einstein and Werner Heisenberg in the construction of a new physics that was to have revolutionary repercussions far beyond the purely scientific realm. Wolfgang Köhler, Max Wertheimer, and Kurt Koffka developed their *Gestalt* psychology that for a while seriously rivaled the Viennese schools of Freud and Adler in popular influence. In the field of academic philosophy the positivism of Mach and Avenarius as well as the vitalism of Hans Driesch receded more into the background. This was the period of a revived Kantianism in the Marburg school of Hermann Cohen, Nicolai Hartmann, Paul Natorp, and Ernst Cassirer. Edmund Husserl's first important statement of his Phenomenology, published in 1913, saw its full flowering in the years of the republic. Catholic philosophy found its spokesman in Max Scheler, with his opposition to all modernity and subjectivism, and in the moving spirituality of Theodor Haecker. More than ever before loomed the influence of Nietzsche, who had now become respectable for academic philosophers as well as for rebels, and who found a legion of interpreters and misinterpreters from the vulgar racialists and more respectable nationalists like Alfred Bäumler to the fusion of Nietzsche and Kierkegaard as the foundation for existentialism worked out by Martin Heidegger and Karl Jaspers.

The universities remained, on the whole, as before the war, strongholds of conservative nationalism. But the republic created two new universities at Cologne and at Hamburg which attracted a far more progressive and liberal faculty. In the older universities too, despite the vehement opposition of the entrenched interests, new and fresh influences came into academic life. Jews, hitherto rarely to be found as regular professors; Socialist scholars, formerly outside the pale of official German culture; and women, now entered the family of German academic life. Distinguished scholars like Ernst Cassirer in philosophy, Erwin Panofsky in the history of art, Emil Lederer and Eduard Heimann in economics, Gustav Mayer in the history of the labor and socialist movements, Hermann Heller and Hermann Kantorowicz in political science, and Karl Mannheim in sociology not only introduced new points of view hitherto not heard in the academic halls of Germany but also enriched German scholarship and university life by opening up new areas of scientific investigation.

The Weimar period saw a special flourishing of the social sciences. Here the influences of Dilthey, Simmel, and Max Weber were of paramount importance. Dilthey's distinction between *erklären* (to explain), which characterized the natural sciences, and *verstehen* (to understand), which was the methodological approach to the social sciences, was taken up to become the basis for the development of the *Geisteswissenschaften*. In some instances, as in the case of the economist Werner Sombart, this led to a quasi-mystical reaction to scientific procedures and to a complete turnabout from his earlier progressive thinking. In political science acute and extremely clever scholars like Carl Schmitt and Robert Michels laid bare the irrational basis of political behavior to such an extent as to destroy any possibility for orderly democratic political organization, and in this way helped prepare the ground for an authoritarian rationale of political organization. What Settembrini said of Naphta, in Thomas Mann's *The Magic Mountain,* may be said of the brilliant political philosophy of Carl Schmitt: "His form is logic but his essence is confusion."

The field of sociology produced the systematic treatises of Ferdinand Tönnies, Franz Oppenheimer, Leopold von Wiese, and Alfred Vierkandt. A school of disciples of Max Weber, following his path in relating changes in intellectual climate to changes in the social situation, developed the field of *Wissenssoziologie,* or sociology of knowledge. Of these the most brilliant representative was Karl Mannheim at Frankfurt. In history, while conservative historians like Erich Marcks, Dietrich Schäfer, and Georg von Below continued in their traditional ways, older distinguished historians like Friedrich Meinecke, Hermann Oncken, and Otto Hintze joined democratic historians like Walter Goetz, Ernst Troeltsch, and Gustav Mayer in making their peace with the republic and also turning more and more to the field of *Geistesgeschichte,* or history of ideas. It was during this time that Meinecke produced his *Idee der Staatsräson,* in which he pointed out the limitations of a political theory based on power, and his monumental *Die Entstehung des Historismus,* in which he left the field of German power aspirations to find the highest form of German spirit in the classical humanistic era and in Goethe. Historical research was directed in an increasing degree to areas of German history hitherto neglected by the dominant Prussian school prevailing up to then. A new generation of liberal historians was being developed in Weimar Germany which was beginning to refashion completely the image of German history current since the nineteenth century until it was cut off in its incipient beginnings by the advent of Hitler.

The Weimar period saw a flourishing of Catholic scholarship in the social sciences. The Görres Gesellschaft carried on a wide variety of research and capped it with a new and large edition of the *Staatslexikon,* in which the various problems of society, government, and economics were treated in a scholarly and on the whole progressive fashion. Jewish scholarship, strengthened by the addition of new intellectual forces from eastern Europe, carried on the distinguished tradition of the older *Wissenschaft des Judentums* but infused it with a greater appreciation of social forces, with more sympathy for Jewish life in eastern Europe, and with a more positive attitude to the Jewish national movement. Martin Buber, emerging as the most representative leader of German Jewry, united with seekers for "mythos" among Protestants and Catholics, to probe the mystical foundations of religion and ethics. And despite frequent and ominous outbreaks of antisemitism there was, at least until 1929, the hope for the development of genuine understanding between Jew and gentile. From the old thirteenth century romantic Jewish cemetery in Worms, standing amidst the battered and half sunken tombstones of ancient Jewish rabbis and martyrs, one could also encompass the view of the beautiful spires of the Worms cathedral. In this esthetic unity of old Jewry and traditional Christianity, open-minded and progressive Jews and gentiles saw the symbol of German-Jewish affinity and harmony.

Observers familiar with German mores and attitudes noted the beginnings of a change in this area of human behavior which was induced by the republic. The traditional sign *Verboten* was still omnipresent, but there was a definite attempt by republican administrators in many areas to transform this "drill sergeant" spirit of police officials, postmen, and civil servants to a more friendly and human attitude, instead of the traditional forbidding manner of stern discipline. Experiments were started in progressive education, and women received not only the vote but also came to participate more actively in public affairs. With greater political freedom came also a more social-minded attitude toward problems of youth, crime, and sex. As usual in such cases, however, genuinely scientific and reform movements carried in their wake gross perversions and vulgarizations that concealed their lewdness under labels of *Kunst* and *Sexualwissenschaft.* Too often these were lumped indiscriminately into the same category with delicate and sensitive creations of art and mind. Germany, too, went through the same developments of mass culture, with all its ugly manifestations, that are the fateful problem of industrialized, urban mass democracy. Large publishing houses like those of Ullstein, Mosse, and Hugenberg put out not only the *Vossische Zeitung,* the *Berliner Tageblatt,* and the *Lokal-Anzeiger* but also a wide variety of intellectual fare for both sexes and all grades of intelligence and age. German typography and book publishing achieved pre-eminence in the production of art books and beautiful illustrated editions at prices low enough for mass consumption.

The German motion-picture industry grew to enormous dimensions and contributed not only artistic and experimental films but outdid Hollywood in producing films for mass consumption that oozed over with sentiment or were filled with violence of passion, horrors of crime, and general catering to bad taste.

The larger cities, especially Berlin and Munich, showed an increased development of gambling, erotic scandals and homosexuality, nudism, jazz mania, and various forms of occult astrology and magical hocus-pocus. A class of society came into being that made its living by providing for these experiences, and another class that found its highest satisfaction in their enjoyment. Socialists, in keeping with their tradition, carried on the battle against alcoholism, while Catholic political parties and youth groups waged war on obscenity, abortions, and lapses from traditional sex mores. Such manifestations of mass culture were not peculiar to Germany. But war, inflation, political disintegration and violence of political strife served to accentuate and exaggerate these tendencies. More significant still was the fact that in Germany these manifestations came to be linked in the public eye with political democracy and thus helped to discredit the republic in the eyes of the staid and conventional burghers.

In the field of imaginative literature the greatest figures were those who carried on their creative work from pre-war days. Rainer Maria Rilke, the imaginative and sensitive lyric poet, lived on to 1926. To the end he led a purely esthetic existence, disillusioned in the grossly nationalistic and militaristic trends which he saw in his native country. The two literary giants of the Weimar period, Gerhart Hauptmann and Thomas Mann, were identified most closely with the Weimar Republic. But the roads taken by the two were almost antithetic to each other. Hauptmann, author of *The Weavers* and idol of the Socialist masses, produced very little of high quality during this period and became increasingly nationalist until he ended up with his notorious "I vote *Ja*" in the Hitler plebiscite of 1933. Thomas Mann, author of *Friedrich und die grosse Koalition* and the *Betrachtungen eines Unpolitischen,* which Paul Alverdes had called "a true handbook for all sworn enemies of parliamentary democracy," slowly and with agonizing difficulty worked his way out of his deeply ingrained apolitical and amoral conservatism to become a defender of liberal humanism and political democracy, and when Hitler came to power he found his way into political emigration. Thomas Mann reached the highest point of his artistic development with his *Der Zauberberg (The Magic Mountain),* which, with its moving discussions between the rationalist humanist Settembrini and the young national romanticists, may justly be called the saga of the Weimar Republic.

In the poetry of Georg Trakl, René Schickele, Johannes Becher, and the young Franz Werfel; in the plays of Georg Kaiser and Ernst Toller, and in the prose writings of Klabund, expressionism, harking back to the pre-war influence of Frank Wedekind, held sway for a number of years as a characteristic manifestation of Weimar culture. With mad frenzy, eruptive intensity, and explosive and flagellant fury, which did not stop before chaotic destruction either of language or of esthetic form, it sought to encompass in yearning embrace either God or humanity and to give expression to what was considered at the time to be "the wildest raging era of human history."

A literary school, oriented toward European liberalism and influenced by the social radicalism of Marx or the psychology of Freud or the literary experimentation of James Joyce, flourished in the novels of Heinrich Mann, Jakob Wassermann, Stefan and Arnold Zweig, Alfred Döblin, and Hermann Hesse. Proletarian literature, closely allied to the Communist movement, was exemplified in the works of Erich Mühsam, Friedrich Wolff, Bertolt Brecht, Theodor Plievier, Oskar Maria Graf, and the earlier works of Ernst Toller. A small group of pacifist, anti-militarist, and anti-nationalist humanitarians gathered around the *Weltbühne,* edited by Carl von Ossietzky, were dedicated to the cause of deflating the pompous façade of the still flourishing Prussianism and of exposing the secret machinations of the old order of officers and Reichswehr. An over-sophisticated cosmopolitan estheticism and intellectualism which infuriated the conservative and conventional circles, but which tickled the sophisticated with its cold casualness, was found in the literary criticism of Alfred Kerr, in the jazzy and clever tunes of Kurt Weill, and in the devastatingly frank and brutal exposé of the "ruling classes" in the illustrations and paintings of George Grosz.

All these various literary currents emanated from, and were concerned chiefly with, urban life and all the social, psychological, and political tensions associated with modern urban society. For large masses of the German people, as well as for many literary critics and writers, such tendencies were alien and strange. They lived closer to the village, to the peasant, to the idyllic image of rural pre-industrial society. Thus grew that curious alignment of literary parties in Weimar Germany, divided between what they called "asphalt" literature and *Scholleliteratur,* or literature of the soil. For many Germans these Western-oriented currents of the more modernist character were all lumped together under slogans like "Americanization" or "cultural Bolshevism." As Carl von Ossietzky wrote in the *Weltbühne: "Kulturbolschewismus"* for many Germans meant "when Klemperer takes tempi different from Furtwängler, when a painter uses a color for a sunset not seen in Lower Pomerania, when one favors birth control, when you build a house with a flat roof, when you admire Charlie Chaplin and Albert Einstein, when you follow the democracy of the brothers Mann and when you enjoy the music of Hindemith and Kurt Weill—all that is 'cultural Bolshevism.' " But there also was more discriminating and more sensitive criticism. Ernst Wiechert, perhaps the most talented as well as the most genuinely sincere of the conservative writers, characterized the literary currents described above as the expression of a decadent epoch. These writers, he said, were not poets or imaginative creators but "historians." They had everything necessary for their job— "a cool, sharp intellect, a cold eye, the capacity for analysis, the incisive knife, the sure hand." They saw life as it was, a naked, pitiless reality, and they laid it bare and then stepped back. They tore down all the old conventions and objects of piety, and "there was little that they shunned in the means they used." They had little shame and were not sentimental. "They did not have what is called 'heart.' A knife has no heart." They were interested in being "clever and sharp and witty" instead of in being good. The fact that many in these circles happened to be Jews helped to add the antisemitic note to the complex of rural, conservative, romantic, and nationalist factors. Writers like Rudolf Binding, Ernst Wiechert, and Hans Carossa were able to cultivate their "closer to the soil" literature on the highest level of creative activity and remain more or less aloof from the political controversies surrounding these problems, although their works were received most enthusiastically by the more nationalist circles. On the other hand there were others like Hans Johst, Hans Blüher, Friedrich Blunck, Paul Ernst, Heinz Hans Ewers, who waged an open and noise-making battle against the "asphalt" literature and its liberal-democratic-bourgeois allies, while another group like Artur Dinter, Alfred Rosenberg, Dietrich Eckart, and Hans Grimm would never have had claim to mention if not for their close identification with the cultural program of the later triumphant Nazism. Hans Grimm's novel *Volk ohne Raum* (A People Without Living Space), first published in 1926, did more than any other single book to implant in the post-war German mind the burning desire to expand and acquire *Lebensraum*. Likewise, Alfred Rosenberg's ponderous and pompous *Der Mythus des 20. Jahrhunderts* established for him a position as ideological and cultural mentor of the National Socialist movement.

Quite apart and physically aloof from all these movements, but none the less spiritually very close to many of them, stood the priest-like, ivory-tower figure of the poet Stefan George and his circle. Stefan George's popularity only became apparent with the celebration of his sixtieth birthday in 1927. No one since Nietzsche had such a profound influence on German youth. In his *Blätter für die Kunst,* which ran from 1892 to 1919, and in the typographically exquisite and very expensive and limited editions of his poetry, in the exclusive "séances" in darkened Berlin salons, "with Rembrandtesque candle-light illuminating his ascetic profile with its projecting chin," in which he recited his poems to his band of disciplined followers, this "poet-priest" developed a cult of *Formkunst,* as opposed to *Stoffkunst,* in which everything was to be subordinated to its use as a vehicle for esthetic and artistic expression. While ostensibly disdainful and hence disinterested in the political affairs of the day, this very non-political disdain became a reactionary influence against the democratic republic. George and his followers were filled with "revulsion" at the "system." In their quest for a combination of aristocratic and Spartan Hellenism with the Germanic ideals of *Gefolgschaft* and heroism and the Catholic ideal of communion, George eliminated from his intellectual constellation all that was liberal, democratic, socialist, rationalist, and individualist. The works of the George circle were the beginnings of a reaction against democratic and socialist "enlightenment." They were, as Troeltsch called them, "revolutionary books against the revolution." It was a new sort of romanticism in which there was much talk of the "new Reich," of the "Führer" idea, of the nobility of "force," of the lower status of woman, of the eros of homosexuality, and above all of disdain for mass culture and mass politics. Out of this circle came the works of Rudolf Borchardt, Albrecht Schaeffer, Friedrich Gundolf, Ludwig Klages, Friedrich Wolters, Ernst Bertram, and Karl Wolfskehl.

This movement was in reality but part of a general reaction to the industrialization and mechanization of life that had already begun before the war. It was present in the pre-war youth movement and was echoed by Walther Rathenau in his *Mechanik des Geistes*. This trend, interrupted by the war, became even more accentuated and exaggerated by the effects of defeat, inflation and psychological tension. More than ever now came the realization that secularization combined with industrialization had resulted in what Max Weber called the *Entzauberung* of the world, and frantic and often pathological efforts were made to replace this void by intellectual food of medieval German mysticism and nineteenth century romanticism, at times also reinforced by the wisdom literature of India and the Far East. There was a trend to the mystical and occult, as evidenced in the anthroposophy of Rudolf Steiner, the philosophy of Ludwig Klages, the revived interest in the mysticism of Meister Eckhart and Jakob Boehme and in the neo-Hasidism of Martin Buber. Above all, the post-war years saw the full flowering of a powerful neo-romanticism that revived the theories of the older romanticists of the early nineteenth century and refashioned them for an attack upon rationalist and liberal humanitarian democracy exemplified by the republic. New editions, both de luxe and popular, were issued of the works of Novalis, Adam Müller, Franz von Baader, Wackenroder and the Schlegels. Catholic, Protestant, and Jew vied with one another in pointing out how romanticism was peculiarly adapted to the German spirit and how it could solve the complex problems of post-war society. Anti-rationalist organismic theories of the state, anti-capitalist critiques of materialism and economic individualism, revived nationalist xenophobia and ethnocentrism constructed upon reinterpretations of Herder, Fichte and Hegel—all these combined with a scorn for logic and reason and an exaltation of the power of the unconscious and of intuition helped to develop a state of mind which became hostile to the liberal democracy of the republic. Words and concepts like *Mythos* and *Schicksal* became popular vehicles for making it easy to avoid facing the hard realities of concrete existence. This joined with an over-exaggerated nationalist sentimentality and self-pity created an emotional state that was ready to be moved to an overflowing of tears and profuse weeping at the very mention of the word *Deutschland*.

It was during the Weimar period too that Germany produced two of the most famous of what Troeltsch called *"Modebücher"*: Count Hermann Keyserling's *Travel Diary of a Philosopher* and Oswald Spengler's *Decline of the West*. These books gave nourishment to the superiority feeling of the Germans, at the same time lending philosophic justification for the inferiority feeling of foreign intellectuals. For a number of years they were current as fashionable topics of conversation among intellectual circles both inside and outside Germany. Count Keyserling, an elegant and sophisticated nobleman of German Esthonian origin, had established a "School of Wisdom" at Darmstadt to heal the world from the diseases of materialism, rationalism, and "plebeian democracy." Following up his *Travel Diary* with further travels, Count Keyserling gained wide audiences for his lectures in which he attacked "Americanization" and advocated a new hierarchical caste system.

Even more responsive to the chiliastic yearnings of post-war Germany was Spengler's *Decline of the West,* which attained international fame in the post-war years. The German reading public of his day, in the words of Troeltsch, demanded "megalomania based on principles, majestic ramming of open doors, solemn proclamations of *carmina non prius audita,* imperious pronouncement of paradoxes and impudent fancy." Spengler gave it to them in this attempt at a grandiose and majestic interpretation of the entire course of human history.

While marked by grand sweep of style and powerful imaginative vistas, Spengler's *magnum opus* is at the same time full of historically false statements, fantastic pronouncements, and steep analogies lacking critical sense. Spengler's weighty treatise, however, made him one of the leading influences in shaping the conservative opposition to the republic. He became a favorite of both the East Prussian landlords and the West German industrialists. In his political tracts he indulged in unrestrained abuse and ridicule of the revolution of 1918 and the attempt to establish Germany upon republican foundations. Spengler intoxicated German youth, even more than did Nietzsche, with grandiloquent, bombastic, and oftentimes entirely unintelligible talk of "Faustian treatment of history" which "enables one to view the whole fact of man from an immense distance . . . as one regards the range of mountain peaks along a horizon." Rejecting all notions of progress and humanitarianism, Spengler taught a doctrine of radical pessimism tinged with biological struggle and animality that made a powerful appeal to German intellectuals already full of Schopenhauer, Nietzsche, and Wagner. Mankind, he wrote, has no aim, no idea, no plan, any more than the family of butterflies or orchids. It is "a zoological expression or an empty word." Life itself is the alpha and omega of all, and life "has no system, no program, no reason; it is here only for and by itself and the profound order in which it realizes itself can only be grasped by intuitive insight and feeling—and then perhaps can be described but cannot be dissected according to principles of good or bad, true or false, useful and desirable." [2]

"We no longer believe," wrote Spengler, "in the power of reason over life. We feel that life rules over reason." We are not interested in ideals but in brute facts. "To remain master over facts is much more important for us than to become slaves of ideals. The logic of the image of nature, the chain of cause and effect appears to be superficial to us: only the logic of the organic, of destiny, of instinct, which one feels, whose omnipotence is seen in the changes that occur, gives evidence of the profound character of its becoming." Compromise, understanding, mutual concession, live and let live—these are all superficial glossings over the "profound" and fundamental condition of man and society—war and conflict. "A true international is possible only through the triumph of the idea of one race over all others. . . . There are no reconciliations in history. . . . There is only one end to the eternal waging of conflict and that is death—death of the individual, death of a nation, death of a culture." Germans, as the "young nation," are comforted with the pronouncement that their end is in the far distant future and that the immediate future for them is world domination and power.

An important element in Spengler's political doctrine was his identification of Prussianism with socialism. Rejecting both the materialism and the internationalism of Marxian socialism, he defined socialism as complete subjection of the individual to the feeling of obedience and duty to the state. The struggle for the welfare not of the individual but of the whole is, according to Spengler, the profoundest idea of socialism, and therefore it was not Marx but the Prussian king Frederick William I who was the first self-conscious socialist. The true socialist state is thus the militarized state where every worker as well as entrepreneur becomes the civil servant of the state, working in the interests of the entire nation under strict discipline and Prussian austerity. It was the disciplined character of the German Social Democratic party under August Bebel that led Spengler to advocate the union of the "worthwhile sections of German labor with the best bearers of the old Prussian state idea, both determined to establish a strictly socialist state . . . both forged together by a unity of sense of duty, by the consciousness of a great mission, by the will to obey in order to rule, to die in order to conquer, by the power to bring enormous sacrifices in order to carry through that for which we were born, that which we are, and which would not be without us." [3]

In the post-war youth movement there was a special kind of conservatism that called itself "revolutionary conservatism." The pre-war youth movement, influenced by the iconoclasm of Nietzsche and the anti-bourgeois revolt of Ibsen, became in the Weimar period increasingly engulfed by romantic conservatism. In the same way in which the early nineteenth century romanticism was a reaction against the *pure* reason of the Enlightenment, so the romantic youth movement was a reaction against the *practical* reason of technology, rationalization, and mechanization. Their rejection of reason as the "whore of the Enlightenment," their romantic yearning for the rural simplicity of nature as opposed to the mechanical complexity of the big city, their search for *Bindung* and

Ganzheit, for attachment to community and leader to replace what they disdainfully called "atomistic individualism," their idealization of the most distant past as being most genuine and pure, their radical break with conventional morality and religion, their quest for heroism and self-sacrifice instead of well-being and progress—all these led them to the various manifestations of nationalist conservatism. A wide variety of small conservative groups began to be formed almost immediately after the end of the war. Publishing houses like those of Georg Müller, Albert Langen, and the Hanseatische Verlagsanstalt, journals like Lehmann's *Deutschlands Erneuerung,* Wilhelm Stapel's *Deutsches Volkstum,* or Hans Zehrer's *Tat,* became focal centers for the dissemination of such intellectual conservatism. They were "the dangerous slumbering sparks which later flamed forth into the destructive blaze."

A particularly influential group was that of the "young conservatives" around the figure of the literary critic Arthur Moeller van den Bruck; Moeller's *Das dritte Reich* became increasingly popular with the increased vogue of National Socialism. Max H. Boehm's *Ruf der Jungen,* first published in 1919, may be taken as the programmatic declaration of this group, which included among its floating membership many of the later leaders of conservative nationalist politics and culture. The young conservatives, like Spengler, spurned the 1918 revolution as nothing but a display of degrading impotence. The young generation, bound together by its experiences during the war, was called upon to effect a genuine revolution that would wipe away the old Germany of technical progress and materialism. While critical of the "fanatical racialists" led by a Frenchman and an Englishman, and while equally critical of the crass methods of the pan-Germans, these more elegant and sophisticated nationalists called for a "truly high-minded racialist feeling" to overcome the "decomposing influences of the Jewish spirit," and for the purification of German life from the scourges of urban influence, "Americanization" and "Westernism." Attacking the "reactionaries" of both the right and the left, they advocated in nebulous form an idealistic and heroic socialism, Prussian in style, as opposed to the "puny" internationalism of Marxian socialism. Corporativism and Führer principle in internal affairs, the struggle for the protection of border Germans and German minorities, and an orientation toward the East—these were the twin poles of Moeller van den Bruck's program for the new and reborn Third Reich.

Closely allied to this group for a time, but later to emerge as the *enfant terrible* of revolutionary conservative youth, was Ernst Jünger, who with much greater literary genius and with more brilliance and *élan* brought post-war German nihilism to its highest literary form. No one in post-war Germany gave vent with such vehemence to the resentment against bourgeois culture and civilization at home and against foreign influence and domination abroad as did Jünger in his writings between

1920 and 1933. In words almost reminiscent of Nechayev and Bakunin, he preached a gospel of heroic struggle and pan-destructionism.

Jünger aspired to be the spokesman for a new type of youth which was to constitute the active elements of the educated youth of his generation. Activity was the most important element in human life, and it reached its highest pinnacle in war and in revolution. But war and revolution are waged neither for particular goals or purposes, nor for political or moral ideas. They possess a dynamic of their own and are justified only for their own sake. That is why Prussianism, with its ideals of self-sacrifice, stern discipline, and militarism as well as the heroic and nihilist elements in Bolshevism, represent, for Jünger, the ingredients for the model Germany of the future. Jünger did not operate with the ideas of mass propaganda of National Socialism, such as antisemitism, Nordic racialism, blood and soil, and so on. His appeal was to the cultural *élite,* and this appeal had an even more destructive influence because of the impression he gave of openness and integrity. Eventually to become an opponent of the Nazi régime, the actual effect of his writings, like those of Spengler and Moeller van den Bruck, was to attract to National Socialism elements of the population that could not have been won over by other means—a cultured and educated youth who strictly speaking did not follow the Hitler program but who combined in an indefinite, nebulous, and purely emotional fashion pan-German and militaristic nationalism with a revolutionary temper bent on decisive action at all costs.

Such was the rich diversity of intellectual movements in the Weimar Republic, ranging through the whole gamut of political, philosophical, and esthetic forms. Such a cultural fare was no problem for a cultural center like Paris, fully accustomed to the battle of ideas and artistic principles and where radical democrats could read the monarchist *Action Française* with intellectual admiration as well as with political disdain. To a Germany accustomed by its historical traditions to disciplined organization of culture as well as of politics, this richness and variety meant also disorder and confusion. Democratic mass culture brought with it a vulgarization and banalization of political and cultural philosophies that abounded in distortions, over-simplification and forced interpretation. Vulgarization of Hegel and Marx, of Nietzsche and Wagner, of Goethe and Kant, filled the intellectual climate, and was designed to meet the slogans and needs of the popular mass movements. The reaction in some circles was a desire to put an end to this welter of confusion by "decisive" action of some kind or other. For the common man, particularly the common man outside Berlin, the "little man" described by Hans Fallada, salvation meant complete escape from all the confusion of ideas, from the shrieking battles of newspapers and billboards, in order to find security for his simple needs and simple wants—security of employment, security for his wife and family, and security for his mind by not being subjected to the tensions of ideological conflict. Economic crisis, political tension, and cultural confusion all converged in the early 1930's to bring about a state of crisis from which there seemed to be no way out. It was this feeling of crisis which provided the climate for the final collapse of the Weimar Republic.

CHAPTER XX

The Road to Dictatorship, 1930-1933

Der Deutsche versteht sich auf die Schleichwege zum Chaos.

NIETZSCHE

The effects of the economic collapse of 1929 and the death of Strese-mann on October 3, 1929, brought to an end the forward movement of republican Germany. The political problem of monarchy versus republic now evaporated before the struggle of the republic against the mounting influence of authoritarianism. The battle against the republic was taken out of the hands of the old-line traditional monarchist conservatives and was now pushed forward by the militant organizations that made their appeal particularly to the youth and to the new political groupings around the National Socialist movement.[1] A host of semi-military and semi-political militant organizations had grown out of the Freikorps movement that followed the close of the war. The group Oberland, started in Munich during the days of the Soviet Republic, later spread to the Rhineland and Upper Silesia. Its goals were the liberation of Germany from foreign oppression, the destruction of the Treaty of Versailles, and the reconstruction of a "Third Reich." The Wehrwolf, organized in 1923 in Halle at the time of the occupation of the Ruhr, set out to fight plutocracy and international capitalism, and was ready to use Bolshevist Russia for these purposes. The Jungdeutscher Orden, organized in Kassel in 1918 by Lieutenant Artur Mahraun, had as its chief aim the fight against Bolshevism. Communists and Socialists followed the same pattern in setting up their own private armies. The Communist Roter Frontkämpfer-Bund was established in 1925 in Halle, and the Reichsbanner Schwarz-Rot-Gold of Socialists and Democrats was organized by Otto Hörsing and Karl Höltermann in Magdeburg in 1924. The two most influential of all these various militant organizations were the Stahlhelm, and the National Socialist movement with its S.A. and S.S.

The Stahlhelm, which was the largest association of German war veterans, was organized by the Magdeburg factory owner Franz Seldte in

467

December, 1918. It allegedly stood above political parties, but from the start it declared itself opposed to the *Schweinerei* of the revolution and became the spearhead of conservative militant opposition to the democratic institutions. In September, 1928, the Stahlhelm came forth with the notorious "declaration of hate," in which it proudly proclaimed its hatred, "with all our soul," of the existing governmental structure and announced that it would battle against the system that was ruling the state.

The National Socialist German Workers' party, organized as but another of the inconspicuous racialist, militarist groups in Munich in 1919 by the now-forgotten Anton Drexler, soon came under the domination of party member Number 7, Adolf Hitler, who extended the movement in southern Germany, while Gregor and Otto Strasser, and later Joseph Goebbels, "conquered" the industrial centers of the north and west for the Nazis. The National Socialists also organized their special private armies—the S.A. in 1921, headed by the ex-Reichswehr officer Ernst Röhm, and the élite S.S. guard in 1925. Secret relations between the Reichswehr and the National Socialists continued almost all through the duration of the republic. Reichswehr leaders like General von Seeckt viewed with positive approbation "the national feeling, the military will, the social understanding—all borne by youthful upsurge striving for reform"—which they discovered in the Nazi movement. Intimate and open relations between the Stahlhelm and the Nazis were established almost from the start, although in the beginning the Stahlhelm was the more reputable and more influential partner. Seldte called the National Socialists the "light cavalry of the army" and the Stahlhelm the "front-line infantry" that was to decide the issues of battle.

The Nazis, in alliance with the racialist movement of Ludendorff, made their first bid for power in the beer-hall *Putsch* of 1923. This attempt proved to be premature. The powerful conservative interests were not ready at that time to throw their weight to these militant enemies of the republic, and in the last moment decided to resist Hitler's move to power. This experience set Hitler and his followers away from the path of putschism to that of attempting to win over the majority of the electorate and gain power by "legal" means. Hitler himself later termed the 1923 attempt as "improvised and premature," and designated its failure as "a wise finger of Providence." In a talk with Hindenburg in 1932, Hitler admitted that the example of Mussolini's march on Rome had led him astray.[2]

While Hitler was in the fortress of Landsberg dictating *Mein Kampf* to Rudolf Hess, Gregor Strasser, a former apothecary equipped with organizational ability and a free railroad pass accorded to him as a Reichstag deputy, was engaged in building up a compact and disciplined political organization in Prussia that also made strong inroads into the proletarian ranks of the larger industrial centers. Exploiting every type of dissatisfaction among the proletarianized middle classes, the unemployed, the workers, the peasants, the disgruntled intellectuals, the idealistic youth, and the militaristic conservatives, the N.S.D.A.P. started its upward rise to power, while the various bourgeois parties showed a steady trend to disintegration and decline, with an increasing tendency to the right. In 1928 Chancellor Hermann Müller, the Socialist head of a large republican coalition, had declared in the Reichstag that the Reich was entering a period of peaceful development and that "the foundations of the German Republic were secure and unshakable." Two years later the republican coalition was disrupted, Müller was forced to resign on March 27, 1930 (the "black day" in the history of the republic), and Weimar Germany had had its last parliamentary government. The People's party, now bereft of the leadership of Stresemann, and chafing under its coalition with the Socialists and Democrats, turned more to the fiery conservative Nationalists now led by the ambitious industrialist Alfred Hugenberg. Hugenberg, who succeeded Count Westarp as the leader of the Conservative party in 1928, was a fanatical enemy of the republic and of the foreign policy of Stresemann, and was prepared to go to all lengths to overthrow the parliamentary democracy of Weimar. The period of nationalist co-operation with the republic was at an end, and the militant assault on democratic parliamentary institutions was initiated.

The new chancellor picked by Hindenburg, on the advice of General von Schleicher, to succeed Müller was the Centrist leader Heinrich Brüning. Born in Münster of a middle-class family in 1884, Brüning was forty-six years old when he became head of the government. He had served in World War I as a machine-gun officer and was a zealous monarchist in November, 1918. Even as chancellor, in a speech to the Reichstag on February 25, 1932, he boasted of the fact that on November 9, 1918, he was at the head of a military unit fighting "to overthrow the revolution," and he told his hearers, "Do not bring me in any way into any connection with the 9th of November." After the war he became secretary to the leader of the Catholic trade-unions Adam Stegerwald, and then general secretary of the Catholic National Trade-Union League. He belonged to the right wing of the Center party, combining the officer's ideal of disciplined leadership with Catholic belief in the need for authority. He had opposed the policies of Erzberger, as he did the acceptance of the Versailles Treaty, and had come to be known as the "rationalist conservative." Elected to the Reichstag in 1924, he became the party's expert on fiscal matters, and in 1929 he was elected head of the Centrist faction in the Reichstag. Quiet in demeanor and pale in countenance, of priest-like asceticism in outward appearance as in his personal way of life, hating phrases, demagogy, and doctrinairism, Brüning wielded greater moral authority in the country than any previous chancellor of the Weimar republic. For the two years that he occupied the post he came to be looked upon, with the seriousness of his mien and in the ever-pained expression of his face, as the very personification of Germany. "He wore upon himself the reflection of the tragedy that weighed down upon postwar Germany, a visible symbol of the demand for the restoration of its honor."

Brüning was not the kind of person, however, to rally the forces of the republic around him. He neither possessed the enthusiasm for the cause nor was his close-fisted personality suitable for evoking the confidence of party leaders or mass following. Guided by the principle that "one should not let either one's contemporaries or posterity see the ultimate motives of one's policy," and also profoundly religious, he had a feeling of almost divine mission, which gave him a strong sense of inner security and conviction but which also made it easy for him to show an almost contemptuous disregard for political opposition and public opinion. On assuming office as chancellor he warned the Reichstag that the "new ministry represented a last attempt to achieve a solution of the nation's pressing problems in conjunction with the people's legislature, and if the Reichstag parties would not co-operate he would look elsewhere for support." This was not responsible parliamentary government but the beginning of the interlude of "presidial governments" which bridged the road between the democratic republic and Nazi dictatorship.

Brüning announced that he was prepared to use the emergency executive powers of Article 48 of the constitution to the limit. Conceiving himself to be responsible not to the Reichstag but "to the nation," he identified the nation with the chief of state, President von Hindenburg. When his financial proposals were defeated by the Reichstag, he put them in force by the use of the emergency powers of Article 48. To the Socialist leader Breitscheid, who warned him that he was "sitting together with men for whom Article 48 was the beginning of a dictatorship," Brüning replied that the use of the emergency decrees through Article 48 was not an act of dictatorship but "a means for the education of the German people to political thinking." When the combined votes of Nationalists, Nazis, Communists, and Socialists passed a no-confidence motion in the Reichstag, Brüning countered with the dissolution of the Reichstag and a call for new elections on September 14, 1930.

The results of these elections brought German parliamentary government to its most grave crisis. A general swing to the right had been expected, but there was universal shock of amazement when in place of the 12 deputies they had had in the previous Reichstag, 107 brown-shirted Nazis, led by Wilhelm Frick, stalked into the halls of the Reichstag. They numbered in their midst a motley group of crude, ruthless demagogues of unsavory reputation, some of them wanted by the law for various breaches of the peace, but now representing over six million voters and constituting the second largest party in the peoples' assembly. As for the other parties, the S.P.D. showed a slight decline but remained the largest single party, with 143 deputies; the Centrists increased their number from 62 to 68 deputies, while the Communists rose from 54 to 77 deputies. The great gains of the National Socialists were made by attracting large segments of the bourgeois conservative parties and by large groups of previous non-voters. Hugenberg was forced into a back seat, while the Bavarian apothecary Gregor Strasser led the Nationalist assault upon the Brüning government. The convening of the new Reichstag on October 13 was accompanied by wild antisemitic outbreaks in the streets of Berlin. Inside the legislative halls the Nazi deputies openly showed their contempt for the Reichstag in general and for Socialist and Communist deputies in particular. Antisemitic vituperation was combined with reactionary demagogy. While Heines, in the Reichstag, openly boasted of being a *Fememörder,* his S.A. followers were engaged in street rioting directed against Jews, "cultural Bolshevism," and political opponents. Communists countered with the slogan "Beat down the fascists wherever you meet them," but were equally, if not even more, violent against the followers of the Social Democrats. During the first nine months of 1931, forty-five persons were killed in Prussia alone as a result of political street battles.

The results of the Reichstag election did not allow for any feasible parliamentary majority capable of governing with the consent of the Reichstag. There was no possible republican majority in which both Socialists and conservatives could join and no conservative majority possible without the inclusion of the National Socialists. Brüning continued to hold office and govern by the use of presidential emergency decrees under Article 48. The former infantry officer seemed to have established an intimate relationship with his former commander in chief. Hindenburg appeared to have developed a feeling of affection and great trust and confidence in the Centrist chancellor. Both had no qualms of conscience about the use of authoritarian power, and both seemed to agree that they could carry on by means of a "presidial cabinet" that was independent of political parties in the Reichstag.

The Social Democrats were placed in a very difficult situation, especially since Brüning's emergency decrees were designed to cut down as much as possible on the social services and were, therefore, extremely unpopular with the Socialist voters. Both trade-union leaders and S.P.D. party leaders exhibited a high sense of national responsibility in this crisis, when yielding to the demands of the Brüning cabinet exposed them to the savage attacks of the Communists. Hans Schlange-Schoeningen, a conservative member of Brüning's cabinet, testifies to this high sense of duty by the Socialist leaders:

No party was called upon to make greater sacrifices in the interests of the whole than the Social-Democratic Party, and no class was called upon to make

greater economic sacrifices than the working class. . . . I remember one of
the famous night sessions—it was probably in May 1932—when the government
was represented by Brüning, Stegerwald and me, whilst opposite us sat workers'
representatives of all shades. Once again the topic of discussion was the government demand that social expenditure be cut. An almost fierce discussion
proceeded for several hours, and the dawn was actually breaking when the
Social-Democratic trade-union chairman, Leipart, said finally: "Well, if there's
no other way to do it . . ." [3]

The Social Democrats were confronted with the agonizing alternative
of either tolerating the Brüning cabinet by refraining from voting against
it or else risking the entire collapse of the republic and the advent of an
openly fascist dictatorship. It was a cruel fate for the Socialist leaders,
and the debates in the Socialist party conferences and in the party press
reveal the excruciating agony as well as the high sense of national responsibility which characterized their deliberations. They were in the
position of trying to steer a course between the Scylla of Article 48 and
the Charybdis of Hitler. It was a conflict, as Rudolf Hilferding described
it, not between one faction in the party and another, but in the soul of
each Socialist party member, asking himself the question, What is the
greater evil? The tragic and almost fatalistic element in the situation
derived from the fact that political emergency coincided with heavy economic crisis. The Reichstag at this time was a parliament against parliamentarism, and was in the paradoxical situation in which the exercise by
the Reichstag majority of its democratic rights could only effect the overthrow of the government. No matter how bad the Brüning cabinet was
from the Socialist viewpoint, its overthrow would result only in the creation of an even more reactionary government. "To affirm democracy,"
wrote Hilferding, "against a majority that rejects democracy, using the
political means of a democratic constitution which presupposes the functioning of a parliament, this task set before the Social Democrats is almost
like the attempt to square a circle—it is a completely new situation."

Under these circumstances the Social Democrats decided to "tolerate"
the Brüning cabinet, to allow it to rule by the use of emergency decrees, and not to press for the convening of the Reichstag, which would
have resulted in the overthrow of the government. The Communists missed
no opportunity to take advantage of this situation to brand the Social
Democrats as allies of "black reaction" and of the "hunger cabinet." [4]

With such passive support by the Socialists, Brüning and his cabinet
were able to carry on for two years. His policy was one of "Spartan simplicity" and thrift at home and of continued demand for "moral and material equality" for Germany at the council table of the nations. His emergency fiscal decrees were designed to reduce the salaries of public officials
and to cut down drastically public expenditures for overhead costs and
for social services. He raised the tariffs on foodstuffs and increased both

direct and indirect taxation. At the same time, however, he carried on the policy of enlarging German armaments openly within the limits of the treaty and secretly beyond treaty limitations. His nationalist foreign policy also inspired him to the attempt to create a customs union with Austria. German dependence on the foreign world, however, was still so strong that he had to back out of this in the face of French and English protests. A Socialist critic like Carlo Mierendorff could at the time take Brüning to task for vying with the Nazis in his nationalist foreign policy and to label this policy as the "foreign policy of nationalism without the swastika" and distinguished from the foreign policy of the Nazis "only in form but hardly at all in content." In the light of the subsequent record of National Socialism it is easy to see how grossly exaggerated Mierendorff's characterization was.

At the same time, however, the economic crisis became more and more aggravated. The deflationary policies of Brüning were very unpopular among the masses of the population, and unemployment rose from 2,258,-000 in March, 1930, to 6,031,000 in March, 1932. Brüning increased government controls over business and industry and increased the number of cartels to make possible an improvement in foreign exports. He was preparing a change of policy to expand credit facilities at home, but he was forced out of office before he could carry through with these policies.

In March, 1932, new elections for President took place. Brüning's proposal to the party leaders to avoid an election by having the Reichstag extend Hindenburg's term was rejected by Hitler, and the voters went to the polls on March 13. It is an irony of history that Hindenburg, the idol of the monarchists, the loyal and devoted servant of the former kaiser, the close friend and confidant of East Elbian Junkers, now became the "protector of the constitution" and the bulwark behind whom the republican elements rallied against the assault from the right. In the first elections Hindenburg polled 18,650,730 votes (49.6 per cent), Hitler 11,339,-285 votes (30.1 per cent), the Communist Thälmann 4,983,197 votes (13 per cent), and the candidate of the Nationalist Stahlhelm, Düsterberg, 2,558,000 votes (6.8 per cent). Since no candidate had polled a majority, a run-off election was held on April 10. Düsterberg dropped out of the race, and Hindenburg now received 19,359,635 votes (53 per cent), Hitler 13,418,051 votes (36.8 per cent), and Thälmann 3,706,655 votes (10.2 per cent). Hindenburg's election was due in no small measure to the indefatigable electioneering in his behalf carried on by Brüning. Only a few weeks after Hindenburg's triumph, however, Brüning was forced to resign. His departure from office was occasioned not only by a defeat in the Reichstag but by the declared lack of confidence in him expressed by the President.

This act by the "wooden Titan" is one of the most notorious instances of political ingratitude in modern history. The entire circumstances surrounding Brüning's ouster have not yet emerged from the shrouds of secrecy and the realm of pure speculation and rumor. In the center of the intrigue that went on behind the scenes was the same General von Schleicher who had suggested Brüning's name to Hindenburg in 1930. A camarilla of East Elbian landlords joined by Hindenburg's son Oskar and State Secretary Meissner apparently worked on Hindenburg to get rid of Brüning, although Meissner has denied being involved in the machinations. Schleicher and the Reichswehr leaders at the time favored a working arrangement with the Nazis. Brüning's attitude on the matter was one of indecision. His defense minister, General Groener, favored a ban on the S.A., but he was forced out of office by the opposition of his own Reichswehr generals. The Prussian landlords were suspicious of Brüning's agrarian plans, and convinced Hindenburg that his chancellor was a Bolshevik. When Brüning came to Hindenburg on May 29, 1932, with emergency decrees for his signature, Hindenburg upbraided him for introducing "Bolshevist" ideas. "My dear Herr Reich Chancellor," said Hindenburg, "we cannot continue in this fashion under any circumstances. We cannot engage in Bolshevist wage laws and Bolshevist colonization schemes. The two trade-union leaders must get out of the cabinet." Hindenburg then went on to specify, "I mean you and Stegerwald!" He suggested that Brüning might enter another cabinet as foreign minister. This Brüning refused to do, saying, "I will not remain a minister with a broken backbone." The following day Brüning brought to the President the official resignation of his cabinet, and said to the old field marshal, "We hereby transmit to you, Herr Reich President, our resignation precisely seven weeks to the day after your re-election." [5] Meissner is perhaps correct in his suggestion that Brüning's wounded personal pride played a role in the situation. Instead of making a fight against his enemies, Brüning stiffened up coldly and offered his resignation. It is also true, however, that Hindenburg had already made up his mind to dismiss his hitherto favorite and trusted chancellor.

With the ouster of Brüning the elements that had pulled the strings of political intrigue from behind the scenes stepped out into the open. All pretense at adherence to the Weimar Constitution was given up. A small, closely knit group of rightist reactionaries made up of East Elbian large landowners, West German giant industrialists, and politically minded officers of the Reichswehr, ready to make use of the nationalist mass movement of Hitler, came to power, headed first by Franz von Papen and followed later by General Kurt von Schleicher. At the Nürnberg War Crimes Trial in 1946, Franz von Papen, no longer the elegant and debonair political adventurer he had been, related on the witness stand how he had become chancellor. On May 26, 1932, he was on his estate in the Saar. Schleicher called him on the phone and asked him to come to Berlin. When he arrived Schleicher said to him: "There is a cabinet crisis; we are looking for a chancellor." Schleicher then told him that Hindenburg wanted him to take the post. In his meeting with Hindenburg, the President said to him: "I did not call you because I wanted the support of any party through you; I called you because I want a cabinet of independent men." The chief political aim of the von Papen cabinet was "to achieve . . . the practical co-operation of the strongest of the opposition parties, the N.S.D.A.P." [6]

Actually, there never was a cabinet during the entire post-war history of Germany that enjoyed less popular support than the von Papen cabinet. Two Reichstag elections held in 1932 gave the parties supporting von Papen a very small percentage of the vote. Socialists and Centrists held pretty much their own, but the extremes on both right and left showed marked increases. In the July elections the National Socialists reached their highest peak during the republic, polling 13,745,800 votes and electing 230 deputies, making them now the largest single party in the Reichstag. They suffered an appreciable decline in the November elections, dropping to 11,737,000 votes and 196 deputies, a fact which gave the democratic elements a slight trace of solace and sense of relief. The Communists captured 89 seats in the July vote and 100 seats in November. Von Papen, on taking over, lifted the ban on Nazi military formations and also called for Reichstag elections in response to the Nazi demand.

On July 20, 1932, von Papen carried out the "rape of Prussia," ousting the Braun-Severing government which had held the reins of Prussian control since 1921. Von Papen acted on the pretext that the Socialist government had proved itself incapable of maintaining order. Actually, this was part of the entire preconceived plan of eliminating the last vestige of democratic administrative power that stood in the way of nationalist control of the Reich. The reactionary clique now in power could not afford to allow the state of Prussia to remain under the control of the "traitorous" Socialists. The Prussian Socialist government was therefore deposed, a state of siege was proclaimed, and a Reich commissar installed. The German Social Democrats have been subjected to severe criticism for having yielded to this flagrant violation of constitutional government, offering no resistance except that of submitting a complaint to the Supreme Court. The Socialist failure appeared all the more glaring when compared to the flamboyantly aggressive warnings given by Socialist leaders in their public declarations. Otto Wels, Severing, and the "strong man" of Prussia, Otto Braun, had all promised to lead the working classes in a fight to the finish against illegal attempts to oust them from power. Now a lieutenant and ten men were all that were necessary to oust the Socialist leaders, who reputedly had the powerful Prussian police in their hands as well as the "Iron Front" and the Republican Reichsbanner.

Carl Severing and other Socialist leaders have defended themselves against these charges by pointing out that (1) the Prussian Socialists could not have counted on the support of a united police force in any action against the Reich. The much touted Prussian police was already heavily infested with Nazi party members and supporters who would never have answered Severing's call to resist the Reich government. (2) The police was not strong enough to resist the Reichswehr, which had heavy weapons. (3) The Reichsbanner had no weapons to speak of. (4) The feat of the 1920 general strike against the Kapp Putsch could not be repeated in 1932. The trade-union leaders reported that there was no chance of getting the workers to resist. Otto Wels had circularized the leaders of the labor unions right after the events of July 20 and had received no encouragement for resistance. With six million unemployed a general strike had little chance of success. (5) The fatal division of the working classes still obtained, and the Communists rejoiced at the ouster of the Prussian Socialist government. (6) The Socialists could count on no support from any of the other parties. True, the Bavarian prime minister, Held, declared that he would know what to do if a Reich commissar ever came to the Bavarian border. But this was no tangible support for Prussia, and it proved to be no more than an empty boast a year later when the Nazis sent down their commissar to take over in Bavaria. A sad commentary on the situation is revealed in the apologia offered by the Socialist editor Friedrich Stampfer. The men of the S.P.D., he wrote, could act in no other way because they had no tendency to "bloody adventure." The German Social Democratic party, said Stampfer, "was for decades a party of peaceful evolution, of reasonable and balanced consideration, of understanding without force. If it had given the signal for violent action, it would have attempted to appear to be what it indeed was not." [7]

The Socialists pinned their hopes on the new Reichstag elections and satisfied themselves with submitting their case to the Reich Supreme Court. The election turned out as tragically disappointing as did the action of the Supreme Court. From the standpoint of theoretical jurisprudence the legal case was of the highest interest. The most brilliant Socialist jurist, Hermann Heller, was pitted against the political philosopher Carl Schmitt, the darling of the conservatives. From a political point of view, however, the legal battle was of no consequence. The spineless German judiciary proved true to its tradition. It delivered an opinion that was a mastery of political and juristic straddling. The action of the Reich government was declared to be in some ways illegal, yet the Socialist government had no claim to recover its administrative competence. In any case, by the time the decision was handed down the maze of political machination and intrigue had stripped the issue of any political consequence.

The harmonious team play of Papen, Schleicher, and Hindenburg, oriented around the idea of eventually incorporating the Nazis into their orbit, did not last long. According to Otto Meissner, the attitude of the Papen cabinet was not uniform. Hindenburg, personally repelled by the

.rude behavior of Hitler, and resentful of his opposition to him during the presidential elections, was confident that the strength of the Nazis would disappear with improvement in the economic situation. On August 13, 1932, he received Hitler at the latter's request. Hitler developed his aims before the President and assured him that he wanted to achieve his goals only by pacific means but that he did not want to share power with anyone else. Hindenburg told Hitler that he was ready to accept him in a coalition cabinet but not alone. This offer Hitler refused. Negotiations continued with Hitler and Göring. According to von Papen's testimony, Schleicher and Papen met with Hindenburg after the November elections. There still was no possible way of establishing a government based on a parliamentary majority. Papen, at this meeting, made a plea for "extraordinary measures"—the recessing of parliament and the immediate preparation of a bill to reform the constitution which was to be submitted either to the Reichstag or to a new National Assembly. This proposal definitely involved the violation of the constitution. Schleicher thereupon said: "Field Marshal, I have a plan which will make it unnecessary for you to break your oath to the constitution, if you are willing to put the government into my hands. I hope that I will be able to obtain a parliamentary majority in the Reichstag by splitting the National Socialist party." Hindenburg, according to von Papen, was inclined to follow von Papen's plan, but Schleicher predicted the outbreak of civil war. Thereupon Hindenburg yielded and said: "I am an old man and I cannot face a civil war of any sort in my country. If Herr von Schleicher is of this opinion, then I must, as much as I regret, withdraw the task with which I charged you [von Papen] last night."

On the other side former Chancellor Brüning has departed from his more customary reticence to lift slightly the veil over the political maneuvering that went on at the time. Brüning claims that the Nazis concocted a plan to utilize Articles 43 and 59 of the constitution to prefer charges against von Hindenburg before the Supreme Court with a view to deposing him from his office. With the aid of the Communists they had the necessary votes in the Reichstag to carry through such action. Von Papen, according to Brüning, countered this threat with a plan to suppress all parties, labor unions, co-operatives, and similar organizations. Hindenburg thereupon sought the advice of Brüning, who counseled naming General von Schleicher as chancellor and a return to the policy of co-operation of the middle parties with the Social Democrats. When a representative of the Reichswehr informed the von Papen cabinet that the attempt to carry out the plan to suppress all parties would lead to a revolt of such dimensions that the Reichswehr would not be able to cope with it, von Papen was forced to resign and Schleicher was named chancellor.[8]

The man who had since the beginning of the republic been instrumental in making and unmaking cabinets was now (December 2, 1932) at the head of the government himself, ready to tackle the most baffling parliamentary situation. The "social general," as he came to be called in those days of December, 1932, devised a plan for bringing together the trade-union elements of the Socialist party under Leipart with the radical left wing of the Nazis under Gregor Strasser and thus split off part of the Nazi movement from Hitler. Strasser was apparently interested in the plan, but he was confronted with swift and drastic action by Adolf Hitler. Before anything could materialize, Strasser was stripped of all his party offices by Hitler and ousted from the party. He thus remained an isolated individual without following and hence useless for Schleicher's plan. Schleicher thus failed to form the coalition cabinet which he had promised.

General von Schleicher was now to receive a taste of the bitter medicine he had hitherto administered to others. Embittered by his failure, he now determined to fight the Nazis. He presented a plan to Hindenburg to dissolve the Reichstag and transform the government into a military dictatorship. Hindenburg expressed grave doubts as to the constitutionality of the plan, and refused to give Schleicher the same emergency powers he had granted to von Papen. The arch-maneuverer was now out-maneuvered and forced to resign. Behind his back von Papen, aided by General von Blomberg, the East Elbian agrarian Oldenburg-Januschau, and Oskar von Hindenburg, had been negotiating with Hitler and at the same time working on the old man to entrust the Nazi leader with the formation of a government. Von Papen finally won over Hindenburg with the argument that the representatives of the other right-wing parties included in the cabinet "would restrict Hitler's freedom of action." Once more, too, the danger of civil war was dangled before the aged President. On January 30, 1933, Adolf Hitler was called by the President to become chancellor. According to Brüning, Hindenburg was influenced to name Hitler because of his fear that the Nazis would carry out their plan to depose him. Otto Braun, on the other hand, denies this claim, and maintains that the threat to bring out into the open the scandals regarding the *Osthilfe,* which would have compromised him, were of more weight in influencing the decisions of the aged President. In any case Hitler had realized his ambition and he had kept his promise. He was Führer of Germany not by a *Putsch* or revolution. He was the "legal" chancellor called to power by the President in accordance with the constitutional powers vested in him by the Weimar Constitution. Thus the Weimar Republic came to an end not by assault from forces without, but—to follow the pattern described by Toynbee—by committing suicide.

CHAPTER XXI

Germany Goes Berserk, 1933-1945

The strange fatality that haunts the times
Wherein our lot was cast, has no example.

THOMAS HARDY, *The Dynasts*

Ich habe Land besessen
Und Meer dazu, wieviel!
Ich habe Menschen gefressen,
Und weiss kein Ziel.

ALBERT EHRENSTEIN,
Der Berserker schreit

To deal adequately with the history of Germany under Hitler, and to describe the diabolical perversity, the wild flights of political fantasy, the enormity of the crimes committed, and the disaster and ruin brought both to Germany and to the entire world, and at the same time to be able to fathom the motivations and psychological stirrings of all the participants in this most terrifying drama in world history would require the historical insight of a Thucydides or a Burckhardt, the capacity for philosophical and esthetic all-embracingness of a Tolstoy, and the prophetic compassion of a Jeremiah. The thirteen years of Nazi rule opened up a chasm of primitive drives and animalic forces that seem to separate the world before and after Hitler by a time span of thousands of years. Hitler's rule lasted only a dozen years, but his proud boast of a "thousand-year Reich" was more than an empty expression in the light of the woes and calamities it bequeathed to the world. Political monsters have appeared before in history as have cruel tyrants and dictators. But never before in history has a political monster been the master of such highly developed technical means to carry out his monstrous designs.[1]

1. THE RISE OF ADOLF HITLER

The National Socialist movement began as one of the many tiny nationalist political and cultural groups that sprang up like mushrooms in

Germany immediately following the close of World War I. In these groups demobilized soldiers, political and economic malcontents, romantic and careerist adventurers, immature idealistic youths, and designing political intriguers joined forces to fight the new Weimar democracy and the West. The National Socialist German Workers' Party was the offspring of the Deutsche Arbeiter Partei, founded on January 5, 1919, by the soon to be forgotten Anton Drexler. In September, 1919, Adolf Hitler became member Number Seven of the political committee of the party, and in March, 1920, this party became officially known as the Nationalsozialistische Deutsche Arbeiter Partei, or N.S.D.A.P.

Drexler, a wood turner by profession, who had been thrown out of his trade-union, developed a violent hatred of Marxism, and combined it, as was usual, with antisemitism. He also preached the by no means novel doctrine of the need to unite German national interests with true "German" socialism. His autobiography, *Mein politisches Erwachen* (1st ed., Munich, 1919; 3rd ed., 1923), is the work of an autodidact who dabbled just enough in history to be able to create garbled versions of it. It is dull and undistinguished, but it is also not especially violent nor aggressive in its appeal. Drexler attracted to his party the antisemitic writer Dietrich Eckart, whose weekly *Auf gut Deutsch* (first issue, December 7, 1918) came to be regarded as the first paper of the Nazi movement, and an economic writer Gottfried Feder, who offered as a panacea for the solution of Germany's troubles his theory of the *"Brechung der Zinsknechtschaft,"* the destruction of the interest bondage. To these was soon added Ernst Röhm, who came from the Freikorps Epp and who brought into the party many of his military friends.

Drexler's and Hitler's party maintained from the start close and intimate relations with German racialist parties in Silesia, Austria, Czechoslovakia, and Poland. The pan-German character of the movement is apparent from the start. Elements of the Pan-German League and the Vaterlandspartei came in. The influence of the Austrians Walter Riehl of Vienna and Rudolf Jung of Troppau was especially marked in these early days. Jung supplied a more theoretical dressing for the movement. His book *Der nationale Sozialismus* (1st ed., Munich, 1920; 2nd ed., 1922), with its theoretical antisemitism and attacks upon the Old Testament, its anti-clericalism and anti-materialism, its program of the pan-German union of all *Volksdeutsche,* and his economic radicalism, which likewise attempted to fuse the concepts of "national" and "social," was considered to be the most authoritative presentation of national-socialist doctrine until superseded by the gospel according to Adolf. The N.S.D.A.P. also absorbed the Deutsch-Sozialistische Partei, founded by Julius Streicher in Franconia, and allied itself with the racialist movement led by General Ludendorff and his wife.

The Hitler-Ludendorff alliance reached its crest in the *Putsch* of November 9, 1923, which sent Hitler for a short term to the fortress of Landsberg and which marked a turning point in the tactics of Hitler's ride to power. Hitler realized that putschism could not arouse the enthusiasm of the German masses nor win the support of the more influential and respectable circles. His way now was to be that of "legality." On numerous occasions he repeated the promise that he would not use violence to secure power. In a strictly technical sense, too, he kept his word. His accession to power on January 30, 1933, came in strictly legal fashion, in accordance with the provisions of the Weimar Constitution and without the aid of violence or insurrection.

Up to September, 1930, the N.S.D.A.P. was still a negligible factor on the political scene. For most Germans the term Nazi was still associated more or less with something like inmates of a lunatic asylum. The elections of September, 1930, which brought 107 Brown Shirts into the Reichstag instead of the previous twelve, changed the entire picture. From then on they became the most dynamic factor in German political life, until their dynamism became the ruling power of Germany.

The person of Adolf Hitler, the central figure in world history from 1933 to 1945, has by now become the subject of a huge literature, but the problems of his biography will undoubtedly continue to haunt historians and psychologists for many years to come. The phenomenon of Hitler is one that defies all rational analysis. That this individual was responsible for effecting a profound transformation in the history of Germany and in that of the world at large can be denied by no one. That this problem defies rational analysis, however, comes not from the complexity of character or profundity of mind and spirit of Adolf Hitler—he had neither—but from the much more unfathomable and fateful question of how an individual with such a combination of mediocrity and perverse brutality could find sufficiently wide support to make himself the idolized leader of Germany and then come terrifyingly close to being the master of all Europe.

Mediocrity was Hitler's most distinguishing characteristic. Perhaps it was precisely this quality which, in an age of mass appeal, attracted so many to his standard. The average German saw himself mirrored in Hitler's person and could identify himself with him. Hitler was semi-educated and sufficiently cultured to make a pretense of profound interest in art and music, but he was a dilettante in everything from art and architecture to politics and military strategy. Hans Frank, in his penitent mood, told the Nürnberg psychologist: "He played art-and-music lover, but he had no conception of art. He liked Wagner, naturally, because he could see himself playing god with dramatic splendor. And his adoration of the nude!—To him the nude represented merely a protest against convention which he was able to understand." [2]

Hitler was an omnivorous reader, although he scarcely ever referred to any books or authors he had read. Unlike Mussolini, who gloried in parading all the great thinkers of the past as his precursors, Hitler scorned any possible identification of himself as an intellectual. Nor did he deign to give anyone credit for having influenced his thinking. His ideas were unrolled as the intuitive apprehension of a demigod who communed only with cosmic forces. His memory was regarded by all as phenomenal, especially his capacity for factual detail. But Erich Kordt adduces evidence to indicate that this supposed mastery of detail was very frequently based on arrogant bluff, with no one present who was himself familiar with the facts or bold enough to correct the mistakes of the Führer.

One book was apparently read by Hitler with the avowed aim of making it his political *vade mecum*. This was Machiavelli's *The Prince*. Hitler's conduct of statecraft followed in a crude way that of the hero of *Il Principe*. He had unbending energy and tremendous will power and drive: he was inordinately vain and sure of himself, stubborn and full of mistrust of everyone. There were only two or three people with whom he was on sufficiently friendly terms to use the intimate form *Du*, and one of these, Ernst Röhm, he had shot on June 30, 1934. Ribbentrop told the psychologist Dr. Gilbert in Nürnberg: "I don't think anybody ever really had a heart-to-heart talk with him as man to man. Not a single one. . . . I don't think he ever really bared his heart to anyone." [3] Although there is no evidence to substantiate the often mentioned claim that he was sexually abnormal, he did prefer to be regarded as chaste and ascetic, and his love affairs, first with his niece and then with Eva Braun, were closely guarded secrets known only to his intimate entourage.

All who had dealings with him agree that Hitler was a pathological liar and at the same time prone to extraordinary and blatant exaggeration. Field Marshal Keitel, at Nürnberg, told how Hitler talked himself into frantic moods of exaggeration. For example, he would ask, "How many light howitzers are we producing per month?" Keitel would reply, "About 160, perhaps." "I order 900," Hitler would shout, even though there was absolutely no possibility of producing that many.[4]

Hitler had absolutely no capacity for appraising moral values. He looked upon these with the cynical disdain of the Machiavellian "realist." That is why he was so incapable of anticipating ultimate world reaction to his continued aggression. Success and triumph, he felt, would soon obliterate all moral revulsion. Kordt tells of standing with him on the Hradcany hill in Prague, immediately after he broke his Munich pledge and occupied Prague, and hearing his comment when told that France and England were not taking any mobilization measures. "I knew it!" he exclaimed. "In fourteen days no one will mention it any more." [5]

Hitler cultivated the lion-and-fox pattern of Borgia. André François-Poncet, French ambassador to Germany up to November, 1938, has provided us with one of the most delicately drawn portraits of Hitler as he found him in that fantastic "eagle's eyrie," six thousand feet high near

Berchtesgaden. "He is changeable, dissembling, full of contradictions, uncertain," writes the intelligent French diplomat. "The same man with the debonair aspect, with a real fondness for the beauties of nature, who discussed reasonable ideas on European politics round the tea table, is also capable of the worst frenzies, of the wildest exaltations and the most delirious ambitions." [6] Like so many of his followers, Hitler combined the most maudlin kind of sentimentality—ready to weep at the slightest provocation—with inhuman brutality and ruthlessness. This was perhaps the most terrifying aspect of the entire psychology of the Nazi mentality. To sit in a drawing room and engage in discussions on Goethe or idealistic philosophy, to indulge in the music of Mozart or Schubert, and then to walk to the telephone and order several hundred hostages to be shot or some other inhuman atrocity to be perpetrated—such was the frightening character of the Nazi behavior that makes it such an appropriate field of study for abnormal psychology and psychiatry.

Hitler's appeal was primarily that of the demagogue. It was something akin to that of sex appeal—and women were among his most fanatical admirers—but perhaps closer to the contagion of hysteria that seized masses of people at the appearance of a false messiah. For to his following he was the messiah who would redeem Germany from all its troubles. *"Der Hitler, der sorgt für uns!"* (Hitler, he is our provider!) was a widespread feeling among the masses of simple folk who joined his standard, and the word "provider," with its accompanying overtones, had very much the feeling of "Providence" in it.

Hitler was an irrational fanatic who was as one "possessed." But as Albert Speer pointed out, his fanaticism was not that of zealous belief in an idea but rather an inordinate and overweening faith in his own greatness. He was, Speer told Gilbert, "a selfish, destructive force that had no consideration for the German people." Terribly solemn, without any trace of humor, his appeal was bathetic. He rode to fame and power not as an organizer or administrator, nor as a military or intellectual leader, but as an orator. Demagogic oratory that utilized the half baked and vulgarized pathos of the romantic German tradition and the soft sentimentality of mass feeling in post-war Weimar Germany was what made him Führer, first of the party and then of the country. He never reasoned with his audience; he demanded that they believe. He was most effective when he spoke of intangibles like "honor," "fatherland," *"Volk,"* "loyalty," and "sacrifice." His speeches were more "philosophical" than political, and it was this dilettantist and charlatanist philosophizing that appealed to the twentieth century mass heirs to the land of "poets and philosophers." There was a primitive savagery in his voice as it mounted from a slow tenor sound to a hoarse and rasping passion. Non-Germans who heard his raving and ranting as it filled the ether waves and came to them over the radio were amused at the "antics" of the "little man with the mustache." But his German hearers not only took his words in deadly earnest but hung on them as upon the message of a savior. "Can't you feel the terrific strength of his personality?" Ribbentrop asked the Nürnberg psychologist. "Can't you see how he swept people off their feet? I don't know if you can, but we can feel it. It is overwhelming!"[7]

Hitler was, in the words of Hjalmar Schacht, "a mass psychologist of really diabolical genius." And he understood the effectiveness of primitive simplicity. "I have the gift," he once told Rauschning, "of reducing all problems to their simplest foundations." And he was right. Radical simplifier that he was, he astounded people when his over-simplification, which more trained minds would never have dared to propose, brought success. But in reckless desperado fashion the same simplicity also led to equally astounding brutality and eventually to disaster.

Hitler was aided in his rise to power and subsequent rule by a band of henchmen who complemented the Führer in various fields of political activity. There was the Bavarian apothecary Gregor Strasser, who became the efficient organizer of party branches throughout the Reich, but especially in northern Germany, and who with his brother Otto developed the "socialistic" side of the Nazi movement. Otto Strasser broke with the Führer in 1930, and Gregor Strasser was forced to resign his party offices in December, 1932, and then met his end in the purge of June 30, 1934. There were Ernst Röhm, former Reichswehr officer who was the organizer of the S.A., and Heinrich Himmler, former chemistry laboratory assistant, who became organizer of the S.S. and then chief of all the institutions of Nazi terror; there were the former aviator and dope fiend, Hermann Göring, who established the liaison with the Reichswehr circles, and Walther Funk and Hjalmar Schacht, who forged the links with German industry and banking; there was the dark little club-footed Dr. Paul Joseph Goebbels, Rhinelander and pupil of the Jewish interpreter of Stefan George, Friedrich Gundolf, who became the master of mass propaganda and the "conqueror of the city streets" for the Nazis and who remained with the Führer until they both perished in Hitler's bunker in April, 1945; there was the blond Baltic German Alfred Rosenberg, who led the anti-Bolshevik and anti-Christian crusade and who served as the Führer's exponent of pompous Nazi *Weltanschauung;* there was Gottfried Feder, whose babbling on "the breaking of interest bondage" served as the official economic program of the Nazis but whose usefulness ended as soon as the party assumed office and took over the responsibility of actually carrying on the country's economy; there was Walther Darré, born in Argentina, who became the expert on peasants, agriculture, and animal husbandry, whose function was to liberate the peasantry from its enslavement to Christianity and to create a new *Bauernadel,* a new peasant aristocracy, by the same methods he used to breed horses and cattle; there was Hans Frank, the Bavarian lawyer who was to perform the acrobatic stunt of harmonizing National Socialism with *Recht* by proclaiming the Führer to be "the greatest lawgiver of German history" and by defining law as "the will of the Führer"; there was the Hohenzollern Prince "Auwi," August Wilhelm, son of William II, who lent aristocratic tone to the movement; and there was the pornographic Julius Streicher of Nürnberg, whose vulgar and violent antisemitism preached in *Der Stürmer* served to rally all the coarser elements in the population; there was the externally modest and diffident Rudolf Hess—born in Egypt and student and confidant of the pontiff of geopolitics Karl Haushofer—who served as the Führer's deputy and the moderator and adjuster in all intra-party squabbles and conflicts until his fantastic airplane flight to England in the midst of the war put an end to his Nazi career.

In addition to these big party bosses and leaders there was a collection of local bosses and gauleiters, each of whom played a Führer role in his own bailiwick, sometimes even quite independently of both Berlin and Munich. They included somewhat more "respectable" figures like the former soldier Ritter von Epp in Bavaria and the civil servant Wilhelm Frick in Thuringia, Karl Kaufmann, the "socialist" Nazi of Hamburg; Erich Koch in Königsberg, who was to help carry out the genocide policy in the Ukraine during the war; Jakob Sprenger in Frankfurt am Main; and terrorists and *Feme* murderers like Edmund Heines in Breslau, Count Helldorff in Potsdam and Berlin, and Manfred von Killinger in Saxony. To all these were added the dead martyrs Albert Leo Schlageter and Horst Wessel to form the élite of the New Germany and the pantheon of "saints" for the "thousand-year Reich." [8]

2. IDEOLOGY AND "MACHT"

National Socialism, while primarily and in its essential features a typically German movement, was indebted also to influences from other countries, especially Italy, Russia, and the United States. The very success of Italian fascism served as a model and a source of inspiration to the Nazi leaders. They also learned from the experiences of Mussolini what to avoid and how fast they could proceed in their consolidation of power. From Italian fascism they borrowed the Nazi salute, the models for youth organizations, for the labor front, and for the recreational *Kraft durch Freude,* the parallel of *Führer* to *Il Duce,* and other such symbols.* The relationship between the two dictators passed through various stages of trust and admiration. In earlier days, before Hitler's conquests, it was Hitler who looked up in admiration to the Italian dictator, while Mussolini gave condescending attention to the "vulgar" and "uneducated" German rabble rouser. Serious differences between the Führer and the Duce ap-

---

* Hitler also attributed the use of the brown shirt to the example of the Italian black-shirt (see *Hitler's Secret Conversations,* p. 8), but the historical precedent of Vater Jahn's gray shirts was no doubt at least of equal influence.

peared in 1934–1935 on German designs in Austria and in connection with the Nazi assassination of Dollfuss. From the period of their joint action in Spain, however, the two dictators established a close personal relationship that placed them shoulder to shoulder against the other Western powers. Now, however, it was Hitler who called the tune, and Italy ultimately became but a vassal state of the Third Reich. Hitler always had nothing but contempt for the Italian people, and especially the Italian soldiers, but his personal loyalty to the Duce persisted to the end, as evidenced in the breath-taking and hazardous venture carried out at his command in order to set Mussolini free after he had been ousted and jailed.

Nazi borrowings from Russia were of a dual character. From the Russian monarchist émigrés who swarmed into Germany after the Bolshevik revolution and who hovered close to the Nazi movement in its early Munich days, the Nazis received additional fuel for their own antisemitism. Most important of all was the diffusion in Germany of the *Protocols of the Elders of Zion,* which was translated into German and which served as an "authoritative" guide to Nazi antisemitism. Violent anti-Bolshevism was likewise fed into the Nazi movement by these émigrés. Alfred Rosenberg, himself an émigré from Russia, acted as the liaison officer between these antisemitic Russian reactionaries and the Nazi movement.

There was also within the N.S.D.A.P. a marked admiration and affinity for the Bolshevist dictatorship. We have already referred to the trend of National Bolshevism in Germany and the relations between Radek and the German nationalists. The so-called "socialist" elements in the party found a certain affinity with Russian communism except for the "internationalism" of the Bolsheviks, which they rejected. The saying current in Germany, that a Nazi was like a beefsteak—brown on the outside and red on the inside—was not far-fetched. The Nazis admired the Soviet system of repression, from the use of the concentration camp to the centralized power of Stalin, the dictator. Göring, in his interrogation at Nürnberg, related how he had conferred with Marshal Stalin and that he "had the impression that something very strong was there . . . because I saw how this one man had these 200,000,000 Russian people in his hand like that." [9] Hitler always referred admiringly to Stalin as Genghis Khan. He told his generals on August 22, 1939: "On the whole there are only three great statesmen in the world: Stalin, myself and Mussolini. Mussolini, the weakest, has not been able to break with either the power of the crown or of the church. Stalin and I are the only ones that see only the future." [10] It was this kind of reasoning that was used on both sides, by Ribbentrop and Molotov, in negotiating the non-aggression pact of 1939. Much of it was of course artificially fabricated; but there was enough of the truth in the analogies of the two systems to make fabrication not too difficult.

From the United States the Nazi movement borrowed a few German-Americans, individuals like Ernst Lüdecke and Ernst "Putzy" Hanfstängl, a Harvard alumnus who was one of the first larger financial contributors to the movement and who became chief of the Foreign Press Division of the party and "court pianist" to the Führer until he fell into disgrace. More important was the influence of American advertising on the techniques of propaganda developed by the Nazi machine. "What would one think of a soap ad which also recognized the value of other soaps?" wrote Hitler in *Mein Kampf*, and the same, he concluded, must also be true for political pronouncements. American revisionist literature on the causes of World War I and on the ills of the Treaty of Versailles was translated into German and became important and weighty grist for the mills of Nazi propaganda. Most important of all was the dissemination of Henry Ford's *The International Jew*. Baldur von Schirach, former Nazi Youth leader, told psychologist Dr. Gilbert in Nürnberg how at the age of seventeen someone made him read Ford's antisemitic tract. "You have no idea," said von Schirach, "what a great influence this book had on the thinking of the German youth, who did not have the maturity to think for itself." And he told the court at Nürnberg: "I read Henry Ford's book *The International Jew* . . . and became antisemitic." [11] Not that antisemitism in Germany had to be imported from the outside—the antisemitic tradition in Germany was much older than contacts with either Russia or the United States, and Nazi antisemitism would, of course, have developed without the stimulus from abroad. But Ford's tract, like the *Protocols* imported from tsarist Russia, nevertheless served to provide "literary" food as well as authority and prestige for Nazi racialist doctrine.

The question as to the role of ideology in the history of National Socialism has been the subject of interesting speculation. Official Nazi spokesmen always vaunted their *Weltanschauung,* and the word *Geist* was one that fell most frequently from their lips. Hitler's *Mein Kampf* devotes a substantial part of its contents to what might be called "ideology." The works of Feder, Rosenberg, Darré, and Count von Reventlow were intended to provide the movement with an official ideology, and these were supplemented by regular publications like the *Nationalsozialistische Monatshefte* and the *Nationalsozialistische Bibliothek* that served as the ideological organs of the party. On the other hand, one of the keenest interpreters of Nazism, Hermann Rauschning, insists that ideology meant little to the Nazi movement. According to Rauschning the so-called "doctrine" of National Socialism was intended only as a façade for the masses. The élite of the party made use of it just for their own purposes. He points out, and rightly so, that *Mein Kampf* was a dull book and difficult to plod through and that while it sold in millions of copies—largely through official pressure—it was merely a symbol and a literary ornament in the home, and was little read. The same held true even more so in the case of the works of Rosenberg and Darré.* According to Rauschning the leaders of the Nazi movement did not have the slightest idea of what they were going to do after they were in power. All they had was boundless confidence. They had "an open mind and no program at all," says Rauschning. The National Socialist philosophy was mainly the "grafting of all sorts of different fruits on the stem of the common crab-apple planted at the time of its first meetings in . . . the beer house in Munich." These fruits came from the Vaterlandspartei, from pan-German racialism, socialism, traditionalism, nationalism, Prussianism, and so on. And the programs always abounded in generalities so that any and every group could read into it whatever it wanted—farmers, workers, industrialists, small shopkeepers, youth, and so on. "Concrete promises divide, generalities unite." Hitler was the man with the authoritarian panacea that was cut to fit all malcontents. Such too is the interpretation held by Ernst Niekisch.[12]

Every movement which exercises power by means of naked force is bound sooner or later to sacrifice whatever ideology it possesses to the needs of maintaining itself in power. This was true of communism in the U.S.S.R. and this also was true of Nazi ideology. To take but one instance: the doctrine of racialism—considered to be the pivot of the entire movement, in which the element of constancy and permanence was the very core of the doctrine—was subjected to compromise from almost the very beginning of the Nazi movement. The original doctrine of Nordic racialism held that the vast majority of Germans were also of mixed blood and therefore racially inferior. It was only in tiny islets of uncontaminated population between the Elbe and the Weser rivers that "racially pure" Nordics were to be found. It was to be the purpose of Nazism to create the élite leadership for the rule of Germany from these "pure Nordic Germans" and to breed them to become eventually the sole population of Germany. But as the Nazi party grew into a mass party it became impossible to tell millions of followers that they were racial mongrels and inferior. This highly "refined" form of racialism, therefore, was abandoned and the terms "Aryan" and "Nordic" were applied to all Germans as the superior race. In the same way the term "non-Aryan" soon came to be identified exclusively with "Jew," and honored positions were found in Nordic racialism first for the Mediterranean Italians and then for the yellow race of Japan.

Despite all of Hitler's scorn for the polyglot, multi-national empire of the Hapsburgs and despite his repeated declarations that he wanted Germany only for Germans, yet when his aggressive designs demanded it in March, 1939, he marched into Prague and made Bohemia and Moravia

---

* Hitler himself confessed that he had found Rosenberg's book difficult to follow and had read only parts of it. (See *Hitler's Secret Conversations*, p 342.)

with their Czech population not a puppet state like Slovakia, but an integral part of the Greater German Reich. Furthermore, when the long years of war created a serious crisis in the supply of labor the racial doctrine was thrown completely to the winds and thousands of Ukrainian and Russian women were brought into Germany to be mated with German men in order to replenish the German labor supply. A document of September 4, 1942, introduced in the Nürnberg trial, tells of an order by Hitler to import 400,000 to 500,000 domestic workers between the ages of 15 to 35 from the Ukraine. The criteria of selection was to be their "conduct and physical appearance." The Führer had explained that "we have to review our school knowledge about people's migrations." The Germans, he declared, had spread far into the East, hence the great number of blond-haired and blue-eyed individuals in the Ukraine. These "descendants of Germans" were to be "re-Germanized" and to receive the same treatment as Germans.[13]

It is, therefore, true that Nazi ideology was always subject to being sacrificed to the needs of power. It is also true that its program was of such a general character as to permit the most diverse groups to read into it their own interests and their own political desiderata. Within the framework of a supreme devotion to the cause of militant nationalism and a lukewarm regard for other things, it was possible to read many things into the program. But it was not possible to read anything and everything into the party ideology. One could not find place in Nazi ideology for the humane virtues of the Sermon on the Mount, for the principles of the French and American revolutions, for democratic parliamentary government, for the principles of toleration and humanity, for the ideals of international co-operation and the dreams of world peace, for either economic or political liberalism, for Locke's rights of the individual, for scientific ridicule of racism, for modern art, for advanced views on education and for Freudian theories of sex. There was no room at all in the Nazi movement, by any stretching of principle, for Jews, Freemasons, Jehovah's Witnesses, pacifists, liberal democrats or futurists. On the other hand Nazi literature showed a fairly constant stress on antisemitism, on nationalism, on fanatical sacrifice, on the glory of the soldier, on authority, and on the supreme place of force in social relations. The Nazi collection of villains in German history included Erzberger, Kurt Eisner, Rathenau, the *Frankfurter Zeitung,* Freud, and Magnus Hirschfeld. The Nazi roster of heroes in German history almost always listed Arminius and Widukind, Luther, Frederick the Great and Bismarck, Fichte, Friedrich List and Adolf Wagner, Lagarde, Houston Chamberlain, Nietzsche and Spengler, Schlageter and Horst Wessel.

Thus it can be seen that ideology was much more developed and occupied a much more significant role in German National Socialism than in Italian fascism. But it did not occupy the same position of dogmatic authority nor did it receive the same degree of technical and scholarly implementation that Marxism received in the Communist dictatorship in Russia. And Nazi ideology was always subservient to the dynamic character of the movement. Rauschning is altogether on sure ground when he points to this dynamic nihilism as being the essential core of the Nazi movement. In the fundamental mainsprings of the movement it was "action pure and simple, dynamics *in vacuo,* revolution at a variable tempo, ready to be changed at any moment." There was the nihilistic destructionism driven by an insatiable dynamism and a thirst for extension of spheres of action and power that knew no bounds or end. This was what Neville Chamberlain and the Munich apologists never understood. They thought they were dealing with diplomats who had certain aspirations which, even though exaggerated and far-reaching in character, could nevertheless be negotiated and eventually satisfied. They did not understand that they were dealing with a movement that was bent on first revolutionizing the world and then conquering it. Nazi demands could never be satisfied because "being satisfied" ran counter to the entire spirit of the movement. This is what the psychiatrist rightly terms the paranoid character of the movement. For it is of the very essence of the paranoiac to be possessed of desires for power that are limitless and insatiable. This is what the conventional diplomats could not understand and why they thought they could stop German expansionism by making concessions, usually at the expense of the smaller nations. It did not work. One Nazi triumph only started a chain of new desires and new demands. The twelve years of Nazi rule saw a succession of hopes and expectations pinned upon the more "respectable" elements to tame and contain the Nazi revolution. First it was Hugenberg and von Papen and the conservative nationalists who engineered the delivery of power to Hitler on January 30, 1933, that were to hold Hitler in check; then it was Hindenburg and the Reichswehr; then Gregor Strasser and the "socialist" Nazis, or Göring and the "moderate" Nazis. All these hopes proved to be illusory. The dynamism of the Nazi movement overwhelmed all these attempts.

National Socialism represented the most extreme manifestation of the twentieth century revolt against reason. Its basic psychological character was anti-intellectualism. Instead of reason, it founded its entire ideological structure on the appeal to emotion and the appeal to force. "We suffer today from over-education," declared Hitler. "What we need is instinct and will." And in *Mein Kampf,* elaborating his approach toward mass propaganda, he wrote:

It is more difficult to undermine faith than knowledge, love succumbs to change less than [to] respect, hatred is more durable than aversion, and at all times the driving force of the most important changes in this world has been found less in a scientific knowledge animating the masses, but rather in a fanaticism dominating them and in a hysteria which drove them forward.[14]

The language used by Nazi orators and writers was permeated with words and phrases intended to evoke stirring and violent emotional reactions—*Sturm, rasen, erwache! Kraft, Glaube, Opfer,* and above all *Schicksal*—the vocabulary of religious revivalism turned political. "What does it mean to be a National Socialist?" asked Goebbels in his little catechism *Der kleine ABC des Nationalsozialismus.* And his answer was: "To be a National Socialist means nothing else but *Kampf, Glaube, Arbeit, Opfer*" (struggle, faith, work, sacrifice). National Socialist speeches were usually very long, sometimes lasting as much as four to five hours. It was necessary to develop ways of maintaining the hearers in a fever pitch (although a skeptical outsider might have suggested making the speeches shorter). Symbols, like the swastika, banners, medals, uniforms, and parades, were used profusely to stimulate emotional reactions. Such emotional appeals were especially effective in winning over a large section of the German women voters. The girls and women flocked in droves to see and admire the Nazi formations in uniform more than to listen to the oratory.

National Socialism, with all its moral nihilism, also knew how to appeal to the idealistic impulse for sacrifice. It was, as a matter of fact, the only large political movement in Germany that gave evidence of genuine idealistic, even though perversely misguided, sacrifice. "The monarchy," declared Hitler in one of his early speeches, "died because not one of its twenty-six monarchs . . . was ready to die fighting on the steps of the throne. The present republic will die the moment none of these democratic republicans, pacifists, and so on, will be ready to fall on the steps of parliament." [15] Hitler was right. No one was ready to die for democracy in Germany. All the idealistic will to sacrifice seemed to be concentrated on the right. This not only gave the movement internal strength but also served to attract a wider and larger following.

With the rejection of reason as the instrument of social action, the only alternative was the acceptance of force. This was not only put into practice by the Nazis but also made an essential element of their doctrine. It was not power (*Macht*), but concrete physical force (*Gewalt*) that they accepted in true Machiavellian style. "The first condition for success," wrote Hitler, "lies in the constant and uniform application of force." Force, he said, following Machiavelli, must be used consistently and with perseverance in order to prevent the suppressed group from reviving and drawing new sustenance from its persecution.

The Nazi dictatorship can be understood in its deeper meaning only if it is realized that this was not a dictatorship of a small clique, but one that rested on a wide mass basis. The question as to whether or not the masses involved constituted a majority of the German population, whether they were 49 per cent or 51 per cent, is not too significant. What is significant is that the Nazi dictatorship, even more than its fascist counterpart in Italy, rested on the following and support of millions of people who represented a true cross section of the German population. It was, in the deeper historical sense of the term, a product of the mass democratic society of the twentieth century. It could never have come into being in the first place without those political developments of modern times which elevated the masses to a position of influence in the body politic. The Nazis, therefore, displayed a sort of ambivalent attitude toward the masses. On the one hand they concentrated their propaganda on winning over the masses. This was what Goebbels called the "conquest of the streets." The street, wrote Goebbels, "is the characteristic feature of modern politics. Whoever conquers the street can also conquer the masses, and whoever conquers the masses thereby conquers the state." This was the task that Goebbels set himself when he became Berlin gauleiter. With the aid of the S.A. and the Nazi press he did indeed carry out his task with a great measure of success. The appeal for mass support continued to be used most effectively after the seizure of power in the demagogic plebiscites that were staged after decisions on major aspects of home and foreign policy had already been carried out. Exaggerated as were the announced majorities received by the government, and influenced as they were no doubt by the use of terror and force, it probably can be safely said that in all cases the government would have received a comfortable majority even without the use of coercion.

Parallel with this appeal for mass support, however, Nazi ideology displayed an open disdain for the masses. It attacked political democracy and popular government, heaped ridicule on majority rule and presented instead the conception of the rule of an élite, capped by the dominant position of the Führer. The very masses that were cajoled and wooed were told in the same breath that they were incapable of deciding for themselves what they wanted and what was to be done. And the amazing fact was that the Nazi masses accepted this role with approbation. The belief inculcated in the German people since the debacle of 1848, that they were incapable of governing themselves, now bore monstrous fruit.

The organization of the S.A. and the S.S. served to gather the élite during the period of the party's struggle for power, and the special Adolf Hitler schools and other S.S. institutions were set up to train the new élite after the Third Reich came into being. "Energy," wrote Hitler in his first published article, "like everything great, slumbers only in the minority of men." [16] The Germanic principle of leadership, without the help of parliamentary majorities but with the Führer's intuitive perception of the will and needs of the people, was set up in contradistinction to the "Western" conceptions of popular government derived from Locke and the French revolution. De Tocqueville's clairvoyant prediction in 1835 of the way in which industrialized and technological democracy would result in the establishment of a new type of despotism came to be realized a century later in Nazi Germany.

Propaganda, next to physical coercion, was thus necessary for the appeal to and the control of the masses. Propaganda, wrote Hitler in *Mein Kampf,* was not intended for intellectuals but for the masses. It should be designed to influence the feelings rather than the understanding, and must never be above the comprehension of the most limited elements among those it is designed to influence. Since their capacity to understand is usually very limited, propaganda should be restricted to only a few points, punctuated with slogans and repeated over and over again. Above all it must never be objective and it must never concede anything whatsoever to the opposition. The slightest concession to possible justice on the other side, declared Hitler, already creates a basis for doubt in the justice of your own cause. People react to feelings, and feelings, said Hitler, are not complex but simple. There is always one positive and one negative, love or hate, right or wrong, true or false, never half and half. Two things impressed Hitler: the failure of imperial Germany to use propaganda effectively during World War I as compared with British propaganda, and the effective techniques for influencing the masses developed by modern advertising. From these he learned to cultivate the most diabolical methods for mass suggestion. Goebbels later became the master propagandist and the first minister for propaganda in the cabinet of the Third Reich.

Nazi propaganda technique also made it necessary to set up enemies and scapegoats on whom to heap abuse and ridicule and especially on whom to place the blame for all of Germany's troubles. The entire world was Germany's enemy, and the geography books continued to define Germany as "a country surrounded on all sides by enemies." But propaganda required more specific and more concrete objects of hatred. A whole series of "enemies" was discovered or manufactured. There were the "November criminals" and the perpetrators of the "stab in the back"; there were the Marxists and the international capitalists; there were the pacifists and the internationalists; there were the Freemasons and the Papist clericals; and there were, above all, the Jews. The Jews became the scapegoat par excellence of the movement; they were responsible for anything and everything that worked counter to Nazi ideals, and antisemitism became the pivot of the whole totalitarian structure of the Third Reich. Antisemitism served as the vehicle not only for the consolidation of power at home but as the instrument of Nazi foreign policy by means of which it was able to stir up discontented elements abroad and find a basis for support in all parts of the world. Antisemitism as an old, deeply rooted and ubiquitous phenomenon in the Western World could serve better than anything else to galvanize and diffuse pro-Nazi sentiment throughout the world. The Nazi slogan "Without a solution of the Jewish problem there is no salvation for mankind" could find sympathetic ears among unscrupulous malcontents everywhere.

The Jew, in Nazi ideology, was the embodiment of all their enemies, all rolled into one. He was the "November criminal" and the traitor; he was both a Marxist and an international capitalist; he was a pacifist and an internationalist; he was a Freemason and, if not a clerical himself, the ally and partner of the clericals. He was above all the debaser of the purity of the German race. The lewd, lascivious, and pornographic antisemitism that pictured the leering Jew lying in wait to ravish the naïve, blond Aryan maiden became one of the most effective images in the Nazi propaganda arsenal. It was used by Hitler and Goebbels as well as by Rosenberg and Darré, but it found its most loathsome expression in the person of the Franconian gauleiter Julius Streicher. Streicher's *Stürmer,* utilizing the lowest forms of mass appeal and of scandal-sheet journalism, was circulated throughout Germany and usually had a special display stand (the *Stürmer Kasten*) in every town and village, where its screaming headlines in black and red and its pornographic cartoons were set in the path of all who passed through the main thoroughfares. Streicher also published special children's books, like *Der Giftpilz,* which poisoned the minds of the young with the doctrine that "the Jew is the devil in human form."

> *Es geht ein Teufel durch das Land*
> *Der Jude ist's, uns wohl bekannt*
> *Als Völkermörder, Rassenschänder*
> *Als Kinderschreck für alle Länder.*

Nazi antisemitism received alleged "scientific" foundation and was biologically grounded in Nazi racialism. This meant two things: a premium placed upon "purity" of race and a dogmatic belief in the undisputed superiority of the so-called Nordic or Aryan race. All civilizations of the past, according to Nazi doctrine, decayed and disappeared because of race mixture. All that is creative in all phases of human endeavor is the product of the Aryan race, the "Prometheus of humanity" and the "founder of culture," as Hitler called it. The cultivation of racial purity, therefore, was, according to Hitler, the real end and purpose of the state. It is a common error to suppose that Nazi ideology followed Hegel in setting up the power of the state as an end in itself and for itself. The Nazi *Weltanschauung,* wrote Hitler in *Mein Kampf,* "sees in the state principally only a means to an end and conceives this end to be the preservation of the racial existence of man." The mission of the German state was to gather and preserve the "most valuable of the original racial elements and gradually and securely to bring them up to the dominant position in the state." The state "must place race as the central point of the life of the community and must guard the preservation of its purity."

Almost all of the Nazi racial doctrine was taken bodily from the writings of Gobineau, Schemann, and in particular from Houston Stewart

Chamberlain's *Foundations of the Nineteenth Century*. But it had its own anthropological specialists too. Eugen Fischer, a physical anthropologist who had made a reputation for himself at the University of Berlin, prostituted his scholarly integrity by providing an aura of scientific respectability to Nazi racialism. Hans F. K. Günther, more the quack than the scientist, served as the official dispenser of "scientific" racialism. Nordicism was dressed up in scientific terminology but most of the time it was presented in a form which defied all the norms of credibility commonly accepted by the world at large. Hermann Gauch, the author of a work *The New Foundations of Racial Study,* seriously projected the theory that "the Nordic race alone can emit sounds of untroubled clearness, whereas among non-Nordic men and races the pronunciation is impure, the individual sounds are more confused and like the noises made by animals, such as barking, snoring, sniffing, squeaking. That birds can learn to talk better than other animals is explained by the fact that their mouths are Nordic in structure."

In 1935, when foreign exchange was badly needed for importing strategic armament supplies, the racial doctrine was used by the Nazi régime to discourage the use of imported lemons and to use more of the native rhubarb in their place. The *Fränkische Tageszeitung* of July 28, 1935, gave its readers the following sample of *Blut und Boden* theory:

> Only the fruits of the German earth—clod earth [declared the Nazi writer]— can create German blood. Through them only are transmitted to the blood, and thence to the body and the soul, those delicate vibrations which determine the German type. The type is unique the whole world over because there is but one German soil on the earth.
>
> Farewell lemon, we need thee not! Our German rhubarb will take thy place fully and entirely. It is so unpretending that we overlooked and despised it, busy with infatuation for foreign things. In all our shires we can have it in masses, the whole year round. We get it almost for nothing; its tartness will season our salads and vegetable dishes. Slightly sweetened it provides us with delicious refreshment, and what is more, it is a blood-purifying and medicinal agent true to German type. Let us make good with German rhubarb the sins we have committed with the alien lemon.
>
> So out with thee, ingrate daughter of the South: out with thee from our German shires and homes! We will not see thee more, thou wanton creature. After all the catastrophes and sufferings into which our dealings with the alien spirit and its products have driven us, let us fashion new German offspring out of the only material which can make them marrowy, true to type, and German —out of the fruits of our German mother earth.

Nazi antisemitism and Nazi racialism laid the groundwork for the Nazi assault upon Christianity. It is true that the official program of the Nazi party declared itself in favor of "positive Christianity." It is also true that in his earlier public speeches, Hitler, who was born a Catholic, exhibited, at least publicly, a certain admiration for "the solitary spiritual hero" of Nazareth. It is likewise true that both before and after Hitler assumed office the N.S.D.A.P. counted among its supporters religious leaders of both the Protestant and Catholic denominations. It was precisely such support that led the eminent theologian Friedrich Heiler to declare in 1932 that nothing in his life had shocked him so much as to see "broad circles" of the Protestant church embrace a doctrine so antipathetic to Christianity as National Socialism. National Socialism took over the theme of Nietzsche's *Genealogy of Morals* and branded Christianity as nothing more than another form of Judaism. Perhaps, as Jacques Maritain pointed out, the Nazi hatred of the Jews really stemmed from the fact that they resented the imposition of Christianity upon them. Their antisemitism was really a "psychopathic form of Christophobia." They rejected Christianity as an essentially alien idea, foreign to the pure racial culture of the primeval Germans. Teuton paganism, particularly as portrayed in the music dramas of Richard Wagner, was the proper religion for German Nordicism. The real hero in the early history of Germany was not the great Karl, Charlemagne, who forced the Germans to embrace Christianity but Widukind, the leader of the pagan Saxons, who resisted the Christianizing efforts of the Frankish emperor. "Antiquity," said Hitler, "was better than modern times because it did not know Christianity and syphilis." [17] He deplored the appearance of Luther's translation of the Bible because it shed a "halo of glory upon the Bible of Satan" (*Satansbibel*) and because it made available to the broad masses the "entire pettifogging" of the Bible.

The brunt of the Nazi attack was leveled at the Old Testament and at Pauline Christianity. Both were regarded as creations of an inferior and alien race. All that remained of Christianity was the figure of Jesus, whom some of the Nazi authorities proclaimed to be "Aryan." But it was not the Jesus of the Sermon on the Mount. Nothing was so contrary to Nazi beliefs and values as the beatitudes enumerated in the Sermon on the Mount. Nazi youth were to be infused with the heroic and militant qualities, not with humility, charity, mercy, meekness, and love. They were to be trained "for death." "I pray to God that I might die with a French bullet in my heart," was the prayer uttered by a young Nazi lad on his first communion. Whatever remained of the figure of Jesus, for those who did accept him, "was a sort of pantheistic mystic or revolutionary who drove the money changers out of the temple with a whip." Christian love was converted to "love of fellow countrymen," and the Protestant Revolt was identified with "Nordic Christianity."

Basically, however, National Socialism, as interpreted by its party leaders and not by fellow-traveling clergymen, was incompatible with Christianity. In a letter by Martin Bormann, chief of the party chancellery, to Alfred Rosenberg on February 22, 1940, Bormann wrote:

Christianity and National Socialism are phenomena that arose out of quite different foundations. Both are so different from each other that it will be impossible to construct a Christian doctrine that could be approved from the standpoint of National Socialist *Weltanschauung,* in the same way that the Christian faiths will never understand how to recognize the full value of National Socialist *Weltanschauung.*[18]

National Socialism, declared Bormann to Rosenberg, cannot recognize the Christian attitude toward race, family, and marriage, the doctrine of immaculate conception, celibacy, and so on. "The churches will be overcome not by a compromise between National Socialism and Christian doctrine but by a new *Weltanschauung* whose advent you yourself heralded in your works." Racial Teutonic paganism was more to the heart of the hardened Nazi than Christian principle. And inscribed more than anything else in their hearts was Hitler's commandment, "Thou shalt have no other God but Germany!"

This letter by the then-deputy Führer of the N.S.D.A.P. put the official stamp of party approval upon the works of Alfred Rosenberg, the assailant of Christianity. For reasons of political strategy, Rosenberg's *Der Mythus des 20. Jahrhunderts* was not published by the official party publishing house. This fact was used at times to demonstrate that the official party attitude toward Christianity was not that of Rosenberg. The whole history of the party, the anti-Christian discipline imposed on S.S. élite guards, the program of the Nazi training schools, and above all the very spirit of both ideology and practice were violently opposed to the principles of Christianity as they were to those of Judaism. That many Germans of intellectual as well as of more simple mentality could at the very same time worship the "God on the Cross" and idolize the Führer is one of those irrational aberrations of the human spirit that can merely be described but not intelligently explained. A crucifix and a framed picture of Hitler, Göring, and Goebbels together on the same wall was the sight that greeted and baffled many an American soldier who marched into the Catholic Rhineland. It is only one of the many instances of distortion of the intelligent and coherent view of life. Hitler himself had no such dual attitude. "One is either a German or a Christian," he told Hermann Rauschning. "You cannot be both." For the future of the German people, "it is decisive whether they acknowledge the Jewish Christ-creed with its effeminate pity-ethics, or a strong, heroic belief in God in Nature, God in our own people, in our destiny, in our blood." [19]

National Socialist ideology incorporated a certain type of socialism into its program. It appealed to the vague anti-capitalist yearnings of the neo-romanticists who still refused to adjust themselves to the new urbanized and industrialized society. It addressed itself to the backward economic groups, the unemployed, the petty shopkeepers, the independent artisans, to those ruined by inflation, to those who attributed their economic distress to modern large-scale capitalism with its chain stores, department stores, and its complex banking and financial structure which they could not understand. These were the people whom Hendrik de Man once described as the *Stehkragenproletariat,* the people who had been ground down economically to the level of the proletarian but who clung tenaciously to their psychological affiliation with their previous status by continuing to wear the "wing collar" and who stubbornly refused to ally themselves with the organized working classes. National Socialism appealed to the peasantry against their "urban exploiters." *Gemeinnutz vor Eigennutz,* the "general good before the individual good," and the "breaking of the interest bondage"—these were the vague and general formulations of the Nazi program of socialism which could be interpreted by each of these economic groups in the light of their own interests and desires.

National Socialism, however, was more socialist than this. It also made a definite bid to the organized workers of Germany and gathered hundreds of thousands of them under its standard. The National Socialists, beginning with Rudolf Jung and Anton Drexler up to Hitler and Gregor Strasser, recognized how deeply rooted the socialist tradition was in German life. Like the early Christian missionaries among the heathen, who tied in their Christian gospel with the deeply rooted customs and beliefs of the pagans, so Hitler too came "not to destroy the law but to fulfill it." To gain access to the hearts of the German worker one had to come as a Socialist. "Arise ye young aristocrats of a new working class!" exclaimed Goebbels to the workers of Berlin. "You are the aristocracy of the Third Reich." "We are Socialists," wrote Gregor Strasser. "We are enemies, deadly enemies of the present-day capitalist economy with its exploitation of the economically weak, with its unjust wage system, with its immoral evaluation of an individual according to property and money instead of according to responsibility and achievement, and we are determined under all circumstances to destroy this system." [20] There was in Nazi circles even a certain admiration for the heroic and disciplined character of the Social Democratic party, especially of the days of Lassalle and Bebel. But Marxism represented for them the corrupted, materialistic, and international form of socialism. The true gospel of socialism was to be the Nazi variety. "I am not only the conqueror, but also the executor of Marxism," Hitler told Rauschning, "of that part of it that is essential and justified, stripped of its Jewish-Talmudic dogma." The difference between him and the Marxists, he said, was,

that I have really put into practice what these peddlers and pen-pushers have timidly begun. . . . I had only to develop logically what Social-Democracy repeatedly failed in because of its attempt to realize its evolution within the framework of democracy. National Socialism is what Marxism might have been if it could have broken its absurd and artificial ties with a democratic order.

Socialism, for the Nazis, did not mean especially a particular set of economic principles. It was not particularly concerned with "such trifles" as the private possession of the means of production.

Of what importance is that [asked Hitler], if I range men firmly within a discipline they cannot escape? Let them own land or factories as much as they please. The decisive factor is that the State, through the party, is supreme over them, regardless whether they are owners or workers. All that . . . is unessential. Our Socialism goes far deeper . . . it establishes the relation of the individual to the State, the national community. . . . Why need we trouble to socialize banks and factories? We socialize human beings.[21]

Observers who identified socialism with traditional Marxian socialism and who did not yet fully realize or were not ready to realize what socialism meant in the Soviet Union seemed confounded by the Nazi appeal to socialism on the one hand and their alliance with industrialists and private property on the other. They therefore concluded that the socialist plank in the Nazi program was merely sham propaganda. They understood neither the deeper meaning of Nazism nor the dark potentialities of an economic Marxism devoid of democratic controls. The "socialist" element of the Nazi program was just as much and just as little "sham" as any other part of their program. And Gregor Strasser could be the leader of the so-called "socialist" wing of the party and at the same time assure the American correspondent of the *New York Evening Post,* H. R. Knickerbocker, on October 11, 1932: "We recognize private property. We recognize private initiative. . . . We are against the nationalization of trade. . . . When we come to power there will be no violent changes."

Most important of all in National Socialist ideology was the element of passionate nationalism. This was the ingredient that cemented and held together all the disjointed and disparate parts of the program, and it was the common denominator of all the different elements that came into the movement. In its vague and generalized form all it had to do was to preach a doctrine of the glory and greatness of Germany. "Ye shall have no other god but Germany!" With the long tradition of the supreme importance of nationalism in German history and with their capacity to combine the appeal of nationalism with that of socialism, the Nazis in their crass and vulgar manner were able to achieve what Friedrich Naumann was never able to do on the basis of the democratic fusion of these two elements. Concretizing their nationalism in terms of the issues confronting Germany after the close of World War I, the Nazis hammered away at "the breaking of the chains of Versailles." They became heirs of the pan-German dream of expansion, translating it into the slogan of *Volk ohne Raum* and expansion eastward, and they took over the mantle of the romantic apostles of a European empire dominated by Germany with their tune of "Today it is Germany, tomorrow ours is the world."

The former Nationalist minister Hans Schlange-Schoeningen, writing in 1948 in retrospect, came to the sad but accurate realization of "how primitive were the weapons with which Hitler fought and won his struggle for power." Without exaggeration, all his speeches can be resolved into one simple formula: "For fourteen years an accursed system has deliberately ruined Germany, but now I will lead you all, every single one of you, to a glorious future. And the German people, distracted by terrible difficulties, gradually let this lying and stupid refrain be driven into their heads until finally they succumbed." [22]

3. HISTORICAL ROOTS OF NAZISM

Neither the leadership nor the program of the National Socialist party would have been sufficient to bring about either the initial triumph of Nazism or its continuance in power until smashed by Allied armies. Weakness and cowardice on the part of the democratic régime and its leaders throughout the history of the Weimar Republic was in a great measure responsible for allowing the movement to develop and to wax powerful. Still more important was the fact that the Nazis received the support—at first tacit and later more active—of large segments of the more "respectable" elements of the population. Otto Meissner, secretary to the Reich President under Ebert, Hindenburg, and Hitler, is much to the point when he insists (it is, of course, part of his own personal *apologia*) that the majority of the German people viewed the accession of Hitler to power "not as the creation of an authoritarian police state but as the dawn of an era of recuperation and regeneration of German community life." Never in the history of democratic party politics anywhere in the world has a candidate for public office unfolded his program with such brutal frankness and never has an elected leader come so near to carrying out his campaign promises. No degree of *ex post facto* rationalizing and apologetics can wash away the fact that the moral and political character of both the National Socialist program and of its leaders stood clearly revealed to the German voters all through the period of its activity. "We shall be hard, ruthless, and brutal," promised Gregor Strasser in December, 1931, "in cleaning up the trash of the past twelve years." Yet they found allies to help them achieve their goal among leaders in industry, in other political parties, among nationalist organizations, among intellectuals, and in the churches. In his concluding address to the International Military Tribunal Justice Robert Jackson said:

It was the fatal weakness of the early Nazi band that it lacked technical competence. It could not from among its own ranks make up a government capable of carrying out all the projects necessary to realize its aims. Therein lies the special crime and betrayal of men like Schacht and von Neurath, Speer and von Papen, Raeder and Dönitz, Keitel and Jodl. It is doubtful whether the Nazi master plan could have succeeded without their specialized intelligence which they so willingly put at its command. . . . Their superiority to the average run of Nazi mediocrity is not their excuse. It is their condemnation.[23]

Walther Funk, one of the Nürnberg war criminals and former minister of economies, testified that he was "encouraged by industry to become active in the Party" (N.S.D.A.P.) and that he was "active as a go-between for the Nazis and big business." [24] Hitler began addressing meetings of the Rhine industrialists in 1930 and 1931. He established friendly relations with Emil Kirdorf, and Fritz Thyssen introduced him to the Rhenish-Westphalian industrial leaders. On January 27, 1932, he addressed the Industrie Klub in Düsseldorf and won the support of the captains of industry. The occasion is noted in official party literature as "a memorable day in the history of the N.S.D.A.P."

Industrialists, Stahlhelm leaders, and leading figures in the Nationalist party joined forces to bring about the accession of Hitler. Dr. Alfred Hugenberg, leader of the Nationalist party and big industrialist; Franz Seldte, head of the veterans' organization (Stahlhelm); and Dr. Hjalmar Schacht, one of the original founders of the Democratic party and then head of the Reichsbank, all joined with Hitler in October, 1930, to form the Harzburg front against the democratic republic. The role of Hugenberg in the fateful months before Hitler's accession to power still remains concealed in obscurity, but it was of no mean proportion. And Dr. Schacht not only added his prestige to the following of the Nazi movement, but served as the financial wizard who made possible the speedy rearmament of Nazi Germany to make her ready for war. "This man" [Hitler], Schacht told the American business leader S. R. Fuller on September 23, 1935, "set about first to raise the moral standard of the nation. That is why I think him a great man; he has raised the moral standard of the people." [25] On the occasion of Schacht's sixtieth birthday on January 21, 1937, the *Völkischer Beobachter* wrote, "The name of Dr. Schacht will remain linked with the transition of the German economy to the new National Socialist methods."

Many of these nationalists and industrialists imagined that they would be able to manipulate the Nazi leaders for their own purposes and, through von Papen, Hugenberg, Schacht, Hindenburg, von Neurath, and the other "conservative" nationalists, hold the radicalism of Hitler in check. They were, however, no match for the dynamism of Hitler. One by one they had to bow out of the picture and take orders from the upstart Hitler. Hugenberg soon fell into oblivion, Thyssen had to flee the country for his life, and Schacht ended up in a Nazi concentration camp. But their historical, if not legal, responsibility for the triumph of Nazism is beyond question.

Intellectuals and religious leaders too joined the band of supporters who helped Nazism come to power and stay in power. Conservative nationalists, technicians, literary figures, and social scientists worked either singly or collectively to undermine the democratic republic. The Ring Kreis, presided over by Heinrich von Gleichen, started out as a sophisticated and fancy gathering of intellectual opposition to modern rationalism and enlightenment and ended up as the Herren Klub from which came the von Papen circle that paved the road for Hitler. The *Tat* Kreis, in its monthly edited by Hans Zehrer, preached the imminent downfall of international capitalism and the advent of a "German socialism." Nationalist journals like *Deutsches Volkstum,* edited by Wilhelm Stapel and Albrecht Erich Günther, that were not quite as rabid or as vulgar as the official Nazi publications, and publishing houses such as the J. F. Lehmanns Verlag in Munich, the Hanseatische Verlagsanstalt in Hamburg, or the Diederichs Verlag in Jena, rallied around them thousands of intellectuals who were at times a bit squeamish about the methods used by Hitler but who welcomed the substitution of real "authority" and German *Volkstum* for the "weak" and "cosmopolitan" parliamentary democracy. With diabolical brilliance the political scientist Carl Schmitt delivered the funeral oration on the "spiritual breakdown of parliamentarism" and heralded the advent of the new authoritarian and corporative state.

Werner Sombart, internationally known economist and historian of modern capitalism, threw overboard all his earlier canons of scientific research, as well as his liberalism, and joined the chorus of disciples of the new "German socialism." At one of the last meetings of the Verein für Sozialpolitik, on June 30, 1935, Sombart proclaimed the end of the era of free discussion as a prerequisite for scholarly work.

This art of discussion is gone [declared Sombart]. Not discussion but decision now dominates the scene. The creation of a political will comes about today by quite another way. It is no longer the indirect way of influencing public opinion but the direct way by the *Führer* principle. This is a fact which may be evaluated in different ways. I, for my part, say, "Thank God, that this is so!" [26]

Sombart was soon joined by numerous other economists of academic stature. Reputable sociologists and social philosophers like Hans Freyer and Eduard Spranger explained to the academic world the new miracle of social science—how the "charismatic Führer" emerges as an "emanation" from the will of the people to impress upon it the new political idea.[27]

Literary figures, not only those of the nationalist right like Hanns Johst, Paul Ernst, Heinz Heinrich Ewers, and Ernst Jünger, but more moderate and more liberal writers like Rudolf Binding and Gottfried Benn came to the defense of Hitler and his policies against the challenge of foreign liberals like Romain Rolland. The dean of German literature and former idol of the radical left, Gerhart Hauptmann, led the millions of non-Nazis to vote "yes" in Hitler's first plebiscite. Hermann Rauschning tells how Hauptmann looked forward to his first meeting with Hitler as though it were "a counterpart of Goethe's meeting with Napoleon," and how after the meeting, which consisted only of a handshake, the great imaginative creator of *The Weavers,* of *The Sunken Bell,* and of *Florian Geyer* told his friends that "it was the greatest moment of my life."

The parade of fawning admirers, cowardly intellectuals, and opportunistic careerists included Nobel-prize-winning physicists, musicians and artists, technologists and scientists. It more than matched the parade of intellectual sycophants before William II in 1913. And it was given a sacred aura of religious blessing by theologians and clergymen, especially Protestant, who saw in the Nazi state the realization of the "German-Protestant" idea of the state, the defense against the "craftiness" of Jesuits and Ultramontanes, the realization of Stöcker's evangelical and anti-semitic "socialism" and the movement that would replace the "moral depravity" of the democratic republic with "German *Zucht*" and morality, with the spirit of sacrifice, the sense of family, authority and fatherland and which would take up the cudgels of religion against materialism and Mammon. Little did they understand the deep contempt and scorn that Hitler had for what he called bourgeois morals and the "prudery and moral snooping" of the "church-going old women" and "virtue peddlers."

National Socialism, however, could neither have gained the allies it did nor, with their help, have succeeded in gaining its ascendancy if it did not have roots in German historical development. Not that Nazism was the inevitable outcome of German historical development. It was no more inevitable than any other political ideology. But neither was it a bizarre and alien grafting upon the German body politic. In its various manifestations it struck a reminiscent chord of one kind or another in German tradition and in German cultural life. Just as the burning of books by political opponents harked back first to the nationalist student book burnings of 1817 and ultimately to Luther's burning of the papal bull in 1520, so the spirit and doctrines of Nazism found much of their antecedents in the record of the German past.

Economic and political conditions in Germany between 1918 and 1933 obviously played a role in creating the climate for Nazism. But neither the Treaty of Versailles nor economic crisis and unemployment were responsible for the triumph of Nazism. The political frustration and economic suffering were the factors that dictated the time for a reaction to take place. But the form assumed by the reaction to unemployment was dictated by the German historical and cultural tradition. There was widespread unemployment and economic misery in Lancashire and Wales as there was in the United States after 1929, but the forms assumed by the reaction were totally different. The German answer to the post-war ills, in keeping with the whole trend of German history since the end of the eighteenth century, was an appeal to more ardent and more intensive nationalism. And the most extreme form of nationalist appeal was Nazism. In its anti-intellectualism, National Socialism drew its inspiration from the tradition of early nineteenth century romanticism, from the neo-romantic revival of the early twentieth century, and from the pre-war youth movement. Its worship of the all-importance of the state and of force as the main instrument of the state could readily be found in Hegel, Bismarck, and the whole tradition of the *Machtstaat*. Anti-democracy could find no better philosopher than Nietzsche and no more exclusive snobbism than that of Stefan George and his circle. Prussianism, not as a geographical or biological characteristic but as a pattern of behavior and set of values, had found its ideal exponents in Frederick the Great, in Treitschke and Spengler. Authoritarian socialism with its ideal of national economic self-sufficiency or autarchy could be concocted out of a mixture of cameralism, Fichte, Marx, Lassalle, and Spengler. Caesarism found its most widely read advocate in Spengler. Moral relativism and a Germanic brand of Machiavellianism was handed down by Frederick II and Hegel. In the youth movement, in Ernst Jünger, and above all in Nietzsche were found the intellectual foundations for widespread nihilism. The pan-Germans supplied the antecedents for Nazi expansionism. Racialism and paganism left a deep impress on the German mind by means of the works of Chamberlain and notably of Richard Wagner. As for antisemitism, it had a long history in Germany going back to the Crusades, to Luther and Eisenmenger, but it found its modern ideologues in Fichte, Dühring, Lagarde, Stöcker, and Houston Stewart Chamberlain, re-enforced by their Austrian allies Schönerer and Lueger.

These are what are often referred to as the "roots" or "intellectual origins" of National Socialism. This does not mean that all these and other such figures in German history were Nazis. Nor does it mean that Hitler and his henchmen were avid students and disciples of all these famous Germans. Nazism was specifically a twentieth century phenomenon and can only be understood as such. Nor is the historical background important in order to trace the "origins" of Nazi ideas and practices. The importance of these intellectual antecedents lies in the fact that the confluence of all these currents and trends created a tradition and a climate in which National Socialism could take hold of and captivate large masses of German citizens. It is not a question of the "responsibility" of Nietzsche or Hegel or Treitschke as it is a question of understanding how the forces of German culture and tradition converged to make Nazism acceptable and popular in German life.

In many instances the tradition as represented by Nazism was a crude vulgarization of the original parent. Nazism was a vulgarized Goethe, a vulgarized Hegel, a vulgarized Marx, most certainly a vulgarized Nietzsche, and even a vulgarized Spengler. That is why Spengler undertook his mild criticism of Nazi policies in his *Jahre der Entscheidung,* published in 1934

4. THE TOTALITARIAN POLICE STATE

The Third Reich as constituted by the Nazis was organized as a totalitarian police state. With lightning rapidity compared to the pace taken by Mussolini, Hitler eliminated first his political opponents and then his political allies and all others who could possibly challenge his power or even share it with him. The first act to set the tone of terror and fear in the Third Reich was the burning of the Reichstag on February 27, 1933. The circumstances surrounding this act are now quite well established. Hitler had expressed a wish to have a large-scale propaganda campaign for the elections to be held in March, and in working on this plan Goebbels conceived the wily plot to set the Reichstag on fire. Goebbels saw the possibility not only to use it for election propaganda but also as the pretext for the promulgation of dictatorial emergency decrees. Goebbels discussed the details of the plan with Göring, but it was Goebbels who arranged for a group of ten S.A. men led by Karl Ernst to enter the Reichstag building by way of Göring's quarters and set the place afire. In the ensuing confusion Göring was to set the police on the wrong trail, and the accusation was then to be made that the act was part of the Communist terror campaign. The role occupied by the Dutchman Van der Lubbe, the only one actually convicted of the crime at the subsequent Reichstag fire trial, still is not clear. According to one version it was the chief of the Gestapo, Diels, who planted him on the scene; according to another version it was the S.A. men who put him there.

The Reichstag fire served the Nazi leaders well. The charges that this was to be the signal for a Communist revolt were swallowed either willingly or unwillingly by the majority of people, and the next day Hitler forced through the Decree for the Protection of People and State, which suspended civil and personal liberties, abrogated the constitutional guarantees of freedom of speech, freedom from illegal search, right to assembly, and the right to protection of property. It was this decree rather than the subsequent Enabling Act that marked the transition to the Hitler dictatorship.

The propaganda value of the Reichstag fire showed itself in the election returns of March 5, 1933, when the Nazis increased their popular vote from 11,737,000 in 1932 to 17,277,200, and the number of deputies from 196 to 288. This was not the clean sweep looked for by Hitler and Goebbels, and it constituted only 43.9 per cent of the electorate. But with the 8 per cent polled by their Nationalist allies they had close to 52 per cent of the popular vote and for the first time since 1930 there was a governing constitutional majority in the Reichstag.

The first act of the new Reichstag, however, was to bury the Reichstag and the constitution. On March 23 the Nazi-Nationalist coalition presented to the Reichstag an "Enabling Law" which transferred the legislative functions of the Reichstag to the Reich cabinet and which allowed also for any deviations from the constitution deemed necessary by the cabinet. According to John Locke and the principles of democratic rule derived from Locke and the Enlightenment, such an act of self-abdication was impossible and illegal. Political suicide by the legislative body was just as contrary to nature as physical suicide by an individual. Not so for the democracy of Weimar. Except for the Social Democrats (the Communist party deputies were not allowed to take their seats), all political parties, including the "democratic" State party and the Catholic Center party, voted for the Enabling Law and rushed "headlong into their chains."

Heinrich Brüning, the Centrist leader, has claimed that the Center party was duped into voting for the Act. The Centrists under Monsignor Kaas, according to Brüning, had been promised a letter signed by Hitler withdrawing the decree of February 28 in return for a vote for the Enabling Act. Hitler and Frick kept assuring Kaas that the letter was on its way, and Hindenburg pressed them to vote for the law under any conditions. The Centrists succumbed to this pressure. To explain the Centrist action solely in terms of naïveté in putting trust in a letter by Hitler (which never came) is hardly tenable in the light of the shrewd leadership of the Center party on other occasions. It is rather a sad commentary on the pusillanimity of the anti-Nazis and their readiness even at such a critical juncture to subordinate political freedom to "national solidarity." The name of Otto Wels, spokesman for the Social Democrats, will live in the history of liberty in Germany as the only man who stood up to face the menacing threats of brown-shirted deputies, to brave Hitler's and Göring's revengeful mien, and to risk the manacles of Gestapo agents by proclaiming Socialist opposition to the law and to the dictatorship. The final vote by the last freely elected Reichstag of the Weimar Republic was 444 votes for, 94 (Social Democrats) against, the act which established the dictatorship.

With Hitler in the top post, Göring in control of the police, and Goebbels in charge of the instruments of propaganda, the Nazi partners in the coalition soon overwhelmed their Nationalist partners by their dynamism and rapidly concentrated political power in their own hands. On May 2, 1933, action was taken against the trade-unions, and all their administrative apparatus, functions, property, and treasury were placed in the hands of the Labor Front headed by Dr. Robert Ley. One by one all other political parties were either outlawed or forced to liquidate, leaving the N.S.D.A.P. as the only legal party in the land and making Germany, like Russia and Italy, a one-party state. The Nationalist allies were either pushed out of the cabinet altogether, as in the cases of Hugenberg and Gereke, shunted off into other honorific posts, as was done to von Papen and Neurath, or intimidated into silent acquiescence. All potential rivals to Hitler's leadership and all possible leaders of disaffected elements were swept away in the omnibus purge of June 30, 1934, in which Hitler's intimate friend Ernst Röhm; his greatest rival for leadership in the party, Gregor Strasser; his predecessor as chancellor, General Kurt von Schleicher; Edgar Jung, von Papen's secretary; and a miscellaneous assortment of S.A. leaders, Catholic leaders, individuals with whom Hitler had old scores to settle, and purely accidental victims, were all shot down in a blood bath that seemed at the time to have shaken the very foundations of the dictatorship. The net result, however, was only to eliminate several hundred personages,* to strike panic and fear into the entire state apparatus, to bring Göring and Himmler into centralized control of the police powers of the Reich, and to make Adolf Hitler the omnipotent dictator which he remained until his end. The old and by now senile President, on whom the anti-Nazi conservatives had pinned their hopes, sent a telegram to Hitler congratulating him on the measures he had taken to guard the safety of the country. The cabinet, with von Papen excused from being present, passed a law legalizing the acts of June 30, July 1, and July 2. On July 13 the Reichstag convened to hear a long, fabricated account by the Führer of what had occurred. "In these twenty-four hours," declared Hitler, "I was the Supreme Court of the land," and thus the blood bath was provided with legal sanctification.

Three weeks later Hitler's henchmen in Vienna murdered the Austrian chancellor Dollfuss. Nevertheless the Führer's position grew stronger. And when Hindenburg died on August 2, 1934, and was consigned by the Führer's funeral oration "to enter into Valhalla," the occasion was used to effect the merger of the offices of president and chancellor, and Hitler assumed the omnipotent title of "Führer und Reichskanzler." In the plebiscite carried out on August 19, this action was endorsed by 38,395,479 Germans out of a total of 45,550,402 eligible voters. There were 4,300,429 Germans who braved S.A., S.S., and Gestapo to vote "no," and 873,787 protested by turning in invalid ballots.

One element still remained as a source of potential danger for the Nazi dictatorship. It was the Reichswehr. In the first year of Hitler's rule the Reichswehr generals relied on von Hindenburg to defend their interests and they maintained an attitude of semi-reserve. Only General von Hammerstein-Equord laid down his post in 1934 because he would not work with Hitler. Then came the rumblings of Röhm and the S.A. and the supposed aspirations of Röhm to merge the S.A. with the Reichswehr. Hitler decided for the professional army against Röhm, but at the same time the honor of the officer corps was besmirched by the murder of two of its leading figures in the purge of June 30—General von Schleicher and Gen-

---

* The exact number of persons slain in the purge of June 30 has never been established. Hitler himself gave the figure as 77; Gisevius in his testimony before the Nürnberg tribunal placed the figure as "no more than 150–200" (vol. xii, p. 253). Rudolf Pechel, also a well informed and reliable source, gives the number as 922, including 28 women (R. Pechel. *Deutscher Widerstand*, Zürich, 1947, p. 78).

eral von Bredow. The Reichswehr leaders, however, were satisfied with the perfunctory clearing of Schleicher by the senile Field Marshal von Mackensen. The measures that Hitler took for rearmament and for the increase in the military services won the enthusiasm and sympathy of the younger Reichswehr officers. Several of the older figures, like Beck and Fritsch, were critical but not moved sufficiently to act against the régime. Fritsch told General von Halder in 1937, in reply to a proposal to overthrow Hitler: "This man is Germany's destiny, and this destiny must pursue its course unto the end." Beck, too, thought at first he could work with Hitler. As late as 1938 he told Halder, "Mutiny and revolution are words that have no place in the lexicon of a German soldier." [28] General von Blomberg, in an affidavit for the Nürnberg tribunal in 1945, declared:

Before 1938–39 the German generals were not opposed to Hitler. There was no ground for opposition since he brought them the successes they desired.

In 1938 two incidents occurred that threw the Wehrmacht into Hitler's hands. On January 12, 1938, General von Blomberg, the war minister, was married in the presence of Hitler and Göring. It soon became generally known that the lady of his choice was a former prostitute who was registered as such in local police records. It seems that Göring, at least, knew of the past history of the lady. The National Socialist propaganda agencies saw to it that the facts became known and the official leadership of the Reichswehr thereby discredited. Blomberg was forced to retire, and General von Fritsch was slated to be his successor. Fritsch, however, was confronted with a Gestapo dossier that contained charges of practice of homosexuality against him. Hitler, without waiting for the convening of the military trial of Fritsch, requested him to resign all his army posts on February 4, 1938. It turned out that the evidence submitted by the Gestapo pertained to another officer named Frisch, and General von Fritsch was exonerated by the military court. But the effect desired by Himmler and Göring was achieved. The Reichswehr was once more discredited. Hitler thereupon assumed personal command of all the armed forces of the Reich, and the Reichswehr was bound to his person by the oath of personal allegiance. It was not until July 20, 1944, that the generals were to act against Hitler, and then in a most ineffectual manner.

Thus was completed the process of *Gleichschaltung,* the co-ordination of the complete life of Germany to the Nazi pattern. The civil service, political administration, and all cultural and educational agencies and institutions were subjected to a "cleansing" of politically unreliable elements. Ministers, mayors, councilors, police presidents, municipal officers, administrators of economic and cultural agencies—national as well as local—all were forced out to make room for the "old fighters" of the party. With this went a vast movement by fearful jobholders into whatever unit of party organization or auxiliary organization they could join—from the élite S.S. and S.A. down to the air-raid wardens or party *Winterhilfe*. The economic sector remained untouched a little longer than the other phases of communal life, but it too eventually succumbed.

The "solution" of the all-important Jewish problem was initiated by a boycott of Jewish shops in Berlin on April 1, 1933. The liquidation of German Jewry then was carried out in a series of steps that now seems tame compared to the eventual and "final solution" of the Jewish problem. Jews were dismissed from political and cultural positions first and allowed some degree of freedom of action in the economic sphere. Those emigrating were allowed at first to take along a good deal of their belongings with them. In September, 1935, came the notorious Nürnberg Laws "for the protection of the racial purity of the state," which reduced German Jews to the role of second-class citizens stripped of all political and civic rights and privileges. In November, 1938, came the heightened intensification of the campaign against the Jews. Up to now the means used had been almost exclusively political. On November 10, 1938, Nazi antisemitism took on all the forms of terror and violence. Acting in retaliation for the assassination of a German embassy official in Paris by a young Jewish lad, the Nazi Gestapo ordered a series of "spontaneous" outbreaks against Jews throughout Germany. At the given signal S.A. and S.S. men began a "spontaneous" looting of Jewish shops, rounding up Jews for arrest, and carrying out acts of vandalism and violence against them. At another signal the "spontaneous" action was brought to an end. During the course of this action 36 Jews were killed and 36 severely wounded; 191 synagogues were set to flames, with 76 of them completely destroyed, and so much physical damage created that Göring complained that the millions of marks of insurance due to the sufferers would work havoc with his economic program. Economic subsistence for German Jews now became almost impossible, and emigration restrictions were made more rigorous. By the time of the outbreak of the war in September, 1939, out of the 500,000 Jews in Germany and the 190,000 in Austria, only about 285,000 were left. The majority of these were either too old to emigrate or were married to non-Jews and therefore preferred to remain in the country. These were soon to share with the millions of Jews in the rest of Europe the fate of mass extermination.

Between 1933 and 1945 a vast literature accumulated both inside and outside Germany on the "government" of the Third Reich. All this is now of but antiquarian interest. We know now that concealed behind the entire façade of the Nazi governmental structure was a "confusion of private armies and private intelligence services" and that the leading politicians of the Nazi state were "not a government but a court." Hitler, it is true, remained sole dictator to the end, but the camarilla around him were engaged in endless machinations one against the other. The legislative powers vested in the Reichstag were transferred to the cabinet, but the cabinet also came into disuse. Government by conference of the ministers was replaced by individual conferences and, more frequently, merely by administrative orders from the Führer. Ministers frequently learned only from newspapers or radio of actions taken by the "Reich government" on decisive issues. Later, during the war, the ministers were forbidden by Hitler to confer with one another. According to the testimony of Baron Steengracht von Moyland, former state secretary of the Foreign Office, "It was almost more difficult for one minister to discuss a question with another minister by telephone than to have had the Angel Gabriel himself come from heaven and speak with one of us." [29]

Government was almost entirely replaced by administration, and the administration was carried out primarily by those in possession of the instruments of power. The administrative structure was used for the purpose of providing jobs and honors for loyal party members. The Reichstag was stripped of all power but was allowed to continue on in order to reward party members with both the honor and the salary of a deputy. It was used as a sounding board to receive "declarations by the government," but witty Berliners soon came to call it an "expensive Singing Society," whose chief task was to sing *Deutschland über Alles* and the Horst Wessel Song. The Law Securing the Unity of Party and State of December 1, 1933, established the duality of party and state, the typical parliamentary fiction of modern dictatorships. The Law of April 7, 1933, integrated the Länder with the Reich and was supposedly intended to do away with the local states. Actually, the administrative structure of the Länder also continued to exist, and for the same reason that the Reichstag did. The "will of the people" was allowed expression in Reichstag elections and in plebiscites. But the elections gave no choice of candidates to the voters except the slate of the N.S.D.A.P., and the plebiscites were carried out only after the decisive action had already been taken. Courageous opposition in each case could only express itself in abstention from the polls.

Behind the supposed Spartanism taught by official Nazi ideology there was a sea of graft, corruption, and venality. The Nazis, violent in their assault on the *Bonzen* of the Weimar Republic, once in power themselves used their position to enrich themselves and to flaunt themselves in luxurious style. Regular money "gifts" by the state, sequestration of the property of political prisoners, Jews, and later of enemy nationals, looting of art treasures and occupation of villas became part of the way of life of the Nazi élite. The leading example of this pattern was Göring with his dozens of villas and hunting lodges scattered over the choicest spots in the Reich, with his dozens of posts to provide him with the excuse for riotous change of uniform and decorations, with art collections looted from the leading galleries of Europe—all designed to give vent to his Gargantuan appetite for luxury and display and for aping the role of the Renaissance despot.

Hitler's appetite was not that lusty, and his taste ran more in the direction of petty-bourgeois *Gemütlichkeit*. But the forced sales of millions of copies of *Mein Kampf*, to which Hitler owned the copyright, made him enormously wealthy, and his passion for famous paintings was also satisfied by looting the galleries of Europe.

Essentially and realistically the government of the Third Reich was a police state. What counted most were the instruments of power and of terror by means of which the inhabitants were held in check. Up to the purge of June 30, 1934, the S.A. played a leading role in the maintenance of mass terror. Organized in the early days of the Nazi movement as a strong-armed band to protect party meetings and break up meetings of opponents, it became the agent of mass revolution for the party. The S.A. was the instrument for mass raids; it carried out house searches; it arranged mass confiscations; it staged mass demonstrations; it acted as auxiliary police; it arranged "spontaneous" mass actions like the boycott of April 1, 1933, or the pillaging of the night of November 10, 1938.

After the purge of June 30, 1934, and the shooting of Röhm, the revolutionary role of the S.A. was reduced to secondary importance. It was the S.S. that now emerged as the concentration of Nazi élite, under the head of Reichsführer S.S., Heinrich Himmler. Important posts in government departments soon came to be manned by the black-shirted members of the S.S., and the concentration camps became their special province. Most important, however, was the fact that Himmler came to concentrate into his own hands the entire police system of the Reich and with it the most active instruments of Nazi terror and violence—Gestapo, criminal police, security police—all later merged into the huge apparatus of the *Reichssicherheitshauptamt* (Reich Security Main Office), with its seven main divisions. This entire police and terror apparatus came to be amalgamated with the S.S., of which Himmler was Reich leader. "Protective custody," secret incarceration, brutal beatings, terror, murder, arson, and pillage became the main instruments for the exercise of justice and the K.Z.—the concentration camp—the arsenal for the protection of the Nazi state against its internal enemies.

Actually, almost all agencies created by the Nazis became instruments for dictatorial control. The Labor Service, the organization of the various crafts and trades, the youth organizations, the air-raid defense, and the elaborate system of block wardens all were utilized as means of spying upon the population and forcing them to toe the line set down by the Führer.

5. GERMAN RESISTANCE

The police state and its instruments of terror, including the concentration camps, were created in the first place to deal with the opposition at home. The very existence of the huge apparatus of suppression devised and developed by Göring, Heydrich, Himmler, and Kaltenbrunner was in it self proof of the existence of elements of resistance among the German people. The suppressed Socialist and Communist parties built up an underground movement that was fed by émigré organizations outside Germany. The *Schwarze Front,* led by Otto Strasser, which was the dissident group that split off from the Nazis in 1930, also carried on its work from outside Germany. Despite claims of widespread influence and manifold activity made by these groups during the existence of the Third Reich, we now know that the actual influence of the émigré opposition, apart from rescuing individual followers and distributing underground literature, was slender.

Within Germany itself there were several centers of resistance. Feeble attempts to put a brake on the more violent aspects of· Nazi rule were made from within government circles. Von Papen's speech at Marburg on June 17, 1934, written by his secretary Edgar Jung, made a plea for greater freedom of expression and freedom of thought. The author of the speech was purged on June 30, 1934, and his superior came dangerously near murder himself. Dr. Schacht's Königsberg address of August 18, 1935, attacked indiscriminate violence against the Jews, but the text of the speech received no dissemination except through limited distribution by the Reichsbank.[30] Throughout the entire twelve years of Nazi rule there was only one instance of a top government official resigning his post because of opposition to Hitler policies. On January 30, 1937, Baron von Eltz-Rübenach, minister of post and transportation, sent a letter of resignation to Hitler in which he declared it impossible for him to join the N.S.D.A.P. because of the conflict with his Christian beliefs.

The most active, most effective and most consistent resistance came from the churches. The repeated Nazi charges and numerous prosecutions of members of the Catholic clergy for immoral behavior, violation of exchange regulations, and treason indicated the existence of a determined effort by Catholic churchmen and lay leaders to resist the inroads of Nazi paganism and moral depravity. A large Catholic cathedral was undoubtedly the most convenient place in Hitler Germany to escape from the raucous, vulgar, and oppressive hand of the dictatorship. Cardinal Faulhaber delivered a series of public sermons in Munich in defense of the Old Testament, and Bishop Count Preysing in Berlin, Bishop Count Galen in Münster, Archbishop Gröber, and lay Catholic leaders like Dr. Klausener, head of Catholic Action, the philosopher Theodor Haecker, and Hermann and Friedrich Muckermann kept alive the spirit of Catholic resistance. The papal encyclical "Mit Brennender Sorge" of 1937 sought to combat especially the principles of Nazi racialism. Many an obscure Catholic priest or nun risked life and limb to give aid or to rescue from the clutches of the Gestapo or concentration camp those victimized by the Nürnberg Laws.

In the Protestant churches the attempt by Nazi leaders to impose a "German Christian" church under Reich Bishop ("Reibi") Ludwig Müller came to naught even though the great majority of the Protestant clergy maintained political obedience to the Nazi rulers. A smaller group, however, under the leadership of Pastor Martin Niemoeller, Bishop Wurm of Württemberg, Pastors Dietrich Bonhoeffer and Hans Christian Asmussen and other church and lay leaders, constituted themselves as the "Confessional Church" and resisted to the point of martyrdom the political and religious pressures of the dictatorship. The most persecuted sect of all Christian denominations, and one that was treated with almost as much cruelty as the Jews, was the Jehovah's Witnesses (*Bibelforscher*). Little has been written regarding this opposition group, but from the standpoint of heroic steadfastness to convictions and courageous and martyred resistance the German *Bibelforscher* occupy a most honored place in the history of German *Zivilcourage*.

The record of German intellectuals during the Nazi epoch was a sad one. But a few bright spots stand out. The Heidelberg group of Karl Jaspers and Alfred Weber and the Freiburg circle around the historian Gerhard Ritter continued to resist intellectual Nazification and later supplied a number of participants to the political resistance movement. The poet Ernst Wiechert, sobered of his youthful nationalist tendencies, braved the Gestapo to talk to the students of the University of Munich in 1937 on lasting moral values and on the eternal truths that mean more than the shrieking fanfare of racial nationalism and the doctrine of the big stick. A small student circle at the University of Munich, under the leadership of Hans and Sophie Scholl and aided by Professor Kurt Huber, organized a resistance group and managed to issue a number of leaflets in which they branded "every word that comes out of Hitler's mouth as a lie" and called for active sabotage of all Nazi efforts from war industries to press and radio. The circle was uncovered and all the leading figures executed in 1943.

The violent outbreak of November 10, 1938, against the Jews shook a number of individuals in the Foreign Office and the military out of their previous loyal co-operation with the régime. The coming of the war in 1939 added more followers to this group, and the turn in the fortunes of the war in 1942–1943 * consolidated the most formidable opposition group within the Reich. Within the foreign service and government administration Ulrich von Hassell, German ambassador to Italy until 1938; Count Werner von Schulenburg, former ambassador to Moscow; the brothers Erich and Theodor Kordt, and the circle around the former Centrist and Prussian finance minister up to 1944, Johannes Popitz, began

---

* Ulrich von Hassell's entry in his diary for January 22, 1943, reads, "One cannot yet say definitely that the war is lost, but it is certain that it cannot be won" (*Vom andern Deutschland*, p. 292).

to think of active resistance to the régime. Some, like Popitz, placed their hopes on the defection of Göring. In the office of military intelligence, the enigmatic and "Bohemian" character Admiral Wilhelm Canaris, together with his chief aid Major General Hans von Oster, gathered a group of military and civilian followers around them to plot the eventual overthrow of the Nazi régime. In the Wehrmacht the leading figures of the resistance, after the death of Fritsch, were Field Marshal Erwin von Witzleben, General Ludwig Beck, former chief of staff, General Friedrich Olbricht, and a number of younger officers, of whom Colonel Claus von Stauffenberg was the most active. Civilian leadership in this group came from the former mayor of Leipzig, Dr. Carl Goerdeler; and elements from the Socialist and Christian trade-unions were drawn into the circle in the persons of Wilhelm Leuschner, Carlo Mierendorff, Julius Leber, Hermann Maas, and Jakob Kaiser. Church leaders like Pastor Bonhoeffer and the Jesuit Father Alfred Delp also assumed an active role. The active heads of this resistance group were Beck and Goerdeler.

In the spring of 1938 Goerdeler went to London to apprise the French and British authorities of the existence of a plot to overthrow the régime and to ask them to hold firm against the Nazi demands. The Munich agreements in September destroyed all these plans. Negotiations were carried on by von Hassell with a British agent in February, 1940, for co-operation to end the war, and in May, 1942, the Protestant leaders Dr. Schönfeld and Pastor Bonhoeffer met with the British Bishop of Chichester in Stockholm to present through him to the British Foreign Office the program of the resistance group. In 1943 contact was established with the American Office of Strategic Services in Switzerland, headed by Allan W. Dulles. These various groups and individuals did not share a common political ideology. Some were monarchists, others republicans; some had worked faithfully for the Nazis, others had a completely clean record; some hoped for success by boring from within, others would have no truck with anything that smacked of Nazism. Some were avowed democrats, others hoped to salvage the "better elements" of National Socialism and establish a military dictatorship of uncorrupted and "genuine" National Socialism; some were oriented toward the Allies in the West, others looked to Stalin and the East. What united them all was a patriotic feeling of apprehension that Germany was being led to destruction and catastrophe, and a religious and moral revulsion at the brutalities of the régime which outraged their basic principles of Christian ethics. More than anything they were anxious to find an "honorable" way of ending the war before Germany collapsed completely.

The crowning effort of the resistance movement was the ill-fated attempt on Hitler's life carried out on July 20, 1944, by Colonel von Stauffenberg. Plans had been carefully laid for a new government to be proclaimed and for a number of military commanders to assume control of the situation in various parts of the Reich and in occupied Europe. The attempted assassination, however, failed of its end. Instead of the usual concrete bunker where Hitler held his conferences, the meeting on July 20 was shifted to a room with walls partly of wood and partly of concrete. The time bomb set by Colonel von Stauffenberg went off, but the air pressure of the explosion found a way out through the wooden parts of the walls. Four persons were killed in the explosion, but Hitler himself escaped with but minor bruises. The news that the attempt on Hitler's life had failed was sufficient to paralyze all the other plans in Berlin and elsewhere for the overthrow of the régime. The leading figures in the plot were arrested and executed by order of the "People's Court." [31]

No exact statistical data are available on the number of German political prisoners and executions for the twelve years of Nazi rule. Rudolf Pechel cites partial figures that give some indication as to numbers. In the state of Saxony there were 16,069 executions of which 6,644 were from Leipzig. The Society of Victims of Fascism had 250,000 persons registered in October, 1946, as survivors of the political terror. Of those implicated in the July 20, 1944, attempt we know of at least 147 persons executed. These included 3 women, 57 military persons, 10 of the diplomatic service, 22 officials and lawyers, 3 Protestant ministers, 2 Catholic priests, 5 Christian trade-union leaders, 7 Social Democrats, 2 Communists, and the rest of miscellaneous affiliation.

The failure of the resistance movement was largely due to the fact that it was too little and too late. Its chances of success would have been much greater if it had taken advantage of the earlier crises in the régime instead of waiting for a time of war. It could not have acted earlier, however, because then as later the resistance movement had no real mass basis of support. It could count on obedience and following only after it had triumphed, but apart from the small group of leaders there were no large German groups ready to hazard a mass uprising against the terroristic police state. In part this was the very result of the terror system. One of the fateful aspects of Gestapo rule was that political martyrdom in Germany produced little or no effect because no one ever learned of the act of martyrdom. The inspiring effect of courageous resistance was, therefore, nullified by the rigid suppression of all news pertaining to such resistance.

No small portion of blame must rest on foreign opinion and foreign governments. The anti-Nazi leaders in and out of Germany could hope for very little influence upon the German masses when at the same time Hitler and his henchmen were being warmly greeted by representatives of the democracies. Foreign governments displayed a degree of accommodation to the Nazi régime between 1933 and 1939 that the republican leaders of Weimar Germany never were able to command. Beginning with the Vatican, the first foreign power to enter into treaty relations with Hitler, and its concordat with the Third Reich in 1933, through the Anglo-German naval agreement of April, 1935, the Munich treaty of September, 1938, and the Nazi-Soviet Pact of 1939, foreign governments contributed to the increased prestige of the Nazi régime. Industrialists and conserva-tives in Britain, like Lord Rothermere, the Marquis of Londonderry, and the "Cliveden set" of Lady Astor hailed the Nazi gangsters as the great "bulwark" against Bolshevism; international industrialists and bankers like Sir Henry Deterding and Sir Montague Norman in England and the Du Ponts in the United States joined in extending the tentacles of German cartels throughout the world; "economic circles," according to Sumner Welles, "in each of the Western European democracies and the New World welcomed Hitlerism"; pacifists and liberals like George Lansbury and David Lloyd George trudged up to Berchtesgaden to lay before the Führer their plans for world peace; renegade socialist intellectuals in France and Belgium fell for his promises of a "new Europe," while naïve and politically immature Americans like Charles A. Lindbergh saw in Nazism "the wave of the future." It took Hitler's open and unprovoked attack, first on Poland, then on the Low Countries, to shake world opinion into a realization of the true character of the new dynamic revolution.

6. ROAD TO WORLD DOMINATION AND RUIN

Nazi economic policy, taking a leaf from the economic policies of the Soviet Union, also adopted the idea of a Four-Year Plan. The chief goals of the two Four-Year plans beginning in 1936 were the preparation of the country for war. In Hitler's memorandum of 1936 on the "Tasks of the Four-Year Plan," he set the following goals: (1) the German armed forces must be ready for combat within four years and (2) the German economy must be mobilized for war within four years.[32] This does not mean that there were no real social gains for the German masses. Unemployment was almost completely eliminated; the national income was increased; a monumental building program, based on Hitler's architectural dreams, was initiated; an enormous development of synthetics in textiles, petroleum derivatives, rubber, light metals, and new materials was realized; and a feeling of economic security was given to the large masses of the German population. All this was achieved by a commandeer economy which subjected capital, labor, business, and agriculture to drastic control and regulation.

Private property was theoretically left intact by the Nazis, although the government entered business and industry in a direct fashion and made the Hermann Göring Works, created in 1937, the largest industrial combination in Europe. But all other commerce and industry were rigidly regulated by the totalitarian state through severe control of foreign exchange, through state allocation of raw materials, through an administered scarcity which gave primacy to armament needs, through a commandeered capital which subjected all new investments to government control, and through the militarization of labor which administered labor supply, wages, conditions of employment and place of employment, prices and profits, in disciplined subservience to the needs of the state. Agriculture was similarly organized into a huge disciplined cartel in which membership was compulsory and which regulated land tenure, trade in agricultural products, prices, and even details in tillage and production. Despite the dire predictions of traditional economists that the country would not be able to stand the financial strain of the huge rearmament program, thanks to the financial wizardry of Dr. Hjalmar Schacht and the technical skill of economic and industrial experts the Nazi economic system continued to thrive. The Nazis controlled both investments and consumption, and they were able, by means of authoritarian control, to expand or restrict activity in these areas as they pleased. They were able to maintain an equilibrium between production and the consumption of the goods produced and to silence by terror whatever grumblings might have developed. The final collapse of Nazi economic policies came from the non-economic dynamic of the movement. It was the political expansionism that found its outlet in making war and in attempting to bring the rest of Europe under its political as well as economic control that brought economic ruin to Germany. In this expansionist policy German business, industry, and banking co-operated to bring to Nazism its short-lasting but spectacular triumphs.

Had Nazism concerned itself solely with internal German problems (of course then it would not have been Nazism) it would never have become a world problem. What made it the central world problem between 1934 and 1945 was its foreign policy. As Justice Jackson said in his summing-up address before the Nürnberg tribunal, "The intellectual bankruptcy and moral perversion of the Nazi regime might have been no concern for international law had it not been utilized to goosestep the *Herrenvolk* across international frontiers." It was foreign policy that revealed the deepest mainsprings of Nazi ideology and Nazi rule.

Nazi foreign policy resumed the threads of German *Weltpolitik* under William II, but magnified them a thousandfold. Like the foreign policy of William II, it too was marked by a dynamic expansionism that had no set limits and knew no definite aspirations or goals to be satisfied. It set up demands which when satisfied only paved the way for new demands. It was not just that Hitler lied when he assured the world that "Germany has neither the intention nor the desire to intervene in the internal politics of Austria, still less to annex Austria," and then proceeded to march into Vienna, or when he solemnly declared that "Germany has no further territorial claims of any sort in Europe," and then proceeded to swallow up Czechoslovakia. He was, it is true, a pathological liar, and used deliberate falsehood as part of his conduct of foreign policy. Much more basic and much more serious, however, was the fact that Nazism was pathologically insatiable. The rationalization for Nazi expansionist policy was the need for "living space" (*Volksraum*). It is psychologically significant that the German word *Raum* evokes quite a different complex of images and thought patterns than the English word "space." "Space" to an English-speaking person connotes a vacant area but within definite bounds or limits. The word *Raum,* on the other hand, calls forth a picture of endless and limitless expanse, without bounds and without measure. This idea of *Raum* became the driving force of Nazi foreign policy.

In a speech to the supreme commanders in November, 1939, Hitler explained that the goal of his foreign policy was the achievement of a "rational relationship between population and living space." The attempt in recent times to achieve this by birth control he termed "national suicide." "I selected another way," he declared—"adaptation of living space to the size of the population," and the only way to accomplish this was by the sword.[33] Nothing else mattered but the expansion of German power. "Europe, the entire world may go up in flames," once declared Ernst Röhm. "What do we care? Germany must live and be free." Solemn pledges and treaties could be violated, declared Göring, as mere "pieces of toilet paper." Assurances of peaceful intentions and of a deep yearning for peace were broadcast to lull the rest of the world into a false sense of security. "Promise peace that you may begin war with advantage," wrote Fichte, harking back to Machiavelli. Hitler took his leaf from both the Florentine and the German.

The huge mass of documentary evidence presented at the Nürnberg trials, and the final judgment pronounced by a court whose fairness and judicial soberness can hardly be questioned, have convicted beyond a shadow of doubt the leaders of the Third Reich of plotting and waging aggressive war. For World War II there should never arise any problem of "war guilt" or the need for "historical revisionism" unless there be a willful desire to falsify history. Even the most flagrant aggressors in history have never left behind such brutally frank confessions of war guilt. The earlier Nazi propaganda on "breaking the chains of Versailles" and rectifying the injustices of that treaty soon gave way to the deeper dynamism of Nazi policy. It was not German minority protection, or *Anschluss,* or Danzig or the Polish Corridor or Alsace-Lorraine or any other "final demand" that propelled the foreign policy of the Third Reich. Each of these issues merely served as a prelude to the next step. The now famous Hossbach Memorandum of the Conference of November 5, 1937, presented at the Nürnberg trials; the Schmundt notes on the Führer conferences, the detailed preparations made for the annexation of Austria and Czechoslovakia—all indicate premeditated and deliberate aggression in order "to solve the German question by force," the German question being synonymous with "expanding our living space."

On November 23, 1939, Hitler, in the full flush of his dazzling military triumphs, reviewed before his generals the history of his foreign policy. "I am convinced of the powers of my intellect and of decision," he confessed with his usual modesty, and "none have ever achieved what I have achieved. . . . I have led the German people to a great height, even if the world does hate us now." Then he recapitulated how he had to refashion everything, beginning with the "national structure" up to the Wehrmacht. He told of the steps in his plan—exit from the League of Nations and the refusal to participate in disarmament, the huge rearmament program, the march into the Rhineland, into Austria, and into Czechoslovakia. "From the first moment," he declared, "it was clear to me that I could not be satisfied with just the Sudetenland. This was only a partial solution." Furthermore, the occupation of Bohemia and Moravia "was the basis for the conquest of Poland." [34]

Germany's withdrawal from the League of Nations and the disarmament conference on October 14, 1933, laid the groundwork for the plans for full-scale rearmament by Germany, unhampered by the provisions of the Versailles Treaty. Not that Hitler started from scratch; in a speech which he never delivered, but which came to light at the Nürnberg trials, the industrialist Krupp recounted the story of the secret rearmament of 1919–1933 and how "through years of secret work, scientific and basic groundwork was laid, in order to be ready again to work for the German armed forces at the appointed hour." [35] Under the Nazis, however, the entire process of rearmament became the chief goal of the national economy. On March 14, 1935, the Luftwaffe was officially created, utilizing all the preparatory work carried on by the civilian Lufthansa. Universal military training was restored on March 16, 1935, and the plea of Charles de Gaulle, unheeded in his own country, was taken up in Germany to create a most up-to-date and highly mechanized modern army integrated with an air force that utilized the latest advances in aviation techniques. Once more Germany the "borrower" achieved superiority precisely because she was not weighed down with technological obsolescence and could utilize the most efficient and most modern armaments. The Nürnberg rally of September, 1935, was proclaimed the "Party Rally of Freedom," but freedom there had nothing to do with political freedom. It meant, as *Freiheit* so often meant in German history, freedom of action in foreign relations.

On March 7, 1936, came the unilateral renunciation of the Locarno Treaty by Germany and the march of German troops into the Rhineland. This, like the preceding "surprises," met with no resistance by the Western powers, even though Hitler and his generals were so uncertain as to French reaction that they issued two sets of orders to the advancing troops, one being to withdraw if the French acted. "Why, they could have chased us out just like that," General Keitel told Dr. Gilbert in his Nürnberg cell, "and I wouldn't have been a bit surprised. But naturally when he saw how easy it was . . ." [36] Each continued instance of weakness by Britain and France only served to hasten Hitler's next move. Following the official signing of the Anti-Comintern Pact with Italy and Japan on November 25, 1936, and active intervention to aid the Franco forces in the Spanish Civil War in which Göring was able to test and train his air force and try out new weapons, came the invasion of Austria and Hitler's triumphal entry on March 12, 1938, into Vienna, the city he so thoroughly despised.

The occupation of Austria paved the way for the Czech crisis and the breath-taking events of September, 1938. Neville Chamberlain and Édouard Daladier brought home with them the solemn pledge signed by Hitler and Mussolini which was going to bring "peace to our time," but which severed the Sudetenland from Czechoslovakia and destroyed the last bastion against Nazi aggression in central and eastern Europe. The moral conscience of the West was humiliated and outraged, but both Daladier and Chamberlain were greeted in Paris and London as home-coming heroes. But even Mr. Chamberlain, after naïvely trusting the pledge and the signature of the Führer, was shaken out of his political insensibility on March 14, 1939, when Hitler marched into Prague and destroyed the last remnants of the Czechoslovak state. Memel was taken over from the Lithuanians on March 21.

Poland was next on Hitler's agenda. But before taking action in that area he stunned the political capitals of the world by announcing the conclusion of a non-aggression pact with his former arch-enemy, Communist Russia, on August 23, 1939. While Stalin kept British and French missions cooling their heels in Moscow, and while the Western statesmen forgot completely the lesson of Rapallo, Ribbentrop went to Moscow, signed a pact which included a secret clause defining German and Russian spheres of influence and dividing Poland between them, and listened to Stalin exclaim as he raised his glass of vodka: "I know how much the German nation loves its Führer; I should therefore like to drink to his health." All evidence points to the fact that the original initiative for the pact came from Stalin. But Hitler seized the opportunity to protect his eastern flank. On August 22, 1939, he told his generals of his impending move. "Since I have found out," he told them, "that Japan does not go with us without conditions and that Mussolini is manacled by a weak-headed king and the treacherous scoundrel of a Crown Prince I have decided to go with Stalin. . . . I shall shake hands with Stalin within a few weeks on the common German-Russian border and undertake with him a new distribution of the world." [37] That he had no intention of keeping this pact any more than he did any other was indicated by his later remarks in the same speech. "In Russia will happen just what I practiced with Poland. After Stalin's death (he is seriously ill) we shall crush the Soviet Union."

Hitler was absolutely certain that the Western democracies at the last moment would shrink from entering into a general war to defend Poland. "I witnessed the miserable worms Daladier and Chamberlain in Munich," he told his generals. "They will be too cowardly to attack. They will not go any further than the blockade." He gave the signal on September 1, 1939, for the "invasion and extermination of Poland." The "propagandist cause" for starting this war was alleged atrocities by Poland against German minorities. "Never mind," Hitler had said, "whether the propagandist cause is plausible or not. The victor shall not be asked later on whether we told the truth or not. In starting and making a war, it is not the right that matters, but victory."

Victory seemed to be all his. Although Britain and France, honoring their pledge to Poland, now declared war against Germany, they were in no position either geographically or militarily to come to Poland's aid. The Polish forces were annihilated in eighteen days, and Russian troops, on September 18, moved in from the east and joined with the Germans in destroying the Polish state. On September 27 Ribbentrop once again journeyed to Moscow, and the Russo-German "friendship treaty" set the seal upon the fourth partition of Poland.

A period of so-called "phony war" in the west was broken on April 9, 1940, with the Nazi invasion of Denmark and Norway and on May 10 with the lightning attack and conquest of Belgium, Holland, and Luxemburg. The way was now open for the final assault upon France after the British evacuation from Dunkirk, and on June 23 France laid down its arms and the Nazi Wehrmacht formations goose-stepped down the Champs Élysées in Paris. The entire civilized world was shaken to its depths as beautiful Paris, the heart of European civilization, lay at the feet of the new barbarians. A heart-rending photograph, circulated by the world news agencies, which showed the entry of the Germans into Paris with a Frenchman looking on and tears streaming down his agonized face, evoked the same tears and agony throughout the world. France, weakened by internal decay, defeatism, treason, and loss of nerve, became the Vichy satellite of the Third Reich. Britain was now left entirely alone to face the savage bombing of the Nazi air force and to brace itself for invasion. The British people, in the words of Winston Churchill, "held the fort alone till those who hitherto had been half-blind were half-ready."

For over three years Hitler went from one triumph to another and stood as the greatest conqueror of modern times. Invading the Soviet Union on June 22, 1941, he was able to crush the completely unprepared Red Army and to push deeper into Russian territory than either Napoleon or Ludendorff had ever done. From the Channel Islands eastward into the heart of the Ukraine and close to the borders of the Caucasus, and from Narvik in northern Norway south to the Aegean Islands in the Mediterranean, the swastika fluttered proudly as the herald of Hitler's thousand-year Reich and of his new order in Europe. The Japanese attack on Pearl Harbor on December 7, 1941, brought the United States officially into the war, but it was still a long way from being prepared to test its strength against the Wehrmacht. It was not until the end of 1942, with the American landing in North Africa, and in February, 1943, with the Nazi disaster at Stalingrad, that the fortunes of the war finally turned to the side of the Allies. The landings in Sicily, followed by the fall of Mussolini on July 25, 1943, and the final storming of "Fortress Europe," begun on the beaches of Normandy on June 6, 1944, coinciding with the continued offensive of the Red Army in the east, at long last brought the war in Europe to an end on May 8, 1945, with the utter collapse of the entire Nazi structure.

Hitler's plans, like all previous German war plans, had called for a short war. The unexpected reaction of the Western democracies to his aggression in Poland and the stubborn resistance of Britain threw off his timetable. But the Nazi leaders were full of confidence for at least the first four years of the war. The new gospel presented to the conquered peoples of Europe was that of a "new European order" with Hitler as the spokesman of the new Europe. The small nations, they said, could have their nationality guaranteed only by the leadership state of Europe under the new messiah Adolf Hitler. In every nation he conquered, Hitler found not only avowed fifth-column groups made up of native or ethnic German Nazis but also large elements of the population who were willing to give ear to this "new gospel." The extent of moral decadence in European countries was never so clearly revealed as in the widespread collaboration with the Nazis by large groups in the conquered states. Only the heroism and shining nobility of the various resistance movements in the occupied countries were able to provide partial atonement for the widespread collaboration.

In Russia the invading Nazi armies were hailed at first by the native peasantry as the long-hoped-for liberators who would free them from the tyrannical slave state of Stalin. It was the ruthless racialist doctrine of the "master race" and the policy of brutal terrorization by the invading German armies that finally sobered the enthusiasm of the Russian and Ukrainian masses and aroused them to the patriotic defense of their own fatherland.[38] Even at that there were thousands of Russian deserters who were organized into a special army under the command of General Vlassov for service with the Germans.

The Nazi attitude toward conquered peoples showed a certain degree of variation in keeping with their racial theories. Flemings, Dutch, and Scandinavians were regarded as fellow Nordics and were accorded the most tolerable treatment. The French occupied a sort of intermediate position in the hierarchy, and policy toward the French seesawed between cruel suppression and wooing blandishments. The Greeks, the Poles, and the Russians were degraded to the lowest rung of slave labor and physical annihilation. In his orders to march into Poland, Hitler told his generals the following:

> Our strength is in our quickness and brutality. Jhengiz Khan had millions of women and children killed by his own will and with a gay heart. History sees only in him a great state builder. What weak western European civilization thinks about me does not matter. . . . I have sent to the east only my "Death Head Units" with the order to kill without mercy all men, women and children of Polish race or language. Only in such a way will we win the vital space that we need. Who still talks nowadays of the extermination of the Armenians? [39]

The commissioner for the Ukraine, Erich Koch, in a speech delivered in Kiev on May 3, 1943, declared, "We are a master race and we must remember that the lowliest German laborer is racially and biologically a thousand times more valuable than the native population here." [40] Himmler, taking issue with Rosenberg's support of the anti-Bolshevik Vlassov army, expatiated on the utter sterility and worthlessness of the Russian people. Except for an Attila, a Genghis Khan, a Tamerlane, a Lenin, or a Stalin, "this Mongol race of Slavs," he said, "is built upon a sub-human race invigorated by a few drops of our blood." Himmler up-braided his S.S. leaders for not having learned how a small minority can terrorize a whole country. [41]

The record of Nazi brutalities is too long and too painful to list here. They were fully described and documented in the war crimes trials. A policy of complete physical destruction of land and people was carried out in Greece and in the eastern countries. All conquered areas served primarily to supply the needs of the master race. The most effective way of protecting themselves against possible resistance was to decimate the élite groups of the population. This too was carried out with special ruthlessness in Greece, Poland, and Russia. Priests, ministers, teachers, and intellectuals were subjected to extermination or torture. All the rest of the population became a huge reservoir of slave-labor supply for the armament industries of the Greater Reich. Resistance was punished unmercifully by execution of hostages or extermination of entire communities, as in the case of Lidice in Bohemia. "Whether nations live in prosperity," Himmler told his S.S. generals, "or starve to death interests me only in so far as we need them as slaves for our *Kultur*." [42]

A special object of Nazi vandalism was the artistic and cultural treasures of Europe. With all their barbarism, the Nazi leaders had the typical jealous admiration and concealed envy of the upstart for the refined culture of his victims. All the Nazi leaders from Hitler and Göring down to the more lowly S.S. leaders engaged in a titanic policy of cultural looting to fill their private as well as public collections with the gems of the art galleries, museums, and libraries of the conquered peoples. Property of Jews, Freemasons, and "the ideological enemies of National Socialism" was designated by a special decree by Hitler in March, 1942, to be the special province of Alfred Rosenberg; and a specially created military formation, known as "Einsatzstab-Rosenberg," accompanied the invading armies and seized such materials. But each of the top leaders had his own agents on the lookout for cultural treasures, and very often it was a race among them as to who would get there first to get hold of the desired objects.

The most gruesome and most tragic fate of all was reserved for the Jews of Europe. According to an estimate attributed to Adolph Eichmann, the chief of the Gestapo Jewish section, at least 6 million Jews were murdered by the Nazis between 1941 and 1944. When the war was over in May, 1945, the Allied armies found only approximately 100,000 Jews left in all of Europe outside the U.S.S.R. Hitler's promise to exterminate the Jews in the event of war was carried out, and the Nazi goal of ridding Europe of the "Jewish pest" was practically realized, despite their own final defeat.

The Nazi treatment of the Jewish problem went through several stages. By the time the war came there were very few Jews left within the Reich itself. The Jewish problem meant the treatment of the millions of Jews in the conquered areas after 1939. Until 1940 Nazi leaders thought of emigration of the Jews as the "final goal of German Jewish policy." Alfred Rosenberg proposed the establishment of a reservation in Madagascar. Emigration would not only rid the Reich of Jews but would help spread antisemitism. In a Foreign Office circular to all German diplomats abroad, the principle was set forth that "a task of the German foreign policy must be to further this wave of antisemitism." [43] The years 1940 and 1941 constituted a sort of period of hesitation. All Jews were concentrated in reservations and ghettos in Poland. By the end of 1941 the decision was taken to carry out the "final solution" of the Jewish problem. "Final solution" always meant extermination. Directives for the action were almost always verbally transmitted from Hitler and Himmler through Heydrich and Kaltenbrunner to the Gestapo chiefs Müller and Eichmann and down the line to the local officials. The extermination of the Jews was a subject usually not discussed by Nazi leaders in public. In a secret session with S.S. generals on October 4, 1943, Himmler reviewed the "clearing out of the Jews." "This is a page of glory in our history," he said, "which has never been written and is never to be written. . . . It shall be said on this occasion, openly here among ourselves, but we shall never speak of it publicly . . . just as we do not talk about June 30, 1934. . . . But we have fulfilled this most difficult task out of love for our people." [44]

Extermination of Jews was carried out first by special Einsatzgruppen that would herd the Jews of a given area into a ditch and shoot them down. Then more refined techniques were devised in the form of death vans in which the victims were gassed while the vehicles were in motion. The capstone of this gruesome chapter of human depravity came with the establishment of specially constructed crematoria and gas chambers that were able to engage in mass slaughter with efficiency and dispatch. According to the testimony of Rudolf Hoess, commandant of the Auschwitz camp, at least 3,000,000 persons were exterminated at Auschwitz alone, of which all but 20,000 Russian prisoners of war were Jews gathered from all the conquered countries of Europe.

German industry co-operated with the Gestapo in running the camps to utilize the slave labor there, to collect the clothing and shoes of the victims, and to utilize their bones for fertilizer. German bankers received the jewelry and gold fillings of the victims and deposited them in the vaults of the Reichsbank. German scientists carried out gruesome medical experiments upon the victims, and toward the end of the war, when the German war economy was hard-pressed, Himmler and Eichmann offered for sale to Jewish leaders in Switzerland Jewish lives in return for ransom money and vehicles, which they badly needed. Dieter Wisliceny, an intimate of Eichmann, testified at Nürnberg that he had last seen Eichmann in February, 1945, in Berlin, contemplating suicide if the war was lost and saying that "he would leap laughing into his grave because the feeling that he had 5 million people on his conscience would be for him a source of extraordinary satisfaction." [45] Genocide, a new political concept developed by the Nazis, here found its perfect realization. "History," in the words of Justice Jackson, "does not record a crime ever perpetuated against so many victims or one ever carried out with such calculated cruelty."

As the war continued and German losses on the front as a result of Allied bombings increased, a contradiction developed between the policy of ruthless extermination of Jews and other conquered peoples and the mounting needs of labor supply. Manpower shortage in World War II, as in World War I, became the most crucial problem for the German war machine. The racial principle, as we have seen, had to be modified or reinterpreted to excuse the importation of domestic workers from the Ukraine. But arms factories and farms required millions of additional workers. Voluntary recruitment and forced labor in labor and concentration camps were resorted to, to meet the needs. By the end of the war there were about 4,795,000 foreign workers in the Reich, and with war prisoners and political prisoners used to fill the gap in labor supply the amount reached 6,691,000. Whereas economic need asserted itself more in the treatment of most foreign workers, in the case of the Jews the antisemitic goal of extermination usually won out over economic necessity. Regular army circles frequently sought to halt deportation and liquidation of Jews, not so much because of their sympathy and humaneness but because these Jews were helping produce some essential materials necessary for the army. Those Jews who remained alive within the conquered areas owed their survival almost entirely to their continued usefulness to the German war machine.

The attitude of the German people toward the war gradually changed from pride in the great triumphs of the Wehrmacht to a dogged and patient fight for the preservation of the Fatherland. Even at the very start of the war there was nothing like the patriotic fervor of August 4, 1914. The overwhelming masses of the German people had been grateful to Chamberlain and Daladier in 1938 for having saved them from war, and they did not enter the contest a year later without misgivings. But as victory piled up on victory, as one European capital after another fell to the armies of the Führer, and as more and more of the choice products of those countries began to pour into Germany the enthusiasm mounted. There was no German resistance or opposition to speak of while German arms were being carried to victory. Not one of the generals or political leaders later active in the July 20th affair dared stand up to Hitler when he unfolded before them his vast plans of world conquest. It was only as the tide turned against Germany and the prospect of defeat seemed not out of the question that the whole tenor of opinion at home began to change. "When did the war impress you as terrible," Ribbentrop was asked at a pre-trial interrogation in Nürnberg. "It became to me terrible," he replied, "I can tell you the exact moment. From the moment of the African landing—I mean of the English-American forces."

The defeat at Stalingrad in February, 1943, served even more to sober German opinion, since for most Germans, military leaders as well as civilian population, the war against Russia loomed largest in the picture. Goebbels' propaganda machine began to turn from the motif of master race and world dominion to that of a battle for survival. The effect of the heavy Allied bombings on German morale was tremendous. Their earlier sense of pride in the fact that all the horrors of modern warfare were being carried out on enemy soil was rudely shattered. In a speech to a group of air-force engineers on March 25, 1944, Field Marshal Erhard Milch told his hearers to go out and look at the bombed districts in Berlin, Frankfurt, or Düsseldorf. "Not that there is any danger of revolution or any such thing as we know it from 1918," he said. "But at a certain point a human being just cannot endure any more. . . . The war of nerves has reached a point which causes us in the leadership group to worry. The people cannot endure that forever." [46]

At no point in the war, up to the very end, was there any evidence of any diminution in the will to fight. True, there was an increased use of terror against the civilian population as the war dragged on, and Heinrich Himmler, head of the S.S., Gestapo and all the police forces of the Reich, became the most powerful figure in the Reich next to Hitler. But Himmler, who more than any other man in Germany had his hand on the pulse of popular opinion, was able to assure his S.S. commanders on October 14, 1943, "Our people, our workers are on the whole so remarkably decent and are so filled with a sense of faithful execution of their obligations in this war that they create no difficulties for us." [47] It is exceedingly doubtful, however, that the Allied call for "unconditional surrender" had much to do with hardening the resistance of the German armies. Hitler and his henchmen knew that for them there was no half way between total victory or destruction, and they were determined, quite apart from Allied demands, to fight to the end. "I shall stand or fall in this struggle," Hitler told his generals at the start of the war, "and I shall never survive the defeat of my people." This remained his attitude all through the war up to the very end. Right after the attack on Russia he told a group of ministers that he would never give up any of the lands he occupied and that "even if it means war for a hundred years there must never be a military power west of the Urals except Germany." [48]

Field Marshal Milch told the Nürnberg court of seeing Hitler on the day after the defeat at Stalingrad. "Hitler on that particular day was very crushed," and he allowed his visitor to talk more than was his usual wont. But after Milch, according to his own testimony, "said that the time was now five minutes past twelve . . . and that the war was lost," Hitler began his tirade, "got more and more excited until he was very cross and knocked on the table: 'I must attack.' " [49]

After 1943 Hitler began to age rapidly. "The Führer seems to have aged fifteen years during the three and a half years of war," wrote Goebbels in his diary. His hands and face in the last years of the war became so pale that they gave the impression of no blood in his veins. He was hardly able to sleep, and became entirely dependent on drugs and injections which a quack doctor administered to him. This Dr. Theodor Morel came to have an enormous influence on him. He used twenty-eight different drugs on Hitler, and during the last two years Hitler received injections daily. But his determination to re-enact the final scene of *Götterdämmerung* remained to the end. "We shall not capitulate—no never," he had told Rauschning. "We may be destroyed, but if we are, we shall drag a world with us—a world in flames." His final orders to Albert Speer were to carry out a huge operation of destruction, and it was only Speer's bold action in ignoring this order that was responsible for saving a great deal of Germany's industrial potential.

Until the very end Hitler treated anyone who dared suggest that the war was lost as a traitor. Albert Speer braved this policy on March 18, 1945, to write to Hitler that the war was lost and that some measures should be taken to preserve the subsistence level of the population. Hitler's reply to Speer was as follows:

If the war is to be lost, the nation also will perish. . . . There is no need to consider the basis even of a most primitive existence any longer. On the contrary it is better to destroy even that, and to destroy it ourselves. The nation has proved itself weak, and the future belongs solely to the stronger eastern nations. Besides, those who remain after the battle are of little value; for the good have fallen.[50]

The last weeks of the war revealed even more than ever before the bizarre and pathological character of the Nazi leaders. As the Allied armies of Eisenhower and Montgomery swept across Central Germany and deep into Thuringia, Czechoslovakia, and Austria, the Red Army under Zhukov drew a noose around Berlin. One by one the chief Nazi ringleaders realized that the end was near, and left Berlin to seek safety in less conspicuous places. Hitler spurned all pleas to retire to the Bavarian mountains and decided to stay in Berlin. With him remained the ever ambitious Martin Bormann and Dr. Goebbels and his family. They entrenched themselves in the elaborately constructed underground bunker under the Reich chancellery, and from there the Führer continued to play the role of the war lord of a conquering army.

Life in the underground bunker during these last weeks, as described by surviving witnesses, was a weird and fantastic alternation of supreme confidence and abject despair, infused with recourse to astrology, horoscopes, and drugs. Almost to the last day Hitler and Goebbels hoped for a division in the Allied ranks between East and West that would play into their hands. On April 19, on the eve of Hitler's fifty-sixth birthday, the Führer declared, "We are now starting a battle as fanatical as that we had to fight for our ascent to power years ago." And Dr. Goebbels, on the same day, broadcast a speech in which he asked Germany never to forget Hitler. "We are witnessing the last acts of a tremendous tragedy," said Goebbels. "The decision is very near. Let us stake our hopes on our lucky star."

A "lucky star" was about all the Nazi leaders could look to. Recourse to astrologers was even more frequent those days than previously. And both Goebbels and Hitler were indeed certain that the death of Franklin D. Roosevelt on April 12 was the work of their "lucky star" and that a turning point in the war would come. "At the moment," said Hitler in his Order of the Day of April 16, "when fate has taken the greatest war criminal of all times from this earth, the war will take a decisive turn."

More isolated from reality than ever before, Hitler continued to issue orders to attack to his vanishing army units and his depleted air force. The last conference he held with his war leaders was on April 22. He raged and shrieked wildly at everyone how all had betrayed him, how all was over and there was nothing left for him but to die. Göring, previously designated as heir apparent in the Nazi line of succession, had gone to Bavaria, and from there, on April 23, he dispatched a telegram to Hitler asking whether it was not time for him to take over the mantle of the Führer. Hitler, infuriated, replied by stripping Göring of all his state and party offices. Himmler, in the north, spurred on by his aide, Schellenberg, began negotiations with the Western Allies through the Swedish Count Bernadotte. Himmler's offer was rejected by the Allies, but as the news of these negotiations came over the radio in the Berlin bunker Hitler was thrown into mad convulsions of rage and despair. To Ritter von Greim, whom he designated as Göring's successor as head of the Luftwaffe, Hitler exclaimed: "Nothing now remains! Nothing is spared me! No loyalty is kept, no honor observed! There is no bitterness, no betrayal that has not been heaped upon me!"

Bombs were now falling in the yard of the chancellery. Communication with the outside world was completely cut off. By the 28th of April Hitler was convinced at last that the end had come. He proceeded to make his will, a political testament for the nation and a private will, and he decided finally to legalize his liaison with Eva Braun, who had remained loyally by his side to the end. There, in the underground bunker, to the musical accompaniment of shells and bombs and witnessed by Goebbels and Martin Bormann, Adolf Hitler took Eva Braun as his lawful wedded wife. In his political testament he proclaimed Göring and Himmler to be ousted from all Nazi affiliations, and designated Grand Admiral Karl von Dönitz as his successor. His final message to the German people was:

Above all I impose on the leadership and following of the nation the obligation to hold fast to the racial laws and to carry on unmerciful resistance to the world poisoner of all nations—international Jewry.

Thus the Nazi movement ended, as it began, with a call to make war on the Jews.

On April 30 the final immolation rites were carried out. Eva took poison and Adolf shot himself. The bodies of both were then carried out to the courtyard of the chancellery and placed upon the funeral pyre. No bones of Hitler or of Eva were actually found in the yard. This has given rise to speculation that they may still be alive. But the overwhelming weight of evidence points to their death on the 30th of April. Their bones most probably became mixed in with the remains of others who also perished in the same way and in the same place.

Goebbels and Bormann attempted a last desperate offer to negotiate with General Zhukov. The Russians replied with the demand for unconditional surrender. Goebbels thereupon followed the example of his Führer. He first gave poison to his six children, then he and his wife shot themselves and all the bodies were burned. As for Bormann, there is no information at all as to what happened to him. He may have been killed in the bombing of the city or may still be at large and in hiding.

Early in the evening of May 1 radio listeners in Germany were told to stand by for an important announcement. At 9:40 P.M. the announcement was repeated and followed by excerpts from Wagner's _Götterdämmerung_. Then came the playing of the slow movement of Bruckner's Seventh Symphony, written for Wagner's death, and a few minutes later Admiral Dönitz, speaking from Hamburg, brought the news to the German people of the death of their Führer.

Dönitz appealed for German unity to carry on the fight against Bolshevism, still hoping to divide the Allies. The unity of the Eastern and Western Allies, however, remained firm in the demand for unconditional surrender, and on May 7 came the final surrender, first at Reims, France, and on the following day ratified in Berlin. "We must face facts squarely," Dönitz told the German people over the Flensburg radio. "The unity of state and party does not exist any more. The party has left the scene of its activities. With the occupation of Germany, the power has been transferred to the occupying powers. It is up to them to confirm me in my function and the government I have appointed or decide whether to appoint a different one." Within a few days Dönitz was being held in Allied custody to be tried as a major war criminal, and the Nazi epoch was brought to a close.

The entire civilized world was jubilant both at the end of the European war and at the final destruction of the Nazi tyranny. From all corners of Europe the oppressed and the tortured came out into the open sunshine of liberation and freedom. The idealism and self-sacrifice of the heroes of the Allied armies and of the resistance movements seemed at last to be rewarded, and while Nazi Germany lay a shambles of ruins, destruction, and dazed disintegration, the free world looked forward to the dawn of a new era of world peace and prosperity. This jubilant optimism, unfortunately, was soon dissipated, and gave way to a new era of tension and crisis that came from another source. In his Victory Order of the Day, General Dwight Eisenhower declared:

> As we celebrate victory in Europe let us remind ourselves that common problems of the immediate and distant future can be best solved in the same conceptions of co-operation and devotion to the cause of human freedom as have made this expeditionary force such a mighty engine of righteous destruction.

Alas, the "same conceptions of co-operation and devotion to the cause of human freedom" never became a reality once the war was over. The common battle against Nazi tyranny gave way to the cold war between the East and West, leaving Germany the chief battleground for this new play of world forces. Nazi pan-destructionism thus bequeathed to Germany and to the world not only a wholesale destruction of physical property and moral values but a complete disruption of the entire political foundation of Europe and a state of political tension and crisis which bears within it the seeds of even more terrible upheavals and greater catastrophe. Hitler's prediction that if he fell he would bring the rest of the world down with him may yet come to realization.

CHAPTER XXII

Germany Under Occupation, 1945-1949

Glaubt nicht an die jahrtausend alte Lüge, dass Schande mit Blut
abgewaschen werde, sondern an lie junge Wahrheit, dass Schande
nur mit Ehre abgewaschen werden kann, mit Busse, mit
Verwandlung, mit dem Worte des verlorenen Sohnes: Vater,
ich habe gesündigt, und ich will hinfort nicht mehr sündigen.

ERNST WIECHERT, *An die deutsche Jugend*

1. CHAOS

For the second time in the century Germany's expansionist dreams lay shattered in ruins, and once again, as in 1918, Germany was the passive object of policy by her conquerors. This time, however, the costs of the adventure were more gigantic and more terrifying than ever before in its history.[1] Furthermore, unlike 1918, there was no political or revolutionary action this time against the former rulers. One of the most fateful aspects of the entire story of this post-war period derives from the fact that the German people failed to do anything themselves to throw off the yoke of the Nazi dictatorship. Even under the impact of the hammering blows of Allied bombings and of Allied armies pushing deeper and deeper into the country, there was not a single instance of Germans rising up to overthrow even local Nazi authorities. Unlike the case of fascist Italy, where, at least in the north, the coming of Allied soldiers was preceded by anti-fascist acts of liberation and where Mussolini was ousted and finally done away with by Italian hands, Germany experienced not a single revolutionary outbreak. The only signs on the walls which greeted the advancing Allied armies were Nazi slogans and calls for a fight to the death under the Führer.

Germany was freed from the shackles of totalitarianism by outsiders, by foreign arms and by foreign sacrifices. Nationalist sentiment, disciplined obedience, and dazed inertia and apathy combined to stay the hands of

532

Germans from doing even as much as the Italians had done. Or was it also the fear of another *Dolchstoss* legend that paralyzed the anti-Nazis? Once again democracy was initiated in Germany with the odds heavily pitted against it. Once again democracy came as the gift of the former enemy and the outsider, and as such had to contend with deep nationalist resistance to its acceptance.

The condition of the country at the close of hostilities in May, 1945, can be described by only one word—chaos, chaos in its most literal and classical sense. Unlike World War I, which ended with German armies everywhere on enemy soil and which left German territory unscathed, World War II bequeathed to Germany, as it did to the rest of Europe, appalling physical destruction. Continuous battering by Allied bombers, despite Göring's proud boast that his Luftwaffe would never permit Allied planes to invade the German skies; violent house-to-house and street-to-street fighting by last-ditch fanatical Nazi formations, and willful destruction of bridges, public buildings, and roads by retreating Nazis, all brought physical decimation to a very substantial part of German territory. There was hardly an important city or town that did not present a spectacle of mounds and mounds of rubble and ruins, of half destroyed buildings, shattered dwellings, battered railroad stations and disorganized public utilities. Of the larger cities only Heidelberg, Celle, and Flensburg remained intact, with Lübeck and Bamberg not too badly hit. But Kassel, Nürnberg, Cologne, Mannheim, Darmstadt, Essen, Coblenz, and Würzburg seemed almost completely destroyed, and Berlin, Dresden, Breslau, Munich, Hamburg, Mainz, and Frankfurt were almost as badly damaged. People lived huddled together in the ruins of houses, in cellars and in bunkers, and trudged in a dazed condition over what they once knew as streets but what were now only heaps of rubble. The stench of dead bodies buried underneath the rubble lingered on for many, many months. The New York *Herald Tribune* correspondent, entering Berlin on May 3, 1945, wrote:

> Nothing is left in Berlin. There are no homes, no shops, no transportation, no government buildings. Only a few walls . . . are the heritage bequeathed by the Nazis to the people of Berlin. . . . Berlin can now be regarded only as a geographical location heaped with mountainous mounds of debris.

The Russian *Pravda* correspondent told of the terrified and starving housewives of Berlin plundering the shops, and described Berlin as a city of desolation and shattered dreams, inhabited by a half mad, half starving population, clawing its frenzied way into battered food shops, slinking for shelter into dark cellars, and currying favor with their conquerors as they emerged from the catacombs, raising their clenched fists and shouting *"Rot Front."* [2]

The breakdown of transportation and communications, the collapse of the banking system, and the resulting financial chaos added to the physical destruction to produce anarchy, especially in the urban centers. Even more important was the disintegration of all government. Nazi government officials, aware of their potential status as war criminals, committed suicide, fled, went into hiding, or were captured by Allied troops. The complete governmental structure of the country, not only at the top but even on the smallest municipal and village levels, collapsed in its entirety. The élite leadership which had held the country in its grip for the preceding decade disappeared abruptly from the scene. Nor was there a new leadership élite to take its place. Anti-Nazi political figures had either been murdered, tortured, or forced into emigration. Some emerged haggard and physically debilitated from liberated concentration camps. A few came back later from exile. But the situation immediately following the cessation of hostilities found Germany completely devoid of any class of political leaders ready to take over the administrative machinery left vacant by the routed Nazis.

The German masses were psychologically unprepared for defeat and the loss of the war. True, there were many who had managed to listen to foreign broadcasts and who after Stalingrad had seen the handwriting on the wall for Germany. There were also many Germans, their numbers unknown, but their lot perhaps the most tragic of all, who with their own kin in the German fighting forces, yet with deep love of humanity, knelt in silent prayer, as Allied bombers came over to destroy their homes and cities, to plead for Allied victory to destroy Nazism.

For most Germans, however, the glory of Hitler's triumphs was too recent in memory to allow for the complete reversal to defeat. The mass of people were mentally stunned by it all. Accustomed as they were to look to orders, direction, and force from above, they floundered about either in complete apathy or in a mad psychological scramble, when their superiors were gone.

Germany at the close of the war became the center of one of the most gigantic population movements in modern history. To the approximately 66,000,000 Germans, were added close to 8,000,000 nationals of other countries liberated from concentration camps and labor camps.[3] These were later joined by thousands of infiltrees who came trekking into Germany—Jews from Poland and the U.S.S.R. and anti-Communists taking advantage of disorganized conditions to flee from the Soviet dictatorship. After 1947 came refugees from other Soviet-dominated countries who found Germany, by virtue of its geographical location and because of the absence of civil government, the most convenient place to find shelter. Added to these were the close to 8,000,000 soldiers of the invading armies of the major powers and the various missions of the smaller powers, making a grand total of over 15,000,000 non-Germans of varying degrees of political status and economic situation who constituted a completely foreign body in the demographic structure of the country.

To these must also be added close to 10,000,000 German refugees (*Flüchtlinge*). These were, in the first place, ethnic Germans (*Volksdeutsche*) expelled from Czechoslovakia, Hungary, Yugoslavia, Rumania, and Poland, in order to cleanse those countries from German minority problems, and, secondly, Germans who fled or were expelled from the former German territories annexed by Poland and the Soviet Union in the east, namely, Silesia and East Prussia. The great majority of these German refugees filtered into Western Germany. Homeless and without means, they came into the rubble-ridden, half starved and congested West German cities as a heavy drain on the physical resources of the native population. The native Germans regarded them for the most part as aliens, and in general resented their coming and the political and cultural baggage which they brought with them.

This huge amorphous population of post-war Germany was further disorganized by the division of the country by the victors into four zones of occupation. In the beginning each of the zones was sealed off tightly from the others. The ruined economy, the disrupted transportation, and the divided families all found further difficulties and complications created by four zones, four occupying powers, four different political and administrative setups, four different mentalities, and four borders to cross.

The effects of the strain of war, the influence of twelve years of nihilistic National Socialist rule, the shock of defeat, and the tensions of occupation combined to bring about a profound moral disintegration and loss of all sense of values. The primary preoccupation of most Germans was with the most elementary problems of food, shelter, and work. There came the days of a wildly flourishing black market, of a tobacco-starved population that threw official currency to the winds and improvised a wildly fluctuating cigarette economy, in which goods and services were traded for cigarettes, often measured not by the carton or even by the pack, but by the single cigarette. There came the *Stummel* period when foreign soldiers and civilians found themselves followed by Germans waiting to pick up discarded cigarette butts. There followed the days of the *"Fräuleins,"* who, whether the official military orders were for or against fraternization, carried on with Allied soldiers in varying degrees of intimacy in return for chocolate bars, nylon stockings, or K rations to supplement the family food rations.

All these manifestations, in part the concomitance of any military occupation, now assumed vaster dimensions than ever before in history. They continued on well into 1947, until by various actions of the Allied powers, such as repatriation of DP's, emigration of others, economic reforms, relief administration, and more rigid control of their own troops, the more shocking and glaring aspects of this occupation period were gradually eliminated. Deep scars of a moral and psychic nature remain, however, to add to the complexity of the problems of the new German state.

2. YALTA AND POTSDAM

German conditions after the close of the war were determined chiefly by the Allies, but the primary fact in Allied policy was the growing cleavage between the United States, Britain, and France on the one side and the Soviet Union and its satellite countries on the other. During the war, despite ominous signs to the contrary, the optimistic feeling prevailed that the powers of the West and the Soviet Union would be able to continue to work harmoniously in the field of international relations despite differences in outlook and disparities between capitalism and communism. The deep suspicion engendered by the Nazi-Soviet Pact of 1939 gave way, under the impact of common danger, to at least a surface spirit of co-operation. Just as final victory over the Nazis was effected only by the combined coalition of East and West, so the solution of post-war problems, it was felt, could only be achieved by the same union of forces. The first two years after the war's end saw repeated efforts to work out a solution to the German problem acceptable to all the powers. These efforts continued to be more and more fruitless and more frustrating. By 1947 the breach between East and West was more than tentative, and the former Germany now remains divided into two tightly sealed-off areas.

During the last years of the war, and especially after Allied victory appeared to be certain, the press and public opinion in Allied countries carried on a lively discussion on what to do with Germany after victory. Alignments were drawn along the lines of a "hard peace" and a "soft peace." The American newspaperman Drew Pearson, on September 2, 1944, told of President Roosevelt's blowing up because of his dissatisfaction with a handbook for dealing with the Germans, prepared by the army. "Feed the Germans," Mr. Roosevelt was quoted as saying. "I'll give them three bowls of soup a day, with nothing in them. Control inflation! Let them have all the inflation they want! Control industry! There won't be any industry to control!" It was during these days that the so-called Morgenthau Plan for reducing Germany to a primarily agrarian country enjoyed a brief period of influence in high official circles. The heads of the American Office of War Information, Elmer Davis and Robert Sherwood, at a press interview on September 21, 1944, declared that the first thing to do after the war was to convince the Germans that they had really lost the war and that they would lose again if they ever tried to start another one. Even opponents of a "hard peace," like the London *Economist,* also agreed that unilateral German disarmament for an indefinite period would be required. Soviet policy likewise wavered between revengeful and passionate hatred for all Germans and a more sober discrimination between Hitlerites and Germans. While Ilya Ehrenburg called on Russians never to forget the destruction wreaked on the Soviet Union by the invading German armies and proclaimed that there was no Germany but rather "a huge gang," he was almost immediately taken to task by G. Alexandrov in *Pravda,* on April 14, 1945, for oversimplifying the problem. "In fulfilling its great liberation mission," wrote Alexandrov, "the Red army is fighting for the destruction of Hitler's army, Hitler's state and Hitler's government, but its purpose never was, nor is it now, to exterminate the German people." Even more lenient was Stalin's statement of October, 1944. "We do not pursue the aim of destroying the entire organized military force in Germany," said Stalin, "for every literate person will understand that this is not only impossible as regards Germany just as it is in regard to Russia, but also inadvisable from the point of view of the victor."

The Soviet Union was the only one of the Allied powers to set up a National Committee to Free Germany to be used for propaganda purposes during the war and for post-war administration. It did not hesitate to use high army officers and Junkers like General von Seydlitz, Marshal von Paulus, the vanquished leader of Stalingrad, and Bismarck's grandson, Count Heinrich von Einsiedel, together with clergymen and German Communists.

Official Allied policy on post-war Germany, worked out in preliminary fashion in the European Advisory Commission in London, received its final formulation in the Yalta agreements of February, 1945, and the Potsdam Declaration of August 2, 1945. These agreements provided the basis for the attempt at common Allied rule of Germany. Disagreement as to interpretation of these protocols laid the groundwork for the eventual break between the U.S.S.R. and the Western powers. It was at Yalta that the decision was made to divide Germany into four separate zones of occupation. Much criticism has been directed at the Yalta agreements. Most of this criticism emanates from the wisdom of hindsight. Critics of Yalta and Potsdam forgot the climate of 1944 and 1945, when the Soviet Union was an ally against Hitler, when military leaders looked to its aid against Japan, and when its co-operation was deemed a primary prerequisite for the establishment of a post-war international order. It is hard to say that any decision other than zones of occupation was either possible or, if possible, would have worked out more satisfactorily than the arrangements made.

Germany, according to these agreements, was divided into four zones of occupation. The Soviet Union gave its assent to a French zone only on the condition that it be carved out of the territories allotted to the United States and Britain. The American zone comprised the states of Bavaria, Hesse, Württemberg-Baden and the enclave of Bremen, which was to serve as the seaport for the American forces, and contained a population of almost 17,000,000 people. The British zone took in North Rhine Westphalia, Lower Saxony, Schleswig-Holstein, and Hamburg, with a population of almost 22,000,000. The French zone included the Rhineland Palatinate, South Baden, South Württemberg, and the Saar, with a population of about 6,000,000. The zone allotted to the U.S.S.R. comprised the states of Saxony, Thuringia, Mecklenburg-Vorpommern, Saxony-Anhalt, and the Mark Brandenburg, with a population of 17,313,000.* East Prussia was divided between the Soviet Union and the new Polish state, and Poland was allowed to take over the former Germany territory east of the so-called Oder-Neisse Line, which comprised Silesia and its capital city of Breslau (now renamed by the Poles Wraclaw), Danzig, eastern Pomerania with the port of Stettin, and eastern Brandenburg. The eastern borders of Germany as thus established were only tentative and were to await official action by a peace conference. Their *de facto* occupation by the Red Army, however, precluded the possibility of any action by the Western powers, short of outright war, to revise these frontiers.

A special status was given to the former German capital of Berlin, with its population of 3,180,000. It, like Vienna in Austria, was to be occupied and ruled jointly by all four powers, as a symbol of the grand alliance that won the war. Berlin became the most sensitive spot in all Germany, if not in all Europe. It was the microcosm of world diplomacy. It was here that the entire drama of East-West tension was enacted. Here the political, economic, military, and propaganda machines of the four powers came into play with one another or more often against one another. But in this play of forces the U.S.S.R. had one supreme advantage. Berlin lay in the heart of the Soviet zone, and the other occupying powers had to pass through the Soviet zone in order to reach their own sectors in Berlin. From the start the Soviet authorities prescribed official and limited air, rail, and road connections to Berlin for the Allies, and forbade any other communication except by means of these limited routes. The Western powers held that the joint occupation of Berlin by all the four powers by and of itself assumed free access to the city. But no specific provisions for such free access were made. General Lucius Clay later revealed that the Western leaders at Yalta did not foresee the seriousness of the problem of access to Berlin. It was still in the heyday of optimism regarding Soviet co-operation, and there was a delicate hesitancy to arouse Soviet suspicions. Only much later could Clay write, "I think now that I was mistaken in not at this time making free access to Berlin a condition to our withdrawal into our occupation zone." This absence of free access to Berlin for the Allies later came to be used by the Soviet Union as a formidable weapon against the Allied West, used most promi-

---

* The former state of Prussia was liquidated as a political entity by action of the Allied powers.

nently in the Berlin blockade of 1948–1949 and continuing to this day to make Berlin the danger zone of all Germany and all Europe.

In this zonal division of occupied Germany the Soviet Union received the great agricultural food basket of Germany, while the more important industrial areas went to the Western powers, notably the Ruhr in the British zone. The Soviet zone was overwhelmingly Protestant, while the three zones of the Western powers were heavily weighted with the Catholic population of Bavaria and the Rhineland. Important urban cultural centers like Leipzig, Dresden, Jena, Weimar, Halle, and Eisenach came into the periphery of Soviet Communist culture, while Munich, Frankfurt, Hamburg, Nürnberg, Bremen, Essen, Mannheim, Stuttgart, Düsseldorf, Baden-Baden, Karlsruhe, Marburg, and Bonn came under the control of the Western occupying powers. The military commander of each zone was designated as supreme authority in each zone, and central authority for all Germany was vested in the Allied Control Council in Berlin made up of the four commanders in chief and bound by a unanimity rule for all decisions. Actually, the Allied Control Council was only an agency for co-ordinating the policies of the four powers as worked out in the Council of Foreign Ministers. The real executive power was vested in each of the Allied commanders in chief acting in his own zone. The administration of Berlin was vested in a Kommandatura made up of the military heads of the forces of the four powers stationed in Berlin. The city of Berlin itself, like the country as a whole, was divided into four sectors, each sector governed by one of the four powers. The division of Germany was thus made complete and unqualified.

The purposes of the Allied German policy, as set forth in the Yalta and Potsdam agreements, were to destroy Nazism and German militarism, and to make sure that Germany would never again disturb the peace. The guiding principles transmitted to the military commanders were denazification, democratization, and decentralization. At Yalta it was resolved (1) that Germany be totally disarmed, (2) that Nazism and militarism be destroyed, (3) that those responsible for war crimes be tried and punished, (4) that all German industry capable of military production be eliminated or controlled, and (5) that Germany make compensation in kind for the damage she caused. But, declared Winston Churchill in his report to Parliament, it was not "the purpose of the Allies to destroy the people of Germany or to leave them without the necessary means of subsistence. Our policy is not revenge. . . . There will be a place one day for Germans in the community of nations, but only when the traces of Nazism and militarism have been effectively and finally extirpated."

The Potsdam declaration of August 2, 1945, reaffirmed the decisions of Yalta and spelled out in more specific terms the main lines of Allied policy. It provided that Germany was "to be treated as a single economic unit," but the four governments were never able to reach an agreement on measures for dealing with Germany as *one* economic unit. The Soviet Union and France both embarked on policies of unilateral exploitation of their zones. The Potsdam declaration also provided for the collection of reparations to be exacted in the form of equipment. This too proved to be one of the major points at issue between the U.S.S.R. and the Western powers. Excessive concentrations of industry were to be broken up and level-of-industry agreements worked out which were to provide for the dismantling of the industries producing armaments, aircraft, shipping, synthetic gas, oil and rubber, roller bearings, heavy machine tools, heavy tractors, war chemicals, and radio transmitting equipment. Crude steel production was to be reduced to 30 per cent of 1936 production.

3. THE NÜRNBERG TRIALS

The most significant instance of co-operation of the four powers in occupied Germany was the trial of the major war criminals by the International Military Tribunal at Nürnberg. The tribunal, set up by a charter of the four powers and consisting of jurists representing each of the major powers, may be called a milestone in the development of international law. Sitting continuously from November 20, 1945, to October 1, 1946, it was presided over by the British justice Sir Geoffrey Lawrence in a model and exemplary display of judicial temper and procedural skill. The transcript of the proceedings and the documents introduced as evidence fill forty-two bulky printed volumes. This huge assembly of evidence brought to the attention of the world a story of conspiracy, aggression, and brutality unparalleled in the annals of civilized governments. Of the important Nazi leaders, Adolf Hitler and Joseph Goebbels perished in their bunker in besieged Berlin; Heinrich Himmler committed suicide soon after he was apprehended; Martin Bormann was never found; Robert Ley committed suicide before the trials began; and Gustav Krupp von Bohlen und Halbach was declared too ill to be tried. Brought to trial at Nürnberg were Hermann Göring, Joachim von Ribbentrop, Alfred Rosenberg, Wilhelm Frick, Julius Streicher, Rudolf Hess, Walther Funk, Constantin von Neurath, Ernst Kaltenbrunner, Hans Frank, General Wilhelm von Keitel, General Alfred Jodl, Admiral Erich Raeder, Admiral Karl Dönitz, Hjalmar Schacht, Franz von Papen, Baldur von Schirach, Fritz Sauckel, Arthur Seyss-Inquardt, Albert Speer, and Hans Fritzsche. All were indicted for conspiracy to commit crimes against peace, war crimes, and crimes against humanity. Indictments were also entered against the Reich cabinet, the leadership corps of the Nazi party, the S.S. and S.D. (Sicherheits Dienst), the Gestapo, the S.A., and the General Staff and High Command of the army.

Of the twenty-one persons tried (Martin Bormann was tried in absentia), Fritzsche, Papen, and Schacht were finally acquitted; Hess, Funk, and

Raeder were sentenced to life imprisonment; Dönitz, Schirach, Speer, and Neurath to lesser terms of imprisonment; and all the rest to death by hanging. Göring, clown and bully all through the trial, succeeded in cheating his hangman by swallowing a vial of poison the day before the sentence was to be carried out. Verdicts of guilty were also handed down on the leadership corps of the Nazi party, on the S.S. and S.D. and on the Gestapo. Each of the four powers also tried various categories of war criminals in their respective zones, and war criminals apprehended in other European countries were tried in those countries.

Considerable difference of opinion began to develop on the juridical competence and validity of the war crimes trials almost from the moment they started. Opponents of the trials adduced a number of arguments. They claimed that the trials constituted *ex post facto* prosecution and as such were not in keeping with a true sense of justice; others argued that the tribunal was not a real court of law since there was no world state and that it was really a political act by victors against vanquished. Germans in particular cast cynical reflection on the character of a court in which at least one power represented in the tribunal could just as well have been sitting in the defendant's box for the commission of aggression, conspiracy, and crimes against humanity. As the years go by and the appalling record of crime revealed in the trial becomes dim in the memory and conscience of the world, there will undoubtedly be more and more so-called "objective" attacks upon the war crimes trials. Yet with all its flaws, with all the inconsistencies inherent in its operation, with all the cynicism justified by the presence of Soviet judges, the Nürnberg trial will remain one of the truly great and constructive acts of the post-war period. For the first time in history, the voice of humanity not only spoke out, but also acted against those who plotted war and aggression. The precedent has been given to the world if it only chooses to follow it.

As for the effects of the trials in Germany, they brought to the German people a detailed and intimate picture of their former rulers and leaders that could not but shock and instruct all but the most hardened. This does not mean that the enshrinement of the Nazi leaders is forever precluded thereby in future Germany. Myths have a way of either evading known facts or else giving the facts a peculiar twist that allows for their growth despite incontrovertible evidence to the contrary. Nevertheless the path of false exaltation has been made much more difficult by the exposition of truth, and the record of the war crimes trials, disseminated in newspapers, periodicals, books, radio, and film, has done more to discredit Nazism than any other factor except that of the loss of the war.

4. DENAZIFICATION AND RE-EDUCATION

Perhaps the most controversial aspect of Allied occupation policy in Germany was that of so-called "denazification." No other issue aroused so much discussion both inside and outside Germany. From the last years of the war there emerged an overwhelming body of suggestions and proposals of how to rid Germany of the poison of National Socialism and how to prevent the former Nazis from regaining their power and influence in post-war Germany. Denazification was proclaimed to be one of the main objectives of Allied policy by the Yalta and Potsdam declarations. When faced with the task of carrying out the policy of denazification, however, the officers of military government ran into enormous difficulties not clearly envisaged before. The attempts at denazification revealed plainly how deeply "Nazified" Hitler Germany had been. It was not just a simple problem of getting rid of several thousand ringleaders who had seized control of the German government. Denazification, if it was to be carried out in thorough accord with the principles and objectives enunciated in the Yalta and Potsdam declarations, involved millions of people. The sheer quantitative aspect itself made it an almost impossible task.

When it is realized too that during the twelve years of Hitler rule all positions of even lesser importance in every administrative, political, economic, cultural, and technological phase of German life had been filled with members of the N.S.D.A.P. or affiliated party organizations and that all incumbents in these positions had been forced to join party organizations in order to hold their jobs; that all younger and newly trained personnel were the products of Nazi schooling and indoctrination; that the largest percentage of competent anti-Nazi technicians had either emigrated, perished in concentration camps or at the front, or else had been rendered inefficient by years of inactivity and persecution, one can appreciate the dilemma presented to the armies of occupation who, on the one hand, were beset by the enormous task of bringing a chaotic and anarchical country back to some degree of normal functioning and on the other were pressed by denazification directives to get rid of the very people most able technically to help restore normal functioning. The pressure for denazification came as a rule from governments and public opinion at home; the pressure to soft-pedal denazification usually came from military officers stationed in the occupied zones. It was between these two poles of political policy and administrative expediency that denazification measures blew hot and cold for at least four years.

Most military government officials in all zones were appallingly ignorant of the German language, of German history, and of the background of the Nazi movement. They were as little aware of what Nazism really meant as their governmental leaders had been in 1939. With more knowledge and more competence they could have used far greater discrimination in their selection of German personnel to help them in the task of bringing order into Germany. Few as the anti-Nazis were, they should have been given enthusiastic support by military government. This was usually not the case. While it was not always apparent whether Nazism paid or not, it became all too apparent from the start that anti-Nazism did not pay. Enthusiastic and warm support of the anti-Nazis should have been concomitant to punishment of Nazis. This, unfortunately, was not made part of Allied policy, especially in the Western zones. The German people, and especially the youth, who needed some incentives other than sermons and lectures on morals and ethics, were never made to feel that their own material and professional future, their very physical existence, were tied up with anti-Nazism. Cynical pretence of "democratic" loyalty and more often vocal profession of "non-political" or "no-party" affiliations came to be the usual defense mechanisms devised by the average German against the denazification pressure that came from Allied sources.

The denazification objectives were variously interpreted by the four occupying powers. The Russians, while always denouncing the Western Allies for failure to carry out effective denazification, from the start identified denazification with enforced affiliation with the Communist-controlled Socialist Unity party and other "united-front" "anti-fascist" organizations. The *Tägliche Rundschau,* official organ of the Soviet authorities, declared editorially that the door must be open to all ex-Nazis who "have not sold themselves to the imperialists and are able to serve the interests of the German people. And these must receive an opportunity to co-operate with democratic elements so that they can 'denazify themselves.' " Many an S.S. man or Gestapo agent hunted in the Western zones found refuge and sanctuary in the Soviet zone by offering his services to the Soviet authorities and by putting himself under the discipline of some "anti-fascist" organization. Many high offices in the Russian zone were filled with ex-Nazis, and wholesale pardons were issued to those who joined the Socialist Unity party. On February 27, 1948, Marshal Sokolovsky ordered that all denazification commissions in the Soviet zone be dissolved by March 10, declaring that the zone had been cleared of all active fascists and militarists and that any remaining Nazis would be handled by the criminal police. The door was thus opened to persecution of political opponents by the criminal police as former Nazis.

The British never pursued denazification very enthusiastically. They investigated the political background of a person nominated for a position only when it was very obvious that consideration of possible Nazi affiliation was urgent. The French made little distinction between Germans and Nazis. They mistrusted all Germans and wrote off the adult generation as lost. They concentrated their attention on the education of the young and were the first to introduce a completely new set of textbooks for German schools in their zones. They also opened a new university at Mainz to establish an academic institution completely free of Nazi background. Generally speaking the French did not take denazification very seriously, but their cultural and educational policies were the most effective and most intelligent of all the occupying powers.

The Americans, with their zeal for reform, with their unbounded faith in the efficacy of education, and with the greatest pressure for the "purging" of Germany by political groups, journalists, and educators at home carried out the most ambitious program of denazification and hence also one that aroused the most criticism and discussion. The American denazification program passed through several phases. The initial program was based on the Joint Chiefs of Staff directive of April, 1945, the Potsdam declaration, and the Allied Control Council directives of January 12 and October 12, 1946. It was designed to purge the German administration of all more than nominal members and followers of the Nazi movement. All Germans applying for jobs in both public and private positions in the American zone were to fill out a highly detailed and complicated questionnaire (*Fragebogen*), which was then to be scrutinized by American security officers. This was a most cumbersome procedure, and criticism poured in from all sides. Denazification to be successful had to be speedy, and the questionnaire method was anything but speedy. Intelligent and sensitive anti-Nazi Germans joined with those more involved and less sensitive in heaping ridicule on the *Fragebogen*. The most serious objection was that the "little Nazis" were being hounded while the top Nazis were able to evade punishment or trial. American officials too soon came to realize that the attempt to keep 7 million party members—and with dependents probably 25 million people—outside the community as outcasts would work more harm than good.

In March, 1946, the American Military Government promulgated the German Law for Liberation from National Socialism and Militarism, and transferred the powers and responsibility for denazification to special German tribunals (*Spruchkammern*). Addressing the German minister-presidents on November 11, 1946, General Clay said: "Let us have no misunderstanding—denazification is a must. . . . I do not see how you can demonstrate your ability for self-government nor your will for democracy if you are going to evade or shirk the first unpleasant and difficult task that falls upon you."

The law required all Germans over eighteen years of age to register and fill out a questionnaire. Five categories of defendants were established: (1) major offenders, (2) offenders, (3) lesser offenders, (4) fellow travelers, and (5) those exonerated by the tribunal. Over $3\frac{1}{2}$ million persons in the American zone, or about 27 per cent of the 13 million registrants, were chargeable under this law. Successive modifications and mass amnesties by American officials reduced this number by 2,373,115. By September 30, 1950, the German tribunals had covered 958,071 cases.[4] Of these about 350,000 were exonerated or amnestied and the rest received varying degrees of punishment from sentence to labor camps to fines and restrictions of employment. By far the overwhelming number of sentences (close to 600,000) resulted in fines. Only about 23,000 major offenders and offenders were held permanently ineligible for public office, and appeals reduced this number to about 18,000. Exoneration by the courts of such prominent controversial figures as Richard Strauss, Hjalmar Schacht, Franz von Papen, and General Halder aroused considerable mistrust abroad of the sincerity of the Germans in carrying out the program.

The official denazification program was well-nigh completed in all zones by the end of 1948. Its lasting effects are still hard to evaluate. Foreigners as well as Germans have condemned it as a huge failure, although for varying reasons. It has been termed an "artificial revolution" that only brought on "renazification," and a "huge farce" and "a complete failure." Conflicting reports on the "German mind" led to conflicting views on the effects of denazification. A popular saying current among Germans in the American zone runs as follows, "Since the democratic sun has been shining on us we have become browner." Pastor Niemoeller, on February 2, 1948, issued a 700-word pastoral letter describing denazification as "a method for hatred and revenge" which surpassed the obligations of atonement, and he called upon all Germans to refuse to co-operate in the program. His call was supported by a large number of other Protestant clergymen. An intelligent and passionately anti-Nazi writer like Eugen Kogon criticized the entire Allied policy of denazification as one that penalizes those whose only crime was to have made a political error.[5]

The top Nazi leaders were undoubtedly removed from German public life either by Allied war crimes trials or by denazification proceedings. Key positions in the press, radio, film, and theater were filled by people who were neither nationalist nor reactionary. Denazification has also acted as a deterrent to render more difficult the outright return of discredited public figures. On the other hand the years after 1947 saw the huge rehiring of former Nazis for important places in the administrative machinery of the new German states. Perhaps the most revealing aspect as to the effect of denazification in Germany is the hostile attitude that has developed toward those Germans who participated in the various agencies for denazification. These individuals began to find it increasingly difficult to secure employment, and have come to form a new class of political and economic outcasts.

Equally problematic are the effects of the Allied attempts at "re-orientation" of the Germans and their "re-education." The zeal of Allied, especially American, educators, social workers, and youth leaders soon was dissipated against the hard realities of the long tradition of German history, of the political and moral apathy of post-war Germany, of the lack of a sufficient number of energetic and effective German workers in the program, and above all against the tensions and difficulties created by the cleavage between the East and the West in the international arena. We may summarize the effects of denazification by saying that there are actually relatively few convinced Nazis left in Germany, but, in the words of a wise and competent reporter: "At the same time it is true that democracy has failed thus far to become a desirable and common aim, and a dangerous spiritual vacuum exists which is apt to foster new forms of nationalism and totalitarianism." [6]

5. THE SEARCHING OF CONSCIENCE

One of the immediate consequences of defeat was a searching of conscience that went on, at least among the less nationalistic elements of the German people. Germans gropingly sought to fathom the causes of the collapse, to adjust themselves to the realities of occupation, and to find some hope and consolation for the future. Among the first publications permitted by the Allied armies were the accounts of their experiences by liberated concentration-camp victims.

Quite apart from the literature of the Displaced Persons, which is not being considered here, German anti-Nazis liberated from Buchenwald, Ravensburg, Dachau, Mauthausen, and other prison and labor camps revealed to their fellow Germans the gruesome details of a phase of Nazi rule which most Germans claimed had been unknown to them. Of these accounts, by far the most authoritative and most balanced is the work of the brilliant Catholic journalist Eugen Kogon, *Der S.S. Staat,* published in Frankfurt in 1946.

As in the years following World War I, but in much more exaggerated form, the eyes of the world were focused on Germany to discern symptoms of moral repentance and contrition. From all sides came a chorus of demands for a "change of heart," for evidences of "shame," and for confessions of guilt. Every traveler, visitor, politician, or soldier who came to Germany looked for such a "change of heart," and usually left with the sad report that he had failed to find such a change. This anxiety was understandable from the standpoint of a world that had suffered so cruelly from Nazi violence and destruction. But a nation does not experience a radical psychological and moral transformation by the switch of a button. In order to be permanent and effective such a transformation must needs be a slow process. Too often, also, the demands for such a "change of heart" were in bad taste and crude. Sensitive anti-Nazi Germans often found themselves berated rudely and violently for the very things which they themselves had fought against at peril to their own lives.*

In this state of torpor and confusion there was a tragic dearth of intellectual and moral leadership. The intellectual classes of Germany had betrayed their trust by selling themselves wholesale to the Nazis. The figure of Karl Jaspers, noted Heidelberg philosopher, emerged in the early

---

* The searching of conscience by Germans, complained Benno Reifenberg, a former editor of the *Frankfurter Zeitung,* in the first issue of *Die Gegenwart,* cannot be commanded. It must come as an act of free will. "The quieter and the more hidden in the innermost recesses of the heart the *peccavi* is, the purer is its worth." *Deutschland unter Alles,* he wrote, is just as senseless as *Deutschland über Alles.*

days as the most prominent spiritual leader of the new Germany. Jaspers was hardly of the mettle to be a leader. Of delicate health and far removed all his life from the maelstrom of politics and society, a typical non-political German intellectual, he was one of the few German thinkers remaining in Nazi Germany who until the end retained a pure and untarnished record of dignified, consistent, and at times heroic resistance to the threats of the Gestapo and of the Nazified academic world. At a time when moral decency, purity, and integrity of mind were the things most needed by a country soiled and stained by twelve years of degradation, the noble figure of Karl Jaspers served as a source of inspiration for intellectuals groping their way back to freedom and humanity.

Aided by Alfred Weber, noted sociologist and brother of Max Weber, and by the vigorous young journalist Dolf Sternberger, Jaspers launched a journal, *Die Wandlung,* in Heidelberg, which was to help Germans orient themselves in the world of moral and intellectual ruins. In the first issue of November 30, 1945, the editors indicated that they were not presenting a plan for the future. "We want to prepare the ground by meditation and discussion, by informative reports and images." The first task was "to find one's self again thoughtfully in this enormous time of need." Besides penetrating and searching articles on political and intellectual problems, *Die Wandlung* made available to German readers for the first time documents like the Potsdam declaration and materials from the Nürnberg trials such as the Hossbach protocol, the account of euthanasia, and the description of the annihilation of the Warsaw ghetto. Jaspers, Weber, and their colleagues set themselves the task of transforming the German mass man "from a patient obedient mass animal to a type of community of independent, self-conscious individuals jealous of their rights to liberty." The periodical continued to be published until 1949. In its last issue Dolf Sternberger, giving a résumé of its career, ends on a note of rueful skepticism on the attainment of any real transformation of such character. Jaspers, partly for reasons of health, but also in part as a result of a profound disappointment with the course of developments in Germany, left his chair at Heidelberg and accepted a call to Basel, Switzerland.

Of the other groups and journals which took the initiative in the political re-education of the German people there were the *Frankfurter Hefte,* edited by two young liberal Catholics, Eugen Kogon and Walter Dirks, who combined their agitation for political democracy with a renunciation of "outworn" laissez-faire economic liberalism; *Die Gegenwart,* started in Freiburg im Breisgau in the French zone as a political bi-weekly by Benno Reifenberg, Albert Oeser, and other former staff editors of the liberal *Frankfurter Zeitung;* and in Berlin the *Deutsche Rundschau,* resuming its long pre-Hitler career under its former editor Rudolf Pechel, who had been close to the resistance movement of July 20, 1944. Pechel and others like him sought to make up for the fact that liberation from Nazi rule came not from the Germans themselves but by Allied victory, by nurturing a cult of the martyrs of the July 20 attempt as well as of the Munich student resisters. Often, however, the scope and importance of this resistance was exaggerated beyond all historical proportions, and writers like Kogon pleaded for a more sober and realistic appraisal of these manifestations.[7]

The Communist group, under the leadership of Wilhelm Pieck and Walter Ulbricht, assumed direction of political and cultural affairs in the Soviet zone and in the Russian sector of Berlin. It started out initially with a united-front program aimed to rally all anti-Nazi intellectuals on an anti-fascist program. The Kulturbund, organized with Russian approval in Berlin, and its organ, the monthly journal *Aufbau,* gathered together many leading intellectuals, from conservatives like Eduard Spranger and the poet Ernst Wiechert to Communists and fellow travelers like Johannes Becher, Hans Fallada, and Heinrich Mann. As the aims of Soviet policy became clear and the cleavage between East and West grew sharper, the Kulturbund also became out-and-out Communist, and the non-Communists withdrew their participation.

Church leaders also assumed an important role in the leadership of postwar Germany. Liberal Catholics in the Rhineland, in Freiburg, and in Frankfurt, and members of the Nazi-persecuted Protestant confessional church took the lead in a call for religious revival and moral regeneration after the decade of paganism and nihilism. Paster Niemoeller, Bishop Wurm in Württemberg, Bishop Dibelius in Berlin and Karl Barth from Switzerland were the most prominent in the Protestant churches. As too often was the case in German Protestantism, some of the leaders of the confessional church soon lapsed into a nationalism that bore no happy omen for the future of German democracy.

Of literary figures the novelists Herman Hesse and Ernst Wiechert occupied a prominent role in the first few years after the cessation of hostilities. Hesse, who had left Germany for Switzerland, repeated the same sort of call for moral regeneration and pacifism that he had pleaded for after the end of World War I. Ernst Wiechert, once himself the idol of the conservative right, had achieved distinction by his openly defiant addresses to the students at the University of Munich during the Nazi epoch and by his call for a return to the lasting and eternal values of humanity. With the majesty and grandeur of a prophet, with the capacity for love of a saint, and with beautiful simplicity of style and language he castigated his fellow Germans for their past and called for a spiritual and moral regeneration. The National Socialist revolution, he said, had swallowed up everything. "In the Reichstag fire it was not only a heap of stone and wood that went up in flames. In this fire it was Right that went up in flames, Truth and Law." In the twelve years of Nazi rule an entire people was corrupted and poisoned and from the heart of its youth was torn all aspirations for a better, more just and nobler world, the pious reverence before the altars of humanity, the chivalrous attitude toward the weak, the suffering, and the vanquished.

> Now, after witnessing the end [wrote Wiechert], we stand before the abandoned house and see the eternal stars sparkle over the heaps of ruins on earth or hear the rain dropping down on the graves of the dead and on the grave of an epoch. We are alone as no other people has ever been alone on this earth, and branded as no other people was ever branded before.

Wiechert called on the post-war generation to recognize the guilt of Germany, which might need a hundred years to be washed away, and he pleaded with them in these words:

> Everything that you do, do in order to relieve suffering. Let those who set their hearts on property dig out their houses and possessions from the rubble of destruction. You should dig out something else, something that is buried deeper than these: you should dig out God from under the heaps of rubble of the Anti-Christ. . . . You should dig out love from under the rubble of hate. And you should once again dig out truth and right and freedom, and you should set up before the eyes of your children once again the pictures toward which the best of all ages looked from the dust of their weary paths.[8]

Both Wiechert and Hesse gave up in despair their hopes for moral regeneration. Soon the works of nationalists like Ernst Jünger and Ernst von Salomon came to the fore to give a more acceptable expression to the mood of the post-war generation.

Former émigrés on the whole have played an insignificant role in post-war Germany. The most famous of all the émigrés, Thomas Mann, refused to return permanently to Germany despite urgent pleas by his former countrymen. By far the largest number of émigrés were Jews, and most of them felt that too great a chasm had been created between Germans and Jews to allow for Jewish participation in German recovery. The writer Alfred Döblin returned; Heinrich Mann did not. Wilhelm Hoegner, Max Brauer, and Ernst Reuter came back to play a role in the political arena, Hoegner as the first minister-president of Bavaria, Brauer as the mayor of Hamburg, and Reuter as the fiery anti-Communist mayor of the Western sectors of Berlin. Only in the Soviet zone did many émigré Communists return to play a prominent role in the new Germany. Otherwise there was reluctance to receive the exiles, and they were not accorded the same trust as those anti-Nazis who had remained at home. Among the more nationalist elements, especially the youth, there was a widespread feeling that both émigrés and former concentration-camp inmates were traitors to their country. This accounts in a great measure for the hesitant attitude among the youth toward the political and cultural leaders of German recovery.

The problem of German guilt was the most acute moral problem during the immediate years following the collapse. The accounts from the Nürnberg trial, disseminated by Allied licensed newspapers and radio, the films revealing the horrors of the concentration camps shown in all German movie houses, the omnipresence of Displaced Persons, the victims of Nazi brutality; the very physical collapse and ruin on all sides—all these reinforced the pressure of world opinion upon Germans to come to grips with the problem of guilt. Everywhere too, as Germans stepped outside, they were confronted with placards posted by the Allied military government: *"Das ist eure Schuld!"* (You are guilty!)

Several issues were involved in the problem of German guilt. These were: (1) responsibility for having allowed the Nazis to come to power, (2) responsibility for the popular and enthusiastic support of the régime, (3) responsibility for the concentration camps, (4) responsibility for World War II and all the havoc it brought, (5) responsibility for the extermination of six million Jews, (6) responsibility for all the suffering and destruction brought to the nations of Europe conquered by the Nazis, (7) responsibility even of those not immediately involved in criminal acts for having closed their eyes to these doings and for not having fought strenuously enough against them. With all the visible evidences, both physical and documentary, that were made available, there was no possibility of denying the facts of both conspiracy and crime. These facts could not be decried as inventions of Allied propaganda. "German atrocities" were a reality that was too stupendous and all-embracing to be shouted down as enemy distortions. There was, therefore, well-nigh general acceptance of the validity of the facts. Most Germans could agree with Rudolf Pechel when he wrote: "It is and remains a fact that Hitler and his régime unloosed the war, hurled the entire world into unspeakable misery, annihilated millions of human lives, attempted to exterminate the Jews with the most gruesome means, and placed all who did not conform to his views under the axe and on the rack of the executioner. The fact remains that the German people are co-responsible for this crime." [9]

While German writers like Friedrich Wilhelm Foerster and some Communist authors joined with foreigners like Lord Vansittart in a wholesale condemnation of the German past and the German people, anti-Nazi intellectuals in Germany looked for a formulation that would be in keeping with the objective facts of history but yet at the same time provide some measure of hope and self-respect for the conscience of Germany. This the noted Heidelberg philosopher Karl Jaspers attempted to do in a series of lectures delivered at the university and then published under the title *Die Schuldfrage* (Heidelberg, 1946).

Jaspers pointed out the urgency of coming to grips with the problem of German guilt and of drawing the necessary consequences. Germans, being first of all men, said Jaspers, cannot remain indifferent to world opinion.

Even more important, the guilt problem is "a question of life and death for the German soul." Only by means of this question can a conversion take place that will bring about the necessary profound renewal of the German soul.

With precise and delicate logic, yet with deep moral conviction and complete absence of casuistry or attempts to evade issues, Jaspers analyzed the problem of guilt in general, and of German guilt in particular. He distinguished between (1) criminal guilt, for which there is punishment by a court; (2) political guilt, for which there is responsibility and the obligation to make good, imposed by force or the power of the conqueror and which involves the loss or diminution of political power and political rights; (3) moral guilt, which can only be a matter between the individual and his conscience and from which come repentance and regeneration; and (4) metaphysical guilt, which rests on the solidarity of mankind and which makes each individual co-responsible for all injustice in the world, especially crimes committed in his presence or within his knowledge, for which God alone is the juridical power. Law can apply only to criminal guilt and to political responsibility, but not to moral and metaphysical guilt. Moreover, a crime is an individual act and there is, therefore, the important distinction between collective and individual guilt. A people as a whole, declared Jaspers, cannot be accused of a crime. Only individuals are criminals. It is also wrong to accuse an entire people of moral guilt. That too is a purely individual problem.

All Germans, concluded Jaspers, are "guilty" in one or another sense. The demands from the outside for punishment, responsibility, and restitution must be recognized and assumed by the German people. The minority guilty of war crimes and political crimes are liable to punishment, and in that sense the Nürnberg and other war crimes trials were not only necessary but just. The modern state is all-embracing and leaves no one outside. All Germans therefore bear the political responsibility "for our régime, for the acts of the régime, for the initiation of the war . . . and the behavior of the leaders we allowed to place themselves at our head." For this all Germans must assume the responsibility and must make good by work and achievements for all the havoc resulting from these acts. Germans must also reconcile themselves to assume the political consequences of such responsibility, which involve complete political impotence and material and physical want, which will last for a long time. But this responsibility as such does not touch the soul. It is moral and metaphysical guilt which involves the soul and which calls for contrition and regeneration. But contrition and regeneration can only come from within. "Against demands from the outside," disdainfully wrote Jaspers, "the only defense is silence."

Practically every German, wrote Jaspers, is subject to moral and metaphysical guilt, but these are for the conscience and solitary reflection of the individual. Each one must ask himself where he erred, where his feelings and thoughts and actions went astray. Each one must look for his guilt in himself and not in others or in the universal aspects of destiny and fate. Each one must make the resolve to turn about and to become better each day. "Without the path of purification out of the depths of a consciousness of guilt there is no truth to be realized by the Germans."

Jaspers himself anticipated the possibility of using his distinctions between political and moral guilt and between collective and individual guilt in order to evade both guilt and responsibility. Such a tendency did actually begin to appear as soon as the immediate shock of the guilt problem wore off. There were none, or very few, who dared as yet to deny the facts of the crimes of 1933–1945, but various types of excuses, partial justifications, and explanations began to appear. The most common justification was that the facts of Nazi crimes were unknown to any but the few in governmental positions. Some exaggerated beyond all proportions the opposition to the Nazis before 1933 and the resistance against them after 1933. Others pointed out that the German people were actually the first ones to be persecuted by the Nazis and that the concentration camp was instituted as an instrument for punitive measures against Germans. Others again directed the question to the Allies that if they trusted Hitler, beginning with the Vatican Pact, the Anglo-German naval treaty, the Munich agreements, and ending with the Nazi-Soviet Pact, why deride the Germans for placing their confidence in him? Still others, donning the mantle of cosmic aloofness, spoke of Nazism as a disease which infected the entire world, or else spoke philosophically and esthetically of *Schicksal* instead of *Schuld,* of destiny instead of guilt, and that Germany was therefore no more guilty of it than others. Here and there too came a suggestion that perhaps the facts had been exaggerated, that perhaps, for example, the figure of six million Jews exterminated was too high (as if a mistake of even several million, even if true, would minimize the savagery and brutality of the crime). By the time Germany became the diplomatic and propaganda battleground between East and West the guilt problem had receded far into the background, Jaspers and Wiechert were forgotten, and practical issues of *Realpolitik,* such as rearmament, the Ruhr, and the Saar, displaced the moral and spiritual problem of guilt and regeneration.[10]

As was the case after World War I, only on a much broader scale, the feeling arose that the plight of present-day Germany required a re-evaluation of the entire German past. Merely to decry Hitler and Hitlerism was not enough. As Karl Barth pointed out: "The real discussion has not even started yet as long as one talks with Germans about Hitler. The neuralgic point is only reached when you go back in your discussion to Bismarck." Political writers and publicists of the first several years of occupation gave voice to a reaction against militarism and Prussianism and against centralism as opposed to federalism. Luther, Frederick the Great, the romanticists, Bismarck, Nietzsche, and others were subjected to a more critical assessment than was usually prevalent in German historiography. Of the prominent historians Gerhard Ritter, associate of Goerdeler in the July 20 conspiracy, and the octogenarian dean of German historians, Friedrich Meinecke, took the lead in a more moderate re-evaluation of the German past. Meinecke's *Die deutsche Katastrophe* (Wiesbaden, 1946) was an interpretative attempt to explain the advent of Nazism and the ensuing catastrophe as a product of long-range forces in modern history in general and in Germany in particular. The inability of Germany to create a harmonious synthesis between *Geist* and *Macht* and between nationalism and socialism was the chief historical basis, according to Meinecke, for the road to ruin that led to Hitlerism.

Only the Communists and their allies, however, pressed for a really revolutionary attitude toward the German past. "A complete break with the past," declared Otto Grotewohl, "is indispensable," and the German education system must be reconstructed anew completely. This call for a complete break with the past fitted in, of course, with the entire anti-bourgeois ideology of the German Communist movement. The fact remains, nevertheless, that they alone advocated the necessary break with the German tradition which helped pave the way for Nazism. In the case of the others, with all their attempts to reinterpret German history, the remnants of national patriotism which glories in the traditional heroes of the German past still remain deeply rooted. Meinecke, while deploring Prussianism and militarism, and while admitting "the kernel of truth" in the Bismarck criticism, still cannot refrain from expressions of admiration for Boyen, for Treitschke, and for Bismarck.

The immediate reaction to defeat and occupation was a widespread feeling that Germany's role as a great power was over. Whatever future there was in store for her lay in the development of her spiritual and cultural heritage. There was a call for a return to Goethe and the classical liberal tradition. Meinecke called for the founding of a network of Goethe clubs throughout the land. Kogon and Dirks advocated a pacifistic Germany that would cultivate a spiritualized socialism and would become a leading partner in European federation. Germany's role, wrote Meinecke, would be like that of Sweden and Holland, both of whom were also formerly great powers. Now Germany was only "a burnt-out crater of great *Machtpolitik.*" This mood likewise underwent radical change after the cold war between Russia and the West came into the open. Now for many the prospects for Germany as a major power in Europe were once more both real and desirable.

6. THE CREATION OF TWO GERMAN STATES

By the end of 1946 the "German problem" was beginning to be entirely overshadowed by the "Russian problem." Attempts to achieve a common policy for Germany by the four occupying powers form a record of failure and frustration. While there were differences, and some of them serious differences, among the United States, Britain, and France, these nevertheless lent themselves to adjustment and compromise and the three Western powers achieved on the whole a unity of purpose as well as of action. No such unity with the Russians was effected.

The Potsdam conference had provided for a Council of Foreign Ministers to work out a common policy for Germany. Meetings of the foreign ministers were held in Paris in April–May and June–July of 1946, in New York in November–December, 1946, in Moscow in March, 1947, and in London in November–December, 1947, but the sessions of all these conferences were devoted almost entirely to endless recrimination and propaganda speeches, and the meetings ended in utter failure to achieve even a modicum of agreement. The sessions of the Allied Control Council in Berlin became more bitter, less frequent, and more fruitless until on March 20, 1948, Marshal Sokolovsky and his delegation stalked out of what was to be the last meeting of the Control Council, and the administrative machinery for four-power rule of Germany was at an end.

On March 31, 1948, the first measures toward a blockade of Berlin were initiated by the Russians, and on June 24th the "cold war" was on for good. All traffic to and from Berlin to the West was halted. The Western powers countered with the almost miraculous air-lift, a shuttle service of huge supply planes that brought in a daily average of 8,000 tons of supplies to the blockaded city. So effective was this Allied countermove that the Russians had to give up after 324 days of blockade, and arrangements were worked out for lifting the blockade and for reconvening the Council of Foreign Ministers in Paris on May 23, 1949. This meeting was no more successful than any of the preceding conferences. Germany seemed to be permanently divided between East and West, with Berlin a sensitive and precarious island in the center.

What was it that made the hoped-for co-operation between the U.S.S.R. and its wartime allies in the solution of the German problem prove so utterly ineffectual? The answer to this question lies not in the issues over which Bevin, Marshall, Acheson, and Schuman on one side, and Molotov and Vishinsky on the other, wrangled. They argued a great deal about reparations, about currency reform, about the Ruhr, about dismantling plants and decentralization, about prisoners of war still held by the Russians, about centralization versus federalization, about Berlin. All of these issues allowed for compromise, adjustment, and agreement. Even the most troublesome issue of all, that of the eastern borders of Germany and the territories annexed by Poland, which the Western Allies refused to accept as final, need not have been an insuperable obstacle to agreement. But behind all these issues was the ominous and portentous fact of imperialist expansionism of Soviet Communism after the war. The hopes engendered in the years 1941–1945 that the Soviet Union would be content with "socialism in one country" and would abandon its dream of "world revolution" began to disappear as the Cominform was established to take the place of the previously dissolved Comintern, as one by one Poland, Hungary, Rumania, Bulgaria, Albania, and Czechoslovakia went through the typical pattern of united front, people's democracy, Communist coup, and Soviet dictatorship. Yugoslavia was saved from the final stage of this cycle only through the effective resistance of Marshal Tito.

The activity of the Communist parties in Greece, Italy, France, and the Soviet zone of Germany bore witness to the fact that the Leninist dream of world revolution had not been abandoned, but rather transformed into a policy of imperialist expansionism based on a union of propaganda and enormous military power. Germany, with its rich industrial and technical potential, was more than ever before a most desirable prize for the Soviet Union. The Soviet Union, therefore, was not at all interested in arriving at any agreement with the Allies which would allow Germany to develop peacefully as a reunited and independent nation as long as it could hope to bring it within the orbit of the Communist-dominated Iron Curtain.

The Soviet Union could afford, for propaganda purposes, to call for "German unity" and for the evacuation of all foreign troops. This would place her forces directly behind the German border while the Allied forces were hundreds and thousands of miles away. A Communist coup could then repeat the pattern of the "peoples' democracies," and a "united Germany" would be under the heel of Soviet dictatorship. This the Western allies could not and dared not allow. They could not agree to "German unity" until they were sure that this would also mean independent sovereignty for Germany. To Molotov's proposal at the London Conference in December, 1947, for German unity as a precondition for a peace treaty, General Marshall replied, "Any German government called upon to administer a Germany divided as it is today by the policies of the occupying powers would be a sham and a delusion." Thus Germany remains more than ever tied up with the deeper problems of European and world politics, and the words of Gentz that the destiny of Europe is inextricably entwined with the destiny of Germany remain more true today than they were in 1815.

The Western Allies, after several years of separate zonal rule, yielded to American pressure and embarked on a policy which resulted in the creation of a West German federal republic. American policy, beginning with the speech by Secretary of State James Byrnes in Stuttgart on September 6, 1946, became increasingly intent on helping Germany to economic recovery and to political stability. Several factors entered into the modifications of American policy. As the power bearing the major share of occupying costs, and as the chief instigator of the European Recovery Program, the United States was interested in easing as much as possible the burdens on the American taxpayer by integrating German and European recovery. "The United States," declared General Marshall at Moscow on March 31, 1947, "is opposed to policies which will continue Germany as a congested slum or an economic poorhouse in the center of Europe." But the United States as the chief opponent to Soviet aggression was also forced to divert its fears from the dangers of a revived Germany to the more immediate danger of Soviet expansionism. Not that American authorities discounted the grave potential dangers still inherent in a revived Germany. Dean Acheson at the Paris Conference in June, 1949, declared that "one of the chief guarantees against a resurgence of German militarism would have been an agreement among the four powers" and that the absence of such an agreement created "a serious problem of security." But the policies of the U.S.S.R. forced the United States to risk the dangers emanating from the German problem in order to protect itself against the more imminent threat that came from the east. Reorientation of the German mind, denazification, re-education and democratization began to give way to economic reconstruction, political organization, and possible rearmament. General Eisenhower, who in 1945 had come "as a conqueror and not as a liberator," visited Frankfurt again in January, 1951, and told his German hearers that the German soldier as such did not lose his honor and that it was time to "let bygones be bygones."

Britain, never too greatly preoccupied with the "re-orientation" of Germany, always favored confining itself to diplomatic influence in Germany, and thus fell into line with American policy. It joined in the first step toward the political integration of Germany in the merger of the American and British zones to form the so-called Bizonia, promulgated in a series of agreements and proclamations culminating in the Bizonal Agreement of May 29, 1947.

France, haunted by the age-old fear of Germany, and pre-occupied most acutely with the problem of security, on which no French cabinet dared risk compromises, resisted for some time the pressure toward the creation of a German state. France feared not only the political revival of Germany but even more so the economic recovery of Germany before the rest of Europe. It protested constantly against the American and British measures to raise the level of German production and the policies designed to base European revival on German heavy industry. France refused to allow anything to be done in Germany at the expense of the security of France and the other neighbors of Germany. To the American contention that Germany must be able to pay her way by exports France replied that no European country was as yet able to do so, and the economic rehabilitation of Germany to enable her to do what no other European country could as yet do would again give her the economic primacy of western Europe with the inherent political and military dangers which that involved. By unilateral action, but later with support by both Britain and the United States, France incorporated the Saar region into the economic framework of France, although this policy was to be reversed by a popular plebiscite in 1955, which resulted in the Saar's return to Germany.

The Western Allies adopted the policy of restoring political government to the Germans from the bottom up. While, for purposes of military administration they first re-established the *Länder,* or states, and appointed German minister-presidents for them, self-rule and elections started with the villages and counties. On January 20 and January 27, 1946, the first free elections since Hitler were held in the United States zone for local councils. These were later followed by measures for wider self-government. Upon the failure of the London Conference of Foreign Ministers in 1947 the Western powers decided to proceed alone to deal with the pressing problems in Germany. On February 23, 1948, the foreign ministers of the United States, Britain, and France met in London for this purpose. They were joined by the ministers of the Benelux nations on February 26. As a result of these meetings it was decided to merge the three Western zones, to incorporate West Germany into the European Recovery Program, and to arrange for a German Constitutional Assembly to draw up a constitution for the state. This constitution, the Allied leaders declared,

should be such as to enable the Germans to play their part in bringing to an end the present division of Germany, not by the reconstitution of a centralized Reich but by means of a federal form of government which adequately protects the rights of the respective states, and which at the same time provides for adequate central authority and which guarantees the rights and freedoms of the individual.

Negotiations among the Allies, especially to overcome French hesitation, and conferences with German political leaders, were carried on to lay the basis for the end of military government and the setting up of a West German state. German political leaders were extremely wary of assuming leadership in the creation of a German state. They were afraid that such a move would contribute toward the permanent partition of Germany, and they knew the effectiveness of the propaganda from the Eastern zone that proclaimed, "Woe betide the Germans who help in partitioning our country." On July 19, 1948, the minister-presidents of the *Länder* addressed a letter to the Western powers urging that "everything should be avoided that would give the character of a state to the organization that is to be established." They were also hesitant about using the term "constitution." Both French resistance and German reluctance were finally overcome. On July 26, 1948, the German leaders agreed to launch the state, and on April 8, 1949, the Allied powers agreed to an Occupation Statute to govern the conditions under which the new state was to function. The Occupation Statute was transmitted to the German Parliamentary Council convened at Bonn. Despite opposition by the Socialist leaders it was ratified; and the German constitution was approved on May 8, 1949. With Bonn as the permanent capital, the Second Republic was to become known as the Bonn Republic.

According to the new arrangements Allied military government was to be replaced by three Allied high commissioners. Allied troops were to remain in Germany, and the Allies retained control over German disarmament and demilitarization, over the Ruhr, restitution claims, reparations and decartelization, over the remaining DP's, over foreign affairs, foreign trade and exchange, war criminals, the protection of the basic law of the land, and over press and radio to protect the occupying powers. French uneasiness was allayed by the agreement by the Allies that unanimity of the three powers was necessary for the regulation of these policies as well as for amendments to the federal constitution.

The "basic law" which was worked out by the Parliamentary Council—the word "constitution" was avoided to stress the *provisional* character of the new West German state—carefully avoided the mistakes of the Weimar Constitution. Remembering the baneful role played by President von Hindenburg in the collapse of Weimar, the framers decided to create a weak Presidency with almost exclusively ceremonial functions; to avoid the powerful position implicit in a plebiscitarian mandate, the President was to be elected indirectly by the legislature [11] rather than directly by the people for a five-year term (with one re-election permitted). Neither of the two presidents of the Bonn Republic, Theodor Heuss (1949–1959) and Heinrich Lübke (1959–   ), has played an important political role. To avoid ministerial instability—one of the flaws of the Weimar Republic—the basic law provided for a strong chancellor with clear-cut authority to set the guidelines of policy and the power to appoint and dismiss ordinary Cabinet ministers. The chancellor also received institutional safeguards against too easy dismissal by the legislature: under the terms of the "basic law," parliament must invest a new Chancellor by majority vote before an incumbent chancellor can be dismissed, thereby avoiding the frequent periods without a regular government which had been so characteristic of Weimar and other parliamentary democracies. The drafters of the basic law, remembering the Nazis' abuse of freedom to destroy freedom during the Weimar period, provided for the outlawing, by court action, of all parties hostile to the established democratic order. They intended to eliminate extremist parties of both the right and the left, and this was in fact accomplished by the German Supreme Court when it banned neo-Nazi parties in 1952 and the Communist party in 1956. The ensuing simplification of the West German party structure has proved a boon to the functioning of parliamentary democracy. Of even greater importance in reducing the number of Germany's political parties was an electoral law (not formally part of the basic law, but an essential ingredient of the "working constitution" after 1950) which eliminated splinter parties by making 5 per cent of the total vote a *prerequisite* for any representation in the Bundestag (lower house of parliament). Whereas the Weimar Reichstag counted at times as many as 15 parties, today's Bonn Bundestag contains only three.

Parliamentary democracy was strengthened in still other ways. Half of the Bundestag deputies were to be elected directly from single-member constituencies; this allowed personal contact between deputy and voters and weakened the power of party bureaucracies. After the direct mandates won were subtracted from the total seats due to any party under the proportional principle, the remaining half were distributed on the basis of proportional representation. The result is that Bundestag representation expresses the principle of proportionality as well as did the Weimar Reichstag, but with the above-mentioned advantages of forcing half the deputies to establish direct contact with the voters and making them relatively independent of party bosses (under Weimar *all* deputies entered parliament through the party list, whose composition was completely in the hands of party managers). Parliament was also strengthened through the elimination of the plebiscitarian provisions (for initiatives and referenda which bypassed parliament) which had been abused for demagogic purposes during the Weimar period.

Two other valuable features provided by the Bonn "basic law" were judicial review and an effectively functioning federal system. The German Supreme Court, sitting at Karlsruhe, was given the right to declare laws and executive actions unconstitutional: this was to provide some protection against the arbitrary tendencies of Chancellor Adenauer. A workable federalism, based upon an approximate equilibrium of power among eleven constituent *Länder* of the Federal Republic, replaced the unfortunate system—common to both the Bismarckian and the Weimar constitutions—of *de facto* Prussian domination due to Prussia's exceeding the combined area, population, and wealth of all the other states. The partition of Germany between East and West and the formal dissolution of Prussia in 1947 by the Allied Control Council's fiat eliminated the danger of Prussian hegemony. The popular revulsion against centralization after its abuse by the Nazis (who had reduced the once proud *Länder* to mere provinces) plus strong pressure from the American Military Government, resulted in the restoration of the *Länder* as viable political units exercising important political functions and evoking strong local loyalties. They provided many Socialist leaders—deprived of governmental power on the federal level during the entire Adenauer era—with an opportunity to acquire administrative experience and thus to avoid the political sterility which tends to afflict parties reduced to a permanent opposition role. About a third of the *Länder* usually have Socialist premiers, and several others include Socialists in their governing coalitions. The result has been to make the Socialist part of the West German "establishment" despite their permanent opposition position in Bonn.

The first federal elections were held on August 14, 1949. Two strongly anti-Socialist parties, the Christian Democratic Union (C.D.U.) under Konrad Adenauer and the Free Democratic Party (F.D.P.) under Theodor Heuss, received respectively 139 and 52 seats; the Social Democrats (S.P.D.) under Kurt Schumacher received 131. (There were also several minor parties because the above-mentioned 5 per cent requirement was not yet in effect.) Since no party had received an independent majority in the election, there was some debate concerning what kind of coalition government should be formed; many favored a "Great Coalition" to include both the C.D.U. and the S.P.D., or even an all-party government in view of the perilous condition of German affairs which appeared to make normal partisan politics undesirable. Adenauer, the strongest man of the strongest party, however, insisted upon a predominantly right-wing coalition government based upon the C.D.U., the F.D.P., and several minor parties. He was invested with the chancellorship by a bare majority of 202 to 201. (No one doubted that he had contributed to this result by voting for himself.) Theodor Heuss became the first President as part of the coalition bargain; while never emerging from the political shadow of Adenauer, he was to fill this office with intellectual distinction for the next ten years. Kurt Schumacher became the first leader of the opposition.

Konrad Adenauer assumed power under extremely unpropitious circumstances—a fact to be remembered in evaluating the successes of his government. His personal political position was precarious, as indicated by his narrow majority on the investiture vote. Many viewed him, if only in view of his age (73), as a temporary transition figure. His party, the C.D.U., was highly heterogeneous and by no means unanimously in favor of his right-wing domestic policies. The SPD provided a strong opposition, and there was a widespread feeing that Socialism constituted the inevitable "wave of the future." It must also be remembered that democracy and parliament had little prestige in a country where both had failed egregiously in 1933.

The ruin wrought by World War II in Germany had hardly begun to be repaired during the four years of military occupation. Some ten million refugees from the East, demanding assimilation into the fabric of West German society, constituted a source of bitterness and demoralization. To be sure, economic life had begun to revive dramatically after the currency reform of 1948—but the amenities of life remained virtually unknown, the housing situation was catastrophic, and millions continued to live on the edge of starvation. West Germany did not possess sovereign control of its economic life; the Allied governments were planning the internationalization of the Ruhr, several industries with military potential— for example, aviation and shipbuilding—were formally prohibited, and factories continued to be dismantled for the payment of reparations and to achieve demilitarization. Political sovereignty was similarly restricted under the stringent provisions of the Occupation Statute; this included a specific clause under which the Allied Powers possessed the right of withdrawing the partial self-government conferred in 1949. The Germans were treated, in short, as children who were on probation; their every action was watched with mistrust by a world which could not forget the horrors of a Nazism overthrown but four years earlier.

The Germany of 1949 was divided between a Russian controlled East Zone and the Allied-sponsored new West German Republic. The prospect that the partition would become permanent was increased when the Russians answered the creation of the West German Federal Republic (proclaimed on May 23, 1949) by launching the rival (East) German Democratic Republic on October 7, 1949. The chronological priority of the West German state—and the presumed primary responsibility of the Western Powers for Germany's partition—was to become a key theme in Communist propaganda; though it could be explained by the simple fact that the Russians were interested in perpetuating the post-war chaos in the hope that hunger and despair would drive Germans to communism, whereas the Western Allies were eager to achieve a settled order based upon all four zones if possible but upon the three Western zones if necessary. There was, in any case, a world of difference between the Federal Republic based upon the will of the people as expressed in free elections and the so-called Democratic Republic, which was a Communist puppet state resting upon Russian bayonets. The East German régime was ruled by the Socialist Union Party, which was begotten, under Russian pressure, through the shotgun marriage of Communists and Social Democrats in 1946. Wilhelm Pieck, a former colleague of Liebknecht and Luxemburg and now the elder statesman of German communism, was elected President of the German Democratic Republic; Otto Grotewohl, a former Social Democrat, was elected Premier to symbolize the united front of the two parties; the real center of power was Deputy Premier Walter Ulbricht, a Communist bureaucrat who was to show an uncanny ability to survive changes in the Kremlin line while never lacking in servility to his Russian masters. Several non-Socialist parties were able to function by toeing the Communist party line and allowing their leadership to be infiltrated by Communists and fellow-travelers.

The East German Democratic Republic conformed completely to the pattern of a Communist satellite state. There was manipulation of elections, censorship of information and culture, concentration camps for political opponents, prohibition of contact with the West, and a huge propaganda apparatus aiming at ideological conformity. Key industries were nationalized and the economy was operated in accordance with a central plan; consumer preference was disregarded in favor of the needs of the community as defined by Communist bureaucrats. Junker estates were expropriated, ostensibly to be divided among the peasantry though in fact as a preliminary for establishing collective farms. The churches, both Protestant and Catholic, were harassed through such measures as curtailing traditional state subsidies, discriminating against professed Christians in job promotions, and setting up a Marxist "youth consecration ceremony" (*Jugendweihe*) to compete with confirmation; hostility was inevitable since Christianity was the natural foe of Marxist atheism, and because the churches had been too exclusively identified with the now dispossessed upper classes. The Communists also introduced extensive educational reforms which broke the upper-class character of secondary schools, thereby increasing social mobility for the children of the poor provided they showed proper respect toward the Communist party line.

Some of these measures—for example, the break-up of Junker power—had been long overdue and evidently required a Communist dictatorship to be achieved; but in combination they constituted the imposition of an alien pattern upon the 20 million Germans living in the East Zone, one which was bitterly resented by the vast majority of the population. The discontent of the East Zone was exacerbated by the existence of a free West Berlin in the very center of the country, and a free West Germany across what was a completely arbitrary border. There was no question that most Germans, whether in the East or the West, resented partition and hoped for the reunification of their country. To achieve this reunification became one of the avowed aims of German policy after 1949—and the failure to achieve this goal casts a tragic shadow over the otherwise extremely successful record of the Bonn Republic.

CHAPTER XXIII

The Bonn Republic, 1949-1965

Wandlung der Deutschen? Worin besteht sie?
Sie besteht in der Tatsache einer grundlegenden Wandlung
der deutschen Politik. Die Abkehr der deutschen Politik unserer
Zeit von der nationalstaatlichen Souveränitätspolitik und die
Einfügung des freien Teiles Deutschlands in die Integrations-
gebilde der europäischen und der atlantischen Welt ist ebenso
geschichtlich erwiesene Wahrheit wie die geistigreligiöse Wandlung in Deutschland. Sie hat nicht nur den Staatsbegriff verän-
dert, sondern sie ist in die Tiefe des nationalen Bewusstseins ge-
drungen und hat es verwandelt.

EUGEN GERSTENMAIER

1. CONDITIONING FACTORS

While the situation at the beginning of the Bonn Republic was unpropitious, there were also factors which were favorable to the launching of
Germany's second experiment in liberal democracy. The very fact that
matters looked so bleak in 1949 meant that it was comparatively easy to
achieve some gains for the broad mass of the German population; any
successes won on the road to the "normalization" of life were certain to
redound to the credit of the new regime. Much of the necessary post-war
"dirty work" had been done, moreover, by the Military Government, in
sharp contrast to the situation at the time of the Weimar Republic. The
boundaries of Germany had been determined (for all practical purposes)
at the Potsdam Conference without consulting the German people or any
German government; the Bonn Republic was not at its very beginning
confronted, as the Weimar Republic had been, by the agonizing choice
of whether or not to accept an onerous peace treaty. Whereas the Weimar
government had been widely discredited by its prolonged inability to deal
with the inflation of 1920–1923, the drastic currency reform of 1948,
ending the post-war inflation at the price of much social injustice, was
undertaken by the Military Government. The building of a well-functioning
West German democracy was facilitated also by the growing homogeneity
of the country—the result of Nazism, war, partition, and Military Government. The formerly Junker-dominated East—long a liability to the growth

of democracy—lay outside the territory of the Federal Republic; the war-time evacuations from bombed cities and the refugee innundation of 1945 had diminished regional differences and led to an unprecedented inter-mingling of people from different areas, regions, and classes. With the elimination of Prussia, the German-Prussian dualism had ceased to exist, while Bavarian separatism was tamed when it lost its favorite battlecry, "Resistance to Berlin."

The international situation also proved favorable to the development of German democracy. Nationalism was waning in Europe with the revival of a common European consciousness; there was a widespread willingness to accept "reformed" Germans as good Europeans. Of still greater im-portance was the fact of the Cold War, which dominated world politics after 1947. The Cold War reduced the East Germans to the level of a Russian colony, to be sure, since Russia could not be expected to surrender its most advanced European position, least of all in a period of international tension; but it simultaneously made the West Germans increasingly at-tractive as an alliance partner for the United States. The reversal of America's German policy from its initially vindictive phase, symbolized by the Morgenthau Plan, to one of wooing German friendship, was partly the result of economic necessity—Germany was needed, in view of the historic interdependence of the European economy, to make the Marshall Plan successful—partly the result of strategic expediency—the recognition that Germany was an indispensable partner of any effective anti-Com-munist alliance in Europe. The United States was to prove Germany's helpful ally and benevolent friend on what might have been a hard road to economic prosperity, effective democracy, and international respectability.

One additional factor contributed to the democratic success of the Bonn Republic should be noted: Germans had tried every possible form of government in the previous half century, and all had been found wanting even more than liberal democracy. The authoritarian monarchy of William II had led Germany into World War I; the incompetence of Ludendorff's military dictatorship had led to Germany's defeat in 1918; the presidential dictatorship of the years 1930–1933 had failed to master the economic depression and paved the way for Nazism; and Nazism had resulted in the greatest catastrophe in German history. Communism was discredited by the aftermath of Nazi propaganda, the misconduct of the Russian troops in 1945, and its imposition upon the East Zone by Russian Military Government. The liberal democracy of the Weimar Republic also lacked, to be sure, a brilliant record; but its sins had been those of omission rather than commission. Democracy stood a little bit less discredited than all possible competing systems; its establishment was now, moreover, for the first time in German history, an imperative of foreign policy. The return of Germany into the community of nations required American friendship, and American friendship was unthinkable unless Germany foreswore its authoritarian and Nazi past and became a functioning liberal democracy.

Perhaps the greatest asset of the fledgling Federal Republic was the leadership of Konrad Adenauer. Adenauer, born in 1876, had already been a powerful political figure during the Weimar Republic, serving for sixteen years with great distinction as mayor of Cologne before his dismissal by the Nazis in 1933. He had spent the years 1933 to 1945 in retirement, and had been briefly arrested after the July 20, 1944, conspiracy. Adenauer's personality was, however, not cast for the role of a hero of the resistance; he was far too cautious to have engaged in overt anti-Nazi activity, and while keeping admirably clear of complicity in Nazism he survived to play a role in the post-Nazi era. As a victim of Nazism he was again made mayor of Cologne in 1945 by the Military Government, but his proud independence made him a difficult subordinate; he was fired by the British in 1946, allegedly for incompetence. This proved a great blessing to his subsequent career: to be a victim of *both* Nazism and the Military Government was a good starting position for winning the sympathy of German public opinion in the first post-war years, and his dismissal left Adenauer free to become one of the organizers of the C.D.U., first in the British Zone and eventually in all of Western Germany. He came to the chancellorship in 1949 because he had become the leading figure of the C.D.U; it is unlikely that he would have reached this position if he had remained mayor of Cologne, tied down by local administrative responsibilities.

Adenauer was in many ways ideally suited, both by temperament and by outlook, to the situation of 1949. He was a man of supreme patience and great negotiating skill, two essential qualities in a chancellor whose main task was to wring concessions from the Western Allied Powers. His lifelong dislike of Prussia and Berlin meant that he had little reluctance about building a state whose center of gravity would lie in his native Rhineland. He had always been a good Catholic, a fact which became an advantage in a West German state where the old German—primarily Protestant—establishment played a much diminished role. (The post-1870 ascendancy of Protestantism had been based upon the largely Lutheran territories now behind the Iron Curtain.) He had always been a good European, an asset because German nationalism had "burned itself out" after the Nazi debacle. Although a democrat in the sense that he ruled on the basis of election victories, Adenauer had a strong authoritarian streak in his personality. This not only made him an extremely effective administrator but fitted him—when combined with the patriarchal aura surrounding a vigorous man of advanced years—to become a "father figure" to millions of Germans: a figure much needed during the difficult transition from the Führer state to democratic self-government. These qualities, plus his extraordinary skill at manipulating men and maintaining party unity in the faction-ridden C.D.U., made him succeed in winning elections and wielding power for fourteen years.

One of his greatest qualities was a positive genius for simplifying issues and converting the majority of his fellow-countrymen to his views. This holds especially true of the field of foreign policy, where Adenauer made a clear-cut option for the West. He understood that the challenge of communism could be met only by Western unity, and was convinced that Germany could win acceptance as an equal from its former Western enemies by a frank offer of partnership. He saw that Germany was too small to conduct an independent foreign policy in an age dominated by atomic super-powers, and was never tempted by a seesaw policy between East and West such as Stresemann had conducted in the 1920's. His option for the West was predicated upon the belief that German reunification could not be attained by flirting with the Russians; and in any case he refused to sacrifice the solid advantages of Western partnership to a will-o'-the-wisp pursuit of unification through various schemes of neutralization proposed by the Soviet Union (all of which involved cutting close Western ties). Adenauer's professed belief that reunification could be achieved through Western strength rather than an accommodation with the Russians has not been endorsed by the course of events; it remains uncertain, incidentally, whether this was his *real* belief or whether he felt rather that the intrinsically desirable goal of Western integration required the false colors of reunification in order to have smooth sailing with German public opinion.

2. THE ROAD TO SOVEREIGNTY, 1949–1955

The immediate objective of Adenauer's foreign policy was to win German sovereignty and independence from the restraints imposed by the Occupation Statute of 1949. Regaining sovereignty involved a difficult transition in relations with the Allied Powers from an occupied country to an equal alliance partner. Adenauer believed that everything depended upon the establishment of mutual trust between Germans and Allies: the renegotiation of their contractual relationship would become a relatively simple matter once the Allies accepted Germany as a reliable partner. Adenauer had no difficulty in establishing excellent relations with the United States— two successive secretaries of state, the Democrat Dean Acheson and the Republican John Foster Dulles, became his strong admirers. He never established similar cordiality with the British, but this did not matter seriously because Britain in fact subordinated her German policy to America's. Adenauer's greatest success lay in wooing France. He saw the transcendent importance of burying the Franco-German hatchet as a prelude to European unity, and he won the friendship of successive French governments by a skilful mixture of material concessions and the refusal to haggle over minor matters. Adenauer was willing to negotiate economic agreements under which Germany made most of the sacrifices and France received most of the advantages; for example, the Common Market Fund for assisting the economic development of underdeveloped territories, to which Germany contributed heavily while the money was primarily spent in France's colonies. Adenauer courageously defied German national sentiment in order to achieve the settlement of the long-standing Franco-German dispute over the Saar (1955) described below. He had the satisfaction over the years of seeing the "official friendship" between Paris and Bonn ripen into a genuine reconciliation between the two long-hostile nations.

The Federal Republic won sovereignty through a series of steps which progressively whittled down the Occupation Statute of 1949. The first step was taken by the Petersberg agreement of November, 1949 (named after the Petersberg, a mountain overlooking Bonn, where the Allied High Commissioners had their headquarters). Under its terms West Germany was permitted to establish consular representation abroad, a spur to the revival of foreign trade and an entering wedge for the eventual restoration of sovereignty in the field of foreign affairs. The Allies also agreed to curtail the dismantling of German industry, which had become an obvious anachronism in the new atmosphere of European co-operation inagurated by the Marshall Plan; and they terminated the "ceiling of industry" regulations (establishing a top limit to permissible production) which had survived as an Allied Control Council directive from 1946. In return Adenauer agreed to German participation in (and hence acceptance of) the proposed International Authority for the Ruhr, a dangerous concession from the German national point of view since it involved loss of German sovereignty over its key industrial area without reciprocity by other powers. The Socialist opposition leader Schumacher was so furious about this "surrender" that he attacked Adenauer as "the Chancellor of the Allies."

The wisdom of making this "surrender" became clear, however, when it did not need to be implemented. The French Foreign Minister Robert Schuman, shifting from a policy of bullying Germany to one of seeking genuine Franco-German reconciliation, proposed on May 9, 1950, placing the entire German and French production of coal and steel under a joint high authority (allowing, also, for the participation of other European nations). This multilateral "Schuman Plan" was enthusiastically accepted by Adenauer; he valued it as the cornerstone of European economic unity and appreciated the additional bonus of the plan's terminating the International Ruhr Authority before it was even launched. The European Coal and Steel Authority was joined by Italy and the Benelux countries as well after elaborate negotiations completed in 1951. It went into operation on July 25, 1952, with Luxemburg as the seat of the joint High Authority.

West Germany's resumption of sovereignty was facilitated after the summer of 1950 by the American desire for German rearmament and Adenauer's willingness to go along with the Americans. Few developments were so surprising and so certain to stir up bitter controversy. The Allied Occupation Powers had spent much effort after 1945 to purge all surviving remnants of German militarism, more especially since the Prussian General Staff held a high position in the demonology of German history which dominated so much Allied thinking. The anti-militarism of the Occupying Powers sometimes went to the ridiculous length of insisting upon the removal of monuments to German veterans and the renaming of streets which had commemorated victorious generals and battles. All this changed abruptly when American military planners, seized by near-panic after the outbreak of the Korean War in June, 1950, contemplated the defenselessness of Western Europe in the face of a possible Russian attack. The NATO alliance, formed in April, 1949, was little more than a paper structure; the only way of turning it into an effective defense force appeared to be the rearming of Germany. Were the Germans not a military nation, and did they not have valuable experience in fighting the Russians?

The proposal to rearm Germany raised a hornet's nest of difficulties. The Russians protested with some reason the violation of the Potsdam agreement and denounced the danger of reviving German militarism; many West European victims of Nazi aggression were horrified at the renewed prospect of guns in German hands; while the Germans themselves—to the surprise of many observers—proved genuinely reluctant to rearm. Militarism had been thoroughly discredited by the horrors of World War II; most young Germans were appalled by the prospect of repeating the fate of their older brothers by spending the best years of their lives in the army ("Ohne mich"—"count me out"—became the popular slogan of this age group). Many Germans who cared deeply about the development of democratic institutions (especially in the ranks of the Social Democrats) feared the domestic consequences of rearmament; had not the Reichswehr of Seeckt and Schleicher been a sinister anti-democratic influence during the Weimar Republic? Would not a new army once more imbue young Germans with anti-democratic values? Further difficulties were raised by the possibility of a German civil war. The new West German army would become part of the anti-Communist NATO forces; the East Zone was, meanwhile, raising an army (called, for propaganda reasons, a militarized police force) as an integral part of the Communist anti-NATO forces soon to be formally united in the Warsaw Pact Alliance. Was it fair or politic to ask Germans to shoot against Germans, especially when many West Germans had close relatives living in the East Zone?

All these difficulties did not deter Adenauer from offering to the Americans—without consulting his cabinet—a German contribution to Western defense. Always a realist, he saw that German rearmament was eventually inevitable, and he appreciated its present value for securing an equal status for Germany within the Western alliance. Adenauer made it clear that he expected the substantial restoration of sovereignty as the concomitant of rearmament. The two years from 1950 to 1952 were to be characterized by three parallel negotiations: the establishment of the Schuman Plan Authority; the revision of the Occupation Statute in the form of a new "Germany Treaty" (May 26, 1952) which gave West Germany full sovereignty; and prolonged discussion concerning the details of a European Defense Community (E.D.C.) into which a German military contribution would be integrated. The French were adamant against the recreation of a German national army; Adenauer, never a nationalist, was perfectly willing, indeed eager, to fit German rearmament into a European framework. The treaty establishing the E.D.C., signed in Paris on May 27, 1952 (one day after the new "Germany Treaty"), deferred to French sensibilities by proposing German military units no larger than regimental size.

The years 1952–1954 were years of frustration for Konrad Adenauer. He secured, to be sure, ratification for both the E.D.C. and the "Germany Treaty" from the Bundestag, where he possessed a large majority after the 1953 elections. He could not, however, get the French to take similar action; while successive French governments paid lip service to the E.D.C. they did not dare put the treaty to a vote of ratification. The movement toward greater European integration, virtual German sovereignty, and German rearmament appeared stifled; and it suffered a serious setback when French Premier Pierre Mendès-France, terminating the policy of evasion, presided over the defeat of E.D.C. in the French National Assembly in August, 1954. This defeat was due partly to continued hostility to German rearmament in *any* form and partly to a resurgence of French nationalism which opposed the supra-national features of the E.D.C. which were its particular merits in the eyes of "good Europeans" like Adenauer.

With the E.D.C. killed, conditions obviously could not return to the status of 1950. Some form of German rearmament had become inevitable; so had the conferral of sovereignty upon West Germany. The British Foreign Secretary Anthony Eden, co-operating closely with American Secretary of State John Foster Dulles, found the new formula under which the Federal Republic was encouraged to rearm (now in the form of a national army) in return for a voluntary renunciation of atomic, bacteriological, and chemical weapons (the so-called ABC weapons); received sovereignty except for a continued Allied responsibility for Berlin and for promoting German unification (two restrictions desired by the Germans); and was admitted to membership in the NATO alliance. These plans were implemented through detailed negotiations in the winter of 1954–1955 and secured speedy ratification by the legislatures of all the affected powers. Adenauer was able to proclaim the virtual restoration of German sovereignty—limited, alas, to West Germany—on May 5, 1955, only ten years after the most catastrophic defeat suffered by any power in modern history.

The implementation of the decision for rearmament was one of the main tasks of the Adenauer government in the next few years. The new German army was organized by Defense Minister Franz Joseph Strauss, a burly

Bavarian politician who—unlike the civilian defence ministers of the Weimar Republic—was never intimidated by the generals. A genuine attempt was made to avoid the abuses traditional in German army life, such as the caste consciousness of the officer corps and the brutal treatment of the rank and file. An early case of brutal treatment, involving a sick soldier who was compelled to join a cross-country march and died from overexertion, resulted in the exemplary punishment of the officer responsible. The Bundestag, following a useful Swedish example, appointed a special official (the *Wehrbeauftragte*) charged with receiving confidential complaints about mistreatment and investigating their validity. Recruits were taught to consider themselves "civilians in uniform," and the barracks became at times—to the surprise and horror of traditionalists—centers of democratic indoctrination. The Socialist Party, which had initially opposed rearmament as incompatible with both the democratization and the reunification of Germany, cooperated, fortunately, in planning the internal structure of the new army. The fear that the *Bundeswehr* would provide a threat to the democratization of German life proved ill-founded. Care was taken that the upper officer corps be kept free of generals who had served Hitler too ardently, though the appointment to high command posts of both participants and non-participants in the conspiracy of July 20, 1944, proved inevitable. (The Communist charge that all the senior officers of the new German army had once been "Hitler's generals" was technically correct.) It was one of the greatest achievements of Adenauer and Strauss that the new army became an integral part of the political structure of the Federal Republic; unlike Seeckt's *Reichswehr* in the 1920's, it did not become an authoritarian *imperium in imperio* within the framework of the liberal democratic state.

The German army stood under over-all NATO command; this minimized the danger—which was in any case minute, but served as a scarecrow to anti-Germans—that it might be used by the West German government to secure the forcible reunification of Germany and the reconquest of lost Eastern territories. As the Federal Republic won full acceptance as a NATO partner, German officers were increasingly appointed to high positions in the NATO command structure. Germany's unswerving loyalty to the alliance, her willingness to surrender sovereignty to international NATO bodies, and her absolute firmness in the face of both Russian threats and blandishments made Germany a model NATO member—although resentments born of the Nazi period still caused friction when German officers were placed in command of non-German troops.

One left-over of the past, Franco-German friction over the Saar, was eliminated in the winter of 1955–1956. The French had economically incorporated the Saar (with its valuable coal mines and steel mills) after 1945 while establishing a political puppet régime willing to accept this arrangement. The Bonn government, though far from nationalist in its outlook, could not be reconciled to the loss of the Saar; it was aware, of course, of the precedent which open renunciation would create for the far more important case of the East Zone with *its* puppet regime. The French, realizing the ultimate untenability of the *fait accompli* of 1945 now that Germany was returning to the ranks of independent powers, proposed in 1955 an International Statute for the Saar. Adenauer, placing co-operation with France above the national desire for the return of the Saar, supported the Statute and urged the Saar population to do likewise; it was, however, voted down by a two-thirds majority in a popular referendum on October 23, 1955. The French saw the handwriting on the wall and soon agreed to the Saar's reunion with Germany in return for generous economic concessions offered by Adenauer. It was generally considered one of the Chancellor's finest achievements that he had won a complete victory in the Saar question without antagonizing France in the process.

Adenauer recognized that Germany's "moral rehabilitation" in the world required that material restitution be made to the Jewish victims of Nazi genocide. He proposed to pay reparations to Israel—the representative of world Jewry and the haven of many Jews who had escaped extermination—for the Jewish properties seized by Hitler's government. Adenauer tactfully showed full understanding for the reluctance of the Israelis to enter into direct negotiations with the German government and used American intermediaries to achieve a treaty in 1952. Under its terms West Germany agreed to pay about a billion dollars over a twelve-year period, a sum which proved indispensable for the economic development of Israel. Some critics sneeringly called German reparations "conscience money," but the German government recognized clearly and publicly that economic reparation could never wipe away moral guilt; the agreement was, however, a laudable attempt to repair whatever *material* damage could be repaired. It was voted by a unanimous Bundestag and obviously bore the approval of the great majority of Germans.

3. THE REUNIFICATION QUESTION, BERLIN, AND FOREIGN POLICY

Adenauer's spectacular success in winning sovereignty and Western partnership for the Federal Republic was unfortunately accompanied by the hardening of the partition of Germany as the German Democratic Republic became consolidated. It became a cardinal objective of West German policy to forestall this consolidation by preventing diplomatic recognition by the outside world. The Federal Republic claimed for itself the position of being the *only* legitimate German state, and it refused to enter into any relations with the German Democratic Republic (except for certain technical contacts affecting the mails, telephone service, and arrangements for inter-zonal trade), on the ground that there was no legal or moral equivalency between the West German government, freely elected by the people, and the East German government, imposed by Russian force upon a hostile population. The Bonn government insisted that all states friendly to it maintain a similar policy of non-recognition of the East German government; under the terms of the "Hallstein doctrine"—named after the high official of the Foreign Office who later became president of the Common Market Authority—it threatened to break diplomatic relations with any state which embarked upon the "unfriendly act" of official political relations with East Germany. (An exception was made in the case of Russia, on the ground that it was one of the former occupying powers with a legal obligation to work for the unification of Germany—a special position which obviously required diplomatic relations despite the fact that Russia was the sponsor of Ulbricht's regime.) The doctrine was formally invoked only once—against Yugoslavia—when Tito recognized the German Democratic Republic in 1957; many Asian and African nations have, however, been permitted to circumvent the Hallstein doctrine by the simple device of maintaining embassies in Bonn and commercial consulates —which fall short of the proscribed official *political* relations—in East Berlin.

The West German policy of refusing to take official cognizance of unpleasant realities is also applied to the Polish annexation of formerly German territories lying to the east of the Oder and Neisse rivers. It will be recalled that these territories had been provisionally assigned to Poland at the Potsdam conference in 1945; the German population which had lived there for centuries was expelled, and a Polish population—coming partly from Polish territories in the East ceded to Russia—settled there. All Poles, however much they differed on other political subjects, agreed that these areas had become an integral part of the Polish state recreated after World War II; and there was much international sympathy for this attitude in view of the sufferings inflicted by Germans upon Poles during the Nazi period. Few West Germans believed that the "lost Eastern territories" would ever become German again, and the Federal Republic explicitly renounced the use of force for their recovery. The Bonn government insisted, however, that their final disposition must await a future treaty of peace between a reunited Germany and the victorious powers of World War II. This insistence was motivated partly by the old diplomatic rule that one never surrenders anything without a specific *quid pro quo,* partly by the desire not to antagonize the organized refugee groups (*Landsmannschaften*) who were ready to pounce upon "politicians of renunciation" (*Verzichtpolitiker*). The German Democratic Republic, on the other hand, readily yielded to Russian pressure and formally accepted the Oder-Neisse line as a "peace frontier"; to West Germans this was but another example of the "un-German" character of the East-Zone regime.

The hollow and unpopular nature of the German Democratic Republic was dramatically exposed by the uprising of June 17, 1953. This began with a riot of East Berlin workers against the exacting "work norms" imposed by the Communist government—norms that no Western trade union would have tolerated for a moment, and which constituted sheer exploitation of the workers by the state. The disorders quickly spread to other cities of East Germany; the government of Pieck, Grotewohl, and Ulbricht found itself completely isolated from the population and quite incapable of coping with the situation. The Communist leaders, even as they fled to Russian military headquarters to save their lives from the popular wrath, called for Russian troops to intervene. The Russians obliged by sending in tanks to shoot down the virtually unarmed German working class. These tragic events demonstrated two facts of fundamental significance: the East German Communists were incapable of winning the allegiance of the East German working class, let alone other strata of the population; but also, the Western Allies and the Western Germans were unable and unwilling to do anything on behalf of the East German victims of Soviet tyranny, because intervention would have entailed the serious risk of World War III. The East German population was taught the futility of open opposition; the hope of changing the régime having vanished, its opponents saw no way out but to flee individually to the West. This they did in large numbers: the German Democratic Republic was to suffer, over the next eight years, a refugee drain of more than a million people who "voted for the West" with their feet. These refugees were predominantly young men in whose training the East German state had invested much, or members of skilled professions like doctors and engineers: two groups which the German Democratic Republic could ill afford to lose. Whole districts were threatened with the collapse of medical facilities, and ambitious plans for economic development invariably failed because of the shortage of skilled manpower. The refugees proved, on the other hand, great assets, economically and morally, to the Federal Republic. The West German government alternated between propagandist exploitation of the refugee drain and fear that East Germany might stabilize if denuded of too many opposition elements. The official policy was to discourage the flight of all persons who were not directly threatened in their liberty or property. The East German government, mindful of the manpower drain, made "fleeing the Republic" a severe crime; those caught in the act were punished with well-publicized long prison sentences.

Most of these refugees fled by way of West Berlin—a relatively easy matter since Greater Berlin, including both the western and eastern parts of the city, stood theoretically under Allied Four-Power control, which guaranteed free movement of persons throughout the entire city. Berlin's position as an escape hatch for refugees was one of the reasons why the city was a thorn in the side of the East German regime and its Russian master. Another was the political freedom and economic prosperity of West Berlin, both of which constituted standing reproaches to the tyranny and misery of the surrounding German Democratic Republic. The anomalous position of West Berlin, as a Western enclave in the midst of Russian-controlled territory, symbolized the unsolved character of the German problem; the defense of that position expressed the determination to achieve the restoration of German unity when Berlin would again serve as the capital of a reunited country. All these reasons practically compelled the Russians, on the other hand, to aim at terminating the freedom of West Berlin by expelling the Western garrisons and incorporating the abandoned city into the German Democratic Republic.

A method of harassing the Western Allies was readily available because of the precarious nature of Western communication lines to Berlin. The Western Powers had failed to demand foolproof access guarantees in 1945, in the form of a territorial corridor or a drawing of zonal boundaries so as to make Berlin a border city, when their negotiating position was extremely strong. They had circumvented the blockade of 1948–1949 by launching an airlift instead of defending their right to ground access by force of arms, and they had failed to secure new guarantees when the blockade was lifted in the spring of 1949. This left the Russians in a position where they could threaten new blockades at will and irritate the West Berlin population by a policy of pinpricks and calculated arbitrariness. (For example, West Berliners driving to West Germany in their cars can never know whether border controls will take an hour or a day and whether the road will still be open when they return.) The Russian control of the Berlin access lines (which they delegated in part to the government of the German Democratic Republic in 1955) created an atmosphere of chronic friction and provided the temptation to blackmail the Western allies (and West Germans) into accepting diplomatic contacts with East Germany. The Russians wanted complaints about the functioning of the Berlin access lines to be addressed to the "sovereign" German Democratic Republic, which would have amounted to diplomatic recognition; this the Western Powers refused to do although they reluctantly agreed to accept the East German control authorities as "agents" for the still responsible Russians in certain questions. The distinction between dealing with the East German government as a "sovereign state," or as a "Russian agent," was admittedly a narrow one, but it was essential for maintaining the Western thesis that the West German government was the *only* legitimate German government.

The Berlin situation was marked by various minor crises throughout the 1950's, though the Russian bark usually proved worse than its bite and the West Berlin population became used to living a remarkably normal life in the midst of a highly abnormal situation. A formal ultimatum by the Russian dictator Khrushchev on Nov. 27, 1958, demanding a new Berlin settlement within six months, fell flat: The Western Powers realized that defense of their Berlin position had become the touchstone of their firmness throughout the world, and that retreat from Berlin—no matter how precarious their intrinsic position in this isolated outpost—was politically and psychologically impossible. Everyone understood that there could be no defense of West Berlin by conventional arms in the face of Russia's overwhelmingly superior local power (some twenty divisions stationed in East Germany); the security of West Berlin was completely dependent upon the *credible* threat that Russian aggression would trigger a nuclear holocaust. West Germany's voluntary renunciation of nuclear arms left the defense of Berlin an exclusively Allied (primarily an American) responsibility, though the Adenauer government naturally did everything in its power to press the American government into maintaining an absolutely firm line.

The next major Berlin crisis came in the summer of 1961; it was precipitated by the mounting exodus of East German refugees which threatened to depopulate the German Democratic Republic. The Russians and their German puppets took the drastic step of building a wall through the middle of Berlin on the line which separated the Communist East from the free West, thereby making further escapes virtually impossible (August 13, 1961). The imperative behind this step must have been very strong, for the wall proved, predictably, a grave liability from the point of view of public relations: it demonstrated to the entire world that East Germany was a prison whose inmates had to be prevented from escaping by forcible means. The building of the wall also entailed international risks, for it constituted a unilateral abrogation of the Four Power status of "Greater Berlin." The new American administration of President Kennedy was caught off guard by the wall, a contingency which had not been taken into account despite the "heating up" of the Berlin crises in the spring of 1961. Kennedy decided against direct measures to tear down the wall, although some hotheads suggested that he should use the American garrison in West Berlin for this purpose. (This was certainly a rash proposal in view of the overwhelming local military superiority of the Russians. If the American army suffered a defeat in its invasion of East Berlin—what was the next step to have been?) Kennedy limited the American response to a reaffirmation of the American guarantee of the security and viability of West Berlin and gave credibility to this guarantee by sending additional troops to Berlin accompanied by Vice-President Johnson; he also appointed the tough-minded general Lucius Clay—hero of the 1948 airlift—his personal representative in the city. The upshot of the entire crisis was mixed: the Russians suffered a propaganda defeat by being compelled to build the wall; the Americans suffered a political defeat because they proved unable to prevent the Russians from altering the status of Berlin for the worse. The viability of the city was impaired, though as yet but slightly, by the successful Russian practice of "salami tactics"—i.e., slicing off particular Allied rights piecemeal, tactics aimed at destroying confidence in the West's ability to safeguard the future independence of the city. The

East German regime was undoubtedly stabilized by the closing of the Berlin escape hatch as East Germans told themselves that they had no alternative but to accommodate to a regime which was obviously here to stay and from which they could no longer escape.

The wall was also a personal disaster for Konrad Adenauer, occurring as it did at the height of the election campaign of 1961. It demonstrated the fallacy of his long-standing contention that Western strength would prove the key to reunification: the wall revealed not only that Western strength was insufficient to compel Russian evacuation of the East Zone, but that it did not even suffice to prevent the deterioration of the Berlin position through unilateral Russian action. The chancellor's reaction to the Berlin wall showed, incidentally, that the old man was losing his grip: He failed to appreciate the extent to which the German public had been struck in a very raw nerve, and he antagonized many by continuing to campaign as usual instead of going immediately to Berlin. The focusing of the spotlight upon Berlin also proved a great advantage to Adenauer's opponent Willy Brandt, who combined the double roles of S.P.D. chancellor-candidate and Berlin mayor. The result was that the C.D.U., which had been generally expected to win again the independent parliamentary majority it had possessed since 1957, won only a plurality and was forced to renew its pre-1957 coalition with the F.D.P. This fact, combined with blunders in the *Spiegel* affair described below, was to compel Adenauer's involuntary retirement from the chancellorship in 1963.

The lines of Adenauer's foreign policy had been set, and his main achievements won, before 1955. The eight years after 1955 saw some important details filled in but saw also an increasing inability on the part of Adenauer to adjust to the changing currents of world politics. The main accomplishment was the continued development of European unity in the economic field. The Schuman Plan proved an outstanding success in coordinating and modernizing coal and steel production throughout Western Europe. The next step on the road to European integration was the establishment of a Common Market in 1958, with a common tariff against the outside world for both industrial and agricultural products. It is administered by an international authority located at Brussels. A common European Atomic Authority (*Euratom*) simultaneously began to co-ordinate all European efforts in the peaceful uses of nuclear energy. The European movement achieved little progress, however, in the field of political integration, which remained limited to regularly scheduled meetings of foreign ministers and speeches and non-binding resolutions by parliamentary deputies meeting annually in a Consultative Assembly at Strassburg. The accession to power in France in 1958 by General de Gaulle, an old-fashioned believer in national sovereignty and opponent of all supra-national political institutions, foreclosed any advance toward political integration in the foreseeable future.

De Gaulle's nationalist and anti-American policies presented Adenauer with a difficult problem not previously encountered, and one not soluble by the method of simplification which was his special forte. He now had to maneuver between the United States, the main protector of German security, and France, whose conciliation had been Adenauer's proudest achievement, at a time when these two powers were sharply antagonistic on most questions affecting the NATO alliance. Adenauer refused to make a clear-cut choice between France and America though he became in fact distrustful of the soundness of American foreign policy after the death of his close friend John Foster Dulles in 1959; his personal sympathies obviously leaned toward De Gaulle. The German Chancellor signed a special treaty of friendship with France (January, 1963) just after De Gaulle had vetoed Britain's admission to the Common Market, an entry which was ardently desired by American policy as part of Kennedy's "Grand Design" of fitting an increasingly unified Europe into the larger framework of an emerging "Atlantic Community." Adenauer obviously approved of De Gaulle's conduct—though his government professed to deplore it—because the old man was deeply suspicious of Great Britain, a country in which anti-German feeling remained exceptionally strong, and which was expected to get a Labor government in the near future (as was, in fact, to happen with the election victory of Harold Wilson in the following year). The German Chancellor feared, above all, the well-known British pragmatism in foreign policy—so different from his own fanatical hostility to communism—and the consequent British willingness to consider plans for the neutralization and disengagement of armed forces from Central Europe, which constituted in Adenauer's view a morally flabby "softness towards Communism."

His disenchantment with American policy was due to similar suspicions directed against President Kennedy. Adenauer found it hard to take seriously an American President half his own age (they were born, respectively, in 1876 and 1917), and he distrusted Kennedy's "left-wing" intellectual entourage. He feared the rethinking of military problems connected with the so-called McNamara strategy of increasing conventional fighting capacity to permit delay in the use of atomic weapons in any emergency, a strategy which might reduce the credibility of the American atomic deterrent in future Berlin crises. He disliked various projects for a new Berlin settlement discussed within the Kennedy administration after the building of the wall—projects which contemplated East German participation in an International Authority controlling access to the former German capital. He was highly suspicious of Kennedy's policy of seeking limited agreements with the Russians on such questions as cultural exchanges, the sale of wheat, and the banning of atomic tests. The Moscow Test Ban Treaty of August, 1963, was especially offensive to him because the German Democratic Republic was permitted to sign it—a step which led inevitably to the diplomatic "upgrading" of the East German regime.

The German Chancellor found it hard, in short, to adjust to the new world of the 1960's where the simple formula of the 1950's—building Western strength against a monolithic and aggressive Communist world—had ceased to be adequate. He did not understand that the nuclear parity between Russia and America—once both were able to do mortal injury to one another by the delivery of hydrogen bombs through inter-continental missiles—required a complete rethinking of strategic doctrines. He did not understand that the increasing independence of several Communist states in Eastern Europe, beginning with the relaxation of Russian controls over Poland in 1956, made rigid German policies—the Hallstein Doctrine, for example—obsolete. He did not understand the new importance of the "underdeveloped world" of Africa and Asia in shaping the future of the globe and the necessity of contributing to the building of prosperous, anti-Communist societies in these areas through Western help (West Germany did, however, enter this field belatedly under American pressure in 1960). He revealed his own rigidity by the mental short cut of dismissing Kennedy and his entourage—who were wrestling manfully with all these problems—as immature, if not sinful, children who were straying from the straight and narrow path of fervid anti-communism and contempt for neutralism. Adenauer did not and could not see that he had become an anachronism in a rapidly changing world, an anachronism who appeared increasingly ludicrous as the last and most rigid "Cold Warrior" in a world where the Cold War, though by no means ended, was taking on new forms unsuspected in the early 1950's—a time when Adenauer had been perfectly attuned to the needs of Germany and Europe and the policies of the United States and had won his great achievements in the field of foreign policy. He clung to power longer than was good for his historical reputation—an observation which also applies to his record of domestic rule.

4. DOMESTIC POLITICS DURING THE ADENAUER ERA

The main domestic problem which confronted the German people in 1949 was the building of a viable democratic structure of government—no easy task in a country in which the majority of the people had been enthusiastic Nazis at one time or another. The consciousness of the guilt Germans bore—collectively if not individually—for the Nazi years, though neither as fervid nor as widespread as might be wished, dominated the legislative work of the early years of the Bonn Republic. Apart from the reparations for Israel, far-reaching restitution was voted for the surviving victims of Nazism or the families of the killed. Stringent laws against anti-Semitism were put on the statute book, and the few cases of overt anti-Semitic conduct were punished in an exemplary fashion. The most notorious outbreak of post-war anti-Semitism was the swastika painted on a Cologne synagogue in December, 1959. It received world-wide publicity, and the juvenile offenders were quickly apprehended and punished. Anti-Semitic remarks by schoolteachers—a frequent occurrence, if not a commonplace, in Wilhelmine, Weimar, and, of course, Nazi Germany—now led to immediate dismissal. In any case, the Jewish population of the Federal Republic, numbering only about 30,000, was but a pitiful remnant of the flourishing pre-Nazi community of over half a million. It prospered in material terms and was treated with almost excessive deference by the government, but its full psychological integration into German life was made virtually impossible by the agonizing memories of the recent past. The Jews of Germany resented the attitude of those non-Jewish Germans who did not feel their share of guilt concerning the Nazi genocide; yet at the same time there were difficulties in the way of establishing "normal relations" with Germans who *did* feel such guilt. In short, German-Jewish relations were *bound* to remain problematical for a long time to come.

The German Jews joined many others in deploring the foot dragging shown by the Bonn government in the search for the Nazi criminals unapprehended by Military Government. A central investigative office was finally set up at Ludwigsburg (Württemberg) in 1958 which began a race against the statute of limitations barring punishment for murder after twenty years. It was the general judgment of observers that the belated trials of Nazi criminals which resulted from its investigations were unpopular with large strata of German public opinion: not out of sympathy with Nazi crimes but rather from sheer weariness with an unpleasant subject, fear of skeletons dragged out of closets, and the widespread feeling that the punishment of men who had frequently lived decent lives since 1945 served no useful purpose. The four-year extension of the statute of limitations in March, 1965, by the Bundestag was clearly in response to foreign pressures rather than domestic demands; it permitted the continued search and prosecution of those criminals who were still at large.

Adenauer, while sharply denouncing Nazism and insisting upon the importance of giving restitution to the victims of Nazism, assumed at the same time an attitude of "forgive and forget" toward old party members unless there was something criminal in their records. He readily accepted latter-day conversions to democracy at face value and appointed men with tainted political pasts to high governmental positions. The *Staatssekretär* (highest bureaucratic official) in his own chancellery, the admittedly supremely efficient Hans Globke, was installed despite the fact that he had written an official commentary on the infamous Nürnberg Laws of 1935. Theodor Oberländer, for seven years minister of all-German affairs, had an unfortunate "brown past" and was finally dismissed in 1960 in response to incessant foreign clamor. Why did Adenauer appoint such men in the first place? A certain moral obtuseness and cynicism may have played a role, but these appointments were part of a statesman-like design for healing national wounds and building support for the new democracy. There was genuine danger that the ex-Nazis of Germany—a very sizable group!—would be driven into neo-Nazism if pushed into a ghetto of misery and despair. Given jobs and respectability, the vast majority of this group—who had in any case been disillusioned by the fiasco of 1945—would readily acquiesce in Germany's new democratic institutions. In appears certain that this objective could have been achieved by methods short of cabinet appointments, while Adenauer's policy of welcoming ex-Nazis with open arms had the unfortunate drawback that there was too little public confrontation with Germany's ugly past and too much blurring of moral issues. The over-all policy of "domesticating" ex-Nazis through kindness must, however, be considered a political success: Neo-Nazism has proved a negligible force in the life of the Bonn Republic. (The constitutional provision for the outlawing of neo-Nazism could be effectively enforced because it proved to be virtually unnecessary.)

Another sizable group of potential radicals and malcontents, the ten million refugees from the East, were to a remarkable extent assimilated into West German society in the course of the Adenauer era. There was, initially, a great deal of friction between natives and refugees as the latters' arrival put an intolerable strain upon housing and public facilities. The refugees, needing roofs over their heads, were quartered by governmental fiat in private homes, and since the bombed-out cities were already over-crowded, they were generally assigned to the countryside. The peasants, never noted for their hospitality to outsiders, and fearful of the intrusion of "foreigners" with strange dialects and often a different religious faith into previously homogeneous communities, resented this policy. The fact that the refugees had come primarily to the border sections of West Germany, which also happened to be the poorest (partly because of recent loss of their traditional hinterland in the East Zone), added to the difficulty of the situation; Schleswig-Holstein, known as the "poorhouse" of Germany, reckoned 40 per cent of its population refugees in 1949. One of the first steps of the new Federal Government was to relocate, with the use of federal funds, a large number of refugees into the industrial areas of the Ruhr and Württemberg, where they were readily absorbed by an expanding economy.

The refugees, naturally impatient with their slow assimilation into West German society, formed in 1950 a special party, the *Bund der Heimatvertriebenen und Entrechteten* (League of Those Expelled from Their Homelands and Those Deprived of Their Rights, abbreviated B.H.E.). This party was primarily a pressure group to secure material compensation for the losses suffered by the refugees; but the second part of the title, referring to "those deprived of their rights," was recognized by Germans as a clear-cut appeal to the "victims" of the denazification policies of the

Western Military Governments. Adenauer saw the great danger posed by the potential cooperation of the B.H.E. and the Nazis, and he decided to buy it off by a double policy of taking the B.H.E. leaders into his cabinet in 1953 —at this time the notorious B.H.E. leader and ex-Nazi Oberländer became a federal minister—and passing a law compensating refugees for some of their losses, the so-called *Lastenausgleich* (equalization of burdens). The law was a form of capital levy under which those whose property had survived the war were taxed for the benefit of those who had lost everything. The main factor in the refugees' assimilation proved, however, the "German economic miracle" which began with the currency reform of 1948 and continued steadily thereafter. The refugees turned out to be economic assets in a country which soon began to suffer from a chroni labor shortage; the desperate desire of most refugees to recover their fc mer social and economic status made them eager workers.

Adcnauer's policy of killing the B.H.E. with kindness was rewarded by the election results of 1957, when the party was eliminated on the federal level by its failure to meet the requirements of the 5 per cent clause. While continuing to play some role in *Länder* politics, it has failed to appeal successfully to the majority of the refugees, although these refugees remain in many ways a distinct group. They are organized into so-called *Landsmannschaften* from different "lost provinces," such as East Prussia, Pomerania, and Silesia, which hold annual monster rallies attended by hundreds of thousands. These rallies regularly lead to much irresponsible rhetoric concerning Germany's indelible right to possess the territories beyond the Oder-Neisse frontier; though the use of force to regain possession is explicitly repudiated, the rallies nonetheless provide deplorable exhibitions of chauvinism which stir up fears in Warsaw and Prague. They conceal, moreover, the fact that the refugees have become economically and politically (though not psychologically) fully integrated into the Federal Republic; it is most unlikely that many refugees (not to mention their children) would actually wish to return to their homelands to start life anew in case these provinces were, by a miracle, returned to Germany. The refugee leaders—who frequently make a living out of being refugee leaders—have been remarkably successful, however, in appealing to old sentiments over new economic interests; it is considered extremely bad form in many refugee circles to admit being contented with life in the West Germany of the economic miracle.

This economic miracle has been, next to the gains achieved by Adenauer's foreign policy, the most conspicuous success of the Bonn Republic. A few figures will serve to document West Germany's extraordinary progress from a condition of utter ruin to that of one of the most prosperous countries in Europe. By 1955 the gross national product of West Germany exceeded the 1936 (a comparatively "normal" pre-war year) national product of *all* Germany though it contained only 53 per cent of Germany's former area and 75 per cent of its former population. Average real wages reached pre-war levels in 1950, and they more than doubled in the next fifteen years. There was no hope of making crowded and industrialized West Germany self-sufficient in food after the loss of the predominantly agrarian eastern territories, but a booming foreign trade made this quite unnecessary. Total foreign trade ran to $25.4 billion in 1962, the second highest in the world; the balance of trade was favorable despite a 5 per cent upward revaluation of the mark in 1961; the currency was extremely strong with reserves in gold and convertible currencies (mostly dollars) exceeding $6.4 billion.

The dynamic character of the West German economy, once Allied restrictions were removed, is comparatively easy to explain. German management had retained its traditional efficiency, German labor its docility and capacity for hard work. Trade unions felt that it was more important to increase production than to win a better distribution of the national product for the workers; serious strikes were rare and national strikes unthinkable. The Marshall Plan succeeded in priming the economic pump, and Germany was in an optimum position for using American help to good advantage. The world-wide "Korean War Boom" of 1950 came at exactly the right moment for a Germany eager to recapture lost overseas markets. Two factors which appeared disastrous in the first years after 1945 proved blessings in disguise on the road to economic prosperity. The refugee inundation provided West Germany with a valuable supply of skilled labor. The dismantling of many of West Germany's factories, undertaken by the occupation authorities to provide reparations and promote demilitarization, subsequently forced German employers to install the most modern equipment. Much credit must also be given to the laissez-faire policies of Economics Minister Ludwig Erhard, who preached and practiced the importance of freedom, incentives, and competition in maximizing production —especially in a country like Germany where governmental control of the economy was discredited through Nazi practices before 1945 and Communist practices thereafter, and where an industrious and educated population was ready to take advantage of economic freedom to improve its material position.

It should be noted, incidentally, that while Adenauer and Erhard have been dedicated to the principles of laissez-faire, their government has nonetheless played a large role in the economy. Elaborate welfare-state programs, including the long non-controversial system of national health insurance originally introduced by Bismarck in 1889, have been set up or consolidated since 1949. The German welfare state—like every welfare state—provides for a considerable redistribution of income, since it is financed by taxes borne primarily by the rich while its programs primarily benefit the poor. German farmers—like farmers in all industrial communities—receive heavy subsidies which have, unfortunately, too often merely perpetuated unviable family units instead of being used to modernize viable units. The attack upon the national housing shortage has been led by a newly created Federal Ministry of Housing which has used methods (subsidies, tax exemptions, etc.) unknown to traditional laissez-faire. The export of capital to the so-called developing nations has been underwritten by governmental guarantees. Ludwig Erhard has attempted to launch an attack upon the cartels and monopolies which have dominated the German economic scene since the 1890's, but he has been no more successful in "trust-busting" than the American government has been in enforcing the Sherman Anti-Trust Act. For all these reasons it is quite inaccurate to describe the German "economic miracle" as the exclusive fruit of laissez-faire; Erhard's own favorite phrase of *soziale Marktwirtschaft,* i.e., a free-market economy mitigated by a social conscience, is a far more accurate designation.

The impact of the economic miracle upon the average West German has been spectacular. Automobile ownership, once the status symbol of the rich, is now widespread and is at least the aspiration of every working-class family. The eating of meat, once considered a special Sunday treat by most Germans, has become a daily habit for many. Vacations abroad, once considered only by intellectuals and the rich (apart from the few workers sufficiently well connected to participate in Nazi-sponsored "strength through joy" cruises), have become commonplace for many lower-class Germans; hordes of German tourists can be found—especially in Mediterranean countries from Spain to Greece—at all seasons of the year.

Conflict between classes has been substantially reduced by the attainment of a middle-class standard of living on the part of the erstwhile proletariat. Equally important has been what one can only describe as the psychological assimiliation of the working class into the West German community. The long-standing demand for some working-class influence upon the running of factories was met by the Co-determination (*Mitbestimmung*) Law, introduced by the Adenauer government in heavy industry in 1951. Under it the workers possess direct representation on the boards of the firms for which they work through "labor directors" with full voting rights and access to company books. Industrialists feared initially that co-determination might end their power to run their businesses as they chose; many reformers thought that it might launch a spectacular new era of genuine "industrial democracy." The fear and the enthusiasm proved equally misplaced. The labor directors tended at first to feel intimidated at board meetings in the presence of their social superiors; however, when they began to participate in discussions, they usually shed any distinctive working-class outlook. They represented management's point of view to the workers as frequently as they represented the workers' point of view to management. The much-condemned and much-hailed Co-determination Law has in fact made remarkably little difference in the actual operation of industry, although it has no doubt played a role in creating the excellent industrial climate of the Federal Republic.

The sharp reduction in class conflict has facilitated the remarkable evolution of the Social Democratic Party (S.P.D.) from a party ideologically dedicated to Marxism and politically dedicated to the interests of the working class, to a pragmatic party eager to win support for *all* strata of the population. The course of the S.P.D. has been troubled since it was refounded in 1945 under the inspiring but difficult Kurt Schumacher. Schumacher had been one of the younger leaders of the S.P.D. during the last years of the Weimar Republic; he had been sharply critical of the passivity of the party elders as they faced the Nazi peril. He proudly refused to go into exile in 1933 though he was a marked man for the Nazis and was soon sent to concentration camp. He emerged in 1945 after almost continuous imprisonment as a man "possessing a brain without a body" but filled with an iron resolve to rebuild the S.P.D. and make it the dominant force in German public life. Schumacher was keenly alert to the Communist menace at a time when the Western Allies still had illusions about co-operating with Russia in achieving a mutually satisfactory German settlement; he courageously—though vainly—opposed amalgamation of Socialists and Communists into the Socialist Unity Party in the East Zone and deserves much credit for preventing its extension into the Western Zones. At the same time he was certain that the German people would turn to democratic socialism to clean up the sorry heritage of Nazism; Schumacher was bitterly surprised when they turned instead to the laissez-faire, capitalist policies of Ludwig Erhard and Konrad Adenauer. The Socialist leader was deeply distrustful of Adenauer's foreign policy because it gave priority to Western integration over German unification; his vigorous opposition—couched, incidentally, in extremely nationalistic language— gave expression to the latent hostility felt by many Germans toward the Allied Powers. Most observers believed Schumacher's nationalism to be thoroughly authentic, though it may have owed something to the calculation that the S.P.D. of the Bonn Republic should avoid the fate of its Weimar predecessor of becoming discredited because of its "internationalist" outlook. In any case, the Socialist leader opposed, before his death in August, 1952, the Petersberg Agreement, the Schuman Plan, the European Defence Community, and the "Germany Treaty" of May, 1952.

Kurt Schumacher had helped to break the S.P.D. from its traditional rigidity in matters of doctrine by insisting that Marxism was only *one* road, not *the* road, to Socialism; by making the party abandon its (verbally) anti-nationalist outlook, which in any case had long been a matter of rhetoric rather than practice; and by his keen awareness that the world had not stood still since Karl Marx published *Das Kapital* in 1867. His successor in the leadership, the pleasant but colorless bureaucrat Erich Ollenhauer (1903–1963), was unable to put his specific stamp upon the

S.P.D.; while his attempts to compete with Adenauer for popular favor in the elections of 1953 and 1957 proved a fiasco. The S.P.D. began to look ridiculous as all of its prophecies concerning the inevitable failure of Erhard's economic policies were refuted by Germany's burgeoning prosperity, and as Adenauer's foreign policy of regaining sovereignty through Western friendship proved successful despite S.P.D. opposition (although the S.P.D. contention that this policy would *not* lead to reunification was also vindicated by events). After the party won only 31.8 per cent of the vote in the 1957 elections, the leadership recognized the need for a change in the party program and for a chancellor-candidate more attractive than Ollenhauer if the curse of permanent opposition were to be avoided. Herbert Wehner, the strong man of the party apparatus, was unfortunately unsuited for the leadership because he had been a Communist as late as 1944 and possessed a shy, moody, and non-charismatic personality. He took the lead, however, in forcing a change in party policies in the face of much opposition from traditionalist functionaries. A new program was unveiled at the Bad Godesberg Congress in October, 1959: it jettisoned all Marxist intellectual jargon; foreswore anti-clericalism (long a handicap in appealing to Catholic workers) and nationalisation (long the bogey of the German bourgeoisie); and accepted the basic economic principle of Erhard—the pursuit of profit by free men in a free market—and the foreign and defense policies of Adenauer—Western integration and rearmament within NATO. Wehner proclaimed the loyalty of the S.P.D. to the NATO alliance in a celebrated speech on June 30, 1960.

A new chancellor-candidate was found in the person of Willy Brandt, the popular mayor of West Berlin. Brandt had spent the Nazi years in Scandinavian exile, had taken out Norwegian citizenship, and had worn a Norwegian uniform at the time of the Nazi invasion in 1940—all intrinsically honorable acts but acts which many C.D.U. orators, bent upon appealing to the veterans' and nationalist vote, sought to exploit in a disgraceful fashion. (There has been, incidentally, no limit to the compaign of character assassination directed against Brandt; Adenauer himself has publicly referred to the "innocent" fact that his Socialist opponent was born out of wedlock.) Brandt returned to Germany in 1946 and gradually became a strong figure in the Socialist party of West Berlin. A resolute and effective foe of communism, he became the symbol of West Berlin's resolve to maintain its freedom as mayor after 1957. His position on the Berlin firing line, attractive personality, and an effective publicity build-up quickly made him a world figure, and he appealed to some non-working-class Germans who would ordinarily not dream of voting for a Social Democrat. His aim has been to rebuild—in a close co-operation with Herbert Wehner —the S.P.D. on the model of the pragmatic, flexible, broadly based Socialist parties of Scandinavia and Great Britain. The new program and the new party leader succeeded in raising the S.P.D. vote from 31.8 to 36.2 per cent in the 1961 elections—enough to buttress the position of the reformers within the party. Brandt was confirmed as the chancellor-candidate of the party, and upon Ollenhauer's death in 1963 he was elected party chairman as well.

The virtual acceptance by the S.P.D. opposition of the main policies of Adenauer's government gave West Germany that "consensus in fundamentals" which is characteristic of healthy democracies. The government continued, to be sure, to express doubt concerning the authenticity of the S.P.D. conversion, thereby distracting attention from what was in fact Adenauer's greatest triumph: the fact that he not only put his indelible seal upon the foreign and domestic policies of the Bonn Republic against sharp Socialist opposition, but also that the continuance of these policies was guaranteed even in case the opposition should win a future election.

The C.D.U. has been continuously in power since 1949. Its heterogeneous character has fascinated all observers of the German scene because it incorporates the most diverse strands of pre-1933 German party life. The core of the C.D.U. consisted of the voters of the old Center Party, traditionally the protector of Catholic interests since the time of Bismarck's *Kulturkampf;* most of the surviving Center leaders recognized in 1945 that it would be unfortunate, and unnecessary, to revive a purely confessional party. An alliance with Conservative Protestant elements in a common Christian front appeared natural in view of the strong Communist and Socialist challenge. Most of the voters of the old Nationalist party (D.N.V.P.) rallied to the C.D.U.; so did the majority of old Nazis (now ex-Nazis) and a good many voters of Stresemann's People's Party (D.V.P.) and various Weimar splinter groups. The party's common cement of a vague and undenominational Christianity permitted the adhesion of the most variegated socioeconomic groups, though manufacturing, agrarian, and lower-middle-class interests possessed the major voice; the adherence of a large section of the Catholic working class, however, prevented the C.D.U. from becoming a "bourgeois party" in either composition or policy. The unity of the party was maintained through a successful economic policy which brought gains to all strata of the German population; through the careful distribution of jobs between Protestants and Catholics in equitable proportions; and through Adenauer's superb skill at manipulating men and pressure groups.

The Bavarian contingent of the C.D.U. maintained its autonomy under the label Christian Social Union (C.S.U.), though it co-operated closely with the C.D.U. in the Bundestag. This "party separatism" stood in the tradition—so marked in both Wilhelmine and Weimar Germany—of Bavaria's fear of being amalgamated into a larger unit. The C.S.U. was more Catholic and clerical than the C.D.U., since it was based almost exclusively upon Catholic voters; the Protestant population of Bavaria—which had been considerably increased by the refugee influx of 1945—tended to vote for the F.D.P., S.P.D., or B.H.E. The C.S.U.'s national importance lay, however, primarily in the fact that it provided an impregnable political base for West Germany's most controversial politician, Franz Joseph Strauss. This self-made man—the son of a butcher—has had a meteoric career in West German politics. He entered the cabinet as minister for atomic affairs in 1953, but valued this unimportant position only as a starting point for achieving the crucial post of defense minister in 1956. Strauss was a conspicuous success in this sensitive position; he showed great organizing ability in building the *Bundeswehr* up from scratch, established the principle of civilian supremacy for the first time in German history, and impressed his fellow defense ministers in other NATO countries by his superb mastery of the strategic problems of the nuclear age. His political flair, oratorical skill, commanding intellectual qualities, and willingness to assume onerous responsibilities won him an increasingly respected position in German political life despite his abrasive personal qualities; many began to view him as a future chancellor in the early 1960's. His rashness and untruthfulness in the *Spiegel* affair of 1962—to be described below—by compelling his dismissal as defense minister, put, however, a temporary ceiling upon his career. Yet Strauss retained the loyalty of the C.S.U. and its 50-odd deputies in the Bundestag; many expected that this would provide a sufficient basis for a political comeback in the near future.

For much of the Adenauer era the C.D.U./C.S.U. governed in coalition with the F.D.P. in what was always a friction-laden alliance. The F.D.P. is a curious amalgam of South German democratic liberalism looking back to the traditions of the Frankfurt Parliament of 1848 and a North German Protestant nationalism sometimes tolerant of neo-Nazi elements after 1945. The party was anti-clerical (not to say anti-Catholic) in outlook, a source of constant friction with its C.D.U. coalition partner. Its economic policy stood to the right of the C.D.U's because it did not have any working-class following to take into account. Its foreign policy line basically supported Adenauer's Western orientation while flirting on occasion with the opposite policy of securing a neutralized, reunified Germany by negotiations with the Russians. The F.D.P. was constantly racked by internal dissension on questions of foreign policy and on whether to maintain its governing alliance with the far more powerful C.D.U. The F.D.P. exploited the balance-of-power position between the two great parties in order to secure far more ministerial portfolios than were warranted by its numerical strength. Some observers thought that the F.D.P. leadership consisted primarily of ambitious opportunists bent upon holding office at any price; others thought the party a valuable antidote to the megalomania which tended to strike Adenauer and the C.D.U. after successive electoral victories in 1953, 1957, and 1961.

A strong streak of arbitrary authoritarianism, if not megalomania, was indeed the great flaw in Adenauer's political style. He was not only a born autocrat but had become a complete cynic in his view of human nature after the searing experience of 1933, when many friends had turned away from the once-powerful, now-fallen mayor of Cologne. He was deeply convinced that his foreign policy was the only correct one for Western Germany, and that a victory by the Socialist opposition which opposed it, or the increased strength of the F.D.P. which was an unreliable coalition partner on foreign policy questions, must be avoided at any price. For that reason he did not hesitate to use the most questionable means—ranging from character assassination to intimidation—in order to maintain himself, and his C.D.U., in power: He tended, in fact, to identify both himself and the C.D.U. with the state and to look upon the S.P.D. as a "disloyal opposition." He showed exactly the same ruthlessness to friends as to enemies. Crucial policy decisions were frequently made without consulting either parliament or cabinet; cabinet members were reduced to the role of flunkies and sometimes heard about their dismissal over the radio; unkind remarks made by the chancellor behind the backs of his ministers were the favorite topic of conversation in the German capital. This style of governing proved generally demoralizing and contributed to the widely deplored low moral and intellectual level of public life in the Bonn Republic.

Toward the end of his period of power, the Chancellor, now eighty-six years old, finally overreached himself in the famous *Spiegel* affair of October, 1962. The news magazine *Spiegel* had long been critical of the Adenauer government and more especially of Defense Minister Franz Joseph Strauss. When the *Spiegel* published an exposé of the weaknesses of the West Germany army, as revealed by some recent manueuvers, the government decided to strike back. Though the incriminating article was little more than a collection of previously published information, the government arrested several *Spiegel* editors and launched an indictment for high treason. (It was dismissed by the Supreme Court in 1965 for being *prima facie* unsupported by sufficient evidence, quite apart from the fact that there was obviously no treasonable intent.) The police occupied the editorial office of the *Spiegel* and confiscated the entire archive of the journal in a brazen attempt to find material warranting prosecution *ex post facto* and to intimidate future informants of the magazine. (Any hard-hitting journal must rely upon information acquired by semi-legal methods.) Defense Minister Strauss lied to the Bundestag about his role in the entire affair with an indifference to truth and a contempt for parliamentary dignity singular in a minister. Worst of all was the conduct of Adenauer himself: He used the forum of the Bundestag to denounce Rudolf Augstein, the editor of the *Spiegel,* as a man dominated by a desire to make money out of treason: a remarkable *obiter dicta* to be delivered by the head of the executive while commenting upon a pending judicial case. Adenauer also called upon all advertisers to boycott the *Spiegel,* surely an extraordinary attempt to supplement judicial harassment of an opposition journal by economic strangulation.

The outrageous conduct of the government led, however, to a public outcry which forced Strauss's dismissal from the defense ministry and so discredited Adenauer that he was compelled by his own C.D.U. to retire from the chancellorship within a year. It was a refreshing indication that Germans were learning that eternal vigilance is the price of liberty, for there had been far less protest against the far more arbitrary actions of the Nazis in 1933. The West German press criticized the government with rare unanimity; university professors signed petitions against the Chancellor's conduct, an unprecedented action and one of special importance in a country where university professors still top all other professions in social esteem. The F.D.P. threatened to terminate the coalition unless Strauss were dismissed: a good support for the F.D.P.'s favorite contention that it represented a valuable counterweight to C.D.U. arbitrariness. While Strauss remained a hero to his fellow-Bavarians he ceased to be an active contender for the chancellorship in the foreseeable future. Though Adenauer retrieved his own position temporarily by a skillful maneuver—he began apparently serious negotiations for a "Great Coalition" with the S.P.D. against the F.D.P., though this constituted a complete reversal of his policy since 1949—the charismatic spell of the old Chancellor was broken. The leading figures of the C.D.U. ceased to consider him indispensable, and they forced his retirement in favor of Economics Minister Ludwig Erhard—a man whom Adenauer detested and had publicly declared unfit for the chancellorship—within a year (in October, 1963).

It is too early, perhaps, to make a final assessment of Adenauer's role in German history; but it is probable that he was the greatest German statesman since Bismarck. The foreign and domestic policies of the Bonn Republic were an extension of his powerful personality. His successes in foreign policy have been especially impressive: He took over a country still shackled by alien occupation and achieved sovereignty within six years; a nation that was a moral leper he made a respected member of the Western community of nations. Adenauer achieved rearmament in the face of great foreign and domestic obstacles; he turned a defeated and defenseless Germany into the strongest conventional military power in Europe west of the Iron Curtain. He gave effective support to the development of European unity and Atlantic solidarity. His one great diplomatic failure was that he did not make the slightest progress in the direction of German reunification—but it is virtually certain that reunification was *objectively* unattainable in the post-1949 situation and Adenauer was probably wise in concentrating upon what *was* attainable: West German sovereignty within the Western community of nations. The anachronistic conceptions which dominated the last phase of his foreign policy did not permanently damage Germany's position.

Adenauer's domestic record is almost equally impressive. He presided over the economic transformation of Germany from a ruined country to one of unparalleled and well-distributed prosperity. This prosperity permitted the social assimilation of the ten million refugees who appeared to be an intolerable burden in 1949; and it led, furthermore, to the social and psychological assimilation of the working class into the national community. Adenauer's greatest achievement was, however, to provide prestige for Germany's fledgling liberal-democratic institutions. Hitherto liberal democracy had been identified in the German mind with incompetence and failure. The *Paulskirche* Liberals had confused rhetoric with politics; the National Liberals of the Bismarckian era had cravenly surrendered to the Iron Chancellor and become opportunists; the Progressives, while clinging to liberal principles, had become a doctrinaire sect; the democrats of the 1920's had shown themselves to be incompetent politicians while in power and ineffective defenders of the Weimar Republic against the Nazi challenge. Adenauer, though far from liberal in his personal outlook—we have noted his authoritarian ways and his outrageous defiance of basic principles of law and justice in the *Spiegel* affair—presided over a government which emerged from elections conducted within a basically liberal-democratic order. The successes which he won—most notably in the field of foreign and economic affairs—inevitably gave prestige to that order. Germans began to associate liberal democracy with success in foreign policy, rather than with a series of humiliations beginning with Versailles; with rising prosperity instead of catastrophic inflation and a depression of unprecedented severity; and with strong and stable government, not a kaleidoscopic shifting of weak and ephemeral ministries. Many traditional foes of democracy in Germany began to concede, albeit reluctantly, that a democracy which produced Adenauer, and kept him in power for fourteen years, could not be *all* bad.

5. GERMANY AFTER ADENAUER

A common question throughout much of the Adenauer era was: "How will Germany fare after its great Chancellor retires?" Many foreign observers were frankly skeptical about the future of German democracy under different leadership, a skepticism sometimes encouraged by Adenauer in order to buttress his own indispensability. Many German observers had apprehensions about far-reaching domestic changes—for example, the break-up of the heterogeneous C.D.U.—once the hand of the master was removed. Adenauer himself—who was a kind of biological miracle since his faculties remained intact even after he entered his ninth decade in 1956—refused to make provision for his succession by building up a "crown prince"; he acted as if he believed in his own immortality. He briefly contemplated exchanging the demanding chancellorship for the less strenuous, largely ceremonial presidential office when Heuss's second term expired in 1959; but he withdrew his presidential candidacy when the C.D.U. made clear its intention of nominating Economics Minister Erhard as his successor to the chancellorship. Adenauer's off-and-on dickering for the presidency did considerable damage to the prestige of that office, and it was the first time during Adenauer's ten years' chancellorship that his conduct was condemned with near-unanimity by articulate German public opinion. Adenauer showed his continued tactical mastery, however, in negotiating a new coalition with the F.D.P. after the 1961 elections and in surviving the *Spiegel* affair of 1962. Nevertheless his authority became impaired; he would be eighty-nine by the time the next elections, scheduled for 1965, came around; and his party colleagues felt it necessary to start the early building up of a new chancellor to win those elections. The inevitable successor was Ludwig Erhard, the popular symbol of the much-touted economic prosperity. Adenauer acquiesced in what he could not prevent and retired, after a unique series of farewell honors, on October 15, 1963.

The transition from Adenauer to Erhard took place with complete smoothness. The new Chancellor pledged to continue the policies of the old, though there were inevitable shifts in governmental style. The administrative reins were much relaxed: the new Chancellor was quite free of authoritarian airs, he tolerated lengthy cabinet bull-sessions at which he was sometimes outvoted, and he was both unwilling and unable to use Adenauer's ruthless methods of imposing his will upon party and parliament alike. Erhard's weak handling of the prerogatives of the chancellorship quickly sustained Adenauer's earlier verdict that the new Chancellor, though an excellent minister of economics, lacked the toughness required in a chancellor. Erhard's personal popularity remained, however, very great and was to prove the decisive factor in the C.D.U. election victory in Sept., 1965 which confirmed his hold on the chancellorship.

Ludwig Erhard's paunchiness and radiant idealism made a refreshing contrast to Adenauer's lean figure and misanthropic cynicism. Erhard, an economist by profession, had kept himself completely clear of Nazi entanglements in the years 1933 to 1945; he had been rewarded by being appointed minister of economics in his native Bavaria by the American Military Government in 1945. He moved on to become director for economic affairs at the Frankfurt Economic Council, the embryo of the Federal Government, in 1948. The greatest day of his life was when he presented the Military Government with the *fait accompli* of lifting all rationing and price controls at the time of the Allied-sponsored currency reform in June, 1948. A convinced believer in a free-market economy, he was certain that free enterprise was the one reliable road for Germany's return to prosperity. The Military Government treated his policy with skepticism and the S.P.D. opposition predicted imminent disaster; Erhard's faith was, however, soon vindicated by the dramatic German economic miracle. Adenauer made him

minister of economics in 1949, though he had but recently joined the
C.D.U.; from this post he presided over West Germany's ever-increasing
prosperity until his elevation to the chancellorship in 1963.

The Federal Republic faced many unresolved internal problems in the
mid-1960's—problems too long neglected because of the overriding preoccupation with foreign policy and the somewhat doctrinaire hostility to
governmental "planning." One of the most serious was a mounting crisis
in the universities brought on by the sharp increase in enrollments and the
failure to achieve significant reforms after 1945.

The subject of university reform was talked to death in the early post-
war years while very few reforms were actually achieved. The starting
point was the disgraceful record of the universities during the Nazi period:
the student body had been heavily pro-Nazi even before 1933; the professorate had not protested the curtailment of academic freedom or the
introduction of bogus subjects like "German physics" (denying the "Jewish
physics" of Einstein) and "race theory" (aiming at the "scientific" buttress-
ing of anti-Semitism); Bonn University had formally withdrawn an honorary doctorate conferred upon the anti-Nazi novelist Thomas Mann some
years earlier; and Nobel laureates had expressed sycophantic adulation for
the Führer. This sorry record was, of course, not unusual in the Germany
of 1933 to 1945; yet the world had reason to expect something better from
famous centers of learning. The universities' vulnerability to Nazism was
without question accentuated by several flaws in their traditional structure:
the heavily upper- and middle-class character of the student body; the
authoritarian internal organization; and the political naiveté (to use no
harsher word) of much of the professorate.

The post-war reformers resolved to remedy these structural flaws only
to find that the universities practically defied reform. The upper- and
middle-class character of the student body—in 1965 less than 5 per cent
of the students came from working-class homes—is not *directly* due to the
costs of higher education: These are, in fact, far lower than in the United
States, and a generous program of state-financed fellowships (the *Honnefer
Modell*) was launched in 1957. The problem lies, rather, in the difficulties
experienced by working-class children in securing the *Abitur* (the second-
ary-school-leaving certificate) which constitutes the admission ticket to
the university. Germany's secondary schools (*Gymnasia*) are severely competitive, with the first foreign language starting at age ten (instead of the
fourteen customary in the United States); children from uncultured homes,
or with unsympathetic parents, have little chance of surviving the competition unless they are unusually gifted (it is common knowledge that educated
upper- and middle-class mothers often spend much time helping their less
gifted children with homework or even hire private tutors to make certain
that they make the *Abitur*). *Gymnasia* are, moreover, available only in
cities and medium-sized towns, so that rural or small-town children must

travel long distances to school every day. The result of this situation is that only 6 per cent of Germany's nineteen-year-olds complete the *Abitur*. To raise this number would require revolutionary changes in the structure of secondary education, probably involving a lowering of educational standards. There is little popular demand for such changes and their necessity is questioned by the assertion—which is probably true—that the present system is sufficiently flexible so that few *exceptionally* gifted lower-class children are denied access to higher education.

The authoritarian internal structure of German universities is incarnated in the position of the *Ordinarii* (full professors). This small and self-perpetuating group exercises enormous power in the governing of the university and controls, above all, to an unprecedented degree, the careers of younger men aspiring to professorships; it is a common complaint that it insists too often upon ideological conformity and sycophancy as well as ability. Upon completing his doctorate a young man preparing for a university appointment usually serves several years as an assistant to a professor; at this time he is expected to do whatever he is told, whether it be keeping students off the professor's neck, getting his books from the library, or reading the proofs and making the index of his latest manuscript. While doing all this the assistant must prepare a post-doctoral book (*Habilitationsschrift*) whose acceptance by the faculty frequently depends not only upon the quality of the manuscript but also upon the log-rolling skill of the sponsoring professor.

The German system of university appointments—under which professors are a self-perpetuating body through a process of cooptation restricted to a narrow strata—guaranteed its nationalist and Conservative character in 1945. The appointment of Socialists had been unthinkable before 1919 and rare thereafter; the professorate had been—with the laudable exception of a few figures such as the historian Friedrich Meinecke—hostile to the Weimar Republic and it succumbed easily to Nazism under the naive impression that the Nazis were a fundamentally Conservative force, while only individuals *persona grata* to the Nazis were appointed from 1933 to 1945. The result was that there were few professors with liberal-democratic views in the first years after 1945, and even these were frequently recent converts; hence the reformers won little support from *Ordinarii* in the years when reforms might have been possible. The universities being self-governing bodies, it was impossible for a non-dictatorial state to reform them from the outside.

The hidebound traditionalist outlook of the professorate also showed itself in stubborn resistance to the introduction of new fields of study. History, to give only one example, was usually taught by three *Ordinarii* in ancient, medieval, and modern history, respectively; too little attempt was made to train, or accommodate, men in such "new" fields as Russian and American history, while "area studies" devoted to non-European parts of the world—so conspicuous a feature of America's leading universities since World War II—remained virtually unknown. Political science remained a step-child at most universities, though few countries needed a realistic-empirical approach to politics more than Germany. Law faculties retained their traditional pre-eminence, and a law degree remains practically *sine qua non* for a career in administration or diplomacy.

The Conservative structure of the universities began to be modified only in the late 1950's when the claims of young men trained in the post-war years could no longer be ignored, and an enlargement of the charmed circle of *Ordinarii* became inevitable because of increasing student enrollments and the founding of new universities. The pressing need for more professors inevitably meant a relaxation of traditional Conservative criteria for selection, and it became far more difficult for a professor to exploit his assistants when he had to compete for them with other professors. Able men now began to secure professorships by the time they were thirty, and this "juvenation" of the body of *Ordinarii* began to achieve a silent revolution in university affairs at a time when the complacent outlook of West German society was itself quite unpropitious for *institutional* reform. The generational factor in the outlook of professors was very evident during the *Spiegel* affair: Those under forty were usually outspokenly against the government, those older were at least hesitant about criticizing constituted authority.

University enrollments increased drastically despite the continued low number of working-class children qualifying for admission; the reason was the ever-increasing need for trained personnel in a dynamic industrial society. The student population more than doubled in the fifteen years from 1950 to 1965, from about 120,000 to 250,000; this situation led to a terrible overcrowding of all university facilities, from seminars (where enrollments of 150 were by no means unknown) to dining halls (where long waiting lines were customary and quiet conversation impossible). The expansion took place primarily in the large urban universities like those in Munich, Cologne, and Hamburg, where the anonymity of student life aroused much complaint; on the other hand, the older traditions of student social life—including alcoholic conviviality and the revival of dueling—remained strong in small university towns like Marburg and Heidelberg. The gentleman student out for a good time during the brief interval between parental authority and professional responsibility, diminished notably in numbers; German students become more hard-working, earnest, and, above all, competitive in an increasingly mobile society where training was finally replacing birth as the key to power and wealth.

The straining of university facilities was symptomatic of a general neglect of the "public sector" of Germany's economy—a neglect which showed itself in the over-crowding of hospitals and hopeless traffic jams as well as the inadequacy of educational facilities. This neglect was by no means unique to Germany but was made all the more glaring by Erhard's hostility to planning and—in the specific case of education—the excessively decentralized character of educational responsibility. The terms of the Basic Law of 1949 assigned cultural affairs to the *Länder*, and they have defended their prerogative with a zeal worthy of a better cause. There was, of course, some justification for their attitude: The decentralization of culture, a legacy of Germany's territorial multiplicity, had deep roots in Germany's traditions; the Nazis had shown that centralization of culture could have catastrophic results; and the *Länder* could hope to remain vital political units only if they exercised significant governmental responsibilities. Many of the *Länder* made, in fact, heroic exertions to meet educational needs; but there remained nonetheless a deplorable want of over-all co-ordination in coping with what was clearly a national rather than a *Länder* problem.

German science has recovered only imperfectly from the blight of Nazism. The Nazis drove Jewish scientists into exile and had little use for theoretical science lacking immediate practical application. The wartime isolation of the German scientific community from work done elsewhere, combined with the destruction of laboratories through aerial bombardment, also contributed to the loss of Germany's erstwhile primacy in science. Several factors after 1945 worked against the recovery of scientific excellence. The over-crowding of universities made for heavy teaching demands and distracted scientists from research. The unshaken position of the *Ordinarius*—who generally exercises autocratic control over an institute devoted to a particular science—has prevented the development of the kind of teamwork which is increasingly essential in many modern branches of science. Young researchers have been discouraged by the bad tradition under which the *Ordinarius* takes and receives credit for all the research done in his institute; this fact, plus the thorny path to a *Habilitation,* has induced many young scientists to emigrate to America. The worst obstacle in the way of Germany's reattaining her scientific eminence has been, however, the absence of the military contracts which have led in other countries—most notably the United States—to the indirect state subsidization of scientific research. Germany has voluntarily renounced the manufacture of atomic weapons, and her nuclear program is limited to cooperation with EURATOM. Germany lacks the missile and space programs which play such a great part in American and Russian science. The electronics industry—which developed in the United States through military contracts in the years when Germany was disarmed—remains in its infancy. These facts throw grave doubt upon Germany's scientific future —and, by implication, her industrial future as well, since science and technology are inextricably linked in the modern world. It will require large programs, undertaken by the federal rather than the *Länder* governments, to cope with the crisis in German science, not to speak of the university reforms necessary to provide adequate career opportunities for young scientists.

Chancellor Erhard has shown no more initiative in coping with these problems of education, science, and the neglected "public sector" than had Adenauer. The attention of the government has remained centered upon problems of foreign policy. In this field Foreign Minister Gerhard Schröder had the unenviable task of staying loyal to NATO and the America alliance without completely alienating General de Gaulle, who was hostile to both. Schröder, a leader of the North German Protestant wing of the C.D.U., was an outspoken opponent of Gaullism, but he was constantly embarrassed by the existence of strong pro-Gaullist faction composed primarily of South and West German Catholics headed by no less a figure than Konrad Adenauer, who retained the C.D.U. party chairmanship after leaving the chancellorship. (The obvious connection between regional and confessional groups on the one hand and foreign policy conceptions on the other brought about a crisis within the always heterogeneous C.D.U.) These internal frictions within the governing party resulted in much vacillation of policy: The Federal Republic blew hot and cold on the question of the multilateral atomic force originally sponsored by President Kennedy and opposed by President de Gaulle; and its policy on the European Common Market oscillated between defiance of and surrender to France on such questions as agricultural prices and subsidies. Similar uncertainty could be observed in West Germany's policy towards Eastern Europe and Eastern Germany. Schröder succeeded in transcending the spirit (though not the letter) of the Hallstein Doctrine by the establishment of consular relations with several East European states, including Poland; but a genuine "normalization" of relations was made impossible by the continued revisionist clamor of Germany's refugee groups in the question of the Oder-Neisse frontier. Official relations with East Germany remain taboo; commercial relations, however, have increased, and a temporary agreement for Western visitors to cross the Berlin wall at specified times for family reunions was negotiated (to be sure, between the D.D.R. and the Berlin city government, *not* the government of the Federal Republic). The official doctrines of the untouchability of the D.D.R., and of the attainability of reunification through Western strength, remain intact, though the former has been repeatedly breached in practice and the latter sounds increasingly hollow in theory.

West Germany's two great liabilities in the conduct of foreign policy— the need to maintain the Hallstein Doctrine and the continued shadow of the Nazi past—were both revealed in the Near Eastern crisis of the spring of 1965. This crisis was inaugurated by the Arab discovery that Germany had, under American pressure, secretly shipped arms to Israel for several years to help prepare the Jewish homeland against threatened Arab attack. Nasser, the Egyptian dictator, retaliated by inviting the East German dictator Walter Ulbricht for an *official* visit and began to talk about recognizing the D.D.R.—two steps certain to lead to an upgrading of the East German regime. The West German government thereupon yielded to Nassar's blackmail and canceled further arms shipments to Israel in the vain hope that Egypt would cancel the Ulbricht visit; a policy which not only proved unsuccessful but provoked an anti-German outcry, led by the Israeli government which charged a breach of promise, throughout much of the world. (By unfortunate coincidence the debate about extending the statute of limitations on Nazi crimes occurred at exactly the same time.) The German government then sought to appease Israel by proposing formal diplomatic relations, which it had hitherto refused out of fear that the Arabs might retaliate by recognizing the D.D.R. This appeared to many as a right step taken at the wrong time for the wrong reason. The balance sheet of the crisis showed that Germany had placed herself between all stools. Ulbricht had a triumphant visit to Egypt; the Arabs were angry with the Germans for entering into diplomatic relations with Israel; the Israelis, their defences imperiled by the arms cancellation, were only partially appeased by the latter move. German diplomacy had been marked by a singular weakness and vacillation, the latter produced in part by poor co-ordination between Chancellor Erhard and Foreign Minister Schröder.

The only positive aspect of the affair from the point of view of the Federal Republic was that the Arab states did not, after all, open diplomatic relations with East Germany; they only opened (or intensified) consular relations which did not necessitate invoking the Hallstein Doctrine against them. The Arab moderation, while in part a protest against Nasser's leadership by other Arab leaders, was primarily due to respect for West Germany's formidable economic strength, which made responsible Arab leaders hesitate about taking a step certain to result in the cessation of German economic trade and aid. It appears clear, at least in retrospect, that Germany could and should have taken a far firmer line with the Arabs from the very beginning of the crisis; the panicky cancellation of the arms shipment promised to Israel was clearly a mistake which achieved nothing while gravely damaging Germany's reputation for steadiness and good faith.

The weakness of German foreign policy in this particular instance was symptomatic of the Federal Republic's unsureness on the world stage—an unsureness that has resulted in Germany's carrying far less weight in global diplomacy than appeared warranted by her economic and military strength. West Germany was second only to the United States in the volume of its foreign trade, and it was the strongest military power in Europe west of the Iron Curtain. Yet Ludwig Erhard has counted for far less in world politics than either Charles de Gaulle or Harold Wilson. The Federal Republic's comparative lack of influence is largely due to her preoccupation with the insoluble reunification problem, which made the enforcement of a secondary policy like the Hallstein Doctrine a primary concern; to the general parochialism of German public opinion, which takes little interest in world problems outside Europe; and to the prudent recognition that any strong German policy inevitably evokes memories of the Nazis past.

A special problem was raised in the mid-1960's by the increasing resentment felt by young Germans at the continued "half-ghetto" position in which their country found itself on account of the Nazi past for which they could not feel personally responsible. It is to be hoped that before these resentments get out of hand the rest of the world will recognize the existence of a new Germany and not harp incessantly upon the past; but Germans must also recognize—as too many do not—that the enormity of Nazi crimes, and the desire of too many Germans to forget about them too easily, place grave and continued obstacles in the path of normal relations between Germans and the rest of the world.

6. CONCLUSION

Despite many unsolved foreign and domestic problems the Germany of the mid-1960's is characterized by widespread complacency, mitigated, however, by an uneasy though unspecific feeling that "things are too good to last" and that "normalcy" is an abnormal condition for Germans. West Germans are proud of their newly won respectability and happy in the enjoyment of their unparalleled material prosperity. Their democratic order is based upon a broad political consensus and associated in the public mind with an extraordinary series of successes. Yet Germans somehow cannot feel happy even in the face of these fortunate circumstances: Although most Germans expect prosperity to continue, believe their democracy secure, and know that Germany can rely upon its newly acquired Western friends, many clouds continue to hang over their lives. Like people everywhere they are apprehensive about the danger of nuclear war, which could destroy with one bomb everything they have built since 1949. (The Germans, unlike Americans, know by personal experience that totalitarianism and modern war can quite easily destroy the fabric of civilized life.) They have special reason to be discontented because of the apparently permanent partition of their country, which means that 18 million fellow countrymen are doomed to live under Soviet tyranny. They dimly resent, though not as yet very articulately, the fact that Germany is playing a much smaller role in the world of the 1960's than she played from Bismarck's time to Hitler's. There is an incipient recognition that the "German problem"—for a century the key problem confronting Europe—is becoming peripheral on an enlarged world stage, although it remains as unsolved as ever. On a globe dominated by superpowers with populations reckoned in hundreds of millions and possessing nuclear weapons, Germany has become a secondary power—a fate comparable to Sweden's or Holland's in the late seventeenth century. The psychological adjustment to a new parochial position is hard for a nation but recently in the throes of megalomania.

The consciousness of Germany's provincialism is one factor behind the discontent of many German intellectuals in the 1960's. Another is their frustration concerning internal developments during the Bonn Republic. An influential group of writers, loosely joined together under the name "Group 47" (after the fact that they had first gathered together in 1947) criticizes the Germany of the 1960's in the light of the aspirations of the first post-war years. These years had been bitter with hunger, cold, and disillusionment; but they had also been exhilarating with the hope that *all* things had become possible in a reborn Germany resolved to repudiate her evil past. The eager spirits expected to replace capitalism with socialism, authoritarianism with democratic self-government, class hierarchies with social equality, nationalism with Europeanism, militarism with a new civilian ethos, and materialism with idealism. Their disappointment is acute because the Bonn Republic is notable for a renewed flourishing of capitalism, a democratic structure shot through with authoritarian elements, the continuance of social snobbery by a bourgeoisie more powerful than ever, a new army with an inevitable tendency towards militarism and nationalism, and a national complacency which takes satisfaction in all these developments and refuses to come to grips adequately with the Nazi past.

In fact, however, West Germany has changed far more than the critics are willing to allow. It appears that 1945 does, indeed, constitute a major turning point in German history. The nation was transformed politically and psychologically by the aftermath of Nazism and World War II. In the political field there is no longer any feasible alternative to parliamentary democracy. The new West German state is in the happy position—for the first time in the last three generations—of lacking an opposition which repudiates the fundamental structure of the existing policy. Metternich was confronted by intransigent Liberals; Bismarckian Germany, by Marxist Socialists; Weimar Germany, by Nazis, monarchists, Conservative Revolutionaries, and Communists; Nazi Germany, by the various strands of the resistance movement. The Bonn Republic knows no significant opposition to the established libertarian democracy—and this agreement on fundamentals has been supplemented since the late 1950's by agreement on the main lines of foreign and economic policy as well. This development promises well for the future of German democratic institutions—as do the imperatives of foreign policy and the excellent institutional provisions analyzed above.

A further factor of importance is a fundamental transformation of the psychological temper of most Germans. They prided themselves, for the hundred and fifty years before 1945, on their separation from Western Europe: They were proud of German romanticism, as contrasted with the rationalism and pragmatism of Western Europe; proud of their idealism, as contrasted with "philistine" utilitarianism; proud of their spirituality and mystical "depth," as contrasted with superficial materialism; proud of their capacity for self-sacrifice, as contrasted with the egotistic hedonism imputed to their neighbors. Germans believed that their special psychological qualities demanded a special "organic German state" different from, and superior to, the liberal democracy of Western Europe. The Nazis exploited all these reputedly distinctive qualities—romanticism, idealism, mysticism, self-sacrifice, and the conception of a special German state—to the full as they led Germany to catastrophe. They set the stage for the great disillusionment of 1945.

Germans then became desperately anxious to rejoin the Western world they had so long repudiated and to secure full acceptance by its peoples. This reversal involves a far-reaching (to use Nietzsche's phrase) "transvaluation of values." Romanticism, idealism, and self-sacrifice now appear downright silly to many Germans: Rationality and utilitarianism have become the order of the day. The pursuit of self-interest has become a reputable motive, and the solidity of material values came to be appreciated in the years of deprivation after 1945. Today mystical "depth" is denounced as fuzziness; skepticism is widespread in a country marked by the collapse of old values and a painful breach in national continuity. The result of all these changes is a Germany which is both a healthier and a less interesting country, as well as a Germany whose people are less troublesome to the world, and, above all, to themselves. The prospect of 1965 is for the continuation of a West Germany democratic in structure and proud of its participation in the Western alliance; an East Germany with a Communist puppet government which cannot hope to win popular consent, but will continue to exist barring a total transformation of the global situation; and a world in which both Germanies will play a diminished role and the "German problem" will be but one of several problems which defy solution, yet without too many people—outside Germany—becoming unduly excited about this failure.

APPENDIX A: Reichstag Elections 1871–1912

PARTY	1871 No. Votes	1871 No. Deputies	1874 No. Votes	1874 No. Deputies	1877 No. Votes	1877 No. Deputies	1878 No. Votes	1878 No. Deputies	1881 No. Votes	1881 No. Deputies	1884 No. Votes	1884 No. Deputies	1887 No. Votes	1887 No. Deputies
No. eligible voters	7,975,750		8,523,446		8,943,028		9,124,311		9,088,792		9,383,074		9,769,802	
No. valid votes cast	4,134,299	397	5,259,155	397	5,535,785	397	5,811,159	397	5,301,242	397	5,811,973	397	7,527,601	397
Conservatives	548,877	57	359,959	22	526,039	40	749,494	59	830,807	50	861,063	78	1,147,200	80
Reichspartei	627,229	67	431,976	36	426,637	38	785,855	57	379,347	28	387,687	28	736,389	41
National Liberals	1,171,807	125	1,542,501	155	1,469,527	128	1,330,643	99	746,575	47	997,033	51	1,677,979	99
Progressives	361,150	47	469,277	50	597,529	52	607,339	39	1,181,865	115	1,092,895	74	1,061,922	32
Center	724,179	63	1,445,948	91	1,341,295	93	1,328,073	94	1,182,873	100	1,282,006	99	1,516,222	98
Poles	176,072	13	199,273	14	219,159	14	210,062	14	194,894	18	206,346	16	221,825	13
Social Democrats	123,975	2	351,952	9	493,288	12	437,158	9	311,961	12	549,990	24	763,128	11
Guelphs	60,858	7	92,080	4	96,335	4	102,574	10	86,704	10	96,400	11	112,800	4
Danes	18,221	1	19,856	1	17,277	1	16,145	1	14,398	2	14,400	1	12,360	1
Alsace-Lorraine	234,545	15	234,545	15	199,976	15	178,883	15	152,991	15	165,600	15	233,685	15
Antisemites	......	..	......	..	......	..	......	..	......	..	......	..	11,496	1
Other parties	66,670	..	36,636	..	14,153	..	14,721	..	13,010	..	12,700	..	47,600	2

Reichstag Elections 1871-1912 (Cont.)

PARTY	1890 No. Votes	1890 No. Deputies	1893 No. Votes	1893 No. Deputies	1898 No. Votes	1898 No. Deputies	1903 No. Votes	1903 No. Deputies	1907 No. Votes	1907 No. Deputies	1912 No. Votes	1912 No. Deputies
No. eligible voters	10,145,877		10,628,292		11,441,094		12,531,210		13,352,880		14,441,436	
No. valid votes cast	7,298,010	397	7,673,973	397	7,752,693	397	9,495,586	397	11,262,829	397	12,207,529	397
Conservatives	895,103	73	1,038,353	72	859,222	56	948,448	54	1,060,209	60	1,126,270	43
Reichspartei	482,314	20	438,435	28	343,642	23	333,404	21	471,863	24	367,156	14
National Liberals	1,177,807	42	996,980	53	971,302	46	1,317,401	51	1,637,581	54	1,662,670	45
Progressives	1,307,485	76	1,091,677	48	862,524	49	872,653	36	1,233,933	49	1,497,041	42
Center	1,342,113	106	1,468,501	96	1,455,139	102	1,875,273	100	2,179,743	105	1,996,843	91
Poles	246,800	16	229,531	19	244,128	14	347,784	16	453,858	20	441,644	18
Social Democrats	1,427,298	35	1,786,738	44	2,107,076	56	3,010,771	81	3,259,029	43	4,250,401	110
Guelphs	112,100	11	101,800	7	105,200	9	94,252	6	78,232	1	84,618	5
Danes	13,700	1	14,400	1	15,400	1	14,843	1	15,425	1	17,289	1
Alsace-Lorraine	101,156	10	114,700	8	107,400	10	101,921	9	103,626	7	162,007	9
Antisemites	47,500	5	263,861	16	284,250	13	244,543	11	248,534	16	104,538	3
Other parties	74,600	2	129,000	5	397,500	18	267,142	11	319,574	14	497,252	16

NOTE

1. The number of votes cast is for the "valid" votes cast.
2. The number of votes for the Reichspartei for the first two elections includes also the Liberale Reichspartei.
3. Under Progressives are included the several factions which went under changing names and which were eventually all united into the one Progressive party.
4. The sources for these returns are the *Statistisches Jahrbuch, Statistik des deutschen Reichs, Vierteljahrshefte für Statistik des deutschen Reichs.*

APPENDIX B: Reichstag Elections 1919–1933

PARTY	NATIONAL ASSEMBLY JANUARY 19, 1919			JUNE 6, 1920			MAY 4, 1924			DECEMBER 7, 1924			MAY 20, 1928		
	Total Votes	%	No. Deputies	Total Votes	%	No. Deputies	Total Votes	%	No. Deputies	Total Votes	%	No. Deputies	Total Votes	%	No. Deputies
No. eligible voters	36,766,500		423	35,949,800		459	38,375,000		472	38,987,800		493	41,224,700		491
No. valid votes cast	30,400,300	82.7		28,196,300	78.4		29,281,800	76.30		30,290,100	77.69		30,753,300	74.60	
Majority Socialists	11,509,100	37.9	165	6,104,400	21.6	102	6,008,900	20.5	100	7,881,000	26.0	131	9,153,000	29.8	153
Independent Socialists	2,317,300	7.6	22	5,046,800	17.9	84		...	..	......	...	..	......	...	..
Communist party	......	...	..	589,500	2.1	4	3,693,300	12.6	62	2,709,100	9.0	45	3,264,800	10.6	54
Center	5,980,200	19.7	91	3,845,000	13.6	64	3,914,400	13.4	65	4,118,900	13.6	69	3,712,200	12.1	62
Bavarian People's party	......	...	..	1,238,600	4.4	21	946,700	3.2	16	1,134,000	3.7	19	945,600	3.0	16
Democrats	5,641,800	18.6	75	2,333,700	8.3	39	1,655,100	5.7	28	1,919,800	6.3	32	1,505,700	4.9	25
People's party	1,345,600	4.4	19	3,919,400	13.9	65	2,694,400	9.2	45	3,049,100	10.1	51	2,679,700	8.7	45
Wirtschaftspartei	275,100	0.9	4	218,600	0.8	4	692,600	2.4	10	1,005,400	3.3	17	1,397,100	4.5	23
Nationalists	3,121,500	10.3	44	4,249,100	14.9	71	5,696,500	19.5	95	6,205,800	20.5	103	4,381,600	14.2	73
Christlich-soz. Volksdienst	......	...	..	...	...	..	......	...	..	......	...	..	......	...	..
Landbund	......	...	..	...	...	..	574,900	1.9	10	499,400	1.6	8	199,500	0.6	3
Christlich-natl. Bauern u. Landvolk							...	...	..	......	...	..	581,800	1.8	10
Deutsch-Hannov. Partei	77,200	0.2	1	319,100	0.9	5	319,800	1.0	5	262,700	0.8	4	195,600	0.5	3
Deutsche Bauernpartei	......	...	..	......	...	..	......	...	..	......	...	..	481,300	1.5	8
National Socialists	......	...	..	......	...	..	1,918,300	6.5	32	907,300	3.0	14	810,100	2.6	12
Other parties	132,500	0.4	2	332,100	1.6	..	1,165,900	4.0	4	597,600	2.0	..	1,445,300	4.8	4

Reichstag Elections 1919-1933 *(Cont.)*

PARTY	SEPTEMBER 14, 1930			JULY 31, 1932			NOVEMBER 6, 1932			MARCH 5, 1933			NOVEMBER 12, 1933		
	Total Votes	%	No. Deputies	Total Votes	%	No. Deputies	Total Votes	%	No. Deputies	Total Votes	%	No. Deputies	Total Votes	%	No. Deputies
No. eligible voters	42,957,700		577	44,226,800		608	44,373,700		584	44,685,800		647	45,141,900		661
No. valid votes cast	34,970,900	81.41		36,882,400	83.59		35,471,800	79.93		39,343,300	88.04		42,988,100*	95.2	
Majority Socialists	8,577,700	24.5	143	7,959,700	21.6	133	7,248,000	20.4	121	7,181,600	18.3	120			
Independent Socialists	......	...	..	......	...	..	......	...	..	......	...	..			
Communist party	4,592,100	13.1	77	5,282,600	14.6	89	5,980,200	16.9	100	4,848,100	12.3	81			
Center	4,127,900	11.8	68	4,589,300	12.5	75	4,230,600	11.9	70	4,424,900	11.7	74			
Bavarian People's party	1,059,100	3.0	19	1,192,700	3.2	22	1,094,600	3.1	20	1,073,600	2.7	18			
Democrats	1,322,400	3.8	20	371,800	1.0	4	336,500	1.0	2	334,200	0.8	5			
People's party	1,578,200	4.5	30	436,000	1.2	7	661,800	1.9	11	432,300	1.1	2			
Wirtschaftspartei	1,362,400	3.9	23	146,900	0.4	2	110,300	0.3	1	......	...	..			
Nationalists	2,458,300	7.0	41	2,177,400	5.9	37	2,959,000	8.8	52	3,136,800	8.0	52			
Christlich-soz. Volksdienst	868,200	2.5	14	405,300	1.1	3	412,500	1.2	5	384,000	1.0	4			
Landbund	194,000	0.5	3	96,900	0.2	2	105,200	0.3	2	83,800	0.2	1			
Christlich-natl. Bauern u. Landvolk	1,108,700	3.0	19	90,600	0.2	1	46,400	0.1	..	......	...	..			
Deutsch-Hannov. Partei	144,300	0.4	3	46,900	0.1	..	64,000	0.2	1	47,700	0.1	..			
Deutsche Bauernpartei	339,600	1.0	6	137,100	0.3	2	149,000	0.4	3	114,000	0.3	2			
National Socialists	6,409,600	18.3	107	13,745,800	37.4	230	11,737,000	33.1	196	17,277,200	43.9	288	39,638,800	92.2	661
Other parties	1,073,500	3.1	4	342,500	0.9	1	749,200	2.2	..	136,646	0.3	..			

* No. invalid votes: 3,349,363

604

APPENDIX C: Reich Cabinets of Weimar Republic

CHANCELLOR	TERM OF OFFICE	PARTIES REPRESENTED IN CABINET
1. Scheidemann (S.P.D.)	2/13/19 to 6/19/19	7 S.P.D., 3 Dem., 3 Cent., 1 non-partisan
2. Bauer (S.P.D.)	6/19/19 to 10/3/19	7 S.P.D., 4 Cent.
3. Bauer (S.P.D.)	10/3/19 to 3/26/20	6 S.P.D., 4 Cent., 3 Dem.
4. Müller (S.P.D.)	3/27/20 to 6/8/20	5 S.P.D., 3 Dem., 4 Cent.
5. Fehrenbach (Cent.)	6/20/20 to 5/4/21	2 Dem., 5 Cent., 3 People's, 2 non-partisan
6. Wirth (Cent.)	5/9/21 to 10/22/21	3 S.P.D., 3 Dem., 2 Cent., 2 non-partisan
7. Wirth (Cent.)	10/26/21 to 11/14/22	4 S.P.D., 2 Dem., 4 Cent., 1 non-partisan
8. Cuno (non-part.)	11/22/22 to 8/12/23	2 Dem., 2 Cent., 2 People's, 1 Natlst., 4 non-partisan
9. Stresemann (People's)	8/13/23 to 10/3/23	4 S.P.D., 2 Dem., 3 Cent., 2 People's, 1 non-partisan
10. Stresemann (People's)	10/6/23 to 11/28/23	3 S.P.D., 2 Dem., 3 Cent., 2 People's, 1 non-partisan
11. Marx (Cent.)	11/30/23 to 5/26/24	3 Dem., 3 Cent., 2 People's, 1 Bav. People's, 2 non-partisan
12. Marx (Cent.)	6/3/24 to 12/15/24	3 Dem., 2 Cent., 2 People's, 2 non-part., 1 Bav. People's
13. Luther (non-part.)	1/16/25 to 10/29/25	2 Cent., 2 People's, 5 Natlst., 1 Bav. People's, 2 non-partisan
14. Luther (non-part.)	1/20/26 to 5/18/26	3 Dem., 3 Cent., 3 People's, 1 Bav. People's
15. Marx (Cent.)	5/18/26 to 2/1/27	3 Dem., 4 Cent., 3 People's, 1 Bav. People's
16. Marx (Cent.)	2/1/27 to 6/28/28	3 Cent., 1 Bav. People's, 2 People's, 4 Natlst., 1 non-partisan
17. Müller (S.P.D.)	6/28/28 to 3/29/30	4 S.P.D., 2 Dem., 1 Cent., 1 Bav. People's, 2 People's, 1 non-partisan
18. Brüning (Cent.)	3/29/30 to 10/7/31	4 Cent., 1 Bav. People's, 2 People's, 1 Dem., 1 Natlst., 1 Wirtschaft., 1 non-partisan
19. Brüning (Cent.)	10/9/31 to 5/30/32	2 Cent., 1 Bav. People's, 1 Staatspartei, 5 non-partisan
20. Von Papen (non-part.)	5/31/32 to 11/17/32	No Party Ministers
21. Von Schleicher (non-part.)	12/2/32 to 1/28/33	No Party Ministers

605

APPENDIX D: Election Results 1949–1965

Parties	1949 Seats	1949 %	1953 Seats	1953 %	1957 Seats	1957 %	1961 Seats	1961 %	1965 Seats	1965 %
C.D.U./C.S.U.	139	35	243	51	270	52	242	49	245	48
S.P.D.	131	33	151	31	169	35	190	37	202	39
F.D.P.	52	13	48	10	41	8	67	12	49	9
K.P.D.	15	4	..	4	..	..	..	..	..	..
B.H.E.	..	..	27	4	..	..	..	..	..	..
Minor parties	65	15	15	4	17	5	..	2	..	4
Total deputies	402		487		497		499		496	

NOTE

The total size of Bundestag varies from election to election: It was, for example, 402 in 1949, 499 in 1961 and 496 in 1965. The 5 per cent clause, virtually wiping out minor parties, came into effect in 1953.

General Bibliographical Note

It would hardly be feasible to attempt to provide here a complete bibliographical guide to the literature on modern German history and culture. What
follows is a selected list of works which this author considers to be of most
value for students of German history. We shall list works of a more comprehensive character in this introductory section and cite the more specific literature in the notes to each of the succeeding chapters.

The most detailed bibliographical guide is Dahlmann-Waitz, *Quellenkunde
der deutschen Geschichte,* 2 vols. (9th ed., Leipzig, 1931–1932), to be supplemented by the annual volumes of the *Jahresberichte für deutsche Geschichte*
for the years following 1931. For English readers there is G. M. Dutcher, *et al.,
A Guide to Historical Literature* (New York, 1931). *Germany, A Companion
to German Studies,* ed. Jethro Bithell (4th ed., London, 1947), is a convenient
handbook with selected bibliographies, but is better on literature and art than on
political and social currents. *A Bibliographical Introduction to Nationalism*
(New York, 1935), by Koppel S. Pinson, lists the most important books and
articles on German nationalism with critical evaluations. The most important
specialized encyclopedias for this subject are the *Handwörterbuch der Staatswissenschaften,* 8 vols. (4th ed., Jena, 1921–1929); *Staatslexikon,* 5 vols. (5th ed.,
Freiburg im Breisgau, 1926–1932); Bruno Gebhardt's *Handbuch der deutschen
Geschichte,* 2 vols. (7th ed., Stuttgart, 1931). *The Encyclopaedia of the Social
Sciences,* 15 vols. (New York, 1930–1935), contains a vast amount of material
on modern Germany. Many of the articles were written by outstanding German
scholars, and the editors made a special effort to integrate the results of German
research into the articles and especially into the bibliographies attached to the
articles. The only attempt at a comprehensive collection of source materials for
the entire period is Johannes Hohfeld's *Dokumente der deutschen Politik und
Geschichte von 1848 bis zur Gegenwart,* 6 vols. (Berlin, 1951–1954). It is
scheduled to be in six volumes; but the two volumes on the Nazi period are not
yet published. The selection of materials leans to the traditional school of
German history, with very little attention given to liberalism, labor, socialism,
and social and cultural trends.

Of the larger histories of Germany, the only one that approximates com-
pleteness so far as chronology goes is Karl Lamprecht's *Deutsche Geschichte,*
16 vols. (4th ed., Berlin, 1920–1922). Despite the great erudition of the author
and the huge amount of material assembled, Lamprecht's peculiar methodological approach makes his work almost unusable, especially to Anglo-American readers. Much more valuable are the two uncompleted attempts to write
the story of the nineteenth century in Germany: Heinrich von Treitschke's
Deutsche Geschichte im 19. Jahrhundert, 5 vols. (Leipzig, 1879–1894), in
English translation by Eden and Cedar Paul, 7 vols. (London, 1915–1919), and
especially Franz Schnabel's *Deutsche Geschichte im neunzehnten Jahrhundert,*
4 vols. (Freiberg im Breisgau, 1929–1937, rev. ed., 1948-1951). Worthwhile
chapters on German history are found in the *Propyläen Weltgeschichte,* ed.
Walter Goetz, 10 vols. (Berlin, 1930–1933), especially in vols. vii, viii, and x.
They are accompanied by profuse illustrations and magnificent facsimile
reproductions of many valuable documents. Edmond Vermeil's *L'Allemagne*

Contemporaine, 2 vols. (Paris, 1953) deals mainly with the period since 1890. No serious study of modern German history is possible without the use of the various works by Friedrich Meinecke. Of special importance are his *Weltbürgertum und Nationalstaat* (7th ed., Munich, 1928); *Die Idee der Staatsraison in der neueren Geschichte* (Munich, 1924); *Preussen und Deutschland im 19. una 20. Jahrhundert* (Munich, 1918); *Staat und Persönlichkeit. Studien* (Berlin, 1933).

Of briefer surveys the best are: F. A. Henderson, *A Short History of Germany,* 2 vols. (2d ed., New York, 1916); A. W. Ward, *Germany 1815–1890,* 3 vols. (Cambridge, 1916–1918); W. H. Dawson, *The German Empire,* 2 vols. (London, 1919); Veit Valentin, *German People; Their History and Civilization from the Holy Roman Empire to the Third Reich,* translated from the German (New York, 1946); H. S. Steinberg, *A Short History of Germany* (Cambridge, 1944); H. Lichtenberger, *Germany and Its Evolution,* translated from the French (New York, 1913); A. J. P. Taylor, *The Course of German History* (London, 1945); Ralph Flenley, *Modern German History* (London, 1953); E. Vermeil, *Germany's Three Reichs, Their History and Culture,* translated by E. W. Dickes (London, 1944); Friedrich S. Sell, *Die Tragödie des deutschen Liberalismus* (Stuttgart, 1953). Louis L. Snyder's *German Nationalism: The Tragedy of a People* (Harrisburg, 1952) contains a number of suggestive essays.

For the antecedents of modern Germany the best introduction is G. Barraclough's *The Origins of Modern Germany* (Oxford, 1947). For the regional study of Germany and its geography, see: Robert E. Dickinson, *Germany, a General and Regional Geography* (New York, 1953); J. K. Pollock and Homer Thomas, *Germany in Power and Eclipse* (New York, 1952).

Bibliography of Works in English on Modern German History

SECTION I: 1789–1815

Alexander, Edgar. "Church and Society in Germany," in Moody, Joseph (ed.). *Catholic Social and Political Movements 1789–1950*. New York: 1953.

Anderson, Eugene N. *Nationalism and the Cultural Crisis in Prussia 1806–15*. New York: 1939.

Aris, Reinhold. *History of German Political Thought from 1789–1815*. London: 1936.

Bruford, W. H. *Germany in the Eighteenth Century: The Social Background of the Literary Revival*. Cambridge: 1935.

Butler, E. M. *The Tyranny of Greece over Germany*. Cambridge: 1935.

Coudray, Helene du. *Metternich*. New Haven, Conn.: 1936.

Engelbrecht, H. C. J. *G. Fichte: A Study of His Writings with Special Reference to His Nationalism*. New York: 1933.

Epstein, Klaus. *The Genesis of German Conservatism*. Princeton, N. J.: 1966.

Ergang, R. R. *Herder and the Foundations of German Nationalism*. New York: 1931.

Fisher, Herbert. *Studies in Napoleonic Statesmanship: Germany*. Oxford: 1923.

Ford, Guy Stanton. *Hanover and Prussia 1795–1803: A Study in Neutrality*. New York: 1903.

———. *Stein and the Era of Reform in Prussia*. Princeton, N. J.: 1922.

Gooch, George P. *Germany and the French Revolution*. London: 1927.

Herman, Arthur. *Metternich*. London: 1932.

Kissinger, Henry A. *A World Restored: Metternich, Castlereagh and the Problems of Peace*. Boston: 1957.

Kraehe, Enno. *Metternich's German Policy: The Contest with Napoleon 1799–1814*. Princeton, N. J.: 1963.

Langsam, Walter C. *Francis the Good: The Education of an Emperor 1768–1792*. New York: 1949.

———. *The Napoleonic Wars and German Nationalism in Austria*. New York: 1930.

Mann, Golo. *Secretary of Europe: The Life of Friedrich Gentz, Enemy of Napoleon*. New Haven, Conn.: 1946.

Pinson, Koppel S. *Pietism as a Factor in the Rise of German Nationalism*. New York: 1934.

Pundt, A. G. *Arndt and the Nationalist Awakening in Germany*. New York: 1935.

Rosenberg, Hans. *Bureaucracy, Aristocracy and the Autocracy. The Prussian Experience 1660–1815*. Cambridge, Mass.: 1958.

Seeley, John R. *The Life and Times of Stein*. Cambridge: 1878. 3 vols.

Shanahan, W. O. *Prussian Military Reforms 1786–1813*. New York: 1945.
Simon, Walter M. *The Failure of the Prussian Reform Movement 1807–1819*. Ithaca, N. Y.: 1955.
Sweet, Paul R. *Friedrich von Gentz, Defender of the Old Order*. Madison, Wis.: 1941.

SECTION II: 1815–1850

Berlin, Isaiah. *Karl Marx*. New York: 1939.
Brandes, Georg. *Young Germany*. London: 1903.
Butler, E. M. *The St. Simonian Religion in Germany*. Cambridge: 1926.
Clapham, J. H. *The Economic Development of Germany and France 1815–1914*. Cambridge: 1955.
Engels, Friedrich. *Germany: Revolution and Counter-Revolution*. London: 1933.
Hamerow, T. S. *Restoration, Revolution, Reaction: Economics and Politics in Germany 1815–71*. Princeton, N. J.: 1958.
Henderson, W. O. *The Zollverein*. Cambridge: 1939.
Hook, Sidney. *From Hegel to Marx*. New York: 1935.
Krieger, Leonard. *The German Idea of Freedom, History of a Political Tradition*. Boston: 1957.
Legge, J. G. *Rhyme and Revolution in Germany: A Study in German History, Life, Literature and Character 1813–50*. London: 1918.
Marcuse, Herbert. *Reason and Revelation: Hegel and the Rise of Social Theory*. New York: 1941.
Mayer, Gustav. *Friedrich Engels*. London: 1936.
Namier, Lewis B. *1848: The Revolution of the Intellectuals*. London: 1948.
Price, Arnold H. *The Evolution of the Zollverein*. Ann Arbor: 1949.
Rohr, Donald G. *The Origins of Social Liberalism in Germany*. Chicago: 1964.
Thomas, Richard. *Liberalism, Nationalism, and the German Intellectuals (1822–1847)*. Cambridge: 1951.
Valentin, Veit. *1848: Chapters of German History*. London: 1940.
Walker, Mack. *Germany and the Emigration, 1816–85*. Cambridge, Mass.: 1964.
Wittke, Carl F. *The Utopian Communist: A Biography of Wilhelm Weitling* Baton Rouge: 1950.

SECTION III: 1850–1890

Bismarck, Otto von. *Reflections and Reminiscences*. London: 1898. 2 vols.
Bonnin, G. *Bismarck and the Hohenzollern Candidature for the Spanish Throne*. London: 1957.
Bramsted, Ernest K. *Aristocracy and the Middle Classes in Germany: Social Types in German Literature 1830–1900*. Chicago: 1964.
Busch, Moritz. *Bismarck. Secret Pages of His History*. London: 1908. 3 vols.
Clark, C. W. *Franz Joseph and Bismarck: The Diplomacy of Austria Before the War of 1866*. Cambridge, Mass.: 1934.
Darmstaedter, F. *Bismarck and the Creation of the German Reich*. London: 1948.
Dawson, William H. *Prince Bismarck and State Socialism*. London: 1890.

Dorpalen, Andreas. *Heinrich von Treitschke*. New Haven, Conn.: 1957.
Emerson, Rupert. *State and Sovereignty in Modern Germany*. New Haven, Conn.: 1928.
Eyck, Erich. *Bismarck and the German Empire*. New York: 1950.
Footman, David. *Ferdinand Lassalle*. New Haven, Conn.: 1947.
Friedjung, Heinrich. *The Struggle for Supremacy in Germany: 1859–1866*. New York: 1935.
Fuller, J. W. *Bismarckian Diplomacy at Its Zenith*. New York: 1922.
Howard, Michael. *The Franco-Prussian War*. New York: 1961.
Lord, R. H. *The Origins of the War of 1870*. Cambridge, Mass.: 1924.
Lougee, Robert W. *Paul de Lagarde. A Study of Radical Conservatism in Germany*. Cambridge, Mass.: 1962.
Morris, W. O. *Moltke, a Biographical and Critical Study*. London: 1894.
Mosse, W. E. *The European Powers and the German Question 1848–1871*. Cambridge: 1958.
Oncken, Hermann. *Napoleon III and the Rhine: The Origin of the War of 1870–1871*. New York: 1928.
Pflanze, Otto. *Bismarck and the Development of Germany: 1815–1871*. Princeton, N. J.: 1963.
Robertson, Charles G. *Bismarck*. London: 1918.
Shanahan, W. O. *German Protestants Face the Social Question*. Notre Dame: 1954.
Steefel, L. D. *Bismarck, the Hohenzollern Candidature and the Origins of the Franco-Prussian War*. Cambridge: 1962.
———. *The Schleswig-Holstein Question*. Cambridge, Mass.: 1932.
Sybel, Heinrich von. *The Founding of the German Empire by William I, Based Chiefly upon Prussian State Documents*. New York: 1890–1898.
Taylor, A. J. P. *Bismarck, the Man and the Statesman*. New York: 1956.
Wiegler, P. *William the First*. London: 1929.
Windell, G. O. *The Catholics and German Unity 1866–1871*. Minneapolis: 1954.

SECTION IV: 1890–1918

Anderson, Pauline R. *The Background of Anti-English Feeling in Germany 1890–1902*. Washington, D.C.: 1939.
Bebel, August. *My Life*. London: 1912.
Bernhardi, Friedrich von. *Germany and the Next War*. New York: 1914.
Brandenburg, Erich. *From Bismarck to the World War: A History of German Foreign Policy, 1870–1914*. London: 1927.
Bruck, W. F. *Economic and Social History of Germany from William II to Hitler*. London: 1938.
Bülow, Bernhard von. *Memoirs*. Boston: 1931–1932. 4 vols.
Carroll, E. M. *Germany and the Great Powers 1866–1914: A Study in Public Opinion and Foreign Policy*. New York: 1938.
Cowles, Virginia. *The Kaiser*. New York: 1963.
Crothers, G. D. *The German Elections of 1907*. New York: 1941.
Dehio, Ludwig. *Germany and World Politics in the Twentieth Century*. New York: 1959.
Gatzke, Hans. *Germany's Drive to the West: A Study of Germany's Western War Aims During the First World War*. Baltimore: 1950.

Gay, Peter. *The Dilemma of Democratic Socialism: Eduard Bernstein's Challenge to Marx.* New York: 1952.

Gerschenkron, Alexander. *Bread and Democracy in Germany.* Berkeley, Calif.: 1943.

Haller, Josef. *Philip Eulenburg: The Kaiser's Friend.* New York: 1930. 2 vols.

Hohenlohe-Schillingsfürst, Prince. *Memoirs.* London: 1906.

Kohn, Hans (ed.). *German History: Some New German Views.* Boston: 1954.

Kuczynski, Jürgen. *Short History of Labour Conditions in Germany 1800 to the Present.* London: 1945.

Kürenberg, J. von. *The Kaiser, A Life of William II.* London: 1954.

Laqueur, Walter. *Young Germany: A History of the German Youth Movement.* New York: 1962.

Ludwig, Emil. *William Hohenzollern, the Last of the Kaisers.* New York: 1927.

Massing, Paul. *Rehearsal for Destruction, a Study of Political Anti-Semitism in Imperial Germany.* New York: 1949.

May, Ernest. *The World War and American Isolation.* Cambridge, Mass.: 1959.

Mayer, Arno J. *Political Origins of the New Diplomacy 1917–18.* New Haven, Conn.: 1959.

Meyer, Henry Cord. *Mitteleuropa in German Thought and Action 1815–1945.* The Hague: 1955.

Muncy, L. W. *The Junker in the Prussian Administration 1888–1914.* Providence: 1944.

Ritter, Gerhard. *The Schlieffen Plan. Critique of a Myth.* New York: 1958.

Rudin, Harry. *Armistice, 1918.* New Haven, Conn.: 1944.

Mendelssohn-Bartholdy, A. *The War and German Society.* New Haven, Conn.: 1937.

Nichols, J. A. *Germany After Bismarck.* Cambridge, Mass.: 1958.

Rosenberg, Arthur. *The Birth of the German Republic, 1871–1918.* New York: 1931.

Roth, Guenther. *The Social Democrats in Imperial Germany: A Study in Working-Class Isolation and National Integration.* Totowa, N. J.: 1963.

Schorske, Carl E. *German Social Democracy, 1905–1917.* Cambridge, Mass.: 1955.

Sontag, Raymond J. *Germany and England, Background of Conflict, 1848–1918.* New York: 1938.

Stern, Fritz. *The Politics of Cultural Despair.* Berkeley, Calif.: 1961.

Stolper, Gustav. *German Economy, 1870–1940: Issues and Trends.* New York: 1940.

Tirrell, Sarah. *German Agrarian Politics After Bismarck's Fall.* New York: 1951.

Townsend, Mary E. *The Rise and Fall of Germany's Colonial Empire, 1884–1918.* New York: 1930.

Veblen, Thorstein. *Imperial Germany and the Industrial Revolution.* New York: 1915.

Wertheimer, Mildred. *The Pan-German League 1890–1918.* New York: 1924.

Wheeler-Bennett, John W. *The Forgotten Peace: Brest-Litovsk 1918.* New York: 1938.

Wolff, Theodor. *The Eve of 1914.* London: 1936.

Woodward, E. L. *Great Britain and the German Navy.* London: 1935.

Section V: 1918–1933

Anderson, Evelyn. *Hammer or Anvil: The Story of the German Working-Class Movement.* London: 1945.

Angress, Werner. *Stillborn Revolution. The Communist Bid for Power in Germany 1921–23.* Princeton, N. J.: 1963.

Beck, Earl. *The Death of the Prussian Republic. A Study of Reich-Prussian Relations 1932–34.* Tallahassee: 1959.

Bennett, Edward. *Germany and the Diplomacy of the Financial Crisis 1931.* Cambridge, Mass.: 1962.

Berlau, A. J. *The German Social Democratic Party, 1914–1921.* New York: 1949.

Bowen, Ralph. *German Theories of the Corporative State.* New York: 1947.

Brecht, Arnold. *Federalism and Regionalism in Germany.* New York: 1945.

———. *Prelude to Silence—The End of the German Republic.* New York: 1944.

Bresciani-Turroni, Costantino. *The Economics of Inflation; a Study of Currency Depreciation in Post-war Germany.* London: 1937.

Bretton, Henry L. *Stresemann and the Revision of Versailles.* Stanford, Calif.: 1953.

Carr, E. H. *German-Soviet Relations Between the Two World Wars.* Baltimore: 1951.

Clark, R. T. *The Fall of the German Republic.* London: 1935.

Coper, Rudolf. *Failure of a Revolution. Germany 1918–1919.* Cambridge: 1955.

Craig, Gordon. *The Politics of the Prussian Army 1640–1945.* New York: 1956.

D'Abernon, Viscount. *An Ambassador of Peace. Diary 1920–26.* London: 1929.

Dorpalen, Andreas. *Hindenburg and the Politics of the Weimar Republic.* Princeton, N. J.: 1964.

Epstein, Klaus. *Matthias Erzberger and the Dilemma of German Democracy.* Princeton, N. J.: 1959.

Eyck, Erich. *A History of the Weimar Republic.* Cambridge, Mass.: 1962–1964. 2 vols.

Fischer, Ruth. *Stalin and German Communism.* Cambridge, Mass.: 1948.

Freund, Gerald. *Unholy Alliance; Russian-German Relations from the Treaty of Brest-Litovsk to the Treaty of Berlin.* London: 1957.

Froelich, Paul. *Rosa Luxemburg: Her Life and Work.* New York: 1940.

Gatzke, Hans. *Stresemann and the Rearmament of Germany.* Baltimore: 1954.

Gordon, Harold J. *The Reichswehr and the German Republic, 1919–1926.* Princeton, N. J.: 1957.

Halperin, S. William. *Germany Tried Democracy, 1918–1933.* New York: 1946.

Hertzmann, Lewis. *DNVP. Right-Wing Opposition to the Weimar Republic 1918–24.* Lincoln, Neb.: 1963.

Hilger, Gustav, and Alfred G. Meyer. *The Incompatible Allies—A Memoir-History of German Soviet Relations, 1918–1941.* New York: 1953.

Jordan, W. M. *Great Britain, France and the German Problem.* London: 1943.

Kaufmann, Walter. *Monarchism in the Weimar Republic.* New York: 1953.

Kessler, C. H. von. *Walter Rathenau, His Life and Work.* New York: 1930.

King-Hall, Stephen, and Richard Ullmann. *German Parliaments*. London: 1951
Klemperer, Klemens von. *Germany's New Conservatism: Its History and Dilemma in the Twentieth Century*. Princeton, N. J.: 1957.
Kochan, Lionel. *Russia and the Weimar Republic*. London: 1954.
————. *The Struggle for Germany 1914–45*. Chicago: 1963.
Korbel, Josef. *Poland Between East and West. Soviet and German Diplomacy Towards Poland 1919–33*. Princeton, N. J.: 1963.
Lutz, R. H. *The German Revolution, 1918–1919*. Stanford, Calif.: 1922.
Mitchell, Allan. *Revolution in Bavaria 1918–1919. The Eisner Regime and the Soviet Republic*. Princeton, N. J.: 1965.
Rosenberg, Arthur. *A History of the Weimar Republic*. London: 1936.
Scheele, Godfrey. *The Weimar Republic, Overture to the Third Reich*. London: 1945.
Stresemann, Gustav. *Diaries, Letters and Papers* (ed. by E. Sutton). London: 1935–1940. 3 vols.
Turner, Henry. *Stresemann and the Politics of the Weimar Republic*. Princeton, N. J.: 1963.
Waite, Robert G. L. *Vanguard of Nazism: The Free Corps Movement in Postwar Germany, 1918–1923*. Cambridge, Mass.: 1952.
Waldman, Eric. *The Spartacist Uprising of 1919 and the Crisis of the German Socialist Movement*. Milwaukee: 1958.
Watkins, F. M. *The Failure of Constitutional Emergency Powers Under the German Republic*. Cambridge, Mass.: 1939.

SECTION VI: 1933–1945

Abel, Theodore. *Why Hitler Came into Power; an Answer Based on the Original Life Stories of Six Hundred of His Followers*. New York: 1938.
Arendt, Hannah. *Eichmann in Jerusalem*. New York: 1963.
Baumont, Maurice, J. H. Fried, and E. Vermeil (eds.). *The Third Reich*. New York: 1955.
Blond, G. *The Death of Hitler's Germany*. New York: 1954.
Buchheim, Hans. *The Third Reich. Its Beginnings, Its Development, Its End*. Munich: 1961.
Bullock, Alan. *Hitler, a Study in Tyranny*. New York: 1952.
Butler, Rohan. *The Roots of National Socialism 1783–1933*. London: 1941.
Crankshaw, Edward. *Gestapo: Instrument of Tyranny*. New York: 1956.
Dallin, Alexander. *German Rule in Russia 1941–1945. A Study of Occupation Policies*. New York: 1957.
Dulles, A. W. *Germany's Underground*. New York: 1947.
Edinger, Lewis J. *German Exile Politics; the Social Democratic Executive Committee in the Nazi Era*. Berkeley: 1956.
Fitzgibbon, Constantine. *20 July*. New York: 1956.
Fraenkel, Ernst. *The Dual State; a Contribution to the Theory of Dictatorship*. New York: 1941.
Fromm, Erich. *Escape from Freedom*. New York: 1941.
Gallin, Mary A. *Ethical and Religious Factors in the German Resistance to Hitler*. Washington, D.C.: 1955.
Gisevius, H. B. *To the Bitter End*. Boston: 1947.
Hassel, Ulrich von. *Diaries, 1938–1944*. New York: 1947.
Heiden, Konrad. *Der Führer: Hitler's Rise to Power*. Boston: 1944.

————. *History of National Socialism.* New York: 1935.

Hilberg, R. *The Destruction of the European Jews.* Chicago: 1961.

Irving, David. *The Destruction of Dresden.* New York: 1964.

Jarman, T. L. *The Rise and Fall of Nazi Germany.* New York: 1956.

Klein, B. H. *Germany's Economic Preparation for War.* Cambridge: 1959.

Kochan, Lionel. *Pogrom. 10 November 1938.* London: 1957.

Kogon, Eugen. *The Theory and Practice of Hell.* New York: 1951.

Kolnai, A. *The War Against the West.* London: 1938.

Lehmann-Haupt, Hellmut. *Art Under a Dictatorship.* London: 1954.

Lochner, Louis. *Tycoons and Tyrant; German Industry from Hitler to Adenauer.* Chicago: 1954.

Lowie, Robert H. *Towards Understanding Germany.* Chicago: 1954.

Mau, Hermann, and Helmut Krausnick. *German History 1933–45.* London: 1959.

Mayer, Milton. *They Thought They Were Free.* Chicago: 1955.

Meinecke, Friedrich. *The German Catastrophe. Reflections and Recollections.* Cambridge, Mass.: 1950.

Micklem, Nathaniel. *National Socialism and the Catholic Church.* London, 1939.

Mosse, George L. *The Crisis of German Ideology. Intellectual Origins of the Third Reich.* New York: 1964.

Neumann, Franz L. *Behemoth, the Structure and Practice of National Socialism, 1933–1944.* New York: 1944.

Rauschning, Hermann. *The Revolution of Nihilism.* New York: 1939.

Reichmann, Eva. *Hostages of Civilization. The Social Sources of National Socialist Anti-Semitism.* London: 1950.

Reitlinger, Gerald. *The Final Solution. The Attempt to Exterminate the Jews of Europe, 1939–45.* New York: 1953.

————. *The S.S., Alibi of a Nation 1922–45.* London: 1956.

Ritter, Gerhard. *The German Resistance: Carl Goerdeler's Struggle Against Tyranny.* New York: 1958.

Roberts, S. H. *The House That Hitler Built.* London: 1937.

Rothfels, Hans. *The German Opposition to Hitler.* Chicago: 1948.

Schlabrendorff, F. von. *They Almost Killed Hitler.* New York: 1947.

Seabury, Paul. *The Wilhelmsstrasse: A Study of German Diplomats Under the Nazi Regime.* Berkeley: 1954.

Shirer, William. *The Rise and Fall of the Third Reich.* New York: 1960.

Snell, John L. *Origins of the East-West Dilemma over Germany.* New Orleans: 1959.

Snyder, Louis. *German Nationalism: The Tragedy of a People.* Harrisburg: 1952.

Taylor, Telford. *Sword and Swastika: Generals and Nazis in the Third Reich.* New York: 1952.

Tobias, Fritz. *The Reichstag Fire.* New York: 1965.

Toynbee, Arnold (ed.). *Hitler's Europe.* London: 1955.

Trevor-Roper, Hugh R. *Hitler's Secret Conversations, 1941–1944.* New York: 1953.

————. *The Last Days of Hitler.* New York: 1947.

Viereck, Peter. *Metapolitics. The Roots of the Nazi Mind.* New York: 1941.

Wheeler-Bennett, John W. *Munich, Prologue to Tragedy.* New York: 1948.

————. *Nemesis of Power: The German Army in Politics, 1918–1945.* London: 1953.

————. *The Wooden Titan: Hindenburg in Twenty Years of German History 1914–1934*. London: 1936.
Wiskemann, Elizabeth. *The Berlin-Rome Axis*. London: 1949.
Zimmermann, Erich, and Hans Adolf Jacobsen. *Germans Against Hitler. July 20, 1944*. Bonn: 1960.

SECTION VII: 1945–1949

Almond, Gabriel. *The Struggle for Democracy in Germany*. Chapel Hill: 1949.
Balfour, Michael, and John Mair. *Four Power Control of Germany and Austria 1945–46*. London: 1956.
Clay, Lucius. *Decision in Germany*. Garden City, N. Y.: 1949.
Davidson, Eugene. *The Death and Life of Germany. An Account of the American Occupation*. New York: 1959.
Ebsworth, Raymond. *Restoring Democracy in Germany*. New York: 1961.
Gimbel, John. *A German Community Under American Occupation*. Stanford, Calif.: 1961.
Golay, John. *The Founding of the Federal Republic of Germany*. Chicago: 1958.
Litchfield, E. H. (ed.). *Governing Post-war Germany*. Ithaca, N. Y.: 1952.
Merkl, Peter. *The Origin of the West German Republic*. New York: 1963.
Montgomery, John D. *Forced to Be Free: The Artificial Revolution in Germany and Japan*. Chicago: 1957.
Nettl, J. P. *The Eastern Zone and Soviet Policy in Germany 1945–50*. London: 1951.
Oppen, Beate Ruhm von (ed.). *Documents on Germany Under Occupation 1945–54*. London: 1955.
Pollock, James K., and James H. Meisel. *Germany Under Occupation. Illustrative Materials and Documents*. Ann Arbor: 1949.
Salomon, Ernst von. *Fragebogen (The Questionnaire)*. New York: 1954.
Willis, F. Roy. *The French in Germany 1945–49*. Stanford, Calif.: 1962.
Zink, Harold. *The United States in Germany 1944–55*. New York: 1957.

SECTION VIII: 1949–

Alexander, Edgar. *Adenauer and the New Germany: The Chancellor of the Vanquished*. New York: 1957.
Chamberlin, W. H. *The German Phoenix*. New York: 1963.
Davison, P. W. *The Berlin Blockade*. Princeton, N. J.: 1958.
Deutsch, Karl W., and Lewis Edinger. *Germany Rejoins the Powers: Mass Opinion, Interest Groups, and Elites in Contemporary German Foreign Policy*. Stanford, Calif.: 1959.
Edinger, Lewis J. *Kurt Schumacher. A Study in Personality and Political Behavior*. Stanford, Cal.: 1965.
Freund, Gerald. *Germany Between Two Worlds*. New York: 1961.
Friedrich, Carl J. *The Soviet Zone of Germany*. New Haven, Conn.: 1956.
Gottlieb, Manuel. *The German Peace Settlement and the Berlin Crisis*. New York: 1960.
Grosser, Alfred. *Colossus Again. Western Germany from Defeat to Rearmament*. New York: 1955.

Hartmann, Heinz. *Authority and Organization in German Management.* Princeton, N. J.: 1959.
Heidenheimer, Arnold. *Adenauer and the CDU. The Rise of the Leader and the Integration of the Party.* The Hague: 1960.
Hiscocks, Richard. *Democracy in Western Germany.* London: 1957.
Kitzinger, U. *German Electoral Politics.* London: 1960.
Lusser, R. S. (ed.). *Soviet Economic Policy in Post-war Germany.* New York: 1953.
McGinnis, Edgar, Richard Hiscocks, and Robert Spencer. *The Shaping of Post-war Germany.* New York: 1960.
Mander, John. *Berlin, Hostage for the West.* Baltimore: 1962.
Pinney, E. L. *Federalism, Bureaucracy and Party Politics in Western Germany: The Role of the Bundesrat.* Chapel Hill: 1963.
Pollock, James K. *German Democracy at Work.* Ann Arbor: 1955.
Speier, Hans. *Divided Berlin—The Anatomy of Soviet Political Blackmail.* New York: 1961.
Speier, Hans, and W. Davison. *West German Leadership and Foreign Policy.* Evanston: 1957.
Spiro, Herbert. *The Politics of German Codetermination.* Cambridge, Mass.: 1958.
Stahl, Walter (ed.). *Education for Democracy in West Germany: Achievements, Shortcomings, Prospects.* New York: 1961.
Stolper, Wolfgang, and Karl Roskamp. *The Structure of the East German Economy.* Cambridge, Mass.: 1960.
Szaz, Zoltan M. *Germany's Eastern Frontiers. The Problem of the Oder-Neisse Line.* Chicago: 1960.
Tetens, T. H. *The New Germany and the Old Nazis.* New York: 1961.
Wallich, Henry. *Mainsprings of the German Revival.* New Haven, Conn.: 1955.
Weymar, Paul. *Adenauer. His Authorized Biography.* New York: 1957.
Wighton, Charles. *Adenauer. Democratic Dictator.* New York: 1963.
Windsor, Philip. *City on Leave—A History of Berlin 1945–62.* London: 1963.
Wunderlich, Frieda. *Farmer and Farm Labor in the Soviet Zone of Germany.* New York: 1958.

Important Documentary Collections and Reference Works*

ENGLISH

Arntz, Helmut. *Facts about Germany*. Wiesbaden: Steiner, 1962. A very useful guide for all serious students of modern Germany at the college and university level. Covers years from 1945–1962. Includes statistics and historical background of all life and work in the Federal German Republic, its policy, economy, social structure, and educational and cultural life.

Boeninger, Hildegard R. *Hoover Library Collection on Germany*. Stanford, Calif.: Stanford University Press, 1955. A concise but very informative guide through the important Hoover Library collection of Documents relating to modern German history.

The Bulletin, Vols. 1–13. Bonn: Press and Information Office of the Federal German Government, 1953–1965. A weekly survey of German affairs.

Documents on German Foreign Policy 1918–1945. Excerpts from captured archives of German Foreign Ministry and Reich Chancellery.
(1) Series C: 1933–1937, Vols. 1–4. Washington, D.C.: GPO, 1957–1962.
(2) Series D: 1937–1945, Vols. 5–12. Washington, D.C.: GPO, 1953–1962.

Documents on Germany 1944–1961. Committee on Foreign Relations, United States Senate, Eighty-seventh Congress. Washington, D.C.: GPO, 1961.

Education in the Soviet Zone of Germany. Washington, D.C.: GPO, 1959.

The Evangelical Church in Berlin and the Soviet Zone of Germany. Berlin: Eckart Verlag, 1959.

Germany in Europe. New York: German Information Center, 1965. Report and statistics on the participation of the Federal German Republic in the European organizations GATT, OEEC, EFTA, ECSC, EUTRATOM, and EEC (Common Market of the Six).

Germany 1947–1949. The Story in Documents. Department of State Publication 3556. Washington, D.C.: GPO, 1950.

Germany Reports 1945–1955. Official reports and statistics of the Federal German Government. Bonn: Press and Information Office of the Federal German Government, 1955.

Germany Reports 1955–1960. Official reports and statistics of the Federal German Government. Weisbaden: Steiner, 1961.

Germany—Soviet Zone and East Berlin. Washington, D.C.: GPO, 1959.

Mannig, Richard. *Deutschland und die Deutschen im englisch-sprachigen Schrifttum 1948–1955*. Herausg. von Inter Nationes, Bonn. Gottingen: 1957. Indispensable bibliographical guide to modern German history of English and American books.

---

* This list has been compiled by Dr. Edgar Alexander.

Occupation of Germany, 1945–1946. Policy and Progress. Washington, D.C.: GPO, 1946.

Robinson, Jacob, and Philip Friedman (eds.). *Guide to Jewish History Under Nazi Impact.* Bibliographical Series No. 1. New York: YIVO Institute for Jewish Research, 1960; Jerusalem: Yad Washem Authority, 1960. Forewords by Benzion Dinur and Salo W. Baron. A monumental annotated bibliography of over 3,700 books, pamphlets, and periodicals in Hebrew, French, English, and, mainly, German.

The Roman Catholic Church in Berlin and the Soviet Zone of Germany. Berlin: Morus Verlag, 1959.

The Wiener Library Catalogue Series
(1) *After Hitler. Germany 1945–1963.* London: 1963. A listing of over 2,700 books and pamphlets on the history of post-war Germany.
(2) *From Weimar to Hitler. Germany 1918–1933,* 2nd ed. London: 1964. A listing of over 3,000 books, pamphlets, and periodicals, mostly in German.
(3) *German Jewry. Its History, Life, and Culture.* London: 1958. A listing of over 3,500 books, pamphlets, periodicals, almanacs and yearbooks on the history of German Jewry from 1789 to 1950.
(4) *Persecution and Resistance Under the Nazis,* 2nd ed. London: 1960. A listing of over 2,200 books, pamphlets, and periodicals, mostly in German.

GERMAN

Bulletin des Presse- und Informationsamtes der Bundesregierung. Reports the official communiqués of the German government; topical documents on government actions and decisions; and important speeches by government officials and leading political personalities. The most topical source available for information on German politics.

Dam, H. van, and Ralph Giordano. *KZ-Verbrecher vor deutschen Gerichten.* Frankfurt: 1962. A report and documentary.

Deutsche Politik 1960, 1961, 1962, 1963, 1964. Taetigkeitsbericht der Bundesregiegierung fuer die Jahre 1960 bis 1964. Bonn: Presse- u. Informationsamt, 1961–1965.

Deutschland im Wiederaufbau. Taetigkeitsbericht der Bundesregierung fuer das Jahr 1950–1958. Foreword by Chancellor Konrad Adenauer. Bonn: Presse- u. Informationsamt., 1951–1959.

Deutschland im Wiederaufbau 1949–1959 und Taetigkeitsbericht der Bundesreigerung für da Jahr 1959. Foreword by Chancellor Konrad Adenauer. Bonn: Press- u. Informationsamt., 1960.
These three series of official annual reports of the German Federal Government on its activities in the various fields of national and international policy and economics, along with the extensive statistical material and charts for each year's edition, constitute a veritable library of sources and documents on contemporary German history.

Ellwein, Thomas. *Das Regierungssytem der Bundesrepublik Deutschland.* Köln: 1963. 2 vols.

Erdmann, Karl D. *Die Zeit der Weltkriege (1914–1945).* Stuttgart: 1960.

Flechtheim, Ossip K. (ed.). *Dokumente zur parteipolitischen Entwicklung in Deutschland seit 1945.* Berlin: 1962–1963. 3 vols.

Hofer, Walther. *Die Diktatur Hitlers bis zum Beginn des Zweiten Weltkrieges.* Konstanz: 1960.

—— (ed.). *Die Entfesselung des Zweiten Weltkrieges. Mit Dokumenten.* Frankfurt: Fischer Bücherei, 1960.

—— (ed.). *Der Nationalsozialismus. Dokumente 1933–1945.* Frankfurt: Fischer Bücherei, 1957.

Jacobsen, Hans-Adolf (ed.). *Der Zweite Weltkrieg, Grundzüge der Politik und Strategie in Dokumenten, 1939–1945.* Frankfurt: Fischer Bücherei, 1965.

——, and Otto Stenzl (eds.). *Deutschland und die Welt. Zur Aussenpolitik der Bundesrepublik 1949–1963.* DTV-Dokumente 174/175. München: 1964.

Jenke, Manfred. *Verschwörung von Rechts? Bericht über den Rechtsradikalismus in Deutschland nach 1945.* Berlin: 1961.

Lemberg, Eugen, and Friedrich Edding (eds.). *Die Vertriebenen in Westdeutschland: Ihre Eingliederung und ihr Einfluss auf Gesellschaft, Wirtschaft, Politik und Geistesleben.* Kiel: 1959. 3 vols. A monumental documentary and source book.

Literaturverzeichnis der Politischen Wissenschaften. Bibliographische Jahresberichte der Hochschule fuer Politische Wissenschaften München. München: Olzog, 1952–1964ff.

Melzer, Joseph (ed.). *Deutsch-Jüdisches Schicksal in dieser Zeit.* Wegweiser durch das Schrifttum der letzten 15 Jahre 1945-1960. *Nachtrag 1960–1961.* Köln: 1960–1961. A bibliography containing over 2,600 publications.

Das Parlament. Semi-official weekly with excellent reporting and documentation on the parliament at Bonn as well as on the problems of political education.

Pirker, Theo. *Die blinde Macht. Die Gewerkschaftsbewegung in Deutschland.* München: 1960. 2 vols.

Pross, Harry (ed.). *Dokumente zur deutschen Politik 1806–1870.* Frankfurt: Fischer Bücherei, 1963. Includes commentary by Pross.

—— (ed.). *Die Zerstoerung der deutschen Politik Dokumente 1871–1933.* Frankfurt: Fischer Bücherei, 1959. Includes commentary by Pross.

Regierung Adenauer 1949–1963. Mit einem Geleitwort von Bundeskanzler Konrad Adenauer. Bonn: Presse- u. Informationsamt. 1963. A 983-page document on the Adenauer era that has already become the most important source book existing on the activities and achievements of Adenauer during his chancellorship.

Schneider, Hans (ed.). *Bibliographie zum oeffentlichen Recht in der Bundesrepublik.* München: 1960.

Schrifttum ueber Deutschland 1918–1963. Erster Teil: Das Schrifttum des Inlands. Zweiter Teil: Das Schrifttum des Auslandes. Ausgewählte Bibliographie zur Politik und Zeitgeschichte. Herausg. von Inter Nations, Bonn. Wiesbaden: Steiner, 1964.

Schwartz, Albert. *Die Weimarer Republik.* Konstanz: 1958.

Die Verfolgung nationalsozialistischer Straftaten im Gebiet der Bundesrepublik seit 1945. Unter Mitwirkung der Landesjustizverwaltungen und der Zentralen Stelle zur Aufklärung nationalsozialistischer Verbrechen in Ludwigsburg zusammengestellt im Bundesjustizminsterium. Bonn: July 1964.

Weber, Heinrick (ed.). *Der deutsche Kommunismus: Dokumente.* Köln: 1963.

Notes

CHAPTER I

1 F. Nietzsche, *Beyond Good and Evil*, tr. by Helen Zimmern, Modern Library edition, no. 244; *Werke*, Musarion edition, vol. vii, pp. 208–211.

2 Cf. Franz L. Neumann, *Behemoth* (New York, 1942); Frederick L. Schuman, *The Nazi Dictatorship* (2nd ed., New York, 1936).

3 Cf. Richard Brickner, *Is Germany Incurable?* (Philadelphia, 1943).

4 Cf. Leonard von Muralt, *From Versailles to Potsdam* (Hinsdale, 1948).

5 Cf. Stephen Heinz, *Die Entstehung der Rheinromantik* (Cologne, 1922), and Oscar Walzel, "Rheinromantik," in *Vom Geistesleben des 18. und 19. Jahrhunderts* (Leipzig, 1911), pp. 256–289.

6 It is interesting to note that the cult of Widukind was stressed much more by the pagan ideologists of the Nazi movement, like Rosenberg and Himmler, than by the Führer himself. Hitler was much more impressed by the exercise of bloody power by Charlemagne in extending the frontiers of his empire. (See *Goebbels Diaries*, ed. Louis Lochner [New York, 1947], p. 358; also *Hitler's Secret Conversations* [New York, 1953], pp. 309–310.)

7 Heinrich von Treitschke, "Das deutsche Ordensland Preussen," in *Historische und politische Aufsätze* (5th ed., Leipzig, 1886), ii, 34–35.

8 See F. W. Foerster, *Europe and the German Question* (New York, 1940), pp. 46–62.

9 See Hans Rosenberg, "The Rise of the Junkers in Brandenburg-Prussia 1410–1653," in *American Historical Review*, xlix (1943), 1–22; see also L. W. Muncy, *The Junker in the Prussian Administration* (Providence, 1944).

10 See Friedrich Meinecke, *Das Zeitalter der deutschen Erhebung* (Leipzig, 1942), chap. ii, "Das alte Preussen."

11 Thomas Mann, *Betrachtungen eines Unpolitischen* (Berlin, 1917), p. 15.

12 F. M. Dostoievsky, *The Diary of a Writer,* tr. Boris Brasol, 2 vols. (New York, 1949) ii, 727.

13 *Betrachtungen* . . . , p. 7.

14 *Ibid.*, p. 609.

15 H. Heine, *Die romantische Schule*, in Insel ed. of *Sämtliche Werke* (Leipzig, 1910–1915), vii, 26.

CHAPTER II

1 H. Heine, *Sämtliche Werke,* Insel ed., vii, 291.

2 *Wilhelm Meister's Travels*, Everyman's ed., ii, 216.

3 See F. Meinecke, *Die Entstehung des Historismus*, 2 vols. (Munich, 1936), ii, 601–620; also Meinecke's *Schiller und der Individualitätsgedanke* (Leipzig, 1937).

4 On Herder and nationalism see: R. R. Ergang, *Herder and the Foundations of German Nationalism* (New York, 1931); Hans Kohn, *The Idea of Nationalism* (New York, 1944), pp. 427–451.

5 Herder, *Briefe zur Beförderung der Humanität*, no. 42.

6 "Ueber National-Religionen," in *Sämtliche Werke*, ed. Suphan, vol. xxiv.

7 Cf. E. Cassirer, *Freiheit und Form* (Berlin, 1922), pp. 476–477.

8 Cf. Kuno Francke, *Weltbürgertum in der deutschen Literatur von Herder bis Nietzsche* (Berlin, 1928), pp. 45–47.

9 On this duality in German idealistic philosophy and liberalism, see John Dewey, *German Philosophy and the War* (New York, 1915, rev. ed., 1942); G. Santayana, *Egotism and German Philosophy* (New York, 1916); G. de Ruggiero, *History of European Liberalism*, tr. R. G. Collingwood (London, 1927), pp. 218–220.

CHAPTER III

1 The finest treatment of the entire complex of problems created by the French revolution in Germany is in vol. i of Franz Schnabel's *Deutsche Geschichte im neunzehnten Jahrhundert* (Freiburg im Breisgau, 1929; 4th ed., 1948). Of the older German works the most famous are Ludwig Häusser, *Deutsche Geschichte vom Tode Friedrichs des Grossen bis zur Gründung des Deutschen Bundes*, 4 vols. (4th ed., Berlin, 1869); Treitschke's *History of Germany*, vol. i; Wilhelm Oncken, *Das Zeitalter der Revolution, des Kaiserreiches und der Befreiungskriege*, 2 vols. (Berlin, 1884–1886); and Friedrich Meinecke, *Das Zeitalter der deutschen Erhebung (1795–1815)* (2d ed., Bielefeld, 1913); all these older German works are of the traditional Prussian school. The best treatment of Napoleonic policy in Germany is H. A. L. Fisher's *Studies in Napoleonic Statesmanship: Germany* (Oxford, 1923); see also M. Dunan, *Napoléon et l'Allemagne. Le système continental et les débuts du Royaume de Bavière 1806–1810* (rev. ed., Paris, 1943), and G. S. Ford, *Hanover and Prussia 1795–1803. A Study in Neutrality* (New York, 1903). Interesting material not available in the academic works on this age is found in the Socialist writer Kurt Eisner's *Das Ende des Reichs. Deutschland und Preussen im Zeitalter der grossen Revolution* (Berlin, 1907). The most important source collections are *Berichte aus der Berliner Franzosenzeit 1807–1809*, ed. Hermann Granier and published as vol. lxxxviii of *Publikationen des K. Preussischen Staatsarchiven* (Leipzig, 1913), and above all the invaluable *Quellen zur Geschichte des Rheinlandes im Zeitalter der französischen Revolution 1780–1801*, ed. Joseph Hansen, 4 vols. (Bonn, 1931–1938). Résumé essays on the Hansen collection are found in Hansen's own "Das linke Rheinufer und die französische Revolution 1789–1801," in *Mitteilungen der deutschen Akademie* (1932), pp. 421–455, and in Hermann Oncken's "Deutsche und rheinische Probleme im Zeitalter der französischen Revolution," in *Sitzungsberichte* of the Prussian Academy of Sciences, Phil.-Hist. Klasse (1936), pp. 79–116 and (1937) 65–104. A valuable treatment of conditions in the Catholic ecclesiastical states is found in Edgar Alexander, "Church and Society in Germany" in *Catholic Social and Political Movements 1789–1950*, ed. Joseph N. Moody (New York, 1953).

The reception of the French revolution among the intellectual classes in Germany has been treated in several works. The fullest treatment now available is J. Droz, *L'Allemagne et la révolution française* (Paris, 1949); see also G. P. Gooch, *Germany and the French Revolution* (London, 1927); Alfred Stern, *Der Einfluss der französischen Revolution auf das deutschen Geistesleben* (Stuttgart, 1928); Jean Jaurès, *Histoire socialiste de la révolution française*, ed. Albert Mathiez, vol. v (Paris, 1923); Otto Tschirch, *Geschichte der öffentlichen Meinung in Preussen vom Basler Frieden bis zum Zusammenbruch des Staates, 1795–1806*, 2 vols. (Weimar, 1933–1934). Collections of the political literature of the time are available in Martin von Geismar, *Die politische Literatur der deutschen im 18. Jahrhundert* (Leipzig, 1847), and Jakob Venedy, *Die deutschen Republikaner unter der französischen Republik* (Leipzig, 1870), which contain long extracts from the pro-revolutionary writers. Anti-French literature is found in Robert Franz Arnold's collection *Fremdherrschaft und Befreiung 1795–1815* (Leipzig, 1932); Ernst Müsebeck's *Gold gab ich für Eisen. Deutschlands Schmach und Erhebung in zeitgenossischen Dokumenten 1806–1815* (Berlin, 1913); and R. Vaupel's *Stimmen aus der Zeit der Erniederung*, vol. viii of *Der deutsche Staatsgedanke* (Munich, 1923).

For the Prussian reforms see the collection of documents, *Die Reorganisation des preussischen Staates unter Stein und Hardenberg*, Part i, "Allgemeine Verwaltungs- und Behördenreform," ed. Georg Winter (Leipzig, 1931), and Part ii, "Das preussische Heer von Tilsiter Frieden bis zur Befreiung," ed. Rudolph Vaupel, vol. i (Leipzig, 1938), both volumes published as vols. xciii–xciv of *Publikationen des Preussischen Staatsarchiven*. The best life of Stein still remains the classic work of J. R. Seeley, *The Life and Times of Stein*, 3 vols. (Cambridge, 1878). The voluminous collection of Stein's letters and papers has been edited by Erich Botzenhardt under the title *Freiherr vom Stein: Briefwechsel, Denkschrifte und Aufzeichnungen*, 7 vols. (Berlin, 1931–1937). See also Max Lehmann, *Freiherr vom Stein*, 3 vols. (Leipzig, 1902–1904), which stresses the French influences on Stein and the attack upon Lehmann's position by E. von Meier in his *Französische Einflüsse auf die Staats- und Rechtsentwicklung Preussens im xix. Jahrhundert*, 2 vols. (Leipzig, 1907–1908), and *Die Reform der Verwaltungsorganisation unter Stein und Hardenberg* (2d ed., Leipzig, 1912); G. S. Ford, *Stein and the Era of Reforms in Prussia* (Princeton, 1922); G. Ritter, *Stein, eine politische Biographie*, 2 vols. (Berlin, 1931); Walter Görlitz, *Stein, Staatsmann und Reformator* (Frankfurt a. M., 1950). The only full treatment of Hardenberg still remains Leopold von Ranke's *Hardenberg und die Geschichte des preussischen Staates 1793–1813*, 3 vols. (Leipzig, 1879–1881). For Wilhelm von Humboldt see E.

Spranger, *Wilhelm von Humboldt und die Humanitätsidee* (2d ed., Berlin, 1928) and *Wilhelm von Humboldt und die Reform des Bildungswesens* (Berlin, 1910); B. Gebhardt, *Wilhelm von Humboldt als Staatsmann,* 2 vols. (Stuttgart, 1896–1899); and S. Kähler, *Wilhelm von Humboldt und der Staat* (Munich, 1927). For the military reforms see Max Lehmann, *Scharnhorst,* 2 vols. (Leipzig, 1886–1887); Hans Delbrück, *Das Leben des Feldmarschalls Grafen Neidhardt von Gneisenau* (Berlin, 1880); F. Meinecke, *Das Leben des Generalfeldmarschalls H. von Boyen,* 2 vols. (Stuttgart, 1895–1899); W. O. Shanahan, *Prussian Military Reforms 1786–1813* (New York, 1945).

The literature on German romanticism has grown to tremendous proportions and cannot even be scratched here. Most valuable is the almost forgotten work by the Catholic romanticist Joseph von Eichendorff, *Geschichte der poetischen Literatur Deutschlands,* vol. ii (Padeborn, 1857). The standard classic by Rudolf Haym, *Die romantische Schule,* 4th ed. by O. Walzel (Berlin, 1920), still retains its worth. Useful general surveys are Paul Kluckhohn's *Die deutsche Romantik* (Bielefeld, 1924) and *Persönlichkeit und Gemeinschaft* (Halle, 1925).

German political theory of the period and the development of national feeling are treated in Friedrich Meinecke's masterly *Weltbürgertum und Nationalstaat* (7th ed., Munich, 1928). Important materials from a more general European point of view are found in a number of articles by Hans Kohn: "The Eve of German Nationalism," in *Journal of the History of Ideas,* xii (1951), 265–284; "Arndt and the Character of German Nationalism," in *American Historical Review,* liv (1949), 787–803; "The Paradox of Fichte's Nationalism," in *Journal of the History of Ideas,* x (1949), 319–343; "Father Jahn's Nationalism," in *Review of Politics,* xi (1949), 419–432; and "Romanticism and the Rise of German Nationalism," in *Review of Politics,* xii (1950), 443–472. See also E. N. Anderson, *Nationalism and the Cultural Crisis in Prussia 1806–1815* (New York, 1939). Special treatment of political romanticism is found in the brilliant work by Carl Schmitt, *Politische Romantik* (2d ed., Munich, 1925). See also W. Metzger, *Gesellschaft, Recht und Staat in der Ethik des deutschen Idealismus* (Heidelberg, 1917); V. Basch, *Les Doctrines politiques des philosophes classiques de l'Allemagne* (Paris, 1927); R. Aris, *History of German Political Thought from 1789–1815* (London, 1936); Xavier Léon, *Fichte et son temps,* 3 vols. (Paris, 1922–1927); G. Holstein, *Die Staatsphilosophie Schleiermachers* (Bonn, 1923). The influence of Pietism on the development of German nationalism, with special attention to Novalis and Schleiermacher, is treated in Koppel S. Pinson, *Pietism as a Factor in the Rise of German Nationalism* (New York, 1934), with detailed bibliography.

2 Quoted in G. P. Gooch, *Germany and the French Revolution,* pp. 101–102.

3 This entire phase of German cultural history is treated in the author's *Pietism as a Factor in the Rise of German Nationalism.*

4 J. Hansen, ed. *Quellen zur Geschichte des Rheinlandes,* i (1931), 383–384.

5 Kurt Eisner, *Das Ende des Reichs. Deutschland und Preussen im Zeitalter der grossen Revolution,* p. 35.

6 Hansen, *op. cit.,* i, 912–917.

7 See Eisner, *op. cit.,* p. 39.

8 Gooch, *op. cit.,* p. 50.

9 *Lectures on the History of Literature, Ancient and Modern* (London, 1889), p. 329. For Burke's influence in Germany, see F. Braune, *Edmund Burke in Deutschland* (Heidelberg, 1917), and Droz, *op. cit.,* pp. 348–370.

10 Joseph Görres, "Resultate meiner Sendung nach Paris," in *Gesammelte Schriften,* Görres Gesellschaft ed., i (Cologne, 1928), 588–589.

11 Quoted in Gooch, *op. cit.,* p. 307.

12 *Ibid.,* pp. 278–279. See also Stern, *op. cit.,* chap. vii.

13 H. A. L. Fisher, *op. cit.,* p. 241.

14 For this reaction see Hans Kohn, "The Eve of German Nationalism."

15 Quoted in Geoffrey Bruun, *Napoleon and Europe* (New York, 1935), p. 174.

16 E. Müsebeck, *Gold gab ich für Eisen,* pp. 89–90.

17 Cited in J. R. Seeley, *Life of Stein,* pp. 397–398.

18 R. F. Eylert, *Character-Züge und historische Fragmente aus dem Leben des Königs von Preussen, Friedrich Wilhelm III,* 3rd ed., 2 vols. (Magdeburg, 1843–1846), i, 172–175.

19 From H. C. Engelbrecht, *Johann Gottlieb Fichte: A Study of His Writings with Special Reference to His Nationalism* (New York, 1933), p. 134.

20 Cf. Hans Kohn, "The Paradox of Fichte's Nationalism," and Engelbrecht, *op. cit.*

21 Seeley, *op. cit.,* ii, 244.

22 Quoted in *Library of the World's Best Literature,* ed. C. D. Warner, xxvii (New York, 1896), 10727.

23 *Main Currents in Nineteenth Century Literature* (New York, 1902), ii, 181.

24 Eichendorff, *op. cit.,* ii, 419.

25 *Soliloquies*, tr. by H. L. Friess (New York, 1926), p. 30.
26 *Ibid.*, pp. 16, 22.
27 *Ibid.*, pp. 37, 51–52.
28 Adam Müller, *Vorlesungen über die deutsche Wissenschaft und Literatur*, lectures delivered in 1806, new ed. by A. Salz (Munich, 1920), pp. 165–166.
29 From "Glauben und Liebe," in *Fragmente*, ed. Kluckhohn, no. 33.

CHAPTER IV

1 For the general and comprehensive treatment of the restoration period in Germany, see especially Franz Schnabel, *Deutsche Geschichte im neunzehnten Jahrhundert*, vols. i–iv; see also Heinrich von Treitschke, *History of Germany in the 19th Century;* Friedrich Meinecke, *Preussen und Deutschland im 19. und 20. Jahrhundert*, especially the chapter on "Das Zeitalter der Restauration"; Ernst Heilborn, *Zwischen zwei Revolutionen, 1789–1848* (Berlin, 1927). For a literary treatment of this period, see Karl Immermann's novel *Die Epigonen.*
2 Quoted in Egon Corti, *Ludwig I von Bayern* (Munich, 1937), p. 406.
3 Cf. Ernst Troeltsch, "Die Restaurationsepoche am Anfang des 19. Jahrhunderts," in his *Gesammelte Schriften*, iv, 587–613, and his *Der Historismus und seine Probleme*, vol. i; Georg von Below, *Die deutsche Geschichtsschreibung* (2nd ed., Munich, 1924), chaps. iii–v. On Hegel and his influence, see: Franz Rosenzweig, *Hegel und der Staat*, 2 vols. (Munich, 1920); Hermann Heller, *Hegel und der nationale Machtstaatsgedanke in Deutschland* (Leipzig, 1921); Herbert Marcuse, *Reason and Revelation: Hegel and the Rise of Social Theory* (New York, 1941).
4 "Frankreich und Deutschland" (1832), in Leopold von Ranke, *Geschichte und Politik*, ed. Hans Hoffmann (Stuttgart, 1942), p. 60.
5 Corti, *op. cit.*, p. 316.
6 Cf. Horace Wyndham, *The Magnificent Montez* (New York, 1948).
7 Cf. G. Ferrero, *The Reconstruction of Europe*, tr. Theodore R. Jaeckel (New York, 1941), and *The Principles of Power* (New York, 1942); Ritter von Srbik, *Metternich der Staatsmann und der Mensch*, 2 vols. (Munich, 1925); Peter Viereck, *Conservatism Revisited* (New York, 1949). A good antidote to Srbik's biography is Viktor Bibl's *Metternich in neuer Beleuchtung* (Vienna, 1922). A nicely balanced treatment is found in Franz Schnabel, *Deutsche Geschichte im neunzehnten Jahrhundert*, ii, 57–89.
8 Viereck, *op. cit.*, p. 6.
9 *The Living Thoughts of Mazzini*, ed. Ignazio Silone (New York, 1939), p. 125.
10 Cf. especially Friedrich Meinecke, *Preussen und Deutschland im 19. und 20. Jahrhundert*, chapter on "Friedrich Wilhelm IV und Deutschland," pp. 206–247.
11 F. J. Stahl, *Staatslehre* (Berlin, 1910), p. 85. The best biography of Stahl is the unfinished work of Gerhard Masur, *Friedrich Julius Stahl* (Berlin, 1930).
12 A brief but intelligent account of German liberalism of this period is found in Guido de Ruggiero, *History of European Liberalism*, tr. R. G. Collingwood (London, 1927), chap. iii. A significant contribution to the story of economic liberalism is the unpublished Ph.D. dissertation at Columbia University by David I. Gaines, Young Gustav Mevissen and His Times. A Study in the Rhenish Social Ethics of the 1840s (1952).
13 Letter by Humboldt to G. Forster, June 1, 1792, in his *Gesammelte Werke*, 5 vols. (Berlin, 1841), i, 298.
14 A detailed account of the Seven Professors of Göttingen is found in Treitschke's *History of Germany in the 19th Century*, vol. vi, chap. ix. See also G. de Ruggiero, *op. cit.*, pp. 240–251.
15 The classic work on this phase of German history is Friedrich Meinecke's *Weltbürgertum und Nationalstaat.*
16 For the Burschenschaften movement see Paul Wentzcke, *Geschichte der deutschen Burschenschaft*, 4 vols. (Heidelberg, 1919–1939). For the problem of the colors of the movement, see Wentzcke, "Die deutschen Farben," in *Quellen und Darstellungen zur Geschichte der deutschen Burschenschaft*, ix (1927), 121ff., and E. Zechlin, "Schwarz-Rot-Gold und Schwarz-Weiss-Rot," in *Geschichte und Gegenwart* (1926), pp. 11 f.
17 P. Viereck, "Father Jahn," the First Storm Trooper," in *Metapolitics: from the Romantics to Hitler* (New York, 1941).
18 The best treatment of Young Germany is in Georg Brandes, *Main Currents in Nineteenth Century Literature*, vol. vi.
19 Brandes, *ibid.*, pp. 73ff.

20 *Gesammelte Schriften* (Milwaukee, 1858), v., 31–32.

21 *The Poetry and Prose of Heinrich Heine,* ed. F. Ewen (New York, 1947), p. 485–486.

22 Arnold Ruge in *Hallische Jahrbücher,* Jan. 25, 1838, p. 205.

23 *Poetry and Prose . . . ,* pp. 500–501.

24 Cf. Harry Slochower, "Attitudes Towards Heine in German Literary Criticism," in *Jewish Social Studies,* iii (1941), 355–374.

25 Max Brod, *Heinrich Heine* (Amsterdam, 1934).

26 The best treatment of this group of thinkers is found in Sidney Hook's *From Hegel to Marx* (New York, 1935), although Hook's primary interest is in the relationship of these writers to Marx rather than in their own inherent worth and their place in German history. See also Gustav Mayer, "Die Anfänge des politischen Radikalismus im vormärzlichen Preussen," in *Zeitschrift für Politik,* vi (1913), 1–112, and the same author's "Die Junghegelianer und der preussische Staat," in *Historische Zeitschrift,* cxx (1920), 429–436, as well as David Koigen's *Zur Vorgeschichte des modernen philosophischen Sozialismus in Deutschland* (Bern, 1901). The best contemporary account of this movement is Moses Hess's *"Ueber die sozialistische Bewegung in Deutschland,"* reprinted in his *Sozialistische Aufsätze,* ed. Theodor Zlocisti (Berlin, 1921), pp. 103–134. A mass of valuable material is found in Arnold Ruge's *Sämtliche Werke,* 2nd ed., 10 vols. (Mannheim, 1847–1848), and in his memoirs *Aus früher Zeit,* 4 vols. (Berlin, 1862–1867). On Ruge see Hans Rosenberg, "Arnold Ruge und die Hallischen Jahrbücher," in *Archiv für Kulturgeschichte,* vol. xx (1930). Walter Neher's *Arnold Ruge als Politiker und politischer Schriftsteller* (Heidelberg, 1933) is a pedestrian study.

27 Cf. Friedrich Engels, *Ludwig Feuerbach und der Ausgang der klassischen Philosophie,* ed. H. Duncker (Berlin, 1927).

28 Engels, *Ludwig Feuerbach . . . ,* p. 24.

29 Sidney Hook, *From Hegel to Marx,* p. 249.

30 Moses Hess, *Sozialistische Aufsätze,* p. 111.

31 Ruge, A. "Unsere Klassiker und Romantiker seit Lessing," in *Sämtliche Werke,* i, 11.

32 *Hallische Jahrbücher,* v (1842), 6–7.

33 Cf. vol. vi of his *Sämtliche Werke.*

34 See Ruge's review of Arndt's *Erinnerungen* in *Hallische Jahrbücher,* iii (1840), 1921.

35 Review of Gutzkow's *Börne,* in *Hallische Jahrbücher,* iii (1840), 2422.

36 *Vorgeschichte und Begründung des deutschen Zollvereins 1815–1834,* ed. W. von Eisenhart Rothe and A. Ritthaler, 3 vols. (Berlin, 1934), i, 321–322. This collection contains the most important source materials on the establishment of the Zollverein, and has a valuable introduction by Hermann Oncken. See also W. O. Henderson, *The Zollverein* (Cambridge, 1939); Arnold H. Price, *The Evolution of the Zollverein* (Ann Arbor, 1949); Eugen Franz, *Der Entscheidungskampf um die wirtschafts-politische Führung Deutschlands, 1856–1867* (Munich, 1933), and the same author's "Ein Weg zum Reich; Die Entstehung des deutschen Zollvereins," in *Vierteljahrschrift für Sozial- und Wirtschaftgeschichte,* xxvii (1934), 105–136.

37 For Josef von Baader's part in German railway development, see Johannes Sauter's notes in his edition of Franz von Baader's *Schriften zur Gesellschaftsphilosophie* (Jena, 1925), pp. 851–870.

38 Cf. Carl F. Wittke, *The Utopian Communist: A Biography of Wilhelm Weitling, Nineteenth-Century Reformer* (Baton Rouge, 1950).

39 Friedrich Engels, *Germany: Revolution and Counter-Revolution* (London, 1933), p. 13.

40 *Ibid.,* p. 14.

Chapter V

1 The most exhaustive treatment of the revolution in Germany is Veit Valentin's *Geschichte der deutschen Revolution 1848–49,* 2 vols. (Berlin, 1930–1931), with a comprehensive and analytical bibliography of sources and secondary works. An abridged version of this work was published in English under the title *1848; Chapters of German History* (London, 1940). Valentin wrote from the liberal-democratic viewpoint of the Weimar period, and his work was the product of long and intensive study. Unfortunately, the material is poorly organized and weak from the standpoint of synthesis. The first important comprehensive work on the revolution was *Die deutsche Revolution 1848–49* (Leipzig, 1898) by Hans Blum, son of the democratic martyr of the revolution, Robert Blum. This work was written from a National Liberal point of view, and the son had become much more conservative than his father. Blum's volume is especially valuable for its inclusion

of a large number of facsimile reproductions of revolutionary pamphlets and leaflets. From a National Liberal point of view, but of much more scholarly and scientific caliber, is Erich Brandenburg's *Die Reichsgründung,* 2 vols. (2nd ed., Leipzig, 1922), and his brief survey *Die deutsche Revolution 1848* (2nd ed., Leipzig, 1919). Socialist treatment of the revolution is found in the classic series of articles "ghost-written" for the *New York Tribune* in 1850 by Friedrich Engels for Karl Marx and long taken to be the work of Marx. The edition referred to here is *Germany: Revolution and Counter-Revolution* (London, 1933). The work of Engels was supplemented by numerous articles by Franz Mehring and collected in his *Zur deutschen Geschichte* (Berlin, 1931), pp. 322–439, and *Zur preussischen Geschichte* (Berlin, 1930), pp. 267–290. An interesting and semi-literary treatment is Ricarda Huch's *Alte und neue Götter; die Revolution des 19. Jahrhunderts in Deutschland* (Berlin, 1930); a small but useful collection of source material is Tim Klein's *1848. Der Vorkampf deutscher Einheit und Freiheit* (Leipzig, 1914). A. W. Ward's "The Revolution and Reaction in Germany and Austria 1848–49," in *Cambridge Modern History,* xi (London, 1909), pp. 142–233, is still valuable, especially for English readers. Of the recent centenary articles and studies, the best are Friedrich Meinecke, *1848. Eine Säkularbetrachtung* (Berlin, 1948); Hans Rothfels, "1848—One Hundred Years After," in *Journal of Modern History,* xx (1948), 291–319; L. B. Namier, *1848. The Revolution of the Intellectuals* (London, 1948); and Hans Kohn, "1848—Ein Ende," in *Die Wandlung,* iv (1949), 770–780. Bibliographical references for separate aspects of the revolution will be cited later.

2 E. Silberner, "Charles Fourier on the Jewish Question," in *Jewish Social Studies,* viii (1946), 259–262, and "The Attitudes of the Fourierist School Towards the Jews," *ibid.,* ix (1947), 339–362. See also Zosa Szaikowski, "Jewish Saint-Simonians and Socialist Antisemites in France," *ibid.,* ix (1947), 33–60.

3 R. Postgate, *Revolution from 1789–1906* (London, 1920), document no. 112.

4 Text in Hans Blum, *Die deutsche Revolution 1848–49,* facsimile of leaflet "Was wir wollen."

5 Postgate, *op. cit.,* document no. 113.

6 Cited in Hans Krause, *Die demokratische Partei von 1848 und die soziale Frage* (Frankfurt, 1923), pp. 39–40.

7 The articles of Marx and Engels in the *Neue Rheinische Zeitung* from March to December, 1848, are collected in the Marx-Engels *Gesamtausgabe,* pt. i, vol. vii, ed. V. Adoratski (Moscow, 1935). Cf. also Wilhelm Döhl, *Die deutsche National-Versammlung im Spiegel der "Neuen Rheinischen Zeitung"* (Bonn, 1931), and Franz Mehring, "Die März-Revolution und ihre Folgen," in his *Geschichte der deutschen Sozialdemokratie,* (8th ed., Stuttgart, 1919), ii, 1–207.

8 For the proletarian movement in Berlin, see Eduard Bernstein, *Die Geschichte der Berliner Arbeiterbewegung,* 3 vols. (Berlin, 1907), i, 1–68; Max Quarck, *Die erste deutsche Arbeiterbewegung. Geschichte der Arbeiterbewegung 1848–49* (Leipzig, 1924); Wilhelm Friedensburg, *Stephan Born und die Organisationsbestrebungen der Berliner Arbeiterschaft 1848* (Leipzig, 1923); Stephan Born, *Erinnerungen eines Achtundvierziger* (2d ed., Leipzig, 1898). See also the classic pioneer work of Georg Adler, *Die Geschichte der ersten sozialpolitischen Arbeiterbewegung in Deutschland* (Breslau, 1885).

9 Facsimile of leaflet in *Propyläen Weltgeschichte,* viii, 25.

10 Cf. Eduard Bernstein, *op. cit.,* i, 36–37.

11 *Ibid.,* p. 56.

12 Cf. F. Meinecke, *1848. Eine Säkularbetrachtung.*

13 Quoted in Ernst Kaeber, "Die soziale Frage in der Revolution von 1848," in *Aufbau,* iv (1948), 232–238.

14 The text of this letter is published in Paul Hassel, *Josef Maria von Radowitz* (Berlin, 1905), i, 574.

15 *Ibid.,* pp. 577–578 and p. 588. See also Quarck, *op. cit.,* p. 74.

16 The English version of the complete text is found in Postgate, *op. cit.,* document no. 117.

17 Quoted in Meinecke, *1848,* p. 20.

18 The work of the Frankfurt assembly is best studied in the record of the proceedings of the assembly, *Stenographische Berichte über die Verhandlungen der deutschen constituirenden Nationalsammlung zu Frankfurt am Main,* ed. Franz Jakob Wigard, 9 vols. (Leipzig and Frankfurt, 1848–1849). Selections from the proceedings are found in L. Bergsträsser, *Das Frankfurter Parlament in Briefen und Tagebüchern* (Frankfurt, 1929); Georg Mollat, *Reden und Redner des ersten deutschen Parlaments* (Osterwieck, 1895); W. Petzet, and O. E. Sutter, eds., *Der Geist der Paulskirche* (Frankfurt, 1923); Paul Wentzcke, *Die erste deutsche Nationalversammlung und ihr Werk. Ausgewählte Reden* (Munich, 1922). See also W. Appens, *Die Nationalversammlung zu Frankfurt am Main*

1848–1849 (Jena, 1920), which is especially good for constitutional and administrative aspects, and the classic work of Rudolf Haym, *Die deutsche Nationalversammlung*, 3 vols. (Berlin, 1850).

19 In this classification I have followed W. Appens, *op. cit.*

20 Cf. especially A. J. P. Taylor, *The Course of German History* (London, 1945), chap. iv, and Roy Pascal, "The Frankfort Parliament of 1848 and the *Drang nach Osten*," in *Journal of Modern History*, xviii (1946), 108–122. A critique of this position is found in the above-cited article by Hans Rothfels. See also Alfred Meusel, "Nationale Probleme in der deutschen Revolution von 1848," in *Aufbau*, ii (1946), 771–777.

21 *Stenographische Berichte* . . . , i, 212–214.

22 F. Engels, *Germany: Revolution and Counter-Revolution*, p. 57.

23 *Stenographische Berichte* . . . , ii, 1145–1146.

24 *Ibid.*, iv, 2882.

25 Quoted in Otto Ernst Sutter, *Die Linke der Paulskirche* (Frankfurt, 1924), p. 321.

26 *Ibid.*, p. 34.

27 On the democratic left faction of the assembly, see the valuable series of studies *Die Paulskirche*, published by the liberal *Frankfurter Zeitung* during the Weimar period. The more important of these are Hans Krause, *Die demokratische Partei von 1848 und die soziale Frage*, and Otto Ernst Sutter, *Die Linke der Paulskirche*. See also Robert Blum, *Ausgewählte Reden und Schriften*, ed. Herrmann Nebel (Leipzig, 1879), and H. Mitseli, *Carl Vogt 1817–49* (Zürich, 1938). A sane and intelligent critique of the nationalist expansionism of the assembly is found in Karl Gutzkow's *Deutschland am Vorabend seines Falles oder seiner Grösse* (Frankfurt, 1848).

28 Cf. Herbert Arthur Strauss, *Staat, Bürger, Mensch. Die Debatten der deutschen Nationalversammlung 1848/1849 über die Grundrechte* (Aarau, 1947), and Gustav Radbruch, "Die Frankfurter Grundrechte," in Wilhelm Keil, ed., *Deutschland 1848–1948* (Stuttgart, 1948), pp. 80–88

29 Cf. *Stenographische Berichte* . . . , ix, 6735–6736.

30 *Ibid.*, ix, 6622.

31 *Ibid.*, ix, 6864.

32 On the end of the Frankfurt assembly and the radical uprisings, see Wilhelm Blos, *Der Untergang des Frankfurter Parlaments* (Frankfurt, 1924); A. Fendrich, *Die badische Bewegung der Jahre 1848–49* (Frankfurt, 1924); Charles W. Dahlinger, *The German Revolution of 1849* (New York, 1930); Carl Wittke, *Against the Current: The Life of Karl Heinzen* (Chicago, 1945). Reminiscences of the period are to be found in Carl Schurz, *Reminiscences*, 2 vols. (Boston, 1907); Otto von Corvin, *Erinnerungen aus meinem Leben*, 4 vols. (3rd ed., Leipzig, 1880).

33 F. Engels, *Germany: Revolution and Counter-Revolution*, pp. 111–112.

34 On the political refugees of 1848–1849, see Georg von Skal, *Die Achtundvierziger in Amerika* (Frankfurt, 1923); Carl Wittke, *Refugees of Revolution: The German Forty-Eighters in America* (Philadelphia, 1952); and A. E. Zucker, ed., *The Forty-Eighters: Political Refugees of the German Revolution* (New York, 1950).

CHAPTER VI

1 See Josef von Radowitz, *Nachgelassene Briefe und Aufzeichnungen zur Geschichte der Jahre 1848–1853*, ed. Walter Möring (Stuttgart, 1922); *Schriften und Reden*, ed., with a lengthy introduction, by Friedrich Meinecke (Munich, 1921); and Meinecke's *Radowitz und die deutsche Revolution* (Berlin, 1913).

2 Heinrich von Sybel, *Die Begründung des deutschen Reiches*, ii, 98.

3 For an interesting account of the reaction by a democratic writer of the time, see Aron Bernstein, *Revolutions- und Reaktionsgeschichte Preussens und Deutschlands von den Märztagen bis zur neuesten Zeit*, 3 vols. (Berlin, 1882); see also Arnold Ruge, *Geschichte unsrer Zeit von den Freiheitskriegen bis zum Ausbruch des deutsch-französischen Krieges* (Leipzig, 1881).

4 Quoted in W. H. Dawson, *The German Empire*, i, 91.

5 Sybel, *op. cit.*, ii, 284.

6 For the life of William I, see Erich Marcks, *Kaiser Wilhelm I* (8th ed., Munich, 1918), and Paul Wiegler, *Wilhelm der Erste* (Dresden, 1927), tr. into English (London, 1929).

7 For the political writing during this period, see the excellent summaries of important pamphlet and periodical articles by Hans Rosenberg in his *Die nationalpolitische*

Publizistik Deutschlands, 2 vols. (Munich, 1935); vol. i, chap. i. See also *Deutscher Liberalismus im Zeitalter Bismarcks*, ed. Julius Heyderdorff and Paul Wentzcke, 2 vols. (Bonn, 1925–1926), and H. R. von Srbik, *Deutsche Einheit*, 4 vols. (Munich, 1935–1942), vol. ii, chap. ii, and other literature cited there.

8 H. von Treitschke, *Zehn Jahre deutscher Kämpfe* (2nd ed., Berlin, 1879), p. 79.

9 *Idem, Historische und politische Aufsätze* (5th ed., Leipzig, 1886), ii, 219.

10 *Ibid.*, pp. 220 ff.

11 *Historische und politische Aufsätze*, vol. ii.

12 "Zum Jahresanfang," in *Preussische Jahrbücher*, v (1860), 3.

13 *Ibid.*

14 Karl Bollmann, *Vertheidigung des Machiavellismus* (Quedlinburg, 1858), quoted in Rosenberg, *op. cit.*, i, 4.

15 A. Rapp, *Gross-deutsch, Klein-deutsch* (Munich, 1922), p. 165.

16 Rosenberg, *op. cit.*, i, 153.

17 See Rudolf Haym, *Aus meinem Leben* (Berlin, 1902); Hans Rosenberg, *Rudolf Haym und die Anfänge des klassischen Liberalismus* (Munich, 1933); and Otto Westphal, *Welt- und Staatsauffassung des deutschen Liberalismus, Eine Untersuchung über die Preussischen Jahrbücher . . .* (Munich, 1919).

18 See H. Heller, *Hegel und der nationale Machtstaatsgedanke in Deutschland* (Berlin, 1921).

19 See introduction by G. Küntzel to Ranke's *Zwölf Bücher preussischer Geschichte* (Munich, 1930) for a nice comparison between Ranke and Droysen, vol. i, pp. xciii–clii.

20 Cf. Droysen's *Politische Schriften*, ed. Felix Gilbert (Munich, 1933); see also *Droysen's Briefwechsel*, 2 vols. (Berlin, 1929), and *Aktenstücken und Aufzeichnungen zur Geschichte der Frankfurter Nationalversammlung aus dem Nachlass Johann Gustav Droysen* (Stuttgart, 1924), both edited by Rudolf Hübner. Hübner also edited Droysen's *Historik* (2nd ed., Munich, 1943).

21 See Sybel's "Die deutsche Nation und das Kaiserreich," published in 1862. This and other writings of the same character, as well as answers to Sybel by the pro-Austrian historian Julius Ficker, are found in *Universalstaat oder Nationalstaat*, ed. Friedrich Schneider (Innsbruck, 1941). The publication of this volume, as well as that of Srbik (*Deutsche Einheit*), is an indication of the revival of this problem in Germany after the Nazi annexation of Austria and the development of a new Central European empire.

22 Letter to Bachmann, April 22, 1861, in *Briefe*, ed. Max Cornicelius (2nd ed., Leipzig, 1913–1920), ii, 230.

23 *Historische und politische Aufsätze*, ii, 192.

24 *Ibid.*, iii, 25. We see here, as in so much of the pro-Prussian writing of the time, a recurrent theme of the sense of destiny and inevitability of Prussian expansion. Prussian conquest arises from natural and inherent needs which converge and become identical with the needs of Germany as a whole. It is an obvious variation on the Hegelian theme of "what is real is rational," and thus a very convenient rationalization. The Catholic Bishop of Mainz, von Ketteler, observed this pattern of thinking in his definition of Prussianism. He defined it as "an *idée fixe* regarding the calling of Prussia, an unclear notion of a Prussia to whom had been assigned a world task, joined with the conviction that this calling and task is one of absolute necessity which must be realized with the same necessity that a rock must fall when it is loosened. It is therefore ill-fitting to raise any opposition to this world destiny in the name of right or of history" (*Deutschland nach dem Kriege von 1866* [Mainz, 1867], p. 31).

25 *Briefe*, i, 74–75.

26 Letter in 1863, in Rapp, *op. cit.*, p. 208.

27 *Briefe*, ii, 318.

28 "Deutschland und Österreich," in *Das Jahrhundert* (1859), summarized in Rosenberg, *Die nationalpolitische Publizistik . . .* , i, 33.

29 *Die drei Völker und die Legitimität* (London, 1860), also summarized in Rosenberg, *op. cit.*, i, 224–225.

30 *Was Wir Brauchen. Ein Memento mori für das Preussen des Staatsstreichs* (Bremen, 1861), summarized in Rosenberg, i, 362–363.

31 *An die deutsche Nation* (Hamburg, 1866), summarized in Rosenberg, ii, 950–951.

32 See his *Der italienische Krieg und die Aufgabe Preussens. Eine Stimme aus der Demokratie* (Berlin, 1859); his review of Stahr's work on Frederick the Great and his two essays on Fichte. Lassalle's complex motivation, his controversies with Marx on these problems, and the whole complexity of these issues are analyzed in masterful fashion in Hermann Oncken, *Lassalle, Eine politische Biographie* (3rd ed., Stuttgart, 1920). We shall have more to say on this later on in our discussion of the development of German socialism.

33 Cf. Onno Klopp, *Der König Friedrich II von Preussen und seine Politik* (2nd ed.,

Schaffhausen, 1867); *Offener Brief an den Herrn Professor Hauser in Heidelberg betreffend die Ansichten über den König Friedrich II von Preussen* (Hanover, 1862); *Nachtrag zu den offenen Brief* . . . (Hanover, 1862). For the life of Klopp, see Wiard von Klopp, *Onno Klopp. Leben und Wirken*, ed. Franz Schnabel (Munich, 1951).

34 Quoted in Rapp, *op. cit.*, p. 257.

35 *Preussen oder Oesterreich* (Cassel, 1861), Rosenberg, *op. cit.*, i, 396–397.

36 Rosenberg, *op. cit.*, ii, 668–669.

37 *Das preussische Staatsministerium und die deutsche Reformfrage* (Hanover, 1863), summarized in Rosenberg, *op. cit.*, ii, 668–669.

38 *Briefe über Grossdeutsch und Kleindeutsch* (Hanover, 1863), Rosenberg, *op. cit.*, ii, 644

39 See his "Der deutsche Dualismus und Pangermanismus," in *Berliner Revue* (Aug. 22, 1858), Rosenberg, *op. cit.*, i, 9.

40 *Drei und dreissig Sätze von deutschen Bunde* (Berlin, 1861), Rosenberg, *op. cit.*, i, 413–414.

41 See his *Ahasverus, oder die Judenfrage* (1844); *Nationalliberalismus und Judenherrschaft* (Munich, 1874); *Zwischenbemerkungen zur Judenfrage* (Berlin, 1882); also in *Der Föderalismus als das leitende Prinzip* . . . (Mainz, 1879). An objective and sound analysis of this interesting figure is still lacking. O. Schuchardt's *C. Frantz, Deutschlands wahrer Realpolitiker* (Melsungen, 1896), is antiquated and the work of an uncritical admirer; Max Häne's *Die Staatsideen des Konstantin Frantz* (Gladbach-Rheydt, 1929) is immature; the works of E. Stamm, *Konstantin Frantz's Schriften u. Leben 1817 bis 1856* (Heidelberg, 1907) and *Konstantin Frantz 1857 bis 1866* (Berlin, 1930) unfortunately were not available to me. See also Srbik, *op. cit.*, ii, 315–318.

42 Rapp, *op. cit.*, pp. 218–219.

43 Rosenberg, *op. cit.*, no. 749.

44 For the problem of balancing North and South German sentiment in the Nationalverein, see the letter of Hermann Schulze-Delitzsch to Bennigsen of Nov. 13, 1859 in Schulze-Delitzsch's *Schriften und Reden*, iii, 150–152. "We can hardly conceal the fact that the German north is the core of our movement." Schulze-Delitzsch was a faithful follower of the liberal nationalist philosophy of Herder. See especially his speech of Sept. 3, 1860, in Coburg, published in his *Schriften und Reden*, iii, 170–175.

45 Rapp, *op. cit.*, p. 239.

46 H. Oncken, *Rudolf von Bennigsen*, 2 vols. (Stuttgart, 1910), i, 21–22. This volume by Oncken is still the best source for the history of the Nationalverein. See also Paul Hermann, *Die Entstehung des deutschen Nationalvereins und die Gründung seiner Wochenschrift* (Leipzig, 1932); also Walter Grube, *Die neue Ära und der Nationalverein* (Leipzig, 1933). Valuable source material on the history of the Nationalverein is to be found in vol. iii of Hermann Schulze-Delitzsch's *Schriften und Reden*, ed. F. T. Thorwart, 5 vols. (Berlin, 1910–1913). A picture of the mood and times during the first meeting of the Nationalverein is found in *Gutmanns Reisen*, a novel by Wilhelm Raabe.

47 The most detailed account of the constitutional conflict in Prussia is Fritz Löwenthal's *Der preussische Verfassungsstreit 1862–1866* (Altenburg, 1914). A conservative historian's treatment is that of Adalbert Wahl, *Beiträge zur Geschichte der Konfliktszeit* (Tübingen, 1914), and a critique of the same by L. Bergsträsser, "Kritische Studien zur Konfliktszeit," in *Historische Vierteljahrschrift*, xix (1919), 343–376. See also Heinrich von Sybel, "Die preussische Heeresreform von 1860," in his *Vorträge und Abhandlungen* (Munich, 1897); K. Promnitz, *Bismarck's Eintritt in des Ministerium*, Historische Studien, vol. x (1908); O. Nirnheim, *Das 1. Jahr des Ministeriums Bismarcks und die öffentliche Meinung*, Heidelberger Abhandlungen zur mitteleren und neueren Geschichte, no. xx (1908); L. Dehio, "Bismarck und die Heeresvorlagen der Konfliktszeit," in *Historische Zeitschrift*, cxiv (1931), 31–46, and "Die Taktik der opposition während des Konfliktes," *ibid.*, cx (1924), 279–347; G. Ritter, "Die Entstehung der Indemnitätsvorlage von 1866," in *Historische Zeitschrift*, cxiv (1915), 17–64.

48 Bismarck was quoted as saying that even had the king insisted on a ten-year service he would have followed him in this matter. Cf. Bergsträsser, *op. cit.*, 349.

49 Letter of Gustav Freytag to Schulze-Delitzsch, in Schulze-Delitzsch's *Schriften und Reden*, iv, 105–107.

50 For the life of Bismarck see above all Erich Eyck, *Bismarck*, 3 vols. (Zürich, 1941–1944), and Bismarck's *Gedanken und Erinnerungen*, ed. Gerhard Ritter and Rudolf Stadelmann, vol. xv of Bismarck's *Gesammelte Werke* (Berlin, 1932). See also the older works by Max Lenz, Erich Marcks, Paul Matter and G. C. Robertson.

51 Bismarck, *Gesammelte Werke* (2nd ed., Berlin, 1928), x, 129.

52 Carl Schurz, *Reminiscences*, 3 vols. (New York, 1907–1908), iii, 265.

53 *Ibid.*, iii, 274.

54 Quoted in J. Ziekursch, *Politische Geschichte des neuen deutschen Kaiserreiches*, i, 245.

55 H. Schulthess, ed. *Europäischer Geschichtskalender*, iv (1864), 114.
56 *Briefwechsel Droysens*, ii, 813.
57 Nirnheim, *op. cit.*, p. 70.
58 Schulthess, *op. cit.*, iv, 136.
59 Oncken, *op. cit.*, ii, 594. For this Danzig episode see also R. Haymn, *Das Leben Max Dunckers* (Berlin, 1891), and for Bismarck's version see his *Reflections*, vol. i, chap. xvi.
60 F. Lassalle, *Gesammelte Reden und Schriften*, ed. Eduard Bernstein (Berlin, 1919), ii, 95–96.

CHAPTER VII

1 Wilhelm Müller, *Deutschlands Einigungskriege 1864–1871* (Leipzig, 1889), Preface.
2 For the general history of the creation of the Seoond Reich see: Heinrich von Sybel, *Die Begründung des deutschen Reiches durch Wilhelm I*, 7 vols. (Munich, 1889–1895), English tr. (New York, 1890–1898); Erich Brandenburg, *Die Reichsgründung*, 2 vols. (2nd ed., Leipzig, 1922); Johannes Ziekursch, *Politische Geschichte des neuen deutschen Kaiserreiches*, 3 vols. (Frankfurt, 1930–1932); W. H. Dawson, *The German Empire*, 2 vols. (London, 1919); F. Darmstaedter, *Bismarck and the Creation of the Second Reich* (London, 1948); Ernst Denis, *La Fondation de l'empire allemande 1852–1871* (Paris, 1906).
3 Z., "Preussens nationale Aufgabe und Oestreich," in *Die Grenzboten*, ii (1863), 349–360, 376–386, cited in Hans Rosenberg, *Die nationalpolitische Publizistik Deutschlands*, ii, 643.
4 Émile Ollivier, the French statesman, later commented on the Danish war with the following words: "England failed France and France failed England and both failed Europe. The triumph lay with Bismarck alone. He had laid his hand on the heart of France and detected its weakened movement. He had calculated the inertia of England. He held Russia by the memories of the Polish question" (*L'Empire libéral*, quoted in P. J. Grant, and H. Temperley, *Europe in the Nineteenth Century* [London, 1927], pp. 321–322).
The editor of the *Europäischer Geschichtskalender* for the year 1867, in his summary of the year's events wrote: "Bismarck considered the duchies not as liberated but as conquered territories" (vi, 387). The most authoritative treatment of the Danish war is in Lawrence Steefel, *The Schleswig-Holstein Question* (Cambridge, 1932).
5 Bismarck, *Gesammelte Werke*, vii, 102.
6 *Ibid.*, p. 103.
7 H. Friedjung, *The Struggle for Supremacy in Germany 1859–1866* (London, 1935), p. 86. This work by the distinguished Austrian historian is still the most authoritative treatment of the Austro-Prussian War. Friedjung, even though an Austrian Jew, treats Bismarck as his hero. See also C. W. Clark, *Franz Joseph and Bismarck* (Cambridge, Mass., 1934).
8 Friedjung, *op. cit.*, p. 33.
9 Friedjung, *op. cit.*, pp. 314–315.
10 Brandenburg, *Die Reichsgründung*, ii, p. 134.
11 The Prussian historian Wilhelm Oncken calls this act of Prussia "a declaration of war against Austria and its allies . . . as such was it intended and such was its effect" (W. Oncken, *Das Zeitalter des Kaisers Wilhelm* [Berlin 1890] i, 517). On the whole question of responsibility for this war, the comment by Oncken is characteristic for the Prussian attitude. "The war itself," says Oncken, "was a necessity, not brought about by men and also incapable of being prevented by men. For that reason posterity can pass over the entire exchange of correspondence which has to do with the question as to who was the real 'disturber of peace' " (*ibid.*, p. 522).
12 On Lassalle and Bismarck, see E. Bernstein, *Ferdinand Lassalle* (2nd ed., Berlin, 1920), pp. 263–284, and above all Gustav Mayer, *Bismarck und Lassalle. Ihre Briefwechsel und ihre Gespräche* (Berlin, 1928).
13 Ziekursch, *op. cit.*, i, 203.
14 *Ibid.*, p. 204.
15 L. Pastor, *August Reichensperger*, 2 vols. (Freiburg, 1899), i, 580–581.
16 *Europäischer Geschichtskalender*, vii (1867), 184–185.
17 The French Ministry of Foreign Affairs has published 29 volumes of its materials thus far, *Les Origines diplomatiques de la guerre de 1870* (Paris, 1910–1932). The Prussian and German documents have been published in part in the uncompleted *Die auswärtige*

Politik Preussens 1859–1871. Diplomatische Aktenstücke, issued under the direction of the Historische Reichskommission, eds. E. Brandenburg, O. Hoetzsch, and H. Oncken (Munich, 1932–1939), vols. i–vi, viii–x, and in Hermann Oncken, *Die Rheinpolitik Kaiser Napoleons III von 1863 bis 1870 und der Ursprung des Krieges von 1870–71; nach den Staatsakten von Oesterreich, Preussen und den süddeutschen Mittelstaaten,* 3 vols. (Stuttgart, 1926). The most objective treatment of the origins of the war is R. H. Lord's *The Origins of the War of 1870* (Cambridge, Mass., 1924), which also contains a large collection of new documents from the German archives. The most recent statement of the German case is in the first 121 pages of the above-mentioned work of Oncken. These pages have been issued in English translation under the title *Napoleon III and the Rhine* (New York, 1928).

18 *Op. cit.,* p. 9.

19 Dawson, i, 304.

20 *Ibid.,* p. 305.

21 *Op. cit.,* p. 4.

22 M. Malcolm Carroll, "French Public Opinion on the War with Prussia in 1870," in *American Historical Review,* xxxi (1926), 679–700. See also the same author's *French Public Opinion and Foreign Affairs 1870–1914* (New York, 1931).

23 Carl Schurz, *Reminiscences,* ii, 450–451.

24 Bismarck, *Gesammelte Werke,* vii, 186.

25 Schurz, *op. cit.,* iii, 272.

26 II, 88–89.

27 Published by Harold Temperley in "Lord Acton on the Origins of the War of 1870, with some Unpublished Letters from the British and Viennese Archives," in *Cambridge Historical Journal,* ii (1926), 68–82.

28 Lord, *op. cit.,* p. 42.

29 Lord, *op. cit.,* p. 87. I have followed Lord in the entire description of this day's events.

30 Bismarck, *Reminiscences,* ii, 100–102.

31 The text of Abeken's dispatch from Ems ran as follows: "H.M. the King writes me: 'Benedetti intercepted me on the Promenade in order to request of me in a very insistent manner that I should authorize him to telegraph immediately that I shall obligate myself for all future time never again to give my approval to the candidacy of the Hohenzollerns should it be renewed. I refused to agree to this, the last time somewhat earnestly, telling him that such obligations dare not and cannot be assumed *à tout jamais.* Naturally I told him that I had not received any news as yet and since he had been informed earlier than I via Madrid and Paris he could see that my government was once again out of the affair.'

His Majesty has since then received a communication from the Prince. Since his Majesty had told Count Benedetti that he was expecting news from the Prince, the Sovereign himself, in view of the above demand and on the advice of Count Eulenburg and myself, decided not to receive Count Benedetti again but to let him know through an adjutant: that his Majesty had now received from the Prince confirmation of the report which Benedetti already had had from Paris and that he had nothing further to tell the ambassador. His Majesty leaves it to the judgment of Your Excellency whether or not to communicate immediately the new demand by Benedetti and its rejection to both our ambassadors and to the press."

[Signed] A[beken] 13.7.70

The edited version of the above by Bismarck reads as follows: "After the reports of the renunciation by the Prince of Hohenzollern had been officially transmitted by the Royal Spanish government to the imperial government of France, the French ambassador presented to His Majesty the King at Ems the demand to authorize him to telegraph to Paris that His Majesty the King would obligate himself for all the future never again to give his consent should the Hohenzollerns revive their candidacy. His Majesty the King thereupon refused to receive the French ambassador again and sent word to the latter through his Adjutant that His Majesty has nothing further to tell the ambassador."

(Texts of the two versions are translated from facsimile reproductions in *Propyläen Weltgeschichte,* viii [Berlin, 1930], 248.)

32 Lord, *op. cit.,* pp. 6–7. It is interesting to note in this connection the difference in treatment of the antecedents of this war by French and German historians. While most of the leading French historians, like Sorel, Jaurès, Berton, Tschernoff, La Gorce, and Henri Salomon, have not spared criticism of the policy of the French government, the German historians of this period, except for writers in the Social Democratic press, have all been vehement in their defense of Bismarckian policy.

33 M. Doeberl, *Bayern und die Bismarckische Reichsgründung* (Munich, 1925), p. 42. For the situation in Württemberg see A. Rapp, *Die Württemberger und die nationale Frage, 1863–1871* (Stuttgart, 1910), Darstellungen aus der Württembergischen Geschichte, vol. iv.

34 Dawson, *op. cit.*, i, 364.
35 H. Oncken, *Rudolf von Bennigsen*, i, 20.
36 Rosenberg, *op. cit.*, i, 33.
37 *Politische Schriften*, p. 229.
38 *Droysen's Briefwechsel*, ii, 841.
39 Oncken, *op. cit.*, i, 652.
40 Rosenberg, *op. cit.*, ii, 543.
41 *Ibid.*, p. 960.
42 *Ibid.*
43 On Feb. 9, 1865, he described Bismarck's rule, in the *Wochenblatt*, as "devouring
the life marrow of the state, destroying the moral force of the people, making the state
and the people dishonored and despised in the eyes of the world and in its own eyes"
(Rosenberg, *op. cit.*, ii, 817).
44 *Die Grenzboten*, iv (1864), 233–237.
45 *Droysen's Briefwechsel*, ii, 847–848, June 19, 1864.
46 This essay, "Der deutsche Liberalismus," was first published in the *Preussische Jahrbücher*, xviii (1866), 455–515, 575–628. It was reprinted in Baumgarten's *Historische und
Politische Aufsätze und Reden*, ed. Erich Marcks (Strassburg, 1894).
47 "Politische Correspondenz," Feb. 4, 1867, in *Preussische Jahrbücher*, xix (1867),
224–229.
48 Franz Mehring, *Zur Geschichte der Philosophie* (Berlin, 1931), p. 122.
49 D. F. Strauss, "Preussen und Schwaben," in *Preussische Jahrbücher*, xix (1867),
186–189.
50 For a representative Catholic analysis of political and social conditions in Germany
at the time, see Wilhelm Emanuel Ketteler, *Deutschland nach dem Kriege von 1866*
(Mainz, 1867).
51 See Gustav Mayer, "Die Trennung der proletarischen von der bürgerlichen Demokratie
in Deutschland (1863–1870)," in *Archiv für die Geschichte des Sozialismus und der
Arbeiterbewegung*, ii (1912), 1–67.
52 Hermann Schulze-Delitzsch, *Schriften und Reden*, ed. F. Thorwart *et al.* (Berlin,
1910), iii, 225–226.
53 G. G. Gervinus, *Hinterlassene Schriften* (Vienna, 1872), pp. 23–32.
54 Johann Jacoby, *Schriften und Reden*, 2 vols. (Hamburg, 1872), ii, 307–308.
55 *Ibid.*, ii, 317.
56 For a characteristic socialist treatment of Jacoby, see Franz Mehring, *Zur preussischen
Geschichte* (Berlin, 1930), pp. 391–395, and *Zur Geschichte der Philosophie* (Berlin, 1931),
pp. 155–162.
57 For the best exposition of this view, see Arthur Rosenberg, *The Birth of the German
Republic* (London, 1931).

CHAPTER VIII

1 On the general problems of German constitutional development, see: L. Bergsträsser,
Geschichte der Reichsverfassung (Tübingen, 1914); Hugo Preuss, *Verfassungspolitische
Entwicklungen in Deutschland und Westeuropa*, ed. Hedwig Hintze (Berlin, 1927), and
Staat, Recht und Freiheit, ed. Theodor Heuss (Tübingen, 1926); see also the work by the
erstwhile disciple of Hugo Preuss and later National Socialist political theorist Carl
Schmitt, *Staatsgefüge und Zusammenbruch des zweiten Reiches* (Hamburg, 1934), and the
extensive critique of the same work by Fritz Hartung in *Historische Zeitschrift*, cli (1935),
528–544.
2 Cf. *Stenographische Berichte* of the Reichstag sessions of April 1 and 3, 1871.
3 See W. Stolze, *Die Gründung des deutschen Reiches im Jahre 1870* (Munich, 1912),
and Eduard von Wertheimer, *Bismarck im politischen Kampf* (Berlin, 1930), chap. viii.
4 See W. Frank, *Hofprediger Adolf Stöcker* (2nd ed., Hamburg, 1935), pp. 27–28.
5 Hugo Preuss, *Staat, Recht und Freiheit*, p. 176.
6 *Europäischer Geschichtskalender*, xiii (1872), 75–76. In his speech of Jan. 30, 1872
(see *Gesammelte Werke*, xi, 225 ff.), Bismarck had said: "In a constitutional state we
ministers need a majority that supports our policy completely," and the *Kreuzzeitung*
attacked this as being too similar to the French political theories.
7 *Gesammelte Werke*, xi, 496.
8 On the Prussian-German problem see F. Meinecke, *Weltbürgertum und Nationalstaat*
(7th ed., Munich, 1928), book ii; G. Anschütz, *Das preussich-deutsche Problem* (Tübingen

1922), *Recht und Staat,* no. 22; H. Triepel, *Unitarismus und Föderalismus im deutschen Reiche* (Tübingen, 1907).
9 G. Anschutz, *op. cit.,* p. 9.
10 See Günther Franz, *Bismarcks Nationalgefühl* (Leipzig, 1926). For a different view see Hans Goldschmidt, *Das Reich und Preussen im Kampf um die Führung* (Berlin, 1931).
11 Triepel, *op. cit.*
12 Schmitt, *op. cit.* On the relation of the army to the state, see O. Bielefeld, "Das kaiserliche Heer," in *Archiv des öffentlichen Rechts,* xvi (1901), 280–315; Ludwig von Rüdt von Collenberg, *Die deutsche Armee von 1871 bis 1914* (Berlin, 1922), *Forschungen und Darstellungen aus dem Reichsarchiv,* no. 4, and "Die staatsrechtliche Stellung des preussischen Kriegsministers (1867–1914)," in *Wissen und Wehr* (1927), pp. 293–312.
13 F. Meinecke, *Weltbürgertum und Nationalstaat,* p. 527. For similar expressions of indebtedness to Prussia by recent German historians, see Felix Rachfahl, *Preussen und Deutschland in Vergangenheit, Gegenwart und Zukunft* (Tübingen, 1919); Georg von Below, *Deutsche Reichspolitik einst und jetzt* (Tübingen, 1922); and Adalbert Wahl, *Deutsche Geschichte 1871–1914,* 4 vols. (Stuttgart, 1926–1936), i, 5.
14 Written in 1917 and cited in Below, *op. cit.,* p. 42.
15 On the general history of political parties in Germany, see: Gerhard Ritter, "Allgemeiner Charackter und geschichtliche Grundlagen der politischen Parteibildung," in *Volk und Reich der Deutschen,* ed. B. Harms, vol. iii (Berlin, 1929); Ludwig Bergsträsser, *Geschichte der politischen Parteien in Deutschland* (7th ed., Munich, 1952); Friedrich Naumann, *Die politische Parteien* (Berlin, 1910); L. Parisius, *Deutschlands politische Parteien und das Ministerium Bismarcks* (Berlin, 1878); Oscar Stillich, *Die politischen Parteien in Deutschland,* vol. 1, *Die Konservativen* (Leipzig, 1908); vol. ii, *Die Liberalen* (Leipzig, 1911); O. Klein-Hattingen, *Geschichte des deutschen Liberalismus,* 2 vols. (Leipzig, 1911); F. Salomon, *Die deutschen Parteiprogramme,* 2 vols. (Leipzig, 1912); Sigmund Neumann, *Die deutsche Parteien* (Berlin, 1932) and *Die Stufen des preussischen Konservatismus* (Berlin, 1930). For the older background see A. Wahl, "Beiträge zur deutschen Parteigeschichte in 19. Jahrhundert," in *Historische Zeitschrift,* vol. civ (1910); F. Meinecke, "Zur Geschichte des älteren deutschen Parteiwesens," in *Historische Zeitschrift,* cxviii (1917), 46–63, a critique of Erich Brandenburg's *Die Reichsgründung,* and a reply by Brandenburg in cxix (1919) 63–84. An invaluable collection of source materials is found in the selection of letters by leading political figures in the two volumes edited by Julius Heyderhoff and Paul Wentzcke, *Deutscher Liberalismus im Zeitalter Bismarcks* (Bonn, 1925–1926). For a comparative treatment of Protestant and Catholic political action see Karl Buchheim, *Geschichte der christlichen Parteien in Deutschland* (Munich, 1953).
16 Quoted in Stillich, *op. cit.,* p. 135.
17 F. Naumann, *Von Vaterland und Freiheit* (Leipzig, 1913), p. 57.
18 For Stöcker see Walter Frank, *Hofprediger Adolf Stoecker und die christlichsoziale Bewegung* (2nd ed., Hamburg, 1935). This is by the official Nazi party historian, but is none the less the most authoritative study of Stöcker. See also Paul Massing, *Rehearsal for Destruction* (New York, 1949), chaps. ii–v, viii–ix.
19 Massing, *op. cit.,* p. 41.
20 Quoted in Massing, *op. cit.,* pp. 66–67.
21 On the National Liberals, in addition to previously cited literature, see also H. Oncken, *Rudolf von Bennigsen;* H. Kalkoff, *Nationalliberale Parlementarier 1867–1917* (Berlin, 1917); E. Brandenburg, *50 Jahre Nationalliberale Partei 1867–1917* (Leipzig, 1917).
22 Cf. Eugen Richter, *Im alten Reichstag. Erinnerungen,* 2 vols. (Berlin, 1896); F. Rachfahl, "Eugen Richter und der Linksliberalismus im neuen Reich," in *Zeitschrift für Politik,* v (1911–1912), 261–374; L. Ullstein, *Eugen Richter als Publizist und Herausgeber* (Leipzig, 1930); H. Röttger, *Bismarck und Eugen Richter im Reichstage 1879–90* (Bochum, 1932). An excellent summary of left-wing liberalism is to be found in Theodor Barth, "Was ist Liberalismus?" in *Die Nation,* xxii (1905), 402–404, 423–425, 438–439.
23 M. Harden, *Word Portraits* (London, 1911), p. 122.
24 *Ibid.,* p. 134.
25 Rachfahl, *op. cit.,* p. 371.
26 *Ibid.*
27 On Naumann see the excellent and comprehensive biography by his former secretary Theodor Heuss, *Friedrich Naumann, der Mann, das Werk, die Zeit* (Stuttgart, 1937). A more reserved and sometimes too sharply critical treatment is found in William O. Shanahan's two articles: "Friedrich Naumann: A German View of Power and Nationalism," in *Nationalism and Internationalism, Essays Inscribed to Carlton J. H. Hayes* (New York, 1950), 352–398, and "Friedrich Naumann: A Mirror of Wilhelmian Germany," in *Review of Politics,* xiii (1951), 267–301.
28 *Von Vaterland und Freiheit,* p. 66.

29 *Ibid.*, p. 83.
30 *Ibid.*
31 *Ibid.*, p. 85
32 *Ibid.*, pp. 109–111,

CHAPTER IX

1 For the history of Catholic political action in Germany, see above all Karl Bachem *Vorgeschichte, Geschichte und Politik der deutschen Zentrumspartei,* 9 vols. (Cologne 1927–1932). This is a huge collection of materials by a prominent Catholic publicist and political leader of the Cologne group. While obviously partisan in character and not scholarly in the technical sense, it is written by one who has had such intimate personal contact with the movement and is so detailed that it is indispensable for any study of the Second Reich. An excellent collection of source materials, with a good introduction, is Ludwig Bergsträsser's *Der politische Katholizismus,* 2 vols. (Munich, 1921–1923). See also the biography of August Reichensperger by Ludwig von Pastor, 2 vols. (Freiburg, 1899), and of Windthorst by Edward Hüsgen (Cologne, 1907); see also F. Rachfahl, "Windthorst und der Kulturkampf," in *Preussische Jahrbücher,* vol. cxxxv (1909). A most valuable addition to this literature is the recently published study by Edgar Alexander, "Church and Society in Germany," in *Catholic Social and Political Movements 1789–1950,* ed. Joseph N. Moody (New York, 1953).

2 F. J. Buss, "Die deutsche Einheit und die Preussenliebe," in Bergsträsser, *Politischer Katholizismus,* i, 178.

3 Wilhelm Emanuel von Ketteler, *Deutschland nach dem Kriege von 1866* (Mainz, 1867), pp. 104–105.

4 Bergsträsser, *op. cit.,* i, 111. This was also underscored by Peter Reichensperger in his great speech of April 1, 1871, in the Reichstag. See *Stenographische Berichte* for 1871, pp. 105–106.

5 See Chapter III and the literature cited there.

6 On Görres see W. Schellberg, *Joseph von Goerres* (2nd ed., Munich, 1922); Alois Dempf, *Görres spricht zu unserer Zeit* (Freiburg im Breisgau, 1933).

7 Bergsträsser, *op. cit.,* i, 183–185.

8 Cited in Bergsträsser, *op. cit.,* i, 20.

9 From the Report of the Center group in the Prussian diet to their constituents in 1861, published in Bergsträsser, *op. cit.,* i, 234.

10 Bergsträsser, *op. cit.,* i, 42.

11 For a good analysis in English of German Social Catholicism see Ralph Bowen, *German Theories of the Corporative State* (New York, 1947), pp. 75–118, and Alexander, *op. cit.*

12 A. Bebel, *My Life* (London, 1912), pp. 36–37.

13 Bergsträsser, *op. cit.,* i, 285.

14 *Ibid.,* pp. 302–303.

15 Ketteler, *Die Arbeiterfrage und das Christentum* (4th ed., Mainz, 1890), pp. 2–3.

16 Bergsträsser, *op. cit.,* ii, 27–28.

17 This interesting declaration can be found in *Europäischer Geschichtskalender,* xii (1871), 79–87.

18 *Europäischer Geschichtskalender,* xiv (1873), 481.

19 Adalbert Wahl has done most to demonstrate this connection between the Kulturkampf and Bismarck's foreign policy. See his *Vom Bismarck der 70er Jahre* (Tübingen, 1920) and his *Deutsche Geschichte,* i (Stuttgart, 1926), 136–216. A not too convincing critique of Wahl's thesis is found in Paul Sattler, "Bismarcks Entschluss zum Kulturkampf," in *Forschungen zur brandenburgischen und preussischen Geschichte,* ii (1940), 66–101. See also Georges Goyau, *Bismarck et l'église. Le Culturkampf,* 4 vols. (4th ed., Paris, 1922) H. Bornkamm, "Die Staatsidee im Kulturkampf," in *Historische Zeitschrift,* clxx (1950), 41–72, 273–306.

20 Other important Catholic newspapers were the *Kölnische Volkszeitung; Westfälischer Merkur,* in Münster; *Schlesische Volkszeitung,* in Breslau; *Augsburger Postzeitung; Mainzer Journal; Der Badischer Beobachter,* in Karlsruhe; *Das Deutsche Volksblatt,* in Stuttgart. In 1871 there was a total of 126 Centrist newspapers with a total circulation of 322,000; by 1912 this had increased to 446 papers and 2,624,900 circulation. See Bachem, *op. cit.,* ii, 155.

21 J. Ziekursch, *Politische Geschichte des neuen deutschen Kaiserreiches,* i, 229.

22 *Europäischer Geschichtskalender,* xiii (1872), 52.
23 Quoted in Bachem, *op. cit.,* v, 17.
24 Bismarck, *Gesammelte Werke,* xii, 520–521.
25 *Ibid.,* xiii, 475.
26 The text of this is reprinted in *Bergsträsser,* vol. ii. A very full and interesting account of the discussion aroused by the article is to be found in Bachem, *op. cit.*
27 Peter and August Reichensperger, *Die Fraktion des Centrums. (Katholische Fraktion),* in *Zwölf Briefen* (Mainz, 1861), quoted in Hans Rosenberg, *Die nationalpolitische Publizistik Deutschlands,* i, 200.
28 *Stenographische Berichte über die Verhandlungen, Haus der Abgeordneten,* 1872–1873, i, 633. There also remained, of course, a very strong anti-Catholic sentiment among the ruling Protestant conservative circles. See the quotations from ex-Chancellor Georg Michaelis, General Ludendorff, Count Waldersee, and Emperor William II in Bachem, *op. cit.,* iv, 259–264.

CHAPTER X

1 Cf. F. Hayek, *The Road to Serfdom* (Chicago, 1945); see also W. Röpke, *The Solution of the German Problem,* tr. E. W. Dickes (New York, 1947), pp. 173–177.
2 Oswald Spengler, *Preussentum und Sozialismus* (Munich, 1920), pp. 8, 10. See also A. Moeller van den Bruck, *Das dritte Reich* (Berlin, 1923).
3 See Heinrich König, *Das neue Deutschland und der borussische Sozialismus (Lensch, Plenge, Spengler)* (Essen, 1924), and August Winnig, *Vom Proletariat zum Arbeitertum* (Hamburg, 1930).
4 *Vorwärts,* Feb. 2, 1919.
5 Spengler, *op. cit.,* p. 76.
6 There is as yet no authoritative and comprehensive history of the Socialist movement in Germany. The best all-inclusive account is to be found in Heinrich Herkner, *Die Arbeiterfrage,* 2 vols. (8th ed., Berlin, 1922), ii, 323–462. Franz Mehring's detailed *Geschichte der deutschen Sozialdemokratie,* 4 vols. (12th ed., Stuttgart, 1922), only goes down to 1891; Richard Lipinski's *Die Sozialdemokratie von ihren Anfängen bis zur Gegenwart,* 2 vols. (Berlin, 1927–1928), is a very superficial account by a party functionary. For firsthand material on German Socialism consult the protocols of the party congresses; the files of the *Neue Zeit, Sozialistische Monatshefte,* the Berlin *Vorwärts,* and the *Leipziger Volkszeitung.* See also W. H. Dawson, *German Socialism and Ferdinand Lassalle* (3d ed., New York, 1899). Werner Sombart's *Der proletarische Sozialismus,* 2 vols. (10th ed., Jena, 1924), despite its outwardly imposing structure, is already indicative of the degenerating path of Sombart's scholarship toward metaphysical sociology and eventually to racialist nationalism.
7 *Out of My Life* (London, 1912), p. 45.
8 *Ibid.,* p. 79.
9 A descriptive bibliography of the literature on this period is to be found in Paul Mombert, "Aus der Literatur über die soziale Frage und über die Arbeiterbewegung in Deutschland in der ersten Hälfte des 19. Jahrhunderts," in *Archiv für die Geschichte des Sozialismus und der Arbeiterbewegung,* ix (1927), 169–236.
10 Cf. Dr. Lette, "Zur Geschichte der Bildung und Wirksamkeit des Central-Vereins in Preussen für das Wohl der arbeitenden Klassen," in *Der Arbeiterfreund,* i (1863), 1–25, and "Enstehung, Entwicklung, und Thätigkeit des Central-Vereins für das Wohl der arbeitenden Klassen," *ibid.,* xiv (1876), 85–152.
11 Cf. F. A. Lange, *Die Arbeiterfrage* (4th ed., Winterthur, 1879), and Heinrich Braun, *Fr. Albert Lange als Sozialökonom* (Halle, 1881).
12 See Hans Ebeling, *Der Kampf der Frankfurter Zeitung gegen Ferdinand Lassalle und die Gründung einer selbständigen Arbeiterpartei* (Leipzig, 1931).
13 Unfortunately, Richard Lipinski's *Die Geschichte der sozialistischen Arbeiterbewegung in Leipzig* (Leipzig, 1931) remained unfinished and goes down only to 1857.

16 *Offenes Antwort-Schreiben*, in *Gesammelte Reden und Schriften*, ed. Eduard Bernstein, 12 vols. (Berlin, 1919–1920), iii, 9–92.

17 E. Bernstein, *Von der Sekte zur Partei* (Jena, 1911), p. 10.

18 *Ibid.*, p. 12.

19 On Lassalle's theory of the state, see Salo W. Baron, *Die politische Theorie Ferdinand Lassalles* (Leipzig, 1923); Hans Kelsen, *Sozialismus und Staat* (2nd ed., Leipzig, 1923); Max Adler, *Die Staatsauffassung des Marxismus* (Vienna, 1922).

20 Bernstein, *Der Sozialismus einst und jetzt* (2nd ed., Berlin, 1923), pp. 80–81.

21 *Ibid.*, p. 82.

22 Gustav Mayer, *Bismarck und Lassalle* (Berlin, 1928).

23 *Ibid.*, p. 60.

24 Princess Helene von Racowitza, *Autobiography*, tr. Cecil Mar (New York, 1910), pp. 118–119.

25 Cited in Oncken, *op. cit.*, pp. 341–342. For the relations between Lassalle and Marx, see, besides the literature already cited, F. Mehring, "Ueber den Gegensatz zwischen Lassalle und Marx," in *Neue Zeit*, vol. xxxi, pt. 2 (1913), 445–450.

26 Even Catholic writers of the time recognized this importance of Lassalle. They delighted in his vigorous assault upon economic liberalism. Bishop von Ketteler openly acknowledged his indebtedness to the economic theories of Lassalle and secretly tried to establish relations with him. Joseph Edmund Jörg, the editor of the Catholic *Historisch-Politische Blätter*, said of Lassalle: "This man never for a moment stood on a Christian foundation but . . . he illuminated the darkest depths of modern cultural history with the flashing lightning strokes of his spirit and often spoke a language that was not unworthy of a Christian seer and social philosopher" (*Geschichte der social-politischen Parteien in Deutschland*, Freiburg im Breisgau, 1867, p. 28). "No one can say today," continued Jörg, "how the Lassallean movement will develop, and if it will not some time in the future be recognized as equal in importance to the reformation of the sixteenth century and a corrective to it. Three years ago everyone asked: Who is Lassalle? Today this name is in every one's mouth; . . . no one can ignore him, no one can dispute his fame to have been one of the greatest geniuses of the century. Posterity may perhaps date from him the turning point of the dominance of liberalism. For he truly has touched the spot where liberalism is vulnerable" (*ibid.*, p. 161).

27 *Politische Aufsätze und Reden*, ed. Franz Mehring (Berlin, 1912), pp. 41–42.

28 See Mehring's notes to his collection of Schweitzer's *Politische Aufsätze und Reden*; Gustav Mayer, *J. B. v. Schweitzer* (Jena, 1909); A. Bebel, *My Life*, chap. xii; and in *Neue Zeit*, vol. xxx, pt. i (1911), 180–187.

29 There is as yet no authoritative and scholarly biography of Bebel. All existing biographies are more or less official party publications. Of these the best are: Max Hochdorf, *August Bebel* (Berlin, 1932); Franz Klühs, *August Bebel* (Berlin, 1923); Hermann Wendel, *August Bebel* (Berlin, 1913). See also R. Michels, "August Bebel," in *Archiv für Sozialwissenschaft und Sozialpolitik*, xxxvii (1913), 671–700, and Paul Kampfmeyer, in *Biographisches Jahrbuch*, xviii (1913), 215–229.

30 Cf. Kurt Eisner, *Wilhelm Liebknecht* (Berlin, 1900).

31 Bebel, *My Life*, pp. 284–285.

32 See Karl Marx, *Critique of the Gotha Program*, with appendices by F. Engels and V. I. Lenin (New York, 1933).

33 Cf. *The Correspondence of Karl Marx and Friedrich Engels* (New York, 1935), pp. 332–339. See also B. Nikolajewski, "Marx und Engels über das Gothaer Programm," in *Die Gesellschaft*, vol. iv, pt. 2 (1927), 154–171.

34 Cf. H. Schulthess, ed. *Europäischer Geschichtskalender*, xix (1878), 170–171.

35 For the official record of government action against the Socialists, see Otto Atzrott, *Sozialdemokratische Druckschriften und Vereine verboten auf Grund . . .* (Berlin, 1886), and the supplement (Berlin, 1888).

36 Karl Kautsky, *Das Erfurter Programm* (Stuttgart, 1892). The published English translation of this is not too accurate.

37 The statistical data on the Social Democratic party are taken from Ernst Drahn's article "Sozialdemokratie" in *Handwörterbuch der Staatswissenschaften*, vol. vii (4th ed., Jena, 1926). See Appendix for Reichstag elections figures.

38 Cf. Eduard Bernstein's preface to the 50th anniversary edition (Berlin, 1929).

39 Franz Mehring, "Persönliche Erinnerungen an August Bebel," in *Archiv für Geschichte des Sozialismus*, iv (1914), 306.

40 Cf. Theodor Leipart, "Politisch oder neutral," in *Sozialistische Monatshefte*, vol. xx, pt. 2 (1914), 735–739.

41 Cf. Eduard David, *Sozialismus und Landwirtschaft*, vol. i (Berlin, 1903). See also Eduard Bernstein, "Die Bedeutung von Eduard Davids Agrarwerk," in *Sozialistische Monat-*

;hefte, vol. vii, pt. 1 (1903), 108–115, and the extensive critique by Karl Kautsky in *Neue Zeit*, vol. xxi, pt. i (1903), 677–688, 731–735, 745–758, 781–794, 804–819.

42 A beautiful instance of this sense of relief and exultation is to be found in Friedrich Meinecke's *Erinnerungen* (Stuttgart, 1949), p. 137.

43 The English translation was published as *Evolutionary Socialism* (New York, 1909). See also Peter Gay, *The Dilemma of Democratic Socialism, Eduard Bernstein's Challenge to Marx* (New York, 1953).

44 E. Bernstein, *Von der Sekte zur Partei*, p. 76.

45 Cf., for example, Wilhelm Schröder's "Sozialdemokratie und Heeresverfassung," in *Sozialistische Monatshefte*, xix (1913), 536–542.

46 K. Leuthner, "Volksinteresse und Staatsschicksal," in *Sozialistische Monatshefte*, xviii (1912), 1124.

47 Cf. G. Hildebrand, *Sozialistische Auslandspolitik* (Jena, 1911).

48 *Leipziger Volkszeitung*, Aug. 20, 1907.

49 *Protokoll über die Verhandlungen des Parteitages der Sozialdemokratischen Partei Deutschlands abgehalten zu Essen* (Berlin, 1907), p. 262.

50 This nationalist trend in German Socialism alarmed many of the French Socialists and was the occasion for Charles Andler's writings on German Socialism beginning with his articles of Nov. 10 and Dec. 10, 1912, in the Paris *Action Nationale*. See especially *La Décomposition politique du socialisme allemand, 1914–1919* (Paris, 1919), and *Le Social-:sme impérialiste dans l'Allemagne contemporaine* (Paris, 1918).

51 Ludwig Quessel, "Der alte und der neue Liberalismus," in *Sozialistische Monatshefte*, xv (1911), 898–906.

52 R. Lipinski, *Die Sozialdemokratie*, ii, 180.

53 German Reichstag, *Stenographische Berichte* (1907), p. 1100.

54 A. Bebel, *Unsere Ziele* (10th ed., Berlin, 1893), pp. 20–21.

55 From speech delivered by Jaurès on Aug. 19, 1904, and published in *La Revue socialiste*, x (1904), 303–312. This journal erroneously gives the date of the speech as Aug. 21. For Bebel's reply to Jaurès, see the Berlin *Vorwärts*, Aug. 21, 1904.

CHAPTER XI

1 For general surveys of German economic development in the nineteenth and twentieth centuries, see the following: Werner Sombart, *Die deutsche Volkwirtschaft im 19. Jahrhundert* (7th ed., Berlin, 1927); J. H. Clapham, *Economic Development of France and Germany 1815–1914* (4th ed., Cambridge, 1936); W. H. Dawson, *Evolution of Modern Germany* (London, 1907); A. Sartorius von Waltershausen, *Deutsche Wirtschaftsgeschichte 1815– 1914* (2nd ed., Jena, 1923); Karl Helfferich, *Germany's Economic Progress and National Wealth 1888–1913*, tr. from the German (New York, 1914); *Deutschland unter Wilhelm II*, 3 vols. (Berlin, 1914), wherein vol. ii is devoted to economic progress; W. F. Bruck, *Social and Economic History of Germany 1888–1938* (Cardiff, 1938); W. Röpke, *German Commercial Policy* (London, 1934). The best brief account is in Gustav Stolper's *German Economy 1870–1940* (New York, 1940).

2 For the foreign influences on German economic development, see Pierre Benaerts, *Les Origines de la grande industrie allemande* (Paris, 1933), chap. ix.

3 According to the estimates of Karl Helfferich, taken from *Handwörterbuch der Staatswissenschaften*, viii, 748.

4 *Encyclopaedia of the Social Sciences*, xi, 206.

5 This entire period of 1815–1870 is dealt with in masterly fashion in Benaerts, *op. cit.*

6 Sombart, *op. cit.*, p. 86. In 1913 there was a total of 5,486 *Aktiengesellschaften*, with a capital of about 17.4 billion marks. Cf. K. Helfferich, *Georg von Siemens*, i, 197.

7 Sombart, *op. cit.*, pp. 27–28.

8 Taken from *Statistique Internationale des Grandes Villes* (The Hague, 1931), p. 52.

9 Taken from Clapham, *op. cit.*, p. 278.

10 Sombart, *op. cit.*, p. 423.

11 Stolper, *op. cit.*, p. 41.

12 Helfferich, *Germany's Economic Progress*, p. 17.

13 Quoted in Dawson, *Evolution of Modern Germany*, p. 246.

14 Sombart, *op. cit.*, p. 493.

15 J. M. Keynes, *The Economic Consequences of the Peace* (London, 1919), p. 40.

16 Cf. Bernhard Menne, *Krupp* (London, 1937).

17 Cf. Paul Arnst, *A. Thyssen und sein Werk* (Leipzig, 1925).

18 Taken from Sombart, *op. cit.*, p. 496.

19 Cf. Bernhard Huldermann, *Albert Ballin*, tr. W. J. Eggers (London, 1922).

20 Cf. Theodor Heuss, *Robert Bosch, Leben und Leistung* (Stuttgart, 1948).

21 Heinrich Hauser, *Opel. Ein deutsches Tor zur Welt* (Frankfurt, 1939), p. 145.

22 Cf. F. Pinner, *Emil Rathenau und das elektrische Zeitalter* (Leipzig, 1918).

23 Helfferich, *op. cit.*, p. 30.

24 An absorbing account of the developments of the German chemical industry is found in Richard Sasuly, *I. G. Farben* (New York, 1947). The author was one of the chief of the American army investigators of this industry after World War II.

25 Taken from Stolper, *op. cit.*, p. 52.

26 On the role of German banks in the economic progress of Germany, see: Jacob Riesser, *German Great Banks and Their Concentration in Connection with the Economic Development of Germany*, tr. Morris Jacobson (Washington, 1911); Gerhart von Schulze-Gaevernitz, *Die deutsche Kreditbank* (Tübingen, 1922); Georg Bernhard, *Meister und Dilettanten am Kapitalismus im Reiche der Hohenzollern* (Amsterdam, 1936). Interesting and important material is found in some of the better biographies of leading bankers. Karl Helfferich's *Georg von Siemens*, 3 vols. (2nd ed., Berlin, 1923), is a mine of information on the general economic progress of Germany. See also Hermann Münch, *Adolf von Hansemann* (Munich, 1932), and Hans Fürstenberg, *Carl Fürstenberg* (Berlin, 1931).

27 Riesser, *op. cit.*, pp. 6–7.

28 Schulze-Gaevernitz, *op. cit.*, p. 153.

29 Riesser, *op. cit.*, p. 49.

30 Helfferich, *op. cit.*, i, 207.

31 Thorstein Veblen, *Imperial Germany and the Industrial Revolution*, first published in 1915, new ed. by Joseph Dorfman (New York, 1939).

32 *Ibid.*, p. 194.

33 Article "Cartels" in the *Encyclopaedia of the Social Sciences*, vii, 234.

34 *Wirtschaftsdienst*, July 29, 1927, p. 1122.

35 F. Kleinwächter, *Die Kartelle* (Innsbruck, 1883).

36 Sombart, *op. cit.*, p. 316.

37 *Ibid.*, p. 316.

38 *Verhandlungen des Vereins für Sozialpolitik*, cxvi (1906), 267–268.

39 F. Naumann, *Neudeutsche Wirtschaftspolitik* (3rd ed., Berlin, 1913), p. 278.

40 On Kirdorf, see F. A. Freundt, *Kapital und Arbeit* (Berlin, 1929), by an ardent admirer.

41 Interesting sidelights on this investigation may be found in L. Brentano, *Mein Leben* (Jena, 1931), pp. 231–236.

42 For the attitude of German Socialists toward cartels, see Eduard Reuffurth, *Die Stellung der deutschen Sozialdemokratie zum Problem der staatlichen Kartellpolitik* (Jena, 1930).

43 Richard Calwer, "Kartelle und Sozialdemokratie," in *Sozialistische Monatshefte*, vol. xiii, pt. i (1907), p. 374. See also his *Kartelle und Trusts* (Berlin, 1906).

44 Cf., for example, Frederic C. Howe's *Socialized Germany* (New York, 1915).

45 Stolper, *op. cit.*, p. 77.

46 On German commercial policy see: Joseph B. Esslen, *Die Politik des auswärtigen Handels* (Stuttgart, 1925); Oswald Schneider, *Bismarcks Finanz- und Wirtschaftspolitik* (Munich, 1912); W. Röpke, *German Commercial Policy*.

47 For the wide range of social problems engendered by the industrial revolution and the movements and measures of social reform, the most comprehensive work is the classic treatise of Heinrich Herkner, the successor of Schmoller at the University of Berlin, *Die Arbeiterfrage*, 2 vols. (8th ed., Berlin, 1922). See also the older work by Gustav Schmoller, *Die soziale Frage* (reprinted in Munich, 1918); W. H. Dawson, *The German Workman* (London, 1906); F. Naumann, *Neudeutsche Wirtschaftspolitik*; F. Tönnies, *Die Entwicklung der sozialen Frage bis zum Weltkriege* (4th ed., Berlin, 1926).

48 Dawson, *The German Workman*, p. viii.

49 *Stenographische Berichte* of the Reichstag, 4. Legislaturperiode, IV Session, 1881, Anlagen, vol. iii, Aktenstück no. 41, p. 228.

50 Bismarck, *Gesammelte Werke*, xii, 455.

51 Quoted in H. Rothfels, "Bismarck's Social Policy and the Problem of State Socialism in Germany," in *Sociological Review*, xxx (1938), 92.

52 G. E. Buckle, *Life of Benjamin Disraeli* (London, 1920), vi, 341–342.

53 Bismarck, *op. cit.*, viii, 532.

54 See their speeches at the banquet, recorded in *Schriften des Vereins für Sozialpolitik*, lxxvi (1898), 442–444.

55 *Verhandlungen der Eisenacher Versammlung zur Besprechung der socialen Frage* (Leipzig, 1873), p. 1.

56 *Ibid.*, pp. 5–6.

57 For a full account of the history of the Verein, see its final publication, *Geschichte des Vereins für Sozialpolitik*, by its long-active secretary Franz Bose (Berlin, 1939), vol. clxxviii of the *Schriften des Vereins fur Sozialpolitik*. See also L. Brentano, "Zum Jubiläum des Vereins für Sozialpolitik," in *Schriften des Vereins* . . . , vol. clxiii (1923), 1–22.

58 See H. Treitschke, "Der Socialismus und seine Gönner," first published July 20, 1874, and reprinted in *Zehn Jahre deutscher Kämpfe* (2nd ed., Berlin, 1879); also "Die gerechte Vertheilung der Güter," and "Noch ein Wort zur Arbeiterfrage," included in the same volume.

59 *Politics*, tr. B. Dugdale and Torben de Bille, 2 vols. (London, 1916), i, 42–43.

60 *Ibid.*, p. 43.

61 *Stenographische Berichte* of the Reichstag for the first session, 1881, p. 2.

62 Taken from *Encyclopaedia of the Social Sciences*, xv, 14.

63 For a full treatment of the history of the trade-unions in Germany, see Theodor Cassau, *Die Gewerkschaftsbewegung* (Halberstadt, 1925).

64 Cf. Heuss, *op. cit.*

65 On Baron Stumm, see Fritz Hellwig, *Carl Ferdinand Freiherr von Stumm-Hallberg* (Heidelberg, 1936).

66 *Schriften des Vereins für Sozialpolitik*, cxvi (1906), 289.

67 Cf. Gerhart Kessler, *Die deutschen Arbeitgeberverbände* (Leipzig, 1907), vol. cxxiv of the *Schriften des Vereins für Sozialpolitik*, and H. A. Bueck, *Der Centralverband deutscher Industrieller 1876–1901*, 3 vols. (Berlin, 1902–1905).

68 Herkner, *op. cit.*, i, 432.

69 *Ibid.*, i, 446. The smaller entrepreneurs organized their own association in 1895 under the title of Bund der Industriellen. Their attitude was not as intransigeant as that of the association of heavy industry. Eventually both associations united in 1919 as the Reichsverband der deutschen Industrie.

70 *Schriften des Vereins für Sozialpolitik*, cxvi (1906), 214–215.

71 Helfferich, *Siemens*, i, 193–200.

72 Daniel Ricardo, "Thyssens Lebenswerk," in *Die Neue Rundschau*, vol. xxiii, pt. 2 (1912), p. 1005.

73 Cf. Ernst Kohn-Bramstedt, *Aristocracy and the Middle Classes in Germany: Social Types in German Literature 1830–1900* (London, 1937).

74 For general over-all treatment of German cultural developments in the Second Reich, see: John Theodor Merz, *A History of European Thought in the 19th Century*, 4 vols. (4th ed., Edinburgh, 1923); *Propyläen Weltgeschichte*, viii (Berlin, 1930), 457–540, and x (1933), 3–42; Karl Lamprecht, *Deutsche Geschichte*, vol. xi, and vol. i of the supplementary volumes; Adalbert Wahl, *Deutsche Geschichte*, sections on cultural life in vols. i–iii; Georg Steinhausen, *Deutsche Geistes- und Kulturgeschichte von 1870 bis zur Gegenwart* (Halle, 1931); Theobold Ziegler, *Die geistigen und sozialen Strömmungen des 19. Jahrhunderts* (Berlin, 1911); *Germany in the 19th Century*, Manchester University Series, first series (Manchester, 1912); second series (Manchester, 1915); *German Culture*, ed. W. P. Patterson (London, 1915); Curt Gebauer, *Deutsche Kulturgeschichte der Neuzeit* (Berlin, 1932); Rohan D'Olier Butler, *The Roots of National Socialism* (London, 1941).

For the natural sciences see Gustav Abb, ed. *Aus Fünfzig Jahren deutscher Wissenschaft* (Berlin, 1930). Philosophical trends are best studied in F. A. Lange, *The History of Materialism*, tr. E. C. Thomas (London, 1925), and Ueberweg's *Grundriss der Geschichte der Philosophie*, 12th ed., vol. iv (Berlin, 1923). The Nietzsche literature is a vast one. Walter A. Kaufmann's *Nietzsche: Philosopher, Psychologist, Antichrist* (Princeton, 1950), provides a balanced treatment and a detailed bibliography. See also Karl Jaspers, *Nietzsche* (Berlin, 1936), and Crane Brinton, *Nietzsche* (Boston, 1941). The best introduction to Dilthey is H. A. Hodges, *Wilhelm Dilthey* (New York, 1944); see also Hajo Holborn, "Wilhelm Dilthey and the Critique of Historical Reason," in *Journal of the History of Ideas*, xi (1950), 93–118 and Gerhard Masur, "Wilhelm Dilthey and the History of Ideas," *ibid.*, xiii (1952), 94–107.

For German historiography and the social sciences, the introductory articles in vol. i of the *Encyclopaedia of the Social Sciences* are useful, as are the articles on the various disciplines and the article "Geisteswissenschaften"; see also G. P. Gooch, *History and Historians in the 19th Century* (2nd ed., New York, 1952); Georg von Below, *Die deutsche Geschichtsschreibung von den Befreiungskriegen bis zu unseren Tagen* (2nd ed., Munich, 1924); Friedrich Meinecke, *Die Entstehung des Historismus*, 2 vols. (2nd ed., Munich, 1946); Ernst Troeltsch, *Der Historismus und seine Probleme*, vol. iii of his *Gesammelte Schriften* (Tübingen, 1922); H. von Srbik, *Geist und Geschichte vom deutschen Humanismus bis zur Gegenwart*, 2 vols. (Munich, 1950–1951); Albert Salomon, "German Sociology," in *Twentieth Century Sociology*, ed. Georges Gurvitch and W. E. Moore (New York, 1945), pp. 586–614; Max Weber, *Essays in Sociology*, tr. and ed. H. H. Gerth and

C. Wright Mills (New York, 1946), which contains a biographical introduction and selections from the works of Max Weber on science and politics, power, religion, and social structures. Friedrich Meinecke's *Staat und Persönlichkeit* (Munich, 1933) contains beautifully written essays on F. T. Vischer, Schmoller, Weber, and Troeltsch.

For German belles-lettres see Jethro Bithell, *Modern German Literature* (London, 1939); Alfred Biele, *Deutsche Literaturgeschichte*, vol. iii (Munich, 1930); Franz Mehring, *Zur Literaturgeschichte von Hebbel bis Gorki* (Berlin, 1930); Josef Nadler, *Literaturgeschichte der deutschen Stämme und Landschaften*, vol. iv (3rd ed., Regensburg, 1932). This edition of Nadler is less racialist than the 4th edition published under Nazi rule in 1938. For painting and sculpture see F. Haack, *Die Kunst des XIX. Jahrhunderts* (Esslingen, 1913), and Max Sauerlandt, *Die Kunst der letzten 30 Jahre* (Berlin, 1935). For music see Paul Henry Lang, *Music in Western Civilization* (New York, 1941). The classic works on Wagner are Ernest Newman's *The Life of Richard Wagner*, 4 vols. (New York, 1933–1946), and *Wagner as Man and Artist* (New York, 1924); see also Thomas Mann, "Sufferings and Greatness of Richard Wagner," in his *Essays of Three Decades* (New York, 1947), pp. 307–371.

[75] F. Meinecke, *Staat und Persönlichkeit*, p. 61.

[76] *Ibid.*, p. 63.

[77] *Le Progrès de la conscience dans la philosophie occidentale*, p. 431, quoted by Julien Benda in his *Treason of the Intellectuals* (New York, 1928), pp. 229–230.

[78] Walther Rathenau, *Gesammelte Schriften*, ii (1918), 13–14, from his "Zur Mechanik des Geistes" (1912).

[79] Hans Blüher, *Gesammelte Aufsätze* (Jena, 1917), p. 53.

CHAPTER XII

[1] On Frederick III consult the following: Martin Philippson, *Das Leben Kaiser Friedrichs III* (Wiesbaden, 1900); Eugen Wolbe, *Kaiser Friedrich: Die Tragödie des Übergangenen* (Hellerau, 1931); Werner Richter, *Kaiser Friedrich III* (Zürich, 1938); Andreas Dorpalen, "Emperor Frederick III and the German Liberal Movement," in *American Historical Review*, liv (1948), 1–31.

[2] Quoted in Adalbert Wahl, *Deutsche Geschichte*, ii, p. 485.

[3] Quoted in Dorpalen, *op. cit.*, p. 22.

[4] *Geschichte der Frankfurter Zeitung* (Frankfurt, 1911), p. 445.

[5] Cf. L. Bamberger, *Bismarcks grosses Spiel. Die geheimen Tagebücher Ludwig Bambergers*, ed. Ernst Feder (Frankfurt, 1932).

[6] Dorpalen, *op. cit.*, p. 22.

[7] *Ibid.*, p. 30.

[8] For the personal biography of William II, see especially: Ehrich Eyck, *Das persönliche Regiment Wilhelms II* (Zürich, 1948); Emil Ludwig. *Kaiser Wilhelm II*, tr. E. C. Mayne (London, 1926); K. F. Nowak, *Kaiser and Chancellor* (London, 1930) and *Germany's Road to Ruin* (London, 1932), tr. E. W. Dickes; William II, *The Kaiser's Memoirs*, tr. T. R. Ybarra (New York, 1922).

[9] Walther Rathenau, *Der Kaiser* (Berlin, 1921), p. 27.

[10] Quoted in H. W. Steed, *Through Thirty Years*, 2 vols. (London, 1924), i, 21–24.

[11] William's letter was first published in the *Oesterreichische Rundschau*, lviii (1919), 100ff. An English translation is available in Nowak, *Kaiser and Chancellor*, pp. 227–238. The third volume of Bismarck's *Gedanken und Erinnerungen* was published by the J. G. Cotta'sche Buchhandlung of Stuttgart and Berlin in 1921; an English translation was published under the title *The Kaiser vs. Bismarck*, tr. Bernard Miall (London, 1921). The most important historical accounts of Bismarck's dismissal are: Wilhelm Schüssler, *Bismarcks Sturz* (3rd ed., Leipzig, 1921); Ernst Gagliardi, *Bismarcks Entlassung* (Tübingen, 1927); Wilhelm Mommsen, *Bismarcks Sturz und die Parteien* (Stuttgart, 1924); Hans Delbrück, "Bismarcks Entlassung," in his *Vor und nach dem Weltkriege* (Berlin, 1926); Nowak, *Kaiser and Chancellor*. See also Wahl, *op. cit.*, vol. ii, chap. 10.

[12] Hans Delbrück, *Government and the Will of the People*, tr. Roy S. MacElwa (New York, 1923), p. 49. Support for the general lines of Delbrück's thesis is found in Egmont Zechlin, *Staatsreichpläne Bismarcks und Wilhelm II. 1890–1894* (Stuttgart, 1929).

[13] Quoted in Nowak, *op. cit.*, pp. 273–274.

[14] *Geschichte der Frankfurter Zeitung*, p. 655.

[15] From Max Weber, *Politische Schriften* (Munich, 1921), p. 138, and cited in J. P. Mayer, *Max Weber and German Politics* (London, 1944), p. 59.

16 On the history of the Wilhelmian epoch see: Eyck, *op. cit.;* Arthur Rosenberg, *The Birth of the German Republic,* tr. Ian F. D. Morrow (New York, 1931); Johannes Ziekursch, *Politische Geschichte des neuen deutschen Kaiserreiches,* 3 vols. (Frankfurt, 1930–1932); Wahl, *op. cit.,* vols. ii–iv.

17 Theodor Barth, "Briefe über deutsche Politik," in *Die Neue Rundschau,* xvii (1907), 1516. See also Charlotte Sempell, "The Constitutional and Political Problems of the Second Chancellor, Leo von Caprivi," in the *Journal of Modern History,* xxv (1953), 234–254.

18 *Die Zukunft,* lvii (1906), 46.

19 Cf. M. Harden, "Gegen den Kaiser," in *Die Zukunft,* lxv (1908), 207–215, 245–263, 285–304.

20 Eyck, *op. cit.,* p. 499.

21 Ferdinand Tönnies, "Politische Reife," in *Die Neue Rundschau,* xx (1909), 161.

22 Steed, *op. cit.,* i, 385. Steed covered the trial for the *Times.*

23 *Die Nation,* xxi (1903), 2–3.

24 See F. Naumann, "Die Stellung der Gebildeten im politischen Leben," in *Patria,* vii (1907), 80–99.

25 Samuel Saenger, "Kulturpolitik: Gedanken, Ziele, Wege," in *Die Neue Rundschau,* xix (1908), 166.

26 Walther Rathenau, "Kritik der Zeit," in his *Gesammelte Schriften,* i, 206–220.

27 The literature on the history of German foreign policy is tremendous, and no attempt will be made to list all the monographic studies and the vast array of memoir and biographical literature. Of the general treatments the following are the most significant: Eyck, *op. cit.;* J. V. Fuller, *Bismarck's Diplomacy at Its Zenith* (Cambridge, Mass., 1922); Bernadotte Schmitt, *The Coming of the War, 1914,* 2 vols. (New York, 1930); Pierre Renouvin, *Les Origines immédiates de la guerre* (2nd ed., Paris, 1927), tr. T. C. Hume (New Haven, 1928); G. P. Gooch, *Recent Revelations in European Diplomacy* (4th ed., London, 1930); Sidney B. Fay, *The Origins of the World War,* 2 vols. (2nd ed., New York, 1930); Otto Hammann, *The World Policy of Germany, 1890–1912,* tr. M. A. Huttman (London, 1927); Erich Brandenburg, *From Bismarck to the World War,* tr. A. E. Adams (London, 1927); Theodor Wolff, *The Eve of 1914,* tr. E. W. Dickes (London, 1936); E. M. Carroll, *Germany and the Great Powers, 1866–1914* (New York, 1938).

28 *Geschichte der Frankfurter Zeitung,* p. 867.

29 Bernhard von Bülow, *Imperial Germany,* tr. Marie A. Lewenz (London, 1914), p. 20.

30 *Ibid.,* p. 35.

31 For the story of German colonial development see: Mary E. Townsend, *The Origins of Modern German Colonization, 1871–1885* (New York, 1921), and *The Rise and Fall of the German Colonial Empire, 1884–1918* (New York, 1930); A. J. P. Taylor, *Germany's First Bid for Colonies* (London, 1938); Royal Institute of International Affairs, *Germany's Claim to Colonies,* Information Department Papers, no. 23 (London, 1938); W. O. Henderson, "The German Colonial Empire," in *History,* xx (1935–1936), 151–158.

32 Quoted by Wahl, *op. cit.,* iii, 63.

33 *Ibid.*

34 H. Delbrück, "Über die Ziele unserer Kolonialpolitik," in *Preussische Jahrbücher,* cxlvii (1912), 503–513.

35 Erich Brandenburg, *From Bismarck to the World War,* p. 206.

36 Wahl, *op. cit.,* iii, 268–269.

37 Cf. W. F. Bruck, *Social and Economic History of Germany from William II to Hitler, 1888–1938* (Cardiff, 1938), pp. 120–121.

38 Richard von Kühlmann, *Thoughts on Germany,* tr. Eric Sutton (London, 1932), p. 33.

39 *Ibid.,* p. 38. On German navalism, see Eckart Kehr, *Schlachtflottenbau und Parteipolitik 1894–1901* (Berlin, 1930).

40 B. Schmitt, *op. cit.,* i, 46.

41 Sir Edward Grey, *Twenty-five Years,* 2 vols. (New York, 1925), i, 290.

42 Cf. "Deutschland und die allgemeine Weltlage," reprinted in Delbrück's *Vor und nach dem Weltkriege* (Berlin, 1926), p. 132.

43 Johannes Haller, *Aus dem Leben des Fürsten Philipp zu Eulenburg-Hertefeld* (Berlin, 1924), p. 114, tr. by E. C. Mayne as *Philip Eulenburg: The Kaiser's Friend,* 2 vols. (New York, 1930).

44 Quoted in Ernst Jäckh, *Kiderlen-Wächter der Staatsmann und Mensch,* 2 vols. (Berlin, 1924), ii, 236–237. See also Take Jonescu, *Some Personal Impressions* (New York, 1920), pp. 74–75.

45 Sir Edward Grey, *Twenty-five Years,* i, 312–313, and ii, 50.

46 Theodor Wolff, *The Eve of 1914,* pp. 619–620.

47 B. Guttmann, *Bethmann-Tirpitz-Ludendorff* (Frankfurt, 1919), p. 7.

48 Schmitt, *op. cit.,* i, 29.

49 Cited in Bernhard Huldermann, *Albert Ballin,* tr. from the German (London, 1922), p. 164.

50 Quoted in Steed, *op. cit.,* i, 23.

51 Quoted from M. Paléologue, *Un grand Tournant de la politique mondiale,* in Eyck, *op. cit.,* p. 434.

52 Schmitt, *op. cit.,* ii, 324.

53 Rathenau, *Der Kaiser,* p. 8.

54 Steed, *op. cit.,* i, 28.

55 Quoted in Eyck, *op. cit.,* p. 250.

56 On the Pan-German League see Mildred S. Wertheimer, *The Pan-German League, 1890–1914* (New York, 1924); Friedrich Hertz, *Nationalgeist und Politik* (Zürich, 1937), pp. 439–479; F. C. Endres, *Die Tragödie Deutschlands* (Munich, 1922); Martin Hobohm and Paul Rohrbach, *Die Alldeutschen* (Berlin, 1919); Heinrich Class, *Wider den Strom* (Leipzig, 1932).

57 Class, *op. cit.,* pp. 290–292.

58 Valentine Chirol, *Fifty Years in a Changing World* (London, 1928), p. 274.

59 Cited in Eyck, *op. cit.,* p. 773.

CHAPTER XIII

1 Bernhard von Bülow, *Memoirs,* tr. Geoffrey Dunlop, 4 vols. (Boston, 1932), iii, 48.

2 Another such person was the subsequent Prussian Minister of Justice, Hugo am Zehnhoff, who told Erzberger on Aug. 4, 1914, that the war would end with a German defeat. See M. Erzberger, *Erlebnisse im Weltkrieg* (Stuttgart, 1920), p. 4.

3 The most important materials on the internal developments in Germany during the period of World War I are to be found in the reports and proceedings of the Fourth Subcommittee of the National Assembly and the Reichstag, edited by Albrecht Philipp and published under the title *Die Ursachen des deutschen Zusammenbruchs im Jahre 1918,* 12 vols. (Berlin, 1928). Extracts from this collection are available in English translation in the *Causes of the German Collapse,* selected by R. H. Lutz (Stanford, 1934), although one may take issue with the basis of selection made by the editor. Another valuable collection of materials is *The Fall of the German Empire, 1914–1918,* 2 vols. (Stanford, 1932), also edited by Lutz. The most important memoir literature for this period is the works of the chancellors Bethmann-Hollweg, Michaelis, Hertling, and Prince Max of Baden, and the works of party leaders Philipp Scheidemann, Matthias Erzberger, Conrad Haussmann, and Friedrich von Payer; also the recently published *Erinnerungen* by Richard von Kühlmann (Heidelberg, 1948). The best general surveys are: Arthur Rosenberg, *The Birth of the German Republic, 1871–1918,* trans. Ian D. Morrow (New York, 1931); G. P. Gooch, *Germany* (New York, 1927), chaps. vi–vii; K. F. Nowak, *Chaos* (Munich, 1923); and *The Collapse of Central Europe,* trans. P. Lochner and E. W. Dickes (London, 1924).

4 Max Weber, *Gesammelte politische Schriften* (Munich, 1921), p. 458; the same sentiment is repeated in a letter to his mother on April 13, 1915 (*ibid.*).

5 Cf. J. P. Bang, *Hurrah and Hallelujah,* trans. from the Danish by J. Brochner (New York, 1917), and Gooch, *op. cit.,* pp. 117–125.

6 *Die Ursachen des deutschen Zusammenbruchs,* vii, 176.

7 Max Scheler, *Krieg und Aufbau* (Leipzig, 1916).

8 See Hermann Hesse's "O Freunde, Nicht diese Töne," written in Sept., 1914, and republished in his *Krieg und Frieden. Betrachtungen zu Krieg und Politik seit dem Jahr 1914* (Zurich, 1946).

9 M. Erzberger, *Erlebnisse im Weltkrieg,* p. 56.

10 Lutz, *Fall of the German Empire,* i, 498.

11 *Die Ursachen . . . ,* vii, 28.

12 Lutz, *Causes of the German Collapse,* p. 8.

13 *Der deutsche Reichstag im Weltkrieg,* completed in 1926 and published as vol. viii of the series *Die Ursachen . . .* Debates on this report are found in vol. vii, pts. i and ii. Translations of extracts are found in Lutz, *Causes of the German Collapse.*

14 *Verhandlungen des Reichstages,* May 25, 1916, pp. 1290–1291.

15 *Die Ursachen . . . ,* vii, 189.

16 Karl Mühsam, *Wie wir belogen wurden* (Munich, 1918), p. 24. This work gives a detailed account of the operations of the German censorship during the war.

17 For the story of German economy during World War I, see: Leo Grebler and Wilhelm Winkler, *The Cost of the World War to Germany and Austria-Hungary* (New

Haven, 1940), and Albrecht Mendelssohn-Bartholdy, *The War and German Society* (New Haven, 1937), both in the Carnegie Series of the Economic and Social History of the World War. See also Gustav Stolper, *German Economy, 1870–1940* (New York, 1940).

18 See Rathenau's address of Dec. 20, 1915, before the Deutsche Gesellschaft, on "Germany's Provisions for Raw Materials," of which an English translation is published in Lutz, *Fall of the German Republic*, ii, 77–91.

19 Cf. the account of the Reichstag debates on the National Service Law in Schulthess, *Europäischer Geschichtskalender*, vol. lvii, pt. i (1916), pp. 551–553, 562–588, 591–598; also Paul Umbreit's "Die deutschen Gewerkschaften im Kriege" in *Der Krieg und die Arbeitsverhältnisse* (Stuttgart, 1928), vol. vi of the German series of the Carnegie Economic and Social History of the World War.

20 A good description of these two points of view is found in Ernst Troeltsch's wartime essay "Der Imperialismus," in *Die Neue Rundschau*, vol. xxvi, pt. i (1915), pp. 1–14.

21 *Die Ursachen . . .* , i, 403.

22 The best accounts of German war aims are to be found in the records of the Reichstag Commission of Inquiry, especially Volkmann's "Die Annexionsfragen des Weltkrieges" in vol. xii, pt. i; Bredt's "Der deutsche Reichstag im Weltkrieg," in vol. viii; and Herz's "Die allgemeine Ursachen und Hergänge des inneren Zusammenbruches," in vol. v.

23 *Die Ursachen . . .* , vii, 280, and Lutz, *Causes of the German Collapse*, p. 279. In Erzberger's version of this incident, the emperor is quoted as saying that the present war would end with an understanding with France, and then the entire European continent under his leadership would "wage the real war, the second Punic War, against England." See Erzberger, *Erlebnisse im Weltkrieg*, p. 53.

24 Lutz, *Causes of the German Collapse*, p. 260.

25 Lutz, *Fall of the German Empire*, ii, 323.

26 These extracts are taken from Schäfer's "Kriegs- und Friedensziele," in *Schwarz-Weiss-Rot Kalender* (1918).

27 O. Czernin, *Im Weltkriege* (Berlin, 1919), p. 334.

28 Lutz, *Causes of the German Collapse*, p. 89.

29 *Die Ursachen . . .* , iv, 159.

30 Philipp Scheidemann, *Der Zusammenbruch* (Berlin, 1921), p. 25.

31 F. Meinecke, *Strassburg, Freiburg, Berlin* (Stuttgart, 1949), pp. 209–210. "This was considered modest at that time," is Meinecke's comment in 1949.

32 Karl Kautsky, "*Die Sozialdemokratie im Kriege*," in *Neue Zeit*, vol. xxxii, pt. ii (1914), pp. 1–2; see also the issue of Aug. 21, 1914, p. 844.

33 *Verhandlungen des Reichstages*, cccvii, 890.

34 *Europäischer Geschichtskalender*, lvii (1916), 432–434.

35 Cf. A. Joseph Berlau, *The German Social Democratic Party, 1914–1921* (New York, 1949), pp. 136–137.

36 See the testimony by Wilhelm Dittmann in *Die Ursachen . . .* , vii, 335.

37 Wilhelm Kolb, "Sekte oder Partei," in *Neue Zeit*, vol. xxiv, pt. i (1915), p. 60. Cf. also Rudolf Hilferding's critique of Kolb's book and Kolb's reply in vol. xxiii, pt. ii (1915), pp. 489–499 and 631–640.

38 K. Haenisch, *Die deutsche Sozialdemokratie in und nach dem Weltkriege* (4th ed., Berlin, 1919), pp. 132–134.

39 "Persönliche Ueberzeugung und Parteidisziplin" and "Freiheit der Meinungsäusserung und Parteidisziplin," in vol. xxxiv, pt. 1 (1915).

40 For accounts of the split in the Social Democratic party see: Eduard Bernstein, "The Rift in Social-Democracy," in Lutz, *Fall of the German Empire*, ii, 45–56; Haenisch, *op. cit.*; Berlau, *op. cit.*; Eugen Prager, *Geschichte der U.S.D.P.* (Berlin, 1921); Hugo Haase, *Reichstagreden gegen die deutsche Kriegspolitik* (Berlin, 1919); Charles Andler, *La Décomposition politique du socialisme allemande, 1914–1918* (Paris, 1919); E. A. Bevan, *German Social-Democracy during the War* (London, 1918).

41 Berlau, *op. cit.*, p. 154.

42 N. Lenin, *Collected Works*, xix, 201ff.

43 Quoted in Rosenberg, *The Birth of the German Republic*, pp. 149–150.

44 Cf. especially the testimony of Dr. Bell before the Reichstag Inquiry Commission, vii, 308, and Erzberger, *op. cit.*

45 The text of this letter was first published in *Welt am Montag*. Cf. *Die Ursachen . . .* , vii, 390.

46 For the treaty of Brest Litovsk see: J. W. Wheeler-Bennett, *The Forgotten Peace* (New York, 1933); Bredt, in vol. viii of the Reichstag Inquiry, pp. 218–240; Lutz, *Fall of the German Empire*, i, 766–801; James Bunyan and H. H. Fisher, *The Bolshevik Revolution 1917–1918: Documents and Materials* (Stanford, 1934), pp. 476–540; Leon Trotsky, *My Life* (New York, 1930), pp. 362–394; E. H. Carr, *The Bolshevik Revolution*,

iii (New York, 1953), pp. 3–58; Ruth Fischer, *Stalin and German Communism* (Cambridge, Mass., 1948), pp. 28–51. The Reichstag debates were held during the sessions of Feb. 20, Feb. 22, for the treaty with the Ukraine, and March 18, 19, 22, for the Russian treaty.

47 *Verhandlungen des Reichstages*, cccxi, 4217.

48 *Die Ursachen* . . . , i, 446; viii, 239.

49 Trotsky, *My Life*, p. 382.

50 Lenin, *Ausgewählte Werke* (Berlin, 1925), 493.

51 *Ibid.*, p. 490.

52 Bunyan and Fisher, *op. cit.*, p. 501.

53 *Ibid.*, p. ɔ19.

54 Wheeler-Bennett, *op. cit.*, p. 261.

55 Lutz, *Causes of the German Collapse*, pp. 241–242.

56 *Vossische Zeitung*, April 19, 1915; also quoted in *Sozialistische Monatshefte*, xlv (1915), 385.

57 Max Cohn, "West oder Ost," in *Sozialistische Monatshefte*, xvii (March, 1917), 231–236.

58 "Deutsch-russische Wirtschaftsbeziehungen in Vergangenheit und Zukunft," in *Sozialistische Monatshefte*, xlvii (1917), 568–575. Other articles in the same journal of the same character are Schippel's "Deutschland, England und Russland," in xlv (1915), 380–386; "Russland und Wir," in xlvii (1917), 339–346; Max Cohn, "Russische Revolution und deutsche Politik," xlvii, 353–356; August Winnig, "Russland, Frankreich und Deutschland," xlvii, 403–407. A critique of this school of political thinking was given in Stresemann's speech in the Reichstag on the Ukrainian treaty. Cf. *Verhandlungen des Reichstages*, cccxi, 4020.

59 Lutz, *Fall of the German Empire*, ii, 481.

60 *Die Ursachen* . . . , ii, 455. The Socialist Dr. Quessel testified that the Supreme Command had declared publicly as late as Sept. 14, 1918, that it was confident of victory (i, 405).

61 Lutz, *Fall of the German Empire*, ii, 457.

62 *Ibid.*, ii, 461–462.

63 *Ibid.*, ii, 378. It must also be pointed out that Prince Max "inquired first of the Supreme Command whether they agreed to his appointment as chancellor." (See Scheidemann, *Memoirs of a Social-Democrat*, ii, 483.) Interesting in this connection too is the furor caused by the publication in Switzerland on Oct. 9 of a copy of a letter written by Prince Max to his cousin Prince Alexander von Hohenlohe. In this letter Max expressed himself as being opposed "to western parliamentarianism for Germany" and likewise hostile to the Reichstag peace resolution. Scheidemann and Ebert prepared to resign from the government, and only the importunate pleading of the other party leaders and a statement by Max in which he claimed to have been misinterpreted caused the Socialist ministers to withdraw their resignation. (Cf. *Memoirs* of Prince Max of Baden, 2 vols. [London, 1928], i, 198–200; ii, 76–83.

64 Lutz, *Fall of the German Empire*, ii, 403.

65 Rosenberg, *op. cit.*, p. 245.

66 Lutz, *Fall of the German Empire*, ii, 464–465.

67 Cf. Frederick Maurice, *The Armistices of 1918* (London, 1943); see also Harry R. Rudin, *Armistice 1918* (New Haven, 1944).

68 F. C. Endres, *Die Tragödie Deutschlands* (Munich, 1922), pp. 436–437.

69 *Ibid.*, p. 235.

70 Published in Lutz, *Fall of the German Empire*, ii, 521–524.

71 *Die Ursachen* . . . , v, 95.

72 Wheeler-Bennett, *The Wooden Titan* (New York, 1936), p. 187. Is it possible that Adolf Hitler recalled these sentiments by General Groener when he met his death in the bunker in Berlin in 1945?

73 Lutz, *Fall of the German Empire*, ii, 537.

74 From Dreeling's *Das religiöse und sittliche Leben der Armee unter dem Einfluss des Weltkrieges*, as given in Lutz, *Fall of the German Empire*, ii, 268–269.

75 Erich Maria Remarque, *The Road Back*, tr. A. W. Wheen (Boston, 1931), p. 25.

76 *Ibid.*, pp. 214–215.

77 "Das Reich," reprinted in Hesse's *Krieg und Frieden* (Zürich, 1946), p. 118.

78 *Ibid.*, p. 173.

79 Ernst Jünger, *Der Kampf als inneres Erlebnis* (Berlin, 1925; 4th ed., 1929), pp. 2, 3, 76–77. See also the autobiographical novel by Ernst von Salomon, *Die Geächteten* (Berlin, 1930).

CHAPTER XIV

1 There is as yet no thorough and full history of the German revolution of 1918. The treatment here presented is based for the most part on the files of German newspapers, periodicals, and other source literature. The following are the most important general accounts: Eduard Bernstein, *Die deutsche Revolution* (Berlin, 1921), the most objective account, but unfortunately never completed; Hermann Müller, *Die November Revolution. Erinnerungen* (Berlin, 1921); F. Stampfer, *Die vierzehn Jahre der ersten deutschen Republik* (Carlsbad, 1936); Arthur Rosenberg, *A History of the German Republic,* tr. from the German (London, 1936); Richard Müller, *Vom Kaiserreich zur Republik* (Berlin, 1928) and *Der Bürgerkrieg in Deutschland* (Berlin, 1925); E. O. Volkmann, *Revolution über Deutschland* (Oldenburg, 1930; reprinted 1936), written from the anti-revolutionary point of view but containing a great deal of valuable material; *Illustrierte Geschichte der deutschen Revolution* (Berlin, 1929), the official history by the German Communist party; E. Troeltsch, *Spektator Briefe* (Tübingen, 1924). For collections of documents on this period, see E. Buchner, *Revolutionsdokumente* (Berlin, 1921); R. H. Lutz, ed. *The Fall of the German Empire, 1914–1918,* 2 vols. (Stanford, 1932); *Die Ursachen des deutschen Zusammenbruchs im Jahre 1918,* 12 vols. (Berlin, 1928), and English translations of selections from the same in R. H. Lutz, ed. *Causes of the German Collapse* (Stanford, 1934).

2 See his poem "Deutsche Einheit" in the conservative *Deutsche Tageszeitung* of Dec. 7, 1918.

3 Cf. Emil Barth, *Aus der Werkstatt der deutschen Revolution* (Berlin, 1919); Richard Müller, *Vom Kaiserreich zur Republik,* and Ledebour's statements at his trial, to be found in *Der Ledebour Prozess* (Berlin, 1919), pp. 22–30. The testimony of these writers has to a large extent been discredited. Barth "was only the court-fool of the revolution and not its maker. This will be attested to by anyone who has had anything to do with this gentleman." (Arthur Rosenberg before the Reichstag Inquiry Commission on Dec. 2, 1925. Cf. *Die Ursachen . . . ,* iv, 110.)

4 Scheidemann, *Der Zusammenbruch,* p. 210.

5 Lutz, *Causes of the German Collapse,* p. 112.

6 For vivid descriptions of this mood, see E. Troeltsch, *Spektator Briefe,* and F. Meinecke, *Strassburg, Freiburg, Berlin* (Stuttgart, 1949).

7 For the sailors' revolts, the best sources are vols. ix and x of the Reichstag Inquiry Commission's *Die Ursachen des deutschen Zusammenbruchs.* These contain a long report by the Independent Socialist Dittmann, detailed discussions by the members of the commission and other witnesses, and above all the valuable diary of the sailor Richard Stumpf, in vol. x, pt. ii. See also Gustav Noske, *Von Kiel bis Kapp* (Berlin, 1920), and his testimony in the *Dolchstoss Prozess* (Munich, 1925); also sailor Karl Funk's account, "Wie es zur Matrosenerhebung in Kiel kam," in the *Frankfurter Zeitung,* Dec. 10, 1918, morning edition, and "Wie es kam," in the Berlin *Vorwärts,* Nov. 14, 1918, evening edition.

8 G. Noske, *Von Kiel bis Kapp,* p. 11. See also his testimony in the *Dolchstoss Prozess,* p. 179.

9 From Kurt Ahnert, *Die Entwicklung der deutschen Revolution . . .* (Nürnberg, 1918), for Wednesday, Nov. 6.

10 *Münchner Neueste Nachrichten,* Nov. 9, 1918, no. 566.

11 *Ibid.,* Nov. 16, 1918, no. 580. See also Eisner's speech on "Socialization" of Jan. 22, 1919, reported in *Die Neue Zeitung,* Jan. 24, 1919.

12 There is as yet no full-length biography of Kurt Eisner. His political secretary Felix Fechenbach wrote a short appreciation, *Der Revolutionär Kurt Eisner* (Berlin, 1929). A hostile treatment by the Progressive leader Ernst Müller-Meiningen is found in his *Aus Bayerns schwersten Tagen* (Berlin, 1923). There are also no complete collections of Eisner's writings and speeches. All the volumes are highly selective. Pre-war writings are gathered in *Gesammelte Schriften,* 2 vols. (Berlin, 1919), and the post-war speeches in *Die neue Zeit,* 2 vols. (Munich, 1919). But significant statements, articles, and speeches must be culled from Eisner's own newspaper, *Die Neue Zeitung,* the organ of the Munich U.S.D.P., which began to appear on Dec. 20, 1918, and in the other U.S.D.P. papers such as the *Freiheit* and *Die Republik.*

13 From the account of Eisner's funeral in the *Frankfurter Zeitung,* Feb. 27, 1919. A full description of the funeral and also the complete text of Landauer's moving eulogy is to be found in the *Münchner Neueste Nachrichten,* of Feb. 27, 1918. This bourgeois paper was at this time under the direction of the Central Council of the Workers and Sailors.

14 From a Berlin dispatch of Nov. 7 to the *Frankfurter Zeitung* of Nov. 8.

15 According to the recollections of Prince Max, it was not von Payer but Solf who asked the question. The dialogue, according to Prince Max, was as follows:

Prince Max: "Are you ready to take over the post of chancellor of the Reich?"
Ebert: "It is a difficult post, but I will take it over."
Solf: "Are you ready to carry on the government within the framework of the constitution?"
Ebert: "Yes."
Solf: "Also within the monarchical constitution?"
Ebert: "Yesterday my answer would have been an unconditional yes; today I must first consult my friends."
Prince Max: "Now we must solve the question of the regency."
Ebert: "It is too late."

And his party comrades repeated after him: "Too late, too late" (Prince Max of Baden, *Erinnerungen und Dokumente* [Berlin, 1927], p. 638).

16 Quoted in Philipp Scheidemann, *Memoirs of a Social-Democrat*, 2 vols. (London, 1928), ii, 572–573, from Prince Max's *Erinnerungen und Dokumente*, p. 632. Chap. 14 of the latter volume deals with the events of Nov. 7.

17 Scheidemann, *op. cit.*, ii, 582–583. It is an extremely difficult and complex problem to decide how far the Majority Socialists had control over the events and how much they were pushed by the radical demonstrators in the streets. The left Independents like Müller, Barth, Ledebour, and Däumig maintain of course that the Majority Socialists jumped into the revolutionary situation to cash in on what had been prepared by the radical Independents and the Spartacists. Even the more moderate Haase declared in the National Assembly on Feb. 15, 1919, that the Majority Socialists had been against the revolution and he pointed to the Ebert proclamation of Nov. 9 to clear the streets. "On the same day," declared Haase, "he was brought to revolutionary power by the street" (*Die deutsche Nationalversammlung*, i, 235). The facts are, however, that the Majority Socialists had ordered out their followers to a general strike on the morning of Nov. 9, and Ebert's call to clear the streets came only after Prince Max had turned over his office to Ebert. That radical pressure played a role in pushing the Socialist leaders to more energetic action, however, seems to be incontestable.

18 Eduard Bernstein, *Die deutsche Revolution*, p. 33.

19 E. Buchner, *Revolutionsdokumente*, for Nov. 10, 1918.

20 *Spektator Briefe*, pp. 22–24.

21 This subject is best treated by Walter Jellinek in his section "Revolution und Reichsverfassung," in *Jahrbuch des öffentlichen Rechts der Gegenwart*, vol. ix (1920).

22 Reported in the *Neue Zürcher Zeitung*, Nov. 18, 1918.

23 The text of this statement is taken from the *Frankfurter Zeitung*, Nov. 23, 1918, no. 325. This is more reliable and accurate than the version cited in the books on the revolution.

24 *Europäischer Geschichtskalender*, lix (1918), 517; also *Freiheit* of Nov. 26, 1918.

25 Bredt, in *Die Ursachen . . .* , viii, 371.

26 There is no adequate and comprehensive treatment of the question of the soviets in the German revolution. The ideological aspects are treated by Franz Guttmann in his *Das Räte-System. Seine Verfechter und seine Probleme* (Munich, 1922).

27 From the concluding remarks at the Congress of Workers' and Soldiers' Councils, as reported in *Republik*, Dec. 20, 1918.

28 Ernst Däumig, *Das Rätesystem* (Berlin, 1919), p. 5.

29 *Republik*, Dec. 20, 1918.

30 Hermann Müller, *op. cit.*, p. 185.

31 *Protokoll . . . des Parteitages der S.P.D. in Weimar, June 10–15, 1919* (Berlin, 1919).

32 *Vorwärts*, Dec. 1, 1918.

33 Hermann Müller, *op. cit.*, p. 182.

34 Scheidemann, *Memoirs of a Social-Democrat*, ii, 545.

35 Cf. Stampfer, *op. cit.*, pp. 58–59; Hermann Müller, *op. cit.*, pp. 74–76.

36 "An die Mitglieder der Arbeiter und Soldatenräte," in *Vorwärts*, Nov. 22, 1918.

37 Hermann Bousset, *Das Spartakus Programm im Wiedergabe und Widerlegung* (Berlin, 1919), p. 8.

38 *Protokoll . . . des Parteitages der S.P.D. Weimar, June 10–15, 1919*, pp. 140, 200, 234.

39 U.S.D.P., *Protokoll . . . des Parteitages in Halle, October 12–17, 1920* (Berlin, 1920), p. 192.

40 There is as yet no complete biography of Haase nor a complete collection of his writings. Ernst Haase's *Hugo Haase, sein Leben und Wirken* (Berlin, 1929) is entirely inadequate both as to biographical data and as to the selection from his speeches, letters, and articles.

41 U.S.D.P., *Protokoll . . . des Parteitages in Halle, October 12–17, 1920*, p. 84.

42 U.S.D.P., *Parteitag . . . 1919*, p. 317.

43 See especially the proceedings of the Deutscher Sozialistentag, *Protokoll der Konferenz für Einigung der Sozialdemokratie, Berlin, June 21–23, 1919* (Berlin, 1919). Kurt Eisner, according to Eduard Bernstein, pleaded for two hours with Liebknecht on Nov. 24, 1918, to stop splitting the Socialist groups, but in vain. During the Spartacist uprising in Jan., 1919, Bernstein and several other Independents likewise attempted to mediate and stop the fratricidal conflict. Here too they were unsuccessful.

44 See the *Protokoll . . . des ausserordentlichen Parteitages in Halle. Von 12 bis 17. Oktober 1920* (Berlin, 1920).

45 Bernstein, *op. cit.*, p. 171.

46 *Freiheit*, Dec. 17, 1918.

47 *Rote Fahne*, Dec. 14, 1918; reprinted in Paul Fröhlich, *Rosa Luxemburg, Gedanke und Tat* (2nd ed., Hamburg, 1949), pp. 316–317.

48 *Bericht über den Gründungsparteitag der Kommunistischen Partei Deutschlands (Spartakusbund) von 30. Dezember–1. Januar 1919* (Berlin, 1919), p. 25.

49 Fröhlich, *op. cit.*, p. 313.

50 Bernstein, *op. cit.*, p. 101.

51 A detailed and objective account of these events is given by Eduard Bernstein, *op. cit.*, pp. 100–121. Richard Müller's *Der Bürgerkrieg* and Emil Barth's *Aus der Werkstatt der deutschen Revolution* give the story from the point of view of the left Independents.

52 The most detailed account of the January uprisings is to be found in the report of the Investigating Commission of the Prussian Diet, published in the proceedings of the Prussian diet. See also the works of Bernstein, Hermann Müller, and Richard Müller. Eichhorn has given his version of the events in a small pamphlet, *Eichhorn über die Januar-Ereignisse* (Berlin, 1919); Ledebour's account is available in the *Ledebour Prozess;* the materials regarding the murder of Karl Liebknecht and Rosa Luxemburg are contained in *Der Mord an Karl Liebknecht und Rosa Luxemburg. Zusammenfassende Darstellung des gesamten Untersuchungsmaterials mit ausführlichem Prozessbericht* (Berlin, 1920).

53 *Vorwärts*, Dec. 27, 1918.

54 Dr. Doyè reported to the Prussian Investigating Commission that 196 persons were killed in the January riots and 1,175 in the March insurrection (See *Vorwärts*, April 9, 1919). On the March insurrection in Berlin, see the Report of the Prussian Minister of Interior to the Investigating Commission of the Prussian Diet, pp. 8176–8191; the speech of Noske to the National Assembly on March 13, 1919; the account published by the Independent Socialists, *Die Wahrheit über die Berliner Strassenkämpfe* (Berlin, 1919); and the version put out by the Majority Socialists, *Die Berliner Spartakus Unruhen in März 1919* (Berlin, 1919).

55 *Die Neue Zeitung*, Feb. 21, 1919.

56 The history of the civil war in Bavaria has thus far been treated only by partisans of the opposing factions. The most comprehensive account of the events is by Ernst Müller-Meiningen, *Aus Bayerns schwersten Tagen* (Berlin, 1923). The author, one of the leaders of the Progressive party, is violently hostile to Eisner and to the radicals. From an even more conservative point of view are Georg Escherich's *Der Kommunismus in München*, 6 vols. (Munich, 1921), and Max Gerstl's *Die Münchener Räte Republik* (Munich, 1919). The latter is especially valuable for its collection of documents, proclamations, newspaper accounts and other such source materials. Ernst Toller's *I Was a German* (New York, 1934) and *Letters from Prison* (London, 1936) are most valuable. For materials on the other radical leaders see Erich Mühsam, *Von Eisner bis Leviné* (Berlin, 1929); Eugen Leviné, *Skizzen, Rede vor Gericht und anderes* (Berlin, 1925) and Rosa Leviné, *Aus der Münchener Rätezeit* (Berlin, 1925).

57 E. O. Volkmann, *Revolution über Deutschland*, p. 121.

58 Cf. Ernst von Salomon, *Das Buch vom deutschen Freikorpskämpfer* (Berlin, 1938), which contains reminiscences by a large number of former members of these formations and which provides a good picture of the widespread role of the *Freikorps* in all parts of Germany. See also the most recent study by Robert G. Waite, *Vanguard of Nazism. The Free Corps Movement in Post-War Germany, 1918–1923* (Cambridge, Mass., 1952).

59 Cf. Gustav Noske, *Von Kiel bis Kapp*, and his *Erlebtes. Aus Aufstieg und Niedergang einer Demokratie* (Offenbach, 1947). See also the passionate defense of his policy he made before the Social Democratic Party Congress of 1919 (*Protokoll*, pp. 200–207) and before the National Assembly on Feb. 15, 1919, and March 27 (*Die National Versammlung*, i, 261ff., and iii, 1814–1822).

CHAPTER XV

1 *Vorwärts*, Dec. 1, 1918.

2 Richard Müller, *Vom Kaiserreich zur Republik*, ii, 84–85.

3 Cf. *Deutsche Tageszeitung*, Dec. 16, 22, 1918.

4 Cf. Otto Nuschke, "Wie die deutsche Demokratische Partei wurde . . . ," in Anton Erkelenz, ed. *Zehn Jahre Republik* (Berlin, 1928), pp. 24–41.

5 The official text of the deliberations of the Weimar National Assembly have been incorporated into the official government publications of the Reichstag proceedings as vols. 326–333, under the title of *Verhandlungen der verfassunggebenden deutschen Nationalversammlung* (Berlin, 1919–1920). An abbreviated record of the proceedings is *Die deutsche Nationalversammlung im Jahre 1919–1920 in ihrer Arbeit für den Aufbau des neuen deutschen Volksstaats*, ed. E. Heilfron, 9 vols. (Berlin, 1919–1920). The latter edition is more convenient to use in some respects. Its tables of contents of each session are fuller; it has a detailed index; and it also has an interesting introductory section in vol. i on the background of the assembly, party platforms, reproduction of campaign posters, and other such materials. For a history and analysis of the work of the Assembly, see Wilhelm Ziegler, *Die deutsche Nationalversammlung 1919–1920 und ihr Verfassungswerk* (Berlin, 1932).

6 This character of the Assembly was bemoaned by the neo-romanticists of the time. See the essay "Die Nationalversammlung," by Eugen Diederichs in his *Politik des Geistes* (Jena, 1920).

7 An exchange of views on the union of the two Socialist parties by the more sober elements of the two groups was published in the *Freiheit* of Feb. 9 (Rudolf Hilferding's "Die Einigung des Proletariats") and the reply to Hilferding in the *Vorwärts* of Feb. 10.

8 E. O. Volkmann, *Revolution über Deutschland*, p. 303.

9 Schulthess, *Europäischer Geschichtskalender*, vol. lx (1919), pt. i, p. 272. The paper was suppressed because of this inflammatory appeal.

10 Quoted in Berlau, *The German Social Democratic Party 1914–1921*, p. 303, from *Verhandlungen*, vol. cccxxvii, pp. 1408–1409.

11 On the drafting of the constitution, see Walter Jellinek, "Entstehung und Ausbau der weimarer Verfassung," in *Handbuch des Staatsrechts* (Tübingen, 1929); Otto Meissner, "Die Entstehung der Reichsverfassung von Weimar," in *Zehn Jahre deutsche Geschichte* (Berlin, 1928), pp. 39–54; Wilhelm Ziegler, *op. cit.*; and Eugen Schiffer, *Sturm über Deutschland* (Berlin, 1932). On Hugo Preuss, see Carl Schmitt, *Hugo Preuss, sein Staatsbegriff und seine Stellung in der deutschen Staatslehre* (Tübingen, 1930); Hedwig Hintze, "Hugo Preuss, eine historisch-politische Charakteristik," in *Die Justiz*, vol. ii (1926–1927); Walter Simmons, "Hugo Preuss," in *Meister des Rechts* (Berlin, 1930). For an interpretation of the constitution see René Brunet, *The New German Constitution*, tr. from the French by Joseph Gollomb (New York, 1922); Johannes Mattern, *Principles of the Constitutional Jurisprudence of the German National Republic* (Baltimore, 1928); the collection of essays on constitutional problems in *Volk und Reich der Deutschen*, ed. Bernhard Harms, 3 vols. (Berlin, 1929), ii, 227–275; E. Vermeil, *La Constitution de Weimar et le principe de la démocratie allemande* (Strasbourg, 1923). The standard commentary on the constitution is by Gerhard Anschütz.

12 Cf. G. Anschütz, *Drei Leitgedanken der weimarer Verfassung* (Tübingen, 1923).

13 Cf. G. Anschütz, *Das preussisch-deutsche Problem* (Tübingen, 1922); and Friedrich Meinecke, *Weltbürgertum und Nationalstaat*.

14 Heilfron, *op. cit.*, ii, 476.

15 *Ibid.*, p. 630.

16 See Chapter XVIII.

17 The full text of the letter of resignation is found in *Freiheit*, April 9, 1919.

18 *Protokoll über die Verhandlungen des ausserordentlichen Parteitages vom 30. November bis 6. Dezember 1919 in Leipzig, U.S.D.P.* (Berlin, 1920), p. 55.

19 Hugo Haase, "Unsere Beziehungen zu den andern Völkern," in *Freiheit*, April 20, 1919.

20 Heilfron, *op. cit.*, iv, 2289.

21 Friedrich Meinecke, *Strassburg, Freiburg, Berlin*, p. 265.

22 W. M. Knight-Patterson, *Germany, From Defeat to Conquest* (London, 1945), p. 227.

23 The appeal was published in the *Vorwärts* of Dec. 14, 1918. The text of a resolution condemning antisemitism introduced by Max Cohen-Reuss and passed by the Vollzugsrat is published in Hermann Müller, *Die November Revolution*, p. 109.

24 *Verhandlungen der verfassunggebenden deutschen Nationalversammlung*, cccxxviii (1920), 1969.

25 *Ibid.*, p. 1970.

26 Cf. Klemens von Klemperer, "Towards a Fourth Reich? The History of National Bolshevism in Germany," in *Review of Politics*, xiii (1951), 191–210; see also *Schlageter, Eine Auseinandersetzung*, by Karl Radek, Paul Fröhlich, Ernst Reventlow, and Moeller van den Bruck (Berlin, n.d.).

27 Quoted in *Republik*, April 9, 1919.

28 For the Kapp Putsch consult: Richard Bernstein, *Der Kapp-putsch und seine Lehren* (Berlin, 1920); Karl Brammer, *Fünf Tage Militärdiktatur* (Berlin, 1920); and especially E. O. Volkmann, *Revolution über Deutschland*, whose account I have followed in the main. The debates on the Kapp Putsch in the National Assembly took place in the 156th session, on March 18, 1920. For the role of General von Seeckt, see Alma Luckau, "Kapp Putsch: Success or Failure?" in *Journal of Central European Affairs*, vii (1947–1948), 394–405. For participants see Max Bauer, *Der 13 März 1920* (Munich, 1920), and Walther Lüttwitz, *Im Kampf gegen die November Revolution* (Berlin, 1934). On the activities of the monarchists, see Walter H. Kaufmann, *Monarchism in the Weimar Republic* (New York, 1953).

CHAPTER XVI

1 For general accounts of the Weimar Republic, see the following: Ferdinand Friedensburg, *Die weimarer Republik* (Berlin, 1946); Friedrich Stampfer, *Die vierzehn Jahre der ersten deutschen Republik* (Carlsbad, 1936); Arthur Rosenberg, *A History of the German Republic*, tr. from the German (London, 1936); Bernhard Harms, ed. *Volk und Reich der Deutschen*, 3 vols. (Berlin, 1929); *Zehn Jahre deutsche Geschichte 1918–1928* (2nd ed., Berlin, 1928); S. William Halpern, *Germany Tried Political Democracy: A Political History of the Reich from 1918 to 1933* (New York, 1946); Hugh Quigley and R. T. Clark, *Republican Germany* (London, 1928); R. T. Clark, *The Fall of the German Republic* (London, 1935); Georg Bernhard, *Die deutsche Tragödie* (Prague, 1933). A useful collection of documents is Ernst Forsthoff's *Deutsche Geschichte 1918–1938 in Dokumenten* (Leipzig, 1935), although published under the Nazi régime and hence subject to ideological pressure. For the relation of the army to politics, see J. W. Wheeler-Bennett, *The Nemesis of Power, The German Army in Politics* (London, 1953).

2 For the history of political parties during the republic, see: L. Bergsträsser, *Geschichte der politischen Parteien in Deutschland* (7th ed., Munich, 1952); Anton Erkelenz, ed. *Zehn Jahre deutsche Republik* (Berlin, 1928), for the Democratic party; Karl Anton Schulte, ed. *National Arbeit, Das Zentrum und sein Wirken in der deutschen Republik* (Berlin, 1929); Max Weiss, ed. *Der nationale Wille* (Leipzig, 1928), for the German Nationalists. The history of the Social Democratic party is best studied in the protocols of its party congresses and in the handbook *Sozial-demokratische Partei-korrespondenz für die Jahre 1923 bis 1928* (Berlin, 1930). For the activities of the Communist party see Ossip K. Flechtheim, *Die kommunistische Partei Deutschlands in der weimarer Republik* (Offenbach, 1948); Ruth Fischer, *Stalin and German Communism* (Cambridge, 1948); Paul Merker, *Deutschland, sein oder nicht sein?*, 2 vols. (Mexico City, 1944–1945), a Communist party account.

3 For the record of the German courts in political crimes, see E. J. Gumbel, *Verräter verfallen der Feme. Opfer, Mörder, Richter* (Berlin, 1929).

4 Gustav Mayer, *Erinnerungen* (Munich, 1949), pp. 308–309.

5 Cf. Klemens von Klemperer, "Towards a Fourth Reich? The History of National Bolshevism in Germany," in *The Review of Politics*, xiii (1951), 191–211.

6 *Deutsche Geschichte von 1918 bis 1938 in Dokumenten*, pp. 155–157.

CHAPTER XVII

1 Walther Rathenau, *Briefe*, 2 vols. (2nd ed., Dresden, 1927), ii, 75.

2 For German foreign policy during the Weimar period, see: W. M. Jordan, *Great Britain, France and the German Problem 1918–1939* (New York, 1944); Erich Koch-Weser, *Deutschlands Aussenpolitik in der Nachkriegszeit* (3rd ed., Berlin, 1930), tr. into English (Philadelphia, 1930); Harry Kessler, *Walther Rathenau* (New York, 1930); Viscount D'Abernon, *The Diary of an Ambassador*, 3 vols. (Garden City, 1929–1931);

Gustav Stresemann, *Vermächtnis*, 3 vols. (Berlin, 1932–1933), English ed. by Eric Sutton (New York, 1935); Julius Curtius, *Sechs Jahre Minister der deutschen Republik* (Heidelberg, 1948); W. M. Knight-Patterson, *Germany from Defeat to Conquest* (London, 1946), extreme in its anti-German orientation but useful for copious extracts from source materials. A thoughtful defence of the Treaty of Versailles is found in E. Mantoux, *The Carthaginian Peace* (New York, 1952).

3 U.S. Department of State, 862.00/1073.

4 Rathenau, *Gesammelte Reden* (Berlin, 1924), p. 211.

5 *Ibid.*, pp. 203–204.

6 July 6, 1922, p. 3.

7 Techow, later, experienced a genuine moral conversion. As expiation for his crime, he became a leading figure in the anti-Nazi underground movement in France active in rescuing Jews from the clutches of the Gestapo. Cf. the fascinating story of his career in *Harper's Magazine*, April, 1943.

8 According to a conversation between Max Weber and Gustav Stolper in Munich in 1920, reported in Stolper, *This Age of Fable* (New York, 1942), p. 318 n.

9 Cited in E. Jackh, *War for Man's Soul* (New York, 1943), pp. 3–4.

10 Friedrich von Rabenau, *Seeckt. Aus seinem Leben 1918–1936* (Leipzig, 1940), pp. 197–198.

11 Cf. J. H. Morgan, *Assize of Arms. The Disarmament of Germany and Her Rearmament (1919–1939)* (New York, 1946).

12 For the text of this agreement see Carl Severing, *Mein Lebensweg*, 2 vols. (Cologne, 1950), ii, 129–130.

13 On the subject of German rearmament during the Weimar Republic, see: Morgan, *op. cit.*; O. Lehmann-Russbueldt, *Aggression. The Origin of Germany's War Machine 1919–1933* (London, 1942); Walter Görlitz, *Der deutsche Generalstab. Geschichte und Gestalt 1657–1945* (Frankfurt, 1950); Rabenau, *op. cit.*; the files of the *Weltbühne*. For relations between the Reichswehr and the U.S.S.R., see Cecil F. Melville, *The Russian Face of Germany, Account of the Secret Military Relations Between the German and Soviet Russian Governments* (London, 1932); G. W. Hallgarten, "Gen. Hans von Seeckt and Russia, 1920–1922," in *Journal of Modern History*, xxxi (1949), 28–34; *S.P.D. Partei Korrespondenz 1923–1928* (Berlin, 1930).

14 Knight-Patterson, *op. cit.*, p. 491.

15 Cf. M. Margaret Ball, *Post-War German-Austrian Relations. The Anschluss Movement, 1918–1936* (Stanford, 1937).

16 Stresemann, *Diaries*, ed. E. Sutton, iii, 386–387.

17 For the treatment of the question of German minorities, see: Ralph F. Bischoff, *Nazi Conquest Through German Culture* (Cambridge, 1942). See also K. C. von Loesch, ed. *Volk unter Völkern* (Berlin, 1925) and *Staat und Volkstum* (Berlin, 1926), published by the Deutscher Schutzbund, and Karl C. von Loesch and M. H. Boehm, eds. *Zehn Jahre Versailles. Die grenz- und volkspolitischen Folgen des Friedenschlusses* (Berlin, 1930), for materials by German leaders in this movement. See also Georg Schmidt-Rohr, *Die Sprache als Bildnerin der Völker* (Jena, 1932).

18 For Russo-German relations under the Weimar Republic, see: Max Beloff, *The Foreign Policy of Soviet Russia 1929–1941*, 2 vols. (London, 1947), i, 56–69; Ernst Fraenkel, "German-Russian Relations in Soviet Diplomacy Since 1918," in *Review of Politics*, ii (1940), 34–62; E. H. Carr, *German-Soviet Relations Between the Two World Wars 1919–1939* (Baltimore, 1951); Hans von Seeckt, *Deutschland zwischen West und Ost* (Hamburg, 1933); Gustav Hilger's memoirs, *The Incompatible Allies: A Memoir-History of German-Soviet Relations 1918–1941* (New York, 1953).

19 Cf. especially Moeller van den Bruck's *Rechenschaft über Russland*, ed. Hans Schwarz (Berlin, 1933). See also Woldemar Fink, *Ostideologie und Ostpolitik* (Berlin, 1936).

20 Cf. Thomas Mann's "Russische Anthologie" (1921), in his *Gesammelte Werke*, ix, 227–243, and his "Goethe und Tolstoi" in x, 9–140.

21 *Report of Court Proceedings in the Case of the Anti-Soviet "Bloc of Rights and Trotskyites"* (Moscow, 1938), p. 263.

22 *Briefe*, i, 279.

23 Cf. Rabenau, *op. cit.*, pp. 305–320. See also Hallgarten, *op. cit.*

CHAPTER XVIII

1 For economic conditions under the Weimar Republic, see: Gustav Stolper, *German Economy 1870–1940*; J. W. Angell, *The Recovery of Germany* (rev. ed., New Haven,

1932); W. F. Bruck, *Social and Economic History of Germany from William II to Hitler,* *1888–1938* (Cardiff, 1938); Bernhard Harms, *Strukturwandlungen der deutschen Volks-* *wirtschaft,* 2 vols. (Berlin, 1929); Fritz Sternberg, *Der Niedergang des deutschen Kapitalis-* *mus* (Berlin, 1932); Carl Bergmann, *The History of Reparations,* tr. from the German (London, 1927); J. W. Angell, "Reparations," in *Encyclopaedia of the Social Sciences,* vol. xiii (1934); Felix Pinner, *Deutsche Wirtschaftsführer* (Berlin, 1924); Gaston Raphaël, *Hugo Stinnes, der Mensch, sein Werk, sein Wirken,* tr. from the French (Berlin, 1925); H. Wickel, *I.G. Deutschland, ein Staat im Staate* (Berlin, 1932); Hermann Levy, *Industrial* *Germany* (London, 1935); R. B. Brady, *The Rationalization Movement in German Industry* (Berkeley, 1933); Nathan Reich, *Labour Relations in Republican Germany, 1918–1933* (New York, 1938); L. Preller, *Sozialpolitik in der weimarer Republik* (Stuttgart, 1949); Wilhelm Röpke, *German Commercial Policy* (London, 1934); Alexander Gerschenkron, *Bread and Democracy in Germany* (Berkeley, 1943).

CHAPTER XIX

1 For cultural life under the Weimar Republic, the best sources are the files of the liberal-democratic literary review *Neue Rundschau* and the conservative-nationalist *Deutsche* *Rundschau.* See also Jethro Bithell, *Modern German Literature, 1880–1938* (London, 1939); Werner Mahrholz, *Deutsche Literatur der Gegenwart* (Berlin, 1931); Ernst Wiechert, *Jahre* *und Zeiten* (Munich, 1951); Friedrich Franz von Unruh, "Stefan George und der deutsche Nationalismus," in *Neue Rundschau,* xliii (1932), 478–492; Karl Mannheim, "German Sociology 1918–1933," in *Politica* (1934), pp. 13–33; *Die Wissenschaft der Gegenwart,* a series of volumes on historiography, medicine, philosophy, jurisprudence, education, and economics, in which leading figures in these fields present accounts of their own work, 17 vols. (Leipzig, 1921–1930); Ernst Troeltsch, *Gesammelte Schriften,* vol. iv (Berlin, 1925), which contains penetrating book reviews on many important post-war books; Hans Ostwald, *Sittengeschichte der Inflation* (Berlin, 1931); Hermann Hass, *Sitte und Kultur im* *Nachkriegsdeutschland* (Hamburg, 1932); E. Vermeil, *Doctrinaires de la révolution alle-* *mande (1918–1938)* (Paris, 1938); Rohan D'Olier Butler, *The Roots of National Socialism* (London, 1941); R. Bie, *Die deutsche Malerei der Gegenwart* (Weimar, 1930); George N. Shuster, *The Germans* (New York, 1932).

2 *Preussentum und Sozialismus,* p. 81, reprinted in *Politische Schriften* (Munich, 1933), p. 86.

3 From *Preussentum und Sozialismus,* reprinted in his *Politische Schriften,* p. 105.

CHAPTER XX

1 For an account of the various currents of revolutionary conservatism, see: Armin Mohler, *Die konservative Revolution in Deutschland 1918–1932* (Stuttgart, 1950); Ernst H. Posse, *Die politischen Kampfbünde Deutschlands* (2nd ed., Berlin, 1931); Walter Gerhardt [Waldemar Gurian], *Um des Reiches Zukunft. Nationale Wiedergeburt oder* *politische Reaktion* (Freiburg, 1932); F. W. Heinz, *Die Nation greift an* (Berlin, 1933); Robert G. L. Waite, *Vanguard of Nazism. The Free Corps Movement in Postwar Ger-* *many, 1918–1923* (Cambridge, Mass., 1952).

2 Cf. Otto Meissner, *Staatssekretär unter Ebert, Hindenburg, Hitler* (Hamburg, 1950), p. 128.

3 Hans Schlange-Schoeningen, *The Morning After,* tr. Edward Fitzgerald (London, 1948), p. 48.

4 On Social Democratic policy under Brüning, see: Rudolf Hilferding, "Im Krisennot," in *Die Gesellschaft,* viii (July, 1931), 1–8; Carlo Mierendorff, "Tolerieren—und was dann?" in *Sozialistische Monatshefte* (April 13, 1931), pp. 315ff.; and above all the de-bates of the Leipzig Parteitag of 1931.

5 This account is taken from the *Frankfurter General Anzeiger* of June 8, 1932.

6 International Military Tribunal, Trial of the Major War Criminals, *Proceedings,* xvi, 244–245.

7 *Vierzehn Jahre Republik,* p. 579.

8 Cf. Heinrich Brüning, "Ein Brief," in *Deutsche Rundschau,* lxx (July, 1947), 1–22. See also comment on this letter by Otto Braun in the same journal, lxxi (Aug., 1948), 107–112.

CHAPTER XXI

1 The literature on the various aspects and phases of National Socialism is tremendous, and it is impossible here to give more than a highly selective list of works. A detailed and critical bibliography of the vast literature is one of the prime needs for the study of this period. The only bibliographical guide available at present is the semi-official guide to Nazi literature edited by Ehrich Unger, *Das Schrifttum des Nationalsozialismus* (Berlin, 1934).

Of primary importance for the study of Nazism are the huge collections of materials presented at the trials of the Nazi war criminals. First and foremost is the full record of proceedings and texts of all documents presented in evidence in the *Trial of the Major War Criminals Before the International Military Tribunal*, 42 vols. (Nürnberg, 1947–1949). In addition there are the abbreviated records of the twelve trials conducted by the United States Military Tribunals in Nürnberg against the medical, legal, racial, economic, military, and political officials, 16 vols. (Nürnberg, 1946–1951). A specially selected collection of the materials, including some captured documents not admitted as evidence at the trials and also containing valuable summaries of Nazi policy and Nazi organization, is found in *Nazi Conspiracy and Aggression*, issued by the office of the United States Chief of Counsel for Prosecution of Axis Criminality, 7 vols. (Washington, 1946). A very interesting companion volume to these records is the account of conversations with the major war criminals by the prison psychologist G. M. Gilbert, *Nuremberg Diary* (New York, 1947). A selection of documents from the captured archives of the German Foreign Office is being published jointly by a group of American, British, and French scholars in German, English, and French versions. The American edition is appearing under the title *Documents on German Foreign Policy 1918–1945* (Washington, 1949–   ). The documentary material pertaining to the outbreak of World War II has been summarized in Peter de Mendelssohn's *Pattern of Aggression* (New York, 1947).

Hitler's own major contributions to the literature of National Socialism are: *Mein Kampf*, of which the best English version is the Reynal and Hitchcock edition (New York, 1939); *Hitler's Speeches 1922–1939*, ed. Norman Baynes, 2 vols. (London, 1942); *My New Order*, ed. Raoul de Roussy de Sales (New York, 1941); *Hitler's Tischgespräche im Führerhauptquartier 1941–1942*, ed. H. Picker (Bonn, 1951) and the English version of the same material, but in fuller and better form, *Hitler's Secret Conversations 1941–1944* (New York, 1953). A convenient collection of extracts from National Socialist literature is *Thus Speaks Germany*, ed. W. W. Coole and M. F. Potter (New York, 1941). The most comprehensive biography of Hitler is Allan Bullock's *Hitler* (London, 1952).

On the history of the earlier phases of National Socialism the following are useful. the several works of Konrad Heiden, the first historian of the movement, *Geschichte des Nationalsozialismus* (Berlin, 1932), *Geburt des dritten Reiches* (Zürich, 1934), both combined in abridged form in *A History of National Socialism* (New York, 1934); *Der Führer* (Boston, 1944); Henri Lichtenberger and Koppel S. Pinson, *The Third Reich* (New York, 1937), which contains a valuable collection of Nazi documents; Frederick L. Schuman, *The Nazi Dictatorship* (2nd ed., New York, 1936); Stephen H. Roberts, *The House That Hitler Built* (New York, 1938); and the extremely interesting and valuable works by Hermann Rauschning, especially *The Revolution of Nihilism* (New York, 1939), *The Voice of Destruction* (New York, 1940), *Men of Chaos* (New York, 1942). The economic aspects of Nazi policy are best treated in Franz Neumann, *Behemoth* (New York, 1942), and Max Ascoli and Arthur Feiler, *Fascism for Whom?* (New York, 1938).

The intellectual origins of National Socialism are best treated in Rohan D'Olier Butler, *The Roots of National Socialism, 1789–1933* (London, 1941). See also the valuable article by Carl Mayer, "On the Intellectual Origins of National Socialism," in *Social Research*, ix (1942), 225–247.

For educational and religious problems, see: G. Ziemer, *Education for Death* (New York, 1941); W. Gurian, *Hitler and the Christians* (New York, 1936); A. S. Duncan-Jones, *The Struggle for Religious Freedom in Germany* (London, 1938); H. Hermelink, ed. *Kirche im Kampf 1933–1945* (Tübingen, 1950); Arthur Frey, *Cross and Swastika: The Ordeal of the German Church* (London, 1938); Johann Neuhäusler, *Kreuz und Hakenkreuz* (Munich, 1950); Nathaniel Micklem, *National Socialism and the Roman Catholic Church* (London, 1939); Alfred P. Delp, *Christ und Gegenwart*, 3 vols. (Frankfurt, 1948–1949), and *Im Angesicht des Todes* (Frankfurt, 1950).

For the relations of the army to the Nazi regime, see J. W. Wheeler-Bennett, *The Nemesis of Power: The German Army in Politics 1918–1945* (London, 1954), and Telford Taylor, *Sword and Swastika* (New York, 1952). There is as yet no adequate and comprehensive treatment of Nazi policies against the Jews. The most useful works thus far published are: G. Warburg, *Six Years of Hitler* (London, 1939); *Nazi Germany's War Against the Jews* (New York, 1947); Max Weinreich, *Hitler's Professors* (New York, 1946); Léon Poliakov, *Bréviaire de la Haine: Le IIIe Reich et les Juifs* (Paris, 1952); Eva G. Reichmann, *Hostages of Civilization* (Boston, 1951); Gerald Reitlinger, *The Final Solution* (London, 1953). The final act of the Nazi drama is vividly presented in H. Trevor-Roper, *The Last Days of Hitler* (2nd ed., London, 1950).

2 Gilbert, *op. cit.*, p. 21.

3 *Ibid.*, p. 108.

4 *Nazi Conspiracy and Aggression,* Supplement B, pp. 1289–1291.

5 Erich Kordt, *Nicht aus den Akten* (Stuttgart, 1950), p. 298.

6 *The French Yellow Book* (New York, 1940), p. 26.

7 Gilbert, *op. cit.*, p. 66.

8 For accounts of these top Nazi leaders, see: Hermann Rauschning, *Men of Chaos* (New York, 1942); *Nazi Führer sehen dich an* (Paris, 1934); Edgar von Schmidt-Pauli, *Die Männer um Hitler* (Berlin, 1932); Paul Schwarz, *This Man Ribbentrop* (New York, 1943); Willi Frischauer, *The Rise and Fall of Hermann Goering* (Boston, 1951), and *Himmler* (Boston, 1953).

9 *Nazi Conspiracy and Aggression,* Supplement B, p. 1243.

10 *Nazi Conspiracy and Aggression,* vii, 753.

11 Gilbert, *op. cit.*, p. 23; International Military Tribunal, hereafter cited as I.M.T. *Proceedings,* xiv, 368.

12 Cf. Hermann Rauschning, *The Revolution of Nihilism,* and Ernst Niekisch, *Hitler— ein deutsches Verhängnis* (Berlin, 1932).

13 *Nazi Conspiracy and Aggression,* iii, 68.

14 *Mein Kampf,* Eng. ed., p. 468.

15 *Die Nationalsozialistische Weltanschauung,* ed. H. de Vries de Heekelingen (Berlin, 1932), p. 96.

16 *Völkischer Beobachter,* Jan. 1, 1921.

17 *Trials of War Criminals Before the Nuremberg Military Tribunals,* xiii, 422.

18 I.M.T. *Documents,* xxv, 192–193, no. 098–PS.

19 Rauschning, *The Voice of Destruction,* p. 49.

20 Gregor Strasser, in *Der Nationalsozialismus. Die Weltanschauung der 20. Jahrhunderts,* by Gregor Strasser, Otto Strasser, Reventlow, Jung, Herbert Blank, and Reinhold Muchow (Berlin, 1930).

21 Rauschning, *Voice of Destruction,* pp. 186, 191, 193.

22 Hans Schlange-Schoeningen, *The Morning After* (London, 1948), p. 23.

23 I.M.T. *Proceedings,* xix, 417–418.

24 *Ibid.*, xiii, 144.

25 I.M.T. *Documents,* xxxvi, 524.

26 Franz Boese, *Geschichte des Vereins für Sozialpolitik 1872–1932* (Berlin, 1939), pp. 283–284, vol. clxxxviii of *Schriften des Vereins für Sozialpolitik.*

27 See Hans Freyer's *Revolution von Rechts* (Jena, 1931) and Eduard Spranger's "Zum gegenwärtigen geistigen Lage in Deutschland," in *Sitzungsberichte* of Prussian Academy of Sciences, Philos.-Hist. Klasse (1933), p. 821.

28 Cf. Peter Bor, *Gespräche mit Halder* (Wiesbaden, 1950), pp. 112–113. Although Pechel is correct in his generally critical attitude toward Halder, there is no reason to doubt the veracity of this testimony by Halder.

29 I.M.T. *Proceedings,* x, 114.

30 The texts of von Papen's speech are available in I.M.T. *Documents,* xl, 543–558; Schacht's Königsberg speech is Document 433–EC in xxxvi, 507ff.

31 The fullest and on the whole most objective account of the German resistance movement is Rudolf Pechel's *Deutscher Widerstand* (Zurich, 1947). Pechel, editor of the *Deutsche Rundschau,* was himself close to the conservative opposition. The works by H. B. Gisevius (*Bis zum Bittern Ende,* 2 vols., Zurich, 1946, English tr., *To the Bitter End,* Boston, 1947) and Ulrich von Hassell (*Vom andern Deutschland,* Zurich, 1946, English tr., *The Von Hassell Diaries 1938–1944,* Garden City, 1947) are valuable but must be used with caution. Gisevius tends to exaggerate his own role in the resistance and to shield some of his friends, and von Hassell served the Nazis faithfully until 1938. The best account of the plot of July 20 is in Wheeler-Bennett, *The Nemesis of Power,* pp. 634–693; see also G. Weisenborn, *Der lautlose Aufstand* (Hamburg, 1953); E. Zeller, *Geist der Freiheit* (Munich, 1953); Allen Welsh Dulles, *Germany's Underground* (New York,

1947), and Fabian Schlabendorff and Gero Gaevernitz, *They Almost Killed Hitler* (New York, 1947).

32 *Trials of War Criminals,* The Ministries Case, xii, 430–439.
33 I.M.T. *Documents,* xxvi, 329.
34 *Ibid.,* xxvi, 329.
35 *Ibid.,* xxv, 68–69.
36 Gilbert, *op. cit.,* p. 93.
37 *Nazi Conspiracy and Aggression,* vii, 753.
38 Cf. the political report by Dr. Paul W. Thomson, of the University of Posen, of Oct. 19, 1942, submitted as Document 303–PS in the Nürnberg trial (I.M.T. *Documents,* xxv, 343), which makes the claim that before the mistreatment began, the German armies were "greeted as liberators by at least 75 percent of the population."
39 *Nazi Conspiracy and Aggression,* vii, 753.
40 I.M.T. *Documents,* xxvii, 10.
41 *Ibid.,* xxix, 118.
42 *Ibid.,* xxix, 123.
43 *Ibid.,* xxxiii, 237–245, Document 3358–PS.
44 *Ibid.,* xxix, 146.
45 I.M.T. *Proceedings,* iv, 371.
46 *Trials of War Criminals,* Milch Case, ii, 533–534.
47 I.M.T. *Documents,* xxxvii, 502, Document 070–L.
48 *Ibid.,* xxxviii, 86, Document 221–L.
49 *Trial of War Criminals,* Milch Case, ii, 666–668.
50 Quoted in Trevor-Roper, *op. cit.,* p. 82.

CHAPTER XXII

1 The material in this chapter is based chiefly on the press of Germany and the United States and on the author's personal observations. Quite valuable studies and reports are to be found in the files of the following important political journals in Germany: *Die Wandlung, Frankfurter Hefte, Die Gegenwart, Deutsche Rundschau,* and *Aufbau.* American occupation policy is best studied in the regular reports of the Office of Military Government for Germany and its successor, the office of the U.S. High Commissioner for Germany. Of the secondary literature the following are the most useful: Lucius D. Clay, *Decision in Germany* (New York, 1950); *This Is Germany,* ed. Arthur Settel (New York, 1950); *The Struggle for Democracy in Germany,* ed. Gabriel A. Almond (Chapel Hill, 1949); James Stewart Martin, *All Honorable Men* (Boston, 1950); Edward H. Litchfield, *et al., Governing Postwar Germany* (Ithaca, 1953); Hoyt Price, and Carl E. Schorske, *The Problem of Germany* (New York, 1947); Anglo-Jewish Association, *Germany's New Nazis* (London, 1951); J. P. Nettl, *Eastern Zone and Soviet Policy in Germany 1945–50* (London, 1951). A convenient handbook for factual data is the *Deutschland Jahrbuch,* ed. Klaus Mehnert and Heinrich Schulte.
2 *New York Times,* April 30, 1945.
3 General Clay, in *Decision in Germany,* gives the figure 6,500,000 (p. 231). The 9th Quarterly Report of the U.S. High Commissioner for Germany of Oct. 1–Dec. 31, 1951, gives the figure of 8,000,000. The larger figure is also given in *UNRRA: The History of the United Nations Relief and Rehabilitation Administration,* ed. George Woodbridge, 3 vols. (New York, 1950), ii, 469.
4 U.S. High Commission, 5th Quarterly Report, Oct. 1–Dec. 31, 1950.
5 Cf. E. Kogon, "Das Recht auf politisches Irrtum," in *Frankfurter Hefte,* ii (1947), 641.
6 Clara Menck, "The Problem of Reorientation," in *The Struggle for Democracy in Germany.*
7 Cf. E. Kogon, "Die deutsche Revolution. Gedanken zum zweiten Jahrestag des 20 Juli 1944," in *Frankfurter Hefte* (July, 1946). See also the critical analysis of the July 20 opposition in the Berlin *Tagesspiegel* of Jan. 4, 1947, p. 2.
8 Ernst Wiechert, *Rede an die deutsche Jugend 1945* (Munich, 1945). See also Wiechert's beautifully written and moving autobiography *Jahre und Zeiten* (Munich, 1951).
9 R. Pechel, "Tatsachen," in *Deutsche Rundschau* (Dec., 1946).
10 Besides Jaspers, see also the following on the guilt problem: P. Küble, *Die Konzentrationslager* (Singen, 1946); H. Zipperlen, *Die Stunde des Gerichts* (Stuttgart, 1946); Wiechert, *op. cit.;* Pechel, *op. cit.;* W. Dirks, "Der Weg zur Freiheit," in *Frankfurter Hefte* (July, 1946); Martin Niemoeller, "Ich, Du, Wir Alle," in *Deutsche Rundschau* (no. 8,

1946); F. Meineckc, *Die deutsche Katastrophe*. Examples of the "unrepentant" German literature are: Heinrich Hauser, *The German Talks Back* (New York, 1945), and Hans Grimm, *Answer of a German* (Dublin, 1952). A German critical view of the war-crimes trials is found in the work by the former chief counsel of the I.G. Farben, August von Knieriem, *Nürnberg. Rechtliche und menschliche Probleme* (Stuttgart, 1953).

11 Technically, by the *Bundesversammlung*, consisting of the Bundestag (lower house of parliament) and delegations from the *Länder* legislatures. It meets only once every five years for the specific purpose of electing the President.

Index